Alvah Hovey

An American Commentary on the New Testament

Alvah Hovey

An American Commentary on the New Testament

ISBN/EAN: 9783337285616

Printed in Europe, USA, Canada, Australia, Japan

Cover: Foto ©Lupo / pixelio.de

More available books at **www.hansebooks.com**

AN

AMERICAN COMMENTARY

ON THE

NEW TESTAMENT.

EDITED BY

ALVAH HOVEY, D.D., LL.D.

———— · · ·· ————

PHILADELPHIA:
AMERICAN BAPTIST PUBLICATION SOCIETY,
1420 CHESTNUT STREET.

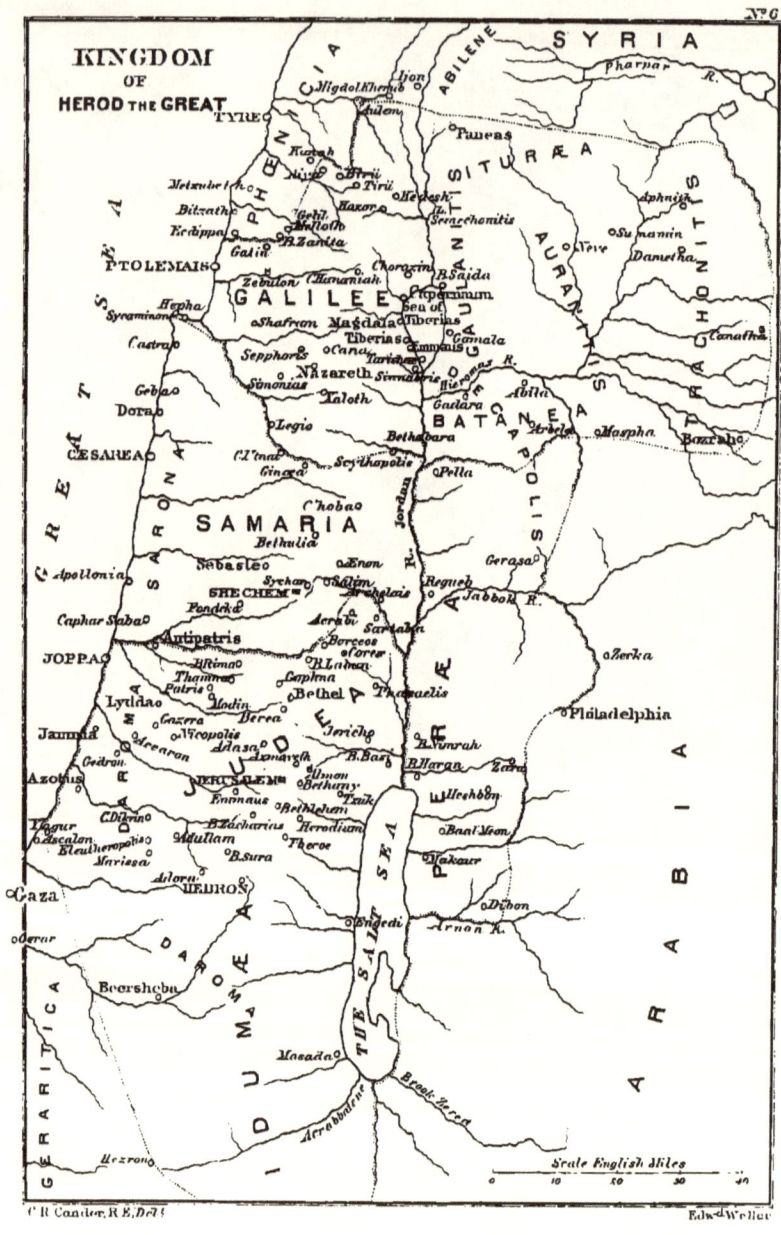

KINGDOM
OF
HEROD THE GREAT

SYRIA

PHŒNICIA

ABILENE

ITURÆA

AURANITIS

TRACHONITIS

TYRE

Migdol Kherub
Ijon
Abel
Pharpar R.

Kedah
Ibrin
Paneas

Metzubeh
Giscalia
Tyrü
Kedesh
Aphnis

Bitzatha
Gebil
Hazor
Serachonitis
Sumanin

Ecdippa
Meloth
B.Zanita
Teve
Dametha

PTOLEMAIS
Galil

Hepha
Zebulon
Chananiah
Chorazin
B.Saida

Syraminon
GALILEE
Capernaum
Sea of

Shafran
Magdala
Tiberias

Castra
Cana
Gamala

Sepphoris
Tiberias
Tarichea
Campsis

Geba
Nazareth
Simonias
Sinnabris
Dion

Dora
Taloth
Gadara
Abila

Legio
Bethabara
Abila
Mospha
Barabic

CÆSAREA
Cl'ina
BATANEA

Ginæa
Scythopolis
Pella

Chobao
DECAPOLIS

SAMARIA
Bethulia

Sebasteo
Enon
Gerasa

Apollonia
Sychar
Salim
Regueb

SHECHEM
Archelais
Jabbok R.

Caphar Saba
Pondrid
Aceth
Sartaba

Antipatris
Borceos
of Forts

JOPPA
B.Rimon
Laban

Thamna
Lapma

Lydda
Patris
Modin
Bethel
Thanaelis

Jamnia
Gazera
Berea
Jericho
Philadelphia

Neopolis
Adasa

Gedron
Adasa
Anava
Anavath
B.Bas
A.Ranah

Azotus
JERUSALEM
Bethany
B.Haran
Zara

Emmaus
Bethlehem
Tsuk
Heshbon

C.Dilrino
B.Zacharias
Herodium
Baal Meon

Vagur
Adullam
Theroe

Ascalon
B.Sura

Eleutheropolis

Marissa
Ailora

Gaza
HEBRON

Dibon

Gerar
Engedi
Arnon R.

Beersheba

Masada

Hezron

Arrabatene
Brook Zered

IDUMÆA

GERARITICA

THE SALT SEA

ARABIA

Scale English Miles
0   10   20   30   40

C.R.Conder, R.E.Del?

Edw.d Weller

N.º 6

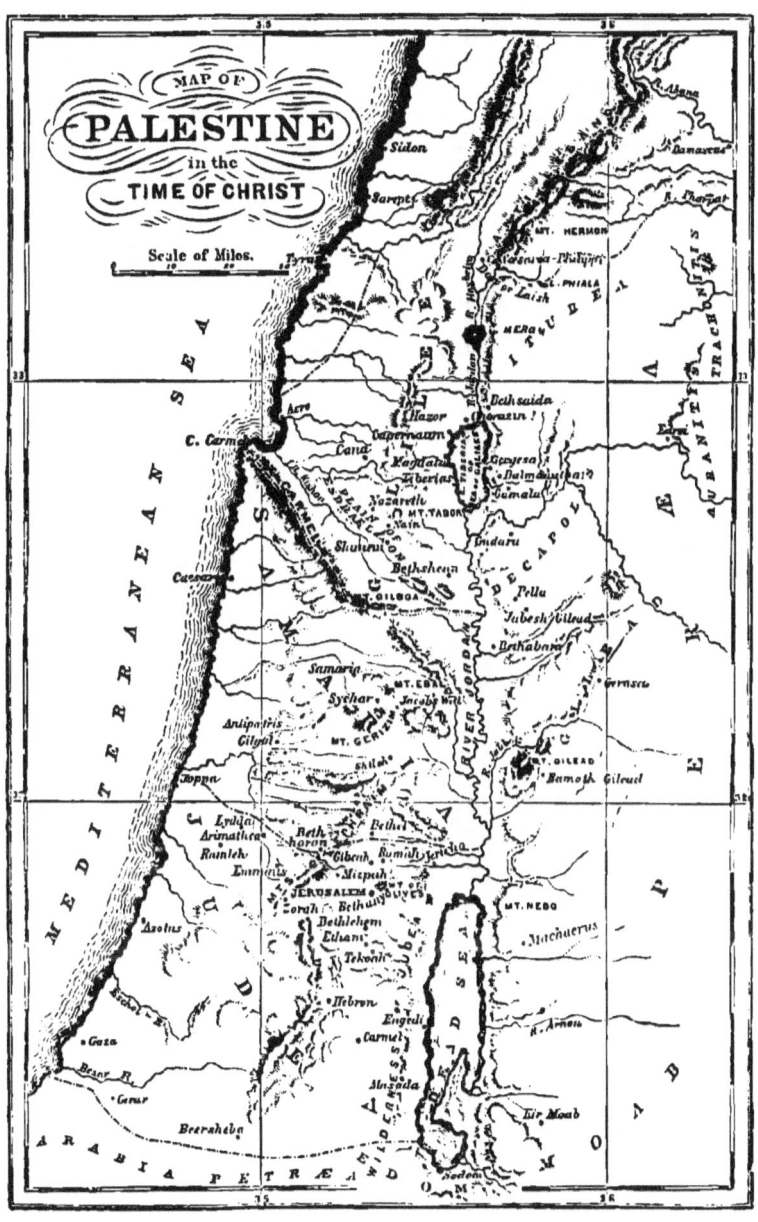

MAP OF

PALESTINE

in the

TIME OF CHRIST

Scale of Miles.

ELECTROTYPED BY
WESTCOTT & THOMSON,
PHILADELPHIA.

PREFACE.

MOST unexpectedly, it falls to my lot to send out the earliest volume in this Commentary on the New Testament. I regret that instead of following I am compelled to lead the way, for I have no doubt that some of my colaborers, with greater learning and experience, are in possession of methods that would make an opening volume better suited to its place. But under the wise leadership of the General Editor each writer, if I may judge from my own experience, is allowed a genuine liberty in modes of working, subject only to some excellent general counsels. The method of exposition that appears in this volume is therefore my own, and other writers are in no sense pledged to follow it. If the reader sees faults in it, he need not fear that they will be perpetuated in subsequent volumes.

As to the method of exposition that I have followed, the Commentary will speak for itself; and yet an introductory word may not be amiss. The reader will find here, I trust, no personal fancies or exegetical refinements. It has been my aim to give the plain, straightforward, practical exposition of reverent common sense. If the method is more homiletical than critical, it is to be remembered that the work is the work of a preacher. I have sought to omit what is needless, and so I have usually given the results of labor without the processes by which they were reached. It has not seemed necessary to spend much time in combating views that I did not accept, or in discussing the claims of various interpretations. Not much, therefore, of a controversial kind will be found here. Nor have I usually made reference to authors whose views I accepted. No man can write without indebtedness to others, but in such a work as this it does not seem desirable to be always citing authorities. My largest indebtedness is of course to Meyer, and my next is, I think, to Dr. Plumptre, who has done admirable work on the synoptical Gospels in Bishop Ellicott's *New Testament Commentary for English Readers.*

I have labored throughout on the principle of faith in the richness of Scripture —in the richness, not of what men may say about Scripture, but of Scripture itself. Especially do I believe in the intrinsic richness of the Gospels. If reverent interpretation can bring out what is really there, it will be plain that there is no

5

need of human additions or supplements, or even of elaborate development of thought, in order that the true light may be seen. The glory of God shines in the face of Jesus Christ, and the knowledge of Jesus Christ is the means to the vision of that glory. As in his life and death his true Divinity and his true humanity were adequately expressed, so in the records of his life and death the living evidences of his true Divinity and his true humanity are to be found; or, rather, there is he himself to be discerned, true man and very God, bringing life and salvation. Hence it is the office of an expositor of the Gospels—and especially of an expositor of this simplest and most vivid of the Gospels, the Gospel of our Lord's visible personality—to exhibit Christ, representing with all possible clearness the portraiture of the living Saviour. For this purpose the expositor should seize upon every means of making the life and its details and the character and its qualities real and living to the reader; for the true subject of his work is not Mark or the Gospel of Mark, but Christ himself. With the desire to show forth his excellence this Commentary has been written. It is one man's humble and willing contribution to the understanding of the holy word and—if God will—to clearness and trueness of thought concerning him whom God hath sent. Many before me have wrought in this divine labor, and many have wrought with so much wider range of knowledge and of power than I that my offering seems but a trifling one; yet in setting forth the excellence of our Saviour no man's earnest labor is in vain. May this tribute, gratefully laid at his feet, be graciously accepted and made helpful to the purposes that he holds dear!

W. N. CLARKE.

OCTOBER 31, 1881.

INTRODUCTION TO THE GOSPEL OF MARK.

THE WRITER OF THIS GOSPEL.

No one of the Gospels except the Fourth contains any internal evidence that helps directly in identifying the author. We are dependent, therefore, upon traditional sources of information; that is, upon information that has been preserved outside of the New Testament. The uniform testimony of Christian tradition is that this book is rightly called the Gospel of Mark, and that the Mark (or Marcus) whose name is associated with it is the Mark who appears in the apostolic history and Epistles. There appears to be no reason for calling this testimony in question.

Mark is first mentioned at Acts 12 : 12, a passage brief but extremely rich in information. We learn, first, that he bore the Hebrew name John (Jochanan), and that a Latin surname—not a Greek—was added to it; from which we infer, though vaguely, some connection, by residence or by social ties, with some Latin-speaking place or people. We learn, further, that his mother was named Mary, and (by implication) that she was a widow. The common English version in Col. 4 : 10 makes her to have been the sister of Barnabas, the companion of Paul ("Marcus, sister's son to Barnabas"); but the word (anepsios) means, more broadly, a cousin—not a nephew—and does not closely define the relation. The connection with Barnabas, however, establishes a connection on some side with the tribe of Levi (Acts 4 : 36). Returning to Acts 12 : 12, we learn from it that the house of Mary was the house to which Peter betook himself when miraculously delivered from prison, and that many were gathered there when he arrived, and were praying; whence we infer that it was a favorite place of resort for the Christians in Jerusalem. It probably contained an "upper room" that was used for worship, possibly the "upper chamber" of Acts 1 : 13, already consecrated by the establishment of the Lord's Supper within its walls. The connection with Barnabas is a fact full of suggestiveness. The house would naturally be his home when he visited Jerusalem. He was there, apparently, and Saul—not yet called Paul—was with him (Acts 11 : 29-30; 12 : 25), at the time of Peter's deliverance; and they, as well as Mark, may have been present when Peter came from the prison. All the Christian leaders would be known at the house of the kinsfolk of Barnabas. The expression "Mark my son" used by Peter (1 Pet. 5 : 13) is commonly taken to show that Mark had been converted through the influence of Peter, probably in early life at his mother's home. The inference may be called probable, but cannot be regarded as certain, for the title might be merely a term of endearment and a testimony to the intimate relations that existed between the two men. It is a conjecture adopted by some that Mark was himself the young man whom he mentions, without naming him, at ch. 14 : 51, 52, who came forth from his bed to join Jesus and his company in the garden.

After the visit of Barnabas and Saul to Jerusalem, they returned to Antioch, and took Mark with them to serve as a companion in Christian labor. When they went out

on their first missionary-journey Mark went with them (Acts 13 : 5) as their "attendant" (*hyperetês*). His office must have been to make necessary arrangements for the
journey, and doubtless to aid in the spiritual work, perhaps to baptize the converts. He
went with them to Cyprus, and thence to Perga in Pamphylia, on the coast of Asia
Minor, but there he departed from them, and returned to Jerusalem. His motives in
returning are nowhere distinctly stated, but Paul long regarded him as worthy of blame
in the matter. It is very certain that Mark "went not with them to the work"—a
fact which Paul probably attributed to fickleness or timidity. On setting out upon the
second journey Barnabas wished to take Mark again, but Paul was unwilling, for the
reason just mentioned; and the disagreement caused the unhappy separation of the two
apostles (Acts 15 : 36—40). Mark became the companion of Barnabas, who returned to
Cyprus, his own country (Acts 4 : 36). We see Mark no more until he appears in company with Peter, who is writing his First Epistle from Babylon. Undoubtedly, this is
not Rome, as some have imagined, interpreting the name mystically, but the ancient
Babylon of the East, where there was a considerable Jewish community, to which Peter
may have been making a missionary-visit. Thus was renewed the relation that was
begun probably in Mark's own home at Jerusalem. There is no reason to suspect that
any alienation had come in between Peter and Mark, or that it was by the alienation
between himself and Paul that Mark was driven back to Peter. He returned before
long to Paul, and next appears in company with him at Rome during Paul's first imprisonment (Col. 4 : 10; Philem. 24). To the Colossians, Paul spoke of him with approval,
as one of the few that were "of the circumcision" who had been "a comfort to him."
At the same time he spoke of Mark as not unlikely to visit Colossæ. Still later, when
Paul was in his last imprisonment, Mark seems to have been with Timothy at Ephesus,
for Paul wrote (2 Tim. 4 : 11), "Take Mark, and bring him with thee, for he is useful
to me for ministering"—*i. e.* "he is such a companion and helper as I need."

This is the latest mention of Mark in the Scriptures. The traditions concerning him
are inconsistent and uncertain. It is alleged that he was at Rome with Peter, serving
as his secretary, but this may be merely an inference from the mystical interpretation
of "Babylon" in 1 Pet. 5 : 13. It is also said that he founded the church in Alexandria,
became the Bishop of it, and suffered martyrdom there in A. D. 68, a few years after the
martyrdom of the two apostles with whom he had labored.

GENUINENESS OF THIS GOSPEL.

There has never been any reasonable doubt that we have in the existing book the
Gospel that Christian antiquity attributed to Mark. The line of historical evidence is
unbroken from very early times. Within the present century it has been questioned
whether the orderly book that we possess is truly described by the language of Papias
that is relied upon for the identification; but the question has not disturbed, and need
not disturb, the confidence of the church in the genuineness of this Christian treasure.
As to the genuineness of the last twelve verses of the book, however, there has long
been doubt. The reasons on each side, and the conclusions that the present writer is
compelled to adopt, will be given in the note on that passage.

PLACE AND TIME OF COMPOSITION.

Of the place, nothing definite is known. Tradition mentions Rome, and no important
variation from this testimony exists; but the mention of Rome is so connected with the
traditions concerning close superintendence from Peter as scarcely to amount to independent testimony. The place must be left in uncertainty.

As to the time of composition there are conflicting traditions. Irenæus distinctly places it after the death of Peter and Paul, but the more general tradition is that the work was done with the knowledge of Peter, and under more or less close supervision from him. It has frequently been noticed that when Paul speaks of Mark to the Colossians (Col. 4 : 10), he introduces him as one who has been a comfort to himself, and as a kinsman of Barnabas; and it has been thought that he would not have confined himself to these particulars if Mark had then had the distinction of a biographer to the Lord Jesus, and especially if his work had represented the remembrances of so highly-honored an apostle as Peter. The argument can scarcely be called conclusive, but it is not without weight. The date of the Epistle to the Colossians, which this argument would make to precede the publication of Mark's Gospel, is, according to Conybeare and Howson, A. D. 62—according to Farrar, 63. The Gospel was certainly published before the destruction of Jerusalem, A. D. 70.

Internal evidence is favorable to the belief in a comparatively early date. The Gospel of Mark contains the record of our Saviour's ministry in the simplest form. While we give no credence whatever to the theory of the gradual growth of the existing Gospels by accretion round a very small nucleus of genuine history—a growth to which reverence and imagination contributed more, perhaps, than memory—still, it appears natural that the simplest and briefest of the Gospels should be the product of the earliest gathering of facts. That each Gospel is independent of the others is certain. But this book reports merely the ministry of Jesus, omitting all that precedes it, and not following the narrative beyond his resurrection. Even within these limits, narrower than those of any other Gospel, it deals mainly with events rather than with teachings. The other Gospels—and most decidedly the latest of them—reveal a purpose in the selection and arrangement of materials—a purpose that corresponds with destination to a certain class of readers. Something of the same is apparent in the Gospel of Mark, but less than in any of the others. Mark betrays less than any other evangelist of any consciousness beyond that of a reporter of the facts. It is impossible to tell precisely at what date any Gospel of the four was sent forth among the Christians, or was written out; but we have little hesitation in speaking of Mark's as the earliest Gospel. Whether or not it is in its present form the earliest-written of the Gospels, it is inwardly the earliest, representing the earliest collation of facts about the life of Jesus.

THE LANGUAGE AND THE READERS.

There is no reason to doubt that the book was originally written in Greek. Suggestions of a Latin original have been made, mainly by Roman Catholic writers, but the idea is probably nothing more than a conjectural inference from the supposed connection of Mark with Rome, which is itself largely dependent for historic support upon the supposed relations of Peter with Rome. In view of the relations of the Latin language to the early churches, it is scarcely possible that an original Gospel in that tongue should have perished and left no trace of its existence.

That Mark designed his Gospel for Gentile readers is established beyond the possibility of doubt by internal evidence. The differences between this book and the Gospel of Matthew are exactly such as would exist between a book for Gentiles and a book for Jews. Mark omits the genealogy of Jesus, which Matthew traces back as far as to Abraham, the father of Israel. He omits the spiritual interpretation of the law, which Matthew preserves in the Sermon on the Mount. Mark never uses the word *nomos*, "law," or, *nomikos*, "lawyer." Never, except in his opening sentence, does he refer in his own person to the Old Testament. The entire structure of the First Gospel reveals a purpose that is wholly wanting in the Second—the purpose to appeal to the Jewish mind in the special conditions of the first Christian age. On the other hand, Mark inserts many words of explanation that would never be needed or thought of in writing for Jews. Notice especially the elaborate account of the customs of "the Pharisees and all the Jews" regarding ablutions, which is by itself sufficient to establish the fact that Mark was writing for Gentiles. Notice also "the river Jordan" (1 : 5), which would scarcely be written for Palestinian readers; the remark that at the time of the Passover "it was not the season of figs" (11 : 13); the mention of the fact that the Mount of Olives was "over against the temple" (13 : 3); the closer definition of the Prætorium (15 : 16); and the only clear definition of "the Preparation" (15 : 42). Notice also that while Mark delights to employ the very words, in the Aramaic tongue, that fell from the lips of Jesus, he uniformly translates them—a thing that he would not do for Jewish readers, a thing that Matthew never does, except in the case of the weighty utterance of Jesus on the cross. (See Mark 5: 41; 7: 11, 34.) The doctrine of the universality of the Gospel, or its destination to all men, is a less striking characteristic feature of Mark's book than of Luke's, but it is more prominent here than in Matthew. Mark, like Luke, had journeyed and labored widely among the Gentiles, and it is plain that for Gentile readers he designed his Gospel.

More closely than this it is impossible to define with certainty the readers for whom this book was prepared. Tradition does something toward connecting the name of Mark with the Christian community at Rome, though its testimony is not so definite and independent as to be unquestionable, and it has often been thought that the Latinisms that Mark uses are confirmatory of the belief that he was writing for Roman Christians. Latinisms are somewhat more frequent in Mark than in the other evangelists, but the inference that he was writing for Romans is too precarious to be trusted. It has already been noticed that the surname of the writer, Marcus, was Latin, and not Greek, and that that fact vaguely suggests some association of his family with some Latin-speaking people or place. Such a connection would account for all Mark's Latinisms. Yet so few are they, and so widely diffused was the Latin tongue, that they scarcely need to be accounted for. In view of the relations that the Greek-speaking countries sustained to the Roman government, there must have been Latinisms everywhere in the Greek of the people, and in writers who were themselves of the common people they would inevitably be found. As a matter of fact, the Gospel of Mark contains eleven words that are Latin words borrowed into Greek. Of these, four—namely, *legeōn*, *kenturiōn*, *spekoulatōr*, and *praitōrion*—are words that came in with the Roman army; two—*dēnarion* and *kodrantēs*—are names of Roman coins; one—*phragelloun*—is the verb that denotes a Roman military punishment; and one—*kēnsos*—is the name of the tribute paid to the Roman government. Thus eight of the eleven words had come into common speech by the presence of the Roman power. Of the remaining three, two are names of objects of daily use—*krabbatos*, "bed," and *xestēs*, "cup"—and the third, *poiēsai to hikanon*, is a Greek equivalent for the Latin verb *satisfacere*. Of these eleven, moreover, only four are peculiar to Mark—namely, *kenturiōn*, *spekoulatōr*, *xestēs*, and *poiēsai to hikanon*. The other seven are found in the other Gospels. In the other Gospels these seven Latin words occur twenty-seven times; in Mark, they occur thirteen times. In such an array of Latinisms there is certainly nothing unusual: Mark merely uses a little more of the everywhere-present foreign phraseology than the others; and no inferences can be drawn from the fact. It may be true that he wrote for the Roman Christians, but it is not proved by his Latinisms.

THE RELATION OF PETER TO THIS GOSPEL.

Christian tradition attributes this book to Mark, and in the comparative obscurity of his name in the apostolic history there is a strong confirmation of its testimony.

To a man who had played so subordinate a part in the history, and a part not entirely creditable, the composition of a Gospel would not be attributed without reason. But Christian tradition is equally uniform in asserting that the book was composed under some influence, less or greater, from the apostle Peter. This belief can be traced back to very early times. Eusebius, of the fourth century (*Hist. Eccl.*, 3, 39), quotes from Papias, Bishop of Hierapolis in Phrygia, who wrote probably before the middle of the second century. He quotes, in turn, from a certain John, whom he calls "the presbyter," whom he cites as having been a disciple of the Lord, and whom he apparently intends to distinguish from John the apostle. Much discussion has arisen about this man, some doubting whether he is to be regarded as any other than the apostle himself. (See the various opinions in *McClintock and Strong's Cyclopædia*, article "John the Presbyter.") The following is the passage from Papias, as translated by Westcott (*Introduction to the Study of the Gospels*, pp. 191, 192, American edition): "This also, then, was the statement of the elder"—*i. e.* of the presbyter: "Mark, having become Peter's interpreter, wrote accurately all that he (Peter) mentioned, though he did not [record] in order that which was either said or done by Christ. For he neither heard the Lord nor followed him; but subsequently, as I said, [attached himself to] Peter, who used to frame his teachings to meet the wants [of his hearers], but not as making a continued narrative of the Lord's discourses. So Mark committed no error, as he wrote down some particulars as he narrated them; for he took heed to one thing, to omit nothing of things he heard, and to make no false statement in [his account of] them."

Other early witnesses to the connection of Peter with this Gospel are Clement of Alexandria, Irenæus, Origen, and Tertullian. Justin Martyr is thought also to allude to this tradition. In Clement the story takes a different form from that which it bears in Papias. When Peter had preached the word in Rome, many hearers of his words requested Mark, as one who had long been with him and remembered what he said, to record what he had stated. Mark did so, and delivered the book to those who had asked for it, Peter neither hindering nor encouraging him in the work. Origen says that "Mark made his Gospel as Peter guided him;" and Tertullian, that "the Gospel of Mark is maintained to be Peter's, whose interpreter he was, ... for it is possible that that which scholars publish should be regarded as their master's work." The tradition naturally grew more definite as time passed, and Jerome said that the Gospel was composed, "Peter narrating and Mark writing." Irenæus, an early authority, having written late in the second century, departs from the general course of the tradition in representing that the book was written after the death of Peter and Paul.

Thus the ancient tradition is not constant or consistent in its representation of details, but it is quite constant in asserting the relation of Peter with this Gospel. The meaning of the word translated, "interpreter," in the passage from Papias, has been much discussed, but the means of obtaining a close definition of it are wanting. It seems most likely that Papias meant to say that Mark became by this writing the interpreter of Peter to the church, the reproducer of Peter's version of the Master's life and deeds. As for the growing definiteness of the tradition, and the gradual extension of the influence attributed to Peter, that would be the natural result of the desire to find apostolic authority for the sacred writings. On the whole, the testimony of Christian antiquity is sufficiently strong and clear to prepare us to find in the book itself the evidences of influence from Peter.

When we come to the internal evidence, we do not find the tradition confirmed in its later and more definite form. There is no sufficient evidence of dictation, or of anything that is virtually equivalent to direct authorship, on the part of Peter. It has been expected that the references to Peter in this Gospel would furnish evidence that his personal feeling had to do with the insertion or omission of matters that related to himself. But while some passages are found that seem favorable to this view, as the notes will show, still it cannot be claimed that in the references to Peter, considered as a whole, there is anything decisively peculiar or characteristic. The real evidence in support of the ancient tradition is found in the fact that the Gospel of Mark manifestly preserves the remembrances of an eye-witness, and of an eye-witness whose relations to Jesus were like those of Peter.

The evidence that this Gospel was enriched by the remembrances of an eye-witness will be presented in detail in the notes, and will be mentioned in general below in the paragraph on the characteristics of this Gospel. It consists in the many graphic details that could scarcely have been brought into the narrative at second-hand. These are often touches of description, especially of the acts, looks, and motions of our Lord himself. Again, they are citations of names and other details that others omit, and of the very words in the Aramaic tongue to which our Lord gave utterance. All these are signs that some one had given to Mark, who was not personally a follower of Jesus, the results of his own keen observation. The evidence of the presence of an eye-witness is found in the whole style of the book and on almost every page.

It is almost equally plain that this eye-witness was some one whose relations with Jesus resembled those of Peter. He was a close companion of Jesus whose opportunities of observation were constant. One of the passages in which the characteristic style of an eye-witness is most apparent is the one that contains the description of the Transfiguration, at which there were present with Jesus only Peter, James, and John. Another is the narrative of the raising of the daughter of Jairus, where no disciples were present except the same three. Moreover, it is a very striking fact that the peculiarly graphic touches of description that are so abundant in the greater part of the Gospel are almost entirely wanting after the record of Peter's denial of his Master. That record stands at the end of the fourteenth chapter. The favorite word *eutheōs* does not occur after ch. 15 : 1. The materials of the story of the Passion, from that point, are much more exclusively than before the same that are used by Matthew, and the characteristic peculiarities, whether of substance or of style, are far less frequent than elsewhere. The proof of this statement may be found in the reading of the narrative in the Greek. Advancing to that part of the book from the preceding part, and reading it in comparison with the other Gospels, one can scarcely fail to be impressed that the keen eye-witness is no longer at his side—an impression that accords perfectly with the belief that the eye-witness was Peter, who was at that time separated in grief and shame from his Master.

Thus, although there is no demonstrative proof of the connection of Peter with the Gospel of Mark, there is a strong probable argument for it. The tradition of the church and the traits of the Gospel fit each other like the parts of a tally.

RELATION TO THE GOSPELS OF MATTHEW AND LUKE.

It has been maintained that the Gospel of Mark was the original source from which Matthew and Luke obtained much of the material for the compilation of their Gospels, and, on the other hand, that the Gospel of Mark is merely an epitome, made by condensation and recasting, of what they had written. But the facts do not correspond to either theory. Each Gospel contains abundant proofs of independence, Mark's not less than the others. It is beyond question, however—indeed, to say so is to utter a truism —that all the evangelists drew upon previously existing materials in compiling their narratives. These materials, ready to their hand, were the substance of the apostolic preaching. In the Gospels—*i. e.* in the Synoptical Gospels—we have "the story" as the Christian preachers were accustomed to tell it. It may already have been written out in part: that question has been warmly discussed—whether the immediate sources of our present Gospels were oral or written. But, in whatever form it may have existed, there was a mass of facts known about the life of Jesus that was common to all the evangelists and to many more. Of these facts, known to them all, forming what has been called a "common tradition," each evangelist evidently made use of such as his purpose required, and added to them such other facts, known perhaps to himself and not to all, as he felt himself justified in adding. It is plain that Mark, aided no doubt by the remembrance of Peter, possessed the facts of the "common tradition" in the most graphic forms, and recorded them more strikingly than the others; but he added to them less than any other evangelist. There are some indications, indeed, that he was careful not to add largely to them—a fact which, if established, would enhance the historical credit of what he did record. It has been suggested, with much reason, that this relation of Mark to the "common tradition" may have had to do with the abrupt ending of his Gospel, and explains the facts about the last twelve verses. (See note there.)

It is worthy of notice that the harmonists of the Gospels usually follow almost entirely the order of Mark, inverting the order of the other evangelists, and making his the basis of their arrangement. Hence in the exposition of this Gospel there is less discussion of questions of order than in treating of the others.

CHARACTERISTICS OF THIS GOSPEL.

In the wisdom of God we are blessed with four portraitures of our Saviour, each with a character of its own. The Fourth Gospel, it is true, differs largely from the others in purpose and method, and even occupies a place by itself in the records of divine revelation; and yet perhaps the Second, the Gospel of Mark, is the one that bears its character most unmistakably upon the surface, and most readily impresses its conception of the Saviour on the reader's mind. Scarcely does a more thoroughly intelligible and self-interpreting piece of literature exist anywhere than the Gospel of Mark. Yet the clearness does not seem to result mainly from high skill in the author. This is not so much a triumph of art as a masterpiece of nature; that is to say, a genuine and natural utterance, under divine guidance, of what a man of clear sight and picturesque language knew about Jesus. It is a picture out of real life, so clear and recognizable because of its reality. As we read we do not need to be told how the writer got his vivid impressions: we know that they are the genuine impressions of actual experience.

The Gospel of Matthew portrays our Saviour in his relation to the Old Covenant, and especially to the new kingdom, long promised, that was now coming to take its place. This is the Gospel of the kingdom. The Gospel of Luke represents him in his wide and tender human relations as the blessing of mankind. The Gospel of John reveals him in his divine glory, coming forth to the world, doing battle, by self-revelation, with its sin and darkness, and spiritually glorified as the Son of God, though rejected and slain by men. The Gospel of Mark presents him to our sight in the midst of the intense activity of the life to which his divine mission brought him. The order of the four as they stand in our Bible is a happy thought of the church. First stands the Gospel of the Messiah, and of the kingdom that he brought into the world. Then comes the Gospel of the mighty Worker, exhibiting the abundant energy that made his life among men great and beneficent. Next follows the Gospel of the Son of man, overflowing with tenderness and love to the race unto which he came. Then, to crown the whole, comes the Gospel of the Son of God, bringing the revelation of One who is at once the ancient glory of the heavens and the sufficient hope and joy of the earth.

Coming to the Second Gospel, with which we are concerned, we may note the following as some of its characteristics: (1) It is the briefest of them all. It is so partly because it is the narrowest in its historical limits. It does not touch upon the birth or early life of Jesus, but meets him at his baptism. It follows him only through his ministry, and, strictly, only through his Galilæan ministry, passing over, like the other Synoptists, the early ministry in Judæa. It breaks off abruptly just after the announcement of the resurrection. It confines itself exactly within the limits proposed by Peter in speaking of the choice of a new apostle, and observed by him in instructing the household of Cornelius (Acts 1 : 22; 10 : 36–43). It has to do solely with the period of our Saviour's activity. (2) As between the words and deeds of Jesus, the division of matter is very different from that of the other Gospels. Mark records about as many miracles as Matthew or Luke: they have twenty each, and he, with his smaller space, has nineteen. But, while Matthew records fifteen parables and Luke twenty-three, Mark records only four, one of which has been preserved by him alone. He does not preserve the Sermon on the Mount, and alludes in other connections to but very few of the sayings that it contains. The address at the sending out of the apostles he greatly abbreviates. Of the great circle of parables delivered on the last journey to Jerusalem, recorded by Luke, he has nothing. Only in recounting the prophetic discourse on the Mount of Olives does he approach to the others in fulness; and even here he is the briefest of the three. His book is emphatically a book of deeds, not of words. It is the Gospel of action. It makes us feel that when God was manifested for us men and our salvation there was for him no rest. An appropriate motto for the Gospel has been said to be the saying of Peter to Cornelius: "Jesus of Nazareth, how that God anointed him with the Holy Ghost and with power; who went about doing good, and healing all that were oppressed of the devil; for God was with him." But in deeper truth his own saying could be taken for the motto of this Gospel: "My meat is to do the will of him that sent me, and to accomplish his work." (3) Although Mark's record is the briefest, it is given with a fulness and richness of detail that imparts to it a peculiar value. He scarcely mentions any event without adding something to our knowledge of it. These additions are made partly by the particularity of his statements, and partly by the picturesqueness and expressiveness of his language. The former fact bespeaks the presence of an eye-witness—the latter, the fact that the eye-witness had a genius for vivid description. We owe to Mark, on more than one occasion of intense interest, our knowledge of the very look and expression of our Saviour's face, of the very words that he uttered in the Aramaic tongue, and of the lifelike and instructive details in many a picture. It is impossible to tell which Gospel we could best spare. Many readers would say, perhaps, "The short Gospel of Mark; that contains so little matter that is not provided to us by the others." Happily, we are not called to choose; and if we were, we might well be extremely sorry to part with this fresh, living, pictorial Gospel, from which we have derived far more than we are aware of the distinctness of our conception of our Saviour. The bright, enlightening words that reveal our Master to our hearts will be pointed out in the notes as we come to them, and it seems scarcely necessary to enumerate any of them here.

THE

GOSPEL ACCORDING TO MARK.

CHAPTER I.

THE beginning of the gospel of Jesus Christ, the[a] Son of God.
2 As it is written in the prophets,[b] Behold, I send my messenger before thy face, which shall prepare thy way before thee.

1 THE beginning of the gospel of Jesus Christ, [1]the Son of God.
2 Even as it is written [2]in Isaiah the prophet, Behold, I send my messenger before thy face, Who shall prepare thy way ;

a Heb. 1 : 1, 2....*b* Mal. 3 : 1.——1 Some ancient authorities omit *the Son of God*....2 Some ancient authorities read *in the prophets*.

Ch. 1 : 1-8. MINISTRY OF JOHN THE BAPTIST. *Parallels*, Matt. 3 : 1-12 ; Luke 3 : 1-18.—The earliest of the four Gospels begins latest in the life of our Lord, and concerns itself exclusively with his public ministry, the sole preface being a brief account of the work of his forerunner. This is due partly, perhaps, to the fact that it was the earliest—for the first thought would naturally be to gather up the record of his words and deeds among men— but probably more to the fact that it was composed far from the land of the Jews, and for people who would have little interest in the genealogy of Jesus, or in anything but the work by which he had become precious to them. So, while John begins from eternity, Matthew from Abraham, and Luke from the events that preceded the birth of the forerunner, Mark finds the forerunner already at work, and introduces Jesus at the time of his baptism. It is noticeable, in view of the traditional belief that this Gospel was composed under the influence of Peter, that its limitations of time correspond with those mentioned by Peter in Acts 1 : 21, 22, where he says that the successor of Judas in the apostolate must be one who has been with them all the time, "beginning from the baptism of John." Mark and Peter begin from the same point.

1-4. INTRODUCTION. ANNOUNCEMENT OF THE GOSPEL.—**The beginning of the gospel of Jesus Christ, the Son of God.** The word "gospel" is probably not yet used of the written record, as "the Gospel of Mark." Rather is it here the good news of the kingdom, regarded as proclaimed; and "the beginning of the gospel" means, in its connection here, "Thus began the glad tidings of Jesus Christ to be proclaimed, as the prophets foretold : John came baptizing in the wilderness." The gospel of Jesus Christ is the gospel, or good news, concerning him, of which he is the substance. Jesus ("saviour") is the personal name, and Christ ("anointed") is the official title ; but the two form in Scripture virtually a double name, which is not exactly represented by

2

"Jesus the Christ." It is a very significant fact that his religion has taken its name, "Christian," from his official title, and not from his personal name. In whatever way the name may first have been given, it has been recognized as true to the facts ; and the Founder of the faith has thus been accepted as not only the Son of Mary, but the Messenger of God, and his relation to the eternal purpose has been exalted even above his personality. If the words "the Son of God," which are omitted in some manuscripts, are genuine, they obtain a special significance and interest from the confession of Peter, "Thou art the Christ, the Son of the living God" (Matt. 16 : 16).

As it is written, etc., is not to be connected grammatically with verse 4 ("As it is written, John did baptize, etc."), but rather with verse 1. It is an expansion of the idea of the beginning, or a statement of the way in which the beginning had been announced. Instead of **in the prophets,** the best text reads "in the prophet Isaiah." There are two quotations from the prophets placed in one paragraph, of which only the second is from Isaiah, the first being from Malachi (Mal 3 : 1 and Isa. 40 : 3). The quotation from Isaiah was perhaps the more prominent in the writer's mind, and in rapid style the one name is used instead of two. Possibly when he wrote the name he may have intended to make only one quotation, but the other may then have flashed into his mind as a suitable introduction to the one of which he was thinking.—Malachi had declared that before the sudden coming of Jehovah to his temple he would send a messenger who should prepare his way before him. In the conception of the evangelist the prediction is addressed to the Messiah himself. **Before thy face, who shall pre-pare thy way.** "Before thee" should probably be omitted. The authority for applying this prediction to John the Baptist is Jesus himself, in Matt. 11 : 10 ; Luke 7 : 27. The other passage that is cited here was quoted by the Baptist himself as descriptive of his office (John 1 : 23), and is definitely applied to him by the other

15

3 The voice of one crying in the wilderness, Prepare ye the way of the Lord, make his paths straight.
4 John⁶ did baptize in the wilderness, and preach
the baptism of repentance for the remission⁶ of sins.

3 The voice of one crying in the wilderness,
Make ye ready the way of the Lord,
Make his paths straight;
4 John came, who baptized in the wilderness and
preached the baptism of repentance unto remission

a Isa. 40 : 3 ....*b* Matt. 3 : 1; Luke 3 : 3; John 3 : 23....*c* Acts 22 : 16.

three evangelists, Luke quoting it at greater length than the others. In its original connection it was not as definite an historical prediction as the one from Malachi, but beyond doubt the Divine Spirit in the prophet was looking forward to the advent of the Messiah and the preparation for it. As an Oriental king sent his herald before him, calling on all to make ready the way for his royal progress and to build or put in order the roads through the country that he must pass, so the coming of the Messiah should be prepared by the summons to spiritual readiness. The grouping of these two passages makes a fine paragraph for the writer's purpose. He thus opens his book by connecting the glad tidings with the ancient Scriptures; but the destination of his book to Gentile readers is plainly seen in the fact that these are the only quotations from the Old Testament that the evangelist himself makes in the whole book, chap. 15 : 28 being omitted from the best text. He records citations by our Lord, but he makes none of his own.

Now comes the announcement of the "beginning" itself. **John did baptize in the wilderness.** Westcott and Hort's text reads "John the baptizer came (*egeneto*) in the wilderness;" the definite article being inserted before the participle, making it virtually a proper name, and almost equivalent to the "Baptist." Mark omits all preliminary account of John, as he does of Jesus, and introduces him thus abruptly as a well-known personage. His silence is compensated by the remarkable fulness of Luke's narrative concerning the birth of John and of Jesus. There is no reason to suppose that Mark was ignorant of the facts that he omitted. Throughout his book he is the evangelist of action, and the omission of all preliminaries is entirely characteristic.—**John** was the near kinsman of Jesus, six months his senior, whose office it was (Luke 1 : 17) "to make ready a people prepared for the Lord." This preliminary work he was to accomplish by announcing the approach of the Messiah, calling the people to repentance, and pledging them through baptism to a new and holy life. Josephus speaks of him under the name of John the Baptist (*Ant.* 18. 5. 2), saying of him, "He was a righteous man, and called the Jews to be baptized and to practise virtue, exercising justice to men and piety to God." Ablutions

for the purpose of purification were well known to the Jews, and the washing with water had long had among them its natural symbolic significance as a sign of spiritual cleansing. But it had been used by divine authority only in certain cases of ceremonial purification, as in the consecration of priests (Ex. 29 : 4) and the purification of lepers (Lev. 14 : 8). It has been claimed that such ablution, or immersion, was in use before John appeared, as an initiatory act for proselytes, but the historical evidence does not prove that the custom was established so early. The baptism of John attached itself to the idea of purification by ablution, and was popularly understood by the help of that idea; but it was peculiar in being detached from all other ritual forms, removed from all special occasions in the life, and enjoined upon all the people. To all comers it was proposed as an act of confession corresponding to an inward change of mind and purpose respecting sin. It is here described, as to its meaning, by two expressions : (1) It was a **baptism of repentance** —*i. e.* it solemnly pledged him who received it to repentance. Repentance is a deep change of mind and purpose respecting sin—a change that includes forsaking as well as regret, a change that will have, if genuine, its appropriate "fruits." John not only called the people to repentance, but gave them this outward act in which to profess it and pledge themselves to the corresponding life. (2) It was **for the remission of sins**—*i. e.* the obtaining of forgiveness for a sinful life was the end to which submission to baptism was one of the means. Not that pardon was promised or expected upon submission to baptism, in itself regarded; but this act, in which repentance was confessed and reformation of life was promised, was evidently a suitable act for one who wished to forsake his sins and be forgiven. If a man honestly sought full remission, it was only right that he should perform this act: so Peter said on the day of Pentecost (Acts 2 : 38); and so it could fitly be called a baptism for, or with reference to, the remission of sins.

Of the form of the act nothing is here said, except by the use of the word *baptize* (*baptizo*). In Grimm's *New Testament Lexicon*, after the general definition of the word (which is, 1. To immerse repeatedly, to immerse, to submerge; 2. To wash by immersing or submerging; 3.

5 And there went out unto him all the land of Judæa, and they of Jerusalem, and were all baptized of him in the river of Jordan, confessing[a] their sins.

6 And John was clothed with camel's hair, and with a girdle of a skin about his loins; and he did eat locusts[b] and wild honey.

5 of sins. And there went out unto him all the country of Judæa, and all they of Jerusalem ; and they were baptized of him in the river Jordan, confessing their

6 sins. And John was clothed with camel's hair, and *had* a leathern girdle about his loins, and did eat

---

a Lev. 26 : 40–42 ; Ps. 32 : 5 ; Prov. 28 : 13 ; 1 John 1 : 8.....*b* Lev. 11 : 22.

To overwhelm) the following statement of the New-Testament use is given: "In the New Testament it is used principally of the solemn rite of sacred washing first instituted by John the Baptist, afterward received at the command of Christ by the Christians and adapted to the subject-matter and character of their religion— *i. e.* immersion performed in water, in order that it might be a sign of vices and sins removed (*abstersorum*), received by those who, led by the desire of salvation, wished to be admitted to the benefits of the Messianic kingdom." It formerly seemed necessary to prove that John's baptism was immersion; but now no writer touches the subject without assuming that fact, and one may be pardoned for passing lightly over the evidence. The time has fully come when the form of John's baptism should no longer need to be discussed.

In the wilderness. Matthew, "in the wilderness of Judæa." No place is more closely specified as the chief seat of John's labors. He doubtless baptized in several places, but probably the only one that would be found in "the wilderness of Judæa" was at the lower ford of the Jordan, or near it, not far from Jericho. That "wilderness" included the wild country on the west of the Jordan and north of the Dead Sea. This would be a convenient place for the multitudes from Judæa and Jerusalem who flocked to him. On the place where Jesus was baptized, see notes on verse 9.

5. EFFECT OF JOHN'S WORK.—The preaching of John was the **beginning of the gospel** as Mark proposed to tell of it, and the result was a great popular movement.—**There went out to him all the land of Judæa, and they of Jerusalem.** Hyperbolical language, meaning that men of all classes, in great numbers, went out to him.—**Were baptized**—imperfect tense, "were being baptized." The verb does not assert, as it would in the aorist, that all who went out received baptism.—**Baptized of him.** He was the only administrator. He was alone in his office, and there is no evidence that he ever divided his work with any. After his death others may have taken up his preaching of repentance, not knowing or not accepting Jesus, and may have baptized under his name (Acts 19 : 3). Of his

manner in immersing, probably, Western practice would give us very little correct conception. In Oriental lands such a rite would be less formal and deliberate than with us.—**Baptized in the river of Jordan.** A definite statement corresponding exactly with the meaning of the word "baptize"—*immersed in the river.* Perhaps we have in the word "river" one of the explanations that Mark added for the benefit of Gentile readers not familiar with the localities of which he wrote.— **Confessing their sins.** A somewhat emphatic expression in the Greek, which apparently refers to something more than an indeterminate "*Peccavi*"— "*I have sinned.*" John was thoroughly practical, and probably he drew out from those who came to him a practical confession. Yet not all who came confessed and were baptized: some refused, and some were refused. Not all who were baptized were truly penitent; but the approved disciples of John, as a class, were truly penitent men before they left him to follow the greater Master. The effect of his teaching is seen in the readiness with which some of his disciples turned from him to Jesus. (See John 1 : 35–51, but not Matt. 4 : 18–22. See notes below.) When baptism was first proclaimed, there was no one to question that it must be an intelligent and deliberate act. To propose the baptism of unconscious human beings, or of one person in view of another's repentance, would have been too plain a contradiction of the whole spirit and aim of John's mission. Yet surely his mission was not more distinctly spiritual than that of his Master.

6. DESCRIPTION OF JOHN'S MANNER OF LIFE. —**Clothed with camel's hair.** of which a coarse, rough cloth was made. The garment was probably the burnouse, or mantle, which the Bedouins still wear; and the leathern girdle was such as the poor use to this day. His figure reminds one of the prophet in whose "spirit and power" John had come, and they are probably right who suppose that John intentionally assumed the appearance and habits of Elijah (2 Kings 1 : 8), in which some of the later prophets also had resembled him—at least, as to the texture of garments (Zech. 13 : 4).—His food was **locusts and wild honey.** Locusts, which are very abundant in that land, were

2

7 And preached, saying, There* cometh one mightier than I after me, the latchet of whose shoes I am not worthy to stoop down and unloose.

7 locusts and wild honey. And he preached, saying, There cometh after me he that is mightier than I, the latchet of whose shoes I am not 'worthy to stoop

a Matt. 3 : 11 : John 1 : 27 ; Acts 13 : 25.——1 Gr. *sufficient.*

"clean" according to the law of Moses (Lev. 11 : 22), and formed, as they still do form, a part of the food of the poor, although it is said that at present they are somewhat despised, as the food of the very poorest. Some travellers have affirmed that they found them palatable when cooked as the people cook them—oftenest by boiling. Wild honey was also abundant, deposited sometimes in trees, as at 1 Sam. 14 : 25, and sometimes in crevices of the rocks (Deut. 32 : 13 ; Ps. 81 : 16). These few details, given in almost identical words by Matthew and Mark,

LOCUSTS.

make up almost the whole of our picture of the personal life of John ; yet our picture is very distinct and lifelike. It includes the main points in the living of an ascetic—a home in the wilderness ; no need of helps or appliances, or provision from beyond his immediate locality ; no dependence on men ; rough clothing, such as the sternest of the prophets had worn, and such as men have often worn for the sake of doing penance ; and such food as nature offered to a hermit. This was no new way of life to John when his ministry began. His aged parents probably died while he was still young, and he "was in the deserts" (Luke 1 : 80), most likely in some such life as this, from his youth to his ministry. Many of his hearers may have brought their luxuries, or at least

their comforts, with them to his preaching ; but John was still the ascetic.

7, 8. John's Preaching.—Mark's report is only a fragment, but a fragment that is perfectly characteristic of him and of his Gospel. This is the Gospel of action. The messenger before the Messiah has come, and now he is in the act of announcing the One who is to come after him. The call to repentance is omitted, as already implied, and only the proclamation is given. **There cometh one mightier than I after me,** or "behind me"—not merely "one," but the one "mightier than I," for the definite article points out a definite individual. It is the superior spiritual power of the Messiah that is here joyfully announced by the forerunner. John may have felt with pain his own inability to change the heart, and even so to read the heart as to avoid being deceived by men ; and so he may have loved to think of the Messiah as the mightier One by whom the things impossible to him should be done.—Before one so much mightier John takes the humblest position. **The latchet of whose shoes I am not worthy to stoop down and unloose.** The latchet was the thong or strap by which the sandal was bound upon the foot ; and, as it was the office of a servant to bear the shoes (Matthew), so it was perhaps a still humbler duty of his to loosen them from the Master's feet. **I am not worthy,** says John— "I am not *hikanos*—suitable, a fit person—to do for him even this most menial service." This is not to be taken as a bold figure of speech on John's part, going perhaps beyond his feeling. It was an honest utterance of humility, from one of the most humble men that ever lived. This was his sincere opinion of the difference between himself and the Messiah whom he had not seen.

Verse 8 illustrates that surpassing spiritual power of the Messiah before which John stands in reverence. The means of illustrating it John finds in his own baptism.—**I have baptized**

8 I indeed have baptized you with water: but he shall baptize⁸ you with the Holy Ghost.

9 And it came to pass in those days, that Jesus came from Nazareth of Galilee, and was baptized⁶ of John in Jordan.

8 down and unloose. I baptized you ⁷in water; but he shall baptize you ⁷in the Holy Spirit.

9 And it came to pass in those days, that Jesus came from Nazareth of Galilee, and was baptized of John

a Joel 2 : 28; Acts 1 : 5; 2 : 4; 10 : 45; 11 : 15, 16; 1 Cor. 12 : 13....6 Matt. 3 : 13; Luke 3 : 21.——1 Or, with

you with water. Aorist, not perfect. Matthew and Luke, "I baptize you," present tense. Mark conceives of John as addressing those whom he has already baptized.—**But he shall baptize you with the Holy Ghost.** As baptism, administered by John, is an overwhelming in water, so shall that which the Messiah imparts be an overwhelming in holy, spiritual influences. He shall merge and whelm men as John has done, and that, too, in a cleansing element; but not in water. Mightier is he, and mightier cleansing influences attend him. He shall do by the Holy Spirit that actual work of renewal and purification of which the baptism of John has been only the symbol. "His work shall surpass mine," says John, "as far as the Holy Spirit surpasses water in actual power to purify." This is to predict for the Messiah a real work, an actual whelming of men in the life-giving, holy influences of the Divine Spirit. The fulfilment of this prediction is not to be found in any gift or gifts peculiar to the apostles: the language of the passage forbids that, as well as the sense of the prediction. The object of the verb in both clauses is the indefinite "you"—"I baptized you, he will baptize you"—and the natural reference is to all who receive his influences. This is a general description of the spiritual work of Christ. The baptizing in the Holy Spirit is not any single act or event in the history of Christ's kingdom; the figure is a noble characterization of the quality and power of his work. It was illustrated on the day of Pentecost, and in the miraculous gifts of the apostolic age (Acts 11 : 16, where Peter recognized an illustration of it), and in the graces that were better than miraculous gifts (1 Cor. 13). It is illustrated still whenever Christ through the Holy Spirit makes new creatures of men and sanctifies his people. Christ is still, as "John the baptizer" called him (John 1 : 33), "the baptizer in the Holy Spirit" (ho baptizōn en pn. hag.). Luke (3 : 16) omits en before hudati and reads, "I baptize you with water," instead of "in water," the dative being the instrumental dative. On this difference Winer remarks (Grammar of the N. T., Thayer's edition, p. 412): "Sometimes we find in parallel passages a preposition now inserted and now omitted. This difference of phraseology does not affect the sense, but each form of expression rose from a different conception. Baptizōn en hudati signifies, 'baptize in water' (immersing); baptizein hudati, 'baptize with water.' Here the identity of the two expressions in sense is manifest; yet we must not consider one as put for the other." Observe, however, that, with pneumati, en is always used: it is always "baptize in the Holy Spirit," never "with." Mark omits the baptism in fire by which in Matthew and Luke the Baptist completes the representation of the superior might of the Messiah.

9-11. THE BAPTISM OF JESUS. Parallels, Matt. 3 : 13-17; Luke 3 : 21, 22.—Matthew alone tells of the hesitation of the Baptist; otherwise, the three reports differ but very slightly.

9. In those days. The time is indefinite, nor is it plainly identified in the other records. The place of the baptism is indicated by John 1 : 28, which says John was at that time baptizing at "Bethabara"—or by the best text Bethania, "beyond Jordan." The Palestine Exploration Fund identifies this as one of the upper fords of the Jordan, still known as 'Abarah, within a day's journey of the early home of Jesus. It is thought that Bethania is meant for Batanea, a name given to the district on the east of the river.—**Jesus came.** Thus informally does Mark introduce to his story the One but for whom it would never have been written. He writes for those who already know him; but so do those who prepare more elaborately for his entrance to their story. Mark is pressing forward to the story of action.—**From Nazareth of Galilee.** His quiet home for nearly thirty years. The impression made by the record is that he came alone, not in a caravan of comers, and directly from his own abode. The moment of his withdrawal from the long retirement was determined in his own heart, which was guided, no doubt, partly by what he heard of the work of the Baptist. In the great movement of godly reformation, when the people were awakened somewhat to holy things, he was drawn to go out and cast in his lot and life with the work, and so to take his appointed place. There is no wrong in thus recognizing the influence of the movement in calling him out. But why was he baptized? Not with the baptism of repentance for the remission of sins, but with the baptism of consecration to the work that lay before him. He was a man and was living under the limitations of. humanity, and he

| 10 And straightway coming up out of the water, he saw the heavens opened, and the Spirit,[a] like a dove, descending upon him: | 10 [b]in the Jordan. And straightway coming up out of the water, he saw the heavens rent asunder, and the |

a Isa. 42 : 1 ; John 1 :32.——1 Gr. into.

would not fail to "fulfil all righteousness"—
i. e. to do all that a man ought who was going
forth to a great work for God and his kingdom.
He was "made like unto his brethren " (Heb. 2:17),
and the step that was suitable to a man was suitable to him—not arbitrarily, but because what
had a meaning to a man had a meaning to him.
As men could consecrate themselves to a holy
life and work in baptism, so could he; and so
he did, pledging himself to the higher activity
of that Messianic life on which he was only
then entering. Moreover, as men may seek
strength for work that is before them by "fulfilling all righteousness"—*i. e.* by obediently
submitting to the ordinances of God—so could
he; and so he did, taking this as one step in
the way by which he was to be "made perfect"
as the "Captain of salvation." The difficulties
that have been suggested by the fact that he
submitted to baptism are due, in great measure,
to the instinctive but erroneous and unscriptural impression that the Son of God must
have been separated in some way from the
common lot of humanity. On the contrary,
he was perfectly identified with the common
lot of humanity ; and that fact, when we learn to
understand it, will tend to make his life at once
far more intelligible and far more adorable—more
truly human and more gloriously divine.—Jesus
came, and **was baptized of John in Jordan.**
Literally, not "in," as in verse 5, but "into"
(*eis*)—a phrase that is as suitable as the other
to the meaning of *baptizō.* It is the very act
of immersion into the river that is represented.

10. The Visible Sign of Acceptance.—Here
first we meet with Mark's characteristic word,
euthus, which, with its cognate *eutheōs,* he uses a
little more than forty times, the words being
variously translated "immediately," "forthwith," "straightway," in the English version.
Coming up out of the water, after the baptism. The best text has *ek,* "out of," instead of
apo, "from."—**He saw**—*i. e.* Jesus. John also
saw the vision (John 1:32-34), but there is every
reason to believe that no others saw it.—**The
heavens opened,** or, rather, "rent open."
The same word as in Matt. 27:51: "The rocks
were rent." It is a present participle here, indicating that he saw the very process of opening. Matthew and Luke use the common word
for "opened," and so the strong, graphic word
is peculiar to Mark. Luke says that he was
praying. Exactly what is meant by "the

heavens rent asunder" who can tell? We are
reminded of Stephen's vision (Acts 7 : 55, 56) and
of the longing of the prophet (Isa. 64 : 1) : "Oh
that thou wouldest rend the heavens, that thou
wouldest come down!"—Whether the Son of God
saw any vision in the opened heavens we cannot know ; but from the opened heavens he saw
**the Spirit, like a dove, descending upon
him.** Mark and the Baptist himself (John 1 : 32) say
"the Spirit ;" Luke, "the Holy Spirit ;" Matthew,
"the Spirit of God."—**Like a dove**—*i. e.* in a
dovelike form, and not merely, as some have
understood it, with a dovelike motion, as a dove
descends. The Baptist adds, "And it abode upon
him." The descent of the dovelike form was of
course symbolic—a visible picture of an unseen
spiritual reality. If this unquestionable statement is admitted, it follows at once that there
was then granted to the God-man some fresh
impartation of the Divine Spirit. The whole
subject is in the realm of mystery, and must
remain there; and yet the recognition of the
human limitations in the life of Jesus may
contribute something to the understanding of
it. It is the work of the Spirit in man to convince concerning sin, and concerning righteousness, and concerning judgment—*i. e.* to awaken
great and controlling convictions concerning
moral evil and moral good, and the discrim-
ination that is made between them in the government of God. These were the convictions,
residing in the divine mind, out of which came
the counsel of redemption. It was necessary
that the mind of Jesus, so far as it was human,
should be brought into perfect accord with these
convictions of the divine mind; and so we can
see how there was reason that the Spirit should
be given to him—"not by measure" (John 3 : 34),
but in unlimited fulness. It is the work of the
Spirit in man, also, to inspire the sense of sonship (Rom. 8 : 16; Gal. 4 . 6) and the spirit of filial
prayer (Rom. 8 : 26, 27); and plainly it was possible
and desirable for the human spirit of Jesus to
be raised to the divine standard in these respects.
If the language of Gal. 4 : 6 is true of us, "Because ye are sons, God hath sent forth the Spirit
of his Son into your hearts, crying, Abba,
Father"—if the Spirit that constrains to the
filial cry is sent to us "because we are sons"—
was there not still greater reason why the human spirit of Jesus should be visited by the
same Spirit of filial love? He "was a son,"
and needed the perfect sense of sonship. Just

11 And there came a voice from heaven, *saying*, Thou art my beloved Son,*a* in whom I am well pleased.
12 And immediately the Spirit driveth him into the wilderness.

11 Spirit as a dove descending upon him: and a voice came out of the heavens, Thou art my beloved Son, in thee I am well pleased.
12 And straightway the Spirit driveth him forth into

a Ps. 2 : 7.

now he was at the threshold of his great work, and this was the moment when he most needed whatever endowments were to come upon him from above. Here alone is the Holy Spirit represented by a dove. The symbolic meaning has been variously interpreted; perhaps it was not meant to be minutely understood. The thought may be that the Divine Spirit is a Spirit of gentleness, or that the Father looks tenderly upon the Son who does always the things that please him and sweetly sends upon men his helpful influence, but, besides all the meaning of the event for Jesus himself, it was intended as a sign whereby John should identify the Messiah (John 1 : 32-34).

11. THE AUDIBLE SIGN OF ACCEPTANCE.—A voice from heaven, Thou art my beloved Son, in whom I am well pleased. Literally, "I delighted."—Thou art. So Mark and Luke; Matthew, "This is."—In whom. For this the best text reads "in thee."—I delighted. Aorist, not present; so in all three. Jesus heard the voice; John certainly did not hear it. The descent of the dove had been given him beforehand as a sign, and he recognized it and used it for evidence. If he had heard the voice, it is very strange that he mentioned the dove and omitted to mention this, which would have served his purpose of identifying the Messiah still better. There is no proof that the voice was ever appealed to as evidence or was meant for evidential use. The voice seems to have been meant for Jesus only, and to have been heard by him alone. It was probably intended as a sign of acceptance to Jesus himself. Accordingly, it is "Thou art" rather than "This is" my beloved Son. The utterance at the transfiguration, plainly evidential in its purpose, was, "This is my beloved Son." At the baptism the public work was at hand, and the new impartation of the Spirit had come; and the moment was a fitting one for a cheering word. As for the force of the communication, the English version obscures it by rendering *eudokēsa* like a present, when it is an aorist: "Thou art my beloved Son; in thee I delighted." When? See John 17 : 24 : "Thou lovedst me before the foundation of the world." The voice from heaven at the beginning of the ministry is the counterpart of this claim in the prayer at the end. At this important hour the Father assures Jesus anew of his identity

with the pre-existent Logos, in whom God from eternity delighted. The ministry would be full of trials, and the quickly-impending temptation might suggest doubts of his own identity with the Holy One of God. By this utterance the identification was completed for the consciousness of Jesus, and there is no reason to suspect that any doubt of it ever crossed his mind in any of the trials of his life or the agonies of his death. Of course, the whole subject of our Lord's consciousness must remain mysterious to us; but this view rests upon the fact that he was subject to the limitations of human growth, and that there was a progress in his consciousness of what he was, which progress was crowned by the full conviction that he now received. What he learned thereafter was (Heb. 5 : 8) how to live and die as God's beloved Son in the purpose of working out salvation for men.

12, 13. THE TEMPTATION OF JESUS. *Parallels*, Matt. 4 : 1-11; Luke 4 : 1-13.—Mark's report is the merest outline, barely serving to put the temptation in its proper place in the history. The evangelist of action presses on to the public ministry, merely outlining what precedes. But he cannot draw an outline that is not lifelike, and this swift sketch is a graphic one. Immediately is to be taken literally: the next event after the baptism is the temptation, and after John had baptized Jesus he saw him no more till after the forty days.—The Spirit driveth him, or thrusts, or urges, him out. Matthew and Luke say, with a milder word, that he was " led " by the Spirit. (Same as in Rom. 8 : 15.) Mark's word tells of a strong irresistible impulse; doubtless such an impulse as he had never felt before, for the Spirit was already doing new work in him. Mark does not say that he was urged forth "to be tempted," but only that he was urged forth to the wilderness. Neither does Luke and Matthew's language does not declare that he went intending or expecting to meet temptation. From Mark we should infer that he went out to be alone, desiring solitude for his own sake. The place is undetermined, but was probably somewhere in the wilderness of Judæa.—If Mark's account had been intended for a full statement, it might perhaps seem to be in conflict with the fuller record of Matthew and Luke, for it reads as if the temptation continued through

13 And he was there in the wilderness forty days, tempted of Satan; and was with the wild beasts; and the angels ministered unto him.

14 Now after that John was put in prison, Jesus[b]

13 the wilderness. And he was in the wilderness forty days tempted of Satan; and he was with the wild beasts; and the angels ministered unto him.

14 Now after that John was delivered up, Jesus came

a Matt. 4 : 1 ; Luke 4 : 1, etc....*b* Matt. 4 : 23.

the **forty days ;** but if it is taken as a concise statement that does not attempt details, we need feel no difficulty.—Even in this brief outline there is one fresh detail not given elsewhere. **And was with the wild beasts.** No description could more vividly set forth his deep retirement and his utter seclusion from men. Of the wild beasts Plumptre says: " In our Lord's time these might include the panther, the bear, the wolf, the hyena, possibly the lion and the serpent." It is a wonder that this scene has not been seized upon in apocryphal Gospels as the foundation for stories about the power of our Lord's purity and gentleness in restraining and subduing the wild animals.— **And the angels ministered unto him.** After the conflict, as we learn from Matthew. In this brief record the great conflict is not detailed, but we have the scene, the deepest wilderness; the contestants, Jesus and Satan; the only spectators, the wild beasts; the helpers of the victorious Christ, the angels. The absence of men is far more strongly emphasized than in the other records. Observe that the narrative of the temptation must have come to the evangelists from the Lord himself. When he was tempted he had no disciple to "tarry and watch" with him (Matt. 26 : 38). The proposals of Satan as to the way to found a kingdom were repelled when no soul of man had believed on him. Faith and righteousness had to be their own witnesses to his soul.

The discussion of the temptation does not belong in this volume. It may not be amiss to say, however, that such thoughts as would throng upon the Christ at this point in his career would be the very ones for the tempter to seize upon if he wished to destroy the virtue of the Son of God. This is the moment of his life at which there is the greatest natural fitness in such a transaction. The place of the story, therefore, is one of the facts that commend it to us as a true part of the biography of Jesus.

14, 15. THE BEGINNING OF THE MINISTRY OF JESUS IN GALILEE. *Parallels,* Matt. 4 : 12-17; Luke 4 : 14, 15; John 4 : 1-3, 43-45.—The return to Galilee here mentioned is not the first return, which occurred not long after the temptation. Mark, with the other synoptists, omits all reference to the first visit to Galilee and the early Judæan ministry, and

resumes the story at the time of the imprisonment of the Baptist. The events here passed over are narrated in John 1 : 19-4 : 42. They may be summarized thus: After the temptation Jesus returns to John, who publicly bears witness to him as the Lamb of God; several disciples of John attach themselves to Jesus, who, accompanied by them, goes to Galilee, attends the wedding at Cana, where the first miracle is wrought, and spends a few days at Capernaum; at the time of the passover he returns to Jerusalem, purifies the temple, performs miracles, and is visited by Nicodemus; he leaves Jerusalem for some other part of Judæa, where he baptizes, by the hands of his disciples, many who believe on him; John, who is still baptizing, again bears testimony to him as the One at whose coming he is glad to retire; now John is thrown into prison (an event that is nowhere recorded in its own order, but comes in only by allusion, mentioned by Luke in anticipation, and by Matthew and Mark as a reminiscence), and Jesus, his fame still spreading, leaves Judæa and returns to Galilee, as recorded in verse 14; on the way he passes through Samaria, meets the Samaritan woman at the well, and spends two days among her neighbors; after which he comes "in the power of the Spirit into Galilee" (Luke) and preaches, as Mark proceeds to tell. John, who reports so fully the preceding period, including the Judæan ministry and the northward journey, is brief in his account of this ministry in Galilee, telling only of the welcome that Jesus received, of his visit to Cana, and of the healing of the nobleman's son. This narrative is peculiar to John; peculiar to Luke is the report of our Lord's visit to Nazareth and preaching in the synagogue there, only to be rejected; then follows a group of events in Galilee, recorded by all the synoptists, the record extending in Mark from chap. 1 : 14 to 2 : 22. From the synoptists we should never suspect that there had been an early Judæan ministry; while from John we should never have learned the extent of this ministry in Galilee.

14. For the imprisonment of John see chap. 6 : 17 and notes there. The word here is not properly **put in prison,** but "delivered up"— the same word that is constantly applied to the deed of Judas and translated "betrayed." Hav-

came into Galilee, preaching the gospel^a of the kingdom of God.

15 And saying, The time^b is fulfilled, and the kingdom of God is at hand: repent^e ye, and believe^d the
gospel.

16 Now^e as he walked by the sea of Galilee, he saw
Simon, and Andrew his brother, casting a net into the
sea, (for they were fishers.)

---

15 into Galilee, preaching the gospel of God, and saying, The time is fulfilled, and the kingdom of God
is at hand: repent ye, and believe in the gospel.

16 And passing along by the sea of Galilee, he saw
Simon and Andrew the brother of Simon casting a

---

a Luke 8 : 1....b Dan. 2 : 44 ; 9 : 25 ; Gal. 4 : 4 ; Eph. 1 : 10....c Acts 2 : 38....d Rom. 16 : 26....e Matt. 4 : 18, etc. ; Luke 5 : 4, etc.

---

ing heard of the event (Matthew). Jesus returned to Galilee.—**Of the kingdom** should
probably be omitted, and we should read
"preaching the gospel of God," the glad tidings which God was now sending by the Messiah. There is no evidence that Jesus proclaimed the glad tidings in Galilee during his
brief visit there soon after his baptism. This
is not his first preaching, however, as a reader
of Mark might suppose, for he had been some
months laboring in Judæa.

15. The time is fulfilled. Literally, "has
been fulfilled." The "fulness of time" has
come; the moment chosen and foretold has
arrived.—**The kingdom of God.** The reign
of God over men in the Messiah, the predicted
establishment of a spiritual power in the world
—misunderstood, however, and supposed to be
the establishment of a great national power by
divine authority.—**Is at hand.** Literally, "has
come near." It has approached in point of
time, and it has approached through the agency
of preaching; it is here offered to the Galileans,
ready to be received as to the spirit of it, and
they will see more and more of its spiritual
glory as the Messiah's work goes on.—In saying, **Repent ye,** the Messiah takes up the
word of his forerunner, and continues the
preaching that the multitudes have heard by
the Jordan. If the kingdom is at hand, the
only right work for men is to break off their
sinful life and bring forth fruits worthy of repentance. Here there is no contrast or difference between the forerunner and the Christ.
The word "repent" is sometimes supposed to
belong to the law, and repentance is conceived
of as something preparatory to the gospel; but
repentance is an evangelical experience, and
only in the light of the gospel, with its promise
of new spiritual life, does the call to repentance
become intelligible as a word of grace.—**And
believe the gospel.** Literally, "believe in
the gospel"—a peculiar form of expression
found here alone : "Put your trust, repose
your confidence, in the good news of God."
The preaching thus briefly reported was done
quite widely through Galilee, and was widely
accepted with joy: so Luke informs us. John
attributes the welcome that Jesus received to

the knowledge of his miracles which the Galileans had obtained at the passover. Doubtless
the warmth of the welcome was increased by
"the gracious words that proceeded out of his
mouth" and the mighty works that soon appeared.

16-20. THE RE-CALLING OF FOUR DISCIPLES.
Parallel, Matt. 4 : 18-22.—Luke 5 : 1-11 appears
to be parallel as a narrative of the calling of
these disciples, but there are considerable difficulties in the harmony, and no one who looks
for a rigid correspondence in the narratives can
think for a moment that Luke was recounting
the same event. There are difficulties in either
view, but it seems most probable that the three
evangelists had the same event in mind.

16. Jesus had returned to Nazareth, but after
his rejection there he had made Capernaum his
home (Luke 4 : 31). **Simon and Andrew.** By
a common oversight, this is often spoken of as
the first call of the two brothers, and their
readiness to follow Jesus is attributed to the influence of the Baptist in preparing them for
him. But they had been among his very earliest followers, had witnessed his first miracle,
had been with him at the passover, had been
his companions in labor in Judæa, even baptizing disciples for him, and had come with
him through Samaria into Galilee. (See note
above.) To Simon, Jesus had long ago given
the name "Cephas," the equivalent of "Peter"
(John 1 : 42). After coming up through Samaria
to Galilee his followers seem to have scattered
to their homes—a proceeding for which no reason is given. But he had left Judæa to escape
hostile observation, and perhaps he thought it
best to begin in Galilee alone, and gather his
circle again when he was ready ; or it may have
been for reasons connected with their affairs
that he let them go. In any case, no doubt
they expected to be called again to follow him.
—Now he came upon them by the shore of the
lake, **casting their net into the sea,** or
"casting about in the sea," as in the best
text—*i. e.* casting their net now on one side
of the boat, and now on the other. If Luke
5 : 1-11 is parallel, the word strikingly illustrates the answer of Simon : "Master, we have
toiled all the night and have taken nothing."

17 And Jesus said unto them, Come ye after me, and I will make you to become fishers of men.
18 And straightway they forsook their nets, and followed him.
19 And when he had gone a little further thence, he saw James the son of Zebedee, and John his brother, who also were in the ship mending their nets.
20 And straightway he called them: and they left their father Zebedee in the ship with the hired servants, and went after him.
21 And they went into Capernaum: and straightway

17 net in the sea: for they were fishers. And Jesus said unto them, Come ye after me, and I will make you to become fishers of men. And straightway
19 they left the nets, and followed him. And going on a little further, he saw James the son of Zebedee, and John his brother, who also were in the boat
20 mending the nets. And straightway he called them: and they left their father Zebedee in the boat with the hired servants, and went after him.
21 And they go into Capernaum; and straightway on

It even shows them in the midst of the fruitless toil.

17. Fishers of men. "Ye shall gather men in great numbers for the kingdom of God." They knew from their own experience what he meant, and could well believe the promise. Jesus utters no call without a promise.

18. It was already a case of "my sheep hear my voice, and I know them, and they follow way that he had gone when he met James and John. John had certainly been with him as long as Simon and Andrew, and so, probably, had James. (See note on chap. 3 : 17.) In the boat were Zebedee, his two sons, and some hired servants. The mention of the servants proves the family to have been above poverty. Out of the five or more in the boat, only two were called. It does not appear whether Zebedee ever became a disciple, but his wife, Salome,

SITE OF CAPERNAUM.

me" (John 10: 27). The renewing of the call indicates that, imperfect as they had been, they had on the whole been true, and that he saw in them "chosen vessels" (Acts 9: 15) for his purpose. Their alacrity is a sign that they were not unwilling to hear again the familiar voice and to resume the place of disciples. It was "immediately" that they left their nets and followed him; so that they were with him when, a little farther along the shore, he came upon the other pair of brothers, their old companions, "both in the flesh and in the Lord."

19, 20. Mark adds that it was only a little afterward followed Jesus in such circumstances as to suggest that she had before that become a widow.—Mark's graphic style appears in the final picture. **They left their father Zebedee in the ship with the hired servants, and went after him.** Did he grudge them to Jesus? Parents sometimes wish him not to lay too exacting a hand upon their children.

21-34. THE EVENTS OF A SABBATH IN CAPERNAUM. 21-28. THE HEALING OF A DEMONIAC IN THE SYNAGOGUE. Parallel, Luke 4 : 31-37.—**They went** or enter) **into Capernaum,** as one company whose lot is hence-

on the sabbath-day he entered into the synagogue, and taught.
22 And* they were astonished at his doctrine; for he taught them as one that had authority, and not as the scribes.
23 And* there was in their synagogue a man with an unclean spirit; and he cried out,
24 Saying, Let *us* alone; what have we to do with thee, thou Jesus of Nazareth? art thou come to destroy

the Sabbath-day he entered into the synagogue and 22 taught. And they were astonished at his teaching: for he taught them as having authority, and not as 23 the scribes. And straightway there was in their 24 synagogue a man with an unclean spirit; and he cried out, saying, What have we to do with thee, thou Jesus of Nazareth? art thou come to destroy

a Matt. 7:28.....b Luke 4:33, etc.

forth cast together, the call having taken place outside the town.—**Straightway on the Sabbath-day**—*i. e.* at the first opportunity, on the first Sabbath that came. The **straightway** or "immediately" expresses Mark's sense of the promptness of his action—losing no time, hastening to his work.—**He entered into the synagogue, and taught.** Literally, in the best text, "He taught into the synagogue"—*i. e.* having entered the synagogue, he taught. It was the best way of reaching the people in their religious hours. There was no exclusive office of teaching in the synagogues. In Nazareth he indicated his desire to speak, and it was granted (Luke 4:16); and at Antioch in Pisidia, Paul and Barnabas were asked if they had any word of exhortation (Acts 13:15).

22. They were astonished at his doctrine. An unfortunate translation which has helped to render distant, vague, and unreal the popular conceptions of our Lord's life and influence. It was his "teaching," not his doctrine, that amazed them. The remark is identical with the one that Matthew places at the end of the Sermon on the Mount. No wonder that such amazement more than once arose.—**For he taught them,** or "was teaching them"—*ēn didaskōn*, almost identical with the imperfect, but containing somewhat more of the descriptive element.—**As one that had authority, and not as the scribes.** A broad contrast, most accurately drawn by these few words. It was by the freshness and independence of his teaching that they were so profoundly impressed. He spoke as one who knew that he had a right to speak. The scribes were mere copyists and interpreters; everything came at second-hand; they neither had nor claimed any independent authority. In the midst of their small and narrow questionings and their stale utterances of second-hand opinion the strong and positive preaching of Jesus came in like a breath of morning air. "We speak that we do know," he said of himself (John 3:11). His "I say unto you" was such a word as they had never before heard. No wonder that they drew the contrast with the scribes; and yet the scribes held the multitude in a bondage that he did not

break. "Ye receive not our witness," he said, positive and true though it is.

23-26. A man with an unclean spirit. Mark's first mention of a demoniac. The difficulties that beset the whole subject of demoniacal possession are very great, and perhaps they will never be entirely removed. The recorded cases are all essentially alike, and in examining this one, the earliest, it will be well simply to look at the recorded facts and see what is given us as the material for a judgment upon the nature of the evil. The word "devil" is never right; it is always "demon." Here the man is said to be *en pneumati akathartō,* "in an unclean spirit"—*i. e.* in such a spirit as the element in which he lived; in the power of such a spirit. "Unclean" means unholy, malign, defiling. Luke calls this "a spirit of an unclean demon." As for the state of the man, it is plain that in this case he was not so wild as to avoid society or so violent as to be restrained from entering the synagogue. Whether he had friends present does not appear. The man spoke out, perceiving and knowing Jesus, without having been addressed; and so it was by his own act that he came under the notice of Jesus. In his address the authorities are divided as to whether *ea*, "let alone," should be retained (in Mark; it is unquestioned in Luke), and between "I know thee" and "we know thee" (in Luke, "I know thee"). In his excited cry three elements appear—recognition, repulsion, dread. The repulsion is first expressed, then the dread, and then the recognition of character, which is of course the foundation of both. If the reading is accepted that gives the plural, "we know thee" (as it is by Tischendorf), the form of speech will indicate that this utterance of one is made in behalf of many, or by one as the representative of a class.—**What have we to do with thee, Jesus of Nazareth** (or Nazarene)? Literally, "What to us and to thee?" There is no question about the plural here. Here is powerful repulsion, the feeling that the two belong to opposite kingdoms and have nothing whatever in common. The language reappears exactly in another case to which the same character is ascribed (chap. 5:7). In calling Jesus a

us? I know thee who thou art, the Holy One of God.
25 And Jesus rebuked him, saying, Hold thy peace, and come out of him.
26 And when the unclean spirit had torn him, and cried with a loud voice, he came out of him.
27 And they were all amazed, insomuch that they questioned among themselves, saying, What thing is this? what new doctrine is this? for with authority commandeth he even the unclean spirits, and they do obey him.

us? I know thee who thou art, the Holy One of God. 25 And Jesus rebuked ¹him, saying, Hold thy 26 peace, and come out of him. And the unclean spirit, ²tearing him and crying with a loud voice, 27 came out of him. And they were all amazed, insomuch that they questioned among themselves, saying, What is this? a new teaching! with authority he commandeth even the unclean spirits, and they

1 Or, it....2 Or, convulsing

Nazarene it is quite credible that a hostile mind may have been willing to gratify its own bitterness by seizing upon any well-known term of reproach.—**Art thou come to destroy us?** Here is dread of the mission of Jesus regarded as a powerful enemy, and dread that apparently extends throughout the class to which the speaker conceives of himself as belonging. This instinctive cry, if it is really such, betrays their expectation of great evil from his coming. This language also is reproduced, substantially, in the similar case just mentioned.—**I know thee**—or "we know thee"—**who thou art, the Holy One of God.** The ground of the repulsion and dread. All Jews would recognize this as a title of the Messiah; and the sentence declares that the speaker, or else the class that he represents, has recognized Jesus as the long-expected Deliverer of men, and feels that men are now to be delivered from demoniac power. At the same time, his holiness is the quality that suggests the name that shall express the hatred.—**The reply of Jesus is simply Hold thy peace,** or "Be silent," **and come out of him.** Here, as always in such cases, he distinctly assumes that there is a personality that can be addressed apart from that of the man, and is able to leave the man. Whatever demoniacal possession may have been, nothing is more certain than that Jesus did thus address demons as resident in men and command them out. He further refuses to allow the testimony that this personality offers to him as the Messiah; so, still more distinctly, in other cases, as at verse 34. Apparently he assents, in the spirit of it, to the "What have we to do with thee?" To this word of Jesus there is a response as of a conscious person—a movement as of rage at being compelled to leave the victim, a final convulsing of the victim's body, a final cry as of inarticulate rage; so, still more distinctly, in other cases, as chap. 9 : 26. But the most evident and significant response is obedience to the command to "come out of him," for the victim is quickly left free from the evil power.

Concerning these representations it may be said, (1) The conduct of the man, taken by it-

self, could be accounted for on the ground of mere insanity; it is not questioned that, if there was genuine possession, it produced insanity. (2) The conduct of Jesus, taken by itself, cannot naturally be accounted for on that theory; he assumes something different from insanity—namely, the presence of an evil spirit. (3) When the conduct of the man is regarded in the light of that of Jesus, all comes into harmony: the man acts as one so possessed might be expected to act, and the intruder is treated as such an intruder would by Christ be treated. (4) Though such possession is unexplained, it cannot be shown to be impossible. (5) The only alternative belief to that of the reality of possession is that Jesus allowed the popular belief in the reality of possession to pass uncontradicted, and acted as if it were true, because he knew that the people were not prepared for any other way of dealing with the subject. The principle of accommodation in divine teaching is scriptural (Matt. 19 : 8), but this theory presents it in an extremely difficult form, appearing even to cast doubt on the moral sincerity of our Saviour. It is a modern fashion to scoff at the reality of demoniacal possession, but the difficulties that attend the denial of it in the recorded cases seem to be quite as great as those that are involved in accepting it. (For further illustration, see notes on chap. 5 : 2-13 and 9 : 14-27.)

27, 28. The teaching and the miracle awakened astonishment and inquiry. **What thing is this?** etc. The text in verse 27 is to be changed; but after the true reading has been ascertained there is some question as to the punctuation of the sentence. Some connect the words **with authority with he commandeth the unclean spirits.** It seems more natural, especially in view of what is said in verse 22, to connect it with the teaching. Tischendorf's text may be translated thus: "What is this? New teaching with authority; and the unclean spirits doth he command, and they obey him." The two answers to the question, "What is this?" refer to the two parts of what had just occurred in the synagogue, the teaching and

28 And immediately his fame spread abroad throughout all the region round about Galilee.
29 And forthwith, when they were come out of the synagogue, they entered into the house of Simon and Andrew, with James and John.
30 But Simon's wife's mother lay sick of a fever; and anon they tell him of her.
31 And he came, and took her by the hand, and lifted her up; and immediately the fever left her, and she ministered unto them.

28 obey him. And the report of him went out straightway everywhere into all the region of Galilee round about.
29 And straightway, [w]hen they were come out of the synagogue, they came into the house of Simon and Andrew, with James and John. Now Simon's wife's mother lay sick of a fever; and straightway they
31 tell him of her: and he came and took her by the hand, and raised her up; and the fever left her, and she ministered unto them.

a Matt. 8 : 14 ; Luke 4 : 38.——1 Some ancient authorities read when he was come out of the synagogue, he came &c.

the miracle. By "new teaching with authority" is meant a teaching that is new in that it has authority: the quality of authority is the new element. To them, accustomed to the endless iteration of the scribes, authority was a novelty, and they exclaimed in wonder when they felt its power. After this had come to mind the miracle was rehearsed, and the wonder at the power of his mere command was renewed. Charms and incantations for the purpose of exorcism were in common use, and apparently they sometimes seemed to be successful (Matt. 12 : 27), but he commanded, and it was done. But observe that the freshness and independence of our Lord's teaching made upon these hearers an impression that even a miracle following it could not efface. As they went home from the synagogue they talked of both, and remembered that such an innovation as authoritative teaching had been introduced in their presence. Observe, too, that no word of this impressive teaching has been preserved to us. We might imagine that the words that have not been preserved for the use of the church were lost. Not so: they had their effect in preparing the apostles to do for the church what they have done; and they entered in also to make up that personal impression of Christ upon the world which rendered Christianity as a living religion possible. If Christ had said less, the apostles would have been less, and the manifested Redeemer would have taken a less powerful hold upon men. No word was lost, and we are still reaping the benefit of utterances of which we have no knowledge whatever.—The fame that went out was the fame both of his teaching and of his mighty works, though doubtless the latter were the greater with those who heard. The best text adds "everywhere" before through-out all the region round about Galilee; and the thought is that his fame spread even beyond Galilee, to the surrounding regions generally.

29-31. Healing of Peter's Wife's Mother.—From the service in the synagogue directly to the house of the disciples. Mark

alone indicates, by one of his quick and unstudied references, that the brothers Simon and Andrew lived together, and that James and John went home with them from the worship in the synagogue as friendly guests—a pleasant glimpse of social and family life, with Jesus in the midst. "A man's foes shall be they of his own household" (Matt. 10 : 36), but by no desire of Jesus. The way in which he constituted the band of apostles put high honor upon the family. (See notes on chap. 3 : 16-19.) Simon's wife's mother. Of her we know nothing but what is recorded here. "Wife's mother" is the right translation of penthera, which means a "mother-in-law;" used of a husband's mother in Matt. 10 : 35. It distinctly implies that Peter was married; and that his wife was not afterward put away from any feeling in favor of celibacy is evident from 1 Cor. 9 : 5, where it appears that she accompanied her husband in his apostolic journeyings. The same passage shows that "the other apostles" also had wives at that time who journeyed with them; but no wife but Peter's is alluded to in the Gospels.—Lay sick of a fever. Luke calls it a great fever.—Anon once meant "immediately," which is the right word here.—The process of healing is variously described. Luke says, "Standing over her, he rebuked the fever;" Matthew, "He touched her hand;" Mark, more minutely, and he came, and took her by the hand, and lifted her up.—The cure is described by the same word in all. The fever left her, the same as in John 4 : 52.—She ministered unto them. Performed such service as the presence of guests in the house required. Luke says that she rose and went about the work "immediately," calling attention to the instantaneousness of the cure. There is no indication as to whether she had any special faith: none appears to have been asked for by our Lord. She must have known much about him, and may have been of a believing heart; but it cannot be shown that Jesus always required faith in himself as a condition of healing.

32 And at even, when the sun did set, they brought unto him all that were diseased, and them that were possessed with devils.
33 And all the city was gathered together at the door.
34 And he healed many that were sick of divers diseases, and cast out many devils; and suffered not the devils to speak, because they knew him.
35 And in the morning, rising up a great while before day, he went out, and departed into a solitary place, and there prayed.
36 And Simon, and they that were with him, followed after him.
37 And when they had found him, they said unto him, All *men* seek for thee.
38 And he said unto them, Let us go into the next towns, that I may preach there also: for therefore^a came I forth.

32 And at even, when the sun did set, they brought unto him all that were sick, and them that were possessed with demons. And all the city was gathered together at the door. And he healed many that were sick with divers diseases, and cast out many demons; and he suffered not the demons to speak, because they knew him^1.
35 And in the morning, a great while before day, he rose up and went out, and departed into a desert place, and there prayed. And Simon and they that were with him followed after him; and they found him, and say unto him, All are seeking thee. And he saith unto them, Let us go elsewhere into the next towns, that I may preach there also; for to

a Isa. 61 : 1, 2; John 17 : 8.——1 Or, *demoniacs*.....2 Many ancient authorities add *to be Christ.* See Luke iv. 41.

32-34. The Healing of Many at Evening.—This group of miracles belongs really to the same Sabbath, though strictly the Sabbath was over before it began. The general movement to bring him the sick and the possessed was suggested by the healing in the synagogue, but was delayed till after sunset, out of reverence for the Sabbath. Mark adds, characteristically, that **all the city was gathered at the door**, and characteristically omits Matthew's remark that here the prophecy was fulfilled, "Himself took our infirmities, and bare our diseases" (Isa. 53 : 4). The coolness and quiet of the evening—how congruous to the work of healing, especially after the heat and frenzy of demoniacal possession! Mark says that they brought all and he healed many; Matthew, that he healed all; Luke, that he laid his hand on every one of them and healed them.—**He suffered not the devils—demons—to speak, because they knew him.** Implying that they would have spoken, and doubtless in the strain of verse 24. The reason for the prohibition was probably the moral incongruity. "The demons also believe and tremble" (James 2 : 19); but it was not fitting that their testimony to the Holy One of God should be allowed to go among the people as one of the evidences of his mission.

35-39. Jesus Retires to Pray, is Followed by his Disciples, and Enters upon a Wider Ministry in Galilee. *Parallels*, Matt. 4 : 23; Luke 4 : 42-44.—The time is apparently the next morning; so, still more distinctly, in Luke. **A great while before day.** The designation of the hour is peculiar to Mark. "Early, far into the night," is nearly an exact translation. It seems probable that the day just spent was the first day of so intense and prolonged miraculous activity in the life of Jesus.—Very naturally might the thoughts suggested by such an ex-

perience banish sleep and impel him to prayer. So, alone, the darkness still unbroken, he **went out** from the house, leaving his friends to their sleep, and sought **a solitary place**, some uninhabited, lonely spot where he might pray. An impressive illustration of his love of prayer, and of his desire to be alone for communion with his Father.

36, 37. Simon and they that were with him—i. e. Andrew, James, and John, and perhaps some others.—**Followed after him.** The word is a strong compound word that tells us that they followed until they found him. Luke does not tell who the pursuers were, but adds their motive in mentioning the entreaty that he would not depart from them. In Mark it is simply, **all men seek for thee.** The disciples did not go out merely for themselves, but as the messengers of the towns-people, who had begun to inquire where Jesus was, and who wished him to remain among them. As he had gone away quietly, they feared that he did not intend to return, and so sent this message after him.

38. But he had other plans, more in keeping with his mission; he did not intend then to return to Capernaum. After **let us go** should probably be inserted "elsewhere" (*allachou*).—**Into the next,** or neighboring, **towns.** *Komopolcis*—literally, "village-cities"—is found here alone in the New Testament; it well corresponds to our word "towns."—**That I may preach there also.** It is preaching, not the working of miracles, that he proposes as the object in this ministry. In Luke, "In the other cities also must I preach the kingdom of God." In Capernaum he was desired probably for the miracles of healing that he might work, but another kind of labor accorded better with his purpose.—**For therefore came I forth**—i. e. not merely to preach, as distinguished from the working of miracles, but more especially to

39 And he preached in their synagogues throughout all Galilee, and cast out devils.
40 And^a there came a leper to him, beseeching him,

39 this end came I forth. And he went into their synagogues throughout all Galilee, preaching and casting out demons.
40   And there cometh to him a leper, beseeching him,

a Matt. 8 : 2; Luke 5 : 12.

preach elsewhere than in Capernaum, to labor in a wider field.— **Came I forth**—whence? Standing by itself, the language might naturally mean "came forth from the house in Capernaum;" and yet the impression made by the story is that he had gone forth from the house to pray, rather than in order to set out on a new tour of preaching, and that when his disciples joined him, and told of the popular clamor for him in Capernaum, he determined to go elsewhere instead of returning. Some have supposed that he referred to his ministry as a whole, and so to his "coming forth" from his retirement at Nazareth; but Luke quotes him as saying, "Because for this I was sent"— *apestalen*, the word from which "apostle" is derived. If the one passage interprets the other, Jesus tells in Mark for what purpose and kind of work he "came forth" from God, using the word *exelthon* in the same sense as in John 8 : 42 and 16 : 28. This well sets forth the character of his mission: he did not come to fasten himself to any single place and give himself to the service of any single people; he must reach outward, to other regions. An example of the missionary impulse—not only an illustration, but an example. It is not enough for his gospel to bless any Capernaum; it must go out into other regions. His mission has been transmitted to his people (John 17 : 18; 20 : 21), and in their hands it is of the same kind as in his: it allows no sitting down at home and confining the privileges to the privileged. The word of the Master is "Go" (Matt. 28 : 19),—a word which he has illustrated for us by his own example.

39. Accordingly, his tour extended to **all Galilee;** but the language is popular, not exact. Galilee was a crowded region, and he cannot have visited strictly every part. Within this tour probably falls the ministry in Chorazin and Bethsaida, or some part of it (Matt. 11 : 21). None of the mighty works performed in these cities do we see, except the later miracle of Mark 8 : 22-26. The length of this tour has been very variously estimated, but cannot be exactly ascertained; it is safe to say that it must have covered some weeks. The activity of this time was not confined to preaching: he was casting out demons as well. Matthew states it still more strongly: "Healing all

manner of sickness and all manner of disease among the people." Performing miracles in a fresh ministry, on a new field, was a different thing from continuing to perform them in Capernaum, where they were desired as a local honor and advantage.

40-45. WHILE PREACHING IN GALILEE, JESUS HEALS A LEPER. *Parallels,* Matt. 8 : 2-4; Luke 5 : 12-16.—The place and time are unknown; Luke, "When he was in one of the cities." This is the first recorded healing of leprosy; two healings of fever and one of demoniacal possession have been recorded, and one of paralysis immediately follows. Leprosy is minutely described for the purposes of the law in Lev. 13, and the office of the priest in connection with the recovery from the disease in Lev. 14. Leprosy was a frequent disease among the Israelites, from the time of the Egyptian bondage. In the Mosaic code it was recognized as a most suggestive type of sin, and was employed, in a manner that is not entirely plain to us in our ignorance of much that belonged to the disease, as an object-lesson in religious instruction. The principal signs of the disease were the appearance of a white spot or swelling in the flesh, with inflammation and cracking, and the exuding of a humor from the affected part, in connection with which the skin became scaly, hard, and white. While the disease was spreading upon his body the leper was totally "unclean," and was obliged to separate himself strictly from other persons and allow no one to come near him. The provisions of the Mosaic law on the subject were very peculiar, as the study of the two chapters named will show, and our knowledge of the disease is not such as to enable us to account for them all. It is not certain that the fear of contagion will explain them; indeed, there certainly was a religious element in the horror of the disease. Doubtless it was intended that leprosy should teach a lesson respecting moral defilement.

40. There came a leper to him. The ten lepers, in Luke 17 : 12, stood afar off, according to the law, but this man appears to have violated the law by his approach to Jesus. He came and knelt—so near that a stretching out of the hand would reach him. Luke's language places him among the more severely afflicted of

and kneeling down to him, and saying unto him, If thou wilt, thou canst make me clean.

41 And Jesus, moved with compassion, put forth *his* hand, and touched him, and saith unto him, I will; be thou clean.

42 And as soon as he had spoken, immediately⁴ the leprosy departed from him, and he was cleansed.

43 And he straitly charged him, and forthwith sent him away;

44 And saith unto him, See thou say nothing to any man: but go thy way, shew thyself to the priest, and offer for thy cleansing those things⁴ which Moses commanded, for a testimony⁴ unto them.

¹and kneeling down to him, and saying unto him,

41 If thou wilt, thou canst make me clean. And being moved with compassion, and touched him, and saith unto him, I will; be thou

42 made clean. And straightway the leprosy departed

43 from him, and he was made clean. And he ⁵strictly

44 charged him, and straightway sent him out, and saith unto him, ²see thou say nothing to any man: but go, shew thyself to the priest, and offer for thy cleansing the things which Moses commanded, for a

a Ps. 33:9; John 15:3....*b* Lev. 14:2, 32....*c* Rom. 15:4; 1 Cor. 10:11.——1 *Some ancient authorities omit* and kneeling down to him....2 Or, sternly

---

lepers, to whom this was forbidden.—His coming announces his eagerness to be healed; his words indicate that he had confidence in the power of Jesus to heal him, probably from what he had heard or seen; but his words appear to indicate an inferior faith in his willingness. **If thou wilt, thou canst make me clean.** Yet the inferiority of his faith in the willingness can scarcely have been more than apparent. If he had not believed in the willingness of the Healer perhaps more profoundly than he was aware, he would not have been prostrate at his feet. Nevertheless, while he was venturing boldly upon his power, he had not gone beyond the point where he felt that he must humbly entreat the consent of his will. How many there are still who know the Saviour's heart no better!

41. It is Mark that adds **moved with compassion, put forth his hand and touched him.** So all three reports. Of course there was no need of touching him in order to perform the cure; even the Roman centurion knew that (Matt. 8:8). To touch him was not exactly a violation of the law; the violation was rather in the permission of it by the leper. But it was a plain declaration of his indifference to ceremonial defilement. It was done in order to illustrate for the man the depth and freeness of his word, **I will.** That word, **I will, be thou clean,** would have been enough; but if the man had any doubt of the fulness of his consent, no thought of defilement should stand in the way for a moment. Doubts of his power might be dispelled by miraculous works; but doubts of his love must be removed by acts of love. What utterance of consent and willingness could be richer and sweeter than the voluntary touching of the leper? It is interesting that the question and answer and the record of the touch are preserved in the selfsame words by all three evangelists: the beauty of the scene and its value in showing the heart of Jesus did not fail to make a deep impression.

42. The best text omits the words **as soon** **as he had spoken.** The cure was instantaneous, however, and complete. Not in vain had the man ventured upon the power and willingness of Jesus. Did Jesus endeavor to remove the ceremonial defilement that resulted from contact with a leper?

43, 44. He straitly charged the man to be silent, as in Matt. 9:30 and Mark 5:43; but here the word is a very strong one, of which "sternly charged" would be a better translation. It implies severity in tone and manner. The word translated **sent away** is also a strong word, being the common word for "casting out" evil spirits. Jesus urged the man quickly away, with a very stern injunction of silence about the miracle.—Verse 44 contains the substance of the strict charge. Jesus would not have the miracle noised abroad, but he would have the man restored to his place in society. The local and temporary reasons for enjoining silence are of course beyond our reach. **Go thy way, shew thyself to the priest.** The priest had nothing to do with the healing of leprosy, but he was the officer who must certify to the reality of healing before a man could take his place among his friends. He must examine the man, pronounce him clean, receive from him and present in his behalf certain offerings, and perform over him a prescribed symbolic ceremony (Lev. 14). The command of Jesus is that the man shall carry his offerings to the priest and get his certificate of health.—**For a testimony unto them.** Not to the priests, for only "the priest" has been mentioned (alike in the three records), but to the people: "For an evidence to the community that your leprosy is gone." Other interpretations, such as, "For a testimony that, after all, I reverence the law," and "For a testimony that I am the Messiah," proved such by miraculous works," are arbitrary and foreign to the context.—**Offer for thy cleansing.** Better, "on account of it," or "in view of it," not with reference to securing it, as a reader of the English text might suppose.

45 But he went out, and began⁰ to publish it much, and to blaze abroad the matter, insomuch that Jesus could no more openly enter into the city, but was without in desert places; and⁰ they came to hear him from every quarter.

45 testimony unto them. But he went out, and began to publish it much, and to spread abroad the matter, insomuch that ²Jesus could no more openly enter into ³a city, but was without in desert places: and they came to him from every quarter.

CHAPTER II.

A ND again he entered into Capernaum after some days; and it was noised that he was in the house. 2 And straightway many were gathered together, insomuch that there was no room to receive them, no, not so much as about the door : and he preached⁰ the word unto them.

1 And when he entered again into Capernaum after some days, it was noised that he was ¹in the house. 2 And many were gathered together, so that there was no longer room for them, no, not even about the door :

a Ps. 77 : 11, 12 ; Tit. 1 : 10.....*b* ch. 2 : 13.....*c* Ps. 40 : 9.——1 Gr. word....2 Gr. he....3 Or, the city....4 Or, at home.

45. The injunctions of secrecy were usually in vain, and so now : the man could not keep it to himself. **To blaze abroad the matter.** Better, "to publish abroad the story." Perhaps our Lord's discernment of a tendency to such disobedience in the man was the occasion of his special sternness. The man had obtained his heart's desire, but regarded not the desire of his Healer; and too much like him are many whom the same gracious Lord has blessed. Jesus might have said to him, in turn, "If thou wilt, thou canst" obey my commandment.

THE EFFECT.—**He could no more** (consistently with his purpose and the kind of influence he wished to exert) **openly enter** (as before) **into the city** (or, rather, into town—*i. e.* into any city), **but was without, in desert places,** and they came to him from **every quarter** (seeking and finding him even in his retirement). Luke seems to mention here a special time when many sought him to hear and be healed, and he was not to be found, having withdrawn to pray.

1-12. AFTER RETURNING TO CAPERNAUM, JESUS HEALS A PARALYTIC. *Parallels*, Matt. 9 : 1-8 ; Luke 5 : 17-26.—There is no better place than this to notice the impossibility of finding an agreement in the evangelists as to the order of events in this part of our Lord's ministry. This healing of a paralytic is placed by Matthew immediately after the healing of the Gadarene demoniac. But that miracle is not mentioned by Mark until his fifth chapter, where it is followed by the narrative of the raising of Jairus's daughter. Matthew certainly does not follow the order of time, but groups events according to their character. Luke moves, in this part of the history, more nearly along with Mark, yet not perfectly. The only way is to follow Mark's order, which bears the clearest internal signs of being deliberately adopted; but minute harmonizing does not seem to have been intended, and we cannot say very positively that we are sure of the true

arrangement of events. In this volume, therefore, not much labor is spent in discussing questions of order.

1, 2. Luke specifies no place, and Matthew refers to Capernaum as "his own city"—*i. e.* the city that he had made his own, as his residence, since he left Nazareth. This was his only home, and probably the **house** here mentioned —which was most likely the house of Peter and Andrew again (as at chap. 1 : 29)—was his only home within Capernaum. It was when he had just left this home, on his last journey to Jerusalem, that he said, "The Son of man hath not where to lay his head" (Luke 9 : 58). To this home he returned **after some days** (*di'hēmerōn*, a rare form of expression, but plain enough, denoting perfectly indefinite time). Neither here nor in Luke is there any help in measuring the length of the time spent in the circuit through Galilee. According to Luke, there were "sitting"—*i. e.* with him within the house—Pharisees and teachers of the law, who had come from throughout Galilee and Judæa, and even from Jerusalem. "From every village" is a popular expression not to be pressed closely. The presence of some from Jerusalem may perhaps be taken (though not too confidently) as an allusion to the ministry in Jerusalem mentioned by John, but passed over in silence by the synoptists. These men may have come up to Galilee to watch the ministry that had then alarmed them. But the work of Jesus was not yet very well understood : there is no sign of hostile feeling in this story until he announced the forgiveness of sins; and it is quite possible that this was a visit of inquiry, with hostile feeling as yet developed only in part.—Besides the visitors from abroad, there was a throng of the people of the town ; and it is Mark, as usual, who tells us that the report of his presence brought them together, and that they were so many that **there was no room to receive them, no, not so much as about the door.** He tells us that Jesus **preached**, or was speaking, **the word unto them**, when the incident that he relates took place ; and Luke adds the unusual

3

3 And⁴ they come unto him, bringing one sick of the palsy, which was borne of four.
4 And when they could not come nigh unto him for the press, they uncovered the roof where he was; and when they had broken ¹ up, they let down the bed wherein the sick of the palsy lay.

3 and he spake the word unto them. And they come, bringing unto him a man sick of the palsy, borne 4 of four. And when they could not ¹come nigh unto him for the crowd, they uncovered the roof where he was; and when they had broken it up, they let down the ²bed whereon the sick of the palsy lay.

a Matt. 9 : 1, etc. ; Luke 5 : 18, etc.——1 Many ancient authorities read bring him unto him....2 Or. pallet

remark that "the power of the Lord was (present) to heal them," or else, as Tischendorf reads, "The power of the Lord was (present) that he should heal." In either case the expression is peculiar, but in either case the allusion is to the free presence of healing energy in Jesus.

3. Not **one sick of the palsy,** but "a paralytic." Palsy and paralysis are not the same

4. By reason of the crowd about the door they could not come near to Jesus, and were driven to ingenuity as the means of getting within his reach. A flight of stairs led from the ground to the roof of the house, and they bore the sick man up over the head of Jesus. Then they **uncovered**—or, literally, "unroofed"—**the roof,** took a part of the roof away·

LETTING DOWN IN A BED.

disease, though the names have a common origin, and there is no reason for confounding them here.—He was **borne of four,** as Mark alone tells us—i. e. carried on the mattress or thick quilt that formed his couch by one friend at each of the four corners. Cases of local and partial paralysis are of course frequent, but the details of this story seem to show that the patient was thoroughly helpless.

In the lack of any description of the house, we cannot picture the act to ourselves as clearly as we would. Some think that Jesus was in the "upper room" of the house, and some that he was on the ground-floor; while some think he may have been in the open yard, just beside the wall, and that what was removed was the railing around the roof. But Thomson's theory of the matter is very simple, and seems to be suf-

5 When Jesus saw their faith,* he said unto the sick | 5 And Jesus seeing their faith saith unto the sick of
of the palsy, Son, thy sins be forgiven thee.

*Acts 14 : 9; Eph. 2 : 8.

ficient (*The Land and the Book*, 2. 6–8). He
thinks that the house was one of those that
are abundantly illustrated by the ruins in that
region, as well as by existing houses—a low,
one-story house with a flat roof; not a large
house built around a court, but a square house
with the entrance through a recess or entry
under the roof and open to the yard. Whether
Jesus stood, as Thomson thinks probable, in
this entry between the yard and the interior of
the house, or in some room within, the process
would be the same. The roofs of such houses
vary in construction, but can all be broken up
without difficulty. Thomson describes a roof
of the heavier kind, containing a layer of stiff
mortar; and he says the only difficulty in opening such a roof would be the inconvenience arising from a shower of dust. But he speaks of
other roofs, made of boards or stone slabs,
which might be still more easily taken up.
Perhaps Luke's phrase—" through the tiling ;"
literally, " through the tiles "—may be a reminiscence of the actual construction of the roof,
and may remove the difficulty by suggesting
that nothing was necessary but to lift the tiles
with which the building was covered. As for
any serious exertion or need of appliances in
letting the man down, Thomson says, speaking
of similar houses that are still to be seen, " Examine one of these houses, and you see at once
that the thing is natural and easy to be accomplished. The roof is only a few feet high, and
by stooping down and holding the corners of
the couch—merely a thick padded quilt, as at
present in this region—they could let down the
sick man without any apparatus of ropes or
cords to assist them. The whole affair was the
extemporaneous device of plain peasants accustomed to open their roofs and let down grain,
straw, and other articles, as they still do in this
country."

5. When Jesus saw their faith. The
faith of them all, the sufferer and those who
were bringing him. He saw it in their works.
The eagerness and persistency were manifest to
all beholders, but he saw in it their faith. He
can discern faith through all its expressions.
In them all it was faith in his power to heal;
in the paralytic himself there was something
more that qualified him to receive something
more than healing.—**Son,** *teknon ;* here alone
used by Jesus in address.—**Thy sins be—are**
—**forgiven.** Said only here and at Luke 7 :

47, 48. But why did he begin thus? This
was not what was expected of him, either by
the spectators or by those who had come in
faith. Even to the man this would be a surprise. But first, in the answer to the question
" Why?" is the fact that this was a case in
which the man's sins could be forgiven. We
must not think that this utterance was a preparation for something that was to follow, and
was made in order to draw out the thoughts
of the hearers. First of all, this was a true
and honest declaration of real pardon. Hence
it gives us a true glimpse into the man's soul ;
for it assures us that he was a penitent and a
humble man. This is a great word, too, in the
testimony it bears to our Lord himself. Unless
this was all fraud and false show, he did so
read the heart of the man as to know that he
was a fit person to receive the pardon of his
sins. Unless he was deceiving all who heard
him, he knew the man's standing in the sight
of God. He distinctly claimed to know it ; but
he claimed more still : he claimed also to speak
for God in the announcement of pardon. Divine insight and divine prerogative, he openly
assumed that he possessed. To deny that he
made these transcendent claims is to make his
conduct so frivolous and wicked that all our
confidence and interest in him is gone for ever.
To admit that he made these claims and to
deny his right to do so is equally to destroy
our confidence and interest in him. So this one
saying, **Son, thy sins be forgiven,** proves
that Jesus possessed divine powers and divine
prerogatives, or else it proves that he was a
charlatan to whose claims the world ought
never to have paid any attention. This is one
of the cases in which the choice lies between
admitting the presence and action of divine
attributes and making his words blasphemy
toward God and insult to man. But further
reason there must have been for his beginning
with pardon instead of healing, and the special
reason was found in what he saw in the man's
heart. There he saw not only that pardon
could be given to him, but that it was the fitting gift to be offered first. When a soul is
truly ready to be forgiven, nothing will come
between that soul and forgiving grace: the
Lord is " ready to forgive." Sickness, perhaps,
had touched the man's heart, and perhaps conscience told him that to sin the sickness was
directly due.

3

6 But there were certain of the scribes sitting there, and reasoning in their hearts,

7 Why doth this man thus speak blasphemies? Who can forgive sins*a* but God only?

8 And immediately, when Jesus perceived in his spirit that they so reasoned within themselves, he said unto them, Why reason ye these things in your hearts?

9 Whether is it easier, to say to the sick of the palsy, *Thy* sins be forgiven thee; or to say, Arise, and take up thy bed, and walk?

10 But that ye may know that the Son of man hath power*b* on earth to forgive sins, (he saith to the sick of the palsy,)

6 the palsy, [1]Son, thy sins are forgiven. But there were certain of the scribes sitting there, and reasoning in their hearts, Why doth this man thus speak? he blasphemeth: who can forgive sins but

8 one, *even* God? And straightway Jesus, perceiving in his spirit that they so reasoned within themselves, saith unto them, Why reason ye these things

9 in your hearts? Whether is easier, to say to the sick of the palsy, Thy sins are forgiven; or to say,

10 Arise, and take up thy [2]bed, and walk? But that ye may know that the Son of man hath authority on earth to forgive sins (he saith to the sick of the

---

a Isa. 43 : 25 ; Dan. 9 : 9....*b* Acts 5 : 31.——1 Gr. *Child*....2 Or, *pallet*

6, 7. The complaint and challenge is, according to the best text, "Why doth this man speak thus? He blasphemeth: who can forgive sins but God alone?" It came from **certain of the scribes** who were **sitting there.** Doubtless they were narrow-minded and unsympathetic, but can we blame them for this amazement and horror? They understood him to claim the divine prerogative, the incommunicable authority, and how could they fail to be scandalized? Indeed, until they knew by what right he made the claim it was proper for them to be scandalized. Perhaps by this time they ought to have known: at any rate, after this they ought; but until they knew they could not have felt otherwise. The complaint does not seem to have been addressed to Jesus, yet it appears not to have been entirely unspoken. It was passed around among themselves, in their own circle, perhaps in whispers, and was certainly expressed on their dark faces. The solemnity of Jesus' manner, and perhaps his manifest joyfulness, may well have kept the charge of blasphemy from direct and open utterance.

8, 9. Mark plainly intends to represent that Jesus had direct knowledge of their thoughts. As he had seen the spiritual state of the sick man, so he saw the hearts of these objectors. **He perceived in his spirit** that they were reasoning thus. The word **immediately** reminds us whose record we are reading; it is a characteristic word.—The introductory question, **Why reason ye these things in your hearts?** seems to indicate that there was something in the circumstances that might have kept them, from their point of view, from wondering and complaining at his words. What was it? It seems to be found in the fact that they expected of him the word "Arise and walk," or some similar word of power. They were looking for a word of healing that would be either proved to be a word of real power or exposed as a vain assumption by what followed it. But now he reasoned with them.—**Whether is it easier, to say to the**

sick of the palsy—the paralytic—**Thy sins be forgiven thee; or to say, Arise, and take up thy bed, and walk?**—*i. e.* "Looking with your eyes of unbelief, you ought not to wonder, for I have spoken a word which, as a word, is easier to speak than the one that you were expecting. It is easier to announce present pardon of sins than to announce present healing of sickness, because there is no one who can convict me of falsehood if I speak falsehood; whereas every beholder could convict me of falsehood if the man did not arise when I bade him." Observe that he did not bring into comparison the two works themselves, healing and pardon, and ask which is the easier work, but only the announcement of the two, asking which is the easier announcement. From his point of view, and with his knowledge of the meaning of his words, it would be infinitely harder to say what he had said, if he had not the right to say it; but from their point of view, and with their half doubt of his sincerity, they need not have wondered that he had spoken the easier word.

10, 11. But in reality it was not a question of saying, but of doing—not what words he could speak, but what power he had. They said he had blasphemed. Had he? Was he trifling with God and men when he said, **Thy sins be forgiven?** "I wish you to know," he said, "that I have power to do the deed of pardon as well as to announce it. It is a diviner deed than the act of healing, but it cannot be attested to the senses as healing can; therefore I will take the act of healing for the test. Let the visible deed of divine power be the proof of my authority to exercise the divine prerogative in the invisible realm of the spirit, in order that ye may know that the Son of man hath power on earth to forgive sins." The word "authority," however, is better than **power.** The claim is that authority has been given to, or resides in, the Son of man, the Messiah, to forgive, and that this authority is now present in his person **on earth,** there to be exercised at his will and pleasure, and the

11 I say unto thee, Arise, and take up thy bed, and go thy way into thine house.

12 And immediately he arose, took up the bed, and went forth before them all; insomuch that they were all amazed, and glorified God, saying, We[a] never saw it on this fashion.

11 palsy), I say unto thee, Arise, take up thy [1]bed, and 12 go unto thy house. And he arose, and straightway took up the [1]bed, and went forth before them all; insomuch that they were all amazed, and glorified God, saying, We never saw it on this fashion.

a John 7 : 31 ; 9 : 32.——[1] Or, *pallet*

results to be made known, if he so wills it, at once to the men who are forgiven. It was conceded that sins might be forgiven, but only by God, as all agreed, and by him only in heaven, his dwelling-place, from which there was no way to make the act clearly known to the sinner. But Jesus claimed that the authority was on earth in himself—a tremendous claim. The language is closely similar to that of John 5 : 27, where the claim of "authority to execute judgment" is made in the same manner, in connection with the assertion of power to raise the dead and to quicken the spiritually lifeless. It is not improbable that this utterance at Capernaum was intended to recall the earlier discourse at Jerusalem to the memory of some now present who had heard it, or heard of it, there—a discourse either unutterably rich or horribly profane in claims of divine prerogative. Here it is the Messiah on the human side, the Son of man, who claims the authority; there he had claimed divine prerogative both as Son of man and as Son of God. So, if there was an implied reference to the previous discourse, it may have brought back the remembrance of still bolder assumptions.—And now, "in order that ye may know that authority to forgive sins is actually present, to be exercised not merely in the unseen heaven, but on the earth, by me, the Son of man, the Christ of God in humanity,"—after this tremendous prelude comes the act. He saith to the paralytic, **I say unto thee, Arise, take up thy bed, and go thy way into thine house.**

12. If the effect of the first mighty word was invisible, not so was the effect of this. "His word was with power." Mark's description contains little that is peculiar, yet it is perhaps the most graphic of them all. **And immediately he arose, took up the bed, and went forth before them all.** The popular effect is emphatically represented in all the reports, and there is no mention in any of them of any indignation or horror. Apparently it was as at Acts 4 : 14, where the presence of the living proof silenced the cavils. Later in our Lord's ministry, when the opposition was more developed, that would not have kept them back ; and even now, undoubtedly, there was

smouldering indignation, at least in many of those who were spiritually prepared to see no good in him. But the man himself "went to his house glorifying God" (Luke), satisfied with his mercy in a double degree, blessed with health of body and with the deeper healing of the soul. After his other utterance of the pardoning word, Jesus added (Luke 7 : 50), literally, "Go unto peace"—let the lot and life to which thou goest be peace; and unto peace we may well think that this man went. The question arises, Did the miracle thoroughly and legitimately prove the power to forgive? The answer is, (1) to the beholders, yes. It was an *argumentum ad hominem* of the most unanswerable kind. It was a direct exertion of superhuman power, expressly offered as proof of the divine authority in question. No one doubted the reality of the healing, or its quality as a work of beneficence, or the claim that it was divine power that wrought it. Hence no one who saw it was in a situation to deny the claim in support of which the miracle was performed. After it the beholders ought to have felt that the earth was now blessed and consecrated by the presence of divinity. (2) To us who read of it, also yes. If it could be proved that Jesus was a deceiver, a dishonest man, it would not be so; but if it can be shown that Jesus was no deceiver, but a truly honest man, then it is so. This was either a fraud or an honest transaction. If Jesus was merely acting honestly as a man, leaving aside all questions of his divinity, the miracle proved that in support of a superhuman claim he could invoke the action of superhuman power. It was therefore a confirmation of his claim. But we most joyfully confess that to us who know his character such a miracle adds nothing to our confidence in his word. We believe him that he is in the Father and the Father in him, because in seeing him we have "seen the Father;" and so we are not shut up to believing him "for the very works' sake" (John 14 : 11). He is the great miracle, and to those who know him he is self-evidencing.

Of the three narratives of this event it may be noted that they well illustrate the relation of the three evangelists to one another. The three narratives tell the same story without the

13 And he went forth again by the sea-side; and all the multitude resorted unto him, and he taught them.
14 And⁴ as he passed by, he saw Levi the *son* of Alpheus sitting at the receipt of custom, and said unto him, Follow me. And he arose and followed him.

13 And he went forth again by the sea side; and all the multitude resorted unto him, and he taught them. And as he passed by, he saw Levi the *son* of Alphæus sitting at the place of toll, and he saith

a Matt. 9 : 9; Luke 5 : 27.

slightest essential variation; and yet whoever compares them in a Greek harmony, or even in an English harmony, will see that in a multitude of points, as to manner of telling the story, they differ. The differences are not such as to make the slightest difficulty, but they are so real and living as to illustrate, as nothing but differences could, the independence of the writers. Each evangelist has his own word for "bed," Mark's word being *krabbatos*, which is one of his Latinisms. The word is simply the Latin word *grabatus* in Greek form—a word that is said to have been condemned (as a Greek word) by the grammarians, who regarded it as a low word or a word used only by the ignorant. It has been taken—and probably not without reason—as one of the evidences of the low social and intellectual grade of many of the Gentile Christians, for whom Mark wrote his Gospel.

13-17. THE CALL OF LEVI, AND HIS FEAST. *Parallels,* Matt. 9 : 9–13; Luke 5 : 27–32. —This narrative immediately follows, in all the Gospels.

13, 14. By the sea-side. In front of the town, or near it. There the crowd again gathered about him, and we have again to wish for a record that was never made of the "gracious words that proceeded out of his mouth." Matthew and Mark both note that it was **as he passed by** that he saw this man who became his disciple.—**Levi.** So called here and in Luke; in the first Gospel, Matthew; and so always in the lists of apostles. But the peculiar way of approaching the man's name in Matt. 9 : 9, together with the use of the word *legomenon,* "called," seems to indicate a change of name. "Matthew" means "gift of God." The name may have been given him by Jesus, as the surname "Peter" was given to Simon; and possibly the odiousness of the old occupation is silently commemorated in the fact that the name that belonged to the publican period of his life was wholly dropped, and he appeared afterward simply as Matthew, not as Levi-Matthew. (Compare Simon-Peter.) By Mark alone is he called the son of Alphæus. There is no reason to suppose that this was any other Alphæus than the one who is referred to in all the lists of the apostles where we have "James the son of Alphæus." In three of the

lists he stands next after Matthew and Thomas. Matthew and James are thus presumably brothers; and if, as is almost certain, Thomas was the twin-brother of Matthew, Alphæus was the father of three of the twelve. If the word "brother" is rightly supplied before "of James" in Luke 6 : 16 ("Judas the brother of James"), he may have been the father of four.—**At the receipt of custom**—*i. e.* at the custom-house of the town, which is thus said to have been located by the shore of the lake, a natural place for it, since the trade of the town was so largely in fish. "Sitting at the receipt of custom," at his desk or table, actually in his place of business as a publican. The real *publicanus,* in Roman usage, was the man of the Roman knights who undertook to pay a certain sum into the public treasury (*in publicum*) as an equivalent for the taxes of a province. Sometimes he represented himself alone, and sometimes a joint-stock company formed for the purpose. This man usually resided in Rome, but in his province he had chief assistants (of whom Zacchæus may have been one), and lower representatives in every town, to collect directly from the people. These collectors were usually natives of the province, because these would best have access to the people; and these are the publicans (*telonai*) of the New Testament. The system was a wretched one, giving abundant opportunities for extortion. The chief *publicanus* had only one object—to collect as much as possible; and there was no redress for his extortions, the government having been already satisfied for the taxes and claiming nothing to do with the collection of them. The local publicans were the more odious to the Jews, because their presence was a continual reminder of the national humiliation and a seeming proof that Jehovah had given over his land to the oppressor. Moreover, they were often no better than they were expected to be, and deserved much of the opprobrium that was heaped upon them.

In the case of this man we have no traces of any previous acquaintance between him and Jesus. But (1) he may have heard the discourse of verse 13; (2) one or more of his brothers may already have become attached to Jesus, and Levi may himself have begun to incline toward him; (3) he may have been among the publicans who were baptized by John (Luke 3 : 12, 13 ; 7 : 29), and

15 And⁴ it came to pass, that, as Jesus sat at meat in his house, many publicans⁶ and sinners sat also together with Jesus and his disciples: for there were many, and they followed him.
16 And when the scribes and Pharisees saw him eat with publicans and sinners, they said unto his disciples, How is it that he eateth and drinketh with publicans and sinners?
17 When Jesus heard *it*, he saith unto them, Theyᶜ that are whole have no need of the physician, but they that are sick: I came not to call the righteous, but sinnersᵈ to repentance.

15 unto him, Follow me. And he arose and followed him. And it came to pass, that he was sitting at meat in his house, and many ¹publicans and sinners sat down with Jesus and his disciples: for 16 there were many, and they followed him. And the scribes ²of the Pharisees, when they saw that he was eating with the sinners and publicans, said unto his disciples, ³He eateth ⁴and drinketh with 17 publicans and sinners. And when Jesus heard it, he saith unto them, They that are ⁶whole have no need of a physician, but they that are sick: I came not to call the righteous, but sinners.

a Matt. 9 : 10, etc....*b* Luke 15 : 1-5....*c* Matt. 9 : 12, 13; Luke 5 : 31, 32....*d* Isa. 1 : 18; 55 : 7; Matt. 18 : 11; Luke 19 : 10 ; 1 Cor. 6 : 9 11 ; 1 Tim. 1 : 15.——1 That is, *collectors or renters of Roman taxes* : and so elsewhere....2 Some ancient authorities read *and the Pharisees*....3 Or, How is it *that he eateth . . . sinners* ?....4 Some ancient authorities omit *and drinketh*....5 Gr. *strong*.

who were taught by him to do the work of a publican without extortion. There is nothing improbable in this last supposition. In any case, he was in a thoughtful, penitent state, ready to abandon the life of sin at the Master's call.—The invitation **Follow me** must even then have been felt to imply something of selection on the part of Jesus, and something of honor to him who received it. The publican may have welcomed with wondering joy an invitation for which he had scarcely dared to hope.—**He arose and followed him.** Luke adds that he "left all." Doubtless it was not much, but it was all. His life was in his work, and so was his living; but the new Master had taken hold of his heart, and he was content to go.

15. It is Luke who says that " Levi made him a great feast in his " (Levi's) "house," perhaps, though not necessarily, on the same day. In Matthew the allusion (to the great feast) is omitted, which has been noted as a natural mark if Matthew was the author of the Gospel that bears his name. He says also that " he was at table in the house," which has been noted as Matthew's way of referring to his own house. **Jesus sat at meat in his house.** Here the translators introduced the name of Jesus without indicating that it was an inserted word; and so obscured, or rather misrepresented, the sense. Tischendorf's text reads thus: " And it came to pass that he was reclining at table in his house; and many publicans and sinners were reclining with Jesus and his disciples; for there were many, and scribes of the Pharisees were also following him." " He," most naturally, is the man last mentioned—namely, Levi. He was at his own table; the presence of Jesus and his disciples with him there is in the writer's mind from the first, but is mentioned only in an indirect way and by implication. Jesus was the centre of the company ; the guests were largely of Levi's own class, the publicans, with whom the respectable would not associate; and, as it often happens in that land, besides the invited

guests there were others who came in, many of whom were of the abandoned classes in the town. With the publicans these were familiarly at home.

16. The scribes and Pharisees. Tischendorf's text reads, " The scribes of the Pharisees." They were representatives of the law in its extreme strictness. The practice of the scribes—copyists and expounders—tended to literalism and precision, and the self-righteous spirit of the Pharisees excluded mercy. Probably among these were the scribes who had witnessed the healing of the paralytic, and who ever since may have been meditating with less and less pleasure on what Jesus was doing. Scribes would not enter the house of Levi, and we can imagine their scorn as they stood outside and saw the Rabbi within at the same table with publicans and sinners. Their criticism was addressed to the disciples who were nearest them. The complaint is the same as the one to which we are indebted for the group of parables in the fifteenth chapter of Luke—a group so rich as almost to reconcile us to the existence of the cavil.

17. The answer here is briefer, but not less characteristic and decisive. It may be thus rendered: " No need have the strong of a physician, but they that are sick. I came not to call righteous persons, but sinners." **To repentance** is an addition that has scarcely any manuscript authority here, and no sufficient authority in Matthew. The words stand unquestioned in Luke, whence copyists have introduced them in Matthew and Mark. In this reply our Lord first describes his own work figuratively—as a work of healing—and the most natural of all statements is made—namely, that such service is only for the sick ; the strong have no need of it, an allusion, perhaps, to the recent work of healing; in any case, a characterizing of his own mission in a very different tone from all that they would expect—a distinct assertion that his conduct was determined by reference to the purpose of a Healer of souls, and, plain-

18 And the disciples of John and of the Pharisees used to fast: and they come and say unto him, Why do the disciples of John and of the Pharisees fast, but thy disciples fast not?

18 And John's disciples and the Pharisees were fasting: and they come and say unto him, Why do John's disciples and the disciples of the Pharisees

ly, of individual souls. It is simply and unqualifiedly as a **physician** that he announces himself. How could he more deeply surprise the men of national aspirations in his time? But next he describes his own work more literally—as a work of calling. Here the same feeling appears as in the figurative description: mercy and helpfulness are still the great considerations; the needy are first to be remembered: "I came not to call righteous persons, but sinners." It is not **the righteous,** by which form of speech the Pharisees may conceivably have been free to suppose that they were alluded to under an honorable name. The contrast is not at all between designated individuals, but between characters—righteous men and sinful men. Not less than before would he now surprise the men of Israel. To call sinners, and not the righteous? How could any one so speak who had any sympathy with the God of Israel, who was righteous and loved righteousness? Such would be the first thought; but the deeper and truer thought, more full of divinity, is that the righteous God so loves righteousness as to wish to put sin away. Hence, in the mission of his great Messenger, the call is to sinners; it is the lost sheep that is sought. The religionists of that day recognized God's love for righteousness (as many men do) far enough to feel that God must love the righteous; but they did not recognize his love for righteousness as a love that would seek to produce righteousness where it is not. It was God as loving and saving the lost that Jesus had come to reveal; but the thought was so contrary to the pride of self-righteous men that they were sure one who would eat with publicans and sinners could not be a messenger of God. Observe how simple and consistent was the devotion of Jesus to his principle. Sinners were to be helped; therefore they must be recognized. Instead of being despised, they must be treated like men and accepted as companions. He who would save them must not shrink from them, and must make them know what love he had for them; hence Jesus set at naught all ceremonial objections to associating with men defiled, and all social objections to being found in company with the despised. He followed his saving love to its legitimate practical conclusions. Few of his friends have love enough to follow in his footsteps here. The failure is often attributed to want of courage, but it is really due

to the want of love. Love makes courage. Matthew prefixes to this answer the words of the prophet (Hos. 6:6), with a sharp injunction to consider them: "But go and learn what that meaneth, I will have mercy, and not sacrifice." His own mission Jesus declares to be in the spirit of this noble Scripture.

18-22. QUESTION AND ANSWER WITH REGARD TO FASTING. *Parallels,* Matt. 9: 14-17; Luke 5: 33-39.—It is commonly assumed that this questioning occurred at Matthew's feast, just as it is commonly assumed that the feast took place on the day of Matthew's call. It is not certain, however, that the feast was made at once, and it is not certain—though it seems probable—that the conversation about fasting went on around Matthew's table. Matthew (9:18) expressly places it in connection with the coming of Jairus to ask for restoration for his daughter. In any arrangement the harmony is attended with difficulties. Possibly, as Gardiner suggests (*Greek Harmony,* p. 42), the Lord met the same objections more than once, and more than once answered them in the same way; in which case the different reports may have come from different occasions. But the interest and value of what he said is not dependent on our ability to refer it exactly to its actual time and place. These utterances are singularly independent of suggesting circumstances.

18. The speakers, in Luke, are indeterminate; in Matthew, expressly the disciples of John; in Mark, apparently those who have been observing the disciples of John and the Pharisees: various ways of introducing a question suggested by the practice from which Jesus departed. Used to fast. Translate, "The disciples of John, and the Pharisees, were fasting" —*i. e.* at the time of the question. It was one of their fast-days. John himself was in prison, but this reference proves that his disciples kept together as a body by themselves during the ministry of Jesus. (See also Luke 7:18; Matt. 14:12.) It proves also that their observances had much in common with those of the Pharisees. John intended that the spirit of all that sprang from his influence should be utterly unlike that of the Pharisees, and perhaps his disciples were not Pharisaic in heart; but when his personal influence was removed they remained a kind of intermediate body between the old and the new. The Pharisees fasted on the second and fifth days of the week (compare

19 And Jesus said unto them, Can the children of the bride-chamber fast, while the bridegroom[a] is with them? As long as they have the bridegroom with them, they cannot fast.
20 But the days will come when the bridegroom shall be taken away from them, and then[b] shall they fast in those days.
21 No man also seweth a piece of new cloth on an old garment: else the new piece that filled it up taketh away from the old, and the rent is made worse.

19 fast, but thy disciples fast not? And Jesus said unto them, Can the sons of the bride-chamber fast, while the bridegroom is with them? as long as they have the bridegroom with them, they cannot fast.
20 But the days will come, when the bridegroom shall be taken away from them, and then will they fast
21 in that day. No man seweth a piece of undressed cloth on an old garment: else that which should fill it up taketh from it, the new from the old, and a worse

a Matt. 25 : 1.....b Acts 13 : 2.

Luke 18 : 12), and this allusion makes it seem probable that the custom of John's followers was the same. In Luke there is an additional reference to the "making of prayers" as a common trait of the Pharisees and John's disciples. (Compare Luke 11 : 1, where it is implied that John had taught to his disciples some forms of prayer.)—**But thy disciples fast not.** The words might mean "are not fasting"—i. e. to-day, as the questioners are—but naturally they have a wider meaning, and indicate that fasting was not an element in the life of the disciples of Jesus. The words do not prove that he had forbidden fasting, but they do prove that the life of his followers, as observed by others, did not contain this element.

19, 20. The question is answered in all three reports exactly as if asked, as in Matthew, by John's disciples. There is no severity in the reply—a fact that indicates honesty in the inquirers. The first part of the answer is distinctly an *argumentum ad hominem* to those who reverenced John and remembered his words. **Can the children of the bride-chamber—** the attendants in the festivities of the wedding **—fast while—**as long as—**the bridegroom is with them?** See John 3 : 29, where the Baptist called Jesus the bridegroom and spoke of himself as the "friend of the bridegroom," whose office it was to arrange the marriage-feast and bring the bridegroom and the bride together. Here is a "cross-reference" between the synoptists and the fourth Gospel, affording one of the interesting examples of undesigned coincidence that have proved so valuable in illustrating and confirming the evangelical record. The synoptists allude to a remark of the Baptist that is recorded only in the Gospel of John. "This is the time," says Jesus to John's disciples, "to which your Master alluded, when the bridegroom should be present among his friends." For his own part, he withdrew, confessing that the union that he had sought to bring to pass was now about to be formed: the bridegroom was now to have the bride, the Christ and his people were coming together. He said that in this very thing his own joy, as the bride-

groom's friend, was completed. How, then, should there be fasting—the sign of sorrow— "while the bridegroom is among his friends at the marriage"? In this reply there is a sharp though kindly appeal to those who had learned of John: why had they not learned this of him? and why should they not be, as he would have them, among those who were rejoicing in the bridegroom's presence? Should they be found in sympathy with the Pharisees, rather than with the followers of him whom their teacher had announced? Yet this was not the whole matter. Even for the children of the bride-chamber fasting was not impossible. Neither they nor those who beheld them must suppose that they had to come to the final joy. The bridegroom was with them, but not yet to remain for ever.—**Days will come when the bridegroom shall be taken away from them.** A tragic outlook, and the earliest recorded intimation of such sorrow to come. Two or three hints there had been in his early discourses at Jerusalem, as John 2 : 19 and 3 : 14, but they were not distinct and likely to be understood at the time. Here, however, was an indication that the presence of Jesus was not to continue with his friends, and one that they, if they were thoroughly attentive, might understand and treasure up. It was implied, too, that this removal from the midst of them should be a sad rather than a glorious removal.—**Then shall they fast in those days,** but "in that day," according to the best text; Luke, "in those days." The sorrow of the disciples at the removal of their Lord by death should find suitable expression in fasting, but while he was among them such a sign of sorrow would be as incongruous as fasting amid the festivities of the wedding. Observe that in this answer fasting is regarded altogether as an expression of sorrow, and not at all in its religious connections as a means of grace or as representative of a type of worship.

21, 22. Here, however, our Lord advances to the other view of fasting, and speaks of it in reference to its religious significance and value. He has pointed out the circumstances in which

22 And no man putteth new wine into old bottles; else the new wine doth burst the bottles, and the wine is spilled, and the bottles will be marred :ª but new wine must be put into new bottles.

22 rent is made. And no man putteth new wine into old ¹wine-skins: else the wine will burst the skins, and the wine perisheth, and the skins : but *they put* new wine into fresh wine-skins.

a Job 32 : 19 ; Ps. 119 : 80, 83.——1 That is, *skins used as bottles.*

It will come in of itself among his friends, and has allowed it its due meaning as an expression of sorrow. What other place and meaning has it for his people? This question is answered by two illustrations. The first one Luke calls a parable; it proceeds upon the essential principle of parabolic teaching in that it is a comparison instituted for the purpose of illustration. It is by no means necessary that a parable should have the form of a narrative. "No one seweth a patch" (not merely a piece; the word denotes something added or put on—a patch) "of unfulled cloth" (cloth new, strong, and liable to make a strain upon what it is attached to) "upon an old garment: else" (if this rule of common sense is overlooked, and the unfulled patch is put on) "the new patch of the old garment teareth away from it, and a worse rent is made." There is much question both about the text and about the construction in the latter part of this, but there is little difficulty as to the thought, and the construction here given (which is Meyer's) seems to be the best : "And no one putteth new wine" (as yet unfermented) "into old" (and weak) "skins : else" (if this rule is neglected) "the wine will burst the skins" (when the fermentation has begun), "and the wine perisheth, and the skins." The clause, "but new wine must be put into new skins," is omitted by Tischendorf, the manuscript evidence being divided. The clause is found in Matthew and Luke, Matthew adding, "And both shall be preserved." The "skins," or leathern bottles, were such as were constantly in use, and are still found in the East—hides partly tanned, and so fastened together as to retain to some extent the form of the animal. Both illustrations were taken from things extremely familiar; and if these words were spoken at Matthew's feast, the leathern bottles may possibly have been in sight.

The point in the use of the "parables" is that the using of the ill-chosen patch and the unsuitable bottles defeats the purpose of him who resorts to it, and the purpose is defeated because of an unwise uniting of the new with the old. The new is the living, expanding, divinely-vigorous kingdom of Christ; the old is that which pertains to the Jewish dispensation, which was decaying and ready to vanish

away (Heb. 8 : 13). The true use of a piece of unfulled cloth is not to be found by putting it as a patch on an old garment, and the value of new wine will be destroyed by storing it in old bottles. So the new life of Christ's kingdom cannot be expressed in forms of the old dispensation : the forms are inadequate, and to use them is to defeat the ends of Christ's kingdom. New life must have new forms of utterance. There is no system or set of institutions that is able to hold the spirit of the new age : that spirit must make institutions adapted to itself. So the entire Epistle to the Hebrews, where it is affirmed that the new institutions are the fulfilment of the old, in the very sense of Matt. 5 : 17, but not less clearly that they are truly new. The application here is to fasting; and the thought of our Lord is that fasting belongs, in spirit, to the old dispensation. It is one of the institutions that are inadequate to the uses of the new; and if the new makes much of it, it will be to the defeating of its own ends. Therefore, it is implied, he will make no attempt to preserve fasting in his kingdom, as if it were a suitable institution for his purpose. It must rank with other means of religious culture which his kingdom has left behind.

Observe that in this passage (1) our Lord assigns a place to fasting as an expression of personal sorrow. But the place that he thus gives it is only a natural place, not a place appointed : he recognizes fasting as something that will occur, but he does not call for it. (2) He distinctly provides against the Roman Catholic idea—that his church is to be a fasting church. If such had been his intent, he could never have spoken thus. Nor is this statement contradicted by the words of verse 21 : "The days come when the bridegroom shall be taken away from them, and then shall they fast, in that day." Those words teach only that the sorrow over his death should find fit expression in fasting, not that fasting should be the continuous habit of the church after his departure. It is not the teaching of Scripture that after his exaltation the church was to be a widowed church during her earthly career, to whom tears and fastings should be the appropriate expressions. (See Matt. 28 : 20; 1 Pet. 1 : 8.) (3) He draws a broad distinction between the old dispensation and the new, and affirms that to express the

23 Andª it came to pass, that he went through the corn-fields on the sabbath-day; and his disciples began, as they went, to pluckᵇ the ears of corn.
24 And the Pharisees said unto him, Behold, why do they on the sabbath-day that which is not lawful?
25 And he said unto them, Have ye never read what David did,ᶜ when he had need, and was an hungered, he, and they that were with him?
26 How he went into the house of God in the days of Abiathar the high priest, and did eat the shew-bread,ᵈ which is not lawful to eat but for the priests, and gave also to them which were with him?

23 And it came to pass, that he was going on the sabbath day through the cornfields; and his disciples 24 ¹began, as they went, to pluck the ears of corn. And the Pharisees said unto him, Behold, why do they 25 on the sabbath day that which is not lawful? And he said unto them, Did ye never read what David did, when he had need, and was an hungred, he, 26 and they that were with him? How he entered into the house of God ²when Abiathar was high priest, and did eat the shewbread, which it is not lawful to eat save for the priests, and gave also to

a Matt. 12 : 1, etc.; Luke 6 : 1, etc....b Deut. 23 : 25....c 1 Sam. 21 : 6....d Ex. 29 : 32, 33 ; Lev. 74 : 9.——1 Gr. *began to make their way plucking....* 2 Some ancient authorities read *in the days of Abiathar the high priest.*

truth and spirit of the new in the terms of the old is not merely difficult, but impossible. (So Heb. 10 : 1.) He must needs "fulfil" before the law could come to use in his kingdom. (4) He gives us reason to believe that in adopting a cheerful style of personal life, in contrast to the manners of John (Matt.11:19), he was acting with the purpose of illustrating the spirit of his kingdom.

23-28. THE DISCIPLES PLUCK EARS OF GRAIN ON THE SABBATH; OUR LORD'S ANSWER TO QUESTIONS CONCERNING IT. *Parallels,* Matt. 12 : 1-8; Luke 6 : 1-5.

23. There is no hint of the time in Matthew or Mark, except that it was on the Sabbath; and the obscure designation in Luke has proved to be one of the hardest points in the Gospels. Gardiner: "Probably it signifies the first Sabbath after the second day of unleavened bread, from which seven Sabbaths were reckoned to Pentecost." We know, at least, that the time was somewhere between passover and Pentecost, when the grain was ripening, but not yet harvested. The place is wholly unknown, except that it was in Galilee. **He went through the corn-fields on the Sabbath.** The word is, literally, "the sown fields." He went for some purpose, on his way from one place to another, not idly rambling. The paths in that land are unenclosed and run through the fields, as illustrated in the parable of the Sower (Matt. 13 : 4); so the grain might be close on either side as they walked.—**His disciples began, as they went, to pluck the ears.** The expression preferred by some—"his disciples began to make a way " (or "to make their way ") "plucking the ears"—is not entirely plain, and difficulties have been made about it, as if they were said to clear a path through the grain by plucking the ears, while nothing was said of the stalks. But the meaning more probably is simply that as they took their course through the field they began to pluck the ears. It is in Mark that we have this peculiar description, but the other evangelists are not less graphic.

Luke, "They plucked the ears and ate, rubbing them with their hands " to free the grain from the husk. The grain may have been wheat or barley.

24. Whence should the Pharisees be near him in the corn-field? Could he never escape? These may have been of the visitors from Jerusalem (Luke 5 : 17), who had already heard much that they disliked. **Why do they on the Sabbath that which is not lawful?** Matthew, "Behold, thy disciples are doing what it is not lawful to do on the Sabbath." There is no indication that he himself was engaged in plucking the grain. He was called upon to answer for his disciples, just as they (verse 16) had been called to answer for him. There was no objection to their act as a violation of the rights of property, the law (Deut. 23 : 25) expressly permitting such freedom with the standing corn of another. In the law itself there was no objection to their doing it on the Sabbath; but, according to the absurd exaggeration of the Pharisees, it was a violation of the day. They regarded the plucking of the ears as a kind of reaping, and the rubbing off of the chaff as a kind of threshing; and reaping and threshing were, of course, forbidden on the Sabbath. Such was the incredibly contemptible paltering with divine requirements with which our Saviour had to do.

25, 26. The reply, as given by all three evangelists, cites a violation of sanctity on the ground of necessity, and one in which the necessity, as now, is that of hunger. The sanctity is not that of the Sabbath alone, but also that of the shew-bread in the tabernacle. The reference is to 1 Sam. 21 : 1-6: "In the days of Abiathar, the high priest;" the mention of the name is peculiar to Mark, and is not without difficulty. The high priest who is mentioned in the original narrative is not Abiathar, but Ahimelech, his father. Abiathar succeeded his father in office not long after, and was high priest during David's reign; so that his name is constantly associated with

27 And he said unto them, The sabbath was made for man,[a] and not[b] man for the sabbath:
28 Therefore[c] the Son of man is Lord also of the sabbath.

27 them that were with him? And he said unto them, The sabbath was made for man, and not man for the sabbath: 28 so that the Son of man is lord even of the sabbath.

a Neh. 9 : 14 ; Isa. 56 : 13 ; Ezek. 20 : 12, 20....b Col. 2 : 16....c John 9 : 14 ; Eph. 1 : 22 ; Rev. 1 : 10.

that of David in the history. Various attempts have been made to reconcile the difference, some supposing that Abiathar was already assistant to his father at the time of David's visit and was present when he came, although this can be nothing but conjecture; others, that our Lord or Mark was content with mentioning the name of the chief high priest of David's time, and the one that was chiefly associated with David's name, which is the same as to say that absolute accuracy was not aimed at; others, that the name of Abiathar stands in the text of Mark as the result of a copyist's error. The law of the shew-bread is given at Lev. 24 : 5-9. Our Lord's argument is again, as so often, an *argumentum ad hominem*—an appeal to the Pharisees on their own ground. The visit of David to the tabernacle was on the Sabbath, for the previous week's shew-bread was just being changed for the fresh, and this was done on the Sabbath (1 Sam. 21 : 6 with Lev. 24 : 8). So David violated the sanctity of the Sabbath (if the Pharisees were right), and at the same time the law that gave the sacred bread to the priests alone. Here was a double violation on the ground of necessity, and the Scriptures nowhere condemned it; nor would the Pharisees really condemn it. David was no Sabbath-breaker, as they all knew; neither were his disciples Sabbath-breakers for gathering and eating the ears of grain. In Matthew a second illustration is added—of the priests laboring in the temple on the Sabbath without sin; also a second citation of the Scripture quoted in verse 13—"I will have mercy, and not sacrifice"—as appropriate to this case also. The principle throughout is that higher requirements subordinate lower; the application of the principle, that necessity and mercy are of higher rank than any ceremonial or formal duties. The requirement of "mercy" was a rebuke to the spirit of the faultfinders, who were very tender of the Sabbath, but cared nothing for the supplying of the needs of their fellow-men. The principle of Paul, "Love worketh no ill to his neighbor, therefore love is the fulfilling of the law" (Rom. 13 : 10), was to them utterly unknown.

27, 28. For confutation of the Pharisees this answer was sufficient: it had been shown that their own law could not be made to support their extreme demands; but the truth implied in the examples that he had quoted deserved a separate statement, and he seized this occasion for the utterance of one of the most important practical truths that ever fell from his lips. What relation does man bear to the Sabbath, and the Sabbath to man? was the real question. The Pharisees made man a slave to the day, as they did to many other legal provisions and demands; so there was need that he should state the true relation, which he now proceeded to do. **The Sabbath was made for man, and not man for the Sabbath.** Compare the original record of the Sabbath (Gen. 2 : 3): God made man with certain powers and needs, and then gave him a day consecrated to special uses to correspond with those powers and needs. The Sabbath was God's special provision for the highest of his creatures. When man had lost the actual enjoyment of it through his sinfulness, God gave it to him again in the Mosaic law in a form and with sanctions that might prove most favorable to the final recovery of the ideal spiritual Sabbath that sin had spoiled. But from first to last it was for the sake of man that it existed, and it had no use except to bring to him the best blessing. When our Lord came the religionists of his day had the Sabbath, and honored it in a certain way: they held it sacred, and bowed down to it as if they were its slaves. When he said, "The Sabbath was made for man"—*i. e.* it is man's servant, not he its slave—his words were violently revolutionary in their esteem; but he was only asserting for the Sabbath the place that God gave it. The Sabbath is perverted when it does not serve man.

We might expect him to say, "Therefore man is lord of the Sabbath;" but what he did say is, **Therefore the Son of man is Lord also of the Sabbath,** the Son of man, the Messiah, viewed in his relation to mankind. Such is its relation to humanity, and such is his relation to humanity, that he is its Lord. Compare Heb. 2 : 6-9, where the thought is that Jesus is exalted to his sovereignty as the representative of man, and in fulfilment of the predictions of exaltation that were made respecting man. So here his relation to man is said to give into his hands and to place under his sovereignty all that belongs to man or serves his

CHAPTER III.

A ND he entered again into the synagogue; and there was a man there which had a withered hand.

1 AND he entered again into the synagogue: and there was a man there who had his hand withered.

a Matt. 12 : 9, etc. ; Luke 6 : 6, etc.

interest. All man's servants are his servants. The Sabbath, having been appointed for the service of man, comes, by virtue of that fact, under the lordship of the Son of man. He is its Master, Director, Lawgiver; in the use of it men are responsible to him. In speaking thus of the Sabbath (1) he claimed it for humanity. To humanity it was given in the original institution, but, for an educational purpose, it had been made temporarily a national institution of the Jews; and by the Jews it had been made still more narrowly a peculiar possession of their own. But now Jesus expressly claimed it for the humanity of which he was Head, and to which it was given at first. (2) He claimed that henceforth the Sabbath should obey his will; his relation to humanity made him its rightful Lord, and both because it was his right and for the sake of mankind he intended to be its actual Lord. (3) Thus he gave clear indication that there should be a Sabbath in his kingdom—a sabbatic institution taking its law from him, fulfilling all the promise that was given by the Jewish institution, and actually serving man, as the Creator intended that the original Sabbath should. The Jewish Sabbath had never fulfilled the ideal of the day: the law could no more make a perfect Sabbath than it could make a perfect sacrifice (Heb. 7 : 19, "The law made nothing perfect"); but when the Son of man, acting as Lord of the Sabbath, wrought out a Sabbath by the working of his Spirit, then first the true Sabbath for man would have come. The Christian Sabbath is the true; the Jewish was only the preparatory institution, which was not "changed" into the Christian Sabbath, but gave way to it by expiring when its work was done.

Observe how different his treatment of the Sabbath from his treatment of fasting. He permits his friends to fast when their hearts are so sad as to demand it; but fasting, as a religious institution, he expressly classes among the means of religious culture of which the new kingdom cannot make use without defeating its own ends. The Sabbath as defined by the Pharisees he not only disparages, but indignantly condemns; but the Sabbath itself he takes under his own lordship, as an institution that God appointed to serve the humanity of which he is Head and King.

There is a very fruitful thought in the there-

fore of verse 28. The word teaches that everything that was "made for man" is thereby brought under the lordship of Christ. Money was made for man; so were marriage and the life of the family; so were books, amusements, means of pleasure and profit of every kind. If they were made for man, the Son of man is Lord of them, and they must be used only as he wills, under his guidance, according to the spirit of his kingdom.

1–6. ON ANOTHER SABBATH, JESUS HEALS A MAN WITH A WITHERED HAND. Parallels, Matt. 12 : 9–14 ; Luke 6 : 6–11.—All three evangelists connect this work on the Sabbath with the preceding, but only Luke notes the fact that it occurred on another Sabbath. Matthew, from whom we should infer that the Sabbath was the same, has followed his favorite method of grouping events of kindred significance, and has not made his connective word to correspond. Possibly in this case they have all acted on Matthew's principle and placed the two events together from internal reasons, rather than because they occurred at nearly the same time. The narratives of Mark and Luke are closely parallel, but Matthew puts the inquiry about healing on the Sabbath into the mouths of the adversaries, and introduces the comparison of the sheep falling into the pit, which Luke places (though with variation of form) at a later time (Luke 14 : 5).

1. He entered again into the synagogue. As his custom was (Luke 4 : 16) at the beginning of his ministry, and probably through the whole of it. He could not fail to put honor upon the religious use of the Sabbath. The services of the synagogue had no direct authority in the ancient Scriptures, synagogues having sprung up about the time of the Exile, and the system having been developed mainly after the close of the Old-Testament canon. But the existence of the synagogues was in true accordance with the spiritual purpose of the Sabbath; and, though the practice of public worship was by no means perfect or satisfactory, still our Lord must have looked approvingly on the service of the synagogue, and have wished to favor it by his example. He did not hold himself aloof because of the faults of the institution, great as they were, yet what must he have felt sometimes as he listened to the instructions that

2 And they watchedᵃ him, whether he would heal him on the sabbath-day; that they might accuse him.
3 And he saith unto the man which had the withered hand, Stand forth.
4 And he saith unto them, Is it lawful to do good on the sabbath-days, or to do evil? to save life,ᵇ or to kill? But they held their peace.
5 And when he had looked round about on them with anger, being grieved for the hardness of their

2 And they watched him, whether he would heal him on the sabbath day; that they might accuse him.
3 And he saith unto the man that had his hand withered, ¹stand forth. And he saith unto them, Is it lawful on the sabbath day to do good, or to do harm? to save a life, or to kill? But they held their peace.
5 And when he had looked round about on them with anger, being grieved at the hardening of their heart,

a Luke 14 : 1....*b* Hos. 6 : 6.——1 Gr. *Arise into the midst.*

were given in the synagogues! The place of this synagogue is unknown; it was somewhere in Galilee—perhaps in Capernaum. Mark says nothing about the company; Luke mentions the scribes and the Pharisees, who may have been the ones who had come from Jerusalem (Luke 5:17); but our knowledge of the time and order is so limited that we cannot affirm it very positively.—**A man which had a withered hand.** Luke, "His right hand." No hint is given of his previous spiritual state.

2. It is plain that, as at chap. 2 : 1-12, they expected Jesus to heal the man. The sight of suffering had often been sufficient to call his power into exercise, and they knew that it would be sufficient now. But they were no longer watching merely to see what he would do: they were watching with intent to accuse him. "The casuistry of the rabbis allowed the practice of the healing art on the Sabbath in cases of life and death, but the withered hand—a permanent infirmity—obviously did not come under that category" (*Plumptre*). If he healed the man, an accusation before the local court—the "judgment" of Matt. 5 : 21—would be the consequence.

3, 4. Luke says that he knew their thoughts; therefore he fully understood the test. Never did he shrink from such a test, and now he boldly took the case into his own hands, calling the man out into the midst of the assembly. But he really transferred the test from himself to his adversaries. **Is it lawful to do good on the Sabbath-days, or to do evil? to save life, or to kill?** Not "on the Sabbath-days," but "on the Sabbath;" the Greek word is the same as in verse 2 and in chap. 2 : 23. The two contrasted verbs do not mean "to do right" and "to do wrong," but rather "to benefit" and "to injure." In the other pair of verbs, "to save life or to kill," he apparently recognizes the principle that neglect is injury, and that he who does not save life when he has the power destroys it. Yet perhaps the words were chosen with intentional sharpness, the dreadful word "kill" being intended to reveal to them the true nature of their own feeling and the tendency of their practice; as

if he had said, "Would you allow me to save a life on the Sabbath? or would you insist that the man must die rather than be saved at the expense of the Sabbath-day? If you say that the man must be left to die, you say that it is lawful, allowable, to kill on the Sabbath; you make the Sabbath justify you in murder. If I may heal to-day, it is lawful to save life on the Sabbath; if I may not heal, it is lawful to destroy on the Sabbath. Which is the right way? What shall I do?" Thus he put his enemies to the test which they meant for him. They could not forbid him to heal except on grounds that would make the sanctity of the Sabbath a cover for cruelty and murder, and the question was publicly thrust home upon them.—But they would not meet the test like men. **They held their peace.** Peculiar to Mark, though implied in Luke. They were silent from cowardice or from the meanness that would only stand aloof and leave him to himself. As for the appeal of humanity, it never touched them.

5. Luke, "Having looked round about upon them all." Mark omits "all," but adds, **with anger, being grieved for the hardness of their hearts.** The deliberate, searching look, turning from countenance to countenance and seeking in vain for some answering look of manliness and love, impressed itself on the memory of the beholders, and some of them, at least, remembered the anger that was in it, and the grief. The men were evading a simple question of right and wrong, and doing it because they would not place themselves where they would be defeated in a wicked purpose, and he was grieved and angry. Shall we call this human grief and anger and class it with his weariness (John 4:6) and wonder (Matt. 8:10; Mark 6:6) and the limitations of his knowledge (Mark 13:32)? Yes; undoubtedly this was human grief and anger, but it was more. It was identical with that anger and grief of God against similar hard-heartedness of which the prophets are full, and which is not unmentioned in the Gospels—a sad anger or a wrathful grief which is infinitely real. The ancient figment of the impassibility of God ought to

hearts, he saith unto the man, Stretch forth thine hand. And he stretched it out: and his hand was restored whole as the other.

6 And the Pharisees went forth, and straightway took counsel with the Herodians against him, how they might destroy him.

7 But Jesus withdrew himself with his disciples to the sea: and a great[b] multitude from Galilee followed him, and from Judea,

he saith unto the man, Stretch forth thy hand. And he stretched it forth: and his hand was restored.

6 And the Pharisees went out, and straightway with the Herodians took counsel against him, how they might destroy him.

7 And Jesus with his disciples withdrew to the sea: and a great multitude from Galilee followed: and

a Matt. 22 : 16....*b* Luke 6 : 17.

have no place in Christian thinking. If God has not the quickest and most intense of feelings, Christ did not reveal him. (Compare, among many Scriptures, Isa. 1 1–20; Hos. 11 : 8, 9; Jer. 7 : 1–28; Ezek. 18 30–32; Eph. 4 : 30.)—For the hard-hearted ones he had not now a word, but only that never-to-be-forgotten look. The word was for the needy man. **Stretch forth thine hand.** And is this thy way, Lord—to call upon man for what he cannot do, and then to "put strength in him" when he "takes hold of thy strength"? The act was impossible to the man; but if he had not had faith in the Healer to attempt it, we have no reason to think he would have been healed. His attempting it was itself a work of faith, and his success was at once a triumph of faith and a gift of God (James 2 : 17, 18). Every genuine act of faith is just such a venturing upon divine power and grace.—**And he stretched it out, and his hand was restored. Whole as the other** is to be omitted here, having come in from the parallel passage in Matthew.

6. According to Luke, the Pharisees who were thus confuted were "filled with madness." No wonder; for, although their hope of an occasion against Jesus had been realized, their defeat was of the most thorough and terrible kind. They had exhibited themselves in their real character, and had drawn out the fact that his grace was only the highest humanity, after all. Nothing is said of any accusation before the local court for this violation of the Sabbath, but there followed **straightway,** that very day, the first recorded plotting against the life of Jesus.—**The Pharisees ... with the Herodians.** The Herodians appear only here and at Mark 12 : 13 and Matt. 22 : 16, these two passages referring to the same occasion. The Herods were practically half Jews: they were Idumæans, of kindred though alien birth with the Jews, and they professed the Jewish faith, but only in a moderate and compromising way. They had sought the establishment of Jewish national life, and had probably intended to make that life ultimately independent of Rome, though for the time

nothing could be done except under the Roman protection. Thus they were regarded with interest by those who intensely dreaded the domination of Rome as a pagan power, and also by those who were more compromising than rigorous in maintaining the national faith. The Herodians were thus a middle party, without vitality enough to last long or to exert any great influence. They had more in common with the Sadducees; but we find them on both occasions in conference with the Pharisees against Jesus. Probably the combination was a union for special purposes, for the sake of which serious disagreements might be overlooked. Mark alone mentions the Herodians here. He and Matthew say that it was a plot to destroy Jesus—an actual counsel of murder.

7–12. JESUS WITHDRAWS TO THE SEA-SHORE; MANY RESORT TO HIM. *Parallel,* Matt. 12 : 15, 16.—In the following verses (11–21) Matthew illustrates the work of the period from prophecy, and in his chap. 4 : 24, 25 he tells of the great concourse from many quarters that attended upon the ministry in Galilee, and of the great activity in healing. Luke's parallel is at 6 : 17–19.

7, 8. Jesus withdrew himself with his disciples to the sea. Matthew, simply, "Knowing it" (the plotting), "he withdrew thence." This was not a retreating for an hour or a day from the malice of his enemies; by the shore of the Sea of Galilee he established for a time the seat of his activity. He did not wish to arouse hostility, and the city was becoming too full of excitement to be the best place for his work. We have no means, of course, of ascertaining the locality that he chose or the length of time that he spent by the sea.—In verse 7 we have an account of the first multitude, so to speak, by which he was surrounded, and in verse 8 we read of the fresh multitude from other regions that was attracted by the fame of what he was doing. First, **a great multitude from Galilee ... and from Judæa,** where he had been seen and heard—the multitude that he had personally attracted—**followed him** to his new scene of working. Then it is added that a great multitude

8 And from Jerusalem, and from Idumœa, and *from beyond Jordan*; and they about Tyre and Sidon, a great multitude, when they had heard what great things he did, came unto him.
9 And he spake to his disciples, that a small ship should wait on him because of the multitude, lest they should throng him.
10 For he had healed many;ᵃ insomuch that they pressed upon him for to touch him, as many as had plagues.
11 Andᵇ unclean spirits, when they saw him, fell down before him, and cried, saying, Thou art the Son of God.
12 And he straitly charged them that they should not make him known.ᶜ

8 from Judæa, and from Jerusalem, and from Idumæa, and beyond Jordan, and about Tyre and Sidon, a great multitude, hearing ¹what great things he did, 9 came unto him. And he spake to his disciples, a little boat should wait on him because of the crowd, 10 lest they should throng him: for he had healed many; insomuch that as many as had ²plagues ³pressed upon him that they might touch him. 11 And the unclean spirits, whensoever they beheld him, fell down before him, and cried, saying, Thou 12 art the Son of God. And he charged them much that they should not make him known.

from south, east, and north, hearing **what great things he did, came to him.** The verb is in the imperfect tense (" was doing "), and it was the actual report spread abroad that brought these people. Luke says that they came to hear as well as to be healed. They came from Idumæa, or the land of Edom, on the south, mentioned here alone in the New Testament. It was the native land of the Herods, and Aretas, the ruler of the land at that time, had given his daughter in marriage to Herod Antipas, by whom she had lately been divorced to make room for Herodias. Probably these political relations had brought about an increase of intercourse between Idumæa and the land of the Jews. They came from Peræa, or the country beyond the Jordan, on the east, a region afterward visited by our Lord; they came from the country about Tyre and Sidon on the north, a region in which Jesus afterward met his own fame in the eager demand of the Syro-Phœnician woman for the healing of her daughter (chap. 7 : 24-30). It is quite possible that the tidings carried home by these visitors to his company awakened the faith that he found in her, or she may even herself have been there. Of such great assemblages Thomson says that they are eminently characteristic of the people of Palestine : " I have seen hundreds of these gatherings in the open air; and, should a prophet now arise with a tithe of the celebrity of Jesus of Nazareth, there would quickly be immense assemblies about him, from Galilee, and from Decapolis, and from Judæa, and from beyond Jordan. There is an irresistible bias in Orientals of all religions to run after the mere shadow of a prophet or a miracle-worker " (*The Land and the Book*, 2. 84).

9. Here first does a boat appear as a help and convenience in our Lord's ministry. Here it is **a small ship.** Properly, " a boat." Afterward, as in chap. 4 : 1 and Matt. 8 : 23, the Greek is " the boat," though not always so. The mention of

the boat here is peculiar to Mark, and it seems as if it were used only to escape the pressure of the throng, not, as in Matt. 13 : 2, as a pulpit.

10-12. But the motive for which they pressed upon him—surely it must have touched his heart so deeply that he would be out of reach as little as possible. The ministry by the seashore was a ministry of healing, more fully detailed as such in Luke, but plainly such in Mark. The still more full account of manifold healing in Matthew (4 : 24, 25) cannot be so definitely assigned to this occasion. The reason of the thronging upon him was that he had already healed many, and therefore "as many as had plagues pressed"—literally, fell—**upon him, for to touch him.** " For power went out from him," says Luke, "and healed them all." He bore with them with an admirable patience and kindness, but sometimes he must escape. Probably we have no reason to imagine that the going forth of power wearied him, as if it were a kind of effluence that took something from him at every act; but he would not have been truly human if he had not been wearied by so constant and severe a demand upon his sympathies. He sought rest on the quiet waters of the lake, and perhaps in resorting to the mountains beyond for prayer. Indeed, in view of verse 13 (see note there), it is difficult to believe that the boat did not sometimes convey him away from the wearying crowd at nightfall to spend the night in communion with his Father. —It seems to have been the rule in the ministry by the shore that the evil spirits fell down before him and acknowledged him as the Son of God: the verbs in verse 11, all in the imperfect tense, indicate as much. They thus fell down, not when he bade them confess, but **when they saw him.** But, as before (chap. 1 : 25-34), he did not accept their testimony. The natural construction of verse 12 makes the prohibition to be addressed to the demons, though in Matthew (12 : 16) it is addressed to all whom he healed.

13 And^a he goeth up into a mountain, and calleth unto him whom he^b would: and they came unto him.
14 And he ordained twelve, that they should be with him, and that he might send them forth to preach,

13 And he goeth up into the mountain, and calleth unto him whom he himself would: and they went 14 unto him. And he appointed twelve,[1] that they might be with him, and that he might send them

---

a Matt. 10 : 1....b John 15 : 16.——1 Some ancient authorities add *whom also he named apostles.* See Luke vi. 13.

Both may be according to fact, Mark having selected for mention only one class of those to whom the command of silence was given. He rejected the testimony of demons; the appeal that he made to evidence is illustrated in John 5 : 32-37, and his witnesses are the Baptist and his own holy and gracious works, and the Heavenly Father himself. How incongruous in the midst of this would be an appeal to the confession of demons! and how unsuitable that such reports should go out among the people! Possibly the charge of collusion with Beelzebub (**verse 22**) may have been suggested by this testimony of demons.

13-19. JESUS WITHDRAWS TO THE MOUNTAIN AND SELECTS THE TWELVE APOSTLES. *Parallel,* Luke 6 : 12-16.—In Matt. 10 : 2-4 the names of the apostles are given, but not in connection with their appointment. A fourth list is given in Acts 1 : 13, made after the twelve had become the eleven. From Luke it is apparent—as it is not from Matthew or Mark —that the appointment of the apostles was immediately followed by the Sermon on the Mount. Matthew omits the appointment of the apostles, and Mark omits the sermon.

13. He goeth up into a mountain. Properly, "the mountain." It is the same in Matt. 5 : 1. Tradition has selected for the honor of this occasion a mountain called Hattin, to the west of the lake and at a little distance from it— a hill with two peaks or eminences, and hence known as the "Horns of Hattin." It is the most prominent height on that side of the lake, and commands a wide prospect; it is easy of access, yet would offer favorable opportunities of retirement. Tradition may be wrong, but in this case it seems likely that it is right. According to Luke, Jesus went to the mountain at evening, apart from his disciples, though they were near, and spent the night in prayer to God: the more likely, then, that nights in his seashore ministry may have been so spent. A great night was this in the history of his kingdom, a great night in his own history—an example of fervent prayer at a crisis of life. We are not forbidden to imagine him studying the characters of the men whom he had called about him and going through the process of selection. Not at random were the apostles chosen, and not, we may be sure, without care-

ful thought on the part of the Master.—In the morning he calleth unto him whom he would: and they came unto him. Peculiar to Mark; in Luke, simply, "He called his disciples." The scene may be thus imagined: Jesus alone upon a higher place of the mountain, and his disciples, a considerable company, near him, below; Jesus has made his selection and calls the chosen ones up to him from the company below, and they come up and take their places at his side. In all the lists the twelve are arranged in groups of four, the persons in each group being always the same, though the order varies within the group. Perhaps the simplest explanation of this is that he called the twelve up in groups of four. Thus, having made a genuine selection in his own mind, he made one openly, and did not call the mass of the disciples up till he had the twelve about him. By this time the multitude, who had spent the night at Capernaum or elsewhere in the vicinity, had followed him and found him, and were present when he proceeded with that charge to his apostles which we know as the Sermon on the Mount.

14, 15. And he ordained twelve. Literally, he "made," or constituted. The number twelve would remind them of the number of the tribes of Israel, and was undoubtedly intended to do so. See the promise in Matt. 19 : 28 that the apostles should sit on twelve thrones judging the twelve tribes of Israel—a promise that cannot possibly be taken literally, because of the fall of Judas if for no other reason, but one that points to the true symbolism of the number in the apostolic body. The church of Christ is the true Israel, and this body of twelve leaders, corresponding to the twelve patriarchs, founders of the tribes, was intended as an indication of that fact. As the old Israel had its twelve founders, so should the new one have. The twelve are not here called apostles, as they are in the parallel passage in Luke, though Mark employs the word in chap. 6 : 30. Luke's language implies that he then gave the name to the twelve. It means "one who is sent," and hence, more specifically, "an ambassador." The name can hardly have suggested to those who received it any definite ambitions respecting a worldly kingdom, but it would not have been unfavorable to such ambitions if they were already cherished.

4

15 And to have power to heal sicknesses, and to cast out devils:
16 And Simon[a] he surnamed Peter;
17 And James the *son* of Zebedee, and John the brother of James; and he surnamed them *Boanerges,* which is, The sons of thunder:[b]
18 And Andrew, and Philip, and Bartholomew, and Matthew, and Thomas, and James the *son* of Alpheus, and Thaddeus, and Simon the Canaanite,
19 And Judas Iscariot, which also betrayed him: and they went into a house.

15 forth to preach, and to have authority to cast
16 out demons; [1]and Simon he surnamed Peter;
17 and James the *son* of Zebedee, and John the brother of James; and them he surnamed *Boanerges,*
18 which is, Sons of thunder: and Andrew, and Philip, and Bartholomew, and Matthew, and Thomas, and James the *son* of Alpheus, and Thaddeus, and Simon
19 the [2]Canaanæan, and Judas Iscariot, who also betrayed him.

---

a John 1 : 42....*b* Isa. 54 : 1 ; Jer. 23 : 24.——1 Some ancient authorities insert *and he appointed twelve....*2 Or, *Zealot.* See Luke vi. 15 ; Acts i. 13.

Mark alone gives here any account of the apostolic office, and he describes it merely as it was during the ministry of Jesus.—**That they should be with him, and that he might send them forth to preach, and to have power ... to cast out devils.** Properly, "demons." Companionship with him was for their education with reference to work for the future. Of his sending them out to preach we have only one example (Matt. 10 : 1; Mark 6 : 30; Luke 9 : 1, 2). Mark's brief account of the apostolic office probably contains the substance of what Jesus then told them: he did not tell them at once either what suffering or what honor should be associated with the name of an apostle. They "could not bear it now," and the future must make its own revelations. As soon as their association with Jesus had ended and he had been glorified, the apostles themselves began to have a new idea of their own function (Acts 1 : 21, 22). Then they felt that they must tell the story of their Master's work from the baptism of John and bear witness to his resurrection. This was Peter's interpretation and unfolding of the Lord's own instruction in Acts 1 : 8: "Ye shall be witnesses unto me." Accordingly, it was held to be necessary that an apostle should have seen the Lord, and should be an eye-witness to his resurrection. (See Acts 1 : 22; 22 : 14, 15; 1 Cor. 9 : 1.) This development of the office was predicted by the Lord in John 15 : 26, 27, and was the fitting development for a relation that first consisted in personal companionship with him. As their relation to him was peculiar, so was their office. It was an office that belonged to that time, and to no other. That they should have successors was impossible, from the nature of the office.

16-19. According to Tischendorf, the words **and he ordained twelve** should be repeated at the beginning of verse 16. The list follows, differing a little from the parallel lists, but the variations are not such as to make any serious difficulties. Indeed, they are probably of more help than hindrance.

Simon, James, John, and **Andrew** form

the first group of four: so in all the lists. (1) Simon stands first in all; Matthew says, "First Simon." He was the first chosen; first in the mind of Jesus, he was practically first in many respects among his fellow-apostles, often standing as their representative, speaking for the whole circle—sometimes for evil, but often for good. After the Master's departure he was the leader of the apostolic band, and the one to whom it was given to open the kingdom of heaven first to Jews (Acts 2), and afterward to Gentiles (Acts 10). From this day of selection until Paul was raised up to do a wider work than was possible to him he was decidedly the first of the apostles. Mark speaks as if the name Peter ("rock") were now for the first time given to him; so also Luke; but it appears in John 1 : 42 that it was given at the very first interview, at the scene of John's baptism. Yet perhaps the name was merely spoken at first and did not attach itself to the man, and was renewed so emphatically as to become a part of himself at the time of the apostolic appointment. Of his previous life we know scarcely more than that he was the son of Jonah, of whom nothing more is known; that he lived first at Bethsaida (John 1 : 44), and afterward at Capernaum (Mark 1 : 29); and that he was a disciple of John the Baptist. He was a fisherman, and already married (Mark 1 : 30). (2) James, a son—apparently the older son—of Zebedee, a fisherman of Bethsaida or Capernaum, and his wife Salome. The name of the mother is ascertained by comparing Mark 15 : 40 with Matt. 27 : 56. In John 19 : 25 it is said that "there stood by the cross of Jesus his mother, and his mother's sister, Mary the wife of Cleophas" (Clopas), "and Mary Magdalene." The construction of this sentence does not positively determine whether three women or four are meant; whether "his mother's sister" is identical with "Mary the wife of Clopas" or is another person, whose name is not given. If the latter is the case, then doubtless "his mother's sister" is Salome, the wife of Zebedee, who certainly was present. The preponderance of modern critical opinion is strongly in favor of this view: so Wieseler, Lücke, Lange, Ewald, Meyer. If this view is correct, James and John were first-cousins to Jesus. It is not easy to be sure that it is correct, but it may be said to be at least probable. The name "James" is the Hebrew "Jacob." The form of expression in John 1:41 makes it most probable that after the visit of John and Andrew to Jesus each set out in search of his own brother, and each found his brother and brought him to Jesus, Andrew coming first with his, and John following with James. If so, James had been with Jesus from the beginning. He and his brother, too, were fishermen, and were partners with Simon and Andrew (Luke 5:10). James is not mentioned separately in the Gospels, but appears in company with John in an ambitious request (Mark 10:35-37) and an unspiritual call for vengeance (Luke 9:54). He was the first of the apostles to suffer martyrdom, and the only one whose death is recorded in the New Testament (Acts 12:2). (3) John ("gift of God"), the younger son, apparently, of Zebedee and Salome; one of the first to follow Jesus, having been directed to him by the Baptist. He is called in his own Fourth Gospel "the disciple whom Jesus loved," and he was apparently the one of the twelve in whom Jesus found the most congenial spirit. Yet he was of fiery disposition, and not the gentle, affectionate creature that he has often been pictured. He is present, though not prominent, in the early apostolic history. His field of service was Ephesus and the surrounding region of Asia Minor, where tradition affirms that he lived to a great age and composed his Gospel near the end of his life. To him the church is indebted also for three Epistles and the Apocalypse. The name **Boanerges** ("sons of thunder") is an Aramaic compound word: it is mentioned by Mark alone, and only here; and as an Aramaic word it is worthy to rank, as an indication of style, with his "Ephphatha" and "Talitha-cumi." No hint is given of the occasion for the name; it is usually taken (and probably aright) as a mark of the fiery disposition of the two brothers seen in Luke 9:49, 54; Matt. 20:21. The fiery zeal of James may have been the occasion of his martyrdom. It is not necessary to suppose that the name was given as a new one at this time, and the fact that the name did not, like "Peter," cling to those who received it may indicate that it was not meant as an abiding designation. Quite likely we have here a trace of the personal relations of Jesus with his friends, a reminiscence of private inter-

course, in which he addressed them sometimes according to what he saw in them; and this title may have been given as much in quiet reproof as in praise of their temper. As a name that might be an honor or a reproach it was an admirable title for men who were possessed of gifts both dangerous and valuable. These three, Peter, James, and John, were the *ecclesia in ecclesia*—the chosen three, the circle nearest to the Master (Mark 5:37; Matt. 17:1; 26:37). The love of Jesus was a real love, and had its choices, as all love has, and his purpose also led him to selections; so there were twelve out of many, three out of twelve, and one out of three—"the disciple whom Jesus loved." Note that the "one" seems to have been selected by love rather than loved because of selection. (4) Andrew son of Jonas, brother of Simon called Peter, a fisherman of Bethsaida, a disciple of the Baptist, John's companion in the first visit to Jesus, the bringer of Peter to his Master (John 1:35-41). In Matthew and Luke his name stands second on the list, next to his brother's name; in Mark and Acts it follows the first group of three. It is not plain why he was not always with the nearest three, among whom his brother was. Only once does he appear with them (Mark 13:3), and twice besides does he appear in the Gospels (John 6:8; 12:22), but with no special marks of character. He is not mentioned in the Acts, and nothing is known of his subsequent labors, even the voice of tradition concerning him being confused and uncertain. Such is the first group of four.

The second group of four consists of **Philip, Bartholomew, Matthew,** and **Thomas:** so in all the lists, Philip always at the head. The order is identical in Mark and Luke; in Matthew, it is Philip, Bartholomew, Thomas, Matthew; in the Acts, Philip, Thomas, Bartholomew, Matthew. (5) Philip. He was of Bethsaida, was evidently a friend of the first four and a fellow-disciple of the Baptist, and was the first to whom Jesus said, "Follow me" (John 1:43, 44). The fact that Jesus "found" him on that occasion implies that he sought him, and hence that he knew him before. Philip appears three times in the Gospel of John (6:5-7; 12:21, 22; 14:8, 9), but not elsewhere, and early Christian history has nothing certain to tell of him. Clement of Alexandria assumes as a recognized fact that Philip was the disciple who said, "Lord, suffer me first to go and bury my father" (Matt. 8:21); but internal evidence seems unfavorable to his assumption (Smith's *Dictionary*, art. "Philip"). His name, like that of Andrew, is a Greek

4

name; and Philip and Andrew appear together at the coming of the "Greeks" to inquire about Jesus (John 12:21). Possibly the Greek names may have determined the Gentile strangers in the choice of persons to inquire of; but Philip and Andrew were Palestinian Jews, and doubtless they had Hebrew names besides. (6) Bartholomew, a name that tells us the man's parentage and nothing more, like Bar-Jesus (Acts 13:6) and Bar-Jona (Matt. 16:17). It is Bar-Tolmai, "son of Tolmai." In three of the lists he stands next to Philip, and it is generally believed that he is the same as Nathanael of Cana in Galilee, whom Philip introduced to Jesus (John 1:45-51). Of the man before his call we know nothing, except from Jesus' testimony to his character: "Behold an Israelite indeed, in whom is no guile"—a sincere and earnest man, loyal to God. He does not appear again, except among the seven who were fishing in the lake when Jesus showed himself to them after the resurrection; that he too was a fisherman is scarcely to be inferred from that. Here, as at first, he appears as Nathanael, which was doubtless his personal name; but his patronymic must also have been a familiar name in his case, as it alone appears in the lists of apostles. These six are known to have been disciples of John the Baptist, and to have been identified with Jesus from the time of his return from the wilderness after the temptation. They are probably the "disciples" who were at the wedding-feast in Cana, accompanied Jesus to Jerusalem at the first passover of his ministry, baptized for him while he remained in Judæa, and returned with him through Samaria to Galilee (John 2:2; 3:22; 4:2). If there were more than these six, we have no means of knowing who they were. As four of them were called a second time in Galilee, so doubtless the others were. (7) Matthew, the "Levi the son of Alphæus" of chap. 2:14. In the lists of apostles he appears only by what was probably his new name. He is known only as the publican (tax-collector) of Capernaum, who promptly followed Jesus and made him a great feast in his own house. He does not appear again in the Gospels or the Acts. Uniform Christian tradition has recognized him as the writer of the Gospel that bears his name. In his own list of the apostles, and there alone, he is written as "Matthew the publican," the name of reproach being humbly retained, and his name is placed after that of Thomas. As suggested above (chap. 2:14), it is not unlikely that Matthew was a disciple of the Baptist who had learned from him the lesson of Luke 3:12, 13. (8) Thomas.

Not mentioned by the synoptists, except in the lists, but mentioned on four occasions in John's Gospel, three times with the alternative name of Didymus, or "the twin" (John 11:16; 14:5; 20:24; 21:2). His name always stands next to that of Matthew in the lists—before it in all but Matthew's own; and that fact, together with the significant name "Didymus," has led many to the opinion that he was Matthew's twin-brother. Though this opinion cannot be proved correct, it may be accepted as highly probable. Matthew, mentioned first by all but himself, was probably the more prominent of the two, and his brother was the one to receive the name of "twin." Possibly there is some confirmation in the fact that the alternative name is found in the reminiscences of John, who, writing at a later time, might naturally be the preserver of a name that had become current within the circle of the apostles. The few allusions to Thomas give us a clearer view of his character than so few words ordinarily give, and we know him better than any other apostle except the first three—a faithful man, thoroughly loyal to his Master, but slow to be convinced and with a tendency to look on the dark side. Such is the second group of four.

The third group of four presents more material for discussion, but the discussion would add little to our definite knowledge. The names are, in Mark, **James the son of Alphæus, Thaddæus, Simon the Cananite** (Cananæus, Kananaios), **Judas Iscariot**. In Matthew the same, and in the same order, except that Thaddæus is called Lebbæus, with Thaddæus (in some manuscripts; not considered sufficient by Tischendorf) as a surname; in Luke, James the son of Alphæus, Simon Zelotes, Judas (the brother or son) of James, Judas Iscariot; in the Acts, the same, with the omission of Judas Iscariot. (9) James the son of Alphæus, the head of this group in all the lists, but he does not appear again in the Gospels. There is a strong presumption in favor of the identity of this Alphæus with the father of Matthew; and if this presumption is correct, then James and Matthew, and probably Thomas, were brothers. But the wife of Alphæus (Clopas, in John 19:25, being the same name in its Aramaic form) is called in Mark 15:40 the mother of James the Less, or the Little, and of Joses—a designation that we would scarcely expect if she were the mother of Matthew and Thomas, or even of one of them. Hence some find in the James and Joses here mentioned the "brethren of the Lord" of Mark 6:3; but strongly against this is John 7 : 5 and Acts 1 : 14, in the face of which it is impossible to find any of his brethren among the apostles. The question has, perhaps, no fully satisfactory solution. To the present writer it seems rather more probable that there was only one Alphæus, and that the two—and probably three—apostles were brothers. To the association of James with Matthew it is objected that their names never stand together; but if Matthew and Thomas were twins, they would naturally form a pair in the lists, and the next name after theirs is uniformly that of James. (10) Thaddæus, called Lebbæus in Matthew, and Judas of James in Luke and Acts. He appears in the Gospels only as "Judas not Iscariot," asking a question, in John 14 : 22, and nothing more is known of him. His name, apparently, was Judas, and Lebbæus and Thaddæus were surnames or titles conferred upon him for reasons that can only be conjectured. "Judas" was so common a name as to call for some additional designation to him who bore it; but the meaning of these titles is so obscure as scarcely to warrant the attempt at interpretation. Nor is it possible to tell what "Judas of James" means. The phrase "brother of James," at the beginning of the Epistle of Jude, has led to a similar filling up of the ellipsis here; but it is not certain that this Judas was the author of the Epistle, neither is it certain what James is meant. And this filling up of the ellipsis is not the usual one, the word "son" being the one that the phrase ordinarily calls for. In our ignorance of the connecting facts it is best to leave the fragmentary record as we find it, and say that of this apostle little is to be known. (11) Simon the Cananite, or Cananæan—not Canaanite, descendant of the ancient inhabitants of the land. The title is somewhat obscure, but is probably to be interpreted by the parallel word in Luke and Acts, Simon the Zealot, Zelotes. It comes from a Hebrew root which signifies "to be hot," and was undoubtedly the Aramaic equivalent for the Greek word Zelotes, which had been in use since the time of the Maccabees to designate a sect or section of the Jews who were most intensely devoted to the idea of nationality, and of God as the only sovereign whom it was right for Jews to obey, who had no fear of death or trouble in defence of their views, and who toward the end of the Jewish period became reckless and violent even to the extent of crime. (See Josephus, Ant., 18. 1.) About A. D. 6 they followed Judas of Galilee, who led a popular revolt and was regarded by many as the Messiah. This Simon,

of whom we know nothing more, had apparently been associated with this party. The acceptance of Jesus as the Messiah by a man who had been associated with the followers of the fiery Judas is an interesting and significant fact. (12) Judas Iscariot was the son of one Simon who is himself called Iscariot in the best text of John 6 : 71 and 13 : 26. "Iscariot" is "Ish-Kerioth," "man of Kerioth," a village of Judah of uncertain site (Josh. 15 : 25); at least, this is the usual explanation, and probably the best. He seems to have been the only apostle who was not a Galilæan, unless Simon, whose name stands next to his, may have been a Judæan, like himself. As Peter is first in all the lists, so Judas is last. It has been suspected that he was placed at the end after his crime had degraded him, but it is more likely that this was originally his position. Certainly, Jesus from the first knew his character; and if this, as we have no reason to doubt, was a genuine selection, surely Judas must have been the last choice. All the lists mention him as the betrayer, except the one in the Acts, from which, of course, he is omitted. Such is the third and last group of four.

Notice the use that Jesus made of natural relationship in constituting the body of apostles. James and John were brothers, and were probably cousins to himself; Peter and Andrew were brothers; Matthew and Thomas were probably twin-brothers, and perhaps a third member of their family was of the apostolic company. Thus fully half of the twelve were associated with their kindred; and, though "his brethren believed not on him," even Jesus himself was not separated wholly from his kindred.

19-30. INTERFERENCE OF JESUS' FRIENDS, AND CAVIL OF THE SCRIBES; WITH THE ANSWER OF JESUS TO THE LATTER. *Parallels,* Matt. 12 : 22-32 ; Luke 11 : 14-23.—From the choice of the apostles our Lord proceeded to address them in the Sermon on the Mount, of which Mark makes no mention. According to most harmonists, we are to place here also the healing of the centurion's servant, the raising of the widow's son at Nain, the message of John the Baptist in the prison to Jesus, the anointing by a pardoned woman in the house of a Pharisee, and a circuit of Galilee in which Jesus was accompanied not only by the twelve, but by various women whom he had healed. In other words, the whole of Luke's seventh chapter, with the first three verses of his eighth, belongs between the two clauses of this nineteenth verse—between the appointment of the apostles and the "going

20 And the multitude cometh together again, so* that they could not so much as eat bread,
21 And when his friends heard *of it*, they went out to lay hold on him: for they said, He* is beside himself.
22 ¶ And the scribes which came down from Jerusalem said, He* hath Beelzebub, and by the prince of the devils casteth he out devils.

20 And he cometh ¹into a house. And the multitude cometh together again, so that they could not so much as eat bread. And when his friends heard it, they went out to lay hold on him: for they said, He is
22 beside himself. And the scribes that came down from Jerusalem said, He hath Beelzebub, and ²By the prince of the demons casteth he out the demons.

a ch. 6 : 31,...,*b* Hos. 9 : 7 ; John 10 : 20,...,*c* Matt. 9 : 34 ; 10 : 25; 12 : 24 ; Luke 11 : 15 ; John 7 : 20 ; 8 : 48, 52.——¹ Or, *home*....² Or *In*

home" that is mentioned immediately after it.

19, 20. A new sentence and paragraph should begin here. **And they went into a house.** Should be, "And they come home," or, as some of the best manuscripts and Tischendorf, "And he cometh home." "Home" is doubtless Capernaum, and the statement plainly allows for any amount of journeying meanwhile. As soon as he had returned the crowd was about him again.—The vivid description is peculiar to Mark. **So that they could not so much as eat bread.** So at chap. 6 : 31. The activity on our Lord's own part is left to be inferred, but it must have been an intense activity of teaching and healing, continued we know not how long.

21. His friends of verse 21 are " his mother and his brethren " of verse 31. Their coming and calling for him is narrated by Matthew and Luke as well as by Mark, but Mark alone tells of their setting out in search of him and of their motive. Considerably later his brethren did not believe on him (John 7 : 5), and probably they persuaded his mother on this occasion, playing, perhaps, upon the anxiety of maternal love. These "brethren" appear to be the "James and Joses and Juda and Simon" of Mark 6 : 3. The question, What was their relation to Jesus? will probably never be settled with unanimous consent. The data being insufficient to furnish a positive decision, temperament and feeling, as well as theological preposessions, will always be elements in the formation of opinions on the subject. The theories are: (1) That they were children of Joseph and Mary, younger than Jesus; (2) That they were children of Joseph by a former marriage; (3) That they were cousins, probably orphaned, and in some way adopted into the family. The first is rejected by all Roman Catholic interpreters, by all who share their feeling as to the superior holiness of virginity, and by some besides who feel that reverence is best satisfied by regarding the Only-begotten of God as also the only offspring of his mother. Yet the scriptural argument for it is very strong (see it stated at length by Alford, on Matt. 13 : 55), and its adherents claim—probably correctly—that no other view would ever have been thought of but for unscriptural ideas of our Lord's mother. If the first theory is rejected, there is no choice between the second and the third.—His friends heard **of it**—of the great throng that was about him and of the busy life he was living—and **went out** from their home in Nazareth, where they were all living, mother, brothers, and sisters, a little later, when Jesus visited the place (chap. 6 : 1-6). The news reached them there, and brought them down to Capernaum, a distance of perhaps twenty miles. They came **to lay hold on him**—*i. e.* by force, as one who was not fit to take care of himself. They said, **He is beside himself,** insane—a conclusion from the excited life that he seemed to them to be living; perhaps the more plausible from the quietness and placidity of the years that he spent with them at Nazareth. Strangers misapprehended him thus (John 10 : 20), but so did his nearest friends. Unbelief will misapprehend whether its opportunities be small or great. Even the " mother and brethren " cannot know Jesus except they be true " mother and brethren."

22. Mark omits the occasion of this conversation, which is carefully given by Matthew and Luke—namely, the healing of the blind and dumb demoniac (Matt. 12 : 22), which caused many to inquire, " Is not this the Son of David?" —*i. e.* the Messiah. The scene is still "at home," and most probably in the house of Peter. "Pharisees" are present (Matthew), and so (Mark) are **the scribes which came down from Jerusalem.** This language distinctly indicates an embassy, men who had come on purpose to watch and harm him. It is not to be assumed that they were the same as the men mentioned at Luke 5 : 17, for some time had elapsed and meanwhile Jesus had been absent from Capernaum. But, whether the same or not, these were spies.—Indignant at the suggestion that this was the Christ, they were ready with their explanation of his mighty works, the reality of which they thus explicitly admitted. **He hath Beelzebub,** or, as the best manuscripts agree, "Beelzebul." The name has been variously interpreted. The name from which it came was

23 And he called them *unto him*, and said unto them in parables, How can Satan cast out Satan?
24 And if a kingdom be divided against itself, that kingdom cannot stand.
25 And if a house be divided against itself, that house cannot stand.
26 And if Satan rise up against himself, and be divided, he cannot stand, but hath an end.

22 And he called them unto him, and said unto them 24 in parables, How can Satan cast out Satan? And if a kingdom be divided against itself, that kingdom 25 cannot stand. And if a house be divided against 26 itself, that house will not be able to stand. And if Satan hath risen up against himself, and is divided,

Baal-ze-bub, "lord of flies," the god of the Philistines worshipped at Ekron (2 Kings 1 : 2) and consulted as an oracle. The god was named, doubtless, from his supposed control over the swarms of flies and similar insects that torment the East. After a time the Jews, thinking all heathen deities to be evil spirits, adopted this name as a title of the chief of evil spirits, but changed it by one letter, making Beelzebub into Beelzebul. Some think that in this change they intentionally degraded and insulted it, even as a word, by turning it into a name which meant "lord of dung" or "of the dunghill." But others, apparently with better reason, make it mean "lord of the mansion" or "of the dwelling"—*i. e.* lord of the place in which evil spirits dwell, or, substantially, "head of the family of evil spirits," he who rules them as a man rules his household. This sense best corresponds to the form of the word (*Meyer*) and best suits the allusions in the New Testament. So here: "He hath Beelzebul" means "he is possessed by the spirit who is lord of all the rest, and who orders them in and out at his pleasure, as a man commands his servants."—Thus the second clause of their charge is the application of the first. **By the prince of the devils casteth he out devils,** or demons. In the Greek the use of the recitative *hoti* (" that ") before each of these clauses seems to indicate that two separate remarks are quoted. One says, "that he hath Beelzebul." Another, "that by the prince of the demons casteth he out demons." Luke adds that others, tempting him, asked of him a sign from heaven.

23-26. The whole twenty-third verse is peculiar to Mark. He **called them**—the scribes from Jerusalem—bespeaking their attention and bringing them face to face with himself and their own words. The wonderful calmness and self-control of this reply cannot be too distinctly noticed in connection with the fearful charge that had just been brought against him. No more terrible accusation than this was possible; it was the direct charge of a positive and practical league with infernal powers. But he, "when he was reviled, reviled not again : when he suffered, he threatened not" (1 Pet. 2 : 23).—**He said unto them in parables.** In illustrative comparisons. The word does not require a narrative, such as we often associate with it. The point lies in the fact of a comparison. But

here the fact to be confirmed is given in the first question (verse 23); it is then confirmed and illustrated by two comparisons, of the kingdom and the household, in verses 24, 25; and it is restated directly in verse 26.—**How can Satan cast out Satan ?** The principle is that no intelligent power works against itself and defeats its own purposes. Observe what is here assumed : it is assumed that the dominion of Satan is an intelligent dominion, with character and purposes ; that the kingdom of evil is one intelligent kingdom, managed by one mind who knows what he is doing. The individual spirits that torment men are not identified personally with Satan, but they are identified morally with him ; so that their presence is his presence, and when they are cast out he is cast out. Now, it is said that in a kingdom there must be unity of counsel, illustrated first by the case of a kingdom among men. It is notorious that divided counsels, going into action, are the ruin of a state ; divided counsels or, more exactly, contradictory counsels —not between rulers and subjects, but in the government itself. How, then, if the kingdom of "the prince of the demons" be thus divided against itself and act against its own purposes? Illustrated next by the case of a household, regarded, not as made up of individuals, who may disagree, but as under the rule of a "householder," "goodman of the house," "lord of the mansion." If it acts against the character and counsels that govern it, it will be a failure. How, then, if the "lord of the mansion" be thus divided against himself, acting for the defeat of his own work? And now is made the application. If Satan were casting out demons, he would be rising up against himself. His sole purpose is to injure men. If he brings in health, calmness, purity, reason, godly gratitude, piety, to the souls of men, and if he sets them free from the bondage by which they are held away from these blessings, he will be acting directly against his own nature. Such a work as that of Jesus cannot possibly be attributed to him, any more than demoniacal possession can be attributed to God. Judge a work by its moral affinities. If it is good, it is not of the devil, for he never delivers men from evil. If such a rising up of Satan against himself as the work of Christ

27 No man can enter into a strong man's house, and spoil his goods, except he will first bind the strong man; and then he will spoil his house.
28 Verily I say unto you, All[a] sins shall be forgiven unto the sons of men, and blasphemies wherewith soever they shall blaspheme:
29 But he that shall blaspheme against the Holy Ghost[b] hath never forgiveness, but is in danger of eternal damnation:
30 Because they said, He hath an unclean spirit.

27 he cannot stand, but hath an end. But no one can enter into the house of the strong man, and spoil his goods, except he first bind the strong man; and
28 then he will spoil his house. Verily I say unto you, All their sins shall be forgiven unto the sons of men, and their blasphemies wherewith soever they shall
29 blaspheme: but whosoever shall blaspheme against the Holy Spirit hath never forgiveness, but is guilty
30 of an eternal sin: because they said, He hath an unclean spirit.

a Isa. 49 : 21, 26 ; 61 : 1 ; Matt. 12 : 29....b Matt. 12 : 31 ; Luke 12 : 10....c Heb. 10 : 29.

would be were proved real, there would be more than danger to his kingdom. **He cannot stand, but hath an end**, would be the true word. A kingdom so broken would be no kingdom at all.

27. More than this does Christ's work mean. The verse should begin with "but"—But **no man can enter**, etc. Not only does Christ's merciful and holy work prove him to be no ally of Satan, but, if Satan's kingdom is being taken away from him, the fact proves the presence of Satan's conqueror. No one can plunder the property of a strong "lord of the mansion" until he has bound the "lord of the mansion" himself; so, if Jesus is doing a great triumphant work of mercy in setting men free from the inferior agents of Satan's kingdom, he must already be master over Satan himself. The defeat of the Lord precedes the defeat of the servants; if the master were at liberty and had the power, he would not suffer his goods to be spoiled.—Perhaps there is a special touch of triumph in the closing words. **And then he will spoil his house ;** as if Jesus were regarding the end as absolutely sure and the work as actually begun. Compare John 12 : 31 : "Now is the judgment of this world ; now shall the prince of this world be cast out." Here speaks, in Jesus, the consciousness that he is absolutely the conqueror and destroyer of Satan's kingdom. Here, as a transition to the solemn words that Mark adds immediately, Matthew and Luke insert, "He that is not with me is against me; and he that gathereth not with me scattereth abroad." There are only two sides in this conflict, and they are the side of the "strong man armed" and the side of the "stronger than he." Not to be with the conqueror of Satan is to be with Satan.

28-30. But, though he answered the horrible charge so patiently, he did not fail to show how fearful a thing it was, or might be, to make it. In him was no implacable resentment of personal injury ; words spoken against him might be forgiven, and all sins and blasphemies were in general within the reach of pardon. But one sin was beyond the reach of

pardon—the blaspheming against the Holy Spirit.—The announcement of pardon for sins in general is much more elaborate and emphatic in Mark than in Matthew (Luke omits all reference to blasphemies). The grouping of words in the Greek is such as to throw the strongest possible emphasis on "all"—**all sins and blasphemies.** Mark omits, while Matthew mentions, the pardonableness of "speaking a word against the Son of man."—The key for the understanding of the "unpardonable sin" must be sought in the words, **He hath an unclean spirit,** or "He hath Beelzebul," as interpreted above. Jesus did not say that these men had committed the sin that hath no forgiveness, but he did say that that sin lay in the direction in which their sin was leading them. The sin thus suggested is the instinctive attributing of holy divine works to an evil source. It is the denial that good is good. This is the application in the Messianic age of Isaiah's denunciation (5 : 20): "Woe unto them that call evil good, and good evil ; that put darkness for light, and light for darkness; that put bitter for sweet, and sweet for bitter." The Holy Spirit is the supreme agent of good among men ; and when a man commits the sin against him of which Jesus speaks, he calls the Holy Spirit's good, evil, doing it out of a heart that has lost all sense of genuine good and is spiritually blind. No man will commit this sin until the sense of right and wrong, of good and evil, has become utterly perverted and even the holy work of God is without beauty to the soul. When that work appears to a man to be an evil work whose affinities are with hell rather than with heaven, then this sin becomes possible to him.

Hath never forgiveness. Literally, "hath not forgiveness unto the age," *eis ton aiōna*—i. e. *in æternum*, for ever. So John 4 : 14; 11 : 26; 1 Cor. 8 : 13, where the phrase *eis ton aiōna* is used with a negative particle to express the idea of "never" in the strongest manner. So here, "Hath never forgiveness" well represents the thought.—**But is in danger of eternal damnation.** More accurately, "but is guilty

31 ¶ There came then his brethren and his mother, and, standing without, sent unto him, calling him.
32 And the multitude sat about him; and they said unto him, Behold, thy mother and thy brethren without seek for thee.

31 And there come his mother and his brethren; and, standing without, they sent unto him, calling him.
32 And a multitude was sitting about him; and they say unto him, Behold, thy mother and thy brethren

a Matt. 12 : 46–48 ; Luke 8 : 19, 21.

of an eternal sin." (1) The word *kriseōs* (which would mean, however, "judgment," and not "damnation") gives place in the best text to *amartēmatos*, "sin," the same word as in the preceding verse, All sins, etc. It means, not the act of sinning, but the sinful act, the sin committed. (2) "An eternal sin" cannot mean endless transgression, an eternal continuance of sinning, for the reason just given: the word is not "sinning," but "sin." An eternal sin is a sin of eternally abiding guilt. The duration of the sin—*i. e.* of the guilt of the sin—is measured by *aiōnios*, which corresponds to the *eis ton aiōna, in æternum*, to which the unpardonableness of the sin is said to extend. (3) To this corresponds the word *enochos*, which with the dative may mean "in danger of" or "exposed to," as in Matt. 5 : 21, "in danger of the judgment," but with the genitive, as here, it means, most naturally, "guilty of"—"guilty of an eternal sin." Thus the sinner "hath not forgiveness for ever, but shall be guilty," when he has blasphemed against the Holy Spirit, "of an eternally abiding sin"—a sin whose guilt is never removed from his soul by pardon.

As to the quality of unpardonableness, (1) to suppose that God ever arbitrarily selects any sin and says that he will not forgive it is entirely inconsistent with what we know of his character. He always forgives the truly penitent, and no sin is in itself of too great guilt to be pardoned. If any sin is unpardonable, it is so because of its effect upon the sinner's heart, rendering him incapable of receiving pardon. (2) The sin that is here mentioned is a natural and spontaneous act of spiritual insensibility. Even of itself it reveals the fact that the sinner is beyond the reach of spiritual influences. If the Holy Spirit is condemned as the agent of evil, what power is left that can move the heart? When such a state is reached, it is morally impossible that the sinner should be forgiven, because it is morally impossible that he should repent. (3) All such ideas as that this sin is quickly and easily committed or committed unconsciously are in the sharpest opposition to the Scriptures. An unpardonable sin can be nothing less than the sin that comes as the grand result of a sinful life. (4) Any one who fears that he has committed the unpardonable sin has not committed it, for

it implies total indifference to good. No tenderhearted sinner need fear that he is beyond the reach of pardon. (5) Yet it is easy to see that this sin is not impossible. Our Lord did not himself judge the Pharisees as guilty of it or enable us to judge any one, but it is plain that the sin was possible to them, and is possible to others besides them. Sin hardens the heart; and it may so harden the heart that God cannot, consistently with the nature that he has given to man, enter and renew it.

Matthew and Luke record considerable additions to this discourse as given by Mark (Matt. 12 : 33-45 ; Luke 11 : 24-36). The saying about the sin against the Holy Spirit, Luke records in another connection (12 : 10).

31–35. COMING OF OUR LORD'S KINSMEN, AND HIS ANSWER CONCERNING HIS TRUE KINSMEN. *Parallels,* Matt. 12 : 46–50 ; Luke 8 : 19-21.

31, 32. They had come "to take him." (See note on verse 21.) Mark has meanwhile described the scene in which they found him and the conversation in which he was engaged. He graphically shows them coming, standing without, and sending their message in through the crowd which they could not penetrate. **A multitude sat about him.** Not "the multitude." Some manuscripts (and Tischendorf, not the revisers) read, "Behold, thy mother and thy brethren and thy sisters without are seeking thee." The sisters are mentioned at Mark 6 : 3, but we know nothing of their names or history. His mother, coming as his mother, would doubtless have been welcomed ; but an intrusive coming of his kindred to interfere with his work was quite another matter. Now that he was fully "about his Father's business," it was even more necessary than at the beginning of his work (John 2 : 4) that his mother should leave him to his Father's guidance. The moment, too, was a solemn one ; he had just been speaking of the deadly opposition between the two kingdoms, and was in a frame of mind to prize most highly those who were "with him" and were not "scattering abroad." Any attempt to "scatter abroad," to weaken his work, would then be especially painful to his soul, and the more if it came from those who ought to know him well. Yet in their coming (at least, we may be sure, in his mother's) there was kind-

33 And he answered them, saying, Who is my mo- | 33 without seek for thee. And he answereth them, and
ther, or my brethren? | 34 saith, Who is my mother and my brethren? And
34 And he looked round about on them which sat | looking round on them that sat round about him,
about him, and said, Behold my mother, and my | he saith, Behold, my mother and my brethren!
brethren! | 35 For whosoever shall do the will of God, the same
35 For whosoever shall do* the will of God, the same | is my brother, and sister, and mother.
is my brother, and my sister, and mother. |

CHAPTER IV.

A ND[b] he began again to teach by the sea side: and | 1 AND again he began to teach by the sea side. And
there was gathered unto him a great multitude, so | there is gathered unto him a very great multitude,
that he entered into a ship, and sat in the sea; and the | so that he entered into a boat, and sat in the sea;
whole multitude was by the sea on the land. | and all the multitude were by the sea on the land.

a James 1 : 25; 1 John 2 : 17....b Matt. 13 : 1, etc.; Luke 8 : 4, etc.

ness, but kindness how ignorant and mistaken! With what faults of friends he had to bear, as well as with evil in enemies! Not without pain, however, can he have given to his mother this rebuff. It was necessary; but he was a genuine son, and had a son's grateful and loyal heart toward his mother. His dying act of care for her (John 19 : 26) was a more congenial act to his heart.

33–35. Who is my mother, or my breth-ren? As if he did not know any from with-out who might appeal to him in that name.—**He looked round about on them which sat about him.** Literally, "in a circle about him." A graphic touch of Mark, to which Matthew adds another: "Stretching out his hand toward his disciples." The gesture impressed one beholder, the look another. Very full of tenderness and solemnity must the look have been, accompanying such words, for here is the adoption of the obedient.—**Behold** (these are) **my mother, and my brethren! for whosoever shall do the will of God, the same is my brother, and my sister, and mother.** In Luke, "My mother and my brethren are these, who hear and do the word of God." Compare "Every one that heareth these sayings of mine and doeth them" (Matt. 7 : 24). The centre of his true kindred is not the mother, the brother, or the sisters, but the Father. This, he says, is the *only* centre; there is no true unity with him except through spiritual harmony with the will of God: "Whoever would be a brother to me must be a child to him." Without this even natural kinship is as nothing. This, he also says, is the *real* centre—the centre of an actual unity; whoever is doing the will of God is united to Jesus by a tie stronger than any tie of flesh and blood: "Whoever is my Father's own is my own, one of my true kindred, in the closest bonds." Does he not even imply that the relation is as close and tender on one side as on the other?—toward the true brother, sis-ter, and mother as toward the Heavenly Fa-ther? Do not God and they that do the will of God thus come into one family for Jesus, in

which one and the same love reaches out in both directions? He said elsewhere, "As the Father hath loved me, so have I loved you;" and this is almost saying, "As I love my Father, so do I love you." Does this passage make God (or the doing of the will of God) the way to Christ, rather than Christ the way to God? Yes, in a sense. Whoever comes to Christ does the will of God in doing so, and it is in (not by the merit of) the doing of what God appoints that Christ accepts him. In all this Jesus did not disown the ties of kindred or put any slight upon them; rather did he show how highly he esteemed them. What must the natural relations be to him if he can make them the illustration of his relations both to God who sent him and to the people whom he saves?—Notice that the two mis-statements respecting Jesus, "He is beside him-self" and "He hath Beelzebul," are morally very far apart. One was a misunderstanding of his work—an ignorant, mistaken misrepre-sentation in which there was at least room for the anxiety of affection, and in which he was regarded as unfortunate. It implied spiritual ignorance, but not malignity. The other was a malignant refusal to see good in him, and a spontaneous judgment that his highest good was highest evil. The one corresponds to "speaking a word against the Son of man;" while the other at least approaches the unpar-donable sin of blasphemy against the Holy Spirit.—It is a satisfaction to find that after the resurrection of Jesus, Mary, the mother of the Lord, and his brethren were with the apostles in the upper room, where they waited for the fulfilment of Jesus' promise (Acts 1 : 14).

1–25. THE PARABLE OF THE SOWER, AND THE INTERPRETATION OF IT. *Par-allels,* Matt. 13 : 1–23; Luke 8 : 4–18.

1. And he began again to teach by the sea side. As before, at chap. 3 : 7. After the choice of the apostles he had returned to Ca-pernaum, there to find scribes from Jerusalem watching him, to be accused of being in league

2 And he taught them many things by parables,[a] and said unto them in his doctrine,
3 Hearken;[b] Behold, there went out a sower to sow:
4 And it came to pass, as he sowed, some fell by the wayside, and the[c] fowls of the air came and devoured it up.
5 And some fell on stony[d] ground, where it had not much earth; and immediately it sprang up, because it had no depth of earth:

2 And he taught them many things in parables, and 3 said unto them in his teaching, Hearken: Behold, 4 the sower went forth to sow: and it came to pass, as he sowed, some seed fell by the way side, and the 5 birds came and devoured it. And other fell on the rocky ground, where it had not much earth: and straightway it sprang up, because it had no deep-

a ver. 34; Ps. 78 : 2....b ver. 9 : 23; ch. 7 : 16....c Gen. 15 : 11....d Ezek. 11 : 19; 36 : 26.

with Satan, and to be sought by his kindred as a man beside himself. After such a reception he withdrew from the city; according to Matthew, on the very day of the events just recorded.—But he was popular still. When he went out, there **gathered unto him a great multitude.** Literally, in the best text, "A greatest multitude." For his resorting to the boat no reason is apparent besides the sufficient one of a desire to escape the crowd and be able to address them at better advantage. There is no ground for imagining that he wished to be safe from attack, after his exciting words, recorded most fully in Matt. 12. He used the boat before to escape from the crowd, but now as a pulpit.

2. He taught them many things in parables. The phrase **in parables** occurred at chap. 3 : 23, but in the teaching of the same day. "Parable" has not been used earlier in description of his teaching, except in reference to brief comparisons, and thus only twice (Luke 5 : 36; 6 : 39). Now seems to have begun the time of teaching by parables, the language of verses 10 and 13 indicating that this style of instruction was new to the disciples. The name "parable" is given in the New Testament (1) to proverbial sayings, which are usually condensed comparisons, as Luke 4 : 23 (in the Greek); (2) to comparisons without narrative, as Matt. 13 : 31-33; Mark 13 : 28; but chiefly (3) to narratives in which heavenly things are illustrated by means of earthly, as the three parables in Luke 15. Archbishop Trench treats thirty-three passages in the Gospels as parables. These make up about one-third of our Lord's teaching as preserved to us; and in a precise classification of his words various shorter sayings, of which Trench says nothing, would be added. This method of teaching has been widely employed among the Orientals, being well suited to the Oriental mind. It was common among the Jews, and was regarded by them as a means of higher education and an agency unsuited for popular use. It was especially a natural method to Jesus, both because of his keen interest in nature (when was such an appreciation of nature ever expressed as that of Matt. 6 : 29?) and because he "knew what was in man" and was

interested at every turn in human life. Yet his beginning to employ this mode of teaching marks the fact that he was not understood, and did not now expect to be understood very widely or very well. The religious leaders were against him, the misunderstanding of his work was growing malignant, and the people who followed him were led by curiosity more than by intelligent interest. The parabolic form of teaching was "less open to attack, better as an intellectual and spiritual training for his disciples, better also as a test of character, and therefore as an education for the multitude" (*Plumptre*).

Matthew records seven parables in this connection; Mark only three, one of which he alone has preserved, that of the growth of the seed (verses 26-29). It must be left somewhat uncertain whether these were all spoken on one day, as one would infer from Matthew, or whether Matthew has followed his custom of grouping and added something from other occasions to the one day's work.

3-8. The call to attention, **Hearken,** is peculiar to Mark. It has often been remarked that our Lord as he sat in the boat may have seen the sower going forth to his work, and observed all the peculiarities of field and of sowing that enter into his parable. Stanley says (*Sinai and Palestine*, p. 418) that he saw a field close to the shore of the lake that supplied every detail of the description — path, birds, rocks, thorns, and rich soil. Such fields, however, with roads running through them, are not home-fields, but open country, remote from the dwellings of the farmers, to which they literally go forth to sow; thus also in Ps. 126 : 6 (*The Land and the Book*, 1. 115). In this there is perhaps a quiet confirmation of the fact that Jesus had gone out from the town to some retired place of the shore where such a field might be in sight.—**Some fell by the wayside.** By the path running unfenced through the open field, the path itself, of course, was trodden hard, and the margin of it was no good place for grain. The fate of the seed that fell there was to be "trodden down" (Luke) and devoured by the birds.—**On stony ground,** or, rather, rocky ground—ground in which the

6 But when the sun was up, it was scorched; and*
because it had no root, it withered away.
7 And some fell among thorns;$ and the thorns grew
up, and choked it, and it yielded no fruit.
8 And other fell on good* ground, and did yield fruit$
that sprang up and increased, and brought forth, some
thirty, and some sixty, and some an hundred.
9 And he said unto them, He that hath ears to hear,
let him hear.
10 And* when he was alone, they that were about
him with the twelve asked of him the parable.
11 And he said unto them, Unto$ you it is given to
know the mystery of the kingdom of God: but unto

6 ness of earth: and when the sun was risen, it was
scorched; and because it had no root, it withered
7 away. And other fell among the thorns, and the
thorns grew up, and choked it, and it yielded no
8 fruit. And others fell into the good ground, and
yielded fruit, growing up and increasing; and
brought forth, thirtyfold, and sixtyfold, and a hun-
9 dredfold. And he said, Who hath ears to hear, let
him hear.
10 And when he was alone, they that were about him
11 with the twelve asked of him the parables. And he
said unto them, Unto you is given the mystery of
the kingdom of God: but unto them that are with-

a Ps. 1 : 4; James 1 : 11....*b* Jer. 4 : 3....*c* Heb. 6 : 7, 8....*d* Col. 1 : 6....*e* Matt. 13 : 10, etc..../ Eph. 1 : 9.

underlying ledge of rock was but just below the surface. The ledge often protruded in such fields as Jesus had in mind; and where it was just hidden the grain might find a warm bed in the shallow layer of earth, and spring up the more quickly by reason of the shallowness, as the parable says.—But the grain would lack **depth of earth** (Mark); "root" (Matthew); "moisture" (Luke); and "when the sun came up" (Matthew) it must wither. — **Among thorns.** The well-known thorns whose roots remained in the earth and were there before the seed was sown, though they were out of sight. They spring up in clumps with a strong growth, sometimes covering almost whole fields. Grain among them might grow, but would be so overshadowed and shut in as to be fruitless. —**On good ground,** which was abundant in the land of Gennesaret. Every field was certain to have its good part, rich and productive, where the seed might prosper.—**Thirty, sixty, an hundred.** Thirty-fold was the recognized ratio in an ordinary crop, but a larger yield— even so great as a hundred-fold—was not unknown in Palestine, though doubtless rare. Probably the language is partly proverbial and founded upon the record of Isaac's harvest of a hundred-fold when "the Lord blessed him" (Gen. 26 : 12). Thomson speaks of the extraordinary number of stalks that do actually spring from a single root, and says that he has seen in the Plain of Sidon more than a hundred stalks from one root, each with its head filled with grain, making a yield of more than a thousand-fold.—In the main the parable is almost verbally identical in Matthew and Mark; but Mark adds the descriptive words **sprang up and increased** in verse 8, and inverts the order of Matthew in mentioning the ratios of increase. These are sufficient signs of independence, especially the latter. Luke varies from Matthew and Mark very strikingly in the choice of words, though not in the substance of the parable. That he has preserved a separate and independent remembrance of the parable no reader can possibly doubt.

9. Thus, within the narrow compass of less than a hundred words (even in Mark's report, which is the longest), Jesus gave a comparison of indefinite suggestiveness and of inestimable practical worth. **He that hath ears to hear, let him hear** is an emphatic call to attention, always referring to what precedes it. It is thought to have been a familiar phrase in the schools of the rabbis. It is rather a call to attention than an appeal to spiritual discernment, and yet such an appeal is naturally implied. The phrase seems to have been used thrice on this day of parables (see verse 23 and Matt. 13 : 43), and is recorded twice besides in the teaching of Jesus: Matt. 11 : 15; Luke 14 : 35 (Mark 7 : 16 is probably to be omitted). It reappears, slightly altered in form, in the letters to the seven churches, Rev. 1–3, and at Rev. 13 : 9.

10. When he was alone—_i. e._ alone with his friends, apart from the multitude. The place and the exact time of this inquiry it is impossible to ascertain.—**They that were about him, with the twelve.** Here is a sign of the presence of a larger circle of near friends, who shared the intimacy of the apostles with the Lord. Some such have already been mentioned, in Luke 8 : 1–3.—**Asked of him the parable,** or parables, as the best text reads, corresponding to the language of verse 2, indicating, apparently, that more than one parable had already been spoken. It is quite possible that this inquiry, though introduced after the first parable because it drew out the explanation of that parable, was not made until some later time.

11.12. The answer implies some such question as the one recorded by Matthew—"Why speakest thou to them in parables?"—for it includes the reason for adopting this form of instruction. **To know** is omitted here in the best text, though not in Matthew or Luke; but the thought of it is implied here.—**Unto you it is given to know the mystery of the kingdom of God.** Matthew and Luke, "to know the mys-

them that are without,ᵃ all *these* things are done in parables:
12 That⁰ seeing they may see, and not perceive; and hearing they may hear, and not understand; lest at any time they should be converted, and *their* sins should be forgiven them.
13 And he said unto them, Know ye not this parable? and how then will ye know all parables?
14 * The sowerᶜ soweth the word.
15 And these are they by the wayside, where the word is sown; but when they have heard, Satan comethᵈ immediately and taketh awayᵉ the word that was sown in their hearts.

12 out, all things are done in parables: that seeing they may see, and not perceive; and hearing they may hear, and not understand; lest haply they should
13 turn again, and it should be forgiven them. And he saith unto them, Know ye not this parable? and how
14 shall ye know all the parables? The sower soweth
15 the word. And these are they by the way side, where the word is sown; and when they have heard, straightway cometh Satan, and taketh away the

a Col. 1 : 5; 1 Thess. 4 : 12; 1 Tim. 3 : 7....*b* Isa. 6 : 9, 10; John 12 : 40; Acts 28 : 26, 27; Rom. 11 : 8....*c* Isa. 32 : 20; 1 Pet. 1 : 25.... *d* 1 Pet. 5 : 8; Heb. 12 : 9....*e* Heb. 2 : 1.

teries." The word **mystery** is used in the New Testament, not to describe the quality of a truth or a fact as "mysterious," hard to understand. It tells rather of the relations of a truth or fact as once concealed, but now revealed, and yet revealed only within a certain circle, as of the initiated. A mystery, in the New Testament, is a truth that must be made known, if it is to be known, and one that actually is made known, by divine revelation, to those who have spiritual power to receive it. The word is not used in the Gospels except here and in the parallel passages, but it became a favorite word with Paul, and is found several times in the Apocalypse. Thus the gospel in general is called a mystery (Rom 16 : 25), and so is the truth regarding the manifestation and history of Christ (1 Tim. 3 : 16). So, again, is the relation of Christ to his church (Eph. 5 : 32), and the unity of Jews and Gentiles—*i. e.* of all mankind—in Christ (Eph. 3 : 4).—**The mystery of the kingdom of God** here is the revealed truth of the kingdom. This "hath been given," Jesus says, by the counsel of God to the disciples, the inner circle.—**But unto them that are without**—without the circle of Christ—**all things are done in parables. These** should be omitted. In parables do all things come to pass—reach their minds; and parables are a means at once of revealing and of concealing truth—of revealing it to those who "have ears to hear," and of concealing it from those who have not. (Compare Matt. 13 : 16 ; "Blessed are your eyes, for they see; and your ears, for they hear.") The inevitable separation of men, by the teaching of Christ, into those who hear unto life and those who hear unto death is reannounced by the citation of a terrible passage from Isaiah (6 : 9, 10) about the inevitable and fatal blindness of the disobedient. This separation was not an accidental but a necessary, and therefore an intended, result of his ministry (see, especially, John 9 : 39); and the choice of the parabolic form was one of the steps by which the inevitable separation must be accomplished. The

quotation from Isaiah, verbally exact in Matthew, is free and inexact in Mark, and still more so in Luke.

13. **Know ye not this parable?** which is not an obscure one. Then ye have not grasped the principle.—**And how then will ye know all parables** that I intend to give you? The question is peculiar to Mark, and gives us one of his glimpses of the tender thoughtfulness of our Lord for his disciples. Here shines out the quality of the true teacher. This is "a word in season," in view of the course of parables that he intends.

14-20. In the interpretation the language of Mark diverges more from that of Matthew than in the parable itself, though Mark still has rather more in common with Matthew than with Luke. He agrees with Luke, however, in retaining the plural form throughout.

The sower soweth the word. Of course the sower is primarily the Lord himself, and the parable represents the results of his ministry; but the sower is also any "laborer together with him" whom he sends forth to his field. "Here, ye apostles, and all ministers of the word, foresee the results of your ministry."—**The word.** "Of the kingdom," Matthew; "of God," Luke. Four classes of hearers are now portrayed—not ideally, but from real life. Our Lord had already met with them all, and his word had found all these four receptions. He could have named the hearers who belonged to the various classes. The parable obtains a new freshness and interest when we thus think of it as our Lord's testimony to his own experience.

1. **They by the way-side**—*i. e.* they that correspond to the seed sown there. Here the seed comes literally and absolutely to naught, being picked up from the hard ground by the birds. The word also fails. The reason is, in Matthew, that the hearer "understandeth it not;" and, in consequence of this failure to understand, the "evil one" (Matthew)—**Satan** (Mark); "the devil" (Luke)—taketh away—or,

16 And these are they likewise which are sown on stony ground; who, when they have heard the word, immediately receive it with gladness;
17 And have no root* in themselves, and so endure but⁰ for a time: afterward, when affliction or persecution ariseth for the word's sake, immediately° they are offended.
18 And these are they which are sown among thorns; such as hear the word,
19 And the⁴ cares of the world, and the deceitful-

16 word which hath been sown in them. And these in like manner are they that are sown upon the rocky *places*, who, when they have heard the word, 17 straightway receive it with joy; and they have no root in themselves, but endure for a while; then, when tribulation or persecution ariseth because of 18 the word, straightway they stumble. And others are they that are sown among the thorns; these are 19 they that have heard the word, and the cares of the

a Job 19 : 28....*b* Job 27 : 10....*c* 2 Tim. 1 : 15....*d* Luke 14 : 16-20; 1 Tim. 6 : 9, 17; 2 Tim. 4 : 10.

in Matthew, snatcheth away—the word from the heart. Luke adds, " Lest, believing, they should be saved"—an allusion to the thought of the citation from Isaiah. The understanding that is lacking is not chiefly intellectual: it is that moral discernment by which truth is perceived as truth and as divine, and is made the possession of the heart. When the word of God, though heard, is not thus perceived and appropriated, Satan (our Lord says) removes it from the heart. In the parable the variety of the means of removal is noted by the mention of the birds; in the interpretation the unity of the power that controls the means of removal is noted by the mention of Satan. The enemy of good has a thousand means and influences by which he can abstract from the mind truth that has not sunk into the heart. Truth left outside the heart will be stolen away; unappropriated, it will be lost. How much of the truth that is heard is thus left on the surface, spiritually unperceived—the soul not knowing that truth is there—to be taken away by the servants of evil! From such seed a harvest is, of course, literally impossible. Very likely this was the largest class in our Lord's audiences.

2. **Sown on stony ground,** or the rocky places. Luke, " Upon the rock." Here is the sharpest contrast, at first sight, to the first class: no growth and no promise there; quick growth and rare promise here. Those had no perception of the word: it lay outside; but these receive it, receive it immediately, receive it immediately with joy. Yet, notwithstanding their joy and promptness, the word gets no inward hold upon their character; it pleases them, but does not possess them: they have no root in themselves. The truth does not reach far down into their nature. Hence they are temporary— *proskairoi*, a most suggestive word. Not possessed by the truth, they have nothing to hold them to it, and they are offended and repelled as soon as the word becomes the occasion of **affliction or persecution.**—Note the repetition of **immediately.** When trouble comes, desertion is as prompt as was the glad reception of the word. Cases similar to this seem to be

meant in Luke 9 : 57-62. (See also Gal. 5 : 7.) Somewhat such was the earnestness (as far as it went) of the rich young man (Mark 10:17). Many such temporary followers our Lord must have had, and he may easily have found them at first the most enthusiastic of all. Innumerable have they been in the history of his kingdom.—All the intenser activities of his kingdom have this for their dark shadow of evil, the producing, through excitement or temporary zeal, of disciples who **have no root in themselves,** no subduing power of righteousness and love upon the character. So precious is religion that the necessity of "deep root" for it is too easily overlooked: we think it enough if the precious seed is growing. Yet there is no good fruit from religion that does not reach down deep enough to have an enduring life. Root in himself is necessary to a Christian—a life strong enough to outlive any excitement in which it may have sprung up, and to survive hours of severe testing and crises of discouragement (Ps. 139 : 23, 24).

3. **Sown among thorns.** Verse 18 begins, in the best text, " And others are they that are sown among the thorns." Quite another class is now to be introduced. This distinct clause, in Mark, with the word "others," divides the parable into two parts, and now, leaving the seed that does not survive till the time of harvest, our Lord proceeds to that which, with or without fruit, lives through the season. Here is not premature and temporary growth, but overshadowed and enfeebled life. The word is received, perhaps thoughtfully, and the life of obedience to it begins; but the soul is preoccupied, and the word cannot draw to its own service the powers of the man. The thorns represent prepossessions, preoccupations, influences, that absorb the soul and keep it away from devotion to a Christian life. These are: (1) **The cares of this world.** Literally, "Of the age," the current life of man in his present state. The original word for cares (*merimnai*, "drawings in different ways") suggests the distractions of mind that accompany interest in this world's affairs. These cares are not all sinful; but, whether sinful or not, they may absorb the power of the man,

ness* of riches, and the*b* lusts of other things entering in, choke the word, and it becometh unfruitful.*c*

20 And these are they which are sown on good ground; such as hear the word, and receive *it*, and bring forth fruit,*d* some thirty-fold, some sixty, and some an hundred.

¹world, and the deceitfulness of riches, and the lusts of other things entering in, choke the word, and it 20 becometh unfruitful. And those are they that were sown upon the good ground; such as hear the word, and accept it, and bear fruit, thirtyfold, and sixtyfold, and a hundredfold.

---

a Prov. 23 : 5....*b* 1 John 2 : 16, 17....*c* Isa. 5 : 2, 4....*d* Rom. 7 : 4 ; Col. 1 : 10 ; 2 Pet. 1 : 8.———1 Or, *age*

---

and so dwarf his Christian life. (2) **The deceitfulness** (or deceit) **of riches.** The power of wealth, whether possessed or only sought, to blind the mind and hold it by false pretences— the delusive promises that wealth holds out to him who seeks it, and the insinuating deceptiveness of prosperity and plenty. When wealth or the thought of it sets a false standard for the desires; when it obscures the distinction between good and evil in the means of gain; when it generates pride and occasions extravagance; when it gives its possessor an influence that of right belongs only to character,—then it chokes the word of truth and righteousness. (3) **The lusts of other things.** Literally, "The desires concerning the rest of things." In Luke, "The pleasures of life." These are the various longings, the vagrant desires, after the various things that "are not of the Father, but are of the world," "the lust of the flesh, and the lust of the eyes, and the pride of life" (1 John 2 : 16). These influences, **entering in**—taking possession of the soul—**choke the word, and it** (the word) **becometh unfruitful.** The hearers of this class are like grain in the midst of a thorn-clump; it lives through the season, but the thorns have so absorbed the strength of the soil that the grain has no power to mature its fruit. Luke, "They bring no fruit to perfection." they mature nothing and yield nothing. This part of the parable is an expansion of the text, "No man can serve two masters" (Matt. 6 : 24). (See also James 1 : 6-8.) It is a sad and weighty truth that double-mindedness in the hearer may render unfruitful the word of God itself.

4. **On good ground; such as hear the word and receive it.** "Understand it" (Matthew) spiritually, as the first class do not; "keep it," or hold it fast, "in an honest and good heart" (Luke). The good soil is the sincere and obedient heart, which appreciates and appropriates the truth. These hearers "bring forth fruit in patience" (Luke), recognizing that it is not sufficient to endure "for a while." Their fruitfulness has its degrees—**thirty-fold, sixty, and au hundred**—but they are all fruitful to the glory of God. The fruit consists in the character and works of holy virtue which the truth of Christ will produce. (See Gal. 5 : 22,

23; 2 Pet. 1 : 5-8.) The joy of harvest is a joy both to the soul and to the Lord.

It is necessary that the seed (1) take root; (2) take deep root; (3) take deep root in a clear field; (4) take deep root in a clear field of good soil. It is of no use for the truth to fall as it were by the wayside; yet it is not enough to avoid the wayside and receive the truth into the soul. It must not fall upon the rock, it must go deep into the soul; yet it is not enough to avoid the rock and receive the truth to a deep and permanent place in the soul. It must be kept out of the thorns, the repressing influences of worldly and selfish life, and be patiently guarded and obeyed in a good and honest heart. The four classes of hearers are (1) heartless; (2) shallow-hearted; (3) half-hearted; (4) whole-hearted. In the first, the divine life does not spring up; in the second, it springs up, but only to a temporary and disappointing growth; in the third, it springs up to a permanent but stunted and profitless growth; in the fourth, it springs up to a prosperous and productive growth. There are at least three ways to be fruitless, only one to be fruitful. Three classes of our Lord's hearers out of four the word preached did not profit (Heb. 4 : 2); and the case is still the same. The same classes still exist—three fruitless to one fruitful. But then one class out of four was not fruitless; here was the triumph of grace, and here is the triumph still. There is genuine fruit unto God in his field; and the work of the gospel is to be glorious and honorable in enlarging this successful class and diminishing the others. Study the parable from the standpoint of the thorns, already in possession of the soil, and resenting the entrance of the grain; also from the point of view occupied by the soil, supposing it to be intelligent, with the power of directing its nourishing influences to that which it regards as of the highest worth.

21-25. CAUTION AGAINST MISUNDERSTANDING OF HIS PURPOSE IN TEACHING BY PARABLES. *Parallel*, Luke 8 : 16-18.—There is no parallel in Matthew. Almost all of these verses are found in Matthew, but they are scattered here and there, and not brought at all to the illustration of the point for which they are used in Mark and Luke.

21 ¶ And he said unto them, Is a candle brought to be put under a bushel, or under a bed? and not to be set on a candlestick?

22 For² there is nothing hid, which shall not be made manifest; neither was any thing kept secret, but that it should come abroad.

23 If any man have ears to hear, let him hear.

21   And he said unto them, Is the lamp brought to be put under the bushel, or under the bed, *and* not to be put on the stand? For there is nothing hid, save

22 that it should be manifested; neither was *anything*

23 made secret, but that it should come to light. If any

There is nothing strange in this, for these sayings are mainly of the striking, proverbial kind, capable of many applications, and very likely used many times by our Lord. The passage that is here made up from them is so admirably appropriate to the connection that we cannot possibly suppose it to have been made up by compilation: it was certainly spoken thus. In its connection, this is one of the noblest and most far-reaching of all our Saviour's utterances.

21–23. Jesus had now given forth one elaborate parable and expounded it, and he had given his friends to understand that such teaching was thenceforth to be frequent with him. Already, before the exposition, he had told his disciples that it was given to them to know the revealed truth of which a parable was the picture, while to the world outside was given only the parable itself, to be understood or not according to the hearer's heart. Thus parabolic teaching was in an important sense esoteric, and useful only to the initiated. But such counsel to the initiated must not be left unguarded. They must not suppose that they were entrusted with secrets of the kingdom to be guarded as secrets: that would defeat his very purpose. He must make perfectly plain to them the intent for which he gave them a clearer knowledge of his truth than others possessed. Hence this passage, to which perhaps something of their subsequent fidelity in preaching was due; to which, also, we may owe more than we are aware of the records that they made of his life and words. "No permanent secrets in the kingdom; all truth for all men"—this is the thought of the passage.

Is the candle (or lamp) **brought** in order **to be put under a bushel** (the ordinary household measure, holding about a peck, found in every house), **or under a bed** (the table-couch)? Is it not brought that it may be **set on the candlestick,** or, rather," lampstand "? As he himself is the Light of the world (John 8 : 12; 12 : 46), so his truth is light, to whomsoever it may be entrusted. It has the nature and powers of light, and even when entrusted to an inner circle it is destined to the uses of light. In their hands it is a lamp, given, not to be hidden, but to be

placed where it can shine. Though they receive truth in the form of parables, which all cannot now receive, still they must not think it was given them for themselves alone: the light was meant for the lampstand (Matt. 5 : 15, 16).—Verse 22 repeats the lesson. In the best text, literally, "for there is nothing secret, but in order that it may be manifested; nor did anything become hidden, but in order that it may come to light "—*i. e.* there is nothing secret, as the meaning of these parables is secret, except that it may cease to be necessary to have it secret; nor has anything in the course of the Lord's ministry become a hidden thing, as the truth thus expressed is hidden from the many, except in order that it may in due time reach all men. If truth seems to be hidden in being entrusted exclusively to a favored few, it is not so: that method was chosen as the best way for ultimately spreading it abroad. So, perhaps still more strongly, in Matt. 10 : 27: "What I tell you in darkness, that speak ye in light; and what ye hear in the ear, that preach ye on the housetops." Thus the communicating of truth to a few is guarded from misunderstanding. A permanent circle of initiated pupils is declared not to be what Jesus desires; indeed, an inner circle is forbidden to exist. All truth is for all men, and whoever has truth committed to him is required to give it forth. Erasmus paraphrases, "Think not that I wish that which I commit to you to be concealed for ever. A light has been kindled in you by me, that by your ministry it may dispel the darkness of the whole world." "I am the light of the world," "Ye are the light of the world." (Compare Phil. 2 : 15, 16.) Thus Jesus affirms that in teaching by parables he speaks to a few, because that is the best way to reach the many. He teaches an inner circle in order that his circle of learners may become unlimited. There are other examples of similar use of temporary methods; as when God gave his people one sacred place, Jerusalem, in order that he might bring in the religion that was proclaimed in John 4 : 21-24, in which no place is consecrated, because all places are sacred. Here, again, he closes a solemn saying with the formula of attention.

24 And he saith unto them, Take heed what[a] ye hear: With[b] what measure ye mete, it shall be measured to you; and unto you that hear shall more be given.
25 For he that hath, to him shall be given: and he that hath not, from[c] him shall be taken even that which he hath.

24 man hath ears to hear, let him hear. And he said unto them, Take heed what ye hear: with what measure ye mete it shall be measured unto you: 25 and more shall be given unto you. For he that hath, to him shall be given: and he that hath not, from him shall be taken away even that which he hath.

a 1 Pet. 2 : 2....b Matt. 7 : 2....c Luke 8 : 18.

24, 25. Thus far the duty of using the truth as light is used has been grounded in the nature of truth and the purpose of the Teacher; now it is grounded in the law of human life itself. The words, **And he saith unto them,** repeated here, probably indicate, not a new beginning with a change of time and place, but rather the narrator's remembrance of the special emphasis with which all this was spoken, very likely after a solemn pause.—**Take heed what ye hear.** Luke, "how ye hear." Not, "Be careful what you listen to," as if he would warn against dangerous teachers, but, "Carefully consider what you are hearing; observe how important it is; remember how necessary that you make the right use of it." It is almost, "Take heed to what you hear." The reason assigned for this caution is that, according to the universal law, what one does will return to him.—The words **that hear** are to be omitted, and the omission considerably changes the structure of the sentence: "With what measure ye mete, it shall be measured to you, and added to you."—This saying, **With what measure ye mete, it shall be measured to you,** proverbial in form, is applied in the Sermon on the Mount (Matt. 7 : 2) to the retribution that must come upon uncharitableness and self-willed judgment. Here our Lord gives it a quite different application; it is a law of life, and may be applied in many ways. In this case its lesson is, "You will be dealt with, as to truth, as you deal with others. Hide it, and it will be hidden from you; impart it, and it will be imparted to you." How many souls, in dealing with truth as God has given it to them, have found it even so—that concealment was loss, while giving was gain! If the apostles had kept their truth as a private trust, how their souls would have shrivelled!—**Shall more be given** is a promise of a return, which shall be not merely as the gift, but greater. So Luke 6 : 38. (Compare 2 Cor. 9 : 8-14.)—Verse 25 contains what was evidently more or less a proverbial saying with our Lord. **He that hath, to him shall be given,** etc. (See Matt. 25 : 29; Luke 19 : 26.) Here it fits the connection far otherwise than as in the passages referred to—another illustration of our Lord's various use of single important sayings. Here,

5

by a very striking turn of thought, **he that hath** is identified with him who imparts his trust of truth to others, the free giver, the true apostle, messenger of grace and truth; while **he that hath not** is identified with him who keeps his trust of truth to himself, content to be ever a disciple without becoming an apostle. The giver **hath,** the miser **hath not.** How true a description of men, and how true an interpretation of the law of life!—And now it is declared that for these two classes there shall be retribution. **He that hath, to him shall be given.** So Luke 6 : 38—a passage that may serve as a link between this and Matt. 7 : 2: "Give, and it shall be given unto you." (See also Luke 12 : 48.)—**And he that hath not, from him shall be taken even that which he hath.** How is this? He "hath not," and yet he "hath" something that he can lose. Yes; the spiritual miser possesses much in his own esteem; much truth has been entrusted to him; but if he is not a giver of truth, and so a possessor, his possession shall become no possession: what he hath shall be worthless to him. Such instruction may well have made the apostles careful what use they made of the parables. Perhaps, it is due that they were so faithful in putting the lamp on the lampstand, not only by preaching, but also by making record of his words, especially such words as these.

26-29. THE PARABLE OF THE GROWTH OF THE SEED.—Mark's record has no parallel here, he alone having preserved to us this beautiful and suggestive parable. It seems not a little strange that such a parable should find only one out of the four to record it; but the reason why it is so can scarcely be even conjectured.

The key for the interpretation of the parable must be sought in the position which it occupies. It stands, in Mark, immediately after the parable of the Sower—i. e. nothing has intervened except the interpretation and the remarks on the true use of parables. The parable of the Mustard-Seed immediately follows it; but before the parable of the Mustard-Seed comes, in Matthew, that of the Good Seed and the Tares. This parable is thus associated closely with the two in which the work of the Saviour in his kingdom is compared to a sower's work, but its affinities are closer with the former, with which Mark

26 ¶ And he said, So is the kingdom of God, as if a man should cast seed into the ground;
27 And should sleep, and rise night and day, and the seed should spring and grow up, he knoweth not how.
28 For the earth bringeth forth fruit of herself;[a] first the blade, then the ear; after that, the full corn in the ear.
29 But when the fruit is brought forth, immediately he[d] putteth in the sickle, because the harvest is come.

26 And he said, So is the kingdom of God, as if a man
27 should cast seed upon the earth; and should sleep
28 and rise night and day, and the seed should spring
up and grow, he knoweth not how. The earth [b]beareth fruit of herself; first the blade, then the ear,
29 then the full corn in the ear. But when the fruit
[3]is ripe, straightway he [3]putteth forth the sickle,
because the harvest is come.

---

a Matt. 13 : 24....*b* Gen. 1 : 11, 12....*c* Eccles. 3 : 1, 11; Job 5 : 26....*d* Rev. 14 : 15.——1 Or, *yieldeth*....2 Or, *alloweth*....3 Or, *sendeth forth*

---

associates it. In that parable (verses 3–8) the seed, which is the word, is sown, and its various destinies are pictured as they occur in the life and experience of individual hearers. In this, nothing is said of individual conduct or destiny, but the method of advance from sowing to harvest in the field as a whole is set forth. The sower is the same sower as in the first parable; the seed is the same seed, though more broadly regarded, perhaps, as including all the powers and influences of the kingdom. The field is the world. Some have preferred to take the parable as the illustration of the work of the gospel in the individual life, the history of personal Christian growth; but the connection with the parable of the Sower is decidedly against this interpretation. It is far more natural that the two sowers and the two fields should be the same in the two parables; and after the first picture, so full of warning and so suggestive of possibilities of failure, there surely was place for another, in which the destiny of the good seed should be foretold on a wider scale and with reference to the methods of the world-wide work.

26. As if a man should cast seed into the ground. Literally, "the seed," by which must be meant either "his seed,"—the seed that he is sowing; or, "the seed already in mind"—the seed that has been mentioned in the foregoing parable. The latter sense seems to be decidedly preferable; the seed is still the word, and the present parable is an exposition of the parable of the Sower. When the husbandman has cast the seed into the ground he sleeps and rises, night and day—sleeps by night and rises when day comes, according to his wont—and while he is doing nothing to make it germinate, the seed springs up and grows, he knows not how.—**For the earth bringeth forth fruit of herself.** The *for* should be omitted, and the emphasis, as in the original, be marked by commencing with **of herself.**—And the grades of growth are marked; not in a day do the powers and influences of the creation mature the grain. **First the blade,** undistinguishable from grass, yet not grass; **then the ear,** ready for the grain to form, and yet not filled; **after that**

the full corn in the ear, the ripened grain, ready for the garner.—**But when the fruit is brought forth**—or permits, for such is the best translation of *paradoi*—**immediately he putteth in** (or sends forth) **the sickle, because the harvest has come.** The grain is harvested as soon as it is ready.

In the interpretation we must not suppose it our duty to find in this parable the whole truth concerning the kingdom of Christ. No one parable gives us that; and this shows us one aspect, and only one, of the work of Christ among men. It shows us the agency of his word in its relation to the general operation of God in the world. Nor must we suppose that every part of the comparison is significant and closely to be pressed in the interpretation. If that principle were adopted, there could never be a parable. Parables proceed upon the principle of resemblance, not of identity. In the present case there are some parts of the parable that are present only as parts of the imagery by which the central idea is set forth. The kingdom of Christ is set forth in its relation, not to the forces of nature or the natural receptivity of man, but to the general operation of God in the world. As the farmer submits his seed to the operation of the powers of nature, so does the Messiah, whether sowing in person or through the agency of his followers, submit his truth and kingdom to that general operation of God in human history wherein God works in accordance with the nature that he has given to man. Not to nature or to man, but *to the world as ruled by God*, he commits his gospel. It takes its place among other powers in the world, and among them it does its work. **He knoweth not how** does not mean that the Messiah knows not how the true seed grows; it is a part of the picture of spontaneous growth in nature.—**The earth bringeth forth fruit of herself** does not mean that the true seed bears its fruit without divine influences; for even in the parable, as Bengel remarks, the culture of the soil is not excluded, neither are the influences of sun and rain. But the gospel is cast into the world as an element in human life, and it does its work, not by startling divine interpositions, but as grain ma-

30 ¶ And he said, Whereunto shall we liken the kingdom of God? or with what comparison shall we compare it?

31 *It* is like a grain of mustard seed, which, when it is sown in the earth, is less than all the seeds that be in the earth:

32 But when it is sown, it groweth up, and becometh greater[a] than all herbs, and shooteth out great branches; so that the fowls of the air may lodge under the shadow of it.

30 And he said, How shall we liken the kingdom of God? or in what parable shall we set it forth? It is

31 like a grain of mustard seed, which, when it is sown upon the earth, though it be less than all the seeds

32 that are upon the earth, yet when it is sown, groweth up, and becometh greater than all the herbs, and putteth out great branches; so that the birds of the heaven can lodge under the shadow thereof.

a Matt. 13 : 31, 32 ; Luke 13 : 19, 19....b Prov. 4 : 18; Isa. 11 : 9 ; Dan. 2 : 44; Mal. 1 : 11.——1 Gr. As unto.

tures and seeds grow under the fostering influences of Divine Providence. This is the teaching of the parable, and the best commentary on it is found in the history of Christian truth among men. In exactly this way—silently, as seeds grow—has God's kingdom come thus far, and is it coming still. This is a parable of hope, for in the world in which Christ places his seed there are powers at work that render the harvest certain. If this parable is parallel to that of the Sower, the harvest is not primarily [but see Matt. 13 : 30.—A. H.] the gathering of saints to glory, but the gathering of men to Christ. This, the great Husbandman, who reaps as well as sows, will accomplish in due time.

30-32. THE PARABLE OF THE MUSTARD-SEED. *Parallels*, Matt. 13 : 31, 32; Luke 13 : 18, 19.—**Whereunto** (or how) **shall we liken the kingdom of God ? or with what comparison** (or parable) **shall we compare it ?** In using the plural, **we,** our Lord seems to conceive of his disciples as deliberating with him in the choice of a comparison; not that he was in doubt as to how the gospel could be illustrated — comparisons thronged upon him—but because he would have them also on the watch for comparisons. The world was full of them, and they, the teachers of men in higher things, must learn, as well as their Master, to find them. Yet possibly he may sometimes, like any one of them, have had to feel after an illustration in nature that was suited to his thought.—**A grain of mustard-seed.** There seems to be no good reason for looking elsewhere than to the ordinary mustard of the East. Thomson (*The Land and the Book*, 2. 100) has seen it as high as a horse and rider. [See also the beautiful incident in Dr. Hackett's *Illustrations of Scripture*, p. 124.—A. H.] This is the *Sinapis nigra ;* but some have thought that the *Salvadora Persica* was more probably the herb that Jesus had in mind. The former, however, meets all the real requirements of the case, and was the more familiar plant to his hearers. " It (the *Sinapis nigra*) is a small grain producing a large result; the least of the husbandman's seeds, becoming the greatest of the husbandman's herbs. This is the point of the

parable, and gives the only sense in which the kingdom of heaven is like a grain of mustard-seed " (*The Bible Educator*, 1. 121).—**Less than** and **greater than** are not to be pressed to the point of minute precision. There may be smaller seeds in existence without giving us reason to stumble at our Saviour's words. The mustard-seed was commonly spoken of as the smallest of seeds, and that is enough. — **Becometh greater than all the herbs,** Matthew, "is greater than the herbs, and becometh a tree "— *i. e.*, of course, a tree in appearance, not botanically. The **great branches** are such as one

MUSTARD-PLANT.

would think impossible upon an herb that sprang from so small a seed.—The comparison calls for very little explanation, the lesson— small beginnings and great results—being very plain. Such is the kingdom, begun obscurely, with no human prospect of greatness, no seeming possibility of success. It began among the Jews, a disappointed people chafing under foreign masters; it was the smallest of sects among them; it contradicted their ideas, and was rejected by them; it seemed to be powerless at home, and without opportunities abroad; and its Founder died on the cross. Even after the day of Pentecost it seemed but a feeble sect.

5

33 And with many such parables spake he the word unto them,ᵃ as they were able to hear *it*.
34 But without a parable spake he not unto them: and when they were alone, he expounded all things to his disciples.
35 And the same day, when the even was come, he saith unto them, Let us pass over unto the other side.

33 And with many such parables spake he the word 34 unto them, as they were able to hear it: and without a parable spake he not unto them: but privately to his own disciples he expounded all things.
35 And on that day, when even was come, he saith

---

a John 16 : 12.

Yet compare the strong language of Paul in Rom. 16 : 26; Col. 1 : 23 as to the wide extension of the gospel within the apostolic times. Consider also the power of the name and principles of Jesus in the world to-day, and the ever-widening circle of Christian influence. The kingdom has grown out of all resemblance to its humble beginning. Such is the kingdom; and the same rule is to be observed in its agencies. They are often obscure and yet mighty. A single act of a quiet person often seems possessed of a germinant power of usefulness that brings most unexpected fruit to the glory of God. Christian history is full of illustrations. Notice that this comparison does not set forth the greatness of the kingdom absolutely, as destined to fill the earth, but only relatively, in contrast with the insignificance of its apparent promise. **33, 34.** CONCLUSION OF THIS RECORD OF PARABOLIC TEACHING. *Parallel,* Matt. 13 : 34, 35. — **With many such parables.** Mark thus recognizes a larger teaching by parables on that occasion, which he does not report. Matthew places before this point the parables of the Tares and the Leaven, and after it, in the same connection, the exposition of the parable of the Tares, and the parables of the Hidden Treasure, the Costly Pearl, and the Net cast into the Sea. Of this group, only Luke records only the Sower, the Mustard-Seed, and the Leaven; Mark, only the Sower, the Growth of the Seed, and the Mustard-Seed. Mark, doubtless, knew that others were spoken, but why he omitted them we cannot affirm.—**As they were able to hear it**—*i. e.* not in amount proportioned to their ability to receive and understand it—not as in John 16 : 12—but **in parables**, that being the only form in which the people were spiritually **able to hear** what he had to say to them. This was the mode which their limited ability to hear and understand forced upon him.—**And without a parable spake he not unto them.** His public teaching on this occasion was altogether by parables. Not even the expositions were given in the audience of the people. Not improbably, the same practice extended to other occasions at this period of his ministry; so that we have clear indication of a large number of unrecorded parables. Undoubtedly, there must

have been many such, his facility in illustrating from nature and life being enough to render it certain that he was frequently "using similitudes." For the multitude they were intended to awaken curiosity and thoughtfulness; for "his own disciples," to whom he expounded them in private, they were of the very substance of his message—pictures of fundamental truths of his kingdom. Compare 1 John 2 : 21 : "I have not written unto you because ye know not the truth, but because ye know it." Notice that his explanations were not for those who were most dull of apprehension; the explanations were reserved for those who could understand. Here, again, "to him that hath shall be given." The disciples thought they understood this course of parables (Matt. 13 : 51), and, in a sense, they did understand them; yet what a "springing and germinant" meaning had these words of Jesus! Not fully interpreted even yet. The understanding of his truth is progressive; men in every age understand it, yet do not understand it; it is revealed, yet it is ever coming to the mind and heart of man; it is known, yet it is so great as almost to seem unknown.—It is Mark that adds, in his own vein, **as they were able to hear it**, and speaks of the private exposition to his own disciples. Matthew, not less characteristically, has here a quotation from Psalm 78 : 2 as to the utterance of parables and dark sayings. Matthew is the evangelist who constantly connects the new covenant with the old; Mark is the one who constantly views it in itself and pictures the Christ as a peculiar personage, working alone a mighty work among men.

35-41. JESUS STILLS A TEMPEST ON THE LAKE. *Parallels,* Matt. 8 : 23-27; Luke 8 : 22-25.

35, 36. The same day, when the even was come—*i. e.* the day of the parables. Matthew and Luke differ from Mark and from each other as to the time and connection of this event, but their notes of time are not so definite as Mark's, and his order bears the stronger marks of intentional arrangement; hence, as usual, the only course is to follow him.—**Let us pass over unto the other side.** The eastern side of the lake, the starting-point being somewhere near Capernaum.—" Leaving the multitude " is a better sense for *aphentes ton ochlon* here than

35 And when they had sent away the multitude, they took him even as he was in the ship: and there were also with him other little ships.

36 unto them, Let us go over unto the other side. And leaving the multitude, they take him with them, even as he was, in the boat. And other boats were

having sent the multitude away. The purpose was to find rest. How great was the need of it, a backward glance will show. The first words of Matt. 13 : 1 distinctly connect the ministry of parables by the lakeside with the coming of his mother and brethren, and with the bitter charge of the scribes from Jerusalem, as all occurring on the same day. Thus, to find the events of the morning, we are carried back to Mark 3 : 20 or Matt. 12 : 22. Within the day now ending he had been so thronged at home as to have no time to eat; he had healed a demoniac; he had been accused of being in league

been illustrated before him. The only doubt in this enumeration relates to the explanation of the parables, which may not yet have been reached; they may have brought him their question and received their answer or explanation now, as they were going to the other side. Such a day's work as this could not fail to bring a terrible strain upon him in mind and heart. We must not forget how intensely living his own truth was to him, or how deeply he cared for the destinies of his hearers. And this had been a day of rejection for his truth and of hardening for some, at least, of those who

SEA OF GALILEE.

with the evil one, and so of being the worst of demoniacs and the most wicked of men; he had thus met with the most violent rejection of his mission and his goodness; he had been sought by his own kindred as a man beside himself, and had been obliged to repel them, even though his mother was among them; he had changed the method of his teaching, had taken up the use of parables, and had delivered **many** (*verse 33*) to a thronging multitude; he had afterward explained these to his disciples, who were eager and yet not swift to understand him; and all the day the parable of the Sower, with its three fruitless classes to one fruitful, had

heard him. Whether he knew then the experience of his servants in depression and despondency—the "Lord, who hath believed our report?"—we cannot say; but that day was enough to give him full sympathy with his servants in the experience of mental weariness. Far deeper and more consoling is this weariness than that of John 4 : 6, when he was merely "wearied with his journey;" now he was wearied with his work.—They took him, **even as he was in the ship** (or boat)—peculiar to Mark—*i. e.*, probably, because he was utterly weary and would have them spend no time in preparation. He was "in the boat," as

37 Andᵃ there arose a great storm of wind, and the
waves beat into the ship, so that it was now full.
38 And he was in the hinder part of the ship, asleep
on a pillow: and they awake him, and say unto him,
Master,ᵇ carest thou not that we perish?

37 with him. And there ariseth a great storm of wind,
and the waves beat into the boat, insomuch that the
38 boat was now filling. And he himself was in the
stern, asleep on the cushion: and they awake him,
and say unto him, ¹Master, carest thou not that we

a Matt. 8 : 24 ; Luke 8 : 23....*b* Ps. 10 : 1 ; Isa. 40 : 27 ; Lam. 3 : 8.——1 *Or, Teacher*

at verse 1.—That there were also with him
other little ships is peculiar to Mark—the
vivid remembrance of an eye-witness how they
set out upon the lake amid a little fleet of boats,
filled, no doubt, with friends.

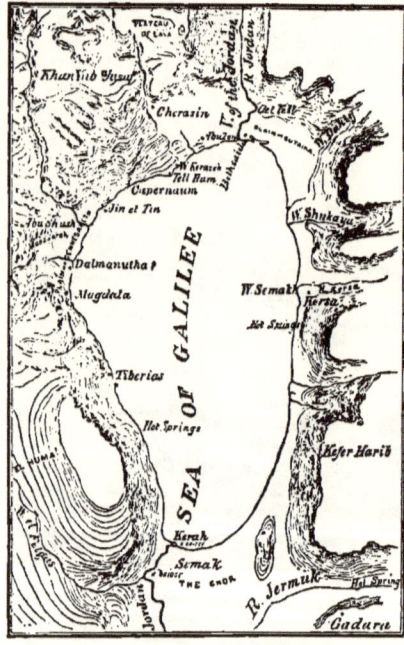

37, 38. A great storm of wind. For a
description of such a sharp, sudden tempest
by night on that lake see Thomson, *The Land
and the Book*, 2, 32, 33. Such storms are frequent
on all inland seas, but especially there. The
level of the lake is six hundred feet below that
of the ocean, yet the altitudes of the surrounding
hills are very considerable. Hence the streams
that cut their way down to the lake gain extraordinary velocity, especially when the snows
are melting and wear for themselves deep water-
courses, which serve as gigantic funnels, through
which the winds rush down upon the lake and
make such sudden and violent disturbances as
occur scarcely anywhere else.—So that it—the
boat—was now filling, not full. Matthew says

"covered with the waves," and Luke adds that
"they were in danger;" but the most graphic
of all the touches is Mark's when literally translated, "The waves beat into the boat, so that
it was now filling."—The pillow, or rather
"cushion," was a part of the furniture of the
boat; not unlikely, from its being at the stern
of the boat, it was the steersman's cushion.
Mark alone mentions it, and tells the part of
the boat in which Jesus lay asleep—asleep so
profoundly in his utter exhaustion as to know
nothing of the tempest. How perfectly natural
a sequence to such a day as has been described!
Yet nothing has been directly said in the narrative of his weariness; we see it rather than
read of it. Not only the weariness do we see,
but the calmness, the trust, as of a little child;
the tempest does not awaken him.—But the
secret of his calmness has not yet taken possession of his friends. The petulant carest
thou not that we perish? is found in Mark
alone; it is a foolish word of distrust, yet
matched—how often!—by the complaints of
later disciples when they are tempted to fancy
that "the Lord hath forsaken the earth." It
indicates, too, a degree, or rather a kind, of
familiarity that ill accords with true reverence. Not yet did they fully know with whom
they had to do. But did they really suppose
that the boat would perish, with all on board,
when the Christ of God was there? They were
not yet fully convinced that he was the Christ, or
such a fear could never have overcome them.
[It is worthy of notice that Mark alone, whose
narrative is believed to have been derived from
Peter, gives the appeal to Jesus the form of a
"petulant" or reproachful question. Compare
Matthew (8 : 26): "Save, Lord, we perish;" and
Luke (8 : 24): "Master, Master, we perish." And
what is more likely than that Peter alone used
the words recorded by Mark? Who else of the
disciples was so likely to give such a turn to his
appeal for help? No one of the twelve save
Peter appears to have reproved the Lord on any
other occasion. But he, in his honest arro-
gance and impetuosity, did this more than once.
And if he alone used the words preserved by
Mark, what more natural than that he alone
was wont to repeat them? For they were
words which he might well remember, and
which, in the excitement of that moment on

39 And he arose, and rebuked the wind, and said unto the sea, Peace, be still. And*a* the wind ceased, and there was a great calm.
40 And he said unto them, Why are ye so fearful?*b* how is it that ye have no faith.
41 And they feared*c* exceedingly, and said one to another, What manner of man is this, that even the wind and the sea*d* obey him?

39 perish? And he awoke, and rebuked the wind, and said unto the sea, Peace, be still. And the wind
40 ceased, and there was a great calm. And he said unto them, Why are ye fearful? have ye not yet
41 faith? And they feared exceedingly, and said one to another, Who then is this, that even the wind and the sea obey him?

---

a Ps. 89 : 9; Lam. 3 : 31, 32....b Ps. 46, 1, 2; Isa. 43 : 2....c John 1 : 10, 16....d John 38 : 11.

---

the lake, in the storm, were probably observed by no one of his associates. This little question, therefore, "Carest thou not that we perish?" confirms the early tradition that Mark's Gospel is at the same time Peter's.—A. H.]

39–41. It is not **he arose,** but "he awoke," or, still stronger, "he was aroused."—He **rebuked the wind.** Matthew, "the winds;" Luke, "the wind and the raging of the water." —But the word of address was to the sea; Mark alone gives it. **Peace, be still,** is not a literal rendering, but is an effective one. The first word is "Be silent;" the second, literally, "Be muzzled," or, in its metaphorical sense, "Be reduced to silence." The second is in the imperative mode of the perfect tense—a rare use in the New Testament—thus explained: "The perfect imperative is used when an action complete in itself is represented as to continue in its effects; as in Mark 4 : 39, in Christ's address to the troubled sea: *pephimōso,* 'be (and remain) *still*'" (*Thayer's Winer,* p. 315). Note the simplicity of this narrative: no attempt to make the style correspond to the sublimity of the act.—Just so of the effect: how could it be more simply described? **The wind ceased.** Literally, "grew weary"—an expressive word for the sudden lull and resting of the raging wind. It was not a gradual dying away of the wind, followed by a long swell of the waters, but a quick cessation, followed almost immediately by a great calm. "Here was a greater than Jonah" (*Meyer*). All theorizing as to the inner nature of the act is of course in vain; but no one who has seen in him the Lord of nature, and has known his other works of power, need feel any difficulty in the narrative. Attempts have, of course, been made to explain away the miracle, some calling it a coincidence and some finding in the story only a mythical representation of the power of Christ to still the tempests of the soul. But the testimony of Meyer is of value here: "It is to be held historically as a miracle, an event that sprang from the divine power that dwelt in Jesus, on account of which it is no more difficult to ascribe to him a mighty work upon the elements than an influence upon the bodily organism." Jesus never raised storms, but he quelled them. Compare the fancy in

Shakespeare's *Tempest*—a fancy ethereal, but not spiritual—of a magician who has power upon the elements. He does not act without a purpose, but he serves his purpose first by raising storms, and then by quelling them. So a wonder-worker would be likely to do, without divine self-control. The apostles could be trusted with miraculous power only because the mind was in them (though imperfectly) that was also in Christ Jesus. It is a tribute to the power of his grace in them that we have no reason to think they ever abused it.

40, 41. In Matthew (not in Luke) the question of verse 40 precedes the rebuke to the winds and address to the sea, the "Why are ye so fearful, O ye of little faith?" being uttered while the storm is still raging. In Mark the remonstrance follows the deliverance. The text is somewhat doubtful, but the reading of the revisers is probably right: "Why are ye fearful? have ye not yet faith?"—faith in him, in his love as well as in his power, which they had half disowned in their **carest thou not that we perish?** but which their experience of him ought to have made fresh and unfailing; and perhaps also faith in God's paternal watchfulness and protection, which enabled him to sleep amid the tempest, while they were half crazed with fear.—**What manner of man** (or, more accurately, "who, then") **is this?** The question of the disciples in Mark and Luke; in Matthew, of "the men" who were with them, in their own boat or in the other boats. Even the apostles had not learned to know him as one from whom such control of nature could be expected, and now they were awestruck in his presence. (Compare Luke 5 : 8, 9.) We may picture the amazement of other persons who may have been upon the lake at the sudden cessation of the wind, for which they knew no reason, and of the astonishment and incredulity with which the true story of it might be received; yet not then, and in that land, with any such incredulity as now, and in the West. The miracles, like other means that God uses, were used at the right time and place. It is the highest evidence of their divine source that they were so perfectly adapted to the age in which they were employed.

CHAPTER V.

A ND⁴ they came over unto the other side of the sea, into the country of the Gadarenes.

1 AND they came to the other side of the sea, into the country of the Gadarenes.

1 AND they came to the other side of the sea, into the country of the Gadarenes.

a Matt. 9 : 28, etc. ; Luke 8 : 26, etc.

1-20. JESUS HEALS A DEMONIAC ON THE EASTERN SHORE OF THE LAKE. *Parallels*, Matt. 8 : 28–34 ; Luke 8 : 26–39.

1. This narrative immediately follows in all three records. The time was the early morning, when they came to land from the nocturnal voyage just described. As to the place, the manuscript readings of the name of the country are full of variation in all the Gospels. The

that either of them did so. In any case, neither of them can have been the "city" mentioned in verse 14, for this was close to the shore. Hence there has been much perplexity about the scene of this miracle, and suggestions have not been wanting that the names were not real names, but had only some symbolic meaning to correspond to a mythical story. Origen declares, however, that in his day there was a

TOMB AT GADARA.

most approved readings are "Gadarenes" in Matthew and "Gerasenes" in Mark; while in Luke authorities are divided between "Gerasenes" and "Gergesenes." Gadara was a city of some repute, sixteen Roman miles east of Tiberias; Gerasa was also an important town, about twenty Roman miles away. Both were east of the lake, and either might conceivably give its name to the district that extended to the lake, though there is no historical evidence

town called Gergesa on the eastern shore of the lake. Thomson (*The Land and the Book*, 2, 34–37) seems to have been the first in modern times to find there a ruined town that bears the name of Kersa, or Gersa. The town stood quite near the water, and all the requirements of the story seem to be sufficiently met by it. The site may be regarded as beyond question, and the discovery removes all difficulty as to the scene of the miracle, except that it does not

2 And when he was come out of the ship, immediately there met him out of the tombs a man with an unclean spirit,
3 Who had *his* dwelling[a] among the tombs; and no man could bind him, no, not with chains:
4 Because that he had been often bound with fetters and chains, and the chains had been plucked asunder by him, and the fetters broken in pieces: neither could any *man* tame him.
5 And always, night and day, he was in the mountains, and in the tombs, crying, and cutting himself with stones.
6 But when he saw Jesus afar off, he ran and worshipped[b] him,

2 the country of the Gerasenes. And when he was come out of the boat, straightway there met him
3 out of the tombs a man with an unclean spirit, who had his dwelling in the tombs: and no man could
4 any more bind him, no, not with a chain ; because that he had been often bound with fetters and chains, and the chains had been rent asunder by
5 had strength to tame him. And always, night and day, in the tombs and in the mountains, he was cry-
6 ing out, and cutting himself with stones. And when he saw Jesus from afar, he ran and worshipped him ;

•

a Isa. 65 : 4....*b* Ps. 72 : 9.

explain the confusion of names in the ancient records. As it is scarcely possible to be sure what was the original reading in any one evangelist, perhaps the divergences can never be perfectly accounted for; but the loss of the site of Gergesa would tend to produce such confusion, more especially as Gadara and Gerasa remained well-known names. The narrative is given in substantially the same way by Mark and Luke, though with some differences of arrangement. Matthew's report is more brief and compendious, and differs from the others chiefly in that he speaks of two demoniacs, while they mention only one. The common conjecture for explanation is that there were two, but that one was so far inferior to the other in violence and prominence as to pass almost unnoticed. Plainly, there is nothing impossible in this conjecture, but it must be remembered that all attempts at reconciliation must be conjectural, the facts being partly unknown to us. In the present narrative we meet with only one demoniac.

2-5. This appears to be the most violent case of demoniacal possession described in the Gospels. It is also the most fully detailed as to its outward manifestations, although the case in chap. 9 is more minutely described as to bodily symptoms. The whole description is in Mark's most vivid style. The man met Jesus **immediately,** on the very shore, as he was leaving the boat; his home was in the city (Luke), but he had long been living in the tombs. These are still to be seen in the mountain back of Gersa—caves in the mountainside, natural or artificial. They might be large enough to give shelter to a man, and, as they were ceremonially unclean (Num. 19:16), one who was insanely shunning human society would be likely to seek them ; no one else, certainly, would resort to them. All maniacs were outcasts as soon as they became violent, for that age had no provision for taking care of them. Institutions of pity for the unfortunate are among the gifts of Christ; antiquity knew nothing of them, or of the spirit that would

produce them. The power of the evil spirit to produce mental insanity in its worst forms is here abundantly illustrated. The disease in chap. 9 is epilepsy ; here it is pure insanity. The victim flees from home; he is sleepless and vociferous (according to the Revision, "always, night and day, in the tombs and in the mountains, he was crying out"); he is given to injuring himself ("and cutting himself with stones"); he is violent toward others ("so that no one was able to pass by that way"); and is unnaturally strong, so that restraint is impossible. The language of verse 3 in the best text introduces the despair that experience has occasioned: "And no one could any longer bind him"—it had been tried again and again, as verse 4 tells, but his preternatural strength had always triumphed—"and no one had strength to tame him." These outward results of demoniacal possession were horrible enough, but the worst was in the consciousness of the victim—a consciousness that seems to have been strangely and horribly divided, now the man and now the demon being the centre.

6-9. The order seems to be, the boat draws to the shore, and Jesus disembarks; the demoniac sees him from a distance, and comes running to the place; Jesus, when he sees him coming, immediately commands the spirit to come out of him (verse 8); the man comes nearer, bows down before him, and cries out as in verse 7; then follow the question and answer of verse 9. **Worshipped him**—*i. e.* bowed down before him, as in adoration. The act must not be confounded here with true worship, of which there certainly was nothing. But there was confession, in exactly the spirit of James 2 : 19: "The devils" (demons) "also believe, and tremble," or "shudder."—The cry of verse 7 was a cry of such shuddering recognition, accompanied by impotent rage. **What have I to do with thee ?** Literally, "What to me and to thee?" exactly as at chap. 1 : 21 —a cry of repulsion corresponding to the eter-

7 And cried with a loud voice, and said, What have I to do with thee, Jesus, *thou* Son of the Most High God? I adjure thee by God that thou torment me not.

8 For he said unto him, Come out of the man, *thou* unclean spirit.

9 And he asked him, What *is* thy name? And he answered, saying, My name *is* Legion:[b] for we are many.

10 And he besought him much, that he would not send them away out of the country.

7 and crying out with a loud voice, he saith, What have I to do with thee, Jesus, thou Son of the Most High God? I adjure thee by God, torment me not.

8 For he said unto him, Come forth, thou unclean spirit, out of the man. And he asked him, What is thy name? And he saith unto him, My name is Legion; for we are many. And he besought him much that he would not send them away out of the

a Acts 16 : 18; Heb. 2 : 14; 1 John 3 : 8....b Matt. 12 : 45.

nal repulsion between the two kingdoms which the two represented.—**Jesus.** The name is inserted in Mark and Luke. If the quotation is exact, the name would seem to indicate that the man had heard of Jesus, perhaps had seen him. To suppose a supernatural knowledge of his human name on the part of the spirit would be to introduce something to the record. —**Son of the Most High God.** This name for God is very ancient (Gen. 14 : 18), and was used in earlier times often along the borderland between the Hebrew faith and other monotheistic religions. So it appears in connection with Melchizedek, with Balaam (Num. 24 : 16), and in the song of Moses (Deut. 32 : 8), at a point where the relation of Israel to other nations is brought in. Plainly, the name **Most High** is one of the simplest expressions of the relation of God to the world, and one in which monotheists of any type might unite with Jews and Christians. In the later Jewish period, when the Jews were scattered among the nations, it became a very frequent word in their writings, being often used in the Greek translation of the Old Testament. " It was one of the words which, in later as in earlier times, helped to place the Gentile and the Jew on common ground" (*Plumptre*). The same writer thinks, though on what authority is not apparent, that the name was often used in exorcism, and that this fact accounts for its appearing in the speech of demoniacs here and at Acts 16 : 17, this being the name of God that they had most frequently heard.—**I adjure thee by God, torment me not.** The adjuration is peculiar to Mark; Luke, "I beseech thee;" Matthew, "Art thou come hither to torment us before the time?" in which the expectation of coming torment is clearly admitted and Jesus is recognized as the person who is to be feared.—The word of adjuration (*orkizō*) is the word from which our word "exorcise" is derived. The evil spirit, in its fear, is trying to match the command of Jesus by a counter-command in the very name that it dreads. Jesus has said, **Come out of the man,** and the spirit demands, in the name of

God himself, to be let alone. How little could an evil spirit conceive of the spiritual unity of Jesus with God! To such a spirit "God" meant only power, and hated power; and the spirit may have dimly thought that the name of God would act as a name of power on Jesus, even as on itself.—The next question of Jesus, **What is thy name?** was an attempt to recall the man to the remembrance of his humanity. —But the answer came from the indwelling power, not from the man, the horrid possessor giving a name that was mockery to the personality of his victim. **My name is Legion: for we are many.** Legion, a Roman troop, varying in number at different times, but well enough represented by six thousand, which was nearly the maximum.—Note the shifting and divided consciousness, first singular and then plural. **My name, . . . for we.** The appropriateness of the name **Legion** seems to be assumed by the evangelist in verse 15, "Him that had the legion." Possibly it was a name that he had often given to himself, and one that had become familiar to those who knew him.

10. From this point there is a change. In verse 2 it was an **unclean spirit;** but now, after the word **Legion** has been uttered, the possessing power is spoken of in the plural—**them,** and in verse 13 **the unclean spirits.** In Luke the man was introduced at the beginning as one who had "demons," but not so in Mark.—In verse 10 the variable consciousness sadly appears again, the man identifying himself and his interests for the time with the destiny of the spirits that have been tormenting him. **He** (the man) **besought him much, that he would not send them** (the spirits) **away out of the country,** the surrounding region. According to Mark, the spirits begged (through the man) to be allowed to linger about the place where they had been dwelling; according to Luke, to be allowed to remain out of "the abyss"—not "the deep," which many readers have confounded with the sea, but the "bottomless pit," the place of their final misery. The same word occurs in Rev. 9 :

11 Now there was there, nigh unto the mountains, a great herd of swine feeding.
12 And all the devils besought⁵ him, saying, Send us into the swine, that we may enter into them.
13 And forthwith Jesus gave° them leave. And the unclean spirits went out, and entered into the swine: and the herd ran violently down a steep place into the sea, (they were about two thousand,) and were choked in the sea.

11 country. Now there was there on the mountain side 12 a great herd of swine feeding. And they besought him, saying, Send us into the swine, that we may 13 enter into them. And he gave them leave. And the unclean spirits came out, and entered into the swine: and the herd rushed down the steep into the sea, *in number* about two thousand: and they were choked

a Lev. 11 : 7, 8; Deut. 14 : 8....*b* Job 1 : 10, 12; 2 : 5, 6....*c* Rev. 13 : 7; 1 Pet. 3 : 22.

1 ; 20 : 1, etc. Even demons were pleading with their Master for mercy. For a hint of the state of lesser misery which they preferred, see Matt. 12 : 43.

11-13. The herd of swine was **nigh unto the mountains,** or "on the mountain-side." In Matthew, "far off"—*i. e.* at some distance; in sight, but not close at hand.—**All the devils,** or "demons," at the beginning of verse 12, is to be omitted; so is **forthwith,** at the beginning of verse 13.—**Send us into the swine, that we may enter into them.** A desperate proposal. Of course, they could not expect him to permit them to enter again into human beings, and this was the only chance they saw of remaining at liberty. Why did Jesus give the permission? We cannot fully answer the question, but we may be sure that it was for some reason connected with the welfare of the man. Perhaps, in view of his divided state, it was necessary that he should see the evil power actually removed from him, and behold the evidence by seeing its mischief wrought in something else, before he could surely believe in the restoration of himself to himself. If it were thus necessary that the evil should be made visible apart from the man, it was right and merciful to allow it to be done in the brutes that were at hand. The act thus comes into likeness with the blighting of the fruitless fig tree for the illustration of spiritual things (Matt. 21 : 18-20).—The effect, however, is a complete surprise. As to the place, the most accurate account of it, from careful observation, is given by J. Macgregor, in the *Rob Roy on the Jordan,* p. 411. On the mountain back of the lake he saw a large herd of animals of various kinds feeding together. Between the base of the mountain and the water is a narrow plain. Macgregor says: "We are told that the whole herd of swine ran violently down a steep place. Literally, it is 'down the steep' in all three reports. It does not say that it was a high place, but steep, and that they ran (not fell) down this into the sea. There are several steeps near the sea here, but only one so close to the water as to make it sure that if a herd ran violently down, they would go into the sea. Here, for a full

half mile, the beach is of a form different from any other round the lake, and from any that I have noticed in any lake or sea before. It is flat until close to the edge. There a hedge of oleanders fringes the end of the plain, and immediately below these is a gravel beach inclined so steep that when my boat was at the shore I could not see over the top even by standing up; while the water alongside is so deep that it covered my paddle (seven feet long) when dipped vertically a few feet from the shore. Now, if the swine rushed along this short plain toward this hedge of underwood (and in the delta of Semakh their usual feeding-place would be often among thick brushwood of this kind), they would instantly pass through the shrubs and then down the steep gravel beyond into the deep water, where they would surely be drowned."

As to the event itself, as it is a surprise to the reader, so it may have been to the spirits. (1) The spirits desired an abode in the swine, to keep them from being driven to the abyss. (2) The drowning of the swine left the spirits without an abode. (3) Hence it cannot have been at the impulse of the spirits that the swine rushed to their death. (4) The natural conclusion is that the spirits failed to effect a union with the powers of the swine, but that the approach of the unwonted disturbing power to the natures of the animals only excited them and caused them to rush to their own destruction. The fact that the ordinary word for entering into a person is used of the approach of the demons to the swine does not disprove this explanation, the evangelists having made no attempt accurately to represent the psychological peculiarities of the transaction. The greater desire of the demons was certainly disappointed, while the less was granted; and there appears no way but this to account for it, unless we suppose that Jesus by his own will drove the swine to death—a much less plausible explanation. Why did Jesus permit the swine to perish? According to this view, they did not perish directly by his act, but as a result of his permission of what proved impossible. The suggestion that he destroyed the swine, or consented to their destruction, for a rebuke and punish-

14 And they that fed the swine fled, and told *it* in the city, and in the country. And they went out to see what it was that was done.

15 And they come to Jesus, and see him that was possessed with the devil, and*a* had the legion, sitting, and clothed, and in his right mind: and they were afraid.*b*

16 And they that saw *it*, told them how it befell to him that was possessed with the devil, and *also* concerning the swine.

17 And they began to pray him to depart*c* out of their coasts.

18 And when he was come into the ship, he that had been possessed with the devil prayed him that he might be with him.

19 Howbeit, Jesus suffered him not, but saith unto him, Go home to thy friends, and*d* tell them how great things the Lord hath done for thee, and hath had compassion on thee.

14 in the sea. And they that fed them fled, and told it in the city, and in the country. And they came to 15 see what it was that had come to pass. And they come to Jesus, and behold *l* him that was possessed with demons sitting, clothed and in his right mind, *even* him that had the legion: and they were afraid. 16 And they that saw it declared unto them how it be-17 fell *l* him that was possessed with demons, and concerning the swine. And they began to beseech him 18 to depart from their borders. And as he was entering into the boat, he that had been possessed with 19 demons besought him that he might be with him. And he suffered him not, but saith unto him, Go to thy house unto thy friends, and tell them how great things the Lord hath done for thee, and *how* he had

Isa. 49 : 25; Col. 1 : 13....*b* Job 13 : 11; Ps. 14 : 5; 2 Tim. 1 : 7....*c* Job 21 : 14; Luke 5 : 8; Acts 16 : 39....*d* Ps. 66 : 16; Isa. 38 : 19.——*l* Or, *the demoniac*

ment upon the guilt of keeping them contrary to the law of Moses is somewhat weakened by the fact that this eastern side of the lake was partly Gentile territory, together with the fact that pork was a staple article of food with the Roman soldiers; so that their presence in the land would inevitably secure the keeping of herds of swine. Nor does it seem like our Lord, who expressly disclaimed all judging of men (Luke 12 : 14; John 5 : 45; 8 : 15; 12 : 47), thus to interfere to execute punishment in behalf of the law of Moses. More likely this was a part of that visible work of the evil power outside of the man which he saw to be necessary to the man's best welfare. "Those who measure rightly the value of a human spirit thus restored to itself, to its fellow-men, and to God will not think that the destruction of brute-life was too dear a price to pay for its restoration" (*Plumptre*).

14-17. The swineherds, and apparently some others (verse 16), had witnessed the event. The swineherds fled, amazed and indignant, and told the story, and the people flocked out from city and country, curiously gazing. "The whole city," Matthew; "the whole multitude of the region of the Gergesenes," Luke. When they had come, the witnesses of the act again repeated the story, both concerning the demoniac and concerning the swine. As to the man, he was **sitting, and clothed, and in his right mind,** "at the feet of Jesus" (Luke); **and they were afraid,** or, as in Luke, "were held with great fear." This was something new and strange; alarming too, though a work of grace, for it startled their dulness. Doubtless we might expect them to be unwilling that such acts as the destruction of the swine should be made frequent among them; but the restoration of the man seems also to have been one of the grounds of their repulsion from Jesus. Instead of "ad-

oration" or "rejoicing," "fear" is the word that describes their feeling; yet this was no holy and fruitful fear. Compare the exorcism at Acts 19 : 13-17, when the resulting fear turned to the magnifying of the name of Jesus. The true song for the man would be that of Ps. 40 : 1-3, but the last words would fail him : "Many shall see it and fear, and shall trust in the Lord." Not so of these people : they saw it and feared, and begged the Lord to depart out of their borders. This was too much like making a reality of divine power, and they did not wish to retain any such element in their life. Jesus seemed to them a disturber; so he is—a disturber of spiritual stagnation, a disturber of the dulness of death; but alas for those who see him only in this character! On similar grounds Jesus is often sent away still, men dreading him as an agitator who threatens to make their life too earnest.

18-20. The request was not made in vain. The case was not unlike that of chap. 6 : 5: there was no sympathy with his aims, and thus no basis in the popular spirit for his great works of mercy. He went back to the boat, apparently, without having gone up to the town at all.— But the man—no wonder that he clung to the Healer at whose word the dreadful incubus had fled and the freshness and sweetness of natural life had returned. No one like Jesus for this man to gaze upon; and he begged for the opportunity to be with him in a life of following, gazing, contemplation. Perhaps, too, he was half afraid that the evil might return if he were left alone.—But the Master knew a more excellent way. **Go home** (to thy house) **to thy friends, and tell them.** Thy house, long deserted for the tombs; thy friends, who have given up all attempts to bind thee—go to them, clothed and in thy right mind, **and tell them how great things the Lord hath**

20 And he departed, and began to publish in Decapolis how great things Jesus had done for him: and
all men did marvel.
21 And when Jesus was passed over again by ship
unto the other side, much people gathered unto him:
and he was nigh unto the sea.

20 mercy on thee. And he went his way, and began to
publish in Decapolis how great things Jesus had
done for him: and all men did marvel.
21 And when Jesus had crossed over again in the
boat unto the other side, a great multitude was

done for thee. The effect ought to be as in
Acts 4 : 14, or, rather, as in Acts 9 : 35–42.—**The
Lord**—*i. e.* God (as in Luke) through the agency
of Jesus. The collocation and comparison of
titles here cannot properly be used to prove the
deity of Christ. From this command it is evident that Jesus desired to be known on that
side of the lake as widely as possible. Himself in person the people were not ready to receive, but this trophy of his power might convince them.—He proclaimed **in Decapolis.**
Specified by Mark alone. The name means
"ten cities," or, rather, "the region of ten
cities." Soon after the Romans took the country (B. C. 65) ten cities—all, or nearly all, east
of the Jordan—were rebuilt by the conquerors
and endowed with certain privileges; and the
district took its name from this fact. The names
of the cities are not given with uniformity by
ancient writers, and the limits of the district
that was called Decapolis cannot be very definitely ascertained. Gadara was one of the ten.
The name "Decapolis" appears in the New
Testament only here and at Matt. 4 : 25 and
Mark 7 : 31.—How extensive the man's grateful
ministry was, of course we cannot tell. Luke
says, "Throughout the whole city;" Mark, **in
Decapolis.** Mark adds that **all men did
marvel,** but it is not said whether any believed. There are no clear signs of any fruitful
ministry among the dwellers on that side of the
lake.—As to the wisdom or folly of sending
Jesus away, the remaining part of the chapter
affords ample illustration of the truth. No
more of the tormented were released in the
country of the Gerasenes, and none of the sick
were healed. The Lord went back to raise the
daughter of Jairus from the dead, and to pour
new life into the body of the woman who
touched the hem of his garment in the throng;
but none of these things were done among the
Gerasenes: they had sent him away. The people could remain in their dulness too, for they
had sent away the only One who threatened to
disturb them with a blessing. Whoever dis-
misses Jesus as an unwelcome disturber may
in like manner be left in quietness, but it is the
quietness that marks the absence of true life,
the peace which is no peace; and there is no
evil like that. Whoever sends him away must
by him be sent away. (Compare Luke 12 : 8, 9
with Matt. 25 : 41.)

**21–43. A WOMAN WITH AN ISSUE OF
BLOOD IS HEALED, AND THE DAUGH-
TER OF JAIRUS IS RAISED FROM THE
DEAD.** *Parallels,* Matt. 9 : 18–26; Luke 8 :
40–56.—Mark and Luke agree in the order
here, expressly connecting this narrative with
that of the healing of the Gerasene demoniac.
Matthew expressly connects it with our Lord's
discourse on fasting (9 : 14–17), which Mark has
already recorded (2 : 18–22), at such a point as to
indicate that a considerable time intervened
between that and this. Of course our Lord
often met the same objections, and may have
encountered the question about fasting on two
occasions and given it twice the same answer.
This would account for the recurrence of the
remarks on fasting in two connections, but
scarcely for Matthew's ignoring of the fact that
there were two connections. As to that, however, it appears that Matthew, in his practice
of grouping events according to an inward
connection rather than in the order of time,
does not always strictly adapt his connective
words to the new place which his method
gives to narratives. It occasionally seems as
if he transferred a finished paragraph, with its
introductory connective word already fitted to
its context, to a new place suggested by his
principle of grouping, without changing the
introductory connective. Especially in the
group of miracles in chaps. 8, 9 is it difficult
to insist upon the appropriateness of his connectives. If we may draw an inference from
his practice, it seems possible that the connective phrase, "While he was speaking these
things" (Matt. 9 : 18), may have been designed to
suit a different context from the one in which
we find it.

21. The miracle on the eastern side of the
lake took place in the early morning, and later
in the day Jesus and his company were back
on the western side, but not in the town of
Capernaum. **He was nigh unto the sea,**
and there the crowd gathered to him, having
been waiting (Luke) for his return. Possibly
the change in his mode of teaching and the
introduction of parables had for the time
quickened the popular curiosity.

**22–24. One of the rulers of the syn-
agogue.** Presumably the synagogue in Capernaum, though nothing positively determines the
place.—The name **Jairus** is the Greek form

22 And,[a] behold, there cometh one of the rulers of the synagogue, Jairus by name; and when he saw him, he fell at his feet,

23 And besought him greatly, saying, My little daughter lieth at the point[b] of death: I pray thee come and lay thy hands on her, that she may be healed; and she shall live.

24 And Jesus went with him; and much people followed him, and thronged him.

25 And a certain woman, which had an issue[c] of blood twelve years,

22 gathered unto him: and he was by the sea. And there cometh one of the rulers of the synagogue, Jairus by name; and seeing him, he falleth at his

23 feet, and beseecheth him much, saying, My little daughter is at the point of death: I pray thee, that thou come and lay thy hands on her, that she may

24 be [1]made whole, and live. And he went with him; and a great multitude followed him, and they thronged him.

25 And a woman, who had an issue of blood twelve

---

a Matt. 9 : 18, etc. ; Luke 8 : 41, etc....b Ps. 107 : 18.....c Lev. 15 : 19, etc.——1 Or, saved

---

of the Hebrew "Jair;" it is the name of one who was a great man at the conquest of Canaan (Deut. 3 : 14), and later of one of the Judges of Israel (Judg. 10 : 3-5). Of Jairus nothing is known except what is recorded here. If, as is probably the case, he was a ruler of the synagogue in Capernaum, he would naturally be one of those who were sent by the centurion who had "built a synagogue" to intercede for him when his servant was sick (Luke 7 : 3). In that case he would be no stranger to the healing power of Jesus, and his confidence would be fully explained.—His eagerness appears in his falling down at Jesus' feet and his entreating him greatly, "much"—i. e. earnestly and persistently.—**My little daughter lieth at the point of death.** The phrase eschatōs echei, paraphrased **at the point of death,** is late Greek, and is said to have been condemned by the grammarians as bad Greek. Luke says that "he had an only daughter, about twelve years of age, and she was dying," not "lay a dying." Thus Mark and Luke agree perfectly in their statement; but, in Matthew, Jairus says, "My daughter just now died." The Greek verb is in the aorist, and "is even now dead" is not a good translation of it: that she has died already is distinctly affirmed. But the discrepancy is much less than one might think. Matthew tells the story compendiously; he omits all reference to the subsequent message from the house, in which the tidings of her death are brought; and he groups the two communications in one, making Jairus tell the whole in a single sentence. He gathers into this first request all the information about the case that was brought to Jesus before he reached the house. In Luke the request is only that he will come to the house; in Mark and Matthew the request is added that he will lay his hands upon her, with the full expression of confidence that that will be the means of restoration—according to the story as it is in Mark, of restoration from the verge of death; according to Matthew, of restoration from death itself. A beautiful example of confident resorting to the grace

and power of the Saviour. It was not in vain; no refusal awaited such an appeal. The request was brought to the lake-shore, where Jesus arrived in the boat. What he was doing we are not told; perhaps he had not had time to begin; or Jairus may even have been among those who were "waiting for him" when he came.—The crowd heard the request, and **followed, as Jesus went with him,** up from the lake-side into the town. He let them follow for a part of the way, not turning them back until his own time had come. He was not helpless in the matter; he did escape from the crowd when he was ready to insist upon it. Both in Mark and in Luke the words that describe the pressure of the throng are very strong words; in Luke, "crowd to suffocation" well represents it. Not much rest for our Saviour after the overpowering weariness of the previous evening—only the sleep on the boat. The healing and the repulse across the lake, a crowd waiting for him on his return, and now a call to go and give life to a dying child! But his compassion never failed, and he never considered himself. We have no reason to imagine that any consideration of himself ever held him back from a deed of love. He was the one perfectly unselfish Being, never false to this divine character. God is the unselfish One, and Christ is the manifestation of God.

25-34. Here is a story within a story, a miracle within a miracle. Between the beginning and the completion of the work undertaken in behalf of Jairus this healing comes in, as if to illustrate the abundance of his power. The whole scene with Jairus is an illustration, on the earthly plane, of the truth of Eph. 3 : 20. Mark and Luke tell this story much alike; Matthew very compendiously, omitting everything but the secret touch and the word of healing. Mark's narrative of this event is one of the best specimens of his graphic style.

(1) The Occasion.—The woman had suffered twelve years, or as long as the child who was dying in the house of Jairus had lived. She had suffered not only from disease, but also from the physicians. That she had spent her

26 And had suffered many things of many phy- | 26 years, and had suffered many things of many physi-
sicians, and had spent all that she had, and was noth- | cians, and had spent all that she had, and was noth-
ing bettered, but rather grew worse, | 27 ing bettered, but rather grew worse, having heard
27 When she had heard of Jesus, came in the press | the things concerning Jesus, came in the crowd be-
behind, and touched[b] his garment; | 28 hind, and touched his garment. For she said, If I
28 For she said, If I may touch but his clothes, I | 29 touch but his garments, I shall be made whole. And
shall be whole. | straightway the fountain of her blood was dried up;
29 And straightway the fountain of her blood was | and she felt in her body that she was healed of her
dried up: and she felt in her body that she was healed |
of that plague. |

a Job 13 : 4 ; Ps. 108 : 12 ; Jer. 30 : 12, 13....b 2 Kings 13 : 21 ; Matt. 14 : 36 ; Acts 5 : 15 ; 19 : 12.——1 Or, *saved*

all upon them is mentioned by Mark and Luke; that she had been injured by them, by Mark alone. It is nothing strange that she **suffered many things** at their hands, for the medical treatment of that day among the Jews was of the most puerile and contemptible description. The illustrations that are given in Geikie's *Life and Words of Christ*, 2. 167–169, present an astonishing mixture of ignorance, superstition, and recklessness. Of many of the recipes, the best that can be said is that they are harmless and foolish; of many the harmlessness cannot be predicated. Among the remedies proposed for such a case as this, of hemorrhage, the following, given in the Talmud, is one of the least injurious: "Set the woman in a place where two ways meet, and let her hold a cup of wine in her right hand, and let some one come behind her and frighten her, and say, Arise from thy flux." In all the remedies that are there detailed this final command, "Arise from thy flux," appears to be an element in which some confidence was reposed. Evidently twelve years of such treatment would be worse than one.—Mark adds that **she had heard of Jesus;** more correctly, "the things concerning Jesus"—*i. e.* the reports of what he had done. Her faith came by hearing; that of Jairus, perhaps, by seeing.

(2) The Approach, and the Touch of Faith.—The woman was ceremonially unclean under the law written at Lev. 15 : 25, and her disease was one that modesty would impel her to conceal. Hence her secret approach, coming **in the press behind.** Hence, also, the slightness of the touch that she ventured upon; she would not do so much as to run the least risk of being discovered.—Yet she had full confidence that even the slightest touch would not be in vain. She said to herself, **If I may touch but his clothes, I shall be whole;** and so she touched "the border"—not "the hem"—of his garment. It was the fringe or tassel which all Jews wore upon their garments, in accordance with the law of Num. 15 : 38, 39. It was given them upon their clothes to serve as a constant reminder of the law of God, which it was their duty to obey. Upon this fringe, hanging upon the back of Jesus' outer garment,

the woman laid her hand. Even such contact as this would render Jesus unclean until the evening (Lev. 15 : 19) if it were understood and strictly interpreted; and perhaps she feared it might be forbidden her if she sought it more openly. So this was a timid act of unquestioning faith. That he could heal she did not doubt; but that there was a better way than this to approach him she did not perceive. How shall we estimate her faith?—as strong or weak? Regarded as confidence in his power to heal, it was strong—as strong, perhaps, as that of Jairus, or of any other whom Jesus blessed by his miraculous working. Even in her timidity, too, there was a certain boldness—the boldness that dared to be persistent—which we cannot but admire. Happy was she that she dared approach Jesus from behind, if she dared not come to him from before. Yet this was inferior faith, not intelligent or highly spiritual. If she shrank from Jesus, then certainly she did not know him, and was not trusting him as he loves to be trusted. She trusted his power, but did not yet know his heart. No one who knows him well will timidly creep up to him from behind. To know him is to believe him when he says, "Him that cometh unto me I will in no wise cast out." It looks, too, as if she had some idea of a magical efficacy about him which would flow out even from his clothes; and it is certain that her faith had as yet done nothing to bring her into the circle of the Saviour's influence, and that even now she was thinking to be healed and then to slip away unobserved, in the spirit of the nine lepers who did not return to give glory to God (Luke 17 : 12-19). On the whole, we must estimate her faith as tenacious and persevering, and in that sense strong, but as ignorant and by no means high in spiritual quality.

(3) The Effect.—Instantaneous healing, instantly perceived in physical sensation.—**She felt in her body that she was healed of that plague.** It was not mere relief, but the inward consciousness that the long-felt disease itself was removed. In Luke, "immediately the flowing of her blood stanched;" in Mark, **straightway the fountain of her blood**

30 And Jesus, immediately knowing in himself that virtue had gone out of him, turned him about in the press, and said, Who touched my clothes?
31 And his disciples said unto him, Thou seest the multitude thronging thee, and sayest thou, Who touched me?
32 And he looked round about to see her that had done this thing.
33 But the woman, fearing and trembling, knowing what was done in her, came and fell down before him, and told[b] him all the truth.

30 ¹plague. And straightway Jesus, perceiving in himself that the power *proceeding* from him had gone forth, turned him about in the crowd, and said, Who touched my garments? And his disciples said unto him, Thou seest the multitude thronging thee, and
32 sayest thou, Who touched me? And he looked round
33 about to see her that had done this thing. But the woman fearing and trembling, knowing what had been done to her, came and fell down before him,

a Luke 6 : 19 ...b Ps. 30 : 2.——1 Gr. scourge.

was dried up—not merely the flow, but the fountain. All this through a mere touch! Twice are similar results of touching, on a wider scale, recorded. (See Luke 6 : 19 and Matt. 14 : 36.) In the latter case healing energy did seem to flow out from him, almost without his own act. (Compare Acts 19 : 12.)

(4) THE INQUIRY OF JESUS.—Here we reach questions that we cannot answer, about his consciousness.—**Jesus knowing.** "Perceiving in himself that the power proceeding from him had gone forth" is the revisers' translation. Both Mark and Luke apparently represent that the touch was unknown to him except through the consciousness of the going forth of the power that was wont to proceed from him. In some way, concerning which conjectures are useless, the touch of faith drew from him the healing energy, and by a sensation that must remain mysterious to us he was inwardly aware of its going forth.—The old translation, **knowing in himself that virtue had gone out of him,** was extremely unfortunate; many a child has understood it to mean that he felt that his power was gone, filched away from him by this surreptitious touch, than which nothing could be farther from the truth.—**Turned him about in the press** is peculiar to Mark, a reminiscence of an eye-witness.—Another is found in the descriptive touch given after the record of his inquiry. **He looked round about to see her that had done this thing.** He was sincere; he was really searching for the person.—**Who touched my clothes?** The answer of the disciples (stronger in Luke, "Thou seest the multitudes press thee and crush thee") was perfectly natural, but him it did not satisfy, and he must still search for the person. Why? Lest the superstitious should learn to attach some magical power to his garments or should suppose that he wished them to do so. Now that this had been done, it was for the interest of all that the truth should come to light. Moreover, it was not good that imperfect faith should creep away in silence without being at once reproved for its timidity and taught the lesson of courage. What an impression of him

the woman would have carried away with her if he had not called her out! So he persisted in the question, though "all denied" (Luke), and the remonstrance of his disciples seemed reasonable. "Some one touched me" (Luke). To press him and to touch him were two different things: the pressure was external, coarse, lifeless; the touch was an act of the soul, and it reached the soul of the Redeemer. "*Isti premunt, illa tetigit. Tangentem quæro, non prementem.*"—"*Those press, she touched. I seek one touching, not pressing*" (Augustine).

(5) THE CONFESSION OF THE WOMAN.—More emphatically and elaborately related by Luke. Mark mentions one motive, **knowing what was done in her,** and Luke another, "seeing that she was not hid"—conscious of her healing, and finding that she was not to be allowed to escape unseen. It is difficult to think that her own heart was not impelling her, spite of all her fears, to grateful confession.—She came **fearing and trembling,** yet she came, and **fell down before him**—not now behind him—**and told him all the truth.** As in Luke, she "declared in the presence of all the people for what cause she touched him, and how she was healed immediately"—a confession most painful for her to make; and yet, if she afterward grew in grace and in the knowledge of Jesus, can she ever have wished that he had permitted her to go away without making it?—Observe that her touch, thus confessed and explained, publicly fastened ceremonial defilement upon Jesus for the remainder of the day; and if there were "strict constructionists" present, the fact can scarcely have failed to be noticed. But who should be in the habit of putting a strict construction upon the law of Moses if not Jairus, the ruler of the synagogue? It is certain that Jesus paid no heed to the defilement, and that Jairus also was willing to disregard it. Whether he would have been willing but for his grief and anxiety, we cannot tell; but this was a case in which his own heart clamored for the "mercy, and not sacrifice," in which Jesus delighted. Jesus had twice demanded it (mercy in preference to

34 And he said unto her, Daughter, thy faith*ᵃ hath made thee whole: goᵇ in peace, and be whole of thy plague.

35 While he yet spake, there came from the ruler of the synagogue's *house* certainᶜ which said, Thy daughter is dead:ᵈ why troublest thou the Master any further?

36 As soon as Jesus heard the word that was spoken, he saith unto the ruler of the synagogue, Be not afraid, onlyᵈ believe.

34 and told him all the truth. And he said unto her, Daughter, thy faith hath ¹made thee whole; go in peace, and be whole of thy ²plague.

35 While he yet spake, they come from the ruler of the synagogue's *house*, saying, Thy daughter is dead: 36 why troublest thou the ³Master any further? But Jesus, ⁴not heeding the word spoken, saith unto the

---

a ch. 10 : 52; Acts 14 : 9....*b* 1 Sam. 1 : 17; 20 : 42; 2 Kings 5 : 19....*c* John 5 : 25; 11 : 25....*d* 2 Chron. 20 : 20; John 11 : 40.——1 Or, *saved thee*....2 Gr. *scourge*....3 Or, *Teacher*....4 Or, *overhearing*

---

strictness), as against narrow and repressive interpretations of the law (see Matt. 9 : 13; 12 : 7), and this was a good illustration of what he meant. Should he give heed to a ceremonial demand when a child lay dying waiting for the touch of his hands? Would the father of the child have him regard it, Pharisee though he was? The whole law, like the Sabbath, was "made for man," and the Son of man would freely treat it as man's servant and forbid man to be its slave.

(6) THE REPLY OF JESUS.—This was made when she had **told him all the truth**, confessed her faith, and acknowledged her Healer.—**Daughter.** So in all three reports; here alone is he said to have addressed a woman by this title. Addressed also to Bartimæus (Mark 10 : 52), to the Samaritan leper who "returned to give glory to God" (Luke 17 : 19), and to the sinful woman in Simon's house who "loved much" (Luke 7 : 50). In three cases (including the present) the words refer primarily to healing; in the fourth, to pardon. It is hard to think that Jesus meant them in this case to convey only the announcement of healing.—**Go in peace.** Literally, "into peace"—*i. e.* The future to which thou goest shall be peace; thou shalt be, and remain, whole, or well, from thy plague, the scourge or torment that has been twelve years upon thee. This is a blessing for the future as well as for the present. The same phrase occurs at Luke 7 : 50 (and there alone), where it stands in connection with the forgiving of sins.

35, 36. The episode ended, the original story is here resumed. A joyful episode it was to the woman; a surprising one to the crowd; a sad and perplexing one it must have been to Jairus. The movement toward his house, slow at the best because of the crowd, had been stopped by the act of the woman, and his request was in abeyance while her case was attended to; and yet his child was dying when he left home to seek the Healer. Now, just as the last words to the woman were spoken, the message came that all was over. The mes-

sengers (or the messenger, as in Luke, "There cometh one") added, **why troublest thou the Master** (Teacher) **any further?** The word rendered **troublest** is a strong word, though not a very frequent one; it is used here by both Mark and Luke. It means, first, "to flay" or "skin;" then "to rend" or "lacerate;" then, metaphorically, "to vex, annoy." It is difficult to resist the conviction that the messengers spoke ironically, in bitter impatience and vexation: "Trouble the Teacher no more: he has given himself so much trouble already! He was sent for in a case of life and death, and he set out to come, with a great crowd around him; but now we find him standing in the road and talking with a chronic invalid whom he has allowed to intrude upon him and detain him; and meanwhile the child has died. Let him go back, now that all is over. He has let the child die: why trouble him any more?" With this interpretation accords the language of verse 36 in the best text, where, instead of *akousas*, we read *parakousas*, a word that occurs in the New Testament only here and at Matt. 18 : 17. There it is found twice, and is translated "neglect to hear," or, by the revisers, "refuse to hear."—It means "to hear without regarding" or "not to heed." According to this reading, Jesus heard what the messengers said to Jairus of him, but took no notice of it, let it pass unanswered. The only heed that he paid to it was in this—that he made it the occasion of an encouraging word to Jairus. **Be not afraid, only believe.** A most appropriate word it was just when all seemed to be lost and the father might be half disposed to take the counsel of the messengers. But what a word! and what an assumption! **Be not afraid**, although the child is dead; **only believe:** faith in my power is not even yet in vain. What calmness, in view of his own power to raise the dead! So, again, in the whole preparation for the raising of Lazarus: no tumult of excitement in his soul, no questioning as to the result, and no wonder at his own ability to perform so divine a work.

37 And he suffered no man to follow him, save Peter, and James, and John the brother of James.
38 And he cometh to the house of the ruler of the synagogue, and seeth the tumult, and them that wept and wailed greatly.
39 And when he was come in, he saith unto them, Why make ye this ado, and weep? the damsel is not dead, but sleepeth.*b*
40 And they laughed him to scorn. But when he had put them all out, he taketh the father and the mother of the damsel, and them that were with him, and entereth in where the damsel was lying.

37 ruler of the synagogue, Fear not, only believe. And he suffered no man to follow with him, save Peter,
38 and James, and John the brother of James. And they come to the house of the ruler of the synagogue; and he beholdeth a tumult, and many weep-
39 ing and wailing greatly. And when he was entered in, he saith unto them, Why make ye a tumult, and
40 weep? the child is not dead, but sleepeth. And they laughed him to scorn. But he, having put them all forth, taketh the father of the child and her mother and them that were with him, and goeth in where

a ch. 9 : 2; 14 : 33.....*b* John 11 : 11-13.

37-40. Mark speaks as if the crowd were now forbidden to go farther, and Peter, James, and John alone were permitted to go beyond where the messengers met the company. From Luke we would infer that the separation was not made till the house was reached. Mark's more exact statement is probably to be preferred. The tidings that the child was dead might reconcile the crowd to turning back. It is true that he had raised the widow's son from the dead at Nain a few months earlier (Luke 7 : 11-17), but the multitude would scarcely be expecting such a work from him, and may have turned back with some sympathy with the impatience of the messengers, or at least with regret that Jesus had not arrived in time. His special three were taken with him; this, however, is their earliest appearance as an inner circle closest to him.—It is a little singular, in view of the short career of James and the long history and great services of John, that John is mentioned oftenest in the Gospels as **the brother of James.** It looks as if, to his contemporaries, James gave promise of being the greater of the two, and as if he were admiringly remembered after his career was cut short by the sword of Herod.—The house was filled with the noise and tumult that in that land follows a death : "As soon as death takes place the female members of the household and the professional mourning-women announce it to the neighborhood by setting up their shrill and piercing cry—called the *tahlil* —which is heard at a great distance and above every other noise, even the din of battle, and is quite characteristic of the East" (Van Lennep, *Bible Lands*, p. 586). Allusions to the lamentation at funerals are numerous in the Old Testament; for example, Eccles. 12 : 5, where the professional mourners are mentioned. In Jer. 9 : 17 the "mourning-women" are called in to assist in giving utterance to grief; in Amos 5 : 16 there is a call for those who are "skilful of lamentation;" in 2 Chron. 35 : 25 the minstrels appear, the mournful singers who were called in to help. Matthew speaks

here of the minstrels—literally, "flute-players" —who were in the house of Jesus to notice, and he noticed it to rebuke it; but it seems a strange rebuke. In Matthew he commands the hired mourners away : "Give place" or "Withdraw."—In all three he says that the child is not dead, but is sleeping. By this he meant, not, as some have tried to make him mean, "This is not real death, but only a sleep that resembles it," and not, "Death ought to be regarded merely as a sleep," but, "This death, since I have been summoned to help, is only a sleep, out of which the child will quickly be awakened." Hence he could say, **Why make ye this ado and weep?**—*i. e.* Why did you not understand that I would dispel the sorrow? After once you had sent for me, why did you send for the minstrels and mourners, as if there were no hope? The fame of the work at Nain had spread widely, and, though the impression had been partly effaced, still they ought to have known that to raise the dead was not beyond his power.—But **they laughed him to scorn.** The language is identical in the three reports. Strange language it seems to us for the house of mourning; but such mourners as these would find it easy to turn from mourning to laughter, and back in a moment again to their wailing. Luke adds, "knowing that she was dead," in which there is a quiet confirmation of the reality of her death, and so of the genuineness of the miracle.—**But when,** etc. Better "But he, having put them all forth." The he is somewhat emphatic (*autos*) in the Greek, and the word for **put out** is a strong word—the same that is used of his act in driving out the intruders to the temple (Mark 11 : 15; John 2 : 15). Thus he enforced the command that is recorded in Matthew and cleared the house of the mourners, whose presence was so sharp a contradiction of his own. As he had rejected the crowd, so he rejected the mourners, and only the six persons entered into the chamber of death.—Of the mother of the child

41 And he took the damsel by the hand, and said unto her, Talitha cumi; which is, being interpreted, Damsel, I say unto thee, Arise.ᵃ

42 And straightway the damsel arose, and walked; for she was *of the age* of twelve years. And they were astonished with a great astonishment.

43 And he chargedᵇ them straitly that no man should know it; and commanded that something should be given her to eat.

41 the child was. And taking the child by the hand, he saith unto her, Talitha cumi; which is, being

42 interpreted, Damsel, I say unto thee, Arise. And straightway the damsel rose up, and walked; for she was twelve years old. And they were amazed straight-

43 way with a great amazement. And he charged them much that no man should know this: and he commanded that *something* should be given her to eat.

a Acts 9 : 40....*b* ch. 3 : 12 ; Matt. 8 : 4 ; 12 : 16-18 ; Luke 5 : 14.

we know only that she knew of her husband's going to bring Jesus, that she had witnessed the child's death during the absence of her husband, and that the mourners had been brought in with her knowledge, and apparently with her consent. Thus she had probably given up hope of any help from Jesus. As for the father, he had been reassured by the words of Jesus, and had witnessed, even while he was impatiently waiting, the evidence of the full power of him who had now come with him. The miracle on the way must have refreshed his faith, as Jesus certainly intended that it should.

41–43. Passing beyond where the minstrels were, the six entered where the child lay dead. The only contact, or sign of any transference of power, was in the taking of her hand, mentioned by all three evangelists. He **said unto her**—Luke, "he called;" Matthew mentions no address—**Talitha cumi.** The words are Aramaic, rightly interpreted by Mark. The **I say unto thee,** however, is Mark's addition, truly representing the spirit of Jesus' address. They were the very words that he spoke, remembered and preserved by one of the three disciples who heard them. Doubtless the tone and manner in which they were spoken lingered, as well as the words themselves, in the mind of Peter. (For other citations of his very words by Mark, bringing in Aramaic speech to Greek writing, see Mark 3 : 17 ; 7 : 11, 34 ; 10 : 51 ; 14 : 36.) Mark translates *talitha* by *korasion*, a word that is not used except familiarly—"little girl" or "my child." It suggests the tone of tenderness that Jesus brought to the scene, and the tenderness itself that was dwelling in his heart. —The imperative word, *egeire*, may be translated either " Arise " or " Awake." After **she is not dead, but sleepeth,** it is far more likely that the latter was in the mind of Jesus, and that he meant to say, " My child, awake "—an utterance far removed from the formal **Damsel, I say unto thee, Arise,** with which we are familiar. Doubtless it was spoken quietly as he took her by the hand. We mistake if we think of power as shining forth in his look and tone in that silent chamber of death. It was

the most simple and quiet of acts in its outward form, and the calm " My child, awake !" came to him, it would seem, as naturally as it might to a mother whose child must be called out of slumber. All the world has a fondness for associating power with signs of power; but what is more sublime than this quiet, natural, affectionate recalling of a departed spirit? Where else do humanity and divinity appear more livingly as one?—The gentle word was sufficient. " Her spirit returned " (Luke) ; she arose and walked. Here it is, at the end, that Mark tells the age of the child, mentioning it, apparently, lest some reader should have been supposing that she was too young to walk. Luke told her age at the very introduction of the story ; Matthew, not at all—as far as it goes, an indication of the independence of the two reports.—**They were astonished with a great astonishment,** but with what eyes did she look upon her Restorer? Had she ever seen him before? and did she know how much it meant? To Lazarus the voice that awakened him to earthly life again was the familiar voice of Jesus, but to the child this may have been a stranger's voice. Did those whom he called back from the dead ever know each other and come into mutual confidence upon these awful experiences?—He would not have the great work talked of, and yet how could it be concealed? Mark and Luke, who record the injunction of silence, do not say that it was disregarded ; but Matthew, who does not mention it, says that the report of this deed went out into all that land. Just so Luke says of the raising of the widow's son ; and the raising of Lazarus spread abroad the fame of Jesus, helped to secure for him his regal entrance into the city of David, and gave his name so divine a character that his enemies were the more determined quickly to destroy him.—Not the least interesting part of the story is the closing word. **He commanded that something should be given her to eat.** Observe in this, (1) Economy of miracle. Not without miracle could the child be restored, but when once life was re-established it must be sustained by natural means, like any other life.. Miraculous

CHAPTER VI.

A ND he went out from thence, and came into his own
country; and his disciples follow him.
2 And⁹ when the sabbath-day was come, he began to
teach in the synagogue: and many hearing *him* were
astonished, saying, From⁶ whence hath this *man* these
things? and what wisdom *is* this which is given unto
him, that even such mighty works are wrought by his
hands?

1 AND he went out from thence; and he cometh
into his own country; and his disciples follow him.
2 And when the sabbath was come, he began to teach
in the synagogue: and ¹many hearing him were
astonished, saying, Whence hath this man these
things? and, What is the wisdom that is given unto
this man, and *what mean* such ²mighty works wrought

---

a Matt. 13 : 54, etc.; Luke 4 : 16, etc....*b* John 6 : 42.——1 Some ancient authorities insert *the*....2 Gr. *powers.*

---

power had no *protégés*, none whom it adopted
to give them permanent care—a fact in which
we see how unweakened by human weakness
were the hands in which that power was held.
(2) The thoughtfulness of common sense. The
child must have food, for the life was truly re-
established, and its needs were just the same as
if no death and no miracle had intervened.
But her friends, in their excitement, might forget it; and so the Healer, always thoughtful,
reminded them. (3) The calmness of one to
whom divine power was simply natural. There
is no wonder in Jesus at what he has done, no
excitement now that a spirit has returned at
his call, no variation in the perfect balance of
his mind. As there was no excitement beforehand, so there is no flurry at the moment, and
no pride afterward. He is just as free and able
to think of necessary practical details as if this
had been an ordinary occurrence of common
life.

**1-6. JESUS VISITS NAZARETH; AGAIN
REJECTED THERE.** *Parallel,* Matt. 13 : 54-58.
—Some, as Alford, regard Luke 4 : 16-30 also as
parallel, thus identifying this visit to Nazareth
with the one that Luke places at the beginning
of the Galilæan ministry. Alford's chief argu-
ments are the improbability of two visits so
similar, the impossibility of our Lord's wondering at the unbelief of his townsmen after it
had once been so violently expressed, and the
fact that the allusion to miracles in Capernaum
at Luke 4 : 23 seems to imply a greater number
of mighty works than had been wrought there
at the early time usually assumed for the visit.
He might have added that the tone of the address in Luke seems to correspond somewhat
better to the fact of growing unpopularity than
to a time of fresh beginning. Yet, on the whole,
it seems quite certain that there were two visits.
There is some apparent difficulty, it is true, in
the fact that the same objection was made to
our Lord twice, and the same answer was given
on both occasions; but see notes below. As to
the early miracles in Capernaum, we are by no
means sure that we have a full record of them;
and as to our Lord's wondering at the unbelief

of the Nazarenes, surely he might wonder that
all the intervening events and a second visit had
done nothing toward removing it. Moreover,
the differences are considerable. Jesus apparently was alone in the first visit, and was accompanied by his disciples in the second. There
is no mention of miracles in the first, and after
the rejection there is no time for them; while
in the second there is mention of healings,
though few, after the rejection. The temper
of the people is not the same: it is violent, uncontrollable rage in the first case, and cool indifference in the second. On the whole, therefore, this is to be taken as a second attempt of
our Lord to win the faith of his townsmen. A
possible motive for this visit has been suggested
in the fact that he had lately been obliged to repel his mother and brethren (chap. 3 : 31-35), and
was anxious to avoid all appearance of wilful
separation from his old friends and neighbors.
To this it should be added that his tender and
faithful heart would certainly impel him to
make a special effort to seek and gain them, if
he had been obliged to treat them with an appearance of unfriendliness. That the scene
with his mother and brethren was quickly followed by a visit to those who had known him
in his youth and had once rejected him was
profoundly and delicately characteristic of our
Saviour.

1. Came into his own country. His
patris—his fatherland, or ancestral home. The
same word is used in Matthew, but neither Matthew nor Mark tells what or where the place
was. The common use of the epithet "Nazarene" is sufficient, however, to identify it.
This is Mark's only direct reference to his connection with Nazareth, but the reference proves
that he knew at least something of the facts recorded by Matthew (2 : 23) and Luke (1 : 26; 2 : 39),
and serves as one of the confirmatory "cross-
references" between the Gospels—the more important, perhaps, as it relates to the period which
lies beyond the limits prescribed to Mark by the
purpose of his Gospel.

2, 3. That he **began to teach in the synagogue** seems to indicate that his visit continued—or, at least, was intended to continue—

3 Is not this the carpenter, the son of Mary, the brother of James,ᵃ and Joses, and of Juda, and Simon? and
are not his sisters here with us? And they were offend-
edᵇ at him.

3 by his hands? Is not this the carpenter, the son of
Mary, and brother of James, and Joses, and Judas,
and Simon? and are not his sisters here with us?

beyond a single day of public worship.—**Many**
—or, as some manuscripts read, "the many,"
the greater part—**hearing were astonished.**
—There is some uncertainty about the punctuation and construction of the questions that
follow. There certainly are three questions,
and the most natural construction seems to be,
not that of the revisers, but, **whence hath
this man these things? and what wisdom is this which is given unto him?**
and are such **mighty works wrought by his
hands?**—*i. e.* can it be that by his hands are
performed the miracles of which we hear? The
question about the wisdom follows upon his
teaching in their presence. On his other visit
"all bare him witness, and wondered at the
words of grace that proceeded out of his
mouth." So in Capernaum (chap. 1 : 27) his teaching made an impression that was not eclipsed
even by a present miracle. In Nazareth, however, there were no miracles before the teaching, and the allusion was to those that were
reported from elsewhere, especially, no doubt,
the recent works in Capernaum, as the raising
of Jairus's daughter.—The question, "Are such
mighty works wrought by his hands?" is perfectly in accord with the inquiry that follows it,
Is not this the carpenter? Equally so is the
question about his wisdom. **The carpenter**
was of humble social position and of limited
opportunities for education (compare John 7 :
15: "How knoweth this man letters, having
never learned?"), and that his should be the
hands by which the mighty works were performed was in their sight almost incredible.—
Observe that on the former occasion his words
were "words of grace," and they wondered;
now they were words of "wisdom," and they
stumbled. This was probably an announcement of the principles of his kingdom, and,
though they admired, they had no heart for
the doctrine.—**The carpenter.** Here alone
is Jesus so called; Matthew, "the carpenter's
son." It was the universal custom for the Jews
to teach trades to their sons. (Compare Acts
18 : 3.) From this word we infer that Joseph
taught Jesus his own trade and Jesus worked
with him as a carpenter in his shop at Nazareth. Justin Martyr says that in his time (the
second century) articles said to have been made
by his hands, such as rakes and harrows, were
preserved and were in demand as sacred relics.

In a country village like Nazareth a carpenter
would be busied mainly with work of no great
magnitude—somewhat with the construction
of houses, but quite as much with the making
of household implements and utensils. Not
unlikely, the bushel and the lampstand and
the couch and the plough of which he spoke
had been fashioned by his hands, and perhaps
to his thoughts they had suggested, while he
was working, some of the illustrative uses that
he made of them. There is evidence in the
manuscripts and in Christian literature that
this name, "the carpenter," and even "the
carpenter's son," came to be regarded as somewhat of a reproach; but how could his friends
have more thoroughly misunderstood his spirit?
In his full and true acceptance of the lot of humanity, he accepted humble and regular labor
as a part of his life. We cannot fail to see that
he thus put a divine honor upon labor. The
popular impression that the necessity for labor
is a part of the penalty of sin is directly contradicted by his example. Among the many
words about the life of our Lord for which we
have reason to be deeply thankful, not the least
is this word, "Is not this the carpenter?"—**The
son of Mary.** The absence of the name of
Joseph has always been taken to show that
Mary was now known apart from her husband
—*i. e.* as a widow. Joseph is mentioned in the
record of the previous visit: "Is not this Joseph's
son?" It would be too much to infer that he
had died between the two visits, but it does
seem probable that he died not long before the
first, if not after it.—**The brother of James,
and Joses, and of Juda, and Simon?** (See
note on chap. 3 : 21.) The same names in
Matthew as here; they are common Hebrew
names.—**His sisters.** Of whom no names
are given, and of whose history we know nothing. The only hint as to their number is found
in the word "all," used by Matthew: "Are not
his sisters all with us?" The word indicates
that they numbered three or four, at least.—
And they were offended at—or in—him.
The same phrase as at Luke 7 : 23. They found
something in him that occasioned stumbling,
caused them to hesitate, and finally to refuse
when asked to believe in him. "Blessed is he"
that does not so; but this blessedness was not
for them.

4. The complaint that was made against him

4 But Jesus said unto them,[a] A prophet is not without honor, but in his own country, and among his own kin, and in his own house.

5 And[b] he could there do no mighty work, save that he laid his hands upon a few sick folk, and healed *them*.

6 And he marvelled[c] because of their unbelief. And[d] he went round about the villages, teaching.

4 And they were [l]offended in him. And Jesus said unto them, A prophet is not without honor, save in his own country, and among his own kin, and in his own house. And he could there do no [2]mighty work, save that he laid his hands upon a few sick 6 folk, and healed them. And he marvelled because of their unbelief.

And he went round about the villages teaching.

---

a Matt. 13 : 57 ; John 4 : 44....b ch. 9 : 23 ; Gen. 19 : 22....c Isa. 59 : 16 ; Jer. 2 : 11....d Matt. 9 : 35 ; Luke 13 : 22 ; Acts 10 : 38.——1 Gr. caused to stumble....2 Gr. power.

---

was precisely the same as at his former visit: his old neighbors had listened to him more patiently, but had nothing different to say. After all that had passed, they were still rejecting him because they had known him so well and in circumstances so humble; they were persistently judging "according to the appearance." Therefore, as they had nothing new to say, neither had he: what was true before was true now—**A prophet is not without honor, but in his own country, and among his own kin, and in his own house:** as much as to say, "This is my hardest field; the strongest prejudices meet me here. I told you so before, and I tell you so again. This is the common lot of prophets and teachers—to be received abroad, but dishonored at home." Compare the experience of Jeremiah with the men of his native Anathoth (Jer. 11 : 21).—The words **among his own kin** are peculiar to Mark's report; they are the words that tell what must have cut most sharply to his loving heart. A constant pain it must have been that his "brethren" believed not on him; and if there was any town in which he would most have delighted to be welcomed in his mission, that town surely was Nazareth. But "he came unto his own, and his own received him not" (John 1 : 11). Similar was the experience of his apostles, especially of Paul, in learning that the Jews, the "own," the kinsfolk, of the Saviour, would not receive him, while the Gentiles, who were strangers from the covenants of promise, were far more ready to believe.

5, 6. Mark alone inserts the **could;** but Matthew distinctly attributes the abstinence from miraculous works to the unbelief of the people. Mark notes the few exceptions that were possible—the healing of a few sick in whom, or in their friends, he may have discerned another spirit. The inability to perform mighty works there must not be conceived of as if there were a kind of outward restraint upon him, a physical repression of his power. The inability was inward and moral. It is true that unbelief or non-belief did not always form a hindrance to his miraculous working; see the case of the demoniacs

in the land of the Gergesenes, where there was no faith, and that of the paralytic (chap. 2 : 1-12), where there was an unfriendly presence, as there was, and sometimes still more terribly, on many other occasions. But the stolid and persistent indifference of the Nazarenes made a moral atmosphere in which he found it difficult and practically impossible to put forth his divine energy. The plain implication is that he would gladly have let his power flow out freely, but was morally shut up from gracious giving. Even he, then, was sometimes under constraint and unable to do as he would, because of the spiritual atmosphere around him —a point at which we find him unexpectedly in sympathy with the experiences of his servants. It was by a real entering to human life that he became a carpenter; but is there not a deeper identification of himself with human conditions in this, that "he could do no mighty work there, because of their unbelief"?—In his wonder at the unbelief we have another glimpse of the resemblance of his thoughts to ours. We do not ordinarily think of wonder as an act or attitude of the divine mind; but Jesus **marvelled because of their unbelief,** just as he had already "marvelled" at the faith of the centurion (Luke 7 : 9). Wonderful was the stupidity and persistence of the unbelief of these Nazarenes, and he truly wondered. Wonderful was the faith of the Roman, comparatively unprivileged, yet surpassing Israel, and he truly wondered. Natural and spontaneous were his thoughts; not, as men have sometimes supposed they must believe, mechanical and unlike those of other thinking beings.

7-13. JESUS INSTRUCTS AND SENDS FORTH HIS APOSTLES. *Parallels,* Matt. 9 : 35-10 : 1; and 10 : 5-16; Luke 9 : 1-6.

6. This undefined tour among the villages in Galilee is mentioned with more detail in Matt. 9 : 35, but its extent is there left as undefined as here, and no incidents of his teaching or contact with the people have been preserved. His feeling, however, in view of the state in which he found the people, is recorded by Matthew, and his pity for the spiritual con-

7 ¶ And he called *unto him* the twelve, and began to send them forth by two and two, and gave them power over unclean spirits;

8 And commanded them that they should take nothing for *their* journey, save a staff only; no scrip, no bread, no money in *their* purse:

9 But be shod[b] with sandals;[c] and not put on two coats.

---

7 And he called unto him the twelve, and began to send them forth by two and two; and he gave them 8 authority over the unclean spirits; and he charged them that they should take nothing for *their* journey, save a staff only; no bread, no wallet, no [1]money in 9 their [2]purse; but *to go* shod with sandals: and, *said*

---

a ch. 3 : 13, etc.; Matt. 10 : 1, etc.; Luke 9 : 1, etc.; 10 : 3, etc....b Eph. 6 : 15....c Acts 12 : 8.———1 Gr. brass....2 Gr. girdle.

---

dition in which they were is assigned as the reason for the act that follows.

7. He called unto him the twelve—the place is unknown—**and began to send them forth.** This had been the second clause in their original commission, "That they might be with him, and that he might send them forth to preach and to have authority to cast out demons;" and now he **began** to assign them work under it. This was their first mission. Matthew chooses this as the time for recording their names; Mark and Luke have recorded them before, in connection with their appointment.—He sent them **by two and two,** according to the sound practical principle that experience has always been teaching. (See Eccles. 4 : 8-12—a passage that one may almost think Jesus cited to the twelve in the course of his preparations for their mission.) Each was thus compelled to be a helper to another, while each was also permitted to lean upon another's help. As for the division of the twelve into pairs, of course we cannot tell positively how it was done; but there is every reason to suppose that the division that is elsewhere given was observed. The pairs were probably Peter and Andrew, brothers; James and John, brothers; Philip and Bartholomew, friends before they met Jesus; Matthew and Thomas, probably twin-brothers; James, the son of Alphæus, and "Judas of James," of whose relation nothing very certain can be said; and Simon the Zealot and Judas Iscariot. May there possibly have been something in the presence of the Zealot at his side from which the evil heart of Judas drew nourishment for a worldly ideal of the Messiah and discontent with Jesus? The six pairs probably went out in as many different directions, very likely not meeting again until their mission was fully accomplished.—Their preaching was to be enforced by miracles, which their Master now gave them authority to perform in his name. Mark mentions only **power over unclean spirits;** Luke adds "diseases;" Matthew, "all manner of sickness and all manner of disease," and he even records the command, "Raise the dead." He gave them full range in the work of healing; but here alone during

his ministry are they said actually to have healed.

8-11. The needful instructions for the journey and the work are given by Mark and Luke only in a very brief and compendious form; by Matthew more fully, though it is not certain that the whole of what is recorded in his tenth chapter was spoken at this time. Verses 8, 9 tell of the preparation they were to make for the journey, and verses 10, 11 of their conduct in the places that they might visit. As for preparation, the point of the commands is that they were to go as they were, not waiting to make themselves ready. For such a journey Orientals in the common walks of life would require far less preparation than men of Western habits would feel to be necessary. **Nothing for their journey, save a staff only.** In Matthew and Luke it is "no staff"—*i. e.* they were not to go to the pains of getting one

SANDALS.

if not supplied already; they were not to trouble themselves about preparation, even so little as that.—**No bread.** They were to depend upon finding food as they went.—**No scrip,** or wallet or small bag. The word is used in Early English of the bag that a traveller carried. It occurs at 1 Sam. 17 : 40, where it refers to the shepherd's bag that David had.—**No money**—literally, brass—**in their purse,** or girdle, the folds or twists of the girdle being the receptacle for the traveller's money.—**Shod with sandals.** The plain, ordinary foot-gear, such as plain people wore. In Matthew it is "no shoes;" but there does not seem to be a contrast intended between shoes and sandals, as if sandals were permitted and shoes forbidden. There is no distinction between the words, and the phrase "no shoes," in Matthew, is governed by the verb "get:" they

10 And he said unto them, In what place soever ye
enter into an house, there abide till ye depart from
that place.
11 And whosoever shall not receive you, nor hear
you, when ye depart thence, shake off the dust under
your feet for a testimony against them. Verily I say
unto you, It shall be more tolerable for Sodom and Gomorrah in the day of judgment, than for that city.
12 And they went out, and preached that men should
repent.[b]
13 And they cast out many[c] devils, and anointed with
oil[d] many that were sick, and healed them.

10 he, put not on two coats. And he said unto them,
Wheresoever ye enter into a house, there abide till
11 ye depart thence. And whatsoever place shall not
receive you, and they hear you not, as ye go forth
thence, shake off the dust that is under your feet for
12 a testimony unto them. And they went out, and
13 preached that men should repent. And they cast
out many demons, and anointed with oil many that
were sick, and healed them.

a Neh. 5 : 13; Acts 13 : 51....b Luke 24 : 47; Acts 2 : 38; 3 : 19....c Luke 10 : 17....d James 5 : 14.

were forbidden to procure anything more than
they already had.—**Not on two coats.**
Strictly, tunics or inner coats. They were not
to encumber themselves with anything superfluous, or even with a change of clothing.
Their habits would make this a far more natural arrangement to them than it would be to
us. Their mission would be mainly to the
poor, and in style adapted to their work they
must go. They were to go, too, in haste and
for actual work, and therefore they must go
unencumbered.—The point of the command
in verse 10 is, "Accept hospitality when it is
offered in good faith, and do not be changing
your quarters in search of greater convenience
or comfort. You will not be long in a place;
do not waste your working-time in trying to
accommodate yourselves." There might be
temptation to do exactly that, and to degrade
their mission besides, if they were to hold
themselves open to invitations from wealthier
men who might receive their word.—**And
whosoever shall not receive you.** The
best text refers, not to person, but place. This
open denunciation was for towns where both
message and messengers should be rejected.
See Luke 9 : 52-56 for a case in point. That,
however, was a Samaritan village, less privileged than the Jewish, and therefore less severely condemned.—**Shake off the dust under your feet.** A symbolic act of renunciation such as Jews were accustomed to perform on crossing the border in returning from
a Gentile country into their own. Thus the
rejecters of the apostles' message were to be
treated as Gentiles—a very fitting symbol,
since this was the message of the true King
of Israel, and they who should disregard it
would not be of the true Israel.—The shaking
off of the dust is to be **for a testimony,** not
against them, but "unto them," although it
might be practically a testimony against them.
It is a testimony to them of the greatness of
him whom they have rejected, and of the terrible nature of their deed. It is even a part
of the preaching: it is one way of announcing

the truth of Christ; and if it should lead the
rejecters to repentance, after all, its highest
purpose would be accomplished. (For illustrations, see Acts 13 : 51 and 18 : 6.)—The latter half of verse 11, comparing the guilt and
doom of such a city with the guilt and doom
of Sodom and Gomorrah, stands unquestioned
in Matthew, but forms no part of the best text
in Mark.

12, 13. Only one word tells of the substance
of the apostles' preaching in this tour: they
preached **that men should repent.** Doubtless the main point of their message was dictated to them by their Master. Observe that
this was not merely the proclamation of the
Christ, but rather the announcement of the
duty of men in view of his coming. They took
up the preaching of John, and of Jesus himself; undoubtedly they said, "Repent, for the
kingdom of heaven is at hand."—Under their
commission to cast out demons they did great
and beneficent work and left many grateful.
Mark alone mentions their healing of diseases.
They **anointed with oil;** and this custom
appears again in Scripture only in James 5 : 14,
where it is evidently in use—at least, among
some Hebrew Christians. Jesus himself sometimes employed physical media in healing, as
in Mark 7 : 33; 8 : 23; John 9 : 6, 7; but these
were apparently exceptional cases with him.
His miracles were free acts of his personality,
which usually rejected all media. (Compare 1
Kings 17 : 21, 22 and 2 Kings 4 : 29-35 for scenes
that illustrate the superiority of his working.)
But when he did use physical media we never
hear of his using oil. In that age oil was regarded as a curative agent; perhaps that is the
very reason why the Lord himself did not employ it. In the hands of the apostles when
they were healing the use of it would be symbolic of their belief in the use of natural means
of healing, in connection with the prayer of
faith and full reliance upon the mighty Name.
It was a suitable symbol for disciples in their
humble consciousness of using only a derived
power, but less suitable to the Lord.—As to the

14 And⁎ king Herod heard *of him;* (for his name was spread abroad;) and he said, That John the Baptist was risen from the dead, and therefore mighty works do shew forth themselves in him.
15 Othersᵇ said, That it is Elias. And others said, That it is a prophet, or as one of the prophets.
16 But when Herod heard *thereof,* he said, It is John, whom I beheaded: he is risen from the dead.

14 And king Herod heard *thereof;* for his name had become known: and ᵇhe said, John ᶜthe Baptist is risen from the dead, and therefore do these powers
15 work in him. But others said, It is Elijah. And others said, *It is* a prophet, *even* as one of the proph-
16 ets. But Herod, when he heard *thereof,* said, John,

a Matt. 11 : 1, etc.; Luke 9 : 7, etc....b ch. 8 : 28; Matt. 16 : 14.——1 Some ancient authorities read *they*.....2 Gr. *the Baptizer.*

length and extent of this tour it is impossible to be certain. Wieseler and Ellicott maintain that it lasted only a day or two; but most authorities insist that it must have been longer—probably some weeks, which certainly seems most likely. According to Matt. 11 : 1, Jesus himself, as soon as he had dismissed his disciples to their work, departed himself, alone, " to teach and preach in their cities." Thus for the time he broke up the one company into seven—an act which cannot fail to be recognized as an aggressive movement toward the more rapid gaining of converts. He had lately entrusted truth especially to his disciples in the form of parables, and he would not fail to give them an early opportunity to set the lamp on the lampstand and make manifest what in their experience he had hidden (chap. 4 : 21, 22). He had lately turned away, in a certain sense, from the people, scarcely expecting to be understood by them, to speak more hopefully to his disciples; yet he would not so leave the people, but would make sure that the word " Repent " was spoken again in their ears, and by men whom some of them might possibly regard when they would not attend to him. With what manner of thoughts did he follow the twelve while they were absent from him?

14–29. HEROD BELIEVES JESUS TO BE JOHN THE BAPTIST, WHOM HE BEHEADED; STORY OF THE BAPTIST'S DEATH. *Parallels,* Matt. 14 : 1–12; Luke 3 : 19, 20 ; 9 : 7–9.

14–16. This **Herod** is Herod Antipas, the son of Herod the Great and Malthace, a Samaritan woman. After the father's death the kingdom that he had founded was divided among the sons, and Antipas received Galilee and Perea as his portion. He bore the name of " tetrarch " as ruler of a fourth part of the Roman province of Syria; and the title **king** was a popular one—a substitute for " tetrarch." He was one of the tributary sovereigns to whom Rome could well afford to grant some gratification of their vanity. His reign covered almost the whole lifetime of our Lord, and continued beyond it, extending from B. C. 4 to A. D. 39.—It is not positively affirmed that Herod heard of Jesus now for the first time, though it is

plainly implied that he had not known much of him, and now obtained more information than he had had before. That he knew little of Jesus is nothing strange, for he was often absent from Galilee; and, what is more important, he was profoundly indifferent to all such matters. As to the means by which he now heard more of Jesus, it is sufficient to remember the mission of the apostles through Galilee with the power of healing: this would cause the name of Jesus to be **spread abroad,** or to " become known " where it had not been known before, and his fame might easily thus reach Herod.—The word **said,** occurring four times in these three verses, is uniformly in the imperfect tense, indicating that it refers, not to what Herod and the others said at some single moment, but to what they " were saying " when Jesus was spoken of. Herod's guilty conscience assented to the opinion of some who said that John the Baptist had risen from the dead (Luke), but he was greatly " perplexed." Others were saying that this was Elijah, who was expected to appear, in accordance with a literal interpretation of Mal. 4 : 5, 6; others, **it is a prophet,** or—more correctly " even "—**as one of the prophets**—*i. e.* he is a new prophet in whom the long-broken line of prophecy has been resumed. In Luke is recorded the further guess that " one of the old prophets is risen again "—not Elijah or some special messenger, but an ordinary prophet returned.—The theory that Jesus was John returned from the dead is given first as Herod's own theory, and is reiterated, after the others have been enumerated, in the literal and intenser form, **whom I beheaded,** " John, this one has risen." Both pronouns, **I** and **he,** or " this one," are strongly emphatic, and Herod's saying is the confession of guilt and fear. It was **when Herod heard** the other theories that he said this; this was his unvarying answer to them all. We have no positive evidence that Herod was in belief a Sadducee, though it is certain that his affiliations were with them rather than with the Pharisees. His character would be most at home among those who " say that there is no resurrection, neither angel nor spirit " (Acts 23 : 8), and probably, if he was sincere in any belief on such subjects, he was sincere in

17 For Herod himself had sent forth, and laid hold upon John, and bound him in prison, for Herodias' sake, his brother Philip's wife: for he had married her. 18 For John had said unto Herod, It is not lawful[a] for thee to have thy brother's wife. 19 Therefore Herodias had a quarrel against him, and would have killed him; but she could not. 20 For Herod feared[b] John, knowing that he was a just man and an holy, and observed him; and when he heard him, he did many things, and heard him gladly.

17 whom I beheaded, he is risen. For Herod himself had sent forth and laid hold upon John, and bound him in prison for the sake of Herodias, his brother 18 Philip's wife: for he had married her. For John said unto Herod, It is not lawful for thee to have 19 thy brother's wife. And Herodias set herself against 20 him, and desired to kill him; and she could not; for Herod feared John, knowing that he was a righteous man and a holy, and kept him safe. And when he heard him, he [1]was much perplexed; and he heard

a Lev. 18 : 16....b Ex. 11 : 3 ; Ezek. 2 : 5-7.——1 Many ancient authorities read did many things.

such scepticism. The more striking, then, his confession. Conscience was too strong for unbelief.—**Therefore mighty works**, etc. The best text reads "Therefore do these powers work in him." "John did no miracle" (John 10:41); but if he had risen from the dead, it would be different, and "these powers" were only what would be expected. In Luke it is rather perplexity than conviction in Herod's mind—perplexity that led him to seek to see Jesus that he might assure himself as to who he was.

17-20. Matthew and Mark relate the story of the imprisonment and death of John by way of explanation of Herod's confession. Luke alludes to the imprisonment at the end of his account of John's ministry, and omits the narrative of his death, alluding to it only in Herod's confession, "John have I beheaded." The death probably took place at about the beginning of the preaching-tour mentioned just above.

Herod himself—emphatic, in correspondence to the emphatic "I" in "John have I beheaded"—**had sent forth.** So he did not seize him on the spot after his bold reproof, but took time to think, and sent out afterward, with greater guilt because with greater deliberateness. The union of Herod and Herodias was condemned by the Jews as incestuous, though it was not more so than the previous marriage of Herodias with Philip. Herod Antipas, Philip, and Aristobulus, who was the father of Herodias, were all half brothers, sons of Herod the Great by different wives. Herodias first married Philip, her half uncle, and then deserted him to become the wife of Antipas, who bore to her the same relation. Antipas had long been married to a daughter of Aretas, the king of Arabia, and was living with her when he determined to marry Herodias. She fled to her father, Aretas, when she saw the shame inevitable, and he came with an army to avenge her and sorely defeated Antipas. Thus on both sides the marriage of Herod and Herodias was unquestionably and unblushingly adulterous. It has been discussed whether

John condemned the marriage rather as incestuous than as adulterous. Perhaps it is impossible to determine, and certainly it is needless: the marriage was equally open to both reproofs. —Of the time and place of his reproof there is no hint, save that the word **said** ("John said unto Herod") is in the imperfect tense, as in verses 14-16, and may indicate that John spoke more than once. He was acting "in the spirit and power of Elijah" (1 Kings 18:17, 18).

Verses 19, 20 are peculiar to Mark. Matthew has a brief account of Herod's feeling—not quite the same as that which appears in Mark, but it may represent a feeling that Herod, fierce and fickle, entertained during some part of the time of John's imprisonment. **Herodias had a quarrel**—more correctly, "set herself"— **against** John, or "had a grudge against him" which his imprisonment did not satisfy, and desired to kill him.—Verse 20 gives us the only favorable glimpse that is given in Scripture of any Herod. The received version says **observed him.** It should be "kept him safe" from the plottings of Herodias.—The question between **did many things** and "was much perplexed" is a question of text; and the reading which the revisers have adopted is one of the happy discoveries of recent textual study. Herod "was perplexed," being impressed with the goodness of John and the righteousness of his cause, and being convicted by his own guilty conscience, and yet being bound by what he had done, and unable, and no doubt really unwilling, to extricate himself.—**And heard him gladly.** Perhaps quite willing to listen, by way of amends to his conscience. Compare the conduct of Felix (Acts 24:23-26). Herod appears at better advantage than Felix, for there is no sign that he was looking for bribes.—John lay in prison probably a year and a half, and his disciples had access to him (Matt. 11:2). The place of confinement is said by Josephus (Ant. 18.5.2) to have been Machaerus, a fortress on the eastern side of the Dead Sea. It is known to have belonged to Aretas, but by some means unknown it had come into the possession of Herod. The place still bears the

21 And when a convenient day was come that Herod on his^a birth-day made a supper to his lords, high captains, and chief *estates* of Galilee;
22 And when the daughter of the said Herodias came in, and danced,^b and pleased Herod and them that sat with him, the king said unto the damsel, Ask of me whatsoever thou wilt, and I will give *it* thee.
23 And he sware unto her, Whatsoever^c thou shalt ask of me, I will give *it* thee, unto the half of my kingdom.
24 And she went forth, and said unto her mother, What shall I ask? And she said, The head of John the Baptist.
25 And she came in straightway with haste unto the king, and asked, saying, I will that thou give me by and by in a charger the head^d of John the Baptist.
26 And the king was exceeding sorry; *yet* for his oaths' sake, and for their sakes which sat with him, he would not reject her.

21 him gladly. And when a convenient day was come, that Herod on his birthday made a supper to his lords, and the ²high captains, and the chief men of
22 Galilee; and when ²the daughter of Herodias herself came in and danced, ³she pleased Herod and them that sat at meat with him; and the king said unto the damsel, Ask of me whatsoever thou wilt,
23 and I will give it thee. And he sware unto her, Whatsoever thou shalt ask of me, I will give it thee,
24 unto the half of my kingdom. And she went out, and said unto her mother, What shall I ask? And
25 she said, The head of John ⁴the Baptist. And she came in straightway with haste unto the king, and asked, saying, I will that thou forthwith give me in
26 a charger the head of John ⁴the Baptist. And the king was exceeding sorry; but for the sake of his oaths, and of them that sat at meat, he would not re-

a Gen. 40 : 20....*b* Isa, 3 : 16.....*c* Esth. 5 : 3, 6 ; 7 : 2.....*d* Ps. 37 : 12, 14.——1 Or, *military tribunes* Gr. *chiliarchs*....2 Some ancient authorities read *his daughter Herodias*....3 Or, *it*....4 Gr. *the Baptizer*.

name of *M'Khaur*. It was visited and identified by Tristram in 1872. (See Tristram's *The Land of Moab*, chap. xiv.) He reports that he found among the ruins of the keep, or central fortress, two dungeons, one of them deep, with its sides scarcely broken in. In the masonry of these dungeons are still visible the holes in which staples of wood and iron were once fastened. "One of these," he says, "must surely have been the prison-house of John the Baptist."

21. From this point Luke is silent, and Matthew's report is brief and compendious. Almost all the living touches of narration we owe to Mark. **A convenient day.** For the purpose of Herodias—a day of opportunity.—Concerning the **birth-day** of Herod, there has been much discussion as to whether the occasion was strictly his birth-day or the anniversary of his accession to the throne, which might be called by the same name. There has been some interest in maintaining the latter, because the day of his accession is known, and such a fixed date would be very useful in settling other dates in our Lord's ministry. But the best recent authorities are generally agreed that this was simply Herod's birth-day. The celebration, however, with such an assemblage, would extend beyond a single day.—The supper or feast was given to **his lords,** or grandees—*megistasin*, a peculiar word corresponding well to "grandees," or "magnates"—and **high captains,** *chiliarchs,* commanders of cohorts in the Roman army, **and chief estates**—literally, "first men"—**of Galilee.** The distance of Machaerus from Galilee occasions no difficulty.

22, 23. **When the daughter of the said Herodias came in**—the daughter of "Herodias herself," of the very queen—**and danced.** The words "of Herodias herself" note the indignation and horror with which a Jew would regard such an act. Dancing-women were abun-

dant, and in such banquets it was common for them to appear, transparently robed, and execute voluptuous and impurely - suggestive dances. This was the Roman fashion—sad and degrading enough, but it was quite another matter to Jewish eyes when the daughter "of Herodias herself" condescended to such an exhibition of her charms for the coarse delight of the company. It was the work of her mother, too, who was adapting her wiles to the man she had to play upon.—The girl **pleased Herod** and the guests—pleased the lowest there was in them—and the king's oath of reward was ready. In form the oath resembles that of Ahasuerus (Esth. 5 : 6). Probably the form had become proverbial, but doubtless Herod had no thought of anything great or serious being asked.

24, 25. Whether the girl was in league with her mother in advance we can only conjecture; but her mother was her counsellor, and she was her mother's ready tool. Her withdrawal and interview with her mother Matthew represents only by the clause, "Being put forward by her mother," with which he introduces the request. She was out but a moment, for her mother needed no time to think; and **she came in straightway with haste unto the king,** her "feet swift to shed blood" (Rom. 3 : 15).—**In** —upon—**a charger**—*i. e.* a platter or plate.— **Immediately.** No delays; a confirmation, too, of the probability that the prisoner was within the walls where they were gathered.— **The head of John the Baptist.** No more half satisfactions to the grudge of Herodias. Her hatred should now be altogether gratified once for all, and her foe should no more stir the conscience of her husband.

26-28. Here was the testing of Herod. He **was exceeding sorry**—sorry to be so caught; sorry to destroy a man whom he knew to be so great and good; sorry to do real violence to his

27 And immediately the king sent an executioner, and commanded his head to be brought: and he went and beheaded him in the prison,
28 And brought his head in a charger, and gave it to the damsel: and the damsel gave it to her mother.
29 And when his disciples heard of it, theyᵃ came and took up his corpse, and laid it in a tomb.

27 ject her. And straightway the king sent forth a soldier of his guard, and commanded to bring his head: and he went and beheaded him in the prison,
28 and brought his head in a charger, and gave it to the
29 damsel; and the damsel gave it to her mother. And when his disciples heard thereof, they came and took up his corpse, and laid it in a tomb.

a Acts 8 : 2.

conscience; sorry to run the risk of enraging the people by destroying one whom they reverenced as a prophet. He was sorry—no doubt sincerely—but the sorrow came to nothing, for his oaths (plural, indicating that he had swaggeringly done great swearing) and his guests. before whom he would not break his oaths, decided the question.—It was the well-known strife between honor and duty: a false sense of honor was waging war against conscience and the best self-interest, and all other good motives. It prevailed too. **He would not reject her.**—Swift again was the movement. **Immediately.** The name of the officer whom he sent (*spekoulatōr*) is a Latin word, *speculator*, "a spy," or "scout;" applied also to members of a body-guard who acted as messengers. This is one of Mark's Latinisms.—**Commanded his head to be brought.** A better reading is "commanded to bring his head." Not unlikely the "bring his head" may be almost an exact quotation of the rough, gruff order of the surly, disgusted king. The command was literally obeyed: the head was the girl's reward for her dancing, and to her it was given, upon the platter; but she knew that the plan was not her own, and loyally delivered the horrid present to her mother. What an ending for a life of holy protesting against sin! No glimpse is given of the scene in the prison. Did John know by what kind of influence he was commanded out of the world? Let us hope that he was spared that horror and indignation. Never did human event look more as if good were only a plaything in the hands of evil; and one would prefer to think that the Baptist was spared the struggle of reconciling this in his dying moments with the goodness of God and the love and righteousness of Jesus. **29. And when his disciples heard of it, they came.** A sign that they were not present, though scarcely to be pressed as a proof that not one of them was there. His disciples cannot have been very numerous, and probably they ceased, upon his death, to exist in Palestine as a body separate from the followers of Jesus; although in Acts 18 : 25 and 19 : 1-7 we find traces of them at a distance after about twenty-five years had passed. Not

improbably, however, these distant influences were borne out from the centre at an earlier date, while John was still at work, and before the position of Jesus in relation to him had become plain.—**And took up his corpse—**having now, as before, free access to the prison **—and laid it in a tomb.** Probably near Machærus, but of which no trace or tradition remains.—Matthew adds that when they had buried his body "they came and told Jesus"—an indication, apparently, that they were now ready to cast in their lot with him. Yet perhaps they had other thoughts besides: it would be strange if they did not sadly wonder why Jesus did not rescue his great forerunner, and question whether he could be sincere in the high praise he gave him. Answers to some such questions they may have desired; and all that their best welfare required, we may be sure, the Master gave them. Some of John's disciples went over to Jesus at the first hint from him (John 1 : 36, 37), and he was willing that more should go (John 3 : 27-30); but toward the last, with his weary questionings in the prison (Matt. 11 : 3) and his sense of desertion, he may not have been so ready to part with them. He may have thought it his duty to keep them about him, or as many of them as he could, till greater certainty about Jesus could be obtained. **30-44. THE APOSTLES HAVING RETURNED, JESUS CROSSES THE LAKE WITH THEM IN SEARCH OF REST, AND THERE FEEDS FIVE THOUSAND.** *Parallels*, Matt. 14 : 13-21; Luke 9 : 10-17; John 6 : 1-14.—Here, and here alone between the beginning of the Galilæan ministry and the week of the Passion, we have four parallel reports. John comes into parallelism with the synoptists at this crossing of the lake, and continues parallel through the record of the return, when Jesus walks on the water, though here we lose our four-fold record by the silence of Luke. John contributes a valuable note of time in the remark that the passover was at hand. The death of the Baptist occurred, therefore, in the spring, and there remained just a year of the ministry of Jesus after the death of the forerunner.

30 Andᵃ the apostles gathered themselves together unto Jesus, and told him all things, both what they had done, and what they had taught.

31 And he said unto them, Come ye yourselves apart into a desert place, and rest a while: for there were many coming and going, and they had no leisure so much as to eat.

32 And they departed into a desert place by ship privately.

33 And the people saw them departing, and many knew him, and ran afoot thither out of all cities, and outwent them, and came together unto him.

30 And the apostles gather themselves together unto Jesus; and they told him all things, whatsoever they had done, and whatsoever they had taught. And he saith unto them, Come ye yourselves apart into a desert place, and rest a while. For there were many coming and going, and they had no leisure so much 32 as to eat. And they went away in the boat to a desert 33 place apart. And *the people* saw them going, and many knew *them*, and they ran there together ¹on

a Luke 9 : 10.——1 Or, *by land*

30. The tidings of the death of John would seem to have reached Jesus while he was still alone; but about the same time his company was again gathered around him by the return of the apostles. Of the tone of the report they brought to him nothing is said—whether cheerful or sad—nor is there anywhere any glimpse of them in the work of this mission. They reported **what they had done ;** Mark adds, **and what they had taught.** In their teaching he would certainly see defects, but his response to their report would be nothing else than cheering: he was training them, and he would not fail to encourage them.

31, 32. The invitation was addressed to the twelve alone. **Come ye yourselves apart into a desert place, and rest a while** —*i. e.* a little while. **A while** is by no means an adequate translation of *oligon*, "a little." He did not expect long rest, but he did hope for a little.—The place was probably Capernaum. After the reunion of the company of Jesus the crowd had returned, and those who were **coming and going** gave them **no leisure so much as to eat.** The whole of verse 31 is peculiar to Mark, and both parts of it are intensely characteristic—the representation of our Lord's feeling and the graphic description of the circumstances.—For the invitation two motives appear, one in Mark and one in Matthew. From Mark we should attribute it to tender care of the apostles, weary from their work, and to his desire to be alone with them for a little. This is one of the touching illustrations of his thoughtfulness toward them. In Matthew it is when Jesus heard of the death of the Baptist that he withdrew privately to the desert place. Joined with the other motive was the desire to be in quiet, that he might have leisure for the thoughts that the death of John suggested. The death of such a man must have been a heavy blow to him, more especially since it was such a death. His personal love for John would make him now a mourner; and the event must also have awak-

ened the thought of Matt. 17 : 12—"Likewise shall also the Son of man suffer of them"— and have brought the certainty of his own death freshly before him. It may also have led him to think of modifying his method thenceforth and giving himself more fully, as he did, to the training of his apostles. Thus the two motives were one in effect, driving him away from the shifting, intruding, exacting crowd to be alone with his own.—They went away, not **by ship,** but "in the boat"—the boat that they were wont to use. They must have gone in the early morning.

33. They succeeded in getting away, but not unobserved. Luke says they went to Bethsaida; John, that Jesus "went up into the mountain;" Matthew and Mark merely that the place was desert—*i. e.* uninhabited. The fact seems to be that they went to Bethsaida, which stood at the extreme north of the lake, where the Jordan enters it (see note on chap. 8 : 22), and thence proceeded a little to the south-east, to some convenient point in the hills that rise from the shore of the lake, where they might hope to be alone. It may be that at Bethsaida itself they did not touch at all, and that Luke's mention of it is meant only for a general designation of the locality. The distance from Capernaum to the vicinity of Bethsaida would not be more than six or eight miles, and could be traversed on foot about as quickly as by boat; if the boat was in no haste, more quickly. In the journey for rest there would be no haste, and the pursuing crowd arrived first. The people were **out of all cities**—*i. e.* from many towns in that region, especially from those that must be passed on the way. The crowd grew in going. John speaks of Jesus already seated in the mountain, lifting up his eyes and seeing the crowd approaching, which may be a reminiscence of the fact that they came, not all at once, but kept streaming in. John also connects the mention of the coming throng with the fact that the passover was at hand. It

34 And Jesus, when he came out, saw much people, and was moved with compassion toward them, because[a] they were as sheep not having a shepherd; and he began to teach them many things.
35 And[b] when the day was now far spent, his disciples came unto him, and said, This is a desert place, and now the time is far passed:
36 Send them away, that they may go into the country round about, and into the villages, and buy themselves bread: for they have nothing to eat.
37 He answered and said unto them, Give ye them to eat. And they say unto him, Shall we[c] go and buy two hundred pennyworth of bread, and give them to eat?

34 foot from all the cities, and outwent them. And he came forth and saw a great multitude, and he had compassion on them, because they were as sheep not having a shepherd: and he began to teach them many things. And when the day was now far spent,
35 his disciples came unto him, and said, The place is
36 desert, and the day is now far spent: send them away, that they may go into the country and villages round about, and buy themselves somewhat to
37 eat. But he answered and said unto them, Give ye them to eat. And they say unto him, Shall we go and buy two hundred [1]shilling-worth of bread, and

may be that some part of the multitude was made up of pilgrims to Jerusalem, who turned aside to see the Prophet of Galilee.

34. He came out. From the boat. The disciples may have been impatient that the ever-present throng was even here; with the Master, however, it was not impatience, but compassion.—The activity of the day was rich and various. The motive, pity for the spiritual state of the multitude, which seems to have been often affecting him with a sad surprise. The shepherd-impulse was strong in his heart, and the sight of sheep unshepherded always drew it forth. So **he began to teach them many things,** or, as in Luke, he "spoke to them of the kingdom of God," into which as a fold he would gather the unshepherded (Luke 15 : 4-6; 19 : 10; John 10 : 16). He also "healed their sick" (Matthew), or, as in Luke, "healed them that had need of healing." Such was the rest that he found, and such the opportunity for quiet meditation. He had had no leisure to eat; but, while he became a shepherd to the shepherdless, no doubt his heart was full of the sentiment of John 4 : 32-34: "My meat is to do the will of him that sent me, and to finish his work."

35-44. In this paragraph the synoptists are quite closely parallel, save that Matthew condenses a little, as usual, and Mark adds his fresh touches of description. John diverges at the beginning in attributing the inquiry about the possibility of feeding the multitude, not to the amazed disciples when Jesus has proposed that they shall do it, but to Jesus himself, as a question intended to test the faith of Philip. If it were necessary, no doubt the two conversations could be woven in together and harmonized with a tolerable degree of plausibility; but it is more satisfactory to leave them as two independent reports of the same event. Perhaps the independence is worth more to us than an unquestionable harmony would be. [This is true, for the value of several narratives, instead of one, must be due to their independ-

ence. Yet harmony is compatible with independence. Nay, if several accounts of the same events are true, they must be in real harmony with one another, though we are sometimes unable to show this. The omission from the narratives of a single connecting act or remark may render it for ever impossible for us to see the exact connection or point out the exact sequence of the things reported. But it is desirable to show the harmony of the different narratives wherever this can be done, or at least to show that the several accounts, though independent, need not be supposed to contradict one another at any point. Compare notes on John 6 : 5 sq.—A. H.]

The suggestion of the apostles (verses 35, 36) seemed not only rational, but the only rational one: the people must not be kept away from the necessary comforts, and the disciples thought that even for Jesus to keep them longer would be no kindness. A startling proposal, **Give ye them to eat.** The words are identical in Matthew, Mark, and Luke, showing how sharply the incisive and startling command entered into the minds of the hearers. Matthew introduces it with the equally astonishing remark, "They need not depart." He proposed that which is impossible to men; but he himself was there. There had been as yet no multiplication of food by his hands, so far as we know, except as the turning of water into wine (John 2 : 1-11) might be called such. The belief of the apostles in his miraculous power ought by this time to have been perfect; but it is to be remembered that he did not propose himself to feed the multitude: he said, **Give ye them to eat.** After that proposal it was only natural that they should think first of their own resources, and inquire how the thing could be done. It was not altogether unbelief that made them speak of buying bread for the people; he had compelled them to look at the matter from that side. They knew that they had nothing adequate, and were equally sure that it was impracticable to buy.—**Two hun-**

38 He saith unto them, How many loaves have ye? go and see. And when they knew, they say, Five, and two fishes.
39 And he[a] commanded them to make all sit down by companies upon the green grass.
40 And they sat down in ranks by hundreds, and by fifties.
41 And when he had taken the five loaves and the two fishes, he looked up to heaven, and blessed,[b] and brake the loaves, and gave them to his disciples to set before them; and the two fishes divided he among them all.

38 give them to eat? And he saith unto them, How many loaves have ye? go and see. And when they knew, they say, Five, and two fishes. And he commanded them that all should [1]sit down by companies upon the green grass. And they sat down in ranks, by hundreds, and by fifties. And he took the five loaves and the two fishes, and looking up to heaven, he blessed, and brake the loaves; and he gave to the disciples to set before them; and the two fishes

a ch. 8 : 6 ; Matt. 15 : 35....b 1 Sam. 9 : 13 ; Matt. 26 : 26 ; Luke 21 : 30.——1 Gr. recline.

dred pennyworth of bread. The proposal to buy is omitted by Matthew, and the quantity by Luke. This quantity is mentioned in Mark without comment, and in John as insufficient. The denarius ("penny" is a very poor translation, or, rather, not a translation at all) was equal actually to about fifteen cents, but relatively to considerably more. In Matt. 20 : 2 it appears as a suitable return for a day's labor.—In Mark alone are the disciples sent to find how many loaves they have. Their investigation and report are represented in the words **when they knew, they say.** Literally, "knowing, they say." One of Mark's telling brevities. The loaves were thin and brittle; from Luke 11 : 5, 6 it appears that three would be required for a meal for a single person. The fishes are called in John (not elsewhere) opsaria, a word that denotes a condiment, something eaten with bread or other staple food. Hence the idea of "small fishes;" but that idea cannot be insisted on, as the word had come to be used of fish generally. After the report of a hopeless quantity, Matthew adds the reply of Jesus: " Bring them hither to me "—the one hope of making the small supply sufficient. This is the one hopeful thing to do with Christian gifts and resources of every kind—offer them to him in whose hands a handful can feed a multitude.

The proposal thus to feed the people was another suggestion of the Shepherd's heart. Bodily wants were not beneath his notice, and yet this act had predominantly a spiritual purpose. Brief though the record is, that had been a great day of power and teaching, and such a day might well close with a climax of convincing might. The people must sit down in order to secure orderly and impartial distribution. Heavenly things must be handled with earthly wisdom ; bread produced by miracle must be distributed in the best human order. The description of the sitting down is peculiar to Mark, and is unlike anything else in the New Testament. **He commanded them to make all sit down by companies**—symposia symposia, "company

by company"—**upon the green grass. And they sat down** prasini prasini—not exactly in **ranks,** but rather in blocks like garden-beds, some in blocks of a hundred and some by fifties. The repetition or doubling of the descriptive words is in the Hebrew style. The change of word from the general symposia, "company," to the purely descriptive prasini, "garden-beds," shows how the scene arose pictorially in the memory of the narrator, and he again saw the people arranged in squares and looking, in their vari-colored clothing, like flower-beds on the grass.—The grass is mentioned by Matthew and John. John says that there was "much ;" Mark alone calls it **green grass**—a part, again, of the pictorial memory of the scene. The word corresponds, too, to the season, the passover-time, in spring.

He looked up to heaven, and blessed. So Matthew and Mark—i. e. he blessed God, praised God in thanksgiving; Luke, " he blessed them," the loaves and fishes—invoked the blessing of God upon them ; John, " he gave thanks." It was simply the grateful prayer before eating, " grace before meat," offered by the host or head of the family. (So Luke 24 : 30; see notes on Mark 14 : 22, 23.) Distribution was made by the hands of the disciples; so expressly in all but John. The separate mention of the giving out of the fishes is a slight link between Mark and John.—In Mark's addition to what Matthew and Luke tell, **and the two fishes divided he among them all,** we see distinctly recorded the deep sense of wonder, and yet the keen observation of an observer close at hand. This story, as told in Mark, can be nothing else than the report of an eye-witness; the evidences are of the plainest and most irresistible kind.—As to the process of the miracle, speculations seem to be in vain. Theories of the acceleration of natural processes have been proposed for such occasions, but they are useless, and when closely examined are absurd. If this work was performed at all, it was done by creative power; and that is enough to say of it. It was no insufficient or halfway work; they

42 And they* did all eat, and were filled.
43 And they took up twelve baskets full of the fragments and of the fishes.
44 And they that did eat of the loaves were about
five thousand men.
45 And straightway[b] he constrained his disciples to
get into the ship, and to go to the other side before
unto Bethsaida, while he sent away the people.

42 divided he among them all. And they did all eat,
43 and were filled. And they took up broken pieces,
44 twelve basketfuls, and also of the fishes. And they
that ate the loaves were five thousand men.
45 And straightway he constrained his disciples to
enter into the boat, and to go before *him* unto the
other side to Lethsaida, while he himself sendeth the

a Deut. 8 : 3....b Matt. 14 : 22; John 6 : 17.

were all satisfied.—In John the command to
gather the fragments is mentioned; in the
others, only the gathering. The word for **baskets** here is not the same as in the record of the
similar miracle in chap. 8 : 8. (See note there.)
The word here is *cophinus*, the source of our
words "coffer" and "coffin." This, apparently, was the wicker provision-basket that was in
common use. The collecting of the fragments
shows again, like the order in the distribution
of the food, the Saviour's purpose that miracles
shall never displace prudence. Though divine
power can produce a superabundant supply,
still it is right "that nothing be lost."—A fresh
sign of the independence of the four narratives
is found in the manner of recording the number of the multitude. That "there were about
five thousand men" is mentioned by Luke in
connection with the hint of the disciples that
it was impossible to buy bread for so many;
by John, in connection with their sitting down,
when their number was ascertained; Mark says
at the very end, just after mentioning the great
store of fragments that was left, that **they that
did eat of the loaves were about five
thousand men** (about, however, is omitted
in the best text); Matthew, at the same point,
says that they were "about five thousand men,
besides women and children." The women and
children would be arranged, according to Jewish custom, separately from the men, and in
such a multitude would be less in number.
Thus there are three different ways of connecting the number with the story, all natural
—a striking proof of independence.
The immediate effect of the great work is reported by John alone (6 : 14): "Then those men, when
they had seen the miracle that Jesus did, said,
This is of a truth the prophet that should come
into the world." Conviction of his greatness, but
conviction of what kind the next section shows.

**45-56. JESUS RETURNS, WALKING ON
THE WATER, AND HEALS MANY.** *Parallels,*
Matt. 14 : 22-36; John 6 : 15-21.—John remains
in parallelism, but we lose our fourfold harmony
by the dropping out of Luke, who says nothing
of this scene. The key to this section is found
in John 6 : 15: "Jesus therefore perceiving that
they were about to come and take him by force

to make him a king, withdrew again into the
mountain himself alone." Instead of "withdrew" Tischendorf reads "fleeth again to the
mountain," on no very great manuscript authority (though the Sinaitic Manuscript supports it), but mainly because this ancient reading is most unlike anything that a corrector
would produce. The order is, (1) After the
miracle there is a rising purpose, more and more
openly expressed, to compel him to take his
place as the King of Israel. This, then, is the
result of his mighty works and of his ministry
in Galilee generally—the temptation of Satan
in the wilderness is renewed by the men of
Israel. This was really the temptation of Matt.
4 : 8-10. (2) Jesus feels the force of the temptation, and sets himself not only to repel it, but
to stop it. (3) Accordingly, he constrains his
disciples to embark for the opposite shore, probably because they are only too ready to fall in
with the movement and must be kept out of
it. (4) He breaks up the assembly, inducing
the multitude to leave him. By what means he
induced them we are not told; but it is almost
a wonder that this scene has not attracted the
imagination of some great painter—Jesus scattering the multitude who are tempting him to accept a crown of worldly sovereignty. (5) **When
he had sent them away**—or, as the Revision
reads, "taken leave of them" (Mark)—he goes
away alone to the mountain for prayer. Tischendorf's reading, "he fleeth," is extremely fresh
and striking, and bears strong internal marks
of genuineness: he flees out of the scene of
temptation to the place of prayer. But he does
not flee to prayer until he has repelled the
temptation and scattered the tempters. (6) He
spends nearly the whole night in prayer, telling his Father of the carnal acceptance and
spiritual rejection that he has met with, and
adjusting his thoughts to the necessities of his
position. After such misconception he must
deliberately and forcibly throw away this false
popularity, which he does next day, in his great
discourse on the bread of life, in the synagogue
at Capernaum (John 6 : 22-71).

45-47. The disciples, apparently, were not
anxious to go; they had to be **constrained.**
—In the words **to the other side unto Beth-**

46 And when he had sent them away, heᵃ departed into a mountain to pray.

47 And when even was come, the ship was in the midst of the sea, and he alone on the land.

48 And he saw them toilingᵇ in rowing: for the wind was contrary unto them: and about the fourth watch of the night he cometh unto them, walking upon the sea, and would have passedᶜ by them.

49 But when they saw him walkingᵈ upon the sea, theyᵉ supposed it had been a spirit, and cried out:

46 multitude away. And after he had taken leave of them, he departed into the mountain to pray. And when even was come, the boat was in the midst of the sea, and he alone on the land. And seeing them distressed in rowing, for the wind was contrary unto them, about the fourth watch of the night he cometh unto them, walking on the sea; and he would have passed by them: but they, when they saw him walking on the sea, supposed that it was an apparition,

a ch. 1 : 35 ; Matt. 6 : 6 ; Luke 6 : 12....b John 1 : 13....c Luke 24 : 28....d Job 9 : 8... e Luke 24 : 37.

saida we have the puzzle as to the site of Bethsaida, since, according to Luke, they had come to Bethsaida in coming over to this the eastern side. But they were now in the hills below Bethsaida, farther down the eastern shore; and Mark's meaning probably is that he sent the disciples on in the boat, bidding them take Bethsaida, at the head of the lake, in their way, and promising to join them there. Many such a geographical puzzle would be solved in a moment if we were familiar with the every-day expressions of the people; in fact, they occur in consequence of the artlessness of the narrative, the writers being frequently unconscious of any need of explanation.—**When he had sent them away.** The word means "to separate one's self;" but in later Greek it is used for saying "Farewell."—**He departed into a mountain to pray,** glad to be alone, temptation behind him and the solitary mountain before.—**When even was come**—i. e. the later evening, extending from six o'clock till night. —**He alone on the land** is peculiar to Mark. A graphic addition, but scarcely equal to John's " It was now dark, and Jesus was not yet come to them," in which it is apparent that they expected him to come.—The violent wind, mentioned incidentally by Matthew and Mark and directly by John, continued from evening till the fourth watch of the night, which included the last three hours before morning. Thomson (*The Land and the Book,* 2. 32) tells of a storm that he encountered in this very place, the wind blowing violently from the north and northeast; so that for three days it would have been impossible for a boat to reach the land at Bethsaida. In such a storm a boat must be driven, just as that of the disciples was, out of its course and across to Gennesaret, south of its destination.

48. We reach a region of mystery in these words, **he saw them toiling in rowing,** or, more accurately, "seeing them distressed in rowing," the "seeing" peculiar to Mark. The word certainly seems to imply more than that he knew from observing the wind that they must be in trouble. It is a word of sensation, and tells that he saw them. According to Mat-

thew, they were in the midst of the lake. Even the full moon of the passover season is not sufficient to account for such seeing, and it certainly appears as if Mark meant to tell of a supernatural seeing from afar.—**He cometh unto them, walking upon the sea.** Why on the sea? The reason for this exceptional work is to be sought in his heart. His friends were in trouble, beating vainly against the storm, and perhaps in danger; they expected him to join them, and he apparently had promised it; they could not reach the shore to take him in; they were out there by his act, he having con**strained** them to go. It was not in his heart to leave them in their perplexity, and there was no way to go to them, except by the exercise of his supernatural power. Moreover, this way of approach would give him one of the best of opportunities to test, and so to educate, their faith. This simple explanation, by which the act is traced to his feeling toward his disciples, certainly seems better than a resort to theories of rapture and half unconsciousness such as have sometimes been proposed.—Observe the pause after **walking upon the sea :** it should be a colon at least, if not a period.—**And would have passed by them**—which is peculiar to Mark—means not merely " he came near passing them," or " he would have been likely to pass them if they had not cried out," but " he wished," or willed, "to pass by them." He was passing, not unconsciously, but deliberately ; he meant to pass them before coming directly to them. Why? Apparently, in order that they might see him in the dim light and have the opportunity to recognize him. He would put their faith and discernment to the test by this indirect approach. They knew that he was alone on the land, and that he was intending to come to them. They knew his power; would they know him in this unwonted approach? Would they be looking for him even in the storm, or would they be supposing that the storm rendered all hope of seeing him vain? A testing of faith and a lesson of faith might be brought out of this for the good of the disciples.

49, 50. Alas for their faith and their spirit-

7

50 For they all saw him, and were troubled. And immediately he talked with them, and saith unto them, ' Be of good cheer:" it is 1; be not afraid.
51 And he went up unto them into the ship; and the* wind ceased: and they were sore amazed in themselves beyond measure, and wondered.
52 For they considered not the miracle of the loaves: for their hearts was hardened.
53 And⁴ when they had passed over, they came into the land of Gennesaret, and drew to the shore.
54 And when they were come out of the ship, straightway they knew him,
55 And ran⁵ through that whole region round about, and began to carry about in beds those that were sick, where they heard he was.
56 And whithersoever he entered, into villages, or cities, or country, they laid the sick in the streets, and besought him that they might touch,ᶠ if it were but the border⁶ of his garment: and as many as touched him were made whole.

50 and cried out: for they all saw him, and were troubled. But he straightway spake with them, and saith unto them, Le of good cheer: it is 1; he not
51 afraid. And he went up unto them into the boat; and the wind ceased: and they were sore amazed in
52 themselves; for they understood not concerning the loaves, but their heart was hardened.
53 And when they had ⁷crossed over, they came to the land unto Gennesaret, and moored to the shore.
54 And when they were come out of the boat, straight-
55 way the proper knew him, and ran round about that whole region, and began to carry about on their ²beds those that were sick, where they heard he was.
56 And wheresoever he entered, into villages, or into cities, or into the country, they laid the sick in the marketplaces, and besought him that they might touch if it were but the border of his garment: and as many as touched ³him were made whole.

a Isa. 43 : 2... *b* Ps. 93 : 3, 4.....*c* Isa. 63 : 17....*d* Matt. 14 : 34....*e* ch. 2 : 1–3; Matt. 4 : 21....*f* ch. 5 : 27, 28; Matt. 9 : 20; Acts 19 : 12....*g* Num. 15 : 38, 39.——1 Or, *crossed over to the land, they came unto Gennesaret*....2 Or, *pallets*....3, Or, *it*

ual sensibility! They thought it was, not a **spirit**, but "a spectre," a phantasm, an apparition, and they cried out.—**For they all saw him**—the reminiscence of an eye-witness; peculiar to Mark—**and were troubled.** No recognition; no inference of faith from the fact that "Jesus was not yet come to them" and might be expected; no thought that he might in the kindness of his heart come in the only possible way, by miraculous power.—His appearing brought them only the instinctive terror that is awakened by the thought of an apparition. They had failed to stand the test; but his heart—how gentle and patient!—sprang up to cheer them even in this needless terror. His heart must have been saddened, but **immediately he talked with them** in the simplest and most unobtrusive language of reassurance.—Wonderful language of self-assertion indeed it is, declaring his power over nature; yet he who walks on the waves and is Master of the storm speaks assuringly to those who have trusted him, and says, **Be of good cheer: it is I**, whom you know so well; it is only I, of whom you have no reason to be afraid. The tenderness, the intimacy of heart with his friends, the desire to be recognized in his love, is far greater in this than the self-assertion.

Matthew here inserts the episode of Peter's walking on the water. He had failed under a test of his Master's choosing, and now, partly for that very reason, he was taken with the idea of putting his faith to this test of his own choosing. Of course he must fail again. In Mark's Gospel is virtually Peter's, the omission of this incident is quite in character. On the one hand, this Gospel omits to record the high honor that was put upon Peter after his great confession (Matt. 16 : 17–19), which corresponds to godly humility; on the other, it records the

rebuke that was administered just after to Peter (Mark 8 : 32, 33), which corresponds to godly honesty. But, as for this walking on the water, it was an episode that Peter would naturally be willing to forget, and that might be omitted without any dishonor to his Master, and so he might pass it by.

51, 52. The wind ceased. Literally, "grew weary." The same word as in chap. 4 : 39, when he had rebuked the wind, and used nowhere else in the New Testament. Here there is no mention of any rebuke.— The amazement of the apostles is condemned in verse 52—which is peculiar to Mark—as the amazement of unbelief. The miracle that they had witnessed, if nothing else, ought to have taught them better, yet they did not understand it.—**Their heart was hardened,** not by the influence of Jesus or by any divine power. "They understood not concerning the loaves," yet they had counted them and knew how many they were; they had distributed them and knew how many they had fed; they had gathered the fragments of them and know how many baskets they filled. Knowledge may be mathematically correct, and yet not be "understanding."

53–56. Gennesaret was the name of the plain that lay on the western side of the lake and gave to the lake its name; Capernaum stood probably near the north end of it. It was an extremely fertile plain, and was then one of the most populous regions in the land. The spot at which the company of Jesus reached the shore is not specified, but the natural impression is that it was not at Capernaum or at any other of the large towns.—In these verses we have an intensely vivid description of the eagerness with which the great Healer was received. The people recognized him, fully believed in

CHAPTER VII.

THEN came* together unto him the Pharisees, and
certain of the scribes, which came from Jerusalem.
2 And when they saw some of his disciples eat bread
with defiled that is to say, with unwashen) hands, they
found fault.
3 For the Pharisees, and all the Jews, except they
wash *their* hands oft, eat not, holding the tradition[b] of
the elders.
4 And *when they come* from the market, except they
wash,[c] they eat not. And many other things there be,
which they have received to hold, *as* the washing of
cups, and pots, and brasen vessels, and of tables.

1 AND there are gathered together unto him the
Pharisees, and certain of the scribes, that had come
2 from Jerusalem, and had seen that some of his disciples ate their bread with [defiled, that is, unwashen,
3 hands. For the Pharisees, and all the Jews, except
they wash their hands diligently, eat not, holding
4 the tradition of the elders; and *when they come* from
the marketplace, except they [bathe themselves, they
eat not: and many other things there are, which
they have received to hold, [washings of cups, and

a Matt. 15 : 1....*b* Gal. 1 : 11; Col. 2 : 8, 22, 23....*c* Job 9 : 30, 31.——[Or, common,...,2 Or, up to the elbow   Gr. with the fist....3 Gr.
baptize. Some ancient authorities read *sprinkle themselves*....4 Gr. baptizings.

his power to heal, and instantly availed themselves of his presence. Peculiarities of Mark
in this swiftly-drawn picture: That the boat
"moored to the shore," not merely **drew to
the shore;** that the people **ran through
that whole region round about** (Matthew,
"sent"); that they **began to carry about in
beds those that were sick, where they
heard he was** (Matthew, "they brought to him
all that were sick"); that **whithersoever he
entered, into villages, or cities, or country, they laid the sick in the streets,** or
"market-places." Scarcely anywhere do Mark's
greater vividness and fulness of detail appear
more strikingly than in this passage. Such a
remembrance can have come only from an
intensely interested eye-witness.—The entreaty
for permission to touch the border of his garment may be an indication of the popular
effect of the secret miracle in the crowd (**chap.
5:25-34**) when once the story had gone abroad.
This activity is said to have begun as soon as
Jesus landed, but this description relates, probably, to the work of more than one day. On
that first day he went to Capernaum and delivered in the synagogue his great discourse on
the bread of life. Probably it was not the Sabbath, for then this great activity in collecting
the sick would not have occurred, or, if it
had, would have been at once and openly
condemned.

**1-23. JESUS CONFUTES THE PHAR-
ISEES, WHO COMPLAIN OF HIS DIS-
CIPLES FOR EATING WITH UNWASHEN
HANDS.** *Parallel*, Matt. 15 : 1-20.—Luke makes
no report of this discourse, but he records a
similar one delivered in a Pharisee's house in
Perea at a later time (**Luke 11 : 37-42**). That discourse resembled this in its occasion and beginning, but it went on to a different application.

1-4. The place is still Capernaum. **Which
came from Jerusalem.** Literally, "having
come." The scribes and Pharisees who are

mentioned here are probably Galileans who
had been at Jerusalem and had just returned
thence. The definite article is wanting before
the participle. Its presence would indicate that
they were a delegation from the capital; but
probably these were Galilæan religionists, who,
returning from Jerusalem, perhaps after consultation there, made it their first work to
"come together to Jesus" and see what he
was doing.—**They saw some of his disciples eat bread with defiled** — literally,
with common—**hands.** With hands in the
ordinary state. Not "with dirty hands"—that
was not the point of objection—but with hands
unwashen, not ceremonially purified according to their ideas of necessity.—**Some of his
disciples** were doing thus, not all of them—
an indication that he had given them teaching
that would render them indifferent to the practice of the Pharisees in this matter, but that
only a part of them had yet been freed from
their scruples on the subject.—Verses 3, 4 are
parenthetical, and the best manuscripts insert
an "and" at the beginning of verse 5, which
disturbs the grammatical construction and
makes a broken sentence. This led copyists
to add **they found fault** in verse 2, to complete the structure; but the addition is cancelled
by all the chief editors of the text.
The parenthetical passage (verses 3, 4) is
wholly peculiar to Mark, and is devoted to
the explanation, for the benefit of Gentile
readers, of the custom of the Pharisees, shared
by the Jews in general, about ceremonial cleansings. **The Pharisees, and all the Jews.**
A loose popular expression to show that this
custom of the Pharisees was widely received;
not to be pressed, as if it declared absolute
unanimity. Many, of course, had no time for
these practices, and the Pharisees despised all
who neglected them for that reason, or for any
other, and thought there was scarcely a hope
for them. (See John 7 : 49 for an utterance of
this feeling.)—**Except they wash their hands
oft,** or diligently, *pugmé*. Literally, "with the

7

5 Then the Pharisees and scribes asked him, Why walk not thy disciples according to the tradition of the elders, but eat bread with unwashen hands?
6 He answered and said unto them, Well hath Esaias prophesied*a* of you hypocrites, as it is written, This people honored me with *their* lips, but their heart is far from me.
7 Howbeit, in vain do they worship me, teaching *for* doctrines the commandments of men.

5 pots, and brasen vessels.¹ And the Pharisees and the scribes ask him, Why walk not thy disciples according to the tradition of the elders, but eat their bread with ²defiled hands? And he said unto them, Well did Isaiah prophesy of you hypocrites, as it is written,
This people honoreth me with their lips,
But their heart is far from me.
7　But in vain do they worship me,
Teaching *as their* doctrines the precepts of men.

---

a Isa. 29 : 13.——1 Many ancient authorities add *and couches*....2 Or, *common*

---

fist." Probably descriptive of the washing of one hand by rubbing it with the other. The Sinaitic Manuscript alone has *pukna*, "frequently," which Tischendorf alone among editors adopts. —**And when they come from the market,** where in the crowd defilement might most easily be contracted.—**Except they wash, they eat not.** The word is *baptizō*, *ean mē baptisōntai*. So in Luke 11 : 38 the Pharisee wondered that Jesus had not first bathed himself (*ebaptisthē*) before dinner. It is not the baptizing of their hands, but of themselves, or, strictly, the being baptized or bathed, that was thus insisted upon. The word "baptize" is used precisely as in 2 Kings 5 : 14, where it is said of Naaman, "He dipped himself seven times in Jordan." From the strict literal signification, to "immerse" or "submerge," it comes naturally in certain connections to acquire the sense "to wash by immersing," "to cleanse," of course only in cases where the dipping is into clean water. (So Grimm, *N. T. Lexicon*.) "Bathe" is an admissible translation in this connection, and any difficulties about giving the word its proper meaning here are purely imaginary. In verse 4 the word for "washings," in **washings of cups,** etc., is from the same root, *baptismous*, a derivative of *baptizo*. But it is not the word that is used to denote the Christian rite, which is a neuter word, *baptisma*, while this is masculine, a form that is found only here and in Heb. 6 : 2; 9 : 10. Its signification is properly given by Liddell and Scott, in their *Greek and English Lexicon*, "a dipping in water." It indicates sometimes, in certain connections, a thorough cleansing by water, which would naturally be made, in the case of the objects here mentioned, by dipping, according to the literal signification of the word. The **cups** (*poteria*) were drinking-cups.—As for the **pots,** the Greek word *xestai* is a corruption of the Latin *sextuarius*, a pot that held about a pint. These were ordinarily wooden vessels.—The **brasen** —or properly bronze—**vessels** were for similar purposes with the wooden. The law provided, at least in certain cases of defilement,

that earthen vessels should be broken, and that wooden ones should be rinsed in water (Lev. 15 : 12).—The word translated **tables** (*klinōn*) cannot possibly mean that; it is "beds" or "couches," and may refer to the platforms on which they reclined around the table, which must often be thoroughly washed for fear of defilement, or to the cushions, which would need washing quite as much, and very likely would be washed oftener. But the words **and of tables** are omitted by some good manuscripts, by Tischendorf, and by the revisers.

The greater part of these minute requirements lay outside of the Mosaic law. These things, Mark says, **they have received to hold ;** and they do them **holding the tradition of the elders,** the interpretations and supplements of the law, brought down orally from the men of an earlier time. Tradition was the ecclesiastical version of the law—the law as it came out of the hands of the great teachers. It was regarded as equally authoritative with the written law itself, and, by some, more so. It was the very life and mission of the Pharisees to keep the traditional interpretations in full force. (See Farrar, *Life of Christ*, 2. 471.) Whoever reads such descriptions as are given by Farrar and Geikie of the ingenious wickedness with which this was attempted will not wonder at the denunciations of our Lord or be surprised that the Pharisees were his natural enemies. This was a part of the bondage from which he came to set men free.

5-7. Of course they must call him to account, and not the disciples—the rabbi, not the pupils. He and they were reproved oftener for neglecting the traditions than for departing from the genuine law. His quotation in reply is almost verbally exact from Isa. 29 : 13 in the LXX., the sole variation—**teaching the commandments of men,** instead of "teaching doctrines and commandments of men"—being identical in Matthew and Mark. Traditionalism has met him in its extreme form, and he does not miss his oppor-

8 For laying aside the commandment of God, ye hold the tradition of men, *as* the washing of pots and cups: and many other such like things ye do.

9 And he said unto them, Full well ye reject the commandment of God, that ye may keep your own tradition.

10 For Moses said, Honor *thy father and thy mother; and, Whoso curseth father or mother, let him die the death.

11 But ye say, If a man shall say to his father, *It is* Corban,*d* that is to say, a gift, by whatsoever thou mightest be profited by me: *he shall be free.*

8 Ye leave the commandment of God, and hold fast the tradition of men. And he said unto them, Full well do ye reject the commandment of God, that ye may keep your tradition. For Moses said, Honor thy father and thy mother; and, He that speaketh evil of father or mother, let him *die the death: but ye say, If a man shall say to his father or his mother, That wherewith thou mightest have been profited

a Isa. 1 : 17....*b* Ex. 20 : 12 ; Deut. 5 : 16....*c* Ex. 21 : 17 ; Lev. 20 : 9 ; Prov. 20 : 20....*d* Matt. 15 : 5 ; 23 : 1°.——*1* Or, *surely die*

tunity to scorch it with the fire of his wrath.—Perhaps the tone of indignation is even stronger in Matthew than in Mark. **Well hath Esaias prophesied of you hypocrites**—*i. e.* concerning such hypocrites as you, in his own age or in any other. He condemned outward worship without heart, the profession of the lips with no inward devotion or obedience.—Isaiah was full of such denunciations (as chap. 1 : 11–20), and so were all the prophets. Often, as here, they declared that it was **in vain;** it was empty, fruitless work; it went for nothing. Besides the heartlessness, and as another reason for rejecting such worship, God condemns the foisting upon his religion of human traditions and commandments. His worship must be upon the basis of his own requirements, and no human arrangement may take its place beside what he has appointed. The introduction of human tradition was the point in which the passage from Isaiah was directly applicable to the Pharisees.

8. For should be omitted at the beginning of this verse, and so should **as the washing of pots and cups: and many other such like things ye do,** at the end. So this strong statement stands alone: laying aside (or leaving) **the commandment of God, ye hold the tradition of men.** He charges them, not with addition, but with substitution. They have forsaken command for tradition, God for men. The elders are their chief authority, not Moses or Jehovah; they are not serving God. So, in spirit, Jer. 2 : 12, 13. The rebuke is there for idolatry; but in the sight of God the sin of the Pharisees was as heinous as that.

9. And he said unto them probably indicates a break in the discourse; caused, perhaps, by indignant interruptions, or by a call for particulars to illustrate so broad and fearful a charge. So their ancestors asked, "Wherein have we despised thy name?" (Mal. 1 : 6; 3 : 8, 13). —Whether called for or not, he was ready with particulars to illustrate the substitution of tradition for command. **Full well**—*i. e.* finely, beautifully, admirably—**ye reject the com-**

mandment of God, that ye may keep your own tradition. The adverb is the same as in verse 6: "Well hath Isaiah prophesied of you." The repetition is intentional, and the word this time is scathingly ironical: "Admirably do you fulfil the word that Isaiah so admirably spoke concerning you." The holy indignation is thoroughly aroused, and he cares not how heavily he lays on the lash.

10-13. Yet his first illustration is not the one that called out the question. Instead of beginning with the traditions respecting defilements by contact and the necessary cleansings, he goes at once to the Decalogue, and convicts them of setting aside the fundamental law of God to Israel. **Moses said, Honor thy father and thy mother.** An exact quotation from the LXX. of Ex. 20 : 12.—He adds a second extract, giving the same law as expounded and applied in the legislation of Moses. **Whoso curseth father or mother, let him die the death.** Emphatic way of saying, "Let him die." Ex. 21 : 17 quoted almost exactly from the LXX. Both passages are quoted from what **Moses said,** but both are adduced as **the commandment of God** (verse 9) and **the word of God** (verse 13). Thus, Jesus recognizes the Mosaic legislation as the law of his Father; and not merely the milder parts of it, but even the provision for the execution of the disobedient and insulting child. This he brings forward as a part of that law that he has come "not to destroy, but to fulfil"—*i. e.* to exhibit and establish in the fulness of its spiritual meaning. The principle of honor to parents he recognizes as of perpetual and universal force, and he intends to set up for universal obedience and reverence the truth that was honored by the Mosaic provision of death for the disobedient. Incidentally, his mode of citing the second passage is itself exegetical. Viewed in the light of the context, that passage must mean that the spirit of the prohibition can be violated without a profane or blasphemous word, and that not to bless parents by such care as a child

12 And ye suffer him no more to do ought for his father or his mother;
13 Making the word of God of none effect through your tradition, which ye have delivered: and many such like things do ye.
14 ¶ And when he had called all the people unto him, he said unto them, Hearken unto me every one of you, and understand:[a]
15 There is nothing from without a man that, entering into him, can defile him: but the things which come out of him, those are they that defile the man.
16 If any man have ears to hear, let him hear.

12 by me is Corban, that is to say, Given to God; ye no longer suffer him to do aught for his father or his mother; making void the word of God by your tradition, which ye have delivered: and many such like
14 things ye do. And he called to him the multitude again, and said unto them, Hear me all of you, and
15 understand: there is nothing from without the man, that going into him can defile him: but the things which proceed out of the man are those that defile

a Prov. 8:5; Isa. 6:9; Acts 8:30....b Matt. 11:15.

can give is to curse them, according to the true intent of this law. Such, then, is the "commandment of God" respecting parents: they must be treated with honor, and no one is at liberty to withhold from them what blessing he can give.—But now for the **tradition of men** respecting parents which the Pharisees are diligently keeping. Translate verses 11, 12, "But ye say, If a man say to his father or mother, Whatever thou mightest receive in aid from me is Corban, that is, a gift (to God), ye no longer permit him to do anything for his father or mother." **Corban** is a Hebrew word meaning **gift**, but appropriated to use with reference to sacred gifts, acts of devotion to the service of God. The simple uttering of the word **Corban**—"Sacred gift"—over a thing was supposed to set that thing apart from all ordinary uses and give it the character of a consecrated thing. (See Ewald, *Antiquities of Israel*, p. 81.) Now, Jesus affirms that they apply this mode of consecration to the unholy purpose of escaping duty to parents. If a man utters the magical word "Corban" over his relation to his parents, and so declares that it is devoted to God, he is no longer held under obligation to them. The "Corban" carries no real consecration to God in such a case; it gives no new character to the man's life: it is only a fictitious arrangement for releasing him from a duty that has become irksome. Thus the tradition of men enables them to annul or virtually repeal the commandment of God. The liberty which the tradition gives them is more agreeable to their selfish hearts than the duty to which the commandment binds them; and so they set aside the commandment, in order that they may keep the tradition. To accept such a tradition was to dethrone Jehovah. (See Prov. 28 : 24.) One is reminded here of Luther's sore conflict as to whether the monastic vow which was urged upon him was consistent with his duty to his aged father, and of innumerable similar cases in the long history of monasticism. True consecration is not the escaping from obligations, but the reacceptance

of all genuine duty from the hands of God. Consecration to God never releases from duty to man. He who consents to an obligation to God thereby consents to all obligations that God has placed upon him. To suppose the contrary, as these men did, is to trifle with all obligation.—**Making the word of God of none effect through your tradition.** The word translated **making of none effect** (*akuroontes*) is found in the New Testament only in this discourse and at Gal. 3 : 17: it means "to deprive of authority or lordship," and so, of a law, "to annul." It implies more than neglect: it tells of actual nullification.—**And many such like things do ye,** which is not genuine in verse 8, is genuine here, and may possibly be the reporter's summary of a further discourse, in which other abuses of a similar kind were treated as sharply as the intrusion of "Corban" to the family. The subsequent discourse seems to imply that something had been said at this very time of the distinction between clean and unclean food. There were abuses enough within reach to justify a long and terrible discourse.

14–16. The calling of the people who were within reach (the best text omits **all**) was a sign that he had something of special weight to utter. Perhaps the word "again," which is found in the best texts, indicates that he had withdrawn from the multitude for this conference with the Pharisees and scribes, or that it occurred in the house when but few were present.—**Hearken unto me every one of you, and understand.** Matthew, simply "Hear and understand;" so that the special emphasis is peculiar to Mark. The utterance that followed was intentionally enigmatical — plain enough, perhaps, "to him that understandeth," but requiring explanation for those who were then about him. In verse 17 it is called **the parable;** and there is scarcely any brief saying of our Lord that better illustrates, by its relation to the hearers, the purpose of parabolic instruction—to call attention to present truth in suggestive forms, and yet to leave the

17 And when *he was entered into the house from the people, his disciples asked him concerning the parable.
18 And he saith unto them, Are ye so without understanding also? Do ye not perceive, that whatsoever thing from without entereth into the man, *it* cannot defile him;
19 Because it entereth not into his heart, but *b*into the belly, and goeth out into the draught, purging all meats?

17 the man.¹ And when he was entered into the house from the multitude, his disciples asked of him the
18 parable. And he saith unto them, Are ye so without understanding also? Perceive ye not, that whatsoever from without goeth into the man, *it* cannot
19 defile him; because it goeth not into his heart, but into his belly, and goeth out into the draught? *This*

---

a Matt. 15 : 15, etc....*b* 1 Cor. 6 : 13.——1 Many ancient authorities insert ver. 16 *If any man hath ears to hear, let him hear.*

---

apprehension of it contingent in part upon the spiritual power of the listener. Jesus must certainly have been aware that this saying would place him in apparent opposition, not only to the traditional interpretation of the law, but to the law itself. To a certain extent the opposition would be real; yet this was not to destroy, but to fulfil. He had it in mind to uncover the truth which the law had half revealed and half concealed, and which tradition had gone far toward concealing altogether.— Instead of **entering into him** and **come out of him,** as in Mark, Matthew has "entering into the mouth" and "coming out of the mouth." The general statement is stronger in Mark than in Matthew; for Matthew says only that nothing entering into a man defiles him, while Mark says that nothing entering into a man **can defile him.** In Mark it is an unqualified statement of the complete impossibility of true defilement to man from food, and of the fact that all real defilement proceeds from within, from the man himself. Verse 16 is of doubtful manuscript authority, and should probably be omitted.

17. REQUEST OF THE DISCIPLES FOR EXPLANATION.—Mark omits what Matthew gives, the somewhat anxious inquiry, "Knowest thou that the Pharisees were offended when they heard this saying?" which showed how far the disciples yet were from possessing their Master's fearlessness. But his answer must have shown even them that he had nothing of their anxiety about offending the Pharisees. (See Matt. 15 : 12-14.) After that answer, Peter (so in Matthew) asked for an explanation of the enigmatical saying. Mark attributes the question to **his disciples,** and adds that it was asked in **the house** in the absence of the multitude. Peter, as usual, spoke for them all.

18, 19. He begins with a reproof, intimating that they at least ought to understand him. If he had detached them, even in part, from allegiance to the Pharisaic folly, this saying ought not to be dark to them. The assertion here is that whatever is of the nature of food received into the body is unable to impart real defile-

ment to the man, **because it entereth not into his heart,** the seat of his affections, but only to his **belly,** to be digested and cast forth in excrementation. The word **heart** is not used, of course, in its physical sense; the belly and the heart are not contrasted as two bodily organs or regions. The heart is here the seat of the affections and the centre of moral life. Inasmuch as from that centre proceeds evil, the heart is the source of real defilement, and the only source (*verse* 21). With such a centre of moral life food can have nothing to do, for it passes through the body without having any opportunity of contact with the moral powers. Anything that is truly to defile a man must be such that it can affect, and must actually affect, his heart, and work moral evil there. This is an unequivocal statement that the only real purity and impurity are moral. What, then, of ceremonial cleannesses and uncleannesses, not merely as developed and exaggerated by the tradition of men, but as marked out by the commandment of God? Is not this to condemn the whole system as essentially groundless, and so to overthrow the Mosaic law? No. The Mosaic laws concerning defilement are not here condemned, but they are interpreted, and are referred to their true place. If there is no defilement but moral defilement, then any defilement that is supposed to be contracted from food, or in any similar way, must be, at the most, of an arbitrary and unreal kind. It may with perfect propriety be recognized as having a symbolic meaning and an illustrative significance, but it is not real defilement, and must not be so regarded. Thus the ceremonial defilements that are recognized by the Mosaic law are remanded to their true place, as belonging to a system of external law devised for a temporary purpose. The principle is that of Heb. 10 : 1—that in the Mosaic ceremonial the eternal realities are not presented, but represented; not seen in substance, but in shadow; not offered to men, but only illustrated. So any supposed defilement from food may be used to illustrate the true defilement, but must not be confounded with it.—We must never fail to

20 And he said, That which cometh out of the man, that defileth the man.

20 *he said*, making all meats clean. And he said, That which proceedeth out of the man, that defileth the

notice illustrations of Matt. 5 : 17 : "I am not come to destroy, but to fulfil;" and this is one of the best of them. Apparently he was setting aside a great class of provisions in the ancient law, and the legalists of the day could not fail to condemn him for it; but in reality he was revealing the truth of which the law had given only the suggestion. Men had long been familiar with the shadow of the truth concerning defilement, and he was now showing them the substance, the body of truth itself. Thus he was completing or fulfilling the law—exhibiting it as a preparatory dispensation by bringing in that for which it had prepared. And here, as everywhere, he led men to the fundamental principle, that all real good and evil dwell in the heart. "God is a Spirit, and they that worship him must worship him in spirit and in truth."

The last clause of verse 19, **purging all meats,** or "making all meats clean," has occasioned great difficulty. The clause is peculiar to Mark. In the received text the participle (*katharizon*) was neuter; but all recent editors of the text agree that it should be masculine (*katharizōn*). With the old reading there was no better way than to make the neuter participle refer to the action represented by the preceding verb, and then the statement would be that the separation of food, within the body, into that which the body used and that which the body rejected rendered all kinds of food clean. With the present reading many have attempted to make the masculine participle refer to **draught,** or "drain," which they conceive of as the logical subject, though not in the nominative case; and they still retain the idea that the separation of the food by means of the drain that receives the excrements is that which renders all food clean: so Alford and Meyer. But there is no authority for making "clean" mean "available for the body," and "unclean" "unavailable for the body," as this interpretation does. Moreover, it is hard to see how this interpretation accords with the reason that our Lord has just given why food cannot defile a man. Because food enters not to the heart, he says, it has no power to defile; therefore there can be no need of any physical process of separation to remove its defiling parts. It has no defiling parts.

Far better is the interpretation happily adopted by the revisers, which refers the participle back to the subject of the sentence—*i. e.* the speaker, Jesus: "This he said, making all meats clean "—*i. e.* declaring by this utterance that all kinds of food are essentially clean. It is true that such an expression is unparalleled in Mark's style, and that the order of the words is, as Farrar says, "a serious stumbling-block;" but these difficulties are much less than those that beset the other interpretation. This is confirmed, moreover, by certain coincidences with the story of Peter's vision at Joppa (Acts 10:15; 11:9). There, and there alone in the New Testament (see Grimm's *Lexicon*), the word *katharizō* is used in the sense required by this interpretation, "to declare clean:" "What God hath cleansed, that call not thou common." Peter was the sole source of information concerning that vision, and from Peter's memory, probably, came to Mark the report of this discourse. Mark alone preserves this saying, "making all meats clean." Peter may not have perceived the full effect of this discourse upon the distinctions of food until new light had been brought to his mind by the vision at Joppa, which, though it had a further purpose, turned upon this very thought, that food has no defiling power. After that vision it may have flashed upon him that in this discourse the Lord had already abolished the distinctions that had been troubling his mind, and his clear perception may have registered itself, so to speak, in this terse and striking comment upon the utterance that he had not before understood. Evidently, this final clause is a true comment or summary. Verse 15 had already declared the intrinsic impossibility of real defilement from food, and so had cleansed all meats. The suspicion of the Pharisees that in all such matters a new era would come if Jesus had his way was incorrect only in being inadequate. Yet whoever should proclaim the abolition of ceremonial defilements by divine authority would fulfil the law, not destroy it. "If Moses comes to judge me," said Luther, "I will motion him away in God's name, and say, 'Here stands Christ.' And at the last day Moses will look on me and say, 'Thou hast understood me aright,' and he will be gracious to me."

20-23. The converse is now presented, that which can and does defile. It comes altogether from the man himself, from within, out of his heart. Matthew, "For those things that proceed out of the mouth come forth from the heart; and they defile the man." The indictment as Mark gives it contains thirteen counts;

21 For from* within, out of the heart of men, proceed evil thoughts, adulteries, fornications, murders,
22 Thefts, covetousness, wickedness, deceit, lasciviousness, an evil eye, blasphemy, pride, foolishness:

21 man. For from within, out of the heart of men,
22 ᵉevil thoughts proceed, fornications, thefts, murders,
adulteries, covetings, wickednesses, deceit, lascivious-

a Gen. 6:5; Ps. 14:1, 3; 53:1, 3; Jer. 17:9.——ᵉ Gr. *thoughts that are evil.*

---

as Matthew, only seven, six of which coincide with Mark's, while one, "false witness," is added. Matthew follows the order of the Decalogue in the second table; Mark's order appears to be accidental. The beginning is a striking confirmation of the general principle that has been laid down. **For from within, out of the heart of men, proceed evil thoughts.** The word is a compound one, and refers rather to thought as organized and connected, rather to trains of thought than to single thoughts. These evil thoughts defile as truly and deeply as evil deeds; yet not so that the deed will add nothing to the guilt. So in Matt. 5 : 27, 28: the deliberate thought of adultery is adultery in the heart. It is a true judgment, theoretically and practically, that sets evil thoughts, without restriction, at the head of the list.— **Adulteries, fornications, murders, thefts.** On manuscript authority the revisers read "fornications, thefts, murders, adulteries." These are acts, and by the use of the plural are set forth as acts rather than portrayed by any abstract reference to their character. But the one fact concerning them to which our Lord would especially call attention is that they come forth from the heart; these outward deeds are really inward deeds, and are to be judged not solely from their outward effect, their effect upon society, but as expressions of the inward man. Coming forth, they reveal the source from which they sprang.—The same desire to particularize appears in the next two cases. **Covetousness,** or covetings, acts of covetousness, still regarded as springing from the heart, and **wickedness,** or rather, more definitely, "malignities," acts or forms of malignity which manifestly are revelations of that which is within. Here there is a double specialization; for the word used (*ponéria*) means malignity in action, and not merely in thought (Trench, *Synonyms of the New Testament,* 1. 60), and our Lord selects the plural of this definite word to express his thought—forms of active malignity. —**Deceit,** or guile, a quality of the habitual thinking that cannot fail to control the conduct. One of the most deep-seated and ineradicable of sins, partly because it deludes its possessor even when it fails to deceive others. The absence of it Jesus joyfully recognized in Nathaniel (John 1 : 47), and the presence of it David felt to have been one of the facts that inter-

fered with the giving of pardon for his great transgression (Ps. 32 : 2).—**Lasciviousness,** or licentiousness, wantonness, or unbridledness. A word that can scarcely be referred to any special form of sin. It is rather the underlying thought or temper of the heart by which many sins are made possible and easy. It is not unchastity alone, to which modern usage almost limits the words "licentiousness" and "lasciviousness;" it is rather the recklessness of spirit that opens the way to unchastity and to many another sin.—**An evil eye** is envy. So Matt. 20 : 15 : "Is thine eye evil because I am good?" —*i. e.* "Art thou envious at my kindness to another?" It is a natural impulse to attribute envy in action to the circumstances that have aroused it, and to blame the object of our envy rather than ourselves; but our Lord was plainly right in tracing it to the heart.—**Blasphemy** is not merely the speaking profanely against God, as one might infer from the modern usage. The scriptural usage is broader: it is evil-speaking in general, defamation, slander, railing. So it is used in Eph. 4 : 31; 1 Tim. 6 : 4. In the Epistles the word refers oftener to evil-speaking against men than to what we call blasphemy, profanity toward God. Here, though he is still quoting the words that refer to actions, Mark changes (not Matthew), and uses the singular instead of the plural, as before. Apparently he thus ceases in part to specialize, and drags to light for condemnation evil-speaking as a practice, instead of suggesting the special acts.—The last two evils to be mentioned are deep parent-vices of the heart, responsible for innumerable transgressions. **Pride,** the false and extravagant estimate of one's self by which all the thoughts and conduct of the life are put upon a false basis. With pride dominant in the heart, no thought about one's self is correct and truthful, and hence no comparison of one's self with others can be just and no true recognition will be made of the claims of God. Pride is the omnipresent poisoner of motive, vitiator of judgment, murderer of virtue; and its seat is in the heart. **Foolishness,** the lack of true wisdom, or rather the state and character that result when true wisdom is absent. Foolishness is by no means a negative vice. "The fear of the Lord is the beginning of wisdom;" and the fear of the Lord does not merely leave a

23 All these evil things come from within, and defile the man.
24 ¶ And from⁼ thence he arose, and went into the borders of Tyre and Sidon, and entered into an house, and would have no man know it: but he⁵ could not be hid.
25 For a *certain* woman, whose young daughter had an unclean spirit, heard of him, and came and fell at his feet:

23 ness, an evil eye, railing, pride, foolishness: all these evil things proceed from within, and defile the man.
24 And from thence he arose, and went away into the borders of Tyre ³and Sidon. And he entered into a house, and would have no man know it: and he
25 could not be hid. But straightway a woman whose little daughter had an unclean spirit, having heard

a Matt. 15 : 21, etc.....*b* ch. 2 : 1.——1 Some ancient authorities omit *and Sidon*.

vacant place for negative vices when it is absent. The "folly" of the book of Proverbs is a positive and various evil, and so is the **foolishness** that here stands at the end of the list of sins of the heart.

All these evil things, says Jesus, **come from within, and defile the man.** Thus he puts upon sin the disgrace that he has just removed from meats. He has released men from all anxiety about defilement from the kind of food they eat, but he has uncovered a far deeper source of anxiety. The sharpest point of all is that he has declared man to be self-defiled, the fountain of his own uncleanness. From the heart these things proceed; and how terrible they are! No need of ceremonial pollutions to establish the necessity for cleansing; so long as the heart remains such a fountain it is certain that man will be defiled. Nor does he leave any one at liberty to say that the defiling power resides either in acts alone or in thoughts alone; for he has dragged to the light both sins of action and sins of thought.

By no conceivable utterance could our Lord have made a deeper or more irreparable break with the Pharisees and the whole spirit of their teaching. Yet what utterance of his whole ministry was more profoundly characteristic than this?

24-30. THE HEALING OF THE DAUGHTER OF A SYROPHŒNICIAN WOMAN. *Parallel,* Matt. 15 : 21-28. — The narrative is given more fully, vividly, and characteristically by Mark; the conversation, by Matthew. Without Matthew's report, indeed, our knowledge of the incident would be comparatively fragmentary. Mark tells the story as from an eye-witness; Matthew, as from an ear-witness.

24. A fresh journey is here announced, into a fresh field. It is a journey **into the borders** - *i. e.* the region, the country—**of Tyre.** The words **and Sidon** should perhaps be omitted here, though the manuscript authority is not decisive. Verse 31 proves, however, that the journey extended as far as to Sidon. Here, and here alone within his ministry, we follow our Saviour beyond the limits of the land of

Israel in a journey of considerable extent through heathen territory. He confined himself, with this exception, to the Jewish land; and during this tour he plainly indicated (Matt. 15:24) that he regarded himself as going beyond the strict limits of his mission. Yet, as Plumptre remarks, Tyre and Sidon were no more truly defiled in his sight than Chorazin and Bethsaida, and possibly he may have gone forth upon this journey with a feeling that all special sanctity was gone from Jehovah's land. As for the motive of the journey, it was probably the desire for rest and for retirement with the apostles. His ministry in Galilee was ending sadly, and now his heart turned to his circle of nearest followers, with the desire to be with them and to prepare them by instruction for their great trust in the future. One effort to be alone with them had just been defeated (chap. 6 : 31-34), and so a new attempt was made by undertaking a journey that would take them much farther from home.—**Entered into an house.** The house of some friend, perhaps, either in the north of Galilee, near the border of Tyre, or in the land of Tyre itself.—**He would have no man know it: but he could not be hid.** All peculiar to Mark, and important because it proves what was the purpose of the journey. He was not preaching or intending or desiring to work miracles; and if a multitude gathered about him, it would be against his wish.

25. The original connective at the beginning of this verse is " But " instead of **For.** The difference in sense is slight, but real, and the vividness of the picture is increased by the change. He could not be hid, but (on the contrary) immediately, as soon as he had arrived, a woman, etc. Matthew says that she "came out of those coasts," or out of that country—*i. e.,* probably, out of the land of Tyre. This is perhaps favorable to the view that Jesus had not yet crossed the border, but was within the limits of Galilee. If Tischendorf's reading, *eiselthousa,* "coming in," which is certainly ancient, is correct, Mark represents that the interview here described took place in the house. There would be no difficulty in combining this with the record of Matthew, who speaks of an interview on the

26 The woman was a Greek, a Syrophenician by nation; and she besought him that he would cast forth the devil out of her daughter.

27 But Jesus said unto her, Let the children first be filled: for[a] it is not meet to take the children's bread, and to cast it unto the dogs.

26 of him, came and fell down at his feet. Now the woman was a [1]Greek, a Syrophenician by race. And she besought him that he would cast forth the demon 27 out of her daughter. And he said unto her, Let the children first be filled: for it is not meet to take the

a Matt. 7 : 6; 10 : 5, 6.——1 Or, *Gentile*

---

road, for he also says that the woman followed them; and it would be only natural, if they were going to the house, that she should follow them thither. Such a fitting together of the two reports makes the story more picturesque and interesting; but it must not be thought that the credibility of the reports depends upon our ability thus to match them together. It has sometimes been thought so, greatly to the weakening of confidence in the Scriptures, and much to the disadvantage of honest exegetical study. We must never put ourselves under special temptation to pervert any passage of Scripture. —This **woman, whose young daughter** (*thugatrion*, the word is a diminutive) **had an unclean spirit, having heard of him**—*i. e.* of the works he had done and the fact of his presence—**came and fell at his feet.** She had not seen him; faith came by hearing.

26. The woman was a Greek. So the word literally means, but by usage among the Jews and in the New Testament it means a Gentile, a non-Jew. It tells nothing of the nationality of him who bears it as a name; not even in such a passage as John 12 : 20 is it decisive.—That in this case it is used in its broader sense is proved by the descriptive addition that follows. **A Syrophenician by nation,** or "by race," *tō genei*. Matthew calls her a Canaanite. The name **Syrophenician** belonged to the part of the Phœnician race that had its home in Syria, as distinguished from the part that dwelt in Libya, on the southern shore of the Mediterranean. (So Strabo, quoted in Meyer.) The emperor Hadrian (A. D. 117–138) divided the province of Syria into three parts, of which the central one, lying north of Palestine, was called Syrophœnicia; and it is probable that the official name chosen for the district was a name previously in use. Tyre and Sidon, Phœnician cities, were in the Syrophœnician country. Mark's rapid narrative passes by the woman's nationality at what we would call the proper place, and introduces it parenthetically in the midst of her entreaty in behalf of her daughter.—**Besought him that he would cast forth the devil,** or demon, **out of her daughter.** Matthew quotes directly: "Have mercy on me, O Lord, thou Son of

David, for my daughter is grievously vexed with a devil."

27. Let the children first be filled. A direct refusal, with reason assigned. Substantially equivalent to "I am not sent but to the lost sheep of the house of Israel," as given by Matthew. By this he meant, "My ministry is to the Jews, who, though so far astray, are God's own flock" (Matthew), or "God's own family" (Mark). "I am not sent, in this my ministry, except to them. So let the children first be filled, fed, satisfied; for they have the first claim, which is indeed, at present, the only claim." By the word **first** he quietly conveys a promise and suggests the principle of Rom. 1 : 16—"to the Jew first, and also to the Greek," or Gentile—but there was no immediate fulfilment even hinted at for the Gentile.—In Matthew this is given as the answer to the woman's prayer, and at the same time to a most unlovely request of the disciples. At first, according to Matthew, he answered her nothing, but she continued to ask. Then the disciples came and joined their prayer to hers, but in a different spirit, saying, "Send her away, for she crieth after us"—*i. e.* Send her away with her prayer granted, for she is troublesome; give her what she wants, and let us be rid of her. It was to this that he replied, "I am not sent, except to the lost sheep of the house of Israel." Yet the woman persisted with her "Lord, help me," and then he added the reason for his refusal, which in Mark immediately follows upon the refusal itself.—The reason, **for it is not meet** —it is not good, or right—**to take the children's bread, and to cast it unto the dogs.** Observe that the word for **dogs** is not the ordinary word; not the word of Matt. 7 : 6, "Give not that which is holy to the dogs;" not the word of contempt, so often applied to the fierce and hated dogs of the East. It is a diminutive (*kunaria*), and refers to the dogs of the family, the dogs that are about the house. His words picture these dogs playing about the house while the family are at table. To bless Gentiles now, he says, would be like taking the children's bread and throwing it to these.— How profoundly touching and suggestive that even now he calls himself and the blessings of his ministry **the children's bread**—this at

28 And she answered and said unto him, Yes, Lord: yet the dogs under the table eat of the children's crumbs.
29 And he said unto her, For this saying go thy way; the devil is gone out of thy daughter.

28 children's bread and cast it to the dogs. But she answered and saith unto him, Yea, Lord: even the dogs under the table eat of the children's crumbs.
29 And he said unto her, For this saying go thy way;

a Rom. 15 · 8, 9; Eph. 2 : 12-14....b Isa. 66 : 2.——1 Or, loaf

the end of a ministry in Galilee in the course of which his popularity has waned and it has become apparent that he is not to be accepted as the Messiah! The children are refusing their bread, yet, with the faithfulness and persistency of love, he will not take it from them and give it to the dogs.—Israel has the first right to him, and Israel shall have him first. **Let the children first be filled.** Yet even the bread so persistently offered, the children utterly refused.

28. Yes, Lord. The woman quickly accepts the position that he gives her, and with ready wit and ready faith turns sharply upon him.—The word **yet,** that follows in the common version, is sadly wrong and has greatly obscured a beautiful answer. In Matthew the connective is "for;" in Mark it should probably be "and," or "even," though here also "for" has some authority. With "even," the thought is, "True; even for the dogs there is provision: they eat the crumbs, just as I am praying that I may do." Richer still is the thought with "for." "True," she says, "it is not well to give the children's bread to the dogs, for the dogs have the crumbs for their portion. They ought not to receive the bread, for they have their provision already; and it is for this that I am asking. I will gladly leave the children their bread if I may but have what is the proper portion of the dogs." Thus with "for" (which one cannot but think to have been the word that she used) she asks for the blessing she desires, expressly on the ground that she is one of the dogs, and that such mere droppings of his abundant grace as she is asking for may be recognized as her fitting portion.—Here is (1) confidence in the fulness of his power: she knows that he is "able to do this" (Matt. 9 : 28). (2) Confidence in the generosity of his heart: she is sure that there is no deep reason in himself why he must absolutely confine his activity to the providing of **the children's bread.** She feels that "there's a wideness in his mercy" by which even she, a Gentile, is justified in resorting to him in her need. Very naturally, it was in a Gentile heart that this confidence first sprang up: his Jewish followers were narrow enough for a long time after this. (3) Confidence in the fairness of his mind: a full con-

viction that it will not be in vain to present to him a case of need, even if it does lie outside of his accustomed circle; conviction that it will not be breath wasted to argue with him and press him to attend to a humble request. This is faith of a rational kind, for it rests upon a true and just conviction as to the character of him to whom it resorts. It is in the spirit of the faith that our Lord commends in Luke 11 : 11-13, where he bids us ground our expectation of success in prayer upon an intelligent conviction respecting the goodness of God. (4) Persistency, that absolutely will not take refusal. Especially as given in Matthew, this is one of the best illustrations of a determined importunity such as our Lord commends in Luke 11 : 5-10; 18 : 1-8. The woman pleads as if she had heard him say that "Men ought always to pray, and not to faint." (5) Humility, that does not shrink from accepting an inferior position. This is not merely a concession of inferiority for the sake of argument, a "Call me what you will, but give me what I want;" it is a recognition of the first claim of Israel, whose Christ he is, and a humble acceptance of the second place. Yet possibly she may perceive that the time is coming when all such distinctions will be swept away by his grace. (6) Shrewdness, quick to seize an advantage and bold to press it. We do not read of any one else who so turned upon our Lord and argued with him out of his own mouth. We can see that she is not afraid of him, though full of reverence. Neither timid nor disrespectful, she grasps at her opportunity to extort what seems to be refused.

29. The answer of Jesus expressly affirms that her prayer was granted because of what she had said. In Matthew, "O woman, great is thy faith: be it unto thee even as thou wilt;" in Mark, still more explicitly, **For this saying go thy way; the devil is gone out of thy daughter.** This reply appears to settle the question respecting the attitude and motive of Jesus in this conversation. It is often assumed that he must have intended from the first to grant the request, and was testing the woman by refusal with the purpose of drawing out and increasing her faith. There are serious difficulties, in any case, about this view of his conduct, as readers of the story

30 And when she was come to her house, she found the devil gone* out, and her daughter laid upon the bed.
31 ¶ And again,* departing from the coasts of Tyre and Sidon, he came unto the sea of Galilee, through the midst of the coasts of Decapolis.

30 the demon is gone out of thy daughter. And she went away unto her house, and found the child laid upon the bed, and the demon gone out.
31 And again he went out from the borders of Tyre, and came through Sidon unto the sea of Galilee,

a 1 John 3 : 8....*b* Matt. 15 : 29, etc.

have often felt. It is hard to see how in repeatedly refusing the request, and in giving the woman and the disciples a reason for refusing, he was sincere and honest, if all the time he meant to give a favorable answer; for this is not a case of mere delay and silent disappointing of hopes, as in John 11 : 6: it is a case of plain refusal. But we are relieved of all such moral difficulties as soon as we give its due weight to this answer of Jesus, in which he says that he performs the healing on account of this saying. He was honest, then, in all that he said before; he did not intend to grant the request; he gave the real reason for the refusal; and he yielded to her bold and skilful argument. It was true that the mission of his earthly ministry was to Israel, and that this was outside of his field. He had come hither not intending to preach or to heal; and only this woman's faith and courage led him to change his purpose.—To some minds, perhaps, the mere mention of a change of purpose in our Lord may be objectionable. If he was divine, must he not have had his complete foreknowledge and his unalterable plans? In this way the recognition of his Divinity has often made his humanity unreal and his conduct mechanical in the esteem of devout souls. It does not satisfy the terms of the problem of his life to say that Jesus Christ was God. That is only a part of the truth, for he was "the Word made flesh," God within the limitations of humanity. The more we are won away from mechanical theories of his life by clearer views of his person, the less difficulty shall we have in recognizing such a change of mind as he himself here announces. The more real Jesus becomes to us as a living person, the more intelligible is he, morally, to our hearts and consciences, and yet the more divinely glorious and the farther removed from the level of our ordinary humanity.—An additional reason why he must at least have been glad to do this work of mercy was the feeling, so unlike his own, that was rising in the disciples. When they said, "Send her away" with her request granted, "for she crieth after us," he must have been glad to turn to a better purpose an event of which they were making so unworthy a use. When they wished to be

rid of a suppliant, he would be the more inclined to be favorable to the request.
30. The word was, **the devil is gone out of thy daughter.** The fulfilment that the woman found at home was (in the order given in the revisers' text), she "found the child laid upon the bed, and the demon gone out." Matthew's report of the result includes no picture of the scene. Not unlikely, one of the disciples may have gone home with her, and that one may have been Peter, in whose report the more graphic description is found.—As for the daughter, did she ever meet her Benefactor? Longfellow, in *The Divine Tragedy*, has a beautiful conjecture that she saw him for the first time when he was making his entry to Jerusalem, and poured out her heart in love and praise.

31–37. A DEAF-AND-DUMB MAN IS HEALED.—Apparently this is one, and not improbably the first, of the great group of miracles mentioned in Matt. 15 : 29–31; but it is the only one of that group of which we have any special mention, and this is detailed by Mark alone. This passage is of peculiar interest as being one of two very graphic and pictorial narratives of the act of healing, given only by Mark, and intensely characteristic of him. Nowhere are the traces of eye-witnessing more unmistakable, and nowhere else do we thus behold the process of healing as well as the result. The other passage is in chap. 8 : 22–26.

31. According to the text adopted by the revisers, the course of the journey is here quite definitely marked out: "And again he went out from the borders" (region) "of Tyre, and came through Sidon unto the sea of Galilee, through the midst of the borders" (region) "of Decapolis." That he visited the city of Tyre itself is not affirmed, but from the course of the journey it seems probable. He did pass through Sidon, which lay, like Tyre, on the shore of the Mediterranean. From Capernaum to Tyre may have been thirty English miles, and from Tyre to Sidon twenty more. Between the two cities were Zarephath (called Sarepta in Luke 4 : 26), where Elijah was preserved alive in famine and restored the widow's son to life (1 Kings 17). His alluding to the event in the syn-

32 And they bring unto him one that was deaf, and had an impediment in his speech; and they beseech him to put his hand upon him.

33 And he took him aside from the multitude, and put his fingers into his ears, and he spit, and touched his tongue;

32 through the midst of the borders of Decapolis. And they bring unto him one that was deaf, and had an impediment in his speech; and they beseech him to 33 lay his hand upon him. And he took him aside from the multitude privately, and put his fingers into his

a ch. 8 : 23 ; John 9 : 6.

agogue at Nazareth is enough to assure us that our Lord did not pass the spot without remembering again how it was a Gentile widow to whom the prophet was sent. From Sidon he turned south-eastward, and crossed the upper Jordan, and came down on the eastern side. But he did not merely make the journey downward along the river; he appears to have extended his tour still eastward—we cannot tell how far—through some part of the region known as Decapolis, probably visiting some of the cities from which that region took its name. (See note on chap 5 : 20.) The reasons that determined the route, of course, cannot be ascertained. Thus he made his way down to the Sea of Galilee, reaching it somewhere on the eastern side. The limits of Decapolis are somewhat uncertain, but its extent was such that his journey may have taken him farther south than his destination; so that it is impossible to tell from what direction he approached the lake or what point of its shore he probably first touched. Of course the length of the journey cannot be measured; but it can scarcely have been, from Capernaum back to the lake, less than one hundred and fifty English miles, and it may have been more. On the east as well as on the north this was a tour into heathen territory, but in no part, so far as we can judge, was it a tour of missionary activity. It was rather an episode in his ministry when he was alone with his disciples. By comparison with Matthew it appears that this miracle was wrought, most probably, on some "mountain" near the lake, where many were gathered about him.

32. They bring unto him one that was deaf. The adjective literally means "stricken," or "smitten" (*kōphos*, from the verb *koptō*, "to strike"); the thought is that the person has been smitten in some of the organs of sensation, so as to be deprived of power. Sometimes it is the organs of speech that are thus conceived of as smitten, and the word then means "dumb;" sometimes it is the organs of hearing, and it then means "deaf," as here. The other descriptive word (*mogilalos*) means "speaking with difficulty;" not "speechless" (*alalos*), as in verse 37. It is used here alone in the New Testament. It cannot be smoothly rendered without

paraphrase, and **had an impediment in his speech** represents it well. Yet the word is used broadly for "dumb" in the LXX. (Is. 35 : 6).—The great Healer was asked to put his hand on the man ; so Matt. 9 : 18 : "But come and lay thy hand upon her, and she shall live." But now, as then, the great Healer had a way of his own.

33, 34. Three peculiarities appear in this act of healing—the privacy of the transaction, the use of signs and physical media, and the unusual vocal utterances of the Healer. These peculiarities all appear again in the other miracle in chap. 8 : 22-26, already alluded to. In studying them in this case it is to be remembered that this is the only detailed report that we possess of the healing of a deaf man ; and, although we may not be justified in inferring that all healings of the deaf resembled this, we may find in the peculiar method now adopted a special significance in connection with the nature of the affliction that was to be removed. In healing the blind, Jesus, so far as we know, always made some appeal to the senses and powers of which the afflicted ones were possessed, drawing out their faith by word or touch or by requiring the performance of some act. (See Matt. 9 : 29; Mark 8 : 23; 10 : 49; John 9 : 6.) So, usually, in healing the lame and helpless. (See John 5 : 6-8; Mark 3 : 3; Luke 17 : 14.) In the case of a deaf man words would be of no avail; and if any such appeal was to be made, it must be done by signs. In the present case Jesus probably saw in the man himself some reason for judging it best that the cure should be private. The withdrawal from the crowd would impress him, though he could not hear its tumult, with a sense of solemnity. Perhaps Jesus saw in him a vanity that would render anything like a public act of healing hurtful to him. In any case, it was a solemn and touching experience to be alone, or almost alone, with Jesus to be healed.—As for the signs and the physical media, they were such as he could well understand. Jesus **put his fingers into his ears.** Not a mere touch, but an insertion—a sign of the impartation or transference of something from one person to the other, with reference now to the powerless organs of hearing. This was the laying on of his hand

34 And looking up to heaven, he sighed,[b] and saith unto him, Ephphatha, that is, Be opened.
35 And straightway[c] his ears were opened, and the string of his tongue was loosed, and he spake plain.
36 And he charged them that they should tell no man: but the more he charged them, so much the more a great deal they published it;
37 And were beyond measure astonished,[d] saying, He hath done all things well: he maketh both the deaf to hear, and the dumb to speak.

34 ears, and he spat, and touched his tongue; and looking up to heaven, he sighed, and saith unto him, 35 Ephphatha, that is, Be opened. And his ears were opened, and the bond of his tongue was loosed, and 36 he spake plain. And he charged them that they should tell no man: but the more he charged them, so much the more a great deal they published it. 37 And they were beyond measure astonished, saying, He hath done all things well: he maketh even the deaf to hear, and the dumb to speak.

a ch. 6 : 41 ; John 11 : 41 ; 17 : 1....b John 11 : 33, 38....c Matt. 8 : 3, 15....d Ps. 139 : 14 ; Acts 14 : 11....e Ex. 4 : 10, 11.

that had been asked for, made definite, appropriate, and instructive by his wisdom. Then he spit, and touched his tongue—i. e. touched the man's tongue with a finger perhaps moistened with his own saliva—another sign of the transference of something from himself to the afflicted man, this time with reference to his injured organs of speech. Then he stood looking up to heaven, to indicate that this was an act that depended upon a heavenly power—an act, indeed, of Heaven upon the earth. Of course there had been no opportunity, because no possibility, of preaching to the man, and in his ignorance he may easily have supposed that this was some influence of a magical kind. He may not have known to what power he was submitting himself, and the reverent heavenward look of Jesus may have been intended silently to lift his heart and faith to God. How better could he show a deaf man that he was receiving a gift from above? Then he sighed, or, rather, "groaned." The word is not used elsewhere of him, but it is found in Rom. 8 : 23 and 2 Cor. 5 : 2, where evidently no less a word than "groan" is needed to represent its meaning. This was no artificial utterance intended for effect: it was a spontaneous utterance of genuine sorrow in sympathy with human suffering. It came from the same source as the tears at the grave of Lazarus. Although the man could not hear the groan, he might be aware of it, for doubtless his eyes were busy in observing what his Benefactor was doing; and if he was aware of it, he must have felt, however dimly, that there was a deep and genuine sympathy in the Healer's heart. This could be no magician's performance to him: this was a deed of love. And then at last he spoke; and, though the man might not hear the word, he may have known, as before, that it was spoken. Ephphatha, that is, Be opened. Here, as in chap. 5 : 41, Mark has preserved the very word in the Aramaic tongue that fell from the lips of Jesus. No other evangelist has done this, except in the case of the utterance on the cross, "Eli, Eli, lama sabachthani." In the other case (chap. 5 : 41) the Ara-

maic words that Mark preserves were spoken when of the disciples only Peter, James, and John were present; and it is not unlikely that the same special three were the only auditors at this time also. Whether others were present or not, this must certainly have come down to us from one who heard it. The Ephphatha, Be opened, was addressed to the man with reference to his organs of sense, which are conceived of as closed.

35. It would seem that the moment of the Ephphatha was the moment of the change. Of course we know that the preceding parts of the transaction were in no sense necessary to the cure, and were introduced for the sake of the man himself; and we may judge that he received no new power of speech or hearing until the symbolic or pictorial part was finished and the word was spoken.—The cure itself is detailed in Mark's peculiar way. The revisers omit straightway, and thus represent the result: "And his ears were opened, and the bond of his tongue was loosed, and he spake plain," or rightly, normally.—The string of his tongue is an unfortunate phrase, from which a reader might suppose that the man was in some way tongue-tied. But the reference is merely to the bond or restraint that was upon his powers of speech, and there is no indication as to the nature of that restraint.—But now the organs of sense were opened, and henceforth all was done (orthōs) in the natural or normal way.

It is worth while to look back at this act and observe how beautifully our Lord brought to light all that was essential in a work of healing. Perhaps the symbolic action was all the more beautiful, because it must be made to do the whole work of words. Two signs of the transferring of power from himself to the afflicted—the upward look to heaven, to indicate the source of power; the deep sigh or groan of genuine sympathy with the suffering that is to be removed—and the word of power by which the deed is done, and the bond is broken. A beautiful story for deaf-mutes.

36, 37. He charged them. Not merely

CHAPTER VIII.

IN those days the multitude being very great, and having nothing to eat, Jesus called his disciples *unto him*, and saith unto them,

2 I have compassion[b] on the multitude, because they have now been with me three days, and have nothing to eat :

3 And if I send them away fasting to their own houses, they will faint by the way : for divers of them came from afar.

1 In those days, when there was again a great multitude, and they had nothing to eat, he called unto 2 him his disciples, and saith unto them, I have compassion on the multitude, because they continue with 3 me now three days, and have nothing to eat : and if I send them away fasting to their home, they will faint in the way ; and some of them are come from afar.

a Matt. 15 : 32, etc.....*b* Ps. 145 : 8, 15; Heb. 5 : 2.

the man himself, but the people who were around. Of course they would quickly know what had been done, and must be included in his prohibition. Often did he thus plead for silence about his works (as in chap. 3 : 12 and 5 : 43), and now, while he was in search of retirement and quietness, the request was especially to be expected. But, as usual, it was all in vain : the gratitude of the healed and the wonder of the spectators were too strong, and the story must be told. It seems probable that this miracle was the means of bringing on the great period of thronging that is described in Matt. 15 : 30, 31. Mark's expressions in description of the abundant proclamation and the excessive amazement are of the very strongest character.—The final testimony of praise seems to have been called out by the many healings that took place, though first suggested by the one. **He hath done all things well** (perfect tense)—he has been gracious everywhere and in everything—**he maketh** (present tense) **both the deaf to hear, and the dumb to speak.—The dumb.** A stronger word than in verse 32.

1-9. JESUS FEEDS FOUR THOUSAND. *Parallel*, Matt. 15 : 32-38.—The connection is unbroken from chap. 7, and the place is still the "mountain" on the eastern side of the lake whither the multitude had come to meet him. It was on the same side of the lake with the scene of the similar miracle (Mark 6 : 35-44), but we cannot affirm that the place was the same. The intense activity of Matt. 15 : 30, 31 continued several days, and delayed the return of Jesus, after his long absence, to the towns on the other side.—It has sometimes been alleged that this is only an altered version or a varied remembrance of the story just referred to, in chap. 6, two events so nearly alike being supposed to be less probable than the repetition of the story with variations. But there is every reason to believe that there were two miracles of feeding the multitude, as both Matthew and Mark affirm. The circumstances of the two, according to the record, were so different as to

render the unfolding of the two stories from one event most improbable. On the first occasion, Jesus had just gone forth from Capernaum ; on the second, he had just returned to that region after a considerable absence. On the first, the multitude had followed him on foot from Capernaum around the end of the lake, because they saw him departing by boat ; on the second, the multitude was gathered by the tidings of his return and of the miracles that he was performing. On the first, the people had been with him only during the day ; on the second, they had been three days in his company. Moreover, in verses 19, 20 of this chapter, Jesus distinctly alludes to the two events, and with a definiteness that is peculiarly conclusive. (See note there.) There is no reason, therefore, for a reader to suspect that a mythical element has entered here and made two stories out of one.

1-3. Very great (*pampollou*). We should read, with the revisers, "again a great" (*palin pollou*), "when there was again a great multitude, and they had nothing to eat."—This time Jesus takes the initiative, and consults his disciples as to what should be done. **I have compassion on the multitude.** His compassion led him on the other occasion to teach them as well as to feed them ; and so doubtless it did now. Matthew's citation of his words is apparently the more precise, as it is the more expressive ; literally, " And send them away fasting I will not, lest they faint in the way."—Mark adds, **for divers of them came from afar.** There is sufficient manuscript authority for substituting "and" for **for.** The connection of thought is that some of them have come from far, and therefore have far to go—so far that compassion forbids sending them away hungry. He does not say that during the three days they have been with him they have had nothing to eat, but only intimates that by this long stay their provisions have become exhausted.—Why did he consult his disciples on the level of earthly necessities and modes of provision, instead of proposing at once to put forth his own power? Perhaps for two reasons : partly in order that reliance upon him might not

4 And his disciples answered him, From whence° can
a man satisfy these *men* with bread here in the wilderness?
5 And he asked them, How many loaves have ye?
And they said, Seven.
6 And he commanded the people to sit down on the
ground; and he took the seven loaves, and gave thanks,
and brake, and gave to his disciples to set before *them*;
and they did set *them* before the people.
7 And they had a few small fishes; and he blessed,^b
and commanded to set them also before *them*.
8 So they did eat, and were° filled; and they^d took
up of the broken *meat* that was left seven baskets.

4 far. And his disciples answered him, Whence shall
one be able to fill these men with bread here in a
5 desert place? And he asked them, How many loaves
6 have ye? And they said, Seven. And he commandeth the multitude to sit down on the ground; and
he took the seven loaves, and having given thanks,
he brake, and gave to his disciples, to set before them;
7 and they set them before the multitude. And they
had a few small fishes; and having blessed them, he
8 commanded to set these also before them. And they
did eat, and were filled; and they took up, of broken

a ch. 6 : 36, 37....*b* Matt. 14 : 19.....*c* Ps. 107 : 5, 6; 145 : 16....*d* 1 Kings 17 : 14, 16; 2 Kings 4 : 2; 7 : 42, 44.——*I* Gr *loaves.*

alienate them from the habit of forethought
even in the matter of caring for these multitudes that gathered about him; and partly to
show them that even he was not above the
exercise of forethought in the employment of
his miraculous power. Not without carefully
taking note of the need of miracles did he perform them; and he would have his disciples
know that he wrought miracles with a wise
forecast, and not as a matter of course, whether
they were needed or not.

4, 5. The answer is one of helplessness and
despair. Here in the wilderness, with no
place of supply near, and the store of the disciples had gone as low as that of the multitude
in the course of the three days. But why did
they not give utterance to faith in his power?
They had but lately seen a multitude fed by
him, and a little later he rebuked them for
not remembering how able he was to do such
works. But their Master had consulted them
on the earthly level, expressing merely his pity
for the people and his desire that they might
be fed before he sent them away. He had already allowed both disciples and multitude to
use up all their food and come to the verge of
exhaustion, just as if he had no intention of
interposing to relieve them by miracle. There
is no evidence that his disciples ever proposed
to Jesus to use his miraculous power, except
by bringing the sick to him; unless Luke 9 :
54 forms an exception, where they themselves
wished to call fire from heaven to destroy those
who insulted him.—In such a case as this they
would feel that the suggestion of a miracle must
come from him. They would probably have
shrunk, as they ought, from saying, "You can
feed them," especially when they had no hint
of his intention. He can scarcely have wished
them to suggest it. Therefore their answer
probably expressed, not stupidity, but their
sense of duty to consider the matter on the
level that he had proposed. In Mark they say,
whence can a man, or, "Whence shall one
be able?" etc.; in Matthew, "Whence should

we have bread?" etc.; as if recognizing that
they had a share in the proposed work (*Bengel*).—How many loaves have ye? Pressing the work home upon them; as if he had
said, "Your share is first: I shall do nothing
till you have done all."—Seven loaves; on the
other occasion, five. Matthew mentions here
the "few small fishes;" Mark only in the account of the miracle itself.—The command to
place them in his hands is not mentioned here,
as it is in the other case (Matt. 14 : 18), but of
course it is implied. This was the one thing
that they could do; although their handful of
food was as nothing, they could bring it to
him to be made effective; and all his servants
can do that with their resources.

6-9. The scene was as before, but is not so
vividly described. No mention of the grass,
or of the divisions of fifty, or of the "flower-
bed" appearance when they had sat down.
The prayer was one of thanksgiving, both in
Matthew and in Mark; it corresponded to our
saying grace or asking a blessing.—This is the
only place in Mark where the few small fishes
are mentioned, and they are introduced as if
they formed a separate course, attended with a
separate prayer or blessing—an impression that
is confirmed by Mark's employment of another
word to describe the prayer over the fishes, the
word *eulogēsas*, which means "having blessed,"
while the former word means "having given
thanks." These are the two words that are
employed in the narratives of the institution
of the Lord's Supper.—The disciples were again
the almoners, receiving the food to give it to
the people. Here, as before, it is quite useless
to speculate as to the process by which food
was multiplied. All talk about a "hastening
of the processes of nature" is nonsense here,
where the product was such as to require artificial processes as well as natural. Unless the
story is purely a myth, here was the exercise
of creative power.—Of fragments, seven baskets. In the other case, twelve. The difference both in the number of loaves and in the

8

9 And they that had eaten were about four thousand: and he sent them away.
10 ⁶ And straightway⁶ he entered into a ship with
his disciples, and came into the parts of Dalmanutha.
11 And the Pharisees⁶ came forth, and began to question with him, seeking of him a sign from heaven,
tempting him.

9 pieces that remained over, seven baskets. And they
were about four thousand: and he sent them away.
10 And straightway he entered into the boat with his
disciples, and came into the parts of Dalmanutha.
11 And the Pharisees came forth, and began to question with him, seeking of him a sign from heaven,

a Matt. 15 : 39....b Matt. 12 : 38 ; 16 : 1, etc. ; John 6 : 30.

number of baskets is another sign, though a
minor one, of the separateness of the two
events. A more striking sign is the difference
in the "baskets" of the two narratives. The
"basket" of the other story is the *cophinus;* of
this, the *spuris.* This distinction, moreover,
Jesus retains in his allusion to the two miracles (*verses* 19, 20). Of course this is either a natural and unstudied allusion to real events or a
neat piece of deliberate invention; there is no
middle ground. The distinction between the
two kinds of baskets is not easily ascertained.
The *spuris* might be large enough to contain a
man (see Acts 9 : 25), though it is not certain
that the *spuris* was invariably the larger. Probably these were the provision-baskets of some
who had come from afar with food that lasted
three days.—What was done with this large
store of fragments? Probably on the next day,
we find the disciples without bread (**verse** 14),
whence we infer that they did not keep it.
Very likely it was put at the disposal of some
of those who **came from afar** and still had a
long journey before them.—**They that had
eaten were about four thousand.** Matthew adds, "besides women and children."—
The dismission of the multitude is mentioned
only by Mark. Doubtless, Jesus had more
satisfaction in their comfortable state in leaving him than they themselves had. Such gen-
erous acts of giving, even on the plane of physical wants, were appropriate symbols of the
love that he brought to men. We should
greatly misjudge him if we thought of his love
as anything less than complete and comprehensive of the whole state and need of man.

10-12. A SIGN FROM HEAVEN IS DE-
MANDED AND REFUSED. *Parallel,* Matt.
15 : 39-16 : 4.

10. The detention on the eastern side of the
lake was at an end, and all was ready for his
return to the towns on the west, which had
not seen him since he set out, a considerable
time before, on the journey toward Sidon. He
embarked with his disciples **straightway,** as
soon as the multitude had left him. It was
not **a ship,** but "the boat," that received
them—the boat which they were accustomed
to use, brought over from the other side, perhaps, by some friend who knew that they were

near.—**Came into the parts of Dalmanutha.** Matthew says, "into the coasts," or
region, "of Magdala," or, as the best manuscripts read, "of Magadan." The names "Magadan" and "Dalmanutha" are both unknown,
except from this allusion. Magdala (the same
name as "Migdol," "a tower") lay a little
south of Capernaum, at the lower end of the
Plain of Gennesaret, and it is thought that
certain ruins that lie about a mile south of
Magdala represent the ancient Dalmanutha.
The use of the two names affords an excellent
illustration of the independence of the two
narratives.

11. **The Pharisees came forth, and began to question with him.**—*i. e.,* came out
from their homes when they heard that he
was there. By some it is assumed that he
went beyond Dalmanutha to Capernaum, and
that this interview took place there; but the
intention of both evangelists apparently was to
tell what happened almost as soon as he had
landed. Hence these were in all probability
Pharisees of Dalmanutha. Matthew associates
Sadducees with them.—**Seeking of him a
sign from heaven.** See similar requests in
John 2 : 18; Matt. 12 : 38; John 6 : 30, all previous to this. What they asked for was something like the manna (so, expressly, in John
6 : 31), or thunder from a clear sky (1 Sam. 12 : 18),
or fire from heaven, such as came to Elijah
(1 Kings 18), or the signs of Joel 2 : 30, 31. There
was a popular impression that, although miracles upon the earth might be spurious and deceptive, signs from heaven could not be coun-
terfeited. It was expected that they would
accompany the coming of the Messiah, and
therefore Jesus was repeatedly asked to fulfil
this expectation. If he was the Christ, they
thought he would certainly be able and willing, and even anxious, to give this proof of his
claim.—But they were **tempting him,** nevertheless—*i. e.,* as in Matt. 19 : 3 and Mark 12 : 13,
they were trying to entangle him, to his own
injury with the people. They knew well
enough that he would not give them a sign
from heaven; all the Pharisees in Galilee must
have known the great refusal recorded in Matt.
12 : 39 and the more recent one of John 6.
He would not give them the sign, but by re-

12 And he sighed deeply in his spirit, and saith, Why doth this generation seek after a sign? verily I say unto you, There shall no sign be given unto this generation. 13 And he left them, and entering into the ship, again departed to the other side. 14 ¶ Now *the disciples* had forgotten to take bread, neither had they in the ship with them more than one loaf. 15 And he charged them, saying, Take heed, beware[a] of the leaven[b] of the Pharisees, and *of* the leaven of Herod.

12 trying him. And he sighed deeply in his spirit, and saith, Why doth this generation seek a sign? verily I say unto you, There shall no sign be given unto 13 this generation. And he left them, and again entering into *the boat* departed to the other side. 14 And they forgot to take bread; and they had not 15 in the boat with them more than one loaf. And he charged them, saying, Take heed, beware of the leaven of the Pharisees and the leaven of Herod.

a Prov. 19 : 27; Luke 12: 1....b Ex. 12 : 20; Lev. 2 : 11; 1 Cor. 5 : 6-8.

peatedly calling for it they might discredit his claims with the people, who expected it of the Messiah. Since they themselves hated him, they must take all measures to prevent Israel from supposing its hopes to be fulfilled in him; so they would play upon false hopes and studiously repress all spiritual expectations. This was his welcome when he landed again on the soil of Galilee. He had been absent long enough to allow calm thought about him, and had now returned after a few days of gracious working just across the lake. This was his reception—the old wearisome demand of spiritual blindness: Give us **a sign from heaven.**

12. At human misery he sighed (chap. 7 : 34); at human sin amounting to criminal inability to discern the truth **he sighed deeply in his spirit**—a touch of personal remembrance peculiar to Mark. This deep sigh, or groan, was the sign of the chafing of his spirit against spiritual barriers. To the physically deaf he could say "Ephphatha," but not to these spiritually hardened and self-imprisoned Pharisees. What voice could reach them? When the rich young man departed sorrowful, he pointed his disciples to the brighter side, saying, "With God all things are possible." But in the case of these proud and hardened men he could only sigh, for the gates of spiritual possibility seemed closed.—**Why doth this generation seek after a sign?** This generation, the men of his time, who had the opportunity to know him—why should they ask for a sign? If there was no spiritual recognition of him, the case was hopeless; signs would teach them nothing. He himself was the true Sign from heaven, the living Witness to the present God. If they did not see that he was in the Father and the Father in him, their blindness must remain. Therefore he told them, with his emphatic **verily I say unto you,** that no sign should be given them.—In Matthew three additions are placed here, all exceedingly significant: (1) He contrasts their quickness in detecting signs of coming changes of weather with their slowness in discerning spiritual signs. (2) He traces their lack of perception of a present

God to spiritual adultery. The prophets represent Israel as the wife of Jehovah, and often as the unfaithful and adulterous wife. This generation, says Jesus, is thus adulterous; it has broken faith with God, and has become carnal and unloving. Therefore it has lost all spiritual sense and consciousness of him, and, instead of discerning his holy presence in him whom he hath sent, must be asking for visible signs and portents to certify his nearness. But for the spiritual adultery there would be felt no need of signs. (3) "There shall be no sign given but the sign of the prophet Jonah," of which he had before spoken (Matt. 12 : 39, 40), and which he seems to have wished to keep in their sight as a suggestive lesson, which might possibly awaken some right questionings in their hearts.

13. Disheartened and repelled by this reception in "his own country," he abruptly turned back, without going on, as it appears, to Capernaum, and re-embarked to return to the eastern shore. It is little to say that he must have gone in sadness. "He was despised and rejected of men, a man of sorrows, and acquainted with grief." We should greatly misread his life if we interpreted such language almost entirely in the light of his latest sufferings. He felt the grief of rejection, not merely as a personal wrong, but more as the rejection of God and goodness and of saving love. Bringing the message of infinite mercy, he must have longed to be accepted; and it could not but be other than a constant grief to him that "he came to his own, and his own received him not."

Not more than a few hours at the most does he appear to have remained on the western shore, and now he is again afloat on the lake with his disciples, setting out on another journey alone with them, not to return until they have visited the region of Cæsarea Philippi.

14-21. WARNING AGAINST THE LEAVEN OF THE PHARISEES. *Parallel,* Matt. 16 : 5-12.

14, 15. The neglect to take a supply of bread was doubtless the result of their haste in again setting out; and, in that view of the matter, **Jesus** himself was responsible for it, since he

8

16 And they reasoned among themselves, saying, *It is because we have no bread.*
17 And when Jesus knew *it*, he saith unto them, Why reason ye, because ye have no bread? perceive* ye not yet, neither understand? have ye your heart* yet hardened?
18 Having eyes,* see ye not? and having ears, hear ye not? and do ye not remember?*
19 When I brake the five loaves* among five thousand, how many baskets full of fragments took ye up? They say unto him, Twelve.
20 And when the seven* among four thousand, how many baskets full of fragments took ye up? And they said, Seven.
21 And he said unto them, How is it that ye do not understand?

16 And they reasoned one with another, *saying, *We have no bread. And Jesus perceiving it saith unto them, Why reason ye, because ye have no bread? do ye not yet perceive, neither understand? have ye
18 your heart hardened? Having eyes, see ye not? and having ears, hear ye not? and do ye not remember?
19 When I brake the five loaves among the five thousand, how many *baskets full of broken pieces took
20 ye up? They say unto him, Twelve. And when the seven among the four thousand, how many *basket-
21 fuls of broken pieces took ye up? And they say unto him, Seven. And he said unto them, Do ye not yet understand?

had hurried them away. It is Mark alone who mentions the one loaf that they had with them in the boat; plainly a touch of definite remembrance from one who was present.—And he charged them. The emphatic word is peculiar to Mark.—Take heed, beware of the leaven of the Pharisees, and of the leaven of Herod. In Matthew, "of the Pharisees and Sadducees." From this grouping it has sometimes been inferred that Herod was a Sadducee; but that seems too definite a conclusion to draw from such premises. Undoubtedly, Herod's position was such as to give him more in common with the Sadducees than with the Pharisees, and the Sadducees may have been the Herodians of Galilee; but Herod Antipas was probably too much of an indifferentist to hold very strongly the doctrines of any Jewish sect. —The leaven is expressly, according to Matthew, the "doctrine" of the Pharisees and Sadducees, or of the Pharisees and Herod. But "doctrine" (*didaché*) is an active word rather than a passive, and refers rather to the teaching than to the substance of what was taught; and when used of Herod it must be substantially equivalent to "influence."—The warning must be understood in the light of what had just occurred, for it must certainly have been suggested by the demand for a sign from heaven. To the corrupting influence of Pharisaism and Sadduceeism or of political Herodianism—i. e. to the spirit that was manifested in these forms —it was due that Israel had departed from God, and had so lost all spiritual sense of him as to be clamoring for signs from heaven. So the warning means, "Beware of the unspiritual, irreligious, godless teaching through which it has come to pass that God is no longer recognized." Reflecting on the conversation that had sent him, disheartened, back from Galilee, he thought of his own disciples, who were but too prone to a similar unbelief; and he said to himself, "They must not be possessed by the

ungodly blindness that cannot perceive a spiritual meaning and is dependent upon signs to show them God and truth. Yet the land is full of it under the influence of this unholy teaching, and it cannot fail to be working as a leaven in their minds." Therefore he spoke in warning.

16. According to the most probable reading, adopted by the revisers, we may translate, And they reasoned, or considered, together, "saying, We have no bread." The common English version, It is because we have no bread, represents the spirit of their utterance perfectly; though not a good translation. They dimly supposed he must mean that food received from the hands of his enemies was to be rejected, because of the unworthiness of those who might offer it: if Pharisees and Herodians were so defiled, they were not fit persons for them to obtain food from. "There is a childish *naïveté* in their self-questioning which testifies to the absolute originality and truthfulness of the record, and so to the genuineness of the question that follows—a question that assumes the reality of the two previous miracles" (*Plumptre*). They tried to understand him, but this low and uncharacteristic meaning was all that they could find, as if he had said, "You will have bread to buy, and you must be careful from whom you buy it," and had forbidden them to eat the bread of his enemies.

17-21. Mark's report here is much more full than Matthew's. The last two questions of verse 17 are peculiar to Mark, and so is the whole of verse 18, with the exception of the last word; so are the responses of the disciples in verses 19 and 20, and so is verse 21. The translation of verses 18, 19, according to Tischendorf's text, is, "Having eyes do ye not see, and having ears do ye not hear, and do ye not remember when I brake the five loaves unto the five thousand, and how many baskets full of fragments ye took up?" The readings of verse

22 ¶ And he cometh to Bethsaida; and they bring a blind man unto him, and besought him to touch him.ᵃ

22   And they come unto Bethsaida. And they bring to him a blind man, and beseech him to touch him.

a Isa. 35 : 5, 6 ; Matt. 11 : 5.

21 vary, but, according to the most probable, the question is simply, " Do ye not yet understand?" These questions of Jesus are sharp and cutting, full of surprise and indignation. So far as the record goes, they are the sharpest words that he ever spoke to the twelve. We can scarcely wonder at his indignation, for he saw already in them **the leaven of the Pharisees,** the same blindness that had just disheartened him, in their inability to perceive a spiritual meaning. They were like the generation that was described in chap. 4 : 12, which, having eyes, saw not, and having ears heard not. Whatever meaning they might have found in his warning, the one that they did find was one that their experience with him ought to have rendered impossible. They had been with him twice when he fed thousands from a handful, yet they were talking perplexedly among themselves, as if he could possibly be thinking of where the food was to come from. His rebuke means, " When you are with me, and I am responsible for your want of food, you need have no anxiety, and you may know that whatever I may say refers to something else than the way in which food is to be obtained." They ought, moreover, to have known that he who had plainly abolished distinctions of food (chap. 7 : 15) would not now set up a new distinction of a personal or sectarian kind, and teach them that they would be defiled by food bought from ungodly men. Surely it would seem to be asking but very little to ask that they should understand him well enough to escape such an idea. Here was indeed the unspiritual heart, upon which the spiritual thought seemed almost wasted. More than in the case of his townsmen at Nazareth, he " marvelled because of their unbelief." If Christian teachers find even their brethren slow of perception in spiritual things, they may hear their Master saying to them, in the spirit of John 15 : 18, " Ye know that they misunderstood me before they misunderstood you."—In Matthew the final question, " Do ye not yet understand?" is expanded into a direct intimation that the warning did not refer to bread. Matthew adds also that they did at last perceive that he was warning them against the teaching or the principles of the Pharisees and Sadducees. But it is quite certain that they did not take in his full meaning, and that when the subject was dropped he knew that his utterance

had not reached its aim. He had had to expend the energy that might have been given to the work of enforcing an idea in the vain effort to get it apprehended, and then to withdraw baffled by the unreceptiveness of his hearers. It was not his method to urge truth upon them faster than they were able to receive it. John 16 : 12 illustrates his real method : " I have yet many things to say unto you, but ye cannot bear them now."—Observe, again, the distinct reference in these questions to the two separate miracles of feeding—a reference which cannot possibly be removed from the passage without utterly destroying one of the most vivid and self-witnessing scenes in the whole Gospel narrative. Observe, again, too, that in referring here to the first miracle Jesus employs the word *cophinus* in mentioning the baskets, and in referring to the second the word *spuris,* preserving the very distinction that has been made in the two narratives of Mark.

22–26. ARRIVAL AT BETHSAIDA, WHERE A BLIND MAN IS HEALED.— The narrative is peculiar to Mark, and is full of interesting resemblances to the story of the healing of the deaf-and-dumb man in Decapolis, at chap. 7 : 32–37. It is one of Mark's most graphic and characteristic pieces of narration, and certainly comes from an eye-witness.

22. And he cometh—or as the revisers, on textual authority, render it, " they come "—**to Bethsaida.** The narrative follows continuously upon the preceding ; from Dalmanutha they proceeded directly by water to Bethsaida, where they landed. Here we reach again, as at chap. 6 : 45, the old puzzle as to the site or sites of Bethsaida. In that passage the company of Jesus seek Bethsaida by boat, going to it from the eastern shore on the way to Capernaum ; and the going to it is identified with going toward **the other side.** Here they seek Bethsaida by boat, going to it, in the opposite direction, from a point near Capernaum ; and again the going to it is identified with going to **the other side.** (Compare verses 13 and 22.) Thus it appears first to have been on the western side of the lake, and then on the eastern. It is no wonder that two towns of the same name were supposed to have been necessary to fulfil these conditions ; but no other evidence of the existence of two such towns was ever discovered, and the manifest improb-

23 And he took the blind man by the hand, and led him out of the town; and when he had spit on his eyes, and put his hands upon him, he asked him if he saw ought.
24 And he looked up, and said, I[b] see men as trees, walking.
25 After that he put *his* hands again upon his eyes, and made him look up: and he was restored, and saw every man clearly.
26 And he sent him away to his house, saying, Neither go into the town, nor tell *it* to any in the town.

23 And he took hold of the blind man by the hand, and brought him out of the village; and when he had spit on his eyes, and laid his hands upon him, 24 he asked him, Seest thou aught? And he looked up, and said, I see men; for I behold *them* as trees, walking. 25 ing. Then again[b] he laid his hands upon his eyes; and he looked stedfastly, and was restored, and saw 26 all things clearly. And he sent him away to his home, saying, Do not even enter into the village.

a ch. 7 : 33.... *b* Judg. 9 : 36; Isa. 29 : 18; 1 Cor. 13 : 11, 12.... *c* Prov. 4 : 18; Isa. 32 : 3; 1 Pet. 2 : 9.

ability of two towns of the same name on the shores of one lake is very great. But all the narratives can be reconciled and all the allusions accounted for by placing the one town of Bethsaida at the northern end of the lake, where the Jordan enters it. This Bethsaida has always been known under the name of "Bethsaida-Julias." It lay mainly on the eastern side of the Jordan, and this eastern part was rebuilt and beautified by Herod the Tetrarch, who gave it the name "Julias," after a daughter of the emperor. This eastern part was not in Galilee; but by the simple and natural supposition that the town lay partly on the western side of the river it is easy to account for the allusions to it as a city of Galilee, as in John 12 : 21. This place would be on the way from the scene of the first feeding of the multitude to Capernaum, and yet would be on **the other side** from Capernaum and Dalmanutha. (See the whole question clearly discussed in *The Land and the Book*, 2. 29–32; see, also, Andrews, *Life of Our Lord*, pp. 211–218.) — The name **Bethsaida** means "house of fish," and indicates the origin and character of the town. It was a fishing-village, and doubtless lay close to the water's edge. This was the home of Peter, Andrew, and Philip (**John 1 : 44**)—*i. e.* the early home, before the days of discipleship. Mark 1 : 29 tells of a home of Peter and Andrew in Capernaum. **—And they bring a blind man unto him.** The request is, as usual, for a touch; but he takes his own way. This miracle is the only one expressly mentioned of the "mighty works" done in Bethsaida to which Jesus referred in Matt. 11 : 21. The mighty works done in Chorazin do not appear at all, except in that allusion; so that this act alone represents the whole double group.

23–26. Concerning the man himself we can gather only that he was not born blind, and that his home was somewhere outside of the town of Bethsaida. In this work of healing (1) do we not see a peculiar tenderness? He **took the blind man by the hand, and led him out of the town,** or, rather, "village." If we picture to ourselves the scene, we see

Jesus leading the blind—actually leading him by the hand and serving as guide to one who cannot see his way. He leads him, the man knows not whither. Here is a touch, which was asked for, but it is not the touch of healing; yet it is an exceedingly precious touch, revealing a tender kindness in which the man may well have found a constraining and helpful influence. Such friendly nearness of the great Healer would surely be a help to the faith which he desired to awaken. (2) Here is privacy amounting to secrecy. As before (**chap. 7 : 33**), he took the man away from the frequented place in the village and wrought the cure in private—perhaps in order to secure the greater impressiveness of solitude and quiet for the man himself—and after the cure he forbade him to go back into the village and sent him in silence to his own home, which was elsewhere. The last clause of verse 26, **nor tell it to any in the town,** should be omitted. The reason for this secrecy was the usual reason, only modified a little by the circumstances—the desire to avoid needless excitement. Rejected afresh in Galilee and now withdrawing again from that region with his disciples, he was naturally inclined to withdraw quietly, and would particularly avoid making any stir about himself and his movements in Bethsaida. (3) Here, again, is the choice of his own peculiar and unexpected means of healing, instead of the means that were proposed. It reminds one of Naaman and Elisha (**2 Kings 5 : 10, 11**). (4) Here is the employment, as in the similar case, of external media, appealing to the senses, and especially to the senses of which the sufferer was possessed. **He . . . spit on his eyes,** signifying thereby the transference of something from himself to the blind man. The man could feel this sign of transference, and could feel it coming directly to the part that needed the gift of healing. There is no allusion here to any supposed healing power in saliva; the use of the saliva is purely symbolic or pictorial, to represent the impartation of something from person to person. The man could also feel, as he had expected to feel, the imposition of the Healer's hands. It must have been a solemn, tender touch, loving as the touch of a mother's hands, in which the sufferer could not fail to perceive as a present reality the Saviour's joy in the act of healing. It is to be observed that only in these two similar miracles, recorded by Mark alone, do the synoptists refer to the use of saliva as an external medium in healing, and that this is a link to connect the Gospel of Mark with that of John, who has a similar narrative (John 9: 6). (5) There is here a singular and quite unparalleled progressiveness in the healing, with an appearance of tentativeness on the part of Jesus. Nowhere else do we find the progress of such a work tested by question and answer. After spitting upon his eyes and placing his hands once upon them, Jesus asked the man **if he saw ought,** as if his work this time were tentatively done and he were watching for the result with an interest like that of a loving physician. May we think that this was done from a kind of tender interest in the act of healing, a loving delight in seeing the lost power, not only restored, but in the very act, as it were, of coming back? Is it wrong to think of our Saviour as sometimes bending delightedly over one whom he was healing, and giving to himself the pleasure of love in watching the progress of his gracious work? If we do admit such a supposition, it will not prevent us from recognizing the other motive—namely, the purpose to make partial healing a help to the man's faith in the coming perfect restoration. (6) The man's answer to the question whether he saw anything is, according to the revisers' text, "I see men; for I behold men as trees, walking" —i. e. "I see men—I know they must be men, because they are beings that walk—but they are large and vague, like trees; I cannot see them clearly." The reply is simply perfect in its naturalness. So fresh and inimitable an answer is one of the strongest possible confirmations of the story; it corresponds perfectly to the state of one whose vision is half restored. The man had seen before; he remembered men and he remembered trees; but thus far his new sight scarcely enabled him to tell one from the other. (7) Something more was needed, and another touch of the Healer's hands was given. **He put his hands again upon his eyes,** intimating, what has not been said before, that the first touch also was upon the eyes. The description of the completed cure is somewhat changed and made more vivid in the best text. Instead of **and made him look up,** etc., we should read, as in the Revision, "and he looked steadfastly, and was restored, and saw" (or be-

gan to see) "all things clearly," or else "afar off." It is difficult to judge between two readings of the final adverb, differing only by a single letter (*télaugōs* and *dēlaugōs*). One means "with clear sight," and the other "with far sight." After the second imposition of the hands the man gave an intense and searching look, which fixed itself ineffaceably upon the memory of the eye-witness whose report is here given; and then he **saw** (imperfect-tense), or began to see, everything (not **every man**) distinctly. The restoration was perfect. (8) The man was sent to his home, not merely to avoid public excitement, but undoubtedly in part for his own sake: he needed quiet rather than the tumult of the town and the risk of being made a public spectacle.—How much did the man understand of all this? Of what kind was his faith? We have no hint of any faith at all, except such as is indicated by his putting himself in the hands of Jesus. We can neither repress nor answer the question, Into what kind of relation to his Healer was he brought by this experience? Is it credible that any whom he had healed were among those who cried, "Crucify him"? Why not? since he certainly healed many who had but the faintest knowledge of his spiritual character and grace. May they not have turned against him?—It is worthy of notice that here, and almost here alone, when Jesus enjoined secrecy after a miracle, we do not read that the injunction was disregarded. It does not appear that any great excitement was awakened in Bethsaida, or that Jesus lingered there.

27-30. JOURNEY TO CÆSAREA PHILIPPI; CONFESSION OF PETER. *Parallels,* Matt. 16 : 13-20; Luke 9 : 18-21.—There is no reason to suppose any delay, at Bethsaida or elsewhere. When Jesus left Dalmanutha he was setting out for a journey that would take him to a distant region, and probably he pressed on at once. It was a sad journey. The ministry in Galilee had ended in the carnal misconceptions that are represented in the events recorded in the sixth chapter of John—the eagerness to make him a king and the stolid ignorance respecting his spiritual truth and purposes. The journey to Sidon had followed, and the reception on his return had been the old demand, promptly renewed, for a sign from heaven—a demand of pure spiritual blindness. Galilee had failed to receive him in his true character; and very little more in Galilee did he ever do. Now he was setting out for another wandering in a distant land, with only his little band of followers, and was leaving, apparently, no large

27 ¶ And Jesus went out, and his disciples, into the
towns of Cæsarea Philippi: and by the way he asked
his disciples, saying unto them, Whom do men say
that I am?
28 And they answered, John*a* the Baptist: but some
say, Elias; and others, One of the prophets.

27 And Jesus went forth, and his disciples, into the
villages of Cæsarea Philippi: and in the way he
asked his disciples, saying unto them, Who do men
28 say that I am? And they told him, saying, John
the Baptist: and others, Elijah; but others, One of

a Matt. 16 : 13, etc.; Luke 9 : 18, etc....*b* Matt. 14 : 2.

satisfactory results of his ministry behind him.
"He was despised and rejected of men." We
shall not understand the events of this journey
unless we thus recognize its actual place in our
Lord's personal history. The whole scene is
presented with great power in *Philochristus*
(chap. xx), though possibly with some exaggeration of this true idea of sadness in the
journey.

**27. Into the towns of Cæsarea Philip-
pi.** The distance from Capernaum to Cæsarea
Philippi was not great—not more than thirty
or forty miles—but the place seemed remote,
because it was at the very border of the Jewish
land, or, strictly, just beyond the border. Jesus
must have passed near it, if not through it, on
his way southward from Sidon a little while
before. It is not expressly asserted here that
the present journey took him to the town itself,
but neither is it denied. He went to **the towns**
—or, rather, "the villages" (Matthew, "the
parts" or region)—**of Cæsarea Philippi**—*i. e.*
to the surrounding villages that were dependent
upon it.—**Cæsarea Philippi,** or "Philip's
Cæsarea." A very ancient place at one of the
sources of the Jordan. There one of the streams
that make up the river springs forth from the
rock at the mouth of a wide and lofty cavern.
This cavern has a long history as a sacred place.
The name of the spot, as given by Josephus, is
Panium, which, doubtless, tells the story that
the cave was once sacred to the god Pan. The
place is not certainly mentioned in the Old
Testament, but is thought probably to be identical with Baal-gad, which appears to have
been a Phœnician or Canaanite sanctuary long
before the Greek god Pan was known there.
There Herod the Great erected a splendid temple of white marble, which he dedicated to the
worship of Augustus Cæsar; and Philip, the
tetrarch of Trachonitis, his son, in whose territory the place lay, rebuilt the town and named
it Cæsarea Philippi, in honor of the emperor
and of himself, adding his own name to distinguish it from the Cæsarea on the shore of the
Mediterranean, so important in the history of
the apostles. The ancient name has returned
in place of the more recent, and the village is
now known as *Banias*. The spot is one of extraordinary natural beauty. In our Lord's time

the town itself was, of course, a gay Roman
town full of paganism. As there is no sign that
he ever set foot within the similar town of Tiberias, near to Capernaum, so it might be conjectured as intrinsically probable that he did
not go beyond the "villages" of Cæsarea Philippi to the city itself. It has often been observed, though of course it is purely conjectural,
that the magnificent temple on the cliff, in
sight as he was speaking, may have suggested
the simile of Matt. 16 : 18: "On this rock I will
build my church."

So far as we have any indication of his motive in
choosing this direction for his journey, we may
judge that he wished to withdraw his disciples
from all the ordinary influences, that they
might be best prepared for this conversation.
The question, **Whom do men say that I am?**
was asked **by the way.** According to Luke,
he had been praying privately, though in the
presence of his disciples. Like other points
that were specially marked by prayer (Luke
3 : 21 and 6 : 12; Matt. 14 : 23 compared with
John 6 : 15), this was an important turning-
point in his life. The first question was preliminary, but essential to his purpose in the
one that was to follow. **Whom do men say
that I am?** or, in Matthew, according to the
text of the revisers, "Who do men say that the
Son of man is?"—*i. e.* What impression is abroad
concerning me? How far have the people gone
toward recognizing me? He was not asking
for information : he knew the truth only too
well. He did not ask because they had opportunities for knowing that he had not. This
was only the preparation for the question concerning their own belief. Both he and they
knew the fact, but he wished them to state it.—
Plainly, here was good reason for his praying.
He was about to look, with his disciples, into
the results of his ministry thus far, that he
might draw out their faith and might prepare
the way for such changes in the tone of his
teaching to them as might be necessary. This
was indeed a crisis in his ministry.

28. Three answers were given, three opinions
concerning him. (1) That he was **John the
Baptist**—of course, John the Baptist risen
from the dead; for the fact of his death was
notorious. This was the suspicion that haunted

29 And he saith unto them, But whom say ye that I am? And Peter answereth and saith to him, Thou* art the Christ.

29 the prophets.   And he asked them, But who say ye that I am?   Peter answereth and saith unto him,

a John 1 : 41-49 ; 6 : 69 ; 11 : 27 ; Acts 8 : 37 ; 1 John 5 : 1.

Herod's guilty conscience, and here it appears again, as at Luke 9 : 7, that it was a rumor among the people somewhat well known. (2) That he was **Elias,** or Elijah, who was expected to appear as the forerunner of the Messiah, according to the common understanding of Mal. 4 : 5, 6. (3) That he was **one of the prophets.** In Matthew, "Jeremiah, or one of the prophets ;" in Luke, "one of the old prophets is risen again." The three answers, closely parallel to chap. 6 : 14, 15, substantially agree in one. The popular sentiment went so far as to see in him some forerunner of the Christ, some great but inferior one ; but they could not tell him that it went farther. Occasional manifestations of a deeper conviction there might be, as in the effort to make him a king (John 6 : 15) ; but even that poor and carnal recognition of the Messiah was beyond the ordinary and habitual feeling of the people. "He was in the world, and the world was made by him, and the world knew him not." They did not yet own or see that he was the Christ.

29. There are some marks of solemn emphasis in this second question. In Mark the pronouns are both expressed in the preparatory sentence, **And he saith unto them,** a somewhat unusual fulness in so simple a statement. Moreover, while the first question is reported with slight variations by the three evangelists, and while the same is true of Peter's answer, important as it is, this second question is identical in words and order in the three reports ; as if the very words had been so uttered by the Lord that no memory could lose them.—**But whom say ye that I am?** with the strongest emphasis on the ye. "Are ye ready to say what the people will not say? Do ye know with whom ye have been walking? Having eyes, do ye see? and having ears, do ye hear? Have I succeeded, or failed, in making myself known to you?" Just before the journey to Sidon, Peter had spoken a satisfactory word of faith (John 6 : 68, 69). That word was spoken, too, in a dark day, when many were going away disheartened at the hard sayings of Jesus ; and that word then represented the convictions and the constancy of the twelve. But now the days were even darker than then ; and were the twelve still sure of their ground? Was their apprehension of him clear and strong enough to command their hearts and hold them to

constancy when, if they were constant, they must stand so nearly alone? It was time, in the progress of his life with them, for the question to be asked, and asked most searchingly. If they were ready, there were some great things to be told them. Moreover, now, in the day of comparative desertion, was the time to lay in them the foundation of such a faith as they had never before had. Now, therefore, if it was in them to do it, they might take a great step forward in apprehending his kingdom, and he in founding it ; or they might give evidence that it was not in them to take such a step. It was a great moment with him, and a critical moment with them, when he asked them, **Whom say ye that I am?** The spirit of the scene is well represented in *Philochristus* (pp. 248, 249) : " We seemed in that moment to have been brought by the hand of the Lord into a place where two roads met and we had to choose one of the two. And if we went by the one, behold we had against us, not only Rome and Greece and the whole inhabited world, but also the princes of our own people, and the priests and the patriots, and the traditions, also, of our forefathers, handed down through many hundreds of years, and the law given unto us by God for which many generations of our countrymen had fought and died ; yea, even Moses himself seemed to be an adversary if we went by that road. But on the other road no one stood against us ; only we saw not Jesus there. So the conclusion seemed to be that we had in that instant to choose between Jesus and all the world. And, as I judge, even for this cause did the Lord lead us into the wilderness together with our Master in sorrow and in exile, to the intent that there, being apart from the world, we might weigh, as it were in a balance, on the one side all the world, and on the other side the Son of man—a man of sufferings and sorrows ; a man of wanderings and exiles, acquainted with rejections and contempts—and then that, having weighed the two, we might prefer the Son of man. because of a certain voice in our hearts which cried within us, 'Whom have we in heaven but thee? and there is none on earth that we desire in comparison of thee.' And this, I judge, was the faith that Jesus desired of us ; and to this faith was the Lord leading our hearts while Jesus was patiently waiting for our answer."

30 And he charged them that they should tell no man of him.
31 And he began to teach them, that the Son of man must suffer many things, and be rejected of the elders, and of the chief priests, and scribes, and be killed, and after three days rise again.

30 Thou art the Christ. And he charged them that 31 they should tell no man of him. And he began to teach them, that the Son of man must suffer many things, and be rejected by the elders, and the chief priests, and the scribes, and be killed, and after three

---

The answer came, as usual from the lips of Peter. **Thou art the Christ.** In Luke, "the Christ of God;" in Matthew, most fully, and, as one cannot help thinking, in the very words that he used, "Thou art the Christ, the Son of the living God." No forerunner, however great; no Elijah, and no prophet; no "messenger before thy face, to prepare thy way before thee;" but the Messiah himself, the Lord come to his temple, the King coming to his throne. Great words were these—words of recognition and allegiance. Great was it in the esteem of Jesus to recognize him in his divine mission. (Compare John 16 : 27, where he gives utterance to this estimate of true recognition : "The Father himself loveth you, because ye have loved me, and have believed that I came out from God.") Quite worthy was such a confession of the joyfully-uttered benediction of Jesus, recorded only by Matthew : "Blessed art thou, Simon Bar-jona : for flesh and blood hath not revealed it unto thee, but my Father which is in heaven." The joy of Jesus and the benediction are in the spirit of Matt. 13 : 16 : "Blessed are your eyes, for they see." This confession, prompted by no public enthusiasm, made in a lonely place and at a time when friends were few, pledged the allegiance of the twelve to Jesus in his highest character. In view of the discouragements of the time, it showed most satisfactorily that they were at least capable of strong spiritual apprehensions. His holy influence had not been enjoyed in vain. By this confession the twelve were identified as the true nucleus of his kingdom, and Peter as their natural leader. Already might Jesus have uttered the words spoken when the seventy returned triumphant and joyful from their mission (Luke 10 : 21): "I thank thee, O Father, Lord of heaven and earth, that thou hast hid these things from the wise and prudent, and hast revealed them unto babes."—Mark and Luke abruptly leave the conversation here, omitting the blessing upon Peter and the words about the founding of the church.

30. All record, however, his ban upon telling of him, Matthew the most fully : "That they tell no one that he was the Christ." For this, doubtless, there were more reasons than one. The fresh enthusiasm of faith might be followed by an impulse of proclamation ; but this was no time for that. His purpose in the

world was not to force recognition, or even to urge it, but rather to give the opportunity for it and to receive and guide it when it came. Israel, on the whole, had not recognized him, and no acknowledgment did he desire but that of genuine recognition. Not during his lifetime did he desire that enthusiastic disciples should proclaim to the unbelieving Israel that he was the Christ; and least of all now, when his friends were but a handful and their faith had only reached the point where it was ready to be trained in the knowledge of his actual purpose. The apostles did recognize him, but their thoughts were still so far from spiritual that they could not then be trusted to proclaim him. They had preached his truth and delivered his message (chap. 6 : 12), but himself they must not preach until they understood him better. It was an act of love to keep them from preaching him too soon. But their time was coming—a time when all their experience with him would be available for their holy purpose (John 15 : 26, 27).

31-9 : 1. JESUS FORETELLS HIS OWN PASSION, REBUKES PETER FOR DOUBTING IT, AND POINTS OUT THE WAY TO FOLLOW HIM. *Parallels*, Matt. 16 : 21-28 ; Luke 9 : 22-27.—In this paragraph belongs the first verse of chap. 9, which has very unfortunately been severed from its connection in Mark by the division of chapters. In the other Gospels the connection is preserved. The revisers have happily restored it here.

31. A disciple with the current notions about his kingdom might suppose that Jesus had drawn out the great confession in order to prepare the way for some aggressive movements. This taking of the oath, he might think, must have some promise in it. True, but not as he might imagine. "From that time" (Matthew) there was a change in the tone of the Master's teaching. This questioning at Cæsarea Philippi meant, not, "Will you go with me to my throne?" but, "Can ye drink the cup that I drink, and be baptized with the baptism that I am baptized with?" From that time they were to hear of his approaching death. Now that they were pledged to him with some degree of intelligence, **he began to teach them** what he expected and what they must expect. The time was short, and as soon as they were at all ready this sad instruction must begin.—

32 And he spake that saying openly. And Peter took him, and began to rebuke him.
33 But when he had turned about and looked on his disciples, he rebuked[a] Peter, saying, Get thee behind me, Satan:[b] for thou savorest not the things that be of God, but the things that be of men.

32 days rise again. And he spake the saying openly. And Peter took him, and began to rebuke him.
33 But he turning about, and seeing his disciples, rebuked Peter, and saith, Get thee behind me, Satan: for thou mindest not the things of God, but the

a Rev. 3 : 19....b 1 Cor. 5 : 5.

Matthew alone mentions the going to Jerusalem to suffer; with this exception the three reports are of the same effect.—The rejection is predicted as the act of the religious leaders of the nation, the elders and the chief priests and the scribes, not as the act of the people. It was very largely accepted as the act of the nation (see Matt. 27 : 25); and more especially remember the attitude of the Jewish nation toward Jesus from the day of his crucifixion till our own time. Yet Jesus charged it, in predicting it, upon the religious guides of Israel, who ought to have had eyes to see the Messiah's grace.—He must be killed—even for this the disciples must be prepared—and after three days rise again. The announcement is the same in all three reports. But the prediction seemed so enigmatical to the disciples that it scarcely took hold upon their minds. Even the anticipation of their Master's death never became a reality to them, and the thought of his resurrection almost wholly failed to affect either their imagination or their faith.—This was the earliest distinct announcement of his Passion. An intimation of it had been given in the synagogue at Capernaum (John 6 : 51), when the carnal enthusiasm of the multitude called for such an utterance of his real purpose and prospects. The intimations grew clearer and the predictions more elaborate, until he reached the saying of Matt. 26 : 2; "Ye know that after two days is the passover, and the Son of man is betrayed to be crucified."

32. From Matthew we learn that such announcements became habitual "from that time;" but what follows in this place relates to the earliest announcements, made soon after the great confession. And he spake that saying openly, or "plainly." Openly might be taken to mean "publicly;" but he was not now speaking in public, but "distinctly," without reserve or concealment. So the word is used in John 16 : 25 and 29. The sentence is peculiar to Mark, and preserves an eye-witness's impression of the terrible intelligibility of his speech; and Peter was a witness who was likely to remember. But to Peter this seemed altogether inconsistent with the divine destiny of the Christ of God: he surely must have a different future from this. So Paul was obliged

to have it for a part of his regular argument, as against the Jews, "that the Christ should suffer" (Acts 26 : 23).—Peter, very naturally, held the notions of the time, and was scandalized by the "offence of the cross" beforehand, as his countrymen were long afterward. He was not alone in this feeling; as his confession represented the twelve, so, no doubt, only too well, did his remonstrance. And Peter took him aside, beckoning or leading him away a little from the company, and began to rebuke him—began, but was not permitted to go far. Matthew alone gives his words: "God have mercy on thee, Lord; this shall not be to thee:" so note of revisers. "As though the thought of the Passion was too terrible to be endured even for a moment, and ought to be dismissed as a dark and evil dream" (Plumptre). Peter supposed that in this remonstrance he was following out the spirit of his great confession, for which he had just been honored. Neither sincerity nor genuine devotion to Christ saved him from a terrible mistake. He was showing to his Master a mistaken kindness, a wrong that his Master never did to him or to any other friend. Mistaken kindness is as real a wrong as mistaken severity.

33. Matthew, simply, "But he turned and said to Peter;" Mark, with characteristic minuteness, "But he, turning about and seeing his disciples, rebuked Peter, and said:" so, correctly, in the Revision. From the brief private interview with Peter he turned back and saw the disciples looking on and listening, and perceived that they knew what Peter was saying to him. That made it more than a private interview, and rendered an open utterance necessary; so he proceeded to make an example of Peter, speaking more sharply, perhaps, though not more plainly, than if they had been alone. The great confession had been made in the presence of all, and in the presence of all he who made it must be reproved.—No reproof could be sharper than the one that he received; human language cannot frame a sharper. Get thee behind me, Satan. Both the name Satan and the sharp command recall the temptation in the wilderness, where Jesus repelled the tempter in almost the self-same language. (See Matt. 4 : 10; Luke 4 : 8.) Peter had made

34 ¶ And when he had called the people *unto him* with his disciples also, he said unto them, Whosoever will come after me, let him deny himself, and take up his cross, and follow me.

34 things of men. And he called unto him the multitude with his disciples, and said unto them, If any man would come after me, let him deny himself, and

a Matt. 10 : 38; 16 : 24; Luke 9 : 23; 14 : 27; Tit. 2 : 12.

a Satan of himself by virtually renewing that temptation. Satan had then solicited Jesus to seek the kingdoms and glory of the world by turning aside from the way of the cross to the way in which he would lead him; and now his own disciple had vehemently protested against the way of the cross as a way of which he must not think. This was no other than the old temptation, and the terrible condemnation was just.—According to Matthew, he added (literally), "Thou art my stumbling-block," in which he may have referred, not to that occasion only, but may have meant that Peter, with his temperament and views, was frequently suggesting such thoughts to him. A near friend and a true may yet be constitutionally a stumbling-block, a suggester of evil or inferior things.— **Thou savorest not**—"thou mindest not" (Revision), or thinkest not of—"the things of God, but the things of men." A faithful indication of the real fault. Peter was judging by human standards and planning for a Messianic career that would satisfy the ideas of men which coincided with his own. God's idea was far different, in accordance with his own nature. The Messiah had been revealed to Peter by the Heavenly Father (Matt. 16 : 17), but God's Messianic idea was yet to be revealed to him. It was the intent of Jesus, after the great confession, to unfold and enforce this divine idea of salvation through self-sacrifice and death on the Messiah's part. This was the first lesson, and this, sadly enough, the first response. But Peter learned it afterward: see his First Epistle (2 : 21-24 and 4 : 12-16).—The word "savor" (**thou savorest not the things that be of God**) is derived from the Latin *sapere*, through the French *savoir*, "to know," and once well enough represented the Greek word *phronein*, which means "to think of," "regard," or "mind," as in Rom. 8 : 5. But that sense of the English word is now obsolete.—It is a very striking fact that in the Gospel which was probably written under Peter's own eye the congratulation of Jesus upon his confession and the assignment of his place in the church are omitted, while this terrible rebuke was inserted. We may learn something from this about the humility and honesty of Peter's spirit as a Christian; and we may also infer with confidence that he knew nothing of any primacy that elevated him above the other apos-

tles, or of any office conferred on him that was essential, practically, in the constitution of Christian churches. Any consciousness of primacy would infallibly have appeared in the Gospel of Mark.

34. The brief address that follows (34-9:1) is given by the three evangelists with verbal identity in a few places, with divergences in many places, but with complete unanimity as to the substance. This address was intended for no inner circle, for Peter or the twelve; this was for all who might have any interest in the nature of his kingdom; so he **called the people unto him with his disciples also.** A statement peculiar to Mark. It indicates that even in this retirement he did not find solitude; groups gathered about him as he went, but doubtless this multitude was less than those he often had about him nearer home. The utterance that follows was a deliberate public proclamation of the substance of what he had just said in private. That death was before him was no longer a fact to be hinted at or half expressed in dark allusions. He had told it to his disciples plainly, and now he would tell it as plainly to all who might be near him with the thought of following him. He would frankly tell them exactly what they had to look for, and would enable them to count the cost. Old disciples and new alike should understand it.

In this view, how indescribably solemn is the opening! With the multitude gathered to hear some great saying, he began. **Whosoever will come after me** (or behind me, go where I am going), **let him deny himself, and take up his cross, and follow me.—Let him deny himself**—*i. e.* let him utterly refuse the first place to thoughts of self-interest, self-exaltation, and everything of the kind; let him not set out to follow me with any such thoughts whatever. There is nothing in my service to encourage or reward the "self" that seeks promotion and satisfaction in such a Messianic kingdom as is commonly desired. Instead of being gratified, all selfish impulses must be resolutely denied and repressed in the life to which I shall lead. It is a self-denying life; no one will rightly enter it or long follow it who is not willing to resist his own heart and live as naturally he would not.—But more: let him **take up his cross and follow me.** Essen-

35 **For whosoever will save his life shall lose it; but
whosoever shall lose his life for my sake and the gospel's, the same shall save it.**

35 take up his cross, and follow me. For whosoever
would save his life shall lose it; and whosoever shall
lose his life for my sake and the gospel's shall save

a Esth. 4 : 14 ; Matt. 10 : 39 ; 16 : 25 ; Luke 9 : 24 ; 17 : 33 ; John 12 : 25 ; 2 Tim. 2 : 11 ; 4 : 6, 8 ; Rev. 2 : 10 ; 7 : 14-17.

tial to the right understanding of this is the fact that this was the first open announcement of his own impending death. Since he had thus definitely confronted and accepted death, he was like a man who is going to the place of execution bearing the cross upon which he is to be crucified. It was as if he were already carrying his cross to Golgotha; he had accepted it, and, spiritually, it was already upon him. This fact he now, for the first time, announced to those who were following him, and he announced it that they might know what it would be to follow. It would be as if each man took upon his shoulders the cross on which he was to be crucified together with Jesus, and walked behind him to the place of death. In Luke, " Let him take up his cross daily." Not as if there were a new cross for every day—such conceptions rest upon a complete misapprehension of the word " cross "—but because the course of life to one who would follow must be a continuous, daily march toward death. Thus the substance of his saying is, " I declare that I am to die, and I accept my death. Whoever wishes to follow me, let him know that he must cast off all thoughts of self-interest and follow as I go—namely, accepting death." A similar saying is recorded in Luke 14 : 26-33, uttered later, when a crowd was following thoughtlessly, though death was nearer. The definite and profound meaning of cross-bearing in these passages puts to shame much of the current modern talk on the subject. The cross was the implement of the most shameful death, not of discomfort or inconvenience or embarrassment, yet it is often mentioned now as if it merely meant something that crossed one's likings or inclinations. To bear the cross is actively to accept (not merely to submit to) shame and suffering for Christ and with Christ.

35. The connective **For** indicates that in this verse the principle is laid down in accordance with which it comes to pass that one who would follow must bear his cross. The principle is that the higher welfare of man can be secured only by subordinating it to the lower.—**Whosoever will save his life**—desires to save it, makes that the decisive question, and in order to save it keeps aloof from Christ—**shall lose it,** or rather, perhaps, will lose it: it is rather a prediction of the inevitable result than a denun-

ciation of doom.—**But whosoever shall lose his life for my sake and the gospel's, the same shall save it.** In Matthew, " shall find it." Self-indulgence as against the claim of Christ will be fatal; self-sacrifice for the sake of Christ and the gospel is the way to life.— Throughout this passage (35-37) one word is used in the Greek (*psyché*), which is rendered in English now by **life** and now by **soul.** The attempt has often been made, as in the Revision, to translate it throughout the passage by one word, but with no very satisfactory result. Neither word expresses the entire idea, while " life " and " soul " do, at least approximately, represent the two aspects of the life of man that are suggested by the word *psyché*. That word is used here, not in two senses, but in two aspects or applications, which the hearers, familiar with such sententious utterances, would well enough understand. As descriptive of human nature, " spirit is life as coming from God; soul is life as constituted in man. Consequently, when the individual life is to be made emphatic, ' soul ' is used " (Laidlaw, *The Bible Doctrine of Man,* p. 60). To the same effect is the definition of *psyché* in Grimm's *New Testament Lexicon :* " As the sting of Christ's gnomic sayings, intended to be left in the minds of the hearers—to find, to save, to lose one's *psyché*, etc.—*psyché* denotes in one member of the antithesis the life which is lived on the earth, and in the other the happy life which is to be spent in the eternal kingdom of God." Under Laidlaw's definition, which seems sufficient, the word *psyché* can plainly have two aspects, a higher and a lower, which are fairly represented by " life " and " soul " in the present passage. Life, as constituted in man, is present to his consciousness in its earthly form as human life; but it has its higher and more serious and enduring interests, which are called, by way of distinction, the interests of his soul, and his constituted life, with reference to them, is called his soul. In this passage the word is used in shifting application : " Whoever desires to save his life "— in the view of it that most quickly appeals to men, as an earthly life—and, so desiring, stands aloof from Christ, " will lose it," as to its higher and abiding interests ; " but whoever shall lose it "—*i. e.* whoever does lose it, as a matter of fact—in the lower sense, " for my sake and the gospel's, shall save it " in the higher sense.

36 For what shall it profit a man, if he shall gain the whole world, and lose his own soul?
37 Or what shall a man give in exchange for his soul?
38 Whosoever therefore shall be ashamed of me, and of my words, in this adulterous and sinful generation, of him also shall the Son of man be ashamed, when he cometh in the glory of his Father, with the holy angels.

36 It. For what doth it profit a man, to gain the whole 37 world, and forfeit his life? For what should a man 38 give in exchange for his life? For whosoever shall be ashamed of me and of my words in this adulterous and sinful generation, the Son of man also shall be ashamed of him, when he cometh in the glory of his

a Luke 12 : 9; 2 Tim. 1 : 8.

36. Following the text of the revisers, and preserving the noun of twofold application, we may translate, for the purpose of illustration, " For what doth it profit a man to gain the whole world, and to forfeit his *psyché*, life, or soul?" The verb **profit** is in the present tense, not the future; the question is general, relating to the present time, as well as to the future life. What profit is there in such a transaction? The last verb is not the same as the one that is translated "lose" in the preceding verse, and ought to have a different word in the translation. Luke brings in both verbs in a very strong combination; literally, "To gain the whole world, but to lose or forfeit himself." As for *psyché* here, either meaning seems to be allowed to it. The remark is transparently true in the lower and ordinary aspect: to gain the whole world is of no profit to a man who loses his life in doing it. How much more profoundly must it be true of life in its higher aspect, where loss means so much more! If life is regarded in its relation to God and eternity, then what can be the profit if one gains the world, but forfeits, lets go, his soul? The value of man to himself is here set above all other values in the world.

37. This high estimate of the *psyché* is now confirmed by the fact that no other possession can buy it back if once lost. The connective word is " For," not Or, in the best manuscripts; and the connected sense of the two verses is, " What doth it profit a man to gain the whole world and lose his soul? For what is there that he can give, out of all his possessions, as a price with which to buy back his soul when once he has lost it?" If he has bartered it away, there is nothing to redeem it with : lost is lost. This may have been a proverbial saying commonly applied to the physical life, with reference to which it is, of course, absolutely true : lost is lost. But how much more profoundly is it true of the soul in its higher interests! Once lost, with what possession can it be regained? Barter away the true life of the soul for temporary good, and it is gone, as many a man has found to his sorrow, and all that has been accepted instead of it is powerless to bring it back.

38. The general statement of the possibility of losing one's self now receives its definite illustration, in connection with what was said at first of boldly following Jesus. The hearers are told how one of them may lose his soul, or, in Luke's phrase, "lose or forfeit himself." The address was directly to our Lord's contemporaries in that generation, the men who had had the opportunity to know him; and to them it was a terribly searching appeal. **Whosoever therefore shall be ashamed of me, and of my words.** This would be the act of self-forfeiture and self-loss, the shame that would keep them away from him; and the temptation to it was on every side.—They lived in the midst of an **adulterous and sinful generation.** Literally, "in this generation, the adulteress and sinner;" adulterous in the sense of Jer. 3 : 20; 31 : 32; Ezek. 16 : 31, 32; Matt. 16 : 4. The union between Jehovah and Israel was symbolized, in the prophets, by marriage, and the unfaithfulness of Israel by the conduct of an adulterous wife. Now Jesus charges his own generation with such adultery : it is false to God, and stands forth "an adulteress and a sinner." Jesus was condemned for having to do with adulterous and sinful persons, but the great adulteress and sinner was the generation that condemned him. Yet even in the midst of such a generation his follower must not blush to come after him bearing his cross. Indeed, the great need of the whole generation was to be delivered from the wrong-heartedness by virtue of which it would be ashamed of such a Christ as he.—Notice the expression, **ashamed of me, and of my words.** Compare **for my sake and the gospel's,** in verse 35. In both, he associates his truth and himself; he does not wish any one to lose his life for his sake apart from the gospel, or for the gospel's sake apart from him. Just so did his person and his words stand together for the men of that generation, to awaken either reverence and love or shame. His **words,** in such a connection, are especially the words that set forth the nature of his kingdom; for of these especially was there danger that men would be ashamed. Observe here that it was just such

9:1 And he said unto them, Verily⁰ I say unto you, That there be some of them that stand here, which shall not⁰ taste of death, till they have seen the kingdom of God come with power.

9:1 Father with the holy angels. And he said unto them, Verily I say unto you, There are some here of them that stand by, who shall in no wise taste of death, till they see the kingdom of God come with power.

a Matt. 16:28; Luke 9:27....*b* John 8:52; Heb. 2:9.

shame in Peter (verse 32) that called out these words. Whoever is ashamed, on him shall the loss of himself fall; for "the Son of man also shall be ashamed of him" (see Revision), and this is loss of one's self. The life, soul, self, of which he is ashamed, is lost. Illustrate by the parable of the Talents (Matt. 25: 14-30). —**When he cometh in the glory of his Father, with the holy angels.** Luke, "When he cometh in his glory and (the glory) of his Father and of the holy angels;" Matthew, "For the Son of man shall come, in the glory of his Father with his angels, and then will he give to each according to his work." The present humiliation of the Son of man was not always to continue; by and by the glory of God and heaven would be upon him, and the difference between cross-bearing for his sake and the gospel's and being ashamed of him and of his words would be manifested in his judgment.

Ch. 9: 1. Probably the separation of this verse from its context in Mark alone is due to the fact that only in Mark is it introduced by the words **And he said unto them.** But that is no sufficient reason for the separation, the words being merely one of Mark's emphatic calls to special attention. This verse is in sense inseparable from the preceding, as one who reads it in Matthew or Luke will see at once. This closing word was intended for solemn warning and encouragement to the men of that generation who had just been put to the test by the words already spoken; as if he had said, "You will not have long to wait. The Son of man will soon be glorified, and his kingdom and glory will be made manifest even among you before death has come to all of you." The verse is perfectly plain in itself, though it may be difficult to fit its teaching into our scheme of thought on the subject of which it treats. Such difficulty is no reason, however, for seeking to evade or conceal the real sense of a passage, and an interpreter has only to deal with what his passage contains. Hence the only task at present is to state the plain sense of these words.—The simplest form of the saying is in Luke: "I say unto you in truth, There are some of those that stand here who will not taste of death till they shall have seen the kingdom of God." Matthew, who has

just said, "The Son of man shall come," now says, "Verily I say unto you, There are some of those that stand here who will not taste of death till they shall have seen the Son of man coming in his kingdom." In Mark it is, **Verily I say unto you, That there be some of them that stand here, which shall not taste of death, till they have seen the kingdom of God** (already) **come with power.** The word is a perfect participle, "having come" or "already come." Thus the three testimonies as to what it is that some of them that stand here shall see are: Luke, "the kingdom of God;" Matthew, "the Son of man coming in his kingdom;" Mark, "the kingdom of God already come." Such language can mean only that some who were then present should live until after the Son of man had come in his glory and the kingdom of God had come in its characteristic power, and then should taste of death. What events were thus predicted? Some, led by the connection of this verse with the ninth chapter, have found a fulfilment in the Transfiguration; but the objections seem fatal that the language is too far-reaching to suit an event that three persons and no others witnessed after six days, and that neither Christ nor the kingdom of God "came" at the Transfiguration. No event that fulfils the description occurred within the lifetime of any who were present, except that setting up of the kingdom which was accomplished by the work of the Holy Spirit and the abolition of the Old Dispensation. If the prediction did not mean this, it was not fulfilled. That establishment of the New Dispensation in place of the Old was witnessed in part by all that generation, in full by a few; it began at the day of Pentecost, and culminated forty years later. (See notes on chap. 13: 24-27, where this series of events is called a coming of the Son of man.) It was in this coming of his kingdom that Christ said he should be ashamed of the man in that generation who had been ashamed of him—i. e., the principles of the kingdom would condemn and reject the man; there was no place for such a man in such a kingdom; the repulsion between Christ and his shame at Christ was mutual and unalterable; so that the kingdom of Christ, with its rich and eternal blessedness, was not

CHAPTER IX.

A ND* after six days Jesus taketh *with him* Peter, and James, and John, and leadeth them up into an high mountain apart by themselves: and he was transfigured before them.

3 And his raiment became shining, exceeding white* as snow; so as no fuller on earth can white them.

2 And after six days Jesus taketh with him Peter, and James, and John, and bringeth them up into a high mountain apart by themselves: and he was transfigured before them: and his garments became glistering, exceeding white; so as no fuller on earth

a Matt. 17 : 1, etc. ; Luke 9 : 28, etc.....*b* Dan. 7 : 9 ; Matt. 28 : 3.

for him. The principle of his rejection is the same as that of the rejection in the final judgment.

2-13. THE TRANSFIGURATION OF JESUS, AND THE CONVERSATION WHICH IT SUGGESTED. *Parallels*, Matt. 17 : 1-13; Luke 9 : 28-36.—Luke omits the subsequent conversation, but reports the event itself rather more fully than Matthew and Mark, and in language somewhat divergent from theirs. They use largely the same forms of expression, but not in such manner as to cast the slightest doubt on the independence of their reports.

2, 3. After six days. So also Matthew; Luke, "after these sayings, about eight days," which some take as an inclusive reckoning, parallel with that by which the time of our Lord's stay in the grave is mentioned as three days; but the word "about" renders the marking of time indefinite, like our "About a week." These six days were probably spent in the same northern region, not far from Cæsarea Philippi. The traditional scene of the Transfiguration is on Mount Tabor, a solitary rounded hill in the midst of Galilee, a few miles nearly south from Capernaum. On this site three churches and a monastery were erected in honor of the event before the end of the sixth century. Thus in Montgomery's hymn of *The Three Mountains*, Sinai, Tabor, and Calvary:

> " When in ecstasy sublime
> Tabor's glorious steep I climb,
> At the too-transporting light
> Darkness rushes on my sight."

But Tabor is now known to have been inhabited in those days and crowned by a fortress, which had been strengthened less than thirty years before this time—a very good illustration of the insufficient grounds upon which tradition has often decided upon sites for sacred events. The true scene of the Transfiguration was probably somewhere on the slopes of Hermon, the great mountain of the north, which rises as a crown above the whole land of Palestine. A walk of from ten to twenty miles beyond Cæsarea Philippi would bring Jesus and his company into the high solitudes of the mountain.—Here, as in the raising of Jairus's daughter, **Peter, and James, and John** are the special three selected to be the Master's companions. From their conduct at this time we can see how little true companionship for his higher thoughts and powers he found even in the best of those who were about him. Yet plainly he prized what he had.—Luke alone tells us that he went up into the mountain to pray, and that it was while he was engaged in prayer that the great change came upon him. It is from Luke's language that we infer, also, that it was evening when they ascended the mountain. Doubtless he went, as at Luke 6 : 12, to spend the night in prayer. The other apostles were spending the night below.—**And he was transfigured before them.** Matthew uses the same word, which is found also in 2 Cor. 3 : 18, "changed into the same image," and in Rom. 12 : 2, "be ye transformed by the renewing of your mind." Luke says simply that "the fashion" or appearance "of his countenance" (literally) "became different," *egeneto heteron*. Thus there is nothing highly descriptive in either of the words that tell us what occurred; yet it is by this scene that the word "transfigure" has become distinguished from "transform," and come to tell of an ideal form or appearance in which that which is outward represents and expresses a true glory that dwells within. As for the outward appearance, the change extended beyond his face and what was strictly of himself, even to his clothing, which glowed, to the disciples' eyes, with a dazzling light. — Mark describes only his raiment. **His raiment became shining, exceeding white (as snow** should probably be omitted)**; so as no fuller on earth can white them.** The whole description is peculiar to Mark, and its naturalness and *naïveté* strongly commend it as a genuine and original reminiscence. This is a beholder's graphic way of setting forth the superhuman brightness that streamed from the whole person of Jesus. Luke's language is similar, but briefer: literally, "his clothing became white, forth-shining"—not the same word as **shining**, or "glistering," in Mark. But this is description attempted on the earthly plane; Mat-

4 And there appeared unto them Elias, with Moses; and they were talking with Jesus.
5 And Peter answered and said to Jesus, Master, it is good for us to be here:ᵃ and let us make three tabernacles: one for thee, and one for Moses, and one for Elias.
6 For he wistᵇ not what to say; for they were sore afraid.

4 can whiten them. And there appeared unto them Elijah with Moses: and they were talking with Jesus.
5 And Peter answereth and saith to Jesus, Rabbi, it is good for us to be here: and let us make three tabernacles; one for thee, and one for Moses, and one 6 for Elijah. For he knew not what to answer; for

a Ps. 63 : 2 ; 84 : 10....*b* Dan. 10 : 15 ; Rev. 1 : 17.——1 Or, *booths*

thew's imagery is nobler : " his face did shine as the sun, and his raiment was white as the light." What was this? the glory of the rising sun reflected from the snows of Hermon? (So—almost—*Philochristus*, p. 261.) No; the seriousness of this whole record condemns such an explanation. Unless it is all a myth—which we can by no means believe—this was a real irradiation of his body, such an irradiation as to justify that derived sense of the word **transfigured**. It was a genuine shining forth of the nature of Christ; not so much an effort of his as a manifestation of himself, a revealing of the divine nature through the human. No other such event is recorded of him, though some have thought they found one in the walking on the sea (Taylor Lewis, *The Divine Human in the Scriptures*). No doubt a nature that so shone forth once could shine forth again, but the Transfiguration stands in solitary grandeur in the record. Its purpose was to reveal the Christ to chosen ones among his disciples as he had never been revealed to them before (see note below), and so to leave for us a view of his glory. Study this glory in comparison with that of the Mount of Beatitudes. As to the inward nature of this wonder, of course we stand wondering, as they did. We know so little either of God or of man that we cannot call it strange if the manifestations of the God-man baffle us. It is a striking fact that in the commentaries and the " Lives " of Christ the treatment of this event is always among the least satisfactory passages. Probably it will always be so, for nowhere are we led farther into an unknown region.

4. There appeared unto them (the three disciples) **Elias, with Moses.** In Matthew and Luke, " Moses and Elijah "—Elijah, one of the greatest of the prophets, and the one whose spirit was to be reproduced in the earliest work of the Messiah's kingdom, yet one whose spirit seems to be half condemned by Jesus as an inferior spirit, which in the new kingdom is to be surpassed (Luke 9 : 51-56).—**Elias, with Moses.** Moses, the mediator of the old covenant (Gal. 3 : 19), by whom was given the law whose meaning Jesus had now come to

fulfil or to complete (Matt. 5 : 17). Both " the law and the prophets " Christ was thus to fulfil; and his reference to the spirit of Elijah illustrates one part of his work, while abundant references to the law of Moses illustrate the other. All prophets and righteous men had an interest in his work (Matt. 13 : 17 ; John 8 : 56 ; Heb. 11 : 13), but Moses certainly, and perhaps Elijah, beyond the rest. Luke adds that they appeared " in glory," corresponding to the outshining glory of Jesus, and that they spoke of " his decease " (literally, his departure, or exodus). " which he should accomplish at Jerusalem." Note the same word (*exodon*, " exodus ") used by Peter in close connection with his allusion to this scene (2 Pet. 1 : 15). One cannot help wondering whether the three disciples caught the word " exodus " in the fragment that they heard of conversation between Jesus and Moses. Or were the two visitants speaking of his exit from life to compare it, as to manner, with their own? Had they anything to tell him of his own approaching death, or was he telling them? Matthew and Mark say merely that they were **talking with Jesus.** Judging as well as we can from his apparent motive in going to the mountain, we must say that this must have been to him an encouraging and helpful conversation; but more we cannot say.

5, 6. From Luke we learn that the three disciples did not witness the whole scene : while their Master prayed they slept, and it was only after the two visitants had come and the conversation had begun that they became aware of what was passing. Awaking, " they saw his glory and the two men that stood with him." From Luke also we learn to place the proposal of Peter at the moment when he saw that Moses and Elijah were withdrawing. Peter's word of address is " Lord " in Matthew; " Master " in Luke; " Rabbi," in the original, in Mark. His words, **it is good for us to be here,** are identical in all the reports.—**Let us make three tabernacles.** Tents or booths woven of the branches of trees. In such booths the children of Israel were required to dwell during the feast of tabernacles; but doubtless a higher association of ideas brought the word to Peter's mind. Perhaps he vaguely remembered how

9

7 And there was a cloud that overshadowed them; and a voice came out of the cloud, saying, This^a is my beloved Son; hear^b him.

8 And suddenly, when they had looked round about, they saw no man any more, save Jesus only with themselves.

7 they became sore afraid. And there came a cloud overshadowing them: and there came a voice out of the cloud, This is my beloved Son: hear ye him.

8 And suddenly looking round about, they saw no one any more, save Jesus only with themselves.

a Ps. 2 : 7 ; Matt. 3 : 17 ; 2 Pet. 1 : 17....b Deut. 18 : 15.

God talked with Moses at the tabernacle soon after the Exodus. At any rate, he wished to detain the glorious visitants, and was hurriedly planning for their entertainment. This seemed to him like a glimpse of real glory, like glory already reached. After the stern predictions of the cross it may easily have seemed like the bright end, unexpectedly reached without passing through the terrible way. If now they could only stay there! At least it was worth an effort, and he would propose it. Notice that there was no inclusion of the three disciples in the plan : three tabernacles, not six.—Peter's proposal receives no comment in Matthew, but it is half apologized for by Luke in his "not knowing what he said" — *i. e.* not knowing whether he was saying the right thing or not— and by Mark when he says, **For he wist not what to say; for they** (all of them) **were sore afraid.** It was a childish proposal, and one that would scarcely have been preserved in connection with a scene so glorious, except in a narrative of exquisite simplicity and truthfulness; yet in spirit it is not to be condemned: he was not wrong in heart; and it is not wrong to wish to remain "on the mount" as long as possible. As for his recognition of the two glorious ones, did he derive it from something that he heard or from something in their appearance? More likely it was instinctive or intuitive, obtained he knew not how. Doubtless all the three shared it, but we cannot say whether his proposal was theirs.

7. No answer to Peter's proposition ; his offer could not be accepted, and he would one day know why. This was not glory for the Messiah ; this was only help to him in pressing on to glory by the only way, the way of the cross. This was another suggestion from Peter that he should not press on to death, but should accept another glory than that to which his Father called him. He could not turn aside on his way to death to be adored on Mount Hermon in company with Moses and Elijah. If he had, his glory would have departed. No answer; but "while he yet was speaking" (Matthew and Luke) **a cloud** (Matthew, "a bright cloud") **overshadowed them.** Not merely Jesus, Moses, and Elijah, for the disciples entered the cloud, and feared as they entered (Luke). The

cloud would remind them of the pillar of cloud and fire at the Exodus (Ex. 13 : 21), of the cloud that filled the temple of Solomon at the dedication (1 Kings 8 : 10), which had also rested on the tabernacle (Ex. 40 : 34), and perhaps of the "smoke" that filled the temple in Isaiah's vision of the divine glory (Isa. 6 : 4). All these had been visible signs of Jehovah's presence; and in later Jewish times the cloud was expressly recognized as the Shechinah, the dwelling of the glory of God. The sweeping of a bright cloud over them at such a moment would certainly bring all this to mind, in vague impressions if not in distinct thought; and, though there was little room for reflection, the awe of God would be upon the three disciples. When **a voice came out of the cloud,** they would receive it as the voice of God.

The voice said, **This is my beloved Son: hear him.** So Mark ; Matthew adds, as at the baptism, "in whom I am well pleased ;" Luke, according to Tischendorf's reading, "This is my elect Son." All agree in the final **hear him.** The utterance resembles the one at the baptism, yet differs from it. (See note on chap. 1 : 11.) That voice was addressed to Jesus himself, to identify him in his humanity to himself; this was addressed to his disciples, and through them to all to whom his words might come. This was the celestial commendation of Christ to men.

8. Matthew mentions the terror of the disciples at the voice, and tells how Jesus "came to them," apparently from the place, a little removed, where they had seen him, and touched them, with a reassuring word. Of the words **suddenly, when they had looked round,** Farrar says, most justly, "One of the many inimitably graphic touches of truthfulness and simplicity — touches never yet found in any myth since the world began—with which in all three evangelists this narrative abounds" (*Life of Christ,* 2. 29). The voice was still and the vision was ended, and they and their Master were alone again. — There is nothing in this verse to furnish **Jesus only** to preachers as a legitimate text for doctrinal or hortatory use.

Mysterious as the Transfiguration is, we are able to understand something of its significance, both for Jesus and for his disciples. We can see that Jesus ascended the mountain for prayer, in

9 And as they came down from the mountain, he charged them that they should tell no man what things they had seen, till the Son of man were risen from the dead.

10 And .ney kept that saying with *.nemselves, questioning one with another what the rising from the dead should mean.ᵃ

11 ¶ And they asked him, saying, Why say the scribes that Elias*b must first come?

9 And as they were coming down from the mountain, he charged them that they should tell no man what things they had seen, save when the Son of man should have risen again from the dead. And tney kept the sa⁀ing, questioning among themselves what the rising again from the dead should mean.

11 And they asked him, saying, ¹The scribes say that

---

a Acts 17 : 18. . . . b Mal. 4 : 5.——1 Or, How is it that the scribes say . . . come ?

---

order to strengthen his soul for the struggle toward which his thoughts had been freshly turned. He was seeking for strength to bear his own cross even to the end, His prayer was heard (as at Heb. 5 : 7), and in response came this special visitation from the heavenly world. Such heavenly aid was granted him at the great crises of his life, as after the temptation in the wilderness (Matt. 4 : 11) and in the agony of the garden (Luke 22 : 43). Comp. Matt. 3 : 17 ; John 12 : 28. Now the cross was drawing nearer to his soul, and now came the great conversation with Moses and Elijah which stands in unique grandeur among his heavenly interviews. It was to him somewhat like the refreshment that Elijah received for his journey from the visit of an angel beneath the juniper tree (1 Kings 19 : 5-8), but more like the blessing that Moses received in his great vision of God at Mount Sinai (Ex. 33 : 12-34 : 9). As for the disciples, this was the response of Heaven to the great confession. "To him that hath shall be given ;" they had discerned the Christ in his obscurity, and to them was given the vision of his glory. But it was given for a purpose, and in answer to a need. They had been told that his way and theirs was the way of the cross. In that dark and painful way unbelief might easily assail them, as doubt had assailed even John the Baptist in the prison (Luke 7 : 19), and they might ask whether they had not followed cunningly-devised fables when they accepted him as the Christ of God and the chosen of their hearts. In this shining forth of his glory there was confirmation for their faith, congenial reward for their confession, fresh witness from heaven to him whom they alone on earth had recognized, and, if their sense of his authority should fail, a solemn **hear him** uttered from heaven to strengthen their loyalty. The whole passage in Peter's Second Epistle (1 : 13-19) is full of allusions to the event, direct and indirect, and all in the spirit of this interpretation. Evidently the Transfiguration was a resting-place for the confidence of the believers ; certainly it was such to the writer of that Epistle. Farrar remarks, on 2 Pet. 1 : 16, "Many have resolved the narrative of the Transfiguration into a myth ;

it is remarkable that in this verse St. Peter is expressly repudiating the very kind of myths (*muthoi sesophismenoi*) under which this would be classed" (*Life of Christ*, 2. 30).

9, 10. A Strict Command to Conceal this Matter until After the Resurrection of Jesus.—As for the people in general, represented in spirit only too faithfully by the scribes and Pharisees of Dalmanutha (chap. 8 : 11), this was not for them. This was a sign from heaven exactly such as the Pharisees had supposed they desired to see. The voice from heaven, if they had heard it, would precisely have satisfied the terms of their request, though it would not have won from them a genuine faith. But the shining of the inner glory and the **hear him** from heaven were not for the adulterous and sinful generation ; they were not even for all the apostles of Christ. The three were bidden to conceal it from the nine ; for this is the evident meaning of the command. The nine were not ready to see the event with spiritual profit, and certainly not to hear of it at second-hand : they would have been perplexed, perhaps unbelieving, and perhaps jealous. For the time this was a strict secret for the elect of the elect, a special trust. But with what joy must they have revealed it after the rising from the dead had unsealed their lips !—The mention of the rising from the dead still perplexed them, and they began **questioning one with another** what it might mean. Such is the most probable grouping of the words, and it tells of anxious and perplexed discussions, in which they still failed to obtain any clear apprehension of the truth.—Peter is undoubtedly the one of the three to whom we owe the narrative as it stands in Mark, and Matthew's version is in general closely similar. The fresh narrative of Luke, differing slightly, may represent the report of one of the other witnesses, possibly that of James. One would like to think so, for we have nothing in the New Testament from the brother of John and the first martyr of the apostles. Yet the language of 2 Peter proves that the writer was familiar with the story in the form in which it stands in Luke.

11. After this prohibition, given on.the way

12 And he answered and told them, Elias verily cometh first, and restoreth all things; and how it is written* of the Son of man, that he must suffer many things, and be* set at naught.
13 But I say unto you, That* Elias is indeed come, and they have done unto him whatsoever they listed, as it is written of him.

12 Elijah must first come. And he said unto them, Elijah indeed cometh first, and restoreth all things: and how is it written of the Son of man, that he should suffer many things and be set at nought?
13 But I say unto you, that Elijah is come, and they have also done unto him whatsoever they listed, even as it is written of him.

a Ps. 22 : 1, etc.; Isa. 53 : 3, etc.; Dan. 9 : 26; Zech. 13 : 7....b Ps. 74 : 22; Luke 23 : 1; Phil. 2 : 7....c Matt. 11 : 14; Luke 1 : 17.

down from the mountain, a question arose about the great event. Elijah had appeared, and had immediately disappeared; he had come late, after the Messiah had been brought into the world, and had vanished without doing or attempting any work in connection with his kingdom. What should they think? According to the constant teaching of the scribes, Elijah **must first come.** This teaching was based on Scripture, in Mal. 4 : 5, 6, but the disciples alluded to the doctrine in its popular form and connections as the more familiar. Had not Elijah come last instead of first, and even then with no popular effect?

12, 13. There is no important difference of reading here, but the punctuation is not universally agreed upon. Probably it should be, as in Tischendorf and Meyer, " Elijah indeed cometh first, and restoreth all things. And how is it written concerning the Son of man? That he should suffer many things, and be set at naught. But I say unto you that Elijah also hath come, and they did unto him whatsoever things they would, as it hath been written concerning him." The punctuation of the revisers seems less satisfactory. Here it is affirmed (1) that the scribes were right in saying that the mission of Elijah must precede that of the Messiah. He **verily cometh first.** The use of the present tense is the indefinite use, as in Matt. 2 : 4, "where the Christ is born." (2) That the work of Elijah is that he **restoreth all things**—a work of restoration. The language comes from the Septuagint of Mal. 4 : 6, where it is said that Elijah "shall restore the heart of father to son, and the heart of man to his neighbor." The Hebrew is similar in meaning, though not identical : "Shall turn the heart of the fathers to the children, and the heart of the children to the fathers." It is a restoration of piety and love that is thus assigned to Elijah as his work; and to say that he **cometh** and **restoreth all things** is to say that he shall make, as far as his influence extends, the restoration that is predicted of him. (3) That Elijah has already come. **Elias is indeed**—i. e. Elijah as well as the Messiah. The true Elijah —forerunner, restorer, preparer of the way of the Lord—has come. Matthew says that the

disciples understood him to be speaking of John the Baptist; and of course we cannot understand him of any other. In John the Baptist, therefore, the prediction concerning Elijah was fulfilled. (4) That it has been written concerning the Son of man that he shall be a despised Messiah and a sufferer; and that in this prediction it is included, by implication, that his forerunner also shall be despised and rejected. What was written of the Christ in this respect was written of the messenger who was sent before him. "It is enough for the disciple that he be as his Master." (5) That the prediction has been fulfilled in the case of John : they "knew him not" as the true Elijah, and treated him as they would. In Matthew it is added, "Thus also shall the Son of man suffer at their hands."—Thus Jesus gave to the three disciples a fair and intelligible interpretation of the relations of the predicted Elijah-ministry to his own. It was to be like his own in being a work of restoration—the restoration and abiding establishment of piety and love; like his own, also, in being a ministry of suffering and rejection; like his own, and yet inferior in both respects—inferior in restoring power (compare chap. 1 : 6, 7) and inferior in suffering. This Elijah-ministry had been performed, and was no longer to be expected; hence any transient appearance of Elijah, such as they had witnessed, need make them no perplexity. He seems plainly to indicate that the prophecy concerning Elijah has been so fulfilled that no further fulfilment of it is to be expected. He distinctly attaches the prediction to the time next before his own ministry, and gives no hint of any other place for it. All the Christian ages have heard more or less of an Elijah yet to come; but there is no hint in prophecy of a coming Elijah, except in Mal. 4 : 5, 6, and our Lord himself tells us that that Elijah has come. If John the Baptist denied that he was Elijah, he denied it of the sense in which his questioners expected an Elijah; and he could not then have given the opposite answer without pledging himself to a thoroughly false view of his own office. It is worthy of notice that Jesus here implicitly applies the name "great and dreadful day of the Lord," in Mal. 4 : 5, just as Peter applies the similar lan-

14 ¶ And when he came to *his* disciples, he saw a great multitude about them, and the scribes questioning with them.

15 And straightway all the people, when they beheld him, were greatly amazed; and running to *him,* saluted him.

16 And he asked the scribes, What question ye with them?

17 And one of the multitude answered and said, Master, I have brought unto thee my son, which hath a dumb* spirit :

18 And wheresoever he taketh him, he teareth him; and he foameth,* and gnasheth with his teeth, and pineth away; and I spake to thy disciples, that they should cast him out; and they could not.

14 And when they came to the disciples, they saw a great multitude about them, and scribes questioning 15 with them. And straightway all the multitude, when they saw him, were greatly amazed, and running to 16 him saluted him. And he asked them, What ques- 17 tion ye with them? And one of the multitude an- swered him, ¹Master, I brought unto thee my son, 18 who hath a dumb spirit; and wheresoever it taketh him, it ²dasheth him down: and he foameth, and grindeth his teeth, and pineth away: and I spake to thy disciples that they should cast it out; and they

a Matt. 12 : 22; Luke 11 : 14....*b* Jude 13.——1 Or, *Teacher....*2 Or, *rendeth him*

guage of Joel 2 : 31 (Acts 2 : 20) to the time of the establishment of his kingdom through the gospel.

14-29. THE HEALING OF THE DE- MONIAC WHOM THE DISCIPLES COULD NOT HEAL. *Parallels,* Matt. 17 : 14-21 ; Luke 9 : 37-43.—The peculiar quality and value of Mark's narrative may well be seen in the fact that in this case it is almost exactly as long as the narratives of Matthew and Luke combined. To it we owe almost all the details of this intensely vivid scene, the other evangelists adding almost nothing to our knowledge. Nearly the whole of verses 14-16 and 21-27 is peculiar to Mark. In all human writing there is no narrative or descriptive passage that bears more unmistakably than this the internal marks of genuineness and truth. It speaks for itself, if narrative ever did. Is it not a little singular that this most intensely vivid and convincing of scenes should centre around a case of demoniacal possession, the very element in the evangelical record upon which most doubt is cast by rationalistic critics?

14-16. The time was the day after the Transfiguration (Luke), and the place was the foot of the mountain. Early in the day, probably, Jesus and the three came down, the three burdened and uplifted by their glorious secret ; thinking, perhaps, how Moses with shining face, and Joshua, came down Mount Sinai. It is to Peter, who was one of them, that we owe the mention of what **he saw** in coming down. (Instead of **he,** the revisers, on manuscript authority, read "they.") It was an excited throng listening eagerly to the discussion of "scribes" (not **the scribes**) with the nine apostles and any other disciples who may have been present. How vivid is the picture of the effect of Jesus' approach!—the excitement, the amazement, the instantaneous turning away from the one object of interest to him.—**Greatly amazed,** or awestruck ; not, so far as we can judge, from any peculiarity in his appear-

ance, as if some light of the glory were still shining in his face, as when Moses drew near to Israel at the foot of the mountain (Ex. 34 : 29-35), for, if that had been the case, we should certainly have heard of it ; and such a shining, too, would have defeated the purpose of concealment. Rather was it because he was the person of whom they were talking, and they were at once delighted and impressed by a certain sense of solemnity by the appearing of him who had never failed in a work of miraculous healing.—The eager interest with which they all turned from futile discussion and failure to the Mighty One appears in their **running to** meet him. But he cared for his own, and came down like a father to his children in trouble, asking the crowd, and especially the scribes, what they were discussing with his friends. He knew their weakness, and saw that they were perplexed and defeated. They were saluting him with welcome after his absence—not the nine only, but the multitude—when he broke in with his question.

17, 18. The answer came from the most interested, and the one who had the best right to tell the story. **One of the multitude.** Matthew says that he "came kneeling," and Luke that he " cried out " with his request.—**I have brought unto thee my son, which hath a dumb spirit**—*i. e.* a spirit that makes its victim dumb; so in Matt. 9 : 32 and 12 : 22. When Jesus addressed the spirit (verse 25), he spoke to it as **dumb and deaf,** perhaps because of what he had observed in addition to what the father told him.—The additional symptoms described in verse 18 are those of violent convulsions, and plainly they are those of epilepsy, which in this case was complicated with insanity. Luke uses the word *sparassein,* "to convulse," and Mark, at verse 20, the stronger compound word *susparassein.* Matthew says that the child was " lunatic," or epileptic ; but he adds that the lunacy was the work of a demon. More particularly, when the demon

19 He answereth him, and saith, O faithless[a] generation! how long shall I be with you? how long shall I suffer you? bring him unto me.
20 And they brought him unto him: and when he saw him, straightway the spirit tare him; and he fell on the ground, and wallowed foaming.
21 And he asked his father, How long is it ago since this came unto him? And he said, Of a child:[b]
22 And ofttimes it hath cast him into the fire, and into the waters, to destroy him: but if thou canst do any thing, have compassion on us, and help us.

19 were not able. And he answereth them and saith, O faithless generation, how long shall I be with you? how long shall I bear with you? bring him unto me.
20 And they brought him unto him: and when he saw him, straightway the spirit tare him grievously; and he fell on the ground, and wallowed foaming.
21 And he asked his father, How long time is it since this hath come unto him? And he said, From a
22 child. And ofttimes it hath cast him both into the fire and into the waters, to destroy him: but if thou canst do anything, have compassion on us, and help

a Deut. 32 : 20; Ps. 78 : 8; Heb. 3 : 10....b Job 5 : 7; Ps. 51 : 5.——1 Or, convulsed

seized the boy he tore him or convulsed him, or, as some explain it, threw him to the ground; and then he foamed and gnashed his teeth, and the consequence was that he pined away or was steadily wasting. These are the symptoms of epilepsy, which was well known among the ancients, and was regarded by the Greeks and Romans as a sacred disease, brought on directly by supernatural power and of evil omen. The word "lunatic," or "moonstruck," is applied to the victim in this case, as often, probably because the attacks were associated with the recurrence of the full moon. The questions, both physiological and psychological, that are connected with the subject of demoniacal possession are full of difficulty; but nothing is more certain than that our Lord on many occasions, and most emphatically on this, recognized the presence of a personality distinct from that of the victim and commanded it away.

The man said, **I have brought unto thee my son**—*i. e.* to the place where he supposed that Jesus was, because his company was there; brought him, apparently, half in hope and half in despair: this was the last resort, and he came to it without much faith.—But Jesus was not there; probably the man came in the cool of the morning, when Jesus and the three were about coming down from the mountain. **And I spake to thy disciples, that they should cast him out; and they could not.** In Luke, "I entreated thy disciples." Their inability is often explained by the fact that Jesus was not with them, but they had cast out many demons in his absence when he sent them forth for such work (chap. 6 : 13). Then, however, they were sent; and perhaps the lack of the consciousness of mission now embarrassed them. The three leading apostles, too, were absent, and perhaps the company at the foot of the mountain felt itself to be really the less, though actually the larger. No doubt, also, the severity of the case gave them pause. Their confidence was not strong enough to bear the sense of publicity and of being tested that came with the challenge; for the scribes at once fol-

lowed up their failure, plying them with questions that must have made them most uncomfortable. The penalty of unbelieving fear is confusion. (See Jer. 1 : 17.) Nor was there much to help them in the faith of the father.

19. He answereth him, and saith. The revisers' text, more correctly, "He answereth them and saith." Not to the afflicted father, but to the inefficient disciples.—**O faithless generation!** Not now "of little faith;" in Matthew and Luke, "Faithless and perverse generation." Here expressly, as in chap. 8 : 18 implicitly, he ranks his own disciples with the generation to which they belong, since he finds in them the ordinary unbelief. They ought, he implies, to have been able to cast out the evil spirit. Perception of the sadness of the case probably repressed their faith; but it ought to have aroused their compassion, and their compassion ought to have increased their sense of the possibility of healing through the grace of Christ. Our Saviour is exacting in the expectation that his friends will be in possession of the spiritual gifts and graces that he offers them. His almost impatient questions mean, "How long shall this generation, whose unbelief I am learning so thoroughly, vex me so? How long must I live among the faithless?"—But he ends with **Bring him unto me.** The Mighty One now takes hold where the weak have failed.

20. The sufferer was brought, but the sight of the great Healer maddened the malign spirit; so that the boy went into a violent convulsion, and **wallowed foaming** on the ground. Was it the dumbness of the victim that prevented such confession as that of chap. 1 : 34; 3 : 11; 5 : 7? There was no confession, and no vocal objection or entreaty on the part of the spirit.

21, 22. The sad sight arrested even the Healer's mind in the midst of his act of mercy. Compassion was prompting the act, and one would think compassion would urge him on to finish it. But nowhere does the true human thoughtfulness of Jesus appear more plainly; he looked on pityingly while the boy suffered, and compassion even stopped him for a moment

23 Jesus said unto him, If* tho canst believe, all things *are* possible to him that believeth.
24 And straightway the father of the child cried out, and said with tears,*b* Lord, I believe; help* thou mine unbelief.

23 us. And Jesus said unto him, If thou canst! All 24 things are possible to him that believeth. Straightway the father of the child cried out, and said*l*, I

a ch. 11 : 23; 2 Chron. 20 : 20; Matt. 17 : 20; Luke 17 : 6; John 11 : 40; Heb. 11 : 6....*b* Ps. 126: 5....*c* Heb. 12 : 2.——*l* Many ancient authorities add *with tears.*

while he tenderly inquired how long the infliction had been upon him.—The naturalness of this pause is inimitable; and not less so is the father's answer. We can hear in it the tones of anxiety and despair, and of eagerness for the utmost that can be done. **Of—or from—a child.** Then, apparently, the boy had passed beyond early childhood, though in verse 24 he is called by the diminutive name *paidion*, "a young or little child."—**And ofttimes it hath cast him into the fire, and into the waters to destroy him.** But it has been baffled thus far. This demoniac had more watchful friends than the one at Gergesa (chap. 5 : 3), who had no home but in the tombs. It was but too common in ancient times so to turn maniacs loose, and this boy was fortunate above many in having care and protection.—For healing at the hands of Jesus the father had strong desire, but very little faith. **If thou canst do any thing, have compassion on us, and help us,** counting himself in with the child as calling for the gift, but looking upon this as a kind of forlorn hope, concerning which he had as much despair as confidence. The disciples had failed; it was supposed that the Master had more power, but who could tell? **If thou canst do any thing** was as much as he could say. Was not this one of the faithless generation? But there was more excuse for him than for the disciples, who had seen so much.

23. As by the revisers, the word **believe** should be omitted. It was doubtless added by copyists, though very early, to complete an imperfect construction and explain a sentence which without some such help they could not understand. With the word omitted, Jesus took up the father's words, "If thou canst do any thing for us," or rather, merely, **If thou canst,** and gave them another application. The presence of the definite article before **If thou canst** indicates, moreover, that the quoted words form grammatically a part of his sentence. We have not an indignant exclamation, as if he had said in amazement, "If thou canst!" and we have not a question, as if he had asked, "Do you say, If thou canst?" rather did he mean, "As for that *if thou canst* of thine, that *ei dunê*, all things are possible (*dunata*) to him that believeth." The play upon the words (*dunê, dunata*) cannot be reproduced in English, except very imperfectly, but it is something like, "As for that *if thou canst* of thine, all things *can be* to him that believeth." By this he means, "You have inquired about ability and whether any help is possible, but you have misplaced the question. The question of ability is in you, not in me. Faith is the secret of ability and of possibility. The power is sufficient on my part; is it on yours? I can give, but can you receive?" Yet the thought is expressed, not so much reprovingly as cheeringly; for the conclusion is not a severe one, but rather the hopeful announcement of the boundless breadth of the possibilities of faith. This is another way of saying, "Believest thou that I am able to do this?" but with a gracious hint that the man will do well to believe. So does the great Object of faith love to encourage faith. He loves to be trusted.

24. The father's answer was a cry strong and eager, but the words **with tears** are of doubtful manuscript authority. **Lord** should quite certainly be omitted, and the insertion of **thou,** which in the Greek is unexpressed, misrepresents the rapidity of the man's utterance in the eagerness of his impassioned prayer. "I believe, help my unbelief." The saying is commonly, perhaps, taken to mean, "I believe, but I desire to believe more worthily; increase my faith." This makes **help** to mean "remove" or "abolish"—a sense for which no good support can be found. If the man had meant to ask that his faith might be rendered equal to the occasion, one would not expect him to ask it in this ambiguous way; and especially is it certain that he would not use the same word, **help,** that he had just employed in quite another sense.—This word is repeated from the former prayer, **have compassion on us, and help us,** and naturally means, as there, "heal my son." So the thought is, "I believe, and yet my faith is scarcely worthy of the name; I hardly dare to call it faith or to plead by it as a believing man. Yet do not wait for something better, but grant my prayer, even to this faith which is no faith. I do believe; but if my belief is no better than unbelief, still heal my son. Do not sternly judge my faith, but help me as I am." There is no contradiction here, and scarcely even paradox, but only deep sincerity in the beginnings of faith, joined with the eager-

25 When Jesus saw that the people came running together, he rebuked the foul spirit, saying unto him, *Thou* dumb and deaf spirit, I charge thee, come out of him, and enter no more into him.
26 And *the spirit* cried, and rent[a] him sore, and came out of him: and he was as one dead; insomuch that many said, He is dead.
27 But Jesus took him by the[b] hand, and lifted him up; and he arose.
28 And when he was come into the house, his disciples asked him privately, Why could not we cast him out?
29 And he said unto them, This kind can come forth by nothing but by prayer[c] and fasting.[d]

25 believe; help thou mine unbelief. And when Jesus saw that a multitude came running together, he rebuked the unclean spirit, saying unto him, Thou dumb and deaf spirit, I command thee, come out of him, and enter no more into him. And having cried out, and [3]torn him much, he came out: and *the child* became as one dead; insomuch that the more part 27 said, He is dead. But Jesus took him by the hand, 28 and raised him up; and he arose. And when he was come into the house, his disciples asked him privately, 29 [2]*saying*, We could not cast it out. And he said unto them, This kind can come out by nothing, save by prayer[3].

a Rev. 12 : 12....b Isa. 41 : 13....c Eph. 6 : 19....d 1 Cor. 9 : 27.——1 Or. *convulsed*....2 Or, How is it *that we could not cast it out ?*....3 Many ancient authorities add *and fasting.*

ness of strong desire for a special gift. This is an early "Just as I am," and a very rich and suggestive one. If the man had paused to study his own faith and to make it sufficient, and withheld his prayer till he could make it satisfactory, would he more have injured himself or grieved the Master? He was pleasing Jesus best when he ventured wholly on him, trusting all the defects of his faith to the mercy from which he was imploring help. "*Just as I am*" is the word most acceptable to him.

25-27. The excitement was rising, and it was time that the scene should be brought to an end, more especially as the father was now ready in heart to receive the gift for which he prayed. The form of exorcism employed in this case was the most elaborate and solemn of all that are recorded in the Gospels. **Thou dumb and deaf spirit.** So addressed with reference to its work upon the child, the effects of its agency.—**I charge thee.** I is emphatic in the Greek—"I, thou knowest who," as the spirit knew at chap. 1 : 24. The emphasis upon the pronoun is our Lord's solemn self-assertion in the spiritual realm.—**Come out of him.** The customary command; but the addition, **and enter no more into him,** is found here alone. It is pleasant to think that this exceptional command sprang from our Lord's perception of the exceptional severity of the case, and the more than usual interest that he seems to have taken in it.—The rage of a hostile will when compelled to yield vented itself in the final cry and convulsion; for here also the word is "convulsed," rather than rent.—How intensely vivid is the narrative in verses 26, 27 —the prostration of the child, the whisperings of the spectators, the kindness of the Healer! He **took him by the hand, and lifted him up; and he arose.** Luke, and he alone, notes the amazement of the beholders at the mighty power or majesty of God. The same word is used in 2 Pet. 1 : 16 of the glory or majesty which the three disciples had seen in

Jesus on the very night before this healing.— This is one of the many cases in which we would be thankful to see what has been hidden, and know the subsequent relations of this father and child to Jesus. Did the child appreciate the Healer and grow up into a holy Christian manhood? Were all the demons exorcised in his soul? Did the father grow in faith, as one ought after such a beginning? —On the general subject of demoniacal possession, see the note on the first case recorded by Mark (chap. 1 : 23-27).

28, 29. This final reference to the failure of the disciples is omitted by Luke and given more fully by Matthew, who adds here a saying about the power of faith similar to that which followed the blighting of the fruitless tree (Mark 11 : 23). **When he was come into the house,** or "home," to the temporary home that the company had in that region.— **Why could not we cast him**—rather, "it"— **out?** The question had already been answered by the exclamation, **O faithless generation!** in verse 19, but they were not quick to take reproof, and this inquiry was one of the many illustrations of their slowness, with which he had to be patient. Yet perhaps unbelief never fully understands its own failures, but supposes there must be some reason for them to be sought.—**This kind** (of demons) **can come forth by nothing but by prayer and fasting** (some manuscripts omit **and fasting**)—*i. e.* This is an extreme case, one that can be made to yield only to faith nourished by the earnest use of all the means of strength. Prayer is recognized as the first great spiritual agency; and if the reference to fasting is genuine, our Lord associates with prayer self-denial, regarded, evidently, as a fitting means of attaining a holy self-command. Fasting in itself, considered as an end, would certainly command his instantaneous and unutterable contempt, as did the many performances of a similar kind that came

30 ¶ And they departed thence, and passed through Galilee; and he would not that any man should know it.

31 For he taught his disciples, and said unto them, The Son of man is delivered into the hands of men, and they shall kill him; and after that he is killed, he shall rise the third day.

32 But they understood not that saying, and were afraid to ask[a] him.

33 ¶ And[b] he came to Capernaum: and being in the house, he asked them, What was it that ye disputed among yourselves by the way?

30 And they went forth from thence, and passed through Galilee; and he would not that any man 31 should know it. For he taught his disciples, and said unto them, The Son of man is delivered up into the hands of men, and they shall kill him; and when he is killed, after three days he shall rise 32 again. But they understood not the saying, and were afraid to ask him.

33 And they came to Capernaum: and when he was in the house he asked them, What were ye reasoning

a John 16 : 19....b Matt. 18 : 1 ; Luke 9 : 46 ; 22 : 24, etc.

under his notice; and fasting in general received from him such comments as showed that he esteemed it not very highly. (See notes on chap. 2 : 18-22.) But prayer and self-control go harmoniously together as the means by which an efficient faith may best be sought.

30-32. THE RETURN TO GALILEE, AND RENEWED PREDICTION OF THE DEATH AND RESURRECTION OF JESUS. *Parallels*, Matt. 17 : 22, 23; Luke 9 : 43-45.—Turning southward from the region of Mount Hermon, Jesus and his company returned to their old home. They **passed through Galilee; and he would not that any man should know it.** All peculiar to Mark. He wished to awaken no public excitement whatever, and the reason is expressly given by Mark alone: **he taught his disciples, and said unto them,** or, literally, "For he was teaching his disciples, and was saying to them," etc. A touching illustration of Matt. 16 : 21, and of the change in teaching that is there said to have come in "from that time"—the time of the great confession at Cæsarea Philippi. It was thenceforth the purpose of Jesus to impress the coming events upon the minds of his disciples; and so, on the homeward journey, he took care to secure all possible quiet and seclusion, that this lesson might, if it were possible, be learned. He knew that in Galilee his friends would be exposed to the influence of the popular ideas, and might be even slower yet to receive such truths as these; therefore while he had them alone he would seize the moment to teach them as much as they could possibly receive. Painful teaching it was, both to the pupils and to the Teacher; but the time was swiftly coming, and the teaching must not be withheld. The deliberate and persistent planning for a secret journey shows how much of this painful teaching must have been done on the way, and how intent the Master's heart was upon it.—**The Son of man is delivered into the hands of men.** Made a victim to their will. Here it is **men** in all three reports; not the religious

leaders of Israel, as in chap. 8 : 31. It is of human malice and wickedness that mention is made, the evil will of men toward the Son of man.—**And they shall kill him; and after that he is killed, he shall rise the third day.** A peculiar mode of expression, which looks as if it were intended to lay special emphasis on the fact and reality of the killing. Of course a brief sentence like this can furnish only the merest hint of the substance of the teaching that occupied them during that quiet journey.—As the Master's attempt to avoid observation illustrates his sense of the importance of this teaching, so it illustrates also the great slowness of the disciples to understand it. Their various and inconsistent feelings are mirrored in the three reports. In Matthew the effect is that they "were very sorrowful," grieved that such a prospect should be offered in place of their high hopes; in Mark and Luke—much more elaborately stated in Luke —**they understood not that saying, and were afraid to ask him.** Perplexity and reserve were the effects of his teaching: it was mysterious to them, and the solemnity and dreadfulness of his words sealed their lips from inquiring what it meant.—But if they **were afraid to ask him,** they failed to understand their Master himself as truly as his dark words. He wished to be understood, and he now wishes the same. He approves and loves the reverently inquiring spirit.

33-50. ARRIVAL AT CAPERNAUM AND CONVERSATION THERE, SUGGESTED BY THE AMBITION AND EXCLUSIVENESS OF THE DISCIPLES. *Parallels*, Matt. 18 : 1-9; Luke 9 : 46-50.—Matt. 10 : 42 is parallel to verse 41, and Luke 17 : 1, 2 to verse 42; but these sayings are assigned by Matthew and Luke to other occasions. Matthew inserts just before this passage, after mentioning the arrival at Capernaum, the story of the miraculous providing of the tribute-money for Jesus and Peter.

33, 34. Jesus had been absent from Capernaum not far from five months. He had departed just after the passover, in April, and now it must have been near the beginning of Octo-

34 But they held their peace: for by the way they had disputed among themselves who *should be* the greatest.

35 And he sat down, and called the twelve, and saith unto them, If *a* any man desire to be first, *the same* shall be last of all, and servant of all.

36 And he took a child, and set him in the midst of them: and when he had taken him in his arms, he said unto them,

34 in the way? But they held their peace: for they had disputed one with another in the way, who *was* 35 the *b* greatest. And he sat down, and called the twelve; and he saith unto them, If any man would be first, he shall be last of all, and minister of all.

36 And he took a little child, and set him in the midst of them: and taking him in his arms, he said unto

a ch. 10 : 43 ; Matt. 20 : 26.——*b* Gr. *greater.*

ber. (See Andrews's *Life of our Lord.*) He had returned once, meanwhile, to the immediate vicinity of Capernaum (chap. 6 : 10), but there is no evidence that he was seen in Capernaum itself. The length of the present visit cannot be ascertained, but it cannot have been great, certainly not more than a very few weeks. It is the last recorded visit to Galilee, and, as most suppose, the last visit. Some think (as Andrews) that there was probably another visit after he had attended the feast of tabernacles at Jerusalem; but the conclusion is inferential, and this is the last sojourn in Galilee concerning which we have any information. From this visit we have the report of a few discourses and of the one miracle mentioned above, but we have no report of any dealings with friends or enemies beyond his own circle, and no indication of the spirit in which he was received after his absence. —**And being in the house,** or "having come into the house." Matthew, "in that hour"— *i. e.* in the hour of the miraculous providing of the tribute-money. Hence, Mark probably means when he had come into the house after that transaction.—**The house.** Most likely the house of Peter, as in chap. 1 : 29.—The discussion as to **who should be the greatest,** to which Jesus now referred, had taken place **by the way;** we know not where, but probably not far back on the journey. Quite certainly, the spirit of it was still present in their minds. They could not escape from their carnal notions of the kingdom. It was plain that some great event was not far off; the Master's words were foreboding, indeed, but in any literal sense they were scarcely intelligible, and they did not interfere much with the carnal hopes; and so the question about rank in the kingdom was natural enough to them. Meanwhile, Jesus had honored Peter at Cæsarea Philippi, and had quickly degraded him again; he had taken the chosen three up the mountain with him and spent the night, and, though the nine did not know how great was the honor that he had then conferred upon them, the three did know; and now he had miraculously paid the temple-tax for Peter and himself. In their sensitive and expectant state all this would be fuel to

the fire of their ambitious strife.—How lifelike the scene of questioning! After all was over, when he had them alone in the house, he asked them what they had been talking of; but they were silent, knowing what their discussion had been, and how unlike the spirit of their Master. Had they supposed that such a discussion would escape his notice?

35. Mark alone shows us the movements by which he called attention to his coming utterance. **He sat down**—so taking the attitude in which the teachers of that land were wont to speak (so Matt. 5 : 1)—**and called the twelve** about him, especially to hear.—Their discussion had evoked a special and weighty word. The saying is not, as a reader of the English text might suppose, a sentence of degradation upon the ambitious. It is not that one who cherishes the desire to be first shall be condemned by way of punishment to the last and lowest place. It is rather a definition of the true desire to be first. The **shall,** or "will" (for the verb is a simple future), means here about the same as "must," or "must if he is to be successful." If any one desires to be first, and wishes to reach the true first rank according to Christian principles, he will willingly become **last of all, and servant** (*diakonos*) **of all.** The highest place must be sought by accepting the lowest. As to his own spirit and temper, the man must take the humblest place; and as to his work, it must be the work of humble and useful service. Humility and unselfishness are the way to high rank in the kingdom of God; nay, they constitute high rank, they are greatness. The chief servant is the Lord, and all servants serving in his spirit not only shall be great, but are great. He reigns who loves and serves. The thought is more fully expressed in chap. 10 : 42–45, where his own example is given as the great argument and illustration. (See notes there.) Possibly it may have been given here intentionally in briefer form as a seed for subsequent growth.

36. Now comes the object-lesson, the familiar illustration, one that would always be before their eyes and might daily recall the truth that he had taught them. **He took a child.** In all three reports it is a little child. In Matthew,

37 Whosoever shall receive one of such children in my name, receiveth me: and whosoever shall receive me, receiveth not me, but him that sent me.
38 ᶜ And John answered him, saying, Master, we saw ᵇ one casting out devils in thy name, and he followeth not us: and we forbad him, because he followeth not us.

37 them, Whosoever shall receive one of such little children in my name, receiveth me: and whosoever receiveth me, receiveth not me, but him that sent me.
38 John said unto him, Master, we saw one casting out demons in thy name: and we forbade him, be-

---

a Luke 9 : 48....b Num. 11 : 26-28.——1 Or, *Teacher*

"Calling to him a little child," which must have been within hearing. Was it the child of one of the dwellers in the house? The child of Andrew or Peter? Not improbable is the conjecture that it was Peter's child.—He set the **child in the midst of them**—Luke, "by his own side"—and then, as Mark alone adds, **when he had taken him in his arms.** The word is the same as at chap. 10 : 16, and a similar expression is used at Luke 2 : 28, where Jesus himself is in like manner embraced by the aged Simeon. Is it wrong to suggest that if this was Peter's child, it would be in Peter's memory that this act of tenderness would most certainly live, and that in Mark's Gospel it would most certainly appear?—Here was the picture for them to remember, the little child in the arms of Jesus, the symbol of true greatness in his kingdom. Matthew, "Whosoever therefore shall humble himself as this little child, the same is great in the kingdom of heaven." Humility, simplicity, trustfulness, are the marks of greatness.

37. But the danger is that this greatness will not be recognized. Any man of the world can appreciate worldly greatness, but to recognize and honor the true Christian greatness is one of the highest of all Christian acts. **Whosoever shall receive one of such children in my name.** Literally, "upon my name"—*i. e.* upon my name as the ground for the action, as the reason for the receiving; so in Peter's discourse (Acts 2 : 38). Literally, "Repent and be baptized, every one of you, upon the name of Jesus Christ," the recognition of him being the ground of the action. In Luke it is, "Whosoever shall receive this child in my name;" in Matthew, "Whosoever shall receive one such child in my name;" in Mark, Tischendorf reads, with some good authorities, "Whosoever shall receive one of these children in my name," instead of **one of such children.** In any case, the thought is sufficiently determined by the explanatory language of Matt. 18 : 6: "One of these little ones that believe in me." The child who is to be received in Christ's name is not the child that stood among the twelve that day, or any other child, regarded as a child. That was only the symbol, as Jesus expressly said. As a symbol, every such child is to be appreciated and loved; but the "child" that he

means is "one of these truly childlike ones of whom I am speaking." To receive such a one "upon his name" is to accept and honor a humble Christian because he is a humble Christian. —Now he tells how great an act such a receiving is. To see and love the divine beauty that dwells in the spirit of a little child is to see and love the divine beauty of Jesus Christ himself; and to receive him is not an act whose meaning ends with itself: it is to see and love the divine beauty of the living God who sent him. The unity of excellence, in man, Christ, and God, is here positively affirmed, and the true Christian ideal of character is declared to be the character of God. Moreover, the character of God is revealed as a character that is to be imitated by humility in man. Similar language occurs in Matt. 10 : 40 and John 13 : 20 ; but the contexts are different, and neither passage contains the full thought of this.

38. The mention of receiving some one on the ground of his bearing Jesus' name and character reminded John of what the disciples had done with one man who at least might be such a one as the Master meant. **We saw one.** Not named, and perhaps not more definitely known ; no impostor, but a true believer, who, instead of joining himself to the company of the apostles, had gone out by himself to do good in the name of Jesus with faith sufficient to control the demons.—One of the profoundly interesting unwritten histories of the gospel would be the story of this man. What can his motives have been in thus taking up an independent mission of healing, instead of joining himself to the Master? Had he more, or less, of the spirit of Jesus than if he had been inclined only to follow him? How well can he have apprehended the higher excellences of our Lord? What class of successes can we think that he obtained? Could he teach the people to whom he was a blessing? How did he first become aware of his power? How long did it last? Did he ever come to follow as a disciple? And what were his subsequent relations to Christ and the gospel? The biography of this unknown man would be a very interesting chapter in the evangelical story.— **We forbad him, because he followeth not us** (Luke, "followeth not with us"). Be-

39 But Jesus said, Forbid him not: for there* is no man which shall do a miracle in my name, that can lightly speak evil of me.
40 For° he that is not against us, is on our part.

39 cause he followed not us. But Jesus said, Forbid him not: for there is no man who shall do a mighty work in my name, and be able quickly to speak 40 evil of me. For he that is not against us is for us.

a 1 Cor. 12 : 3.... *b* Matt. 12 : 30.——1 Gr. *power.*

cause he is not of our company, and is not professing thy name in the right way. They supposed that such power as he was using was reserved as a privilege for those who followed Jesus as they did. Having themselves had a similar mission, they supposed that none could be obtained, except as they obtained it. From this case, however, we learn, as they did, that the power of Jesus flowed out more widely than to the immediate circle of his followers. Their exclusive spirit is too often the spirit of the privileged. God has more ways than one to communicate the gifts of his grace, and his field is wider than we often think.—It is not certain that John was prominent in the forbidding, though he confesses his share in it. Rather does he seem to have had his misgivings about it, and to have been quite willing to lay the case before the Master for his judgment. However this may be, one likes so to interpret his remark, which is too brief to allow of certainty as to its motive.

39, 40. The answer, which is an application of Matt. 7 : 20, "By their fruits ye shall know them," is full of common sense, and not less full of the divine thought toward man. Translate as in the Revision: "Forbid him not: for there is no man who shall do a mighty work in my name, and be able quickly to speak evil of me. For he that is not against us is for us." "Upon my name," as before, in verse 37—upon my name is the ground of confidence that the miraculous work.—The word that has been rendered **lightly** should be translated "quickly" or "soon," though the thought differs not much from that of "easily" or "readily." **Lightly** conveys too much the idea of thoughtlessness, which is not the right idea. **Speak evil** (*kakologēsai*) is scarcely a strong enough word; for the original almost means "curse." The thought in our Lord's answer is somewhat like this: "The question is, Who ought to be received as a friend, and who to be rejected as an enemy? On this question judge not according to the appearance, but judge righteous judgment. If a man has faith enough in me to work a miracle in my name, he cannot readily turn and act the part of an enemy and cast in his lot with those who revile me. Such a man can be trusted as a friend; he is on our side. Do not reject him or forbid him, then. No one

is to be rejected but an enemy, no one forbidden but he who is doing an enemy's work." He did not mean to say that negative friendliness is enough, as if he had said, Count a man a friend if he is not an open enemy. Rather did he mean that this man was a friend just so far as he was doing a friend's work, and therefore deserved to be treated as a friend; and, moreover, there was an element in the doing of Jesus' work that would tend to make it morally impossible for the man to become an enemy. Since he was acting as a friend, and had in some degree a moral certainty of remaining a friend, as a friend he must be recognized. We are reminded of the jealousy of Joshua for Moses, and of Moses' noble reply, "Would God that all the Lord's people were prophets" (Num. 11 : 29), and of Paul's rejoicing that in every way Christ was preached, whether from the best motives or not (Phil. 1 : 18).—The rich lesson of this incident is still too far from having been learned. It is the lesson of charity and mutual recognition. Jesus expressly told his followers to recognize as their brother the man who was doing his work, though he might not follow with them or do it in their way All exclusive sectarianism, as if one's own sect were the whole kingdom of heaven, and all exclusive feeling, as if one's own way of following Jesus were the only way that he could accept, are here not only forbidden, but ruled out alike by common sense and Christian sentiment. We can have our strong conviction that our way of following Christ is the best, just as the apostles may have been sure that it was better then to journey with him than to go out alone. But he calls our attention, as he called theirs, away from the points on which we might condemn our fellow-laborers to the points in which we can recognize them and esteem them as brethren.—The saying in Matt. 12 : 30, "He that is not with me is against me, and he that gathereth not with me scattereth abroad," is the complement of this, not the contradiction. There, also, the test is practical, and he who is not doing the work of Christ is the one who has no place in his company.—There is no indication that Jesus had ever seen this man, or that his remark was framed with special reference to any peculiarities of his case. In fact, the remark is general, **there is no man,** etc.

41 For* whosoever shall give you a cup of cold water to drink in my name, because ye belong to Christ, verily I say unto you, he shall not lose his reward.
42 And whosoever shall offend^b one of these little ones that believe in me, it is better for him that a millstone were hanged about his neck, and he were cast into the sea.

41 For whosoever shall give you a cup of water to drink, ¹because ye are Christ's, verily I say unto you, he 42shall in no wise lose his reward. And whosoever shall cause one of these little ones that believe ²on me to stumble, it were better for him if ³a great millstone were hanged about his neck, and he were

---

a Matt. 10 : 42; 25 : 40....b Matt. 18 : 6; Luke 17 : 1, 2.——1 Gr. *in name that ye are....*2 Many ancient authorities omit *on me....*3 Gr. *a millstone turned by an ass.*

---

41. Here Jesus grounds the preceding instruction in the greatness of himself and his mission. So great a thing is it to belong to him that from this relation the smallest acts obtain a new and surpassing significance. **Whosoever shall give you a cup of cold water to drink in my name**—*i. e.* because of my name, which you bear, **because ye belong to Christ,** or, with the revisers, "because' ye are Christ's." Here is the reason. This is a most significant and instructive word as used after the confession made by Peter in behalf of his fellow-disciples—significant as a probable hint of the kind of remark that abounded in his private discourse with them after that confession. He was laboring to make them know that he must die and they must suffer; but along with this must certainly have gone much instruction respecting their own position as his friends, and the dignity that really belonged to them in spite of all the suffering and disgrace. "Ye are Christ's," the very language of Paul (1 Cor. 3 : 23). It was the charter of greatness : none in the world were like them in honor, and what was done to them as the representatives of him and his kingdom had a greatness of meaning and value. "Because ye are Christ's" the smallest service to you shall be accounted great, and shall not fail of its reward in the Messianic kingdom. But, by parity of reasoning, any service that you may render to any true believer, even though he follow not with you, is equally great and certain of reward. In Matt. 10 : 42, "Whosoever shall give to drink to one of these little ones," whether apostle or solitary exorcist, "shall not lose his reward." Whoever receives any of the little ones receives the Lord : Matt. 25 : 40, "Inasmuch as ye have done it unto one of the least of these my brethren, ye have done it unto me;" and the reward is indicated in the great invitation of the King, "Come, ye blessed of my Father." Such, distinctly, is our Lord's teaching. Not that the **reward** is payment for merit, but that the reception of the Lord in his humble servants has its fitting end in his glory. Thus, by implication, the man who followed not with them was raised to a level with the apostles as one who was to be served by all the brethren. How cheering is this exaltation of little services, and yet how exacting ! since the decisive element is removed from the magnitude of the service to the motive of the heart in its relation to Christ. It is easier to do great works than good works.

42. On the other hand, as it is a great thing to serve one of these little ones, so it is a great thing and a terrible to cause one of them to stumble. Here they are called expressly **these little ones that believe.** To offend such a one, or cause him to stumble, is to lead him into sin or to prevent him from prosecuting the Christian life and work. The rebuking of the solitary miracle-worker might not result in so great an evil as that ; yet it might ; and it certainly would tend toward that evil. The man might be tempted to give up his faith when the very apostles of Jesus said to him, "Thou hast no part in him." As for the genuine completed act of causing such a soul to sin, its enormity is measured by the dignity that has been put upon the soul, which "is Christ's."—To the committing of such an act death were preferable; and death is solemnly described—death by drowning, with a weight around the neck. The **millstone** here is not the stone of the ordinary hand-mill, which was of moderate size and weight, but the stone of the larger mill that was turned by beasts of burden ; literally, an ass-mill stone. Drowning by the use of a heavy weight was not a Jewish punishment, but it was known among the Greeks, Romans, Syrians, and Phœnicians. It was inflicted by order of the Roman emperors in certain cases of infamy, and is said by Jerome to have been inflicted in Galilee. Plumptre suggests that it may have been witnessed there in the insurrection of Judas of Galilee, and so may have had a special fascination of terror in our Lord's time. The Jews, with their fondness for paying funeral honors to the dead, may well have had a great horror of it. This picture of appalling death is the one that Jesus selected to illustrate the evil of causing a believing soul to stumble.

43-48. If occasions of sin to those who believe on Jesus and "are Christ's" are so serious, it follows that each believer must guard against

43 And*a* if thy hand offend thee, cut it off: it is better for thee to enter into life maimed, than, having two hands, to go into hell, into the fire that never shall be quenched;

44 Where*b* their worm dieth not, and the fire is not quenched.

45 And if thy foot offend thee, cut it off: it is better for thee to enter into life, than, having two feet, to be cast into hell, into the fire that never shall be quenched;

46 Where their worm dieth not, and the fire is not quenched.

47 And if thine eye offend thee, pluck it out: it is better for thee to enter into the kingdom of God with one eye, than having two eyes, to be cast into hell-fire;

48 Where their worm dieth not, and the fire*c* is not quenched.

43 cast into the sea. And if thy hand cause thee to stumble, cut it off: it is good for thee to enter into life maimed, rather than having thy two hands to

45 go into ¹hell, into the unquenchable fire.² And if thy foot cause thee to stumble, cut it off: it is good for thee to enter into life halt, rather than having

47 thy two feet to be cast into ¹hell. And if thine eye cause thee to stumble, cast it out: it is good for thee to enter into the kingdom of God with one eye, rather

48 than having two eyes to be cast into ¹hell; where their

a Deut. 13 : 6; Matt. 5 : 29....*b* Isa. 66 : 24 ; Rev. 14 : 11....*c* ver. 44, 46 ; Luke 16 : 24.———1 Gr. *Gehenna*....2 Ver. 44 and 46 (which are identical with ver. 48) are omitted by the best ancient authorities.

them in his own behalf, as well as in behalf of his brethren. There is danger not only that some one outside will allow himself to cause them, but that they will spring up within the soul by means of something that is important and precious to the man himself. It is not now, "If thy brother offend thee," but **if thy hand offend thee,** or **thy foot,** or **thine eye**—if any part or property of thyself lead thee into sin or prevent thee from prosecuting the Christian life and work. These three cases are now treated with the solemn emphasis of repetition, and the command is, **cut off** the hand, **cut off** the foot, **pluck out** the eye, that is the occasion of sin and apostasy.—The reason given for the command is that **it is better to enter into life** (into the kingdom of God, verse 47) **maimed,** or lame, or blind, than, being in possession of all that is natural to man, **to be cast into hell.**—Are these commands of self-mutilation to be taken literally? By no means. No one who had entered at all into the spirit of Christ's teaching could possibly understand him to advise literal self-injury. According to the principle of Mark 7 : 18, 19, dependence upon self-mutilation for the avoidance of sin would rank with dependence upon classification of food for purity. The reason that was given for that case perfectly covers this : "It cannot defile, because it entereth not into the heart"—*i. e.* anything that reaches and affects merely the body fails to reach the seat of sin. Sin dwells in the heart, not in the hand, the foot, or the eye; it is spiritual, not physical, in its nature; and its physical manifestations are merely like the foliage upon the tree, which might fall off and leave the life of the tree unchanged. Self-mutilation has sometimes been tried as a remedy for sin, and less radical ascetic practices have constantly been put to the test; but it has always been found that the great *skandalon* ("cause of offence"), the heart, remained. Not self-mutila-

tion, but self-conquest, is the Christian ideal (1 Cor. 9 : 24-27 ; Rom. 6 : 19; Col. 3 : 1-11). The language is founded upon the supposition of an extreme case : if the hand, the foot, or the eye were found to be " the incurable, incorrigible cause or occasion of transgression against God," even this might better be sacrificed than that the sin should go on. While this will not happen in any such way that the forfeiting of the bodily organs would cure the sin, still the bodily organs are the most convenient illustrations of that which is nearest and most indispensable to man, and hence are well adapted to our Saviour's purpose. His meaning is, "Sacrifice whatever is nearest, dearest, most precious, or most necessary, to thyself, if the sacrifice is essential to the avoiding of sin and the prosecution of the holy life. Better endure the sacrifice than, by avoiding it, lose thyself. Cast thy hand rather than thy whole self to the enemy." The thought is repeated from Matt. 5 : 29, 30, where it has its fitting place in the Sermon on the Mount. The passage is not less exacting than it would be if its language were to be taken literally. The self-denial to which it calls our attention is of the extremest kind, and our Saviour assures us that such self-denial may in some cases be absolutely essential to salvation. There is no difficulty in seeing that he is right, for sinful practices and situations do often become as hard to forsake and sacrifice as a part of one's self.

As to the text of this passage, according to the best manuscript evidence, verses 44 and 46 should be omitted; so that the words **Where their worm dieth not, and the fire is not quenched** occur only once, at verse 48. On the same evidence, the last clause of verse 45, **into the fire that never shall be quenched,** should also be omitted, having been repeated from verse 43; and so should the word **fire,** at the end of verse 47. Nothing is omitted in the best text but the repetitions. The presence of these repetitions is easily accounted for by the terrible solemnity of the passage, and especially by the repetition of the one command, slightly varied, in verses 43, 45, and 47. In such a connection copyists easily took verse 48 as intended for a sort of refrain, and inserted it after each repetition of the command. Verse 48 is quoted word for word, except as to the tenses and the introductory connective, from the Septuagint of Isa. 66 : 24.

The word *Gehenna* occurs thrice here, and here alone in Mark. It is found seven times in Matthew (5 : 22, 29, 30; 10 : 28; 18 : 9; 23 : 15, 33), once in Luke (12 : 5), and once in the Epistle of James (3 : 6). In the common English version it is always translated "hell," and so is the entirely dissimilar word *Hades*, which corresponds to the *Sheol* of the Old Testament. Hades, or Sheol, is simply the place of the departed, and there is no word in the Old Testament that corresponds to *Gehenna* in its New-Testament sense. The confounding of two so dissimilar words in translation, happily avoided in the Revised New Testament, has led to much confusion and misunderstanding, especially in such passages as Matt. 16 : 18; Luke 16 : 23; Acts 2 : 27; Rev. 20 : 13, 14. The word *Gehenna* is the Hebrew word *Ge-Hinnom*, "Valley of Hinnom." This (or sometimes "the Valley of the son," or "of the sons, "of Hinnom") was the name of the narrow gorge or ravine that lay on the south of Jerusalem. The origin of the name is uncertain. "Hinnom" is commonly taken to be the name of some unknown man of early times; but some, as Grimm (*N. T. Lexicon*), make it to be the Chaldee word *Nihom*, "lamentation," transposed. Solomon erected a place of worship for Molech on the hill that overlooked it (1 Kings 11 : 7), and the valley itself was afterward used as the place of human sacrifice by fire to the same horrid god (2 Kings 16 : 3; 2 Chron. 33 : 6), even the kings sometimes sacrificing their children there. In the great reformation of Josiah, the last godly king, the place was deliberately defiled by the king's order in the interest of godliness; he rendered it ceremonially unclean by placing human bones there, that the people might abhor and avoid a place so crowded with horrible and yet fascinating associations (2 Kings 23 : 10). From that time it became the receptacle for the refuse of the city, the stream that flowed through it to join the Kedron probably being relied upon to carry away the liquid sewage. It has often been affirmed that cleansing fires were constantly burning there; but the author-

ities for the statement are insufficient, although some scriptural allusions would be most easily explained by such a fact. The symbolic use of the name *Gehenna* does not appear in the Old Testament; but before the time of Christ the place, so full of all offensiveness and hopelessness, had become the type of the state in which all that is offensive and worthless in the sight of God must be at last. So *Gehenna* came to be the name of the place or state of future punishment—a sense which it bears wherever it is found in the New Testament, except in Matt. 23 : 15 and James 3 : 6, where it denotes the abode of evil rather than merely the place of punishment.

Verse 48 is to be understood in the light of the connection in Isaiah from which it is taken. In Isa. 66 : 24 it is represented that the true worshippers of God are to assemble in the temple, where they can look out upon the dead bodies of the rebellious in Israel, which are in the place of refuse and rejection, **where their worm dieth not, and the fire is not quenched.** That prophecy points forward to the time when the kingdom of Christ shall have been established, and those who have entered it shall know how terrible is the fate of those who have rejected it and have been themselves rejected. The imagery is borrowed from the Valley of Hinnom, familiar to the first hearers, and is entirely physical. The fact represented is the rejection, from the kingdom of God, of men who have rejected that kingdom. Probably the first application of Isaiah's prophecy was to the generation to which our Saviour spoke, and which rejected him. Any man of that generation, Jesus would say, if he preferred hand, foot, or eye to the Messianic godliness, might expect to find himself among those who were utterly rejected from the Messianic kingdom. With our Lord, to **enter into life** and to **enter into the kingdom of God** is not merely to enter the blessedness of the future state. It is expressly something else: it is to enter into the character and the life that constitute the kingdom. (See John 3 : 5; 17 : 3; Luke 10 : 27, 28, etc.) Accordingly, the opposite state is not exclusively the misery of the future existence: it is primarily the state of those who, by rejecting him, have failed to enter into life and into the kingdom, and who, instead of dwelling in the spiritual Jerusalem, are cast into the *Gehenna* outside. The essential quality of this state will inevitably extend, if they do not repent, to an endless future; for the misery of their state has in it a self-perpetuating quality, from

49 For every one shall be salted with fire, and every sacrifice⁴ shall be salted with salt.
50 Salt *is* good; but if the salt⁴ have lost his saltness, wherewith will ye season it? Have⁴ salt in yourselves, and have⁴ peace one with another.

49 worm dieth not, and the fire is not quenched. For 50 every one shall be salted with fire¹. Salt is good: but if the salt have lost its saltness, wherewith will ye season it? Have salt in yourselves, and be at peace one with another.

a Lev. 2:13; Ezek. 43:24....*b* Matt. 5:13; Luke 14:34....*c* Col. 4:6....*d* Ps. 34:14; 2 Cor. 13:11; Heb. 12:14.——1 Many ancient authorities add *and every sacrifice shall be salted with salt.* See Lev. ii. 13.

the nature of their sinfulness.—We are not justified in drawing for ourselves pictures of future punishment from the suggestions of this imagery. Indeed, it is doubtful whether any of the scriptural imagery was intended to suggest to us pictures, properly so called, of future misery. That misery will be spiritual and moral, and the physical images tell us of its reality, but cannot represent its character. Of the scene and scenery of future misery we know absolutely nothing. The undying worm has commonly been taken to represent the ceaseless gnawing of conscience; and the inextinguishable fire, the unalterable righteousness of God. These are inevitable elements in the future misery, but whether our Saviour meant now to suggest them is at least open to doubt.

49. A saying without parallel, and one of the most difficult in the Gospels. Meyer, who cites fourteen different interpretations besides giving his own, thinks it may have been uttered in a connection that gave light upon it, but has not been preserved. Tischendorf, following substantially the authorities that he is accustomed to follow in cases of doubt, omits the words **and every sacrifice shall be salted with salt,** which he thinks have crept into the manuscripts in which they are found, by way of comment, from the Septuagint of Lev. 2:13. The revisers also omit them. But some manuscripts in turn omit the words **For every one shall be salted with fire,** and apparently the great obscurity of the passage has had to do with the corrupting of the text. Accepting the whole as genuine, Meyer finds the key to the passage in the context and in the allusion to Lev. 2:13. **Every one** is every one of those just mentioned, who shall suffer in *Gehenna.* The **salt** is the salt of the covenant of God, with which every sacrifice must be offered (Lev. 2:13), the symbol of the perpetuity of the covenant relation with Jehovah; which covenant relation has its terrible side to the rebellious and its promise of enlightenment and higher wisdom to the pious. The **fire** is the fire of *Gehenna.* The **sacrifice** is the pious and obedient soul (as in Rom. 12:1), who is a pure sacrifice, spiritually, to God. Thus the verse means, "Justly do I speak of their fire; for every one who goes away into *Gehenna* will

still receive, even in its unextinguished fire, the proof of the perpetuity of Jehovah's covenant, that covenant asserting itself in his case as a covenant of wrath upon the rebellious; and, on the other hand, every one who, by piety and obedience, becomes a true sacrifice to God shall receive the proof of the perpetuity of his covenant on its merciful side by possessing its gifts of enlightenment and higher wisdom in the kingdom of the Messiah." The ordinary interpretations are unsatisfactory because they fail to give a consistent meaning throughout the passage to **fire** and to **salt.** But Meyer finds in the passage itself, thus viewed, a reason for giving a twofold application (though not a double meaning) to **salt ;** and **fire** he explains strictly according to the context. No other interpretation seems so satisfactory as this. In this view, it was precisely because of the unalterable relation of the Jew to Jehovah that he must suffer, and even perish, if he rejected the kingdom of the Messiah, and, in the broader field, it is precisely because of the eternal and necessary relation of man to God that he must suffer without end if he finally rejects God from being his God.

50. The first sentence is parallel to Luke 14: 34, and in part to Matt. 5:13. **Salt is good.** The enlightenment, the wisdom, the character of the kingdom, is *kalon,* "noble," "excellent:" the fulfilment of the covenant on its merciful side gives a noble character to man, and one that he must preserve, for his own sake and for that of the world. Jesus reminds his disciples, perhaps by the tacit allusion to the Sermon on the Mount, that they have this salt and are as a salt to the world. But what if salt were spoiled? How could its virtue be restored? They must be careful not to lose the character of the kingdom.—Concerning the salt losing its saltness, see Thomson, *The Land and the Book,* 2. 43, 44. The salt of Palestine is not made from clean salt water, but from marshes along the sea, and is so mixed with impurities as not to keep its quality very well. Dr. Thomson has often seen it when it had become utterly worthless, without taste and without value: "It is not only good for nothing itself, but it actually destroys all fertility wherever it is thrown; and this is the reason why it is cast into the street."

CHAPTER X.

A ND he arose from thence, and cometh into the coasts of Judea, by the farther side of Jordan : and the people resort unto him again ; and, as he was wont, he taught them again.	1 AND he arose from thence, and cometh into the borders of Judæa and beyond Jordan : and multitudes come together unto him again ; and, as he was
2 ¶ And the Pharisees came to him, and asked him, Is it lawful for a man to put away *his* wife? tempting him.	2 wont, he taught them again. And there came unto him Pharisees, and asked him, Is it lawful for a man

a Matt. 19 : 1 ; John 10 : 40.

—With the last sentence, our Lord returns to the question concerning pre-eminence with which the conversation began. **Have salt in yourselves.** Preserve the pure character of the kingdom, the grace that comes by the fulfilment of God's covenant. Keep in yourselves that which makes you the salt of the earth.— **And have peace one with another.** Omit and forget your strifes for pre-eminence; be lowly and loving. The spirit of the little child is the spirit of peace. See 1 Pet. 1 : 22, which, if not intentionally alluding to this instruction of Christ, is in perfect keeping with it: "Seeing ye have purified your souls by obeying the truth through the Spirit unto unfeigned love of the brethren, love one another with a pure heart fervently."

Here ends the discourse as reported by Mark; but Matthew carries his report farther, adding the Lord's words on the importance of the little ones and the shepherd's care for the wandering sheep, the duty of the offended one and of the church in the case of one who has done wrong to another, (a counsel for the future, so far as the church is concerned), and the duty of boundless forgiveness of injuries, illustrated by the parable of the unforgiving servant to whom mercy was in turn refused (Matt. 18 : 10-35).

1. LAST RECORDED DEPARTURE OF JESUS FROM GALILEE, AND JOURNEY TO JERUSALEM. *Parallel,* Matt. 19 : 1, 2.— Here Mark makes a large omission. The chronological order of the events that he passes by is not entirely plain, nor is it certain just where, in the other records, his resumption of the narrative comes in ; but the discussion of these questions belongs in the treatment of the other Gospels. The order adopted in Gardiner's *Harmony* gives substantially the ordinary arrangement, and may be briefly stated here. After departing from Galilee, Jesus sent out the seventy disciples to prepare the people in Peræa for his own intended coming. He then went to Jerusalem to attend the feast of tabernacles—a fact mentioned by John alone (John 7). After the feast he returned to Peræa and visited the places where the seventy had prepared him a welcome. Through Peræa he journeyed slowly back to-

ward Jerusalem, attended by great multitudes. He was present in Jerusalem at the feast of the dedication, which again is mentioned by John alone (10 : 22), and after this feast he went away to the place where John at first baptized. Hence he was summoned to Bethany by the death of Lazarus, and raised him from the dead. From Bethany he retired to a place called Ephraim, where he remained till the pilgrims were going up to Jerusalem for the passover, when he joined them at a point farther back than Jericho, and went on to Jerusalem for the last time.—Opinions differ as to some points included ; for example, as to whether he returned to Galilee in the interval between the feasts. Moreover, if the conjecture respecting the rich young man that will be mentioned below were accepted, it would be necessary to suppose a different order with reference to the raising of Lazarus. The first ascertainable place in the record of Mark is Jericho, to which Jesus comes at chap. 10 : 46. The events recorded before that point in this chapter belong in Peræa, but cannot be more exactly localized. Within this period falls the rich group of instructions, and especially of parables, reported by Luke, many of them by Luke alone, between his chap. 9 : 51 and 18 : 14. Here belong also the sharp controversies of John 7, 8 and the giving of sight to the man who was born blind (John 9). Mark brings us again to the company of Jesus at some undetermined point in Peræa not long before the end of the journey. He was attended by a multitude, as usual, and the fact that he taught them is here mentioned as the customary fact : **as he was wont, he taught them again.** What a mass of unrecorded instruction is suggested here!

2-12. INSTRUCTIONS CONCERNING DIVORCE. *Parallel,* Matt. 19 : 3-12.—Luke 16 : 18 is also parallel to the closing words of this section. There are considerable variations between Matthew and Mark, both in arrangement and in detail, but no essential differences.

2. The questioners are **the Pharisees**— omnipresent tempters!—and the old practice of trying to catch him by questions still survives. **—Is it lawful.** Perhaps not asked in the nar-

3 And he answered and said unto them, What did Moses command you?
4 And they said, Moses^a suffered to write a bill of divorcement, and to put her away.
5 And Jesus answered and said unto them, For the hardness of your heart he wrote you this precept:
6 But from the beginning of the creation God made^b them male and female.
7 For^c this cause shall a man leave his father and mother, and cleave to his wife;
8 And they twain shall be one^d flesh: so then they are no more twain, but one flesh.
9 What therefore God hath joined together, let not man put asunder.

3 to put away *his* wife? trying him. And he answered and said unto them, What did Moses command you?
4 And they said, Moses suffered to write a bill of divorcement, and to put her away. But Jesus said
5 unto them, For your hardness of heart he wrote
6 you this commandment. But from the beginning of the creation, Male and female made he them.
7 For this cause shall a man leave his father and mo-
8 ther, 'and shall cleave to his wife; and the twain shall become one flesh: so that they are no more
9 twain, but one flesh. What therefore God hath

---

a Deut 24 : 1 ; Matt. 5 : 31....*b* Gen. 1 : 27 : 5 : 2 ; Mal. 2 : 15....*c* Gen. 2 : 24....*d* 1 Cor. 6 : 16 ; Eph. 5 : 31.——1 Some ancient authorities omit *and shall cleave to his wife.*

---

rowest technical sense, as if calling for an interpretation of the Mosaic law, but more generally, asking the judgment of the Rabbi: "May a man put away his wife?" The law of divorce in Deut. 24 : 1 was not entirely plain in the statement of the admissible grounds of complaint against a wife, and the ambiguity had occasioned endless discussion. The schools of Shammai, the stricter, and Hillel, the more lax, contended about it, and the people were divided. Therefore, however Jesus might reply, his answer could be trusted to make him enemies. Moreover, he was in the territory of Herod, under whom the Baptist had suffered for his boldness in the matter of an adulterous marriage. Matthew's addition, "for every cause," was as nearly as possible the translation of the current phrase justified by the lax school of Hillel; and so the question meant, "Is the lax school right?"

3, 4. His answer drove them back to their own authorities. The law under which all their discussions were, and ought to be, conducted was the law of Moses, and what he said must be first considered. **What did Moses command you ?** was the first legitimate question. But their answer was evasive. They stated the permission as if it were unlimited, omitting all reference to the occasions of divorce which the law recognized.

5–9. Yet he accepted their report of the law, imperfect as it was, without criticism. They had omitted the crucial point, the determination of occasions for divorce, and so would he. They had spoken of permission ; of permission he would speak. Divorce was a permitted thing, and the permission was so vague that there might be difficulty in defining its limits. It was permitted, but why? **For the hardness of your heart he wrote you this precept.** The preposition means "on account of," or "out of regard for." The noun means "hard-heartedness ;" "spiritual dulness and incapacity ;" "unresponsiveness to God," amounting to inability to accept high motives. Moses

wrote you this precept, said Jesus (in Matthew, "he suffered you to put away your wives"), because you were not up to the level of a better precept. He said that Moses wrote the precept ; but, according to their view of the matter and according to his (see Mark 7 : 13), the legislation of Moses expressed the appointment of God. It was Jehovah himself who permitted them to put away their wives.—But this precept was not given because there was not a better one at hand. A better was provided in the constitution of man. **From the beginning of the creation**—from the very origin of things—**God,** the Creator, **made them male and female.** An exact quotation from Gen. 1 : 27, Septuagint. Verse 7 and half of verse 8 are exactly quoted from Gen. 2 : 24, Septuagint, though in Mark some manuscripts (and Tischendorf) omit **and cleave to his wife.**

This passage from the narrative of the Creation was cited to show that the distinction of sexes was originally constituted the ground of marriage. By this law marriage is the union of a male and a female of the human race; and it is such a union as shall form a new centre of life to both. For this cause—*i. e.* because he created them male and female—a man shall leave the parents, into natural unity with whom he was born, and find the centre for a new unity in his union with a fellow-being of the opposite sex. Thus the distinction of the sexes was given as the foundation of the family.—Now, the duration for which God intended this union may be inferred from his own testimony as to its closeness and completeness. This testimony Jesus now quotes—**and they twain shall be one flesh**—and then he adds his own emphatic restatement of the fact: so **then they are no more twain, but one flesh**—that is, the union that is founded on the relation of the sexes makes the two to be one flesh, makes each to be, physically, part and property of the other. Marriage has wrought

10 And in the house his disciples asked him again of the same *matter.*

11 And he saith unto them,* Whosoever shall put away his wife, and marry another, committeth adultery against her.

12 And if a woman shall put away her husband, and be married to another, she committeth adultery.

10 joined together, let not man put asunder. And in the house the disciples asked him again of this matter.

11 And he saith unto them, Whosoever shall put away his wife, and marry another, committeth adultery

12 against her: and if she herself shall put away her husband, and marry another, she committeth adultery.

a Matt. 5 : 32 ; 19 : 9 ; Luke 16 : 18 ; Rom. 7 : 3 ; 1 Cor. 7 : 10, 11.

an actual unity which is not to be broken. It is the union of one man and one woman, and the blending of life in sexual union establishes between that one man and that one woman a real unity. By establishing such a relation the Creator showed his intention that a union thus formed should be irrevocable and inviolable, to be legitimately terminated only by death.

In verse 9 is given the better precept that springs from this original order. The verb is in the aorist, not in the perfect; and the reference is not to special cases in which God **hath joined together** two given individuals, but to the original constitution of the race, in establishing which he **joined together** in permanent unity every pair who should ever come together in the union of sex with sex.—**What therefore God hath joined together, let not man put asunder.** That one flesh or one body (see 1 Cor. 6 : 16, where Paul expressly recognizes the truth that physical union establishes true and permanent unity) which has been formed in accordance with God's appointment in the creation of man, let not man put asunder.—Note the contrast between **God** and **man :** man may not break what God has made. Man may break this unity, either by personal unfaithfulness to the obligation of marriage or by contradictory enactments permitting dissolutions that God does not permit. Of the possible dissolution, for one cause, he speaks below.

This law of exclusive and permanent union was the original law of marriage; and this law Jesus reaffirms. But a lower law was given in that legislation which Jesus distinctly recognized as the work of God. Now, Jesus declares that that law was given because of the incapacity of men for this. He thus announces the imperfection of the Mosaic law—not only its incompleteness, but its imperfection—and asserts also its educational purpose. It was meant to train men for a better life than they could then accept. Accordingly, there was in the law a certain amount of what is called accommodation. "God often speaks and gives law, not as he himself is able to do, but as we are able to hear" (*Chrysostom, on Ps. 95*)—a sound principle, but always to be accompanied by this :

"When God thus speaks and gives law, it is in order that he may make us able to hear all that he is able to say to us." We need have no difficulty in admitting that God has dealt in rudimentary instruction, and, so far, in inferior instruction, if only we keep steadily in view his purpose of moral education for men.

10-12. Mark alone tells of the later inquiry of the disciples. In Matthew the address to the Pharisees is continued, with the solemn assertion that he who puts away his wife, except for fornication, and marries another commits adultery. In Mark "except for fornication" is omitted; but it is sufficiently implied. The statement in both Gospels is that a man is charged with adultery when he enters into a new sexual union while the first is still unbroken—*i. e.* when he breaks the exclusive unity of flesh with his wife by an act of union with another. Of course an equal union of sexes can be broken by either member; and so the "except for fornication" is implied clearly enough in principle in Mark. Verse 12, indeed, distinctly enforces the principle of equal responsibility. The custom to which it alludes, of the wife putting away the husband, was a custom, not of Jews, but of Romans and of other Gentiles. Possibly Jesus saw that there was danger, under Roman influence, of its coming in among the Jews.—Here, in verses 11, 12, is our Lord's own answer to the original question, whether a man might put away his wife. It is, "No, unless she has already broken her unity with him." Sexual unfaithfulness forfeits the bond, but nothing else does.

The teaching of this passage is strong and conclusive for all who acknowledge the authority of Jesus Christ. The inviolability of marriage is grounded, not in any principles of expediency or advantage, right as these might be, but in its correspondence to the constitution of man as male and female. The sexual element in marriage makes of the two one flesh—*i. e.* it was meant that sexual union should be inseparable from permanent personal unity—and only by sexual unfaithfulness can the unity, once established, be broken. This is not to affirm that sexual unfaithfulness is necessarily more guilty than any other sin—a life-

13 *And* they brought young children to him, that he should touch them: and *his* disciples rebuked those that brought *them*.

14 But when Jesus saw *it*, he was much[b] displeased, and said unto them, Suffer the little children to come unto me, and forbid them not, for of such is the kingdom of God.[c]

15 Verily I say unto you, Whosoever shall not receive the kingdom of God as a little child, he shall not enter therein.

13 And they were bringing unto him little children, that he should touch them: and the disciples rebuked them. But when Jesus saw it, he was moved

14 with indignation, and said unto them, Suffer the little children to come unto me; forbid them not:

15 for to such belongeth the kingdom of God. Verily I say unto you, Whosoever shall not receive the kingdom of God as a little child, he shall in no wise

a Matt. 19 : 13 ; Luke 18 : 15....*b* Eph. 4 : 26....*c* Matt. 18 : 10; 1 Cor. 14 : 20; 1 Pet. 2 : 2; Rev. 14 : 5.——1 Or, *of such is*

long course of drunkenness and abuse may be as guilty—but the sexual relation is the groundwork of the family, and its purity is absolutely essential to the physical and moral welfare of mankind. With good reason, therefore, God has made faithfulness in this relation the determining element in the perpetuity of marriage. To this divine appointment human laws should be made to correspond. Separations for other causes than adultery there may be, but dissolution of marriage, never. If it is said that such a law works hardship in many cases, the answer is that all laws that are for the general good sometimes work hardship while sin continues. But the purity and the permanency of the family are worth so much to mankind that individuals may well afford to suffer hardship rather than contribute to the overthrow of so precious an institution.

13–16. JESUS BLESSES LITTLE CHILDREN. *Parallels*, Matt. 19 : 13-15; Luke 18 : 15-17.—Three records, closely similar, but each with characteristic additions. No one of them would we willingly spare. The scene is still in some unknown place in Perea.

13. If the record in this chapter is strictly continuous, this event occurred **in the house** (verse 10), and before the going **forth into the way** of verse 17. But of this we cannot be perfectly sure. The little children are called by Luke "infants." We are left to conjecture as to their number—which probably was not large—and to infer that they were brought by their parents. The motive may not have been the most intelligent; possibly there was some idea of a magical value in his touch. Matthew alone goes beyond the request that he would touch them to say that he was asked to put his hands on them and pray. But even if the request was an ignorant one and not of the highest order, it was an appeal to his heart, and he had no thought of putting it aside.—The interference of his disciples sprang from reverence for their Master, but it was not unmixed with contempt for the **young children.** What lack of sympathy with Jesus did it reveal! True reverence and contempt never go

together; least of all, reverence for Jesus and contempt for any who are simple and humble. Were the twelve unanimous? Can we not think there was one to plead for the children, as Reuben for Joseph? Was it partly the remembrance of this scene and of the rebuke he received that gave John his fondness for the title, "little children"?

14, 15. The description of the deep feeling of Jesus at the effort of his friends to keep the children back is peculiar to Mark. **He was much displeased.** The same word as in Matt. 21 : 15, where the chief priests and scribes were "sore displeased" at the children in the temple who were crying, "Hosanna to the Son of David!" A fine contrast between his spirit and theirs. No wonder that he was offended; for his friends were interfering to hold his heart back from its pleasure, and to prevent a richly characteristic act. He might have spoken again as at chap. 9 : 19, or almost as at 8 : 33. But the milder tone is more in harmony with the tender beauty of the scene. Luke adds that "Jesus called them to him," implying some such words as "Come, children," spoken to dispel the fear that the sour looks of the disciples may have awakened. Of him they were not afraid.—**Suffer the little children,** etc. The word **Suffer,** though now consecrated by use, has a formality and solemnity about it that his word did not possess. Literally translated, it is simply, "Let the little children come to me; forbid them not." A saying of inexhaustible sweetness. What a tribute to the true humanity of Jesus and to the heart of God that this saying should have been taken everywhere as characteristic of our Lord! All the world loves it, and feels tenderly toward him for giving it to us. It expresses, not merely his interest in the class whom the children suggest,—namely, the humble,—but his interest in the children themselves, because of their spiritual suggestiveness.—**For of such is the kingdom of heaven**—*i. e.* "These are such types as I love to look at of the spirit that belongs to the members of my kingdom. I welcome them, in their tenderness, simplicity,

15 And he took them up in his arms, put *his* hands upon them, and blessed them.

16 enter therein. And he took them in his arms, and blessed them, laying his hands upon them.

and trustfulness, as illustrations of the spirit into which men are to be brought by my renewing grace. For whoever (verse 15) is to enter into the kingdom must receive it in the simple, humble spirit of a little child. Into the kingdom of which I am King there is no other way." So Matt. 18 : 3. The secret of it is given in Matt. 11 : 29: "For I am meek and lowly in heart." (Compare John 3 : 3.) To be born again is to come to this: it is to be made a little child. He does not say that the children are in his kingdom; not, "of these is the kingdom of heaven." Membership in "the kingdom," strictly so called, as he was preaching it and as we must preach it, implies intelligence and personal faith. Here is no allusion to baptism; and here was his golden opportunity if he had wished baptism ever to be associated with infants. This is a case where we are justified in drawing a negative argument from the silence of the Scripture. Neither is there here any direct allusion to the salvation of infants. Yet it is impossible to see how he could have spoken so freely and joyfully over the little ones if he had been hampered by some theories about elect and non-elect infants that have burdened many of his followers.

16. A touch of solemn benediction was asked for; an embrace of personal tenderness was given (Eph. 3 : 20). The act is passed over by Luke and barely mentioned by Matthew; by Mark it is described with a lingering delight. Literally, "Taking them in his arms, he blessed them, putting his hands upon them." The word for **blessed** (*kateulogei*) is a strong compound word used here alone in the New Testament. It is more expressive of fervent intercession for the little children than the ordinary word. In the embrace, the laying on of his hands, and the prayer for them his heart went warmly out. His prayer must have been a request that in their years of responsibility they might still have the spirit that made them so lovely in his eyes—the childlike spirit that would receive the kingdom of God.—The tender happiness of Jesus in this scene is too plain to be overlooked. It is so plain as to make us instinctively reject the old idea that he was "oft known to weep, but never known to smile." He must have smiled on the children, who did not fear to come to **his arms**. He was so tenderly happy in the scene, perhaps, partly because it was like a ray of light in the deepening darkness. Men were rejecting him, but here was frank and joyful trust in him, even if it

were but for a moment. The trustful touch of the little hands was to him like a cup of cold water when he was weary. To these little children it was given to do what prophets and kings might well have been thankful to be allowed to do: they refreshed the spirit of the Saviour on the way to the cross.—What became of them? It is hard to think of them as perishing among the blasphemers at the fall of Jerusalem. Were they not rather, if they lived to see that time, among the Christians who "fled to the mountains" at their Lord's command, and were preserved for further service in his kingdom? Could they escape the remembrance of his prayer and grow up in unbelief?

17-31. THE RICH YOUNG MAN. *Parallels*, Matt. 19: 16-30; Luke 18: 18-30.—Mark, as usual, makes the picture most complete, though it is Matthew that tells us that the man was young, and Luke that he was a ruler—*i. e.*, probably, of the synagogue, the name not being entirely decisive, as is that which is given to Jairus in chap. 5 : 22. Mark alone tells us that the interview took place **when he was gone forth into the way,** and shows us the picture of his earnestness in **running** to meet or overtake Jesus and kneeling before him. Jesus was already departing, and he made haste with his question ere he should be gone. The grouping is very significant here. In all three Gospels this striking example of the failure to attain the childlike spirit immediately follows the scene with the little children.

Can we ascertain who this young man was? No name is given him, but is there anything to warrant and guide conjecture? The only conjecture worth mentioning is that of Dr. Plumptre, in Smith's *Dictionary of the Bible* (Art. "Lazarus"), that he was Lazarus of Bethany. At the outset this would require a different chronological arrangement from that which is given above; but some harmonists, as Dr. Thomson, in Smith's *Dictionary*, adopt an order that admits of this conjecture. In any view, the order is not so certain in this period that we need be disturbed at any proposals of change. As for this conjecture, it can never pass into certainty; but the present writer's experience is that the longer it remains in the mind the more probable does it appear. (1) He is nameless in the record. So are Martha and Mary in the synoptical Gospels, except as they are mentioned in Luke 10 : 38-42, where there is nothing to connect them with Bethany or with any other part of the Gospel narrative. Mary appears in the anointing

17 ⁣And⁣ when he was gone forth into the way, there came one running, and kneeled to him, and asked him, Good Master, what shall I do that I may inherit eternal life?

18 And Jesus said unto him, Why callest thou me good? There is none good but one,ᵇ that is, God.

17 And as he was going forth into the way, there ran one to him, and kneeled to him, and asked him, Good ²Master, what shall I do that I may inherit eternal life? 18 And Jesus said unto him, Why callest thou

---

a Matt. 19 : 16; Luke 18 : 18....*b* Ps. 86 : 5; 119 : 68.——1 Or, *on his way*....2 Or, *Teacher*

(Matt. 26 : 7; Mark 14 : 3) simply as "a woman." The raising of Lazarus, with all that could suggest it, was kept out of sight by the synoptists, evidently of set purpose; and not until John wrote was the concealment removed. If Lazarus were to be mentioned by the synoptists, it would probably be in some such way as this. (2) The young man was rich, and the family at Bethany is proved, by the story of the alabaster box of ointment, to have been of the wealthier class. (3) He had high Jewish standing and connexions. He was a ruler—at least, of the synagogue, and possibly of something higher. He may have been a member of the Sanhedrin. After the death of Lazarus "many of the Jews came to Martha and Mary, to comfort them concerning their brother." With John "the Jews" are always the ruling class, the religious leaders. The family at Bethany therefore had social relations with many of this class, as they would have if one of their number were a "ruler," in either sense. (4) The young man was evidently a Pharisee, and the conversation of Martha after the death of her brother indicates that she had been taught as a Pharisee. (5) The only special hint of personal relations between Jesus and Lazarus is found in the words, "Lord, behold, he whom thou lovest is sick." The only man of whom it is said that Jesus loved him, apart from the circle of the apostles, is this rich young man. The fact that **Jesus beholding him loved him** would certainly, if the young man was Lazarus, reach his sisters and touch their hearts, and might most naturally be taken up by them as an appeal to Jesus when they wished him to come and save their brother's life. If the young man was not Lazarus, he was some one who was situated in life much as Lazarus was; and the coincidences are such as to render the identification at least considerably plausible. It should be remembered that there is evidence of only one visit to the house in Bethany before this time. The signs of intimacy there belong to the closing period of our Lord's life.

17. Good Master, what shall I do that I may inherit eternal life? The question is identical in Mark with that of the lawyer at Luke 10 : 25. In Matthew the young man proposes to himself the doing of some "good

thing." The question is that of Pharisaism. It does not confess any inability or weakness with respect to good, but rather assumes full power and seeks for guidance only in the selection of a course of conduct. The idea of doing something, in order to gain, and even to inherit, life had full possession of the young man's mind, as we might expect from his Pharisaism. The need of doing good works, and full confidence in his own power and willingness to do any needful good work, these are the striking points of the question. Yet a Pharisee must have been touched by an unwonted influence before he would come running to Jesus with this inquiry, addressing him as "Rabbi," and especially as "Good Rabbi," a title unknown among the Jews, and framed by him to suit his thought (*Farrar*, 2. 166, note). The man must have felt that this Rabbi was indeed good and able to teach him concerning the good that he would gladly do.

18. In the answer there is no emphasis on either **thou** or **me.** It is not, **Why callest thou me good?** as if he would say, "What, from your point of view, can such a title mean?" It is not, **Why callest thou me good?** as if he would say, "Why single me out to receive this title?" "Why do you call me good?" read in the ordinary way, exactly represents the answer, and the emphatic word is **good.** In Matthew the true reading of the reply is different, and Jesus asks, "Why askest thou me concerning the good?" Here, though the reference is to the question the man had asked rather than to the title he had employed, the effect is the same in calling his attention to the word **good** and the idea of goodness. In both, his thoughts are called away at once from himself and from the Rabbi whom he is consulting to the word he has used and the true way to find a definition of it. "What of that word 'good'? Do you understand it? Do you know where you must look for a true idea of goodness? No one is good but God alone. You are talking of higher things than you suppose, and you must look up to him for your standard before you can talk or act intelligently about goodness." In this view, our Lord does not disclaim the title **Good,** but rather ignores it as applied to himself, and asserts that the word can never be understood

19 Thou knowest the commandments, Do not commit adultery, Do not kill, Do not steal, Do not bear false witness, Defraud not, Honor thy father and mother.

20 And he answered and said unto him, Master, all these have I observed from my youth.

21 Then Jesus beholding him, loved him, and said unto him, One thing thou lackest: go thy way, sell whatsoever thou hast, and give to the poor, and thou shalt have treasure in heaven: and come, take up the cross, and follow me.

19 me good? none is good save one, even God. Thou knowest the commandments, Do not kill, Do not commit adultery, Do not steal, Do not bear false witness, Do not defraud, Honor thy father and mother.

20 And he said unto him, Master, all these things 21 have I observed from my youth. And Jesus looking upon him loved him, and said unto him, One thing thou lackest: go, sell whatsoever thou hast, and give to the poor, and thou shalt have treasure

a Ex. 20. Rom. 13:9....*b* Isa. 58:2; Ezek. 33:31, 32; Mal. 3:8; Rom. 7:9; Phil. 3:6....*c* James 2:10....*d* Matt. 6:19, 20; Luke 12:33; 16:9.——1 Or, *Teacher*

until one has learned to define it through the knowledge of God. His purpose is to awaken in the man a sense of the inadequacy of his own conceptions; and this he seeks to do by leading him to lift his eyes to the Perfect Goodness.—Our Lord did not disclaim the title; yet we need not have been troubled if by saying, "God alone is good," he had meant, "That title is not for me." He spoke always in human relations—not, indeed, "as man" any more than "as God:" both phrases are wrong; but there was no word upon his lips that did not become the position and standing of a man; and the humility that would disclaim the title **Good** in such a connection as this would argue nothing against either his divinity or his sinlessness.

19. But as for counsel respecting the attainment of life he refers (as in verse 3) to the existing authority, the law under which the man is living. This authority, he says, is already known. **Thou knowest the commandments.** The parts of the law that he cites are from the second table of the Decalogue, and relate to the duty of man to man. Mark alone adds **Defraud not,** which is not, like the other commands, in the Decalogue. Perhaps it may have been meant as a special application, in a rich man's case, of the tenth commandment, "Thou shalt not covet;" as if Jesus would lead him to inquire whether all his wealth had been acquired without defrauding. Matthew inserts instead of it, as a solemn close, "Thou shalt love thy neighbor as thyself." Whether Mark's **Defraud not** is an interpretation of the tenth commandment or an interpolation of a command from elsewhere in Scripture to the midst of the Decalogue, it is a very remarkable instance of free use of Old-Testament language by New-Testament writers, and by our Lord himself. One would think that if exact quotation were to be found anywhere, it would be in the use of the Decalogue by Jewish writers and by our Lord. Yet here is a striking neglect to quote with precision.

20. Master ("Rabbi")—not, again, "Good" (*Meyer*)—**all these have I observed from my youth.** He had not yet found his answer; he was still perplexed at being told to do what he supposed he had always been doing. Was this self-praise? Perhaps not, consciously; it was rather the consciousness of integrity according to an outward law. Judaism was full of that consciousness, sometimes shallow and self-righteous and sometimes devout. But had the young man ever observed the commandments with the full conviction that God alone is good, and with the deep humility and spirituality which that thought should bring? No; and he did not yet comprehend the difference, though he longed for the better thing. Here is the record of a moral and outwardly religious life, with the cry of the soul for something more and the pathetic demand to know what that something is: "What lack I yet?" (Matthew). Compare and contrast his inquiries with the questions in Acts 2:37 and 16:30.

21. Jesus beholding him, loved him. Not merely beholding, but looking with a fixed and earnest gaze, which the beholders did not forget. This exquisite touch of remembrance is peculiar to Mark. The gaze revealed a genuine love, of which the young man must have been aware, and which made itself manifest also to the disciples. Perhaps some word or act completed the expression. There is no need of perplexing ourselves as to the effect of the love on the man's destiny, or of bringing the love into theological relations. Let the story remain sweet and simple. It is enough to say that the heart of Jesus lovingly yearned over the young man in his sincere though Pharisaic seeking after good. If the young man was Lazarus, the remembrance of the love attached itself to his name.—Love is always kind, especially his love, but this time it was severe: severity was kindness. This command was the true utterance of love. **One thing thou lackest.** He does not say one thing alone, but one he mentions. The similarity of this language to that of his quiet rebuke to Martha has been noticed by those who here have Lazarus in mind (Luke 10:42).—The command is twofold, looking

22 And he was sad at that saying, and went away grieved; for he had great possessions.
23 ⸃ And Jesus looked round about, and saith unto his disciples, How hardly shall they that have riches enter into the kingdom of God!
24 And the disciples were astonished at his words. But Jesus answereth again, and saith unto them, Children, how hard is it for them that trust[a] in riches to enter into the kingdom of God!

22 in heaven: and come, follow me. But his countenance fell at the saying, and he went away sorrowful: for he was one that had great possessions.
23 And Jesus looked round about, and saith unto his disciples, How hardly shall they that have riches 24 enter into the kingdom of God! And the disciples were amazed at his words. But Jesus answereth again, and saith unto them, Children, how hard is it [b]for them that trust in riches to enter into the

a Job 31 : 24; Ps. 52 : 7 ; 62 : 10 ; Hab. 2 : 9 ; 1 Tim. 6 : 17 ; Rev. 3 : 17.——1 Some ancient authorities omit *for them that trust in riches.*

back and looking forward; and both parts are intended to reveal to the man whether or not he has a heart for the good. The first part, **sell whatsoever thou hast,** etc., enjoins the breaking off of his old life by an act of extreme self-sacrifice and of genuine usefulness. It was an act, too, that lay directly in the line of his own principles; for almsgiving was great in the esteem of all devout Jews. Only this would be an extreme, self-emptying act that would scatter his worldly store and destroy his pride as a rich man.—Yet there was encouragement. **Thou shalt have treasure in heaven.** The blessing of God on a right deed. (Compare Matt. 6 : 19, 20; 1 Tim. 6 : 17-19; Ps. 112 : 9; and especially Luke 12 : 33.)—The second part, **come, . . . follow me** (the revisers omit, on good authority, **take up the cross**), directs the man to set out in a new life, the life of a disciple. The whole is, "Deny yourself of what you now possess, devote it to doing good, and then join yourself to me." It often seems as if this command were in direct contrast with the characteristic words, "Come unto me, all ye that labor and are heavy laden, and I will give you rest;" but it is not, for this command only points out what it will be for this man, heavy laden with his peculiar burdens, to come and learn of him who is meek and lowly in heart. This is no arbitrary test. The requirement, taken in connection with the man's question, means, "Do you know and love the good well enough to devote to it your wealth and your life?" To obey the command of Jesus would be this man's short course to rest for his soul.

22. The descriptive word **sad,** used in Mark alone, is translated "lowering" in the only other place in the New Testament where it is found (Matt. 16 : 3). No doubt it was chosen in vivid remembrance of the lowering look upon his sad countenance.—He **went away grieved** (Luke, "very sorrowful," as in Mark 6 : 26 and 14 : 34); **for he had great possessions.** For the time at least love was too severe for him, and the good was too exacting. He was an illustration of Luke 2 : 34, 35. Jesus was set for his fall—perhaps also for his rising—but at present the

thoughts of his heart were revealed as the thoughts of a man who was not "fit for the kingdom" (Luke 9 : 62). He was proposing to put his hand to the plough, but he was looking back to the things that were behind. He could count himself a man and keep the commandments in a fair life, but he could not become a little child. Yet we cannot but be glad that he was sorrowful: if he had gone recklessly away, we should have had no hope of him.

23. Now again the deliberate look of Jesus round the whole circle of his disciples, gazing into each face, impressed itself on the memory of Mark's informant. His saying, **How hardly—i. e.** with what difficulty—**shall they that have riches enter into the kingdom of God!** is amply confirmed by experience. Christian men often become rich, but rich men rarely become Christians. The reason is not far to seek: the process of gaining wealth encourages self-seeking, and the possession of it encourages self-importance; but the spirit that can enter the kingdom is the spirit of a little child.

24. This remarkable verse is peculiar to Mark. The astonishment of the disciples was natural, with their ideas of the kingdom. "Hard for rich men! What can he mean?" All the splendid imagery of the prophets (as in Isa. 60) might rise in their minds to contradict him; and the idea of delivering Israel from oppression by a kingdom that rich men could scarcely enter must have seemed to them absurd. But Jesus solemnly repeated his hard saying; yet his mood was tender, as his word **Children** shows, here alone addressed to them. ("Little children," in John 13 : 33.)—According to the common reading, the repetition of the saying explains and softens it by the modification, **How hard is it for them that trust in riches to enter.** But there seems sufficient reason to accept the reading of ancient manuscripts by which the words **for them that trust in riches** are omitted. In that case the repetition of the saying removes it from the special case of rich men and applies the sentiment more widely: **Children, how hard it is to enter into the kingdom of God!**

25 It is easier for a camel to go through the eye of a needle, than for a rich man to enter into the kingdom of God.
26 And they were astonished out of measure, saying among themselves, Who then can be saved?
27 And Jesus looking upon them, saith, With men *it is* impossible, but not with God: for* with God all things are possible.
28 *ᵃ* Then Peter began to say unto him, Lo, we have left all, and have followed thee.
29 And Jesus answered and said, Verily I say unto you, There is no man that hath left house, or brethren, or sisters, or father, or mother, or wife, or children, or lands, for my sake, and the gospel's,
30 But he shall receive an hundred-fold now in this time, houses, and brethren, and sisters, and mothers, and children, and lands, with persecutions; and in the world to come eternal life.

25 kingdom of God! It is easier for a camel to go through a needle's eye, than for a rich man to enter 26 into the kingdom of God. And they were astonished exceedingly, saying ᵗunto him, Then who can 27 be saved? Jesus looking upon them saith, With men it is impossible, but not with God: for all things are 28 possible with God. Peter began to say unto him, Lo, 29 we have left all, and have followed thee. Jesus said, Verily I say unto you, There is no man that hath left house, or brethren, or sisters, or mother, or father, or children, or lands, for my sake, and for 30 the gospel's sake, but he shall receive a hundredfold now in this time, houses, and brethren, and sisters, and mothers, and children, and lands, with persecu-

a Gen. 18 : 14; Job 42 : 2; Jer. 32 : 17; Luke 1 : 37.——ᵗ Many ancient authorities read *among themselves.*

Plainly, such a remark was a natural outcome of the incident, for it was not chiefly his riches, but his heart, that sent the man away sorrowful, and a like heart is in all men. To all men, therefore, rich or poor, it is by nature **hard to enter into the kingdom of God**—hard in itself, since sin is what it is.—Let us not be afraid that such a text will prove too discouraging. It is better to know things as they are; and perhaps the doctrine of free grace has been so used as to lead to an untrue idea of the easiness of salvation.

25. It is easier for a camel to go through the eye of a needle. This comparison may have been proverbial, as the Talmud contains, at a later date, a closely similar saying. The Koran exactly reproduces it from the New Testament. As for the popular explanation—that the small gate in the city wall, too narrow for a camel to pass through, was called the needle's eye—there is no sufficient evidence of the antiquity of such a use of the name. The comparison needs no special explanation; it is a strong way of representing impossibility: " It is so hard for sinful men, rich or poor, to enter the kingdom, that for a rich man—one who is especially involved in the unchildlike habits of the world—to enter is harder than for a camel to go through a needle's eye." This is no contradiction of any gracious and winning Scripture. It is the Saviour's emphatic statement of a fact, parallel to Luke 13 : 24 and 14 : 26–33, and to many other of his words.

26, 27. Astonished before; **astonished out of measure** now.—The inquiry was **among themselves,** a whispering of amazement. **Who then can be saved?** With such a standard, how would the kingdom receive any one? For was not the love of money everywhere? and how could the kingdom live, with a law so strict?—**Jesus looking upon them.** Again Peter remembered his look. The word, both here and in verse 21, is the

same as in Luke 22 : 61: " The Lord turned and looked on Peter."—**With men it is impossible.** Not now difficult, but more. On human principles or by any power of man it cannot be done; the proud man cannot be brought into the kingdom of the humble, or the worldly-minded rich man into the kingdom of the poor in spirit. So in John 3 : 3: " Except a man be born again, he cannot see the kingdom of God."—**But not with God: for with God all things are possible.** He can make new creatures of men; he can impart the spirit of the kingdom. He has command, too, of all means, earthly and heavenly. So he can bring into his kingdom men who are spiritually incompatible with it. (See 1 Tim. 1 : 12–17; 1 Cor. 15 : 9, 10.) The implication is that, even though this case looks so hopeless, God can yet find means of bringing the unwilling rich man to a better mind. In his hands are even life and death.

28. Peter, as usual, speaks for them all, saying, in substance, " We have done what this man would not: we have accepted the kingdom on the right terms at personal sacrifice." The question, " What shall we have, therefore?" added in Matthew, is plainly implied here and in Luke. Here is a frank statement of self-seeking, even in self-renunciation; self-denial in the hope of direct returns. The apostles were still hoping that their special honors in the kingdom would make amends for everything. Yet in the words of Peter now there may be a tone of despair, in view of the depression of their prospects implied in the words just spoken: " What shall we have, what amends, if the kingdom is to be of this exacting and unambitious kind?" No concealment anywhere of the low spiritual tone of the disciples.

29, 30. How tender and wise the answer! There is no distinct rebuke, but there is a silent one in the fact that the promise is made,

31 But^a many *that are* first shall be last; and the last first.

32 ¶ And^b they were in the way going up to Jerusalem; and Jesus went before them; and they were amazed; and as they followed, they were afraid. And he took again the twelve, and began to tell them what things should happen unto him.

31 tions; and in the ¹world to come eternal life. But many *that are* first shall be last; and the last first.

32 And they were in the way, going up to Jerusalem; and Jesus was going before them: and they were amazed; and they that followed were afraid. And he took again the twelve, and began to tell them the

not to the apostles only, but to all who make such sacrifices as they speak of. Apostles have no exclusive claim, nor even an assurance of pre-eminence in this respect. The rewards of the kingdom are for all the faithful, all who, **for my sake, and the gospel's,** have forsaken what they held dear. Note the true suggestion—that the forsaking must be for a person and for a principle. Jesus wishes not to be regarded apart from the gospel, nor can the gospel be regarded as a true object of sacrifice apart from Jesus. So in chap. 8 : 38. The promise seems to mean (for of course the promise of multiplication of goods cannot be taken literally) that all good that is given up for Christ shall be immeasurably more precious to the soul for the surrender. It shall be given back to the soul, if not to the hands, enhanced a hundred-fold in value. It may be given back to the hands—*i. e.* sacrifices may be required in spirit that are not called for in the course of divine providence—and in that case the hundred-fold of new preciousness is always found. But to the soul all that is given up for Christ shall be returned, and thus graciously multiplied. (The possible thoughts of the lad who gave up his loaves and fishes, John 6 : 9.) The principle of self-sacrifice sweetens life instead of embittering it, and the experience of self-denial surprises the soul with unthought-of wealth. So much at present; and in the age that is coming, with its full spiritual rewards, eternal life. So 1 Tim. 4 : 8.—But the warning lies in the solemn reservation, preserved by Mark alone. **With persecutions.** No easy way leads to these honors and rewards (2 Tim. 3 : 12; 2 Cor. 11 : 23-27; 6 : 4-10). Even when outward persecution is not, still the principle is the same: it is no easy way.—The **hundred-fold** will not prevent the persecutions; but neither will the persecutions interfere with the coming of the hundred-fold.

31. A wise caution. "The judgment of God is according to truth," and rank will finally be determined by true judgment and not according to present appearances. Let no man boast; even the rich young man who has gone away sorrowful may possibly yet outrank the apostles. Here, according to Matthew, our Lord

adds the parable of the Laborers (Matt. 20 : 1-16) to illustrate the solemn warning, **many that are first shall be last; and the last first,** to which, at the end of the parable, he returns. The rich young man we see no more, unless under his proper name. Those who think that he may have been Lazarus suggest that his sickness, death, and resurrection, or some part of that great experience, may have been used by God, to whom all things are possible, in bringing him to the spirit of the kingdom. Whoever he may have been, we cannot suppress the hope that he who is said to have loved him did not leave him to himself.

32-34. ON THE JOURNEY JESUS AGAIN FORETELLS HIS DEATH AND RESURRECTION. *Parallels,* Matt. 20 : 17-19; Luke 18 : 31-34.

32. Scarcely do we possess a more impressive portrait of our Lord in action than this, which is drawn for us by Mark alone. The verbs in the first sentence are in the imperfect tense, and might denote that this was a picture of him as he habitually was during that journey; but the connection makes it more probable that they are meant to represent him as he was at the moment when, for reasons that are suggested here, he took his disciples aside and spoke to them. They were **in the way,** and he was going **before them,** walking on in silence in advance of the company. The apostles were near him, and others, probably many, followed. The effect is thus told, as in the Revision: "And they were amazed; and they that followed were afraid." Astonishment seized upon the disciples, and the multitude behind them were stricken with awe and fear. No hint is given of the reason for this; the portrait is not drawn, after all, but only suggested. Yet we cannot be in doubt; it was something in the appearance and manner of Jesus that filled friends and strangers with this solemnity. It must have been the preoccupied, solemn, and determined look with which he was silently pressing on to death. Peter remembered it well, but perhaps he shrank from attempting to describe it, except by its effects. Jesus was consciously pressing forward into the **persecutions,** and he went with his might. All

33 *Saying,* Behold, we^a go up to Jerusalem; and the Son of man shall be delivered unto the chief priests, and unto the scribes, and they shall condemn him to death, and shall deliver him to the Gentiles;

34 And^b they shall mock him, and shall scourge him, and shall spit upon him, and shall kill him: and the third day he shall rise again.

35 ¶ And James and John, the sons of Zebedee, come unto him, saying, Master, we would that thou shouldest do for us whatsoever we shall desire.

36 And he said unto them, What would ye that I should do for you?

37 They said unto him, Grant unto us that we may sit, one on thy right hand, and the other on thy left hand, in thy glory.

33 things that were to happen unto him, *saying,* Behold, we go up to Jerusalem; and the Son of man shall be delivered unto the chief priests and the scribes; and they shall condemn him to death, and shall deliver

34 him unto the Gentiles; and they shall mock him, and shall spit upon him, and shall scourge him, and shall kill him; and after three days he shall rise again.

35 And there come near unto him James and John, the sons of Zebedee, saying unto him, ¹Master, we would that thou shouldest do for us whatsoever we

36 shall ask of thee. And he said unto them, What

37 would ye that I should do for you? And they said unto him, Grant unto us that we may sit, one on thy right hand, and one on *thy* left hand, in thy glory.

a Acts 20 : 22 ... *b* Ps. 22 : 6, 7, 13.——1 Or, *Teacher*

that he commands us he himself has done, and the highest ambition for man is "so to walk even as he walked." To do that may sometimes be to press bravely into the sorrows of the kingdom, as he did. The fear of the followers indicates that they felt the shadow of his dark future falling upon them and shrank from going into it.—**He took again the twelve**—gathered them close about him—**and began to tell them,** having walked till then in silence, **what things should happen unto him at Jerusalem.**

33, 34. The most elaborate of his predictions of the Passion. A new element appears for the first time, the delivering **to the Gentiles,** which enters here into all three of the reports. The details of his Passion, too, are more minutely drawn than before. The resurrection, as before, is barely announced; he never enlarged upon it as he here does on his sufferings. Was this human foresight or divine foreknowledge? The question need not trouble us. It was both: he foreknew it, and he foresaw it—foreknew it from the standpoint of his divine mission, and foresaw it none the less clearly as an interpreter of human events. —It is added in Luke that "they understood none of these things," the old slowness to take his meaning being still upon them. In this failure to understand the prediction, coupled with the "fear" just mentioned, we have a glimpse of their mixed feeling, doubtless full of foreboding, and yet unable to take in the true sense of the coming evil.

35-45. THE AMBITION OF JAMES AND JOHN REPROVED. *Parallel.* Matt. 20 : 20-28. —Here is a living illustration of the slowness of the disciples to understand, not so much some special words as the Lord himself. Apparently, these two thought their Master's depression was but temporary. Is it possible that they even wished to reassure him and refresh his mind by turning his thoughts to the glory to which they were sure he was advancing?

James and John, the sons of Zebedee. They were among the earliest disciples, John having been, with Andrew, one of the first who followed Jesus (John 1 : 36-40), and James having probably been brought by John to Jesus on that same day (John 1 : 41, where the form of expression in the Greek implies that, though Andrew was the first to find his brother, Simon, and bring him to Jesus, John also quickly found his brother, James, and brought him too). James and John were two of the three nearest to Jesus. (See chap. 9 : 2, etc.) In Matthew the request at this time comes from their mother, whose name was Salome (compare Matt. 27 : 56 with Mark 15 : 40), and who was probably the sister of Mary, the mother of Jesus. (See note on Mark 3 : 17.) The request was probably suggested by the words just spoken, and recorded only by Matthew (19 : 28): "When the Son of man shall sit in the throne of his glory, ye also shall sit upon twelve thrones, judging the twelve tribes of Israel." Of course they took this literally, or nearly so; and now the two disciples, or their mother for them, came asking for the two thrones nearest to the King himself. Their personal nearness to him in the apostleship and the early date of their following may have emboldened them to this; and if they were first-cousins to him, as seems probable, this would be another reason for expecting a favorable answer.—Yet, as if they feared failure, they would try, with a genuine human impulse, to pledge the answer in advance. **We would that thou shouldest do for us whatsoever we shall desire,** or, rather, "ask." He gave no pledge, but asked for their request; when, behold, in spite of all that he had said, now of death and before (chap. 9 : 35) of humility, it was the most ambitious request that could be made—a request for the two chief thrones.

38. Personal loyalty was at the bottom of the desire: they had cast in their lot with him and with him they desired to have their portion. Yet it was a childish desire, an ambition

38 But Jesus said unto them, Ye^a know not what ye ask. Can ye drink of the cup that I drink of? and be baptized with the baptism^b that I am baptized with? 39 And they say unto him, We can. And Jesus said unto them, Ye^c shall indeed drink of the cup^d that I drink of: and with the baptism that I am baptized withal, shall ye be baptized: 40 But to sit on my right hand and on my left hand, is not mine to give; but *it shall be given to them for whom it is prepared.*^e

38 But Jesus said unto them, Ye know not what ye ask. Are ye able to drink the cup that I drink? or to be baptized with the baptism that I am baptized with? 39 And they said unto him, We are able. And Jesus said unto them, The cup that I drink ye shall drink; and with the baptism that I am baptized withal shall 40 ye be baptized: but to sit on my right hand or on *my* left hand is not mine to give: but *it is for them* for

---

a James 4 : 3... *b* Luke 12 : 50....*c* Matt. 10 : 25; John 17 : 14....*d* ch. 14 : 36....*e* Matt. 25 : 34; Heb. 11 : 16.

---

for the end in profound ignorance of the way. —**Ye know not what ye ask.** It is like the reply of a father to foolish children. When addressed to men—ambitious men—how humiliating! yet in this case how searchingly appropriate! It is not less appropriate with reference to many of our requests to our Heavenly Father; for often do we pray for the end in ignorance of the way, and often when the way would be by no means acceptable to us.—The principle of his rejoinder is that of Matt. 10 : 24: "The disciple is not above his master." There is but one way to all the thrones, the way the King has taken.—**Can ye drink** (not "drink of") **the cup that I drink**—*i. e.* which I have to drink, and in spirit am already drinking, the cup of utter self-sacrifice, even unto martyrdom. He drinks the cup, he does not merely drink of it; and he proposes the same to them.—**And be baptized with the baptism that I am baptized with?** "that I am already in spirit enduring?" Another simile for the coming death, omitted by Matthew. The baptism is the overwhelming in pain and death; the woe is to come like the rushing of the water over the body of one whom John plunged in the Jordan. Perhaps he could not have found, within the range of their common thoughts, a stronger simile for his purpose; but he seems to have chosen it partly, also, because it was a sacred simile, the sanctity of baptism having given to the form a suggestive character that made it especially suitable for his use. When it comes to this symbolic use of the word, no one doubts that the act which forms the basis of the symbolism is a complete immersion.—The two questions mean the same, and the thought is, "You ask for thrones: can you die, and in spirit suffer death before death, as I do? Can you take up the cross and come after me, and go to the throne by the way that I take?"

39. Their unqualified **We can** contained both good and evil. They knew that they were attached to Jesus, and it was their loyal hearts that spoke. But they knew not themselves, and spoke in ignorant assurance. The third of the special three put himself similarly on record (Luke 22 : 33); so that Peter, James, and John are the men to whom we owe the most remarkable utterances of the confidence that is easy to an ignorant heart. Yet the **We can** of James and John and the profession of Peter came true in later times, when they had learned the secret of their Master more deeply. Their claims of victory were premature, but their hearts already had the secret of future victory.

The kindness of the answer is something wonderful. There is no tone or spirit of rebuke in it, although there was so much room for reproof. On the surface it is a denial of the request—at least, it would put an end to all exclusive expectations. Yet the prediction **Ye shall indeed drink the cup that I drink** is really a promise of all that is precious in what they asked for. If he could truthfully say, "Ye shall suffer in my spirit," the thrones were assured, though no promise was given of the special ones that were ambitiously chosen. "To him that overcometh will I grant to sit with me in my throne" (Rev. 3 : 21). This prediction scarcely amounts to an announcement of martyrdom for each of the two brothers; it might be fulfilled by life in the martyr's spirit. But James drank that cup (Acts 12 : 2) and John suffered, if he did not die (Rev. 1 : 9). Both attained to high seats at the Master's side, but thrones how unlike all that they were thinking of! and by a way how different from all that they expected! In both aspects was the answer true, that they knew not what they asked. The real thrones were more glorious than they thought, and the way was such as they knew not.

40. The remainder of the answer surprises us; for, instead of giving them some reason why they must beware of looking too high or expecting too much, he disclaims the power to grant their request. **To sit on my right hand and on my left hand is not mine to give:** "but it is for them for whom it hath been prepared." So, correctly, in the Revision. Matthew adds "by my Father."—**But** (*alla*) is not equivalent to "except;" as if he had said, "It is not mine to give, except to those for whom

41 And when the ten heard *it*, they began to be much displeased with James and John.

42 But Jesus called them *to him*, and saith unto them, Ye* know that they which are accounted to rule over the Gentiles exercise lordship over them; and their great ones exercise authority upon them.

43 But so shall it not be among you; but[b] whosoever will be great among you, shall be your minister:

44 And whosoever of you will be the chiefest, shall be servant of all.

41 whom it hath been prepared. And when the ten heard it, they began to be moved with indignation

42 concerning James and John. And Jesus called them to him, and saith unto them, Ye know that they who are accounted to rule over the Gentiles lord it over them; and their great ones exercise authority over

43 them. But it is not so among you: but whosoever would become great among you, shall be your 1min-

44 ister: and whosoever would be first among you, shall

a Luke 22 : 25....*b* ch. 9 . 35; Matt. 20 : 26, 28; Luke 9 : 48.———1 Or, *servant*

it hath been prepared." Such a translation, though sometimes proposed, is inadmissible. Two statements are here—that the assignment of the highest rank is the prerogative of the Father, which reminds one of the language of Mark 13 : 32, and that the highest rank shall be assigned by him to those for whom it has been prepared. But who are they for whom the highest rank has been prepared by the Father? (See verses 42–44.) They are the disciples who are most like the Master. The nearest thrones are prepared for the truest followers, just as the crown is prepared for the successful contestant (1 Cor. 9 : 24). Here, again, the last may be the first, and even the chief apostles cannot be sure that some servant of humbler name may not at the end be above them.

41. The ten—the remainder of the apostolic band—**began to be much displeased with James and John.** Began, but were soon interrupted and brought to account by the Master.—**Displeased.** The same word as in verse 14. Why displeased? Had they not all been questioning who should be greatest (chap. 9 : 34)? and would they not all have been glad of the places James and John had chosen? It was human nature: they thought it very wrong when two petitioned for what all would gladly have claimed.

42. Jesus called them—not necessarily the ten—apart from James and John; this word was for all.—First he states the worldly principle of greatness—a principle with which he says they are familiar. **Ye know that they which are accounted to rule over the Gentiles,** or "the nations"—*i. e.* the recognized and accepted rulers of the world—**exercise lordship,** or "lord it." **over them**—that is, over the Gentiles, or nations, their subjects—**and their great ones exercise authority upon them.** This is the ordinary human conception of greatness. Recognized greatness among the nations of the world implies the exercise of dominion over men; the great ones lord it. This is the ideal of greatness and a kingdom which Jesus rejected in the wilderness, and again when the Jews became his tempters (John 6 : 15).

43, 44. But so shall it not be—or, on manuscript authority, "it is not so"—**among you.** Your principle is not the principle of the world, and you have your own type of greatness and your own way of becoming great. Accordingly, he proceeds to tell of the Christian way of becoming great. The verbs in the future tense may best be rendered by "will" instead of **shall**, for Jesus is telling, not what he requires, but what a man will do who intelligently seeks the Christian greatness in the Christian way. Also, instead of **whosoever will be great,** read "whosoever wishes to become great," and, in verse 44, "whosoever wishes to become chiefest," or "first."—What, now, is the Christian principle of greatness and the way by which a wise Christian will seek high rank? The Christian greatness consists in humble service; and a Christian who wishes to be great will seek it, if he seeks as a Christian, only through humble service.—The desire for greatness is here represented in two degrees, "whosoever wishes to become great among you" telling of the general desire for eminence, and "whosoever of you wishes to become first" expressing the still higher desire for pre-eminence. It is not "the first," as if a Christian could distinctly set his ambition on that: it is "first"—that is, a person of first rank, one of the highest.—Observe particularly that our Lord does not forbid or discourage such desires; he does not say that there are no honors in his kingdom or bid us look for a dead-level of spiritual equality; and he does not hint that it is wrong to desire to have a place among the "first." But he proceeds to tell how a Christian, if he intelligently adopts the Christian principle, will act on such a desire. Does he wish to become great? he will be **your minister** (*diakonos*), attendant, or assistant—*i. e.* he will make himself a helper to his brethren. Does his ambition reach higher, so that he wishes to become a man of first rank? he will bow still lower, and be **the servant of all,** a slave (*doulos*) for the service of all to whom he can be useful. There is a threefold climax. "First" is higher than "great," indicating a higher ambition in the aspiring soul.

45 For even the Son of man came not to be minis- | 45 be [a]servant of all. For the Son of man also came
tered unto, but[a] to minister, and to[b] give his life a | not to be ministered unto, but to minister, and to
ransom for many. | give his life a ransom for many.

a John 13 : 14 ; Phil. 2 : 7....*b* Isa. 53 : 11, 12 ; Dan. 9 : 26 ; 2 Cor. 5 : 21 ; Gal. 3 : 13 ; 1 Tim. 2 : 6 ; Tit. 2 : 14.——1 Gr. *bondservant.*

Slave (*doulos*) is lower than minister, attendant (*diakonos*), indicating a deeper humility as the means of reaching the higher honor. **Of all** is broader than " of you," in **your minister,** indicating that the deeper humility will seek and find opportunities of wider as well as greater usefulness. The higher one wishes to rise, the lower will he bend in brotherly service, and the more freely will he give himself to many.—It may be asked whether our Lord's teaching is not self-contradictory here; whether, in practice, we can conceive of seeking first rank by means of humility and service; whether the two motives are not incompatible. Certainly they are incompatible, so long as we hold the worldly conception of thrones and rewards. But the idea of greatness through any elevation that would gratify vanity he has just expressly ruled out, and has placed the honors of the kingdom in something else. The honor in this kingdom consists in being like the King, and the first rank in being most like the King. Whoever seeks this intelligently will seek it exactly as Jesus said, by humble and loving service to many. In this view of the matter it is evident that the honors are not altogether in the future. Whoever is doing the service in the Master's spirit is already of high rank, already on the throne. But the aristocracy in the kingdom is unconscious. They who belong to it are the last to suspect the fact, and any who may suppose themselves to belong to it are wrong (Matt. 25 : 37-39).

45. The great illustration and example is the Christ himself, in whose glory the ambitious disciples were hoping to share. He came to illustrate, not the human idea of greatness by being served, but the divine idea by serving. The great God himself is greatest in his helpfulness of love, and when he came nearest to men to show them his glory he came thus, in the self-sacrificing Son of man.—**Not to be ministered unto.** Not to " lord it " or " exercise authority " over men, after the manner of the Gentiles, **but to minister,** "serve," **and to give his life a ransom for many.** The extreme act of service. Compare the similar teaching at another time, in Luke 22 : 24-27, culminating in the words, " I am among you as he that serveth," and the matchless object-lesson in John 13 : 1-17; also Rom. 15 : 1-3; Phil. 2 : 5-11. In all these passages, and in

many more (as Gal. 6 : 2; 2 Cor. 8 : 1-9; 1 Pet. 5 : 1-4), the footsteps of the Master are shown to the disciples that they may follow. The act of God in providing the propitiation for our sins, and the act of Christ in laying down his life for us, are given as the supreme examples for us in 1 John 4 : 10, 11 ; 3 : 16. This was our Saviour's way to glory; the chief throne was prepared for the chief servant, and it will be found that the king is he who has done the most for his brethren. This is the only way by which any throne in his kingdom can be reached. (See John 12 : 26, spoken when only death remained to him.)—**To give his life a ransom for many.** A ransom is the price paid for the release of prisoners or captives. The word **for,** in the sense of "instead of" ("a ransom *for* many"), is entirely appropriate, since a ransom is naturally conceived of as taking the place of the persons who are delivered by it, or serving instead of them. An idea of vicariousness, or action in the place of others, resides in this word, as well as in the word **ransom** itself. The phrase falls in with the other language of Scripture which represents the giving up of his life as the indispensable means for the deliverance of men from sin; and of this he was thinking when he spoke of the supreme act of service, the giving of his life a ransom for many. In order to **minister** thus to men he came into the world.—We often think of his way to the cross as rich in examples for us; but here the cross itself is made the chief example. So Eph. 5 : 2. Here we are called to the spiritual " fellowship of his sufferings."

46-52. THE GIVING OF SIGHT TO BARTIMÆUS. *Parallels,* Matt. 20 : 29-34 ; Luke 18 : 35-43.—The travelling company had advanced through Perea and across the Jordan to Jericho, which lies on the western side, about twenty miles from Jerusalem. It was then an important town, having been rebuilt and beautified by Herod the Great, and again, after it had been damaged in a rebellion, by his son Archelaus. Its long and richly-suggestive history may well have rendered it peculiarly interesting to our Lord.—Here are two differences between the evangelists. (1) Matthew speaks of two blind men, while Mark and Luke mention only one, to whom Mark gives the name Bartimæus. The discrepancy is unimportant, since one of the blind men, if there were two,

45 ª Andª they came to Jericho: and as he went out of Jericho with his disciples and a great number of people, blind Bartimæus, the son of Timeus, sat by the highway side begging.
47 And when he heard that it was Jesus of Nazareth, he began to cry out, and say, Jesus, *thou* Son of David, have mercy on me.
48 And many charged him that he should hold his peace: but he cried the moreᵇ a great deal, *Thou* Son of David, have mercyᶜ on me.

46 And they come to Jericho: and as he went out from Jericho, with his disciples and a great multitude, the son of Timæus, Bartimæus, a blind beggar,
47 was sitting by the way side. And when he heard that it was Jesus of Nazareth, he began to cry out, and say, Jesus, thou son of David, have mercy on
48 me. And many rebuked him, that he should hold his peace: but he cried out the more a great deal,

a Matt. 20 : 29, etc. ; Luke 18 : 35, etc....*b* Jer. 29 : 13....*c* Ps. 62 : 12.

may easily have been so much better known than the other, or so much more full of striking faith as to throw the other into the shade. (See Mark 5 : 2 and Matt. 8 : 28, where a similar question arises.)—More important is the difference between Luke, who says that the interview occurred as Jesus was approaching Jericho, and Matthew and Mark, who say that it took place as he was leaving the city surrounded by a great multitude. Various attempts have been made to reconcile this difference. [The reader may desire to look at one of the proposed methods of accounting for the difference between Luke and the other two evangelists as to the point in question. Calvin remarks: " I conjecture that when Christ was approaching the city the blind man cried out; but as he was not heard, by reason of the noise, he seated himself by the way which led out of the city, and was there at length heard by Jesus." Ellicott favors this hypothesis, with a slight modification—viz.: " That the one who is mentioned at our Lord's entry into Jericho as having learnt from the crowd who it was that was coming into the city was not healed *then*, but in company with another sufferer when our Lord was leaving the city." Dr. Hackett suggests that " it is not inconsistent with the narrative that the blind man made his first appeal to the Saviour as the latter was entering the city, but, for some reason, was not at first answered. The next morning he stationed himself at the gate through which the Saviour would pass on leaving the city, and renewed his application to him. All difficulty is removed if we suppose the words *on the morrow* to be understood in Luke 18 : 38—thus : 'And [on the morrow] he cried,' etc. So many events are passed over by the evangelists that such ellipses must often be supplied."—A. H.]

46-48. The impression given by Mark is distinctly that this was the departure from the city, apparently on the way to Jerusalem. The revisers read correctly, " the son of Timæus, Bartimæus, a blind beggar, was sitting by the way side." Beggars in Palestine are innumerable, and blind beggars are to be seen in great num-

bers. Luke adds the graphic touch that he heard the multitude passing and asked what it meant; and the answer was, " Jesus of Nazareth passeth by." As to this man's name, *bar* is the Aramaic prefix for *son ;* so that the two designations, Bartimæus and son of Timeus, are identical. But Bartimæus is an unusual compound, Timeus being a Greek name, while the prefix *bar* is usually given only to Aramaic names. Perhaps this peculiarity of the compound word is the reason why both forms came to the writer's mind and were written down together. Both the blind Bartimæus and his father may have been well-known Christians. (Compare Mark 15 : 21, where familiar names are probably introduced in a similar way.)

47, 48. "Great faith," says Bengel, " that the blind man addressed him as the Son of David whom the people were proclaiming to him as a Nazarene." But the faith must already have been waiting in his heart. He had heard that the Nazarene was the Son of David, the Messiah, and evidently he had believed it. Instead of faith new-born, this apparently was faith seizing its opportunity, and doubtless growing strong by its own act. **Jesus, thou Son of David, have mercy on me.** Turn thy mercy hither, leave me not unblessed. The cry was so loud and urgent as to call out a rebuke from **many.** Whether these were disciples or not does not appear; but quite likely the rebuke sprang as much from contempt for the blind beggar as from any reverence or respect for Jesus.—The rebuke was all in vain, however; it only made the cry more loud and urgent. " What right have these men," Bartimæus might ask, " to stand between me and him who can give me my sight ?"

49, 50. If there were **many** in the company who would have the Saviour leave a blind beggar crying for mercy by the roadside, there must be something done beyond the utterance of a word of healing. Read, as in the Revision, " And Jesus stood still, and said, Call ye him." A direct description, characteristic of Mark, of the act by which Jesus rebuked the rebuke.—At once the half-contemptuous charge **that he should**

49 And Jesus stood still, and commanded him to be called. And they call the blind man, saying unto him, Be of good comfort, rise; he calleth thee.
50 And he, casting⁴ away his garment, rose, and came to Jesus.
51 And Jesus answered and said unto him, What wilt thou that I should do unto thee? The blind man said unto him, Lord, that I might receive my sight.
52 And Jesus said unto him, Go thy way; thy faith hath made thee whole. And immediately he received his sight, and followed Jesus in the way.

49 Thou son of David, have mercy on me. And Jesus stood still, and said, Call ye him. And they call the blind man, saying unto him, Be of good cheer: rise,
50 he calleth thee. And he, casting away his garment,
51 sprang up, and came to Jesus. And Jesus answered him, and said, What wilt thou that I should do unto thee? And the blind man said unto him, Rabboni,
52 that I may receive my sight. And Jesus said unto him, Go thy way; thy faith hath ²made thee whole. And straightway he received his sight, and followed him in the way.

CHAPTER XI.

AND⁵ when they came nigh to Jerusalem, unto Bethphage, and Bethany, at the Mount of Olives, he sendeth forth two of his disciples,

1 AND when they draw nigh unto Jerusalem, unto Bethphage and Bethany, at the mount of Olives, he

a John 11 : 26....b Phil. 3 : 7-9....c ch. 5 : 34 ; Matt. 9 : 22....d Matt. 21 : 1, etc.; Luke 19 : 29, etc. ; John 12 : 14, etc.——1 See John xx. 16....2 Or, saved thee

hold his peace was silenced, and the blind man heard the spirit of Jesus in the voices that now addressed him; but doubtless they were new voices, not the same: friends of Jesus now called.—Be of good comfort, rise ; he calleth thee. Notice the haste of hope. He dropped his outer garment (mantle) or threw it back upon the ground rather than stay to wrap it around him—an unwonted act for a blind man, who would ordinarily be most careful to keep his garment within reach. Must he not have expected to see it when he turned back? This mention of the garment is peculiar to Mark, who also says, as in the Revision, that "he sprang up, and came to Jesus."

51, 52. Jesus had given him this to do on his own part, the coming; and now he bade him offer his request. Did not Jesus know what he wanted? and yet the man must ask. Lord (" Rabboni"), that I might receive my sight. " Rabboni," or " Rabbonni," is used only here and at John 20 : 16. It is sometimes taken to mean " my teacher;" but in John 20 : 16 it is expressly rendered by " teacher" (didaskalos). It is an intensified form of " Rabbi."—The word translated receive my sight strictly means to see again, or to recover sight; and it has sometimes been inferred that Bartimæus had not always been blind. But the same word is used in John 9 : 11 of the man who was blind from his birth. There, however, the use of it seems to rest upon the fact that sight is a natural endowment of man, and that he who receives it receives his own, even though he may never have had it before.—The answer was ready; literally it is, " Go ; thy faith hath saved thee." Whether he meant merely hath made thee whole, given thee thy sight, may perhaps be doubted. Did not such faith as his bring him into the circle of our Lord's full saving influence? But prompt healing was included, and he received sight at once. Matthew says (not Mark or Luke) that the act was performed

by a touch. All record that the man followed Jesus. It is in every way probable that he followed Jesus to Jerusalem and was near him to the end, " his new-found gift of sight qualifying him to take his place among the eye-witnesses of the things that were done in the ensuing week" (Plumptre).

A parabolic and spiritual meaning has always been found in this story, and with good reason. It must have been intended as a suggestive picture of spiritual things. Such faith as this is what a sinner needs—faith to recognize the Saviour as mighty to save, whatever others may think or say of him ; faith to beg for mercy ; faith irrepressible and persistent; faith to obey his call and hopefully come to him; faith to press into his presence at his bidding and plead afresh ; faith to take him at his word when he speaks in mercy, and to glorify God and follow Jesus when he has done the saving work. No less justly is this taken as a true and living picture of the attitude of our Saviour toward the souls that cry out for his saving help, so ready, so wise, so mighty to save.

1-11. THE MESSIANIC ENTRANCE OF JESUS TO JERUSALEM. Parallels, Matt. 21 : 1-11; Luke 19 : 29-44; John 12 : 12-19.—Here we have a fourfold record. Mark now enters upon the Sunday, the first day of the week within which fell the day of crucifixion. He has passed by the visit to Zacchæus, in Jericho, and the parable of the Ten Pounds, uttered as a preparation for the events that were coming at Jerusalem (Luke 19 : 1-27). On the day before this Sunday—i. e. on the Jewish Sabbath—Jesus arrived at Bethany, and was entertained in the house of Simon the leper. John's specific note of time fully settles the date of this event, which is narrated by Matthew and Mark out of its proper place. (See note on Mark 14 : 3.)

1. Bethphage is not certainly known. Some manuscripts (and Tischendorf) omit the name in

2 And saith unto them, Go your way into the village over against you: and as soon as ye be entered into it, ye shall find a colt tied, whereon never man sat; loose him, and bring *him*.

2 sendeth two of his disciples, and saith unto them, Go your way into the village that is over against you: and straightway as ye enter into it, ye shall find a colt tied, whereon no man ever yet sat; loose

Mark, though it stands unquestioned in Matthew and Luke. Probably the place was a small hamlet, named from its fig trees. Its location is not definitively known. F. R. and C. R. Conder, *Handbook of the Bible*, p. 326, say: "It appears clear, from a number of passages in the Talmud (Menakhoth 11. 2), that Beth Phagi marked the sabbatical limit east of Jerusalem. This limit was called the 'wall of Bethphagi' (Tal. Bab. Menakhoth 78b), and the position thus

so, very likely John was the other, as in Luke 22 : 8.

2. The village over against you. "The road from Bethany to Jerusalem, as it passed along the Mount of Olives, encountered a deep valley, and made a long *détour* round the head of the valley to avoid the descent and ascent. A short foot-path, however, led directly across the valley, and it was probably from the point where this parted from the road that the disci-

MOUNT OF OLIVES.

indicated would be two thousand cubits from the east wall of Jerusalem. The distance measures to the present village of *Kefr et-Tor* (named from the mountain), on Olivet, which M. Clermont Ganneau therefore proposes to identify with Bethphage."—**Bethphage** means "house of unripe figs;" **Bethany,** "house of dates."— John tells us of a great multitude streaming out of Jerusalem to meet Jesus, drawn by the excitement over the resurrection of Lazarus. Doubtless it was when this new throng was about to join him that he arranged for the triumphal entry. Of the two disciples whom he sent, the particularity of Mark's narrative leads us to suspect that Peter was one. If

ples were sent for the ass to the village on the opposite side where the path again met the road —a site still marked by ruins" (Gardiner's *Greek Harmony*, p. 172). If this is to be accepted, doubtless the Lord and his company had already passed the village, and the disciples were sent, not forward, but back by the short foot-path, to bring an animal that Jesus had seen as he passed it. Having a Messianic entrance in mind, he would notice the animal, while his companions might not.—**A colt.** Not further described; but that it was the colt of an ass would be understood.—**Whereon never man sat.** For cases of beasts of burden that had never worked being used for sacred purposes,

11

3 And if any man say unto you, Why do ye this, say ye that the Lord hath need*b of him; and straightway he will send him hither.

3 him, and bring him. And if any one say unto you, Why do ye this? say ye, The Lord hath need of him; and straightway he [will send him *back

---

a Acts 17 : 25.——1 Gr. sendeth....2 Or, again

---

see Num. 19 : 2; Deut. 21 : 3; 1 Sam. 6 : 7. According to Matthew's more precise record, the mother of the colt was tied and the colt was with her. The disciples brought both and spread their clothes upon both, uncertain which

self, whom the owner knew to be passing. His disciples called him "Lord" in a special sense, and at this moment he was openly performing a kingly act. The owner may have been a friend. The revisers accept (with Tischendorf)

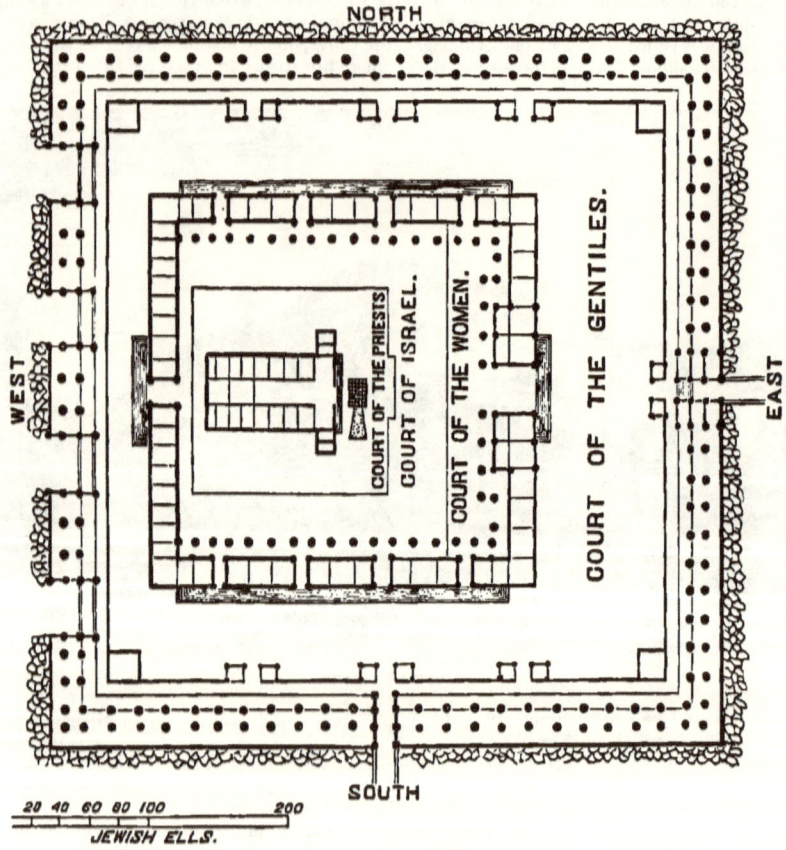

PLAN OF THE TEMPLE.

Jesus would mount: and "they set him thereon," or "he sat upon them"—i. e. upon the clothes thus spread upon the colt.

3. The Lord hath need of him, Lord meaning, possibly, Jehovah, indicating that the animal was claimed for a religious use in the service of God; more probably for Jesus him-

the extremely fresh and beautiful reading, "The Lord hath need of him; and straightway he will send him back hither;" literally, "sendeth him hither again." The reading is well supported, and there is a lifelike quality about it that strongly commends it as a true bit of remembrance. The Lord offered assurance to

4 And they went their way, and found the colt tied by the door without, in a place where two ways met; and they loose him.
5 And certain of them that stood there said unto them, What do ye, loosing the colt?
6 And they said unto them even as Jesus had commanded: and they let them go.
7 And they brought the colt to Jesus, and cast their garments on him; and[a] he sat upon him.
8 And many spread their garments in the way; and others cut down branches off the trees, and strawed *them* in the way.
9 And they that went before, and they that followed, cried, saying, Hosanna; Blessed[b] *is* he that cometh in the name of the Lord:
10 Blessed *be* the kingdom[c] of our father David, that cometh in the name of the Lord: Hosanna in the highest.[d]

4 hither. And they went away, and found a colt tied at the door without in the open street; and
5 they loose him. And certain of them that stood there said unto them, What do ye, loosing the colt?
6 And they said unto them even as Jesus had said:
7 and they let them go. And they bring the colt unto Jesus, and cast on him their garments; and he sat
8 upon him. And many spread their garments upon the way; and others [1]branches, which they had cut
9 from the fields. And they that went before, and they that followed, cried, Hosanna; Blessed *is* he
10 that cometh in the name of the Lord: Blessed *is* the kingdom that cometh, *the kingdom* of our father David: Hosanna in the highest.

a Zech. 9 : 9....*b* Ps. 118 ; 26....*c* Isa. 9 : 7 ; Jer. 33 : 15....*d* Ps. 148 : 1.——1 Gr. *layers of leaves.*

the owner that his property should be returned.

4-6. In a place where two ways met (peculiar to Mark) is a paraphrase founded on the Latin Vulgate (*bivio*), and not on the Greek. The original phrase is obscure. "On the way round" resembles it, but perhaps usage justifies the rendering of the revisers, "in the open street." Farrar makes it mean "in the passage round the house"—*i. e.* tied up at the back of the house; but this scarcely goes well with **by the door.** That we cannot recover the precise allusion occasions no difficulty. Alexander says truly, " The very obscurity of the expression serves to show that it was not a subsequent embellishment, but the vivid recollection of an eye-witness."

7. Their outer garments made a covering for the animal, on which he took his seat. Mark and Luke make no allusion to prophecy, but Matthew and John cite Zech. 9 : 9; and there is no doubt that Jesus was intentionally acting in fulfilment of that prediction. To enter Jerusalem riding on an ass was expressly to declare himself the promised King of Israel. Distinctly foreknowing and foretelling his own rejection (Mark 10 : 33, 34), and perceiving that the time was now at hand, he would not fail to make his claim to the Messiahship openly and unmistakably in the very terms of prophecy. He had not yet been recognized as the spiritual King of Israel; now he would declare himself in such a way that his claim could not be misunderstood, and would be either recognized or rejected as the Messiah. Did they say, " What a King! Riding on an ass, the symbol of peace! How shall this man save us?" He would answer in the words of Zechariah. Such was the King to be, " meek, and having salvation."

8-10. For the moment he was recognized.

As the Messiah the people hailed him, carpeting the road before him with **their garments** and with **branches off the trees.** Read, as in the Revision, " And many spread their garments upon the way; and others branches, which they had cut from the fields." Perfectly accordant with Matthew and Luke, but beautifully fresh and graphic. The multitude cast

OLIVES.

itself about him before and behind and broke forth into song, in the very spirit of Zech. 9 : 9: " Rejoice greatly, O daughter of Zion !"—**Hosanna.** Literally, "Save now"—*i. e.* "God bless him! God save the King !"—**Blessed is he that cometh in the name of the Lord.** Quoted from Ps. 118 :.26.. The re-

11

11 And Jesus entered into Jerusalem, and into the temple: and° when he had looked round about upon all things, and now the even-tide was come, he went out unto Bethany with the twelve.

12 ¶ And° on the morrow, when they were come from Bethany, he was hungry:

13 And seeing a fig tree afar off, having leaves, he came, if haply he might find any thing thereon: and when he came to it, he found nothing° but leaves; for the time of figs was not yet.

11 And he entered into Jerusalem, into the temple; and when he had looked round about upon all things, it being now eventide, he went out unto Bethany with the twelve.

12 And on the morrow, when they were come out 13 from Bethany, he hungered. And seeing a fig tree afar off having leaves, he came, if haply he might find anything thereon: and when he came to it, he found nothing but leaves; for it was not the season

a Zeph. 1 : 12; Ezek. b : 9....b Matt. 21 : 18, etc....c Isa. 5 : 7.

visers correctly omit **in the name of the Lord** in verse 10, and translate, "Blessed is the kingdom that cometh, *the kingdom* of our father David." This was a positive recognition of him as bringing in a kingdom, and of the kingdom as the promised kingdom of David; a strictly Messianic tribute.—**Hosanna in the highest**—not "in the highest degree," but "in the highest regions"—*i. e.* in heaven. "God bless him in heaven, and send the blessing on him here!" Equivalent substantially, though not strictly, to "God in heaven bless him!" This was the Messianic "God save the King!"

Thus the King received the Messianic homage at the gate of his royal city, though doubtless it was ignorant and carnal homage. Even the most intelligent did not know what his kingdom really was.—We cannot repress the inquiry, What would have happened if the Jewish people had received their King? We cannot answer it definitely, but we must not think that the purpose of salvation would have been defeated.—Luke adds the remonstrance of the Pharisees against the loud songs of praise, and our Lord's reply; also the matchless story of his tears over Jerusalem, in view of the terrible future (19 : 39-44). Matthew tells of the commotion in the city when he had entered, the inquiry, "Who is this?" and the weakening of the popular testimony to "this is the prophet Jesus, from Nazareth of Galilee," in which there was perhaps some provincial pride on the part of Galilæan strangers in the city. From the commotion and inquiry, it is plain that Jerusalem was in no mood of acceptance. The royal city had no throne for its King. He came unto his own, and his own received him not.

11. Mark alone follows him to the temple. (See note on verse 15.) But what a conclusion for the Messianic entrance to the royal city! **He looked round about upon all things,** and at evening **went out unto Bethany.** A lame and impotent conclusion it may well have seemed. One must imagine his friends walking out with him at evening bitterly perplexed. They had their national hopes, of the carnal kind, which the event of the morning

must have greatly encouraged; but he had entered the city and done nothing.—Notice the self-control of Jesus in never being driven a step beyond his own purpose by any expectations of his friends.

12-19. THE FRUITLESS FIG TREE BLIGHTED AND THE TEMPLE CLEANSED. *Parallel,* Matt. 21 : 12-22.—These are the events of Monday and of Tuesday morning. It is impossible here to combine the narrative of Mark with that of Matthew and Luke without inverting the order of one or the other. The difference respecting the fig tree is but slight, Matthew compendiously placing together the condemnation of the tree and the discovery that it was withered; while Mark places the condemnation on the morning of Monday and the discovery on the morning of Tuesday. Doubtless, Mark's narrative is the exact one; Luke omits the incident. The difference is greater respecting the cleansing of the temple. From Matthew and Luke we should infer that this work was done on the day of the Messianic entrance; while Mark expressly places it on the day following. Opinions differ as to which order is to be followed. Farrar (*Life of Christ,* 2. 204, note) gives reasons for following Matthew; and no doubt the story in Matthew is more dramatic and impressive, the disappointment after the triumphal entrance having no place in it. But the indications of time in Mark are extremely distinct and positive—far more so than those of Matthew and Luke. Mark is also habitually more exact in arrangement. On the whole, the order of Mark has the stronger evidence, and is to be followed. According to it, Jesus sought and condemned the fig tree on Monday morning, revisited and cleansed the temple on Monday, went out to Bethany Monday night, and, returning on Tuesday morning, found the tree withered.

12, 13. On the morrow. According to Matthew, it was in the early morning.—**He was hungry,** and so it was for himself that he sought food, not for his companions, so far as we know. The principle of Matt. 4 : 4 always governed him; no miracle for himself. He would seek food like any other human

14 And Jesus answered and said unto it, No man eat fruit of thee hereafter for ever. And his disciples heard it.
15 ¶ And they come to Jerusalem; and Jesus went into the temple, and began to cast out them that sold and bought in the temple, and overthrew the tables of the moneychangers,[b] and the seats of them that sold doves;
16 And would not suffer that any man should carry any vessel through the temple.

14 of figs. And he answered and said unto it, No man eat fruit from thee henceforward for ever. And his disciples heard it
15 And they come to Jerusalem: and he entered into the temple, and began to cast out them that sold and them that bought in the temple, and overthrew the tables of the money-changers, and the seats of 16 them that sold the doves; and he would not suffer that any man should carry a vessel through the temple.

a Matt. 21 : 12, etc.; Luke 19 : 45, etc.; John 2 : 14, etc....b Deut. 14 : 25, 26.

being.—Seeing a fig tree. In Matthew, "one fig tree"—i. e. a solitary tree.—Having leaves. Peculiar to Mark. It was this fact that drew him to it.—If haply he might find any thing thereon. The fig tree often produces fruit as early as leaves, or even earlier (Thomson, The Land and the Book, 1. 538); so that the show of leaves justified his search for fruit, although the time of figs was not yet. It was early even for the earliest figs; yet they might already have ripened. Thomson says that he has plucked them in May far in the north, where vegetation is at least a month later than at Jerusalem. It was now the beginning of April; and upon a leafy tree, in some warm spot on the Mount of Olives, it was not unreasonable to look for the first ripening fruit. So there is no just charge against our Saviour, as if he were looking for what he could not expect to find and offended because he did not find it.

14. And Jesus answered and said unto it. As if by its fair and deceptive profession the tree had spoken. It had indeed made reply to his expectations by disappointing them, and now he replied in turn.—The doom of the tree was expressed in terms corresponding to his disappointment. The penalty of fruitlessness was to be fruitlessness. No man eat fruit of thee hereafter for ever. The condemnation of the tree was not an act of anger or of ill-temper. It was a symbolic action, an acted parable. In idea, though not exactly in form, it was the parable of Luke 13 : 6-9 in action. Israel was the fruitless fig tree, or the richly-privileged vineyard that brought forth wild grapes (Isa. 5 : 1-7). Yet, though fruitless, Israel was full of profession, false show of godliness. The leaders of the nation were the most religious of men, yet the least acceptable to him who sought the genuine fruit of goodness. The people had proved themselves unfit to receive their true King. Leaves without fruit, promise without fulfilment—this was the character of Israel; therefore doom must come. This fact was to be revealed finally and most clearly in that day's work, and to form the burden of his prophetic discourse at nightfall. Full of these

thoughts, Jesus saw in the false promise of the tree a living picture of the terrible truth, and used it for illustration. The fruitlessness of the tree should be its ruin. The symbolic act would be plain to beholders who were familiar with the prophets. (See Ezek. 17 : 24; Hos. 9 : 10; Joel 1 : 7; Mic. 7 : 1-4.)—His disciples heard it. Peculiar to Mark, and corresponding to his recognition of the interval between the two parts of the event. Exactly when the tree withered we cannot tell. The "immediately" of Matthew is to be taken relatively, and not

THE FIG.

to mean that the tree withered before their eyes. We only know that it was done before the next morning.

15, 16. This was the second purifying of the temple. (For the similar event, see John 2 : 13-17.) The work probably was begun early in the day. This was the fruit of the looking "round upon all things" of the day before. That was the preliminary inspection; this, the work that was found necessary. Both were regal acts, though the former did not appear so. It was the act of the King to inspect his capital, as well as to purify it. Just three years earlier, at the passover, he had done the same work, claiming unequalled authority at the beginning of his ministry as at the end; but the intrusions had been renewed. Oxen and sheep (for

17 And he taught, saying unto them, Is it not written,ᵃ My house shall be called of all nations the house
of prayer? but ye have made it a denᵇ of thieves
18 And the scribes and chief priests heard it, and
sought how they might destroy him: for they feared
him, because all the people was astonished° at his
doctrine.
19 And when even was come, he went out of the city.

17 And he taught, and said unto them, Is it not written,
My house shall be called a house of prayer for all
the nations? but ye have made it a den of robbers.
18 And the chief priests and the scribes heard it, and
sought how they might destroy him: for they feared
him, for all the multitude was astonished at his
teaching.
19 And ¹every evening ²he went forth out of the city.

sacrifice) are not mentioned now as then, but are
probably included in the traffic of **them that
sold and bought.—Moneychangers,** men
who took the foreign money of worshippers from
other lands, but especially the Roman money
in general use, and gave the half shekel that
was required for the temple-tax. — **Doves.**
Literally, "the doves;" so familiar to fre-
quenters of the temple as to be thus spoken
of. They were the offerings of the poor. (See
Lev. 12 : 6–8.) At the presentation of our Lord
himself in the temple this was the offering
(Luke 2 : 24). When the temple was cleansed before, the dove-sellers were only ordered out (John
2 : 16), not driven out; but now their seats
were overturned, like the tables of the moneychangers, as if in sharper indignation at their
daring to return.—The place of the traffic was
one of the courts, probably the court of the
Gentiles. The excuse, doubtless, was that this
was far less sacred than the inner temple, and
thus it became easy to treat it entirely like un-
consecrated ground. But to Jesus even the
courts of the Lord's house were sacred—too
sacred to be profaned by traffic. This was not
"only a court" to him: it was a part of the
house of God.—**Should carry any vessel
through the temple—**i. e. any of the various
implements of traffic. Very likely (as Plumptre supposes) they made this court a short cut
from one part of the city to another.—There is
no mention of any assistance in driving the
men out, from the disciples or any others. On
the previous occasion he made a scourge for his
own use, but none is mentioned now. In the
fact that he was able to drive them out, the
fact that they retired before him, we have a
most impressive picture of his person, alive
with intense emotion, glowing with the ardor
of holiness, consumed by the zeal of God's
house. Such a scene affords us some conception of the immense personal power of which
he must have been the possessor.

17. He taught, saying unto them. This
is only an extract from larger teaching. Apparently he made the defilement and cleansing
of the temple the text for discourse.—**My house
shall be called of all nations the house
of prayer.** More exactly, as in the Revision,

"a house of prayer for all the nations." The
quotation is an exact one from the Septuagint
version of Isa. 56 : 7. Especially appropriate in
the court of the Gentiles. God meant that Gentiles—i. e. men of all nations—should find here
a sacred place, a house of prayer. This intention, of a wider than national interest in the
sanctity and preciousness of the temple, was
recognized in the prayer of Solomon at the dedication of the first temple in a petition of great
breadth and beauty (1 Kings 8 : 41-43), and became
prominent in the teachings of the prophets. It
is especially prominent, together with its prophetic analogues, in the latter portion of Isaiah.
The popular idea of the exclusiveness of the
old covenant is a somewhat exaggerated idea.—
In contrast to the holy and gracious intent of
God, see what the temple is! **Ye have made
it a den of thieves.** This is far too weak a
phrase. "Den of robbers" is right, and the
thought is almost like that of "murderers' cave."
The denunciation is an allusion to Jer. 7 : 11:
"Is this house, which is called by my name,
become a den of robbers in your eyes? Behold,
even I have seen it, saith the Lord." For that
long-continued desecration of holy things there
was heavy punishment; and Jesus intimated
that the men of his time had placed themselves
where their fathers were in bold sin and in exposure to a fearful doom. No doubt he meant
to condemn not only the traffic in the temple,
but the fraud that went with it, and, still more,
the general indifference to God's true claims by
which the desecration was rendered possible.

18. Here Matthew adds that the blind and
the lame came to him in the temple and were
healed, and that the children sang his praises.
In Mark his popularity is the reason why the
plots against him are carried forward; in Luke,
it is that very popularity that defeats the purpose of the plotters. Both are true, and there
is no contradiction. His enemies began to fear
that he might be taken as the King of Israel,
after all, and the very fact that there seemed to
be reason to fear it increased their difficulties.—
Astonished at his doctrine, or "teaching."
Another hint of considerable unrecorded work.

19. The day ended with his withdrawing
again to Bethany (so Matthew), where his home

20 ⁗ And in the morning as they passed by, they saw the fig tree dried up from the roots.

21 And Peter, calling to remembrance, saith unto him, Master, behold, the fig tree which thou cursedst is withered away!

22 And Jesus, answering, saith unto them, Have faith in God.

23 For verily I say unto you, That whosoever* shall say unto this mountain, Be thou removed, and be thou cast into the sea; and shall not doubt in his heart, but shall believe that those things which he saith shall come to pass; he shall have whatsoever he saith.

20 And as they passed by in the morning, they saw 21 the fig tree withered away from the roots. And Peter calling to remembrance saith unto him, Rabbi, behold, the fig tree which thou cursedst is withered 22 away. And Jesus answering saith unto them, Have 23 faith in God. Verily I say unto you, Whosoever shall say unto this mountain, Be thou taken up and cast into the sea; and shall not doubt in his heart, but shall believe that what he saith cometh to pass;

a Matt. 17 : 20; Luke 17 : 6.

was, doubtless, in the house of Martha. It had been a Messianic day; but Messianic days were fraught with threatening.

20, 21. Here begins the record of Tuesday, which extends (if we include with the day the evening, according to our way of reckoning) to the end of chap. 13. The other records of the day are Luke, chaps. 20, 21, and Matthew, 21 : 20-25, 46. This was the last day of his public ministry. Of no other day have we so full a record, and none that we know of was more significant in his personal history. Now came the great decisive conflict, in which his enemies were openly worsted, one after another, and driven to the desperation of hatred.—But first, on the way to the city, they observed the blighted tree. **Dried up from the roots.** It was no mere injury or weakening, no withering of the foliage; the tree was destroyed and already ruined.—**And Peter, calling to remembrance.** Peculiar to Mark. and doubtless a personal reminiscence of Peter.—Yet here, as elsewhere, he uttered the general thought. **Which thou cursedst**—i. e. which thou didst devote to evil. Beware of associating with the word in the least degree the idea of profanity. The ordinary name for this act, "the cursing of the fig tree," is an unfortunate one. To modern ears it suggests strong language, even profane language, and improper feeling; whereas the language was moderate and the feeling was right. "Blighting," or "destruction," is far better.

22. Have faith in God. Literally, "faith of God," God being conceived of as the object of faith. A very unexpected turn of discourse, the purpose of his act upon the tree being entirely ignored. Why did he not explain the symbolic meaning of the act? And why did he content himself with giving an object-lesson in faith? It was on the principle of John 16 : 12: "I have yet many things to say unto you, but ye cannot bear them now." He preferred to leave the sad symbolic meaning to be perceived at a later time, when they could better understand it. Before the day was

over they might begin to understand it for themselves by observing how Jerusalem treated their Master. If not so, his discourse at evening might begin to open their eyes. For that discourse this act was a kind of text. It did not now need unfolding; it would be opened soon enough. But of a lesson in faith they were in need; and so, instead of telling them why this had been done, he told them how works of faith still greater might be performed.

23. Whosoever shall say unto this mountain, Be thou removed, etc. A similar saying had been given the disciples after their failure to heal the lunatic child (Matt. 17 : 20). Such language cannot possibly have been understood by them or meant by him in any sense but that of hyperbole. (See an allusion to this saying in 1 Cor. 13 : 2.) The thought is that works as impossible to human strength as the moving of the Mount of Olives to the sea shall be possible to faith and shall actually be wrought. "With God all things are possible." For an illustration of Jesus bringing divine possibilities near to human faith, see his words to Martha (John 11 : 23-27).—Undoubting confidence is the secret of such power; but confidence in what? The belief that **those things which he saith shall come to pass** must have some foundation; what is the true foundation? Plainly, the confidence that is here encouraged is the confidence that the proposed act is accordant with the will of God, and that the will of God can and will be done. Such confidence, if it is to be of any value, cannot be blind. It must have its rational and spiritual supports. No man can expect, under this promise, that a mountain will be removed until he is convinced by good reasons that God wishes it to be removed. If he is sure of that, and sure that what God wishes can and will be done, he will believe that the mountain is to be removed. The promise is made to undoubting confidence; but if there is room for question whether the confidence is not irrational, how can it continue undoubting? So this promise gives no encouragement to random, enthusiastic prayers or to

24 Therefore I say unto you, What* things soever ye desire when ye pray, believe that ye receive *them*, and ye shall have *them*.
25 And when ye stand praying, forgive,^b if ye have aught against any; that your Father also which is in heaven may forgive you your trespasses.
26 But^c if ye do not forgive, neither will your Father which is in heaven forgive your trespasses.
27 ° And they come again to Jerusalem: and^d as he was walking in the temple, there come to him the chief priests, and the scribes, and the elders.
28 And they say unto him, By^e what authority doest thou these things? and who gave thee this authority to do these things?

24 he shall have it. Therefore I say unto you, All things whatsoever ye pray and ask for, believe that
25 ye receive them, and ye shall have them. And whensoever ye stand praying, forgive, if ye have aught against any one; that your Father also who is in heaven may forgive you your trespasses.²
27 And they come again to Jerusalem: and as he was walking in the temple, there come to him the chief
28 priests, and the scribes, and the elders; and they said unto him, By what authority doest thou these things? or who gave thee this authority to do these

---

a Matt. 7: 7; Luke 11: 9; 18: 1; John 14: 13; 15: 7; 16: 24; James 1: 5, 6....b Matt. 6: 14; Col. 3: 13....c Matt. 18: 35....d Matt. 21: 23; Luke 20: 1....e Num. 16: 3.——1 Gr. received... 2 Many ancient authorities add ver. 26 *But if ye do not forgive, neither will your Father who is in heaven forgive your trespasses.*

---

selfish petitions. Prevailing prayer is reasonable.

24. Therefore—i. e. because faith is so mighty—**I say unto you**—a sign of special emphasis—**What things soever ye desire when ye pray.** This is given correctly by the revisers: "All things whatsoever ye pray and ask for." **Desire** is a mistranslation for "ask."—"Believe that ye received (them), and they shall be to you." So literally. The verb "received" is in the aorist. The best commentary on this saying is found in Rom. 8: 26, 27, where the acceptable petitions which are destined to be granted are said to have been given to the suppliant by the Holy Spirit, and by him made so strong in the soul as to be unutterable groanings of desire. Thus our Lord says, "Believe that you received these things from the Spirit of God as the materials of prayer; believe that these longings were awakened in you from above; and your requests shall be granted." But this faith, again, cannot be blind, if it is to inherit such a promise. It must have its reasons—so good that the whole man shall be satisfied with them. The reading of the will of God must be rational, as well as the pleading of it. The promise is, in meaning, "When you have reason to believe, and do believe, that your prayer came to your heart from the Spirit of God, you may be sure that an answer to your prayer will also come from God." Compare the profound yet simple testimony concerning prayer in 1 John 5: 14, 15. There, as here, the crucial point is the knowing that we are asking according to his will. But thanks be to God that there is a Spirit who maketh intercession for the saints according to the will of God, working in them that which is well-pleasing in his sight!

25, 26. Forgive, if ye have aught against any; that your Father also which is in heaven may forgive you. This saying is very similar to Matt. 6: 14, 15 and 18: 35. Verse 26 is properly omitted by the revisers as having been added here by free quotation from Matt. 6: 15. The solemn words concerning forgiveness were added, perhaps, partly to prevent misunderstanding of his act upon the fig tree and false inferences from it. Prayer is a tremendous power, but it cannot be used for the gratification of personal resentments. So far from that, the cherishing of such resentments is fatal to prayer itself, being fatal to that full acceptance with God upon which, as a basis, prevailing prayer proceeds. An unforgiving prayer against an enemy would be null and fruitless by its own nature according to this law. Still further, the unforgiving spirit would vitiate all prayer. In this searching law, expressed in verse 26, there is nothing retaliatory or narrow on the part of God. The reason for the law lies in the nature of things. The unforgiving spirit is not the penitent and humble spirit to which forgiveness is promised. Rather is it the hard and self-asserting temper to which the remission of sins cannot be granted. To harbor resentment while pleading for pardon is to cherish the "guile" of Ps. 32: 2. This law, limiting the availability of prayer, makes power contingent upon love: the true Christian relation.—For other illustrations of what things are contingent upon love, study the First Epistle of John. Do not shrink from the Epistle, either. No part of Scripture is more fundamental.

27-33. THE AUTHORITY OF JESUS QUESTIONED. *Parallels*, Matt. 21: 23-27; Luke 20: 1-8.

27, 28. From the blighted fig tree Jesus went to his last searching of the fruitless Israel. This was his last visit to his Father's temple, and the answer of this day to his presence and work was the full revealing of spiritual barrenness.—**Walking in the temple.** Matthew, "teaching;" Luke, "teaching the people and preaching the gospel." Here, even in this full day, is the hint of much unrecorded labor.—The religious leaders of Israel gathered with one accord

29 And Jesus answered and said unto them, I will also ask of you one question, and answer me, and I will tell you by what authority I do these things.
30 The baptism of John, was it from heaven, or of men? Answer me.
31 And they reasoned with themselves, saying, If we shall say, From heaven; he will say, Why then did ye not believe him?
32 But if we shall say, Of men; they feared the people: for* all men counted John, that he was a prophet indeed.
33 And they answered and said unto Jesus, Web cannot tell. And Jesus answering, saith unto them, Neither do I< tell you by what authority I do these things.

29 things? And Jesus said unto them, I will ask of you one ¹question, and answer me, and I will tell 30 you by what authority I do these things. The baptism of John, was it from heaven, or from men? an-31 swer me. And they reasoned with themselves, say-ing, If we shall say, From heaven: he will say, Why 32 then did ye not believe him? ²But should we say, From men—they feared the people: ³for all verily 33 held John to be a prophet. And they answered Jesus and say, We know not. And Jesus saith unto them, Neither tell I you by what authority I do these things.

a ch. 6 . 20; Matt. 3 : 5, 6; 14 : 5....*b* Isa. 1 : 3; 29 : 11; Jer. 8 : 7; Hos. 4 : 6....*c* Luke 10 : 21, 22.——1 Gr. word....2 Or, But shall we say, From men ?....3 Or. for all held John to be a prophet indeed.

to question him as to his authority, a perfectly proper thing to do, except that by this time they ought to have understood his claim. In fact, they did understand it well enough; but the act of yesterday, the interference with the temple, naturally called out a fresh inquiry. His similar act three years before had evoked the same question (John 2: 18). **By what au-thority.** Even a rabbi, according to Jewish custom, must have his credentials from the rabbi who had instructed him, a kind of di-ploma for authority; and Jesus had gone far beyond the assumptions of a rabbi. He had claimed the office of the Lord of the temple. Two questions they put to him, as to his right and the source of his right. **By what au-thority! and who gave thee this author-ity?**

His method of reply would be familiar to them. The rabbis taught largely by question-ing, and the practice of posing an opponent with hard questions was as old as the time of Solomon, and doubtless older. Yet his was not a mere counter-question, a puzzle, intended to put them to silence. Logically, it was a true dilemma; and, like most dilemmas, it had an argument wrapped up in it. It led, too, direct-ly to the answer to their question. If they would admit that John the Baptist was commissioned **from heaven,** they could answer it themselves; for John had declared himself the forerunner of the Messiah, and had expressly borne witness that Jesus was the Messiah. If **the baptism of John** was **from heaven,** the long-expect-ed Christ stood before them, and there was no need of asking by what authority he purified the temple. Hence he said honestly, **Answer me,** "and" (as in Matt. 21 : 24) "I in like wise will tell you by what authority I do these things." If they had said, **From heaven,** he would have completed the argument for them and claimed his right; if they had said, **Of—or from—men,** he would have reproved them for their blindness and declared himself in doing

so.—The sharp **answer me,** both in the ques-tion and repeated at the end, is peculiar to Mark.

31-33. The religious leaders had played fast and loose with John (Matt. 3 : 7; Luke 7 : 30; John 5 : 35), and perhaps they now had no very deep con-victions either way, but only a guilty feeling and a strong dislike of the whole subject. Yet their knowledge must have been such that they could not honestly deny his mission from God. But how natural their consultation under their breath! This is a touch from the life. How perfect, too, the dilemma! To say, **From heaven,** was to invite the question, **Why then did ye not believe him!** That question would be fatal, for it would mean, "Why did ye not accept his testimony to me?" He had used a similar argument concerning their boast-ed faith in Moses (John 5 : 46): "Had ye believed Moses, ye would have believed me." So here, "If John was from God, so am I."—But the other answer was as bad in another way. **But if we shall say, Of men; they fear-ed the people.** Luke, "All the people will stone us"—a strong testimony to the hold that John had upon the popular heart.—The ground of the fear, they all **counted John, that he was a prophet indeed,** whose divine mis-sion was beyond question. Yet not all the peo-ple had received his testimony to Jesus. But this popular estimate of John is fully confirm-ed by Josephus, who says that many of the Jews believed Herod's misfortunes to have come as punishment for his sins against John (Ant. 18. 5. 2).—So one answer would leave them without excuse before Jesus, and the other might expose them to the rage of the people. The only escape was in refusing to answer. **We cannot tell.** This should be, literally, "We do not know"—a false and cowardly evasion, a confes-sion of helplessness.—The dishonesty of the re-ply was a sufficient reason why Jesus should tell them nothing more. To such persons he could make no explanation of himself. **Neither do I tell you.** Notice that he did not say, "I

CHAPTER XII.

AND he began to speak unto them by parables. A* *certain* man planted a vineyard, and set an hedge about *it*, and digged *a place for* the wine-fat, and built a tower, and let it out to husbandmen, and went into a far country.

2 And at the season he sent to the husbandmen a servant, that he might receive from the husbandmen of the*b* fruit of the vineyard.

3 And they caught *him*, and beat him, and sent *him* away empty.

4 And again he sent unto them another servant: and at him they cast stones,*c* and wounded *him* in the head, and sent *him* away shamefully handled.

5 And again he sent another; and him they killed, and*d* many others; beating some, and killing*e* some.

1 AND he begun to speak unto them in parables. A man planted a vineyard, and set a hedge about it, and digged a pit for the winepress, and built a tower, and let it out to husbandmen, and went into another

2 country. And at the season he sent to the husbandmen a *1*servant, that he might receive from the hus-

3 bandmen of the fruits of the vineyard. And they took him, and beat him, and sent him away empty.

4 And again he sent unto them another *1*servant; and him they wounded in the head, and handled

5 shamefully. And he sent another; and him they killed: and many others; beating some, and killing

a Matt. 21 : 33 ; Luke 20 : 9....*b* Cant. 8 : 11 : Mic. 7 : 1 ; Luke 12 : 48 ; John 15 : 1-8....*c* Heb. 11 : 37....*d* Neh. 9 : 30 ; Jer. 7 : 25, etc......*e* Matt. 23 : 37.——1 Gr. *bondservant.*

cannot tell," or "I do not know." He might have spoken as in John 8 : 55: "If I should say, I know not, I should be a liar, like unto you." No time-serving policy was ever treated by him with friendly confidence.—Why did not our Lord avail himself of every opportunity to assert his Messiahship and offer himself as the Christ? Because his spiritual purpose could not thus have been so well served. He came, he said, as a witness to the truth; and his claim was, "Every one that is of the truth heareth my voice." He that had ears to hear would hear. He wished to be recognized, not to force his way. He wished his character and works to be his appeal. Hence his special claims of Messiahship were rare, and the spirit of John 14 : 10, 11 is the spirit of his address to men: "The words that I speak unto you, I speak not of myself: believe me, that I am in the Father and the Father in me."

1-12. THE PARABLE OF THE WICKED HUSBANDMEN. *Parallels*, Matt. 21 : 33-46; Luke 20 : 9-19.—Here follow, in Matthew, three parables most appropriate to the time, all dealing with the facts of ingratitude, unfaithfulness to trust, and the certainty of punishment. They are the parables of the Two Sons, the Wicked Husbandmen, and the Marriage of the King's Son. The nullification of God's command is prominent in the first, the rejection of his messengers and of his Son in the second and third. Mark and Luke give only the second, and both introduce it without any intimation that it was not the first of the series. Mark distinctly recognizes that there were others, however, by his **began to speak unto them by parables**. The three versions of this parable afford us another striking example of the verbal divergences of the evangelists joined with complete substantial agreement. The divergences here are considerable,

and distinctly prove that the three reports were made from memory and were not intended to preserve the very words of Jesus.

1, 2. The first sentence would remind his hearers of Ps. 80 : 8-11, and especially of Isa. 5 : 1-7, where Israel is Jehovah's vineyard. There, as here, the vineyard is provided with wall, tower, and wine-vat. While he does not exactly quote from Isa. 5, his language in both Matthew and Mark is so like that of the passage from Isaiah in the Septuagint as to render certain his intention to bring it to mind.—The **hedge,** or "wall," of the vineyard was sometimes a wall of earth, and sometimes a close-woven fence.—The **wine-fat** was the receptacle for the juice after it was trodden out. It was the lower one of two receptacles, or tanks, dug out of the earth or the rock. The grapes were trodden in the upper one, which was the wine-press, and the juice then flowed down into the vat below. In Matthew's description of the vineyard the wine-press is introduced, instead of the vat.—The **tower** was the place —sometimes literally a tower and sometimes only a cottage (Isa. 1 : 8)—from which the keepers viewed and guarded the property. (For details and illustrations, see Van Lennep's *Bible Lands*, 112-118.)—All this tells of a thorough fitting up of the vineyard, and suggests the language of Isa. 5 : 4: "What could have been done more to my vineyard, that I have not done in it?"—How often, in our Lord's parables, do we meet with this going **into a far country,** representing most vividly an actual trust in the hands of men! But the vineyard was well equipped, and the owner might certainly expect a fair return.—He sent for the fruit **at the season,** the reasonable time. He does not claim fruit before it can have grown.

3-5. A succession of attempts by the owner to secure his rights, and of insulting and abusive repulses by the employed. He sent a ser-

6 Having yet therefore one son, his well beloved, he^a sent him also last unto them, saying, They will reverence my son.
7 But those husbandmen said among themselves, This is the heir: come, let us kill him, and the inheritance shall be ours.
8 And they took him, and killed *him*, and cast *him* out^b of the vineyard.
9 What shall therefore the lord of the vineyard do? He will come and^c destroy the husbandmen, and will^d give the vineyard unto others.

6 some. He had yet one, a beloved son: he sent him last unto them, saying, They will reverence my son.
7 But those husbandmen said among themselves, This is the heir; come, let us kill him, and the inheritance shall be ours. And they took him, and killed him,
9 and cast him forth out of the vineyard. What therefore will the lord of the vineyard do? he will come and destroy the husbandmen, and will give the vine-

a Heb. 1 : 1, 2....b Heb. 13 : 12....c Prov. 1 : 24–31 ; Isa. 5 : 5–7 ; Dan. 9 : 26....d Jer. 17 : 3.

vant—another servant—another—many others. So in Mark; in Matthew, "his servants," "other servants more than the first ;" in Luke, "a servant," "another servant," "a third." But the many others in verse 5 is governed, not by he sent, but by a verb supplied from the sense: "Many others they maltreated, beating some and killing some."—In verse 4 translate, "And him they wounded in the head, and handled shamefully ;" omitting the reference to stoning. The word that is rendered wounded in the head (*kephalaioun*) is nowhere else used in that sense, or as descriptive of any physical action. It ordinarily means "to summarize" or "to sum up." But the physical sense here is scarcely to be doubted.—Evidently, in speaking of the servants, our Lord referred to the long line of the prophets. The true fruit from Israel would have been obedience to God; of which, obedience to his messages through the prophets would have been an important part. But with these words of the prophets are included all other messages and providential calls for faithfulness in the history of Israel. The slowness of Israel to understand from the heart the nature of its trust would have worn out any patience but the divine. As for the prophets, the career of Jeremiah is more fully recorded than any other, and may serve as an example, no doubt, of many; and it fully justifies the picture that is drawn in this parable. (See 2 Chron. 24 : 17–22, for the case of Zechariah, the son of Jehoiada. See also 2 Kings 17 : 13, 14; 2 Chron. 36 : 14–16; Neh. 9 : 26 for general statements on the rejection of the prophets; also the defence of Stephen, Acts 7.)

6. The last appeal, and the highest. One son, his well beloved, remained to the owner of the vineyard; a son, higher than the servants. (See the same thought gloriously unfolded in Heb. 1 : 1–4, and applied by way of exhortation in 2 : 1–4. The rank of him who is the Son is there made the special reason why he must be received.) In Luke, where the tone of deliberation is more marked, the owner says of his son, "It may be they will

reverence him." Of course, God did not say "perhaps," or ask, "What shall I do?" Yet, with reference to obtaining fruit from the Jewish people, the sending of his Son was just such a last resort as this. So the Son himself said (Luke 19 : 42; Matt. 23 : 34–37). If they had received him and rendered the rightful fruit of faith, far different would their lot have been.

7, 8. Let us kill him, and the inheritance shall be ours—*i. e.* by possession. Matthew, "Let us kill him, and let us seize on his inheritance." The fact that he was the heir served them as an argument for violence, not for reverence; for they thought, if he were once out of the way, no one else would trouble them. In this view verse 7 expresses not unfairly the spirit of the Jewish people, or at least of their leaders, respecting Jesus. True, it claims that they had a deeper conviction concerning his relation to God than they ever avowed. But he "knew what was in man," and knew that they were rejecting him because they felt, even though dimly, This is the heir. He was making such a claim on them as they had never felt before, and they dimly perceived that if this could but be silenced they should be left at peace.—They took him, and killed him, and cast him out of the vineyard. Threw his lifeless body over the wall, utterly and insultingly rejected him. In Matthew it is "cast him out of the vineyard and killed him," where some have thought they found a hint of the giving over of Jesus to the Gentiles to be put to death. But the hint, if it exists, is too vague for use, and probably was not intended at all. The parable was framed to teach a lesson broadly, not to provide a prophetic sketch of events. It is not likely that, when Jesus was so anxious to make the one point too plain to be missed, he spent thought on so vague and unimportant a suggestion as this would be.

9. Now comes the important question—a question of life and death to the trusted but unfaithful. What shall therefore the lord of the vineyard do? The obvious answer is

10 And have ye not read this scripture; The* stone which the builders rejected is become the head of the corner:
11 This was the Lord's doing, and it is marvellous in our eyes?
12 And* they sought to lay hold on him, but feared the people: for they knew that he had spoken the parable against them: and they left him, and went their way.
13 * And* they send unto him certain of the Pharisees and of the Herodians, to catch him in *his* words.

10 yard unto others. Have ye not read even this scripture;
The stone that the builders rejected,
The same was made the head of the corner:
11 This was from the Lord,
And it is marvellous in our eyes?
12 And they sought to lay hold on him; and they feared the multitude; for they perceived that he spake the parable against them: and they left him, and went away.
13 And they send unto him certain of the Pharisees and of the Herodians, that they might catch him in

a Ps. 118 : 22....*b* ch. 11 : 18; John 7 : 30....*c* Matt. 22 : 15; Luke 20 : 20, etc.

given in Mark and Luke by Jesus himself; in Matthew, by his auditors. (Compare the case of David, caught by a parable and led to condemn himself, 2 Sam. 12 : 5, 6.) Both may well have occurred, Jesus answering his own question and his answer being supported by their voices. According to Luke, some voices at least dissented, with a deep "God forbid!" These were the voices of the more penetrating, who saw the force of the parable, and who perceived, perhaps, that if it meant anything, it meant that God must destroy his own city and sacred place. But the true answer was too obvious to be escaped.—The disobedient husbandmen, who were robbers (Mat.3:8) and murderers too, must be deprived of their trust, and must receive the extreme punishment; and the vineyard must be entrusted to others, who will be faithful. Only in the answer of the hearers (Matthew) is it added, "who will render him the fruits in their season"—a living sign of their deep interest in the story. The prediction was fulfilled in the destruction of Jerusalem, the scattering of the Jewish people, and the entrusting of the kingdom of heaven to Gentile rather than to Jewish hands. If the ancient husbandmen had been true to their trust, they would not have been so cast out; but now the attitude of Paul and Barnabas at Antioch in Pisidia (Acts 13:46) was the only one that it was possible for a representative of the kingdom to take.

10, 11. The thought is, "But you are overlooking the question, What is to become of the rejected son? He was killed and thrown out of the vineyard: what of him?" Our Lord illustrated this question from Scripture, and Scripture adjacent to that which provided the hosannas of the people a few days earlier. The rejected stone becomes the corner-stone: to him who is now rejected belongs the first place of honor. The quotation is from the LXX, of Ps. 118 : 22, 23.—The corner-stone is no other than Christ himself. (Compare Acts 4 : 11; Eph. 2 : 20; 1 Pet. 2 : 7; and Isa. 28 : 16, from which last passage, probably, the whole group of references to the corner-stone proceeded.)

When he was speaking he was a rejected stone; but his confidence in the future was unwavering.—Verse 11, **This was the Lord's doing, and it is marvellous in our eyes.** Grammatically, "From the Lord did it" (the rejected stone) "become this" (**become the head of the corner**), "and it" (the head of the corner, the corner-stone) "is marvellous in our eyes." As for the origin of this metaphor, it is not necessary to accept, as Plumptre apparently does, the story of an unmarked stone, of strange proportions, rejected as unsuitable by the builders of Solomon's temple, but afterward discovered to be the corner-stone, sent from the quarry fitted to its place—a story that looks suspiciously like one invented to suit the passage. More likely the psalm was composed after the return from the Captivity, and the primary reference is to Israel restored and full of hope: "A people once rejected and of no account is now restored and re-established and counted as a foundation-stone of the temple of God, which he is setting up on the earth" (Kimchi, quoted in the *Bible Commentary*, on Ps. 118 : 22.) In the time of our Lord the passage was commonly referred to the Messiah.

12. His quotation had shown them the purpose of his parable, and now they took it to themselves in anger; not, as David, in penitence. Their anger was violent, but his hold on the people was too evident and too strong to allow them to arrest him. Mark alone adds **and they left him, and went their way.** They were baffled and helpless.

13-17. QUESTION CONCERNING TRIBUTE TO CÆSAR. *Parallels,* Matt. 22 : 15-22; Luke 20 : 20-26.—A consultation followed (Matthew), somewhere in the temple. Luke portrays the deliberate attempt to palm off a trumped-up inquiry as a genuine case of conscience. He also says that this question was intended to bring Jesus into the hands of the Roman Government.

13, 14. The same ill-starred union that was made before in Galilee (Mark 3 : 6) appears now in Jerusalem. **The Pharisees,** intense formal-

14 And when they were come, they say unto him, Master, we know that thou art true, and carest for no man; for thou regardest not the person of men, but teachest the way of God in truth: Is it lawful to give tribute to Cæsar, or not?

15 Shall we give, or shall we not give? But he, knowing their hypocrisy, said unto them, Why tempt ye me? Bring me a penny, that I may see it.

16 And they brought it. And he saith unto them, Whose is this image and superscription? And they said unto him, Cæsar's.

17 And Jesus, answering, said unto them, Render to Cæsar[a] the things that are Cæsar's, and to God[b] the things that are God's. And they marvelled at him.

14 talk. And when they were come, they say unto him, ¹Master, we know that thou art true, and carest not for any one; for thou regardest not the person of men, but of a truth teachest the way of God: Is it

15 lawful to give tribute unto Cæsar or not? Shall we give, or shall we not give? But he, knowing their hypocrisy, said unto them, Why try ye me? bring

16 me a ²denarius, that I may see it. And they brought it. And he saith unto them, Whose is this image and superscription? And they said unto him, Cæsar's.

17 And Jesus said unto them, Render unto Cæsar the things that are Cæsar's, and unto God the things that are God's. And they marvelled greatly at him.

a Matt. 17: 25, 27; Rom. 13: 7; 1 Pet. 2: 17....b Eccles. 5: 4, 5; Mal. 1: 6.——1 Or, Teacher....2 See marginal note on chap. vi. 37.

ists and nationalists, and the **Herodians,** compromisers and time-servers on both points, had no love for each other, but combined against Jesus.—The purpose was **to catch him in his words,** the verb meaning, literally, "to take in hunting." Matthew's word means "to take by a snare."—The messengers must have supposed themselves concealed beyond suspicion, or they would scarcely have attempted this great parade of candor and respect. How elaborate their pretence of confidence in his impartiality! **Is it lawful**—allowable for Jews—**to give tribute to Cæsar, or not? Shall we give, or shall we not give?** Not national tribute, but personal taxpaying, is meant. The word for **tribute** is *kénsos,* Latin *census,* and meant originally the annual tax that was assessed upon property enrolled in the census of the Roman Empire. But in Judæa, at that time, it meant an annual poll-tax of a denarius a head, collected of all subjects. The point of the question was, therefore, " Is it allowable for Jews to acknowledge the Roman power by submitting to its taxation?" No question could be more exciting. The Jewish people were widely affected by the doctrine that, since God was the King of Israel, the land was defiled by the presence of the Roman power, and no true Jew could pay taxes to it. (See Josephus, *Ant.* 18. 1. 1.) On this question fierce insurrections had arisen, attended with bloodshed. The Pharisees hated the tax; the attitude of the Herodians is somewhat doubtful. They had no love for the Romans, but it seems more probable that from motives of policy they maintained the lawfulness of the tax. If so, their agreement with the Pharisees was an agreement on the part of each to throw Jesus, if possible, into the hands of the other; as if each should say, "If he takes your side, he falls into my hands; if mine, into yours." If he opposed the tax, he could be reported to the governor as a rebel; if he consented to it, he would so excite the people that he could be reported to the governor as a dangerous character, even if the peo-

ple did not break out in violence against him and spontaneously do the murderous will of his enemies.

15-17. Before him hypocrisy is a useless mask. How his terse answer contrasts with their palavering question! and how plainly his indignation speaks out! **Why tempt ye me,** putting me to such a test?—**Bring me a penny—denarius—that I may see it.** Matthew, more fully, " the tribute money"—*i. e.* the coin in which the tribute is paid. It was paid in the Roman denarius, a silver coin worth originally about seventeen cents, but

DENARIUS.

reduced in weight before that time to the value of about fifteen cents. No hatred of the Romans sufficed to keep it from common circulation among the Jews. (See Matt. 18 : 28; 20 : 2; Mark 6 : 37; 14 : 5; Luke 7 : 41; 10 : 35.) There is said, however, to have been a coin, made in concession to Jewish prejudice, on which there was no portrait of the emperor. But a denarius with both likeness and legend was not far to seek, even if no one of the company had one, for the moneychangers were near.—**Whose is this image and superscription?** or, rather, "inscription."—**Cæsar's.** "Then you are under the government of Cæsar, and must render to him whatever belongs to the service of a subject. Your current coin acknowledges the Empire, and you are bound to obey its just demands."—Notice the word that he chose, in contrast with their word. They said **give,** *dounai;* he said, **Render,** or "Give back," *apodote.* They thought of the service as voluntary, he as an obligation. The question was not one of giving, but of pay-

18 ¶ Then* come unto him the Sadducees, which say[b] there is no resurrection; and they asked him, saying,
19 Master, Moses wrote[c] unto us, If a man's brother die, and leave *his* wife *behind him*, and leave no children, that his brother[d] should take his wife, and raise up seed unto his brother.
20 Now there were seven brethren: and the first took a wife, and dying, left no seed.
21 And the second took her, and died; neither left he any seed: and the third likewise.
22 And the seven had her, and left no seed: last of all the woman died also.
23 In the resurrection therefore, when they shall rise, whose wife shall she be of them? for the seven had her to wife.

18 And there come unto him Sadducees, who say that there is no resurrection; and they asked him, saying,
19 Master, [1]Master, Moses wrote unto us, If a man's brother die, and leave a wife behind him, and leave no child, that his brother should take his wife, and raise up
20 seed unto his brother. There were seven brethren: and the first took a wife, and dying left no seed;
21 and the second took her, and died, leaving no seed
22 behind him; and the third likewise: and the seven
23 left no seed. Last of all the woman also died. In the resurrection whose wife shall she be of them?

a Matt. 22 : 23; Luke 20 : 27, etc....*b* Acts 23 : 8,....*c* Deut. 25 : 5....*d* Ruth 1 : 11, 13.——1 Or, *Teacher*

---

ing, of discharging a duty. The government gave something to them, and they must give back something to the government. Thus he answered their question in the affirmative, and even went farther than that, asserting that tax-paying was not only allowable, but required.— But the clause that he added searched the heart. **And** (render, or give back) **to God the things that are God's.** "Duty to God stands unchanged; you are still invested with a trust from him, and are bound to return to him the loyalty and the obedience that are his due." The question related to the attitude that the people of God should take toward the Roman Empire. The answer was, " You can be loyal to both, and you must be loyal to both." But the form of the reply suggested the appeal or exhortation : "See that you are loyal to both. You do acknowledge Cæsar by paying his tax ; you do, because you must. Now see that you render to God his tribute, and give him what you owe to him."

Several practical truths are taught by this passage. (1) Established and recognized civil government has a valid claim on its subjects. So also Rom. 13 : 1-7, where Paul (at verse 7) seems to allude to this word of Jesus, using the same language : "Render therefore (*apodote*) to all their due." (2) This claim is partly for value received—a claim of justice for the good that government does. This is implied in the choice of the word " Render." (3) This claim is not inconsistent with the authority of God, but it is rather enforced by his authority. So in 1 Pet. 2 : 13-17, and still more emphatically in Rom. 13. God enforces this claim, partly because it is a claim for just return, and partly because civil government is one of the representatives and means of his own righteous administration among men. (4) This claim is not entirely dependent upon the subject's approval of the character of the chief magistrate. The Cæsar of that day was Tiberius. (5) Loyalty to God, however, occupies a field with

which civil government has nothing to do. God could rightfully require Israel to do its duty to Cæsar, but Cæsar could not rightfully require Israel to do its duty to God. In this field of religious obligation conflicts may arise between human authority and divine; in which case, if Cæsar intrudes, God is first to be obeyed. So, in principle, Acts 4 : 18-20; 5 : 29; Rev. 1 : 9. God built Cæsar's throne, and God's law is highest.

To the discussion of this exciting question of the day Jesus brought a new comprehensiveness. One party paid the tax willingly enough, in worldly indifference to God ; the other resisted it or paid it indignantly, burning with an ignorant zeal for God. It did not occur to either that true zeal for God and cheerful payment of the tax could be united. But he told them that, if they understood God's sovereignty and Cæsar's Empire, they could be loyal to both. Some things are due to Cæsar, and some to God ; and both can be rendered in full consistency. A fine example of new light by comprehensiveness.

The amazement of his questioners (expressed by a strong compound word) can easily be imagined. Instead of falling into the hands of either party, he had actually thrown new light on the question.

18–27. QUESTION OF SADDUCEES CON-CERNING THE RESURRECTION. *Parallels,* Matt. 22 : 23-33; Luke 20 : 27-39.

18. The Pharisees and Herodians having been silenced, it was the turn of **the Saddu-cees** to come forward. Their question is as insincere as the preceding; it was a puzzle upon a doctrine in which they were total un-believers. It proves, however, that the doctrine of the resurrection was everywhere recognized as a doctrine of Jesus.

19–23. This is the so-called Levirate marriage (from Latin *levir*, " a brother-in-law "). (See Deut. 25 : 5-10.) This provision corresponded to the universal desire in Israel for the per-petuation of name and family. So strong was

24 And Jesus answering said unto them, Do ye not therefore err, because ye know not the scriptures, neither the power of God?

25 For when they shall rise from the dead, they neither marry, nor are given in marriage; but^a are as the angels which are in heaven.

24 for the seven had her to wife. Jesus said unto them, Is it not for this cause that ye err, that ye know not 25 the scriptures, nor the power of God? For when they shall rise from the dead, they neither marry, nor are given in marriage; but are as angels in heaven.

a 1 Cor. 15 : 42, 53.

---

the desire that this provision was made for a putative offspring in default of actual. The custom was older than the law, however (Gen. 38 : 8), and exists in many Eastern nations. But the obscure expression in Deut. 25 : 5, " If brethren dwell together, and one of them die," leaves us uncertain in exactly what circumstances the law was applicable. There is no case recorded in the Old Testament, though there is an allusion to the custom in Ruth 1 : 11–13. The transaction of Ruth 4 : 1–8 is of another kind. These questioners stated the law fairly, but their illustration was an extreme one, meant for a *reductio ad absurdum.* The language of verse 19 is awkward, but there is no difficulty about the sense.—**There were seven brethren.** In Matthew, " there were with us," as if the case were fresh from the life. Verse 22 should be, simply, **and the seven left no seed : last of all the woman died also.** Childless by all the marriages, the woman was not linked to any one of the husbands more than to the others.— **In the resurrection, therefore, when they** (the woman and the seven brothers) **shall rise, whose wife shall she be of them?** It is assumed that she must be some one's wife, and how will Jesus judge between the rival claims of the seven?

24. There is something wonderful in the gentleness of the answer, considering the insincerity of the question. He quietly assumed that there was an error, and proceeded to account for it ; he did not even distinctly assert it. **Do ye not therefore** (from this cause) **err**—is it not for this cause that ye err—**because ye know not the scriptures, neither the power of God?** Is not ignorance the secret of your error? Ignorance (1) as to the Scriptures. He did not mean, of course, that the resurrection was mentioned in the Old Testament plainly, as it was mentioned by him. He meant that if they had understood the Old Testament rightly, they would have found the resurrection implied in its teaching, or at least would have been prepared to receive the doctrine. Not unfamiliarity with the Scriptures, but ignorance of their true meaning, kept them from believing in the resurrection. Moreover, a true knowledge of the Scriptures would have prevented their ideas from being so grossly carnal. (2)

As to the power of God. All their conceptions of a resurrection were of a low and carnal kind that underestimated the power of God as shown therein. They thought only of a re-establishment of the present fleshly life. No conception had they of the power of God to make life altogether new in the resurrection-state, but this is what he will do. Now follows the truth on these two points : (1) *The Power of God;* (2) *The Scriptures.*

The Power of God.—**25.** He tells them that they have not understood the resurrection : it is something far nobler than they have supposed, and it will work changes such as they never thought of. **When they shall rise from the dead.** General, and equal to " in the resurrection " of Matthew.—**They neither marry**—contract marriage as husbands—**nor are given in marriage,** by the act of their parents, as wives. In the resurrection-state there will be no marriage. The reason, as expressly given in Luke, is that they " cannot die any more." Marriage, especially as suggested by the Levirate institution, exists for the sake of offspring. But birth and death are correlatives ; they belong in the same world : if one ceases, the other must cease. In that world there is no death ; hence no birth, hence no marriage. The power of God will have brought into being that which Paul calls the spiritual body, in which sexual relations will not continue. Notice that this is not a denial of the perpetuity of those mental characteristics which distinguish the sexes in this world. It is not affirmed that they are excluded from the resurrection-state. It is not said that the holy spiritual relations and personal affinities that may have accompanied marriage will not continue, or that husband and wife will be nothing to each other in the future life. The questioners thought of that life as a continuation of this, with its relations unchanged ; and he simply told them that marriage, in that world, would be out of place. Upon the relations of soul with soul in that world he did not touch.—**But are as the angels which are in heaven.** Not "*are* angels," but "are *as* angels." The most that we know of angels is drawn from such allusions as this. What is here implied concerning them is that they are immortal, and hence

26 And as touching the dead, that they rise; have ye not read in the book of Moses, how in the bush God spake unto him, saying,[a] I am the God of Abraham, and the God of Isaac, and the God of Jacob?
27 He is not the God of the dead, but the God of the living: ye[b] therefore do greatly err.

26 But as touching the dead, that they are raised; have ye not read in the book of Moses, in *the place concerning* the bush, how God spake unto him, saying, I am the God of Abraham, and the God of Isaac, and the God of Jacob? He is not the God of the dead, but of the living: ye do greatly err.

a Ex. 3 : 6....*b* ver. 24.

among them the marriage relation does not exist.

Thus far, Jesus expounded the doctrine of the resurrection. The Sadducees rejected it, but they knew it only in a gross form. Very beautiful is his kindness in thus commending a rejected doctrine by presenting it in a nobler form ; as much as to say, " Would not even you have believed it, if you had known it thus ?" An example to all preachers and teachers. State your doctrine at its noblest ; perhaps those who reject it have never understood it.

The Scriptures.—26, 27. Now he turns to prove the doctrine that he has been expounding—*i. e.* to find it in the Holy Writings. He quoted from the book of the law (the Pentateuch), because from it the question had been drawn ; possibly, also, because the Sadducees prized it above the other Scriptures. The relation of this extract to the doctrine in discussion is somewhat peculiar. The expectation of a life beyond the present was expressed with greater or less clearness here and there in the Old Testament. Many of the writers had shown that they cherished such a hope, though not with the clearness of the gospel. But it was not the hope or expectation that Jesus now wished to bring out : it was the fact. Hence an expression of human desire or aspiration would not suit his purpose, even though it were made under the guidance of the Divine Spirit. He must find a direct utterance of God. This passage, therefore, may be expected to be of unusual importance respecting a future life. To this peculiarity of the case well corresponds Luke's peculiar word : "That the dead are raised, Moses also revealed"—brought to light—"at the bush."—Translate, in verse 26, "have ye not read, in the book of Moses, at the bush, how God spake unto him"—*i. e.* in the section or paragraph where "the bush" is the subject of discourse. (Compare 2 Sam. 1 : 18.)—**I am the God of Abraham, and the God of Isaac, and the God of Jacob.** The citation here is from Ex. 3 : 6, the words of Jehovah to Moses.—The words might be found in many other places of Scripture : no language was more characteristic of the old covenant or more familiar to Jewish ears. He took no recondite passage, but one of the great words of the old dispensation.—In

verse 27, **therefore** is to be omitted. The reading is, **He is not the God of the dead, but the God of the living : ye do greatly err**—*i. e.* ye greatly err in interpreting the text as if he called himself the God of men who do not now exist. If he is any man's God, you may know that that man exists.

How did he draw such an inference? By a fresh and rich principle of interpretation, arguing from the nature of God, and of God's relations to man. The Sadducees took the passage to mean, "I am the God in whom Abraham, Isaac, and Jacob put their trust during their brief existence, which is now for ever ended." But Jesus reasoned thus : "A God who did for the patriarchs what he did would not speak so of himself. He was gloriously their God—so gloriously that he could not call himself their God in such a sense, if their being had been but transient. If men were destined to become extinct, he could not be so gloriously a God to them. That such a God is or can be their God is proof that they are more than mortal." The argument is that the relations into which God enters, or proposes to enter, with men imply their immortality. The richness of man's relation to God is the fact from which Jesus infers his continued existence. See what a God becomes man's God, and it will be plain that he is no creature of a day. Notice that he does not present this as a fact that lies upon the face of Scripture, so that no one can miss it. The Sadducees missed it, and others may ; but Jesus teaches us that they who explore the Scriptures by the light of God's nature will find it.—As if in order to ensure that this should not be taken as an argument for conditional immortality—*i. e.* immortality for Abraham, Isaac, and Jacob as chosen ones—Luke adds that "all live unto him "—*i. e.* in such sense that he is "God of the living" to them, **all** are alive. A distinct statement of the continued existence of all human beings. The relation to God from which the argument is derived is naturally possible to all, if not actual ; and so the conclusion, of immortality, is true of all.—Notice that he draws no distinction here between continued existence and resurrection. The assertion of the former he regards as sufficient to establish the latter. If persons continue to exist, it is

28 ¶ And^a one of the scribes came, and having heard them reasoning together, and perceiving that he had answered them well, asked him, Which is the first commandment of all?

29 And Jesus answered him, The first of all the commandments is,^b Hear, O Israel; The Lord our God is one Lord:

30 And thou shalt love the Lord thy God with all thy heart, and with all thy soul, and with all thy mind, and with all thy strength.^c This is the first commandment.

31 And the second is like, namely this, Thou^d shalt love thy neighbor as thyself. There is none other commandment greater than these.

28 And one of the scribes came, and heard them questioning together, and knowing that he had answered them well, asked him, What commandment is the first of all? Jesus answered, The first is, Hear, O Israel; ¹The Lord our God, the Lord is one: 30 and thou shalt love the Lord thy God ²with all thy heart, and ²with all thy soul, and ²with all thy mind, 31 and ²with all thy strength. The second is this, Thou shalt love thy neighbor as thyself. There is

a Matt. 22 : 35....b Deut. 6 : 4, 5; Luke 10 : 27 ....c Ex. 20 : 2....d Lev. 19 : 18; Matt. 22 : 39; Rom. 13 : 9.——1 Or, The Lord is our God; the Lord is one....2 &c. from.

proper to speak of their resurrection. Compare John 5 : 29, where resurrection is predicted for the two classes that include all men.

Luke adds that after this answer some of the scribes responded, "Rabbi, thou hast well said," being, perhaps, as Farrar says, "pleased by the spiritual refutation of a scepticism which their reasonings had been unable to remove."—The fresh method that he thus introduced, of interpreting Scripture in the light of the nature of God and of his relations to men, is a method of boundless suggestiveness. This one specimen of exegesis is enough to prove the freshness and originality of the Christian light upon the word of God.

28–34. QUESTION OF A SCRIBE CONCERNING THE GREATEST COMMANDMENT. *Parallel*, Matt. 22 : 34–40.—In Matthew this question appears as the result of a conference of the Pharisees, encouraged by the defeat of the Sadducees, though doubtless rendered more respectful by their satisfaction at Jesus' victory. In Mark the questioner alone is mentioned. But Matthew reports only the question and answer, while in Mark the story is a rich chapter out of the personal life of the inquirer.

28. One of the scribes. Matthew says, "a lawyer;" the specialty of the scribes lay among questions of the law. He was an honest man, whose attention was now fastened by the wise and suggestive reply of Jesus to the Sadducees. That a lawyer-scribe should be pleased with that answer, a profound spiritual interpretation of a passage in the law, was itself a special mark of ingenuousness. That answer made him wish to know what Jesus thought on other points in the law.—Which—rather "what;" literally, "of what kind"—is the first commandment of all?—i. e. Of what sort must a commandment be, in order to be the first? What is the decisive quality that gives first rank to a commandment? This was one of the everlasting questions, the relative importance of various commands; but the discussions and decisions were often of the most

trifling kind. (See Farrar, 2. 238.) The qualitative word *poia*, "of what kind," probably indicates that the man was thinking of commands by classes, distinguished from each other by quality and graded according to importance. If so, his idea was a true one, and his view of the law was no means the lowest.

29, 30. Jesus answered him, The first of all the commandments is, Hear, O Israel, etc. Quotation, slightly varied, from the LXX. of Deut. 6 : 4, 5. The first words, Hear, O Israel; the Lord—or Jehovah—our God is one Lord, were a part of the form of morning and evening worship in the temple. No scriptural language was more sacred to Jewish ears.—Out of this affirmation of the reality and unity of the God of Israel ("I am God, and there is none else") naturally flowed the command to regard him with an exclusive and all-controlling love. Thou shalt love the Lord thy God (literally) "out of thy whole heart, and out of thy whole soul, and out of thy whole mind, and out of thy whole strength." The Hebrew (in Deuteronomy) enumerates heart, soul, and strength; but the LXX. rendered "heart" by "mind." Jesus introduces both. This enumeration was not intended by Moses, or by Jesus, as a metaphysical analysis of man, but rather as a cumulative and comprehensive statement of the obligation to love God. Yet there is a fitness in each word. Love to God is to possess the heart, where the affections dwell; the soul, the centre of personality; the mind, or understanding; and the entire active power of the man. The call for such love is the first claim of the law, not merely because such love will lead to obedience to all other commands, but for the deeper reason that such love is the natural and necessary claim of the good God upon moral beings. If there is a God who is worthy to be regarded at all, this is the first duty of men to him. Hence this law is eternal.

31. The second is like, namely this. Omit like, namely. Matthew has "the sec-

32 And the scribe said unto him, Well, Master, thou hast said the truth: for there is one God; and[a] there is none other but he:
33 And to love him with all the heart, and with all the understanding, and with all the soul, and with all the strength, and to love *his* neighbor as himself, is more[b] than all whole burnt-offerings and sacrifices.
34 And when Jesus saw that he answered discreetly, he said unto him, Thou art not far from the kingdom of God. And no man after that durst ask him[c] *any question.*

32 none other commandment greater than these. And the scribe said unto him, Of a truth, Master, thou hast well said that he is one; and there is none 33 other but he: and to love him with all the heart, and with all the understanding, and with all the strength, and to love his neighbor as himself, is much more than all whole burnt offerings and sac- 34 rifices. And when Jesus saw that he answered discreetly, he said unto him, Thou art not far from the kingdom of God. And no man after that durst ask him any question.

---

a Deut. 4:39; Isa. 45:5; 6:14; 46:9....*b* 1 Sam. 15:22; Hos. 6:6; Mic. 6:6, e.... *c* Matt. 22:46.——1 Or, *Teacher*

---

ond is like unto it," whence the word **like** was brought into the text of Mark. The likeness of love to God and love to man is a profoundly suggestive truth too much overlooked in Christian life. A large part of the First Epistle of John is an inspired commentary upon it.—**Thou shalt love thy neighbor as thyself.** Quoted from Lev. 19:18, where it is the climax of a noble series of moral commands in the midst of the book of ceremonies. By the Jews it was held in honor. Compare Luke 10:27, where "a certain lawyer" gave the two commands exactly as Jesus gave them now; but by them it was narrowly interpreted, in the spirit which Jesus condemned at Matt. 5:43-48 and by the parable of the Good Samaritan (Luke 10:30-37). Here he speaks of the second command as the proper sequence of the first, and of the second form of love as the natural result of the first. Love to God will flow out in love to man. Paul speaks of love to man as the fulfilling of the law, so far as man is concerned (Rom. 13:9). James honors this second command as "the royal law"— *i. e.* the king of laws—"according to the Scripture." John traces love to its source, affirming that love is from God and that God is love.—The solemn close of the answer is, in Mark, **There is none other commandment greater than these.** In Matthew, "On these two commandments hang all the law and the prophets." In Mark it is the unrivalled greatness of these that is emphasized; in Matthew it is the fact that these form the very life of God's revelation in the Old Testament. With such a statement of the law as this, we can well understand what our Lord said in Matt. 5:17 of his own teaching as the fulfilment, or completion, of the law; and we have no difficulty in accepting the strong language of the following verse about the eternity of the law. If love is the heart of God's revelation, in its older form as well as in its newer, then he was revealing, first as well as last, an eternal principle and an eternal law. Only its form can change.

32, 33. The remainder of the paragraph is peculiar to Mark. **Well**—*i. e.* finely, beautifully said. Translate, "Well, Rabbi! Truly

saidst thou that he is one, and there is no other besides him."—The scribe repeated the commands from Jesus' lips, only substituting **understanding** for **mind.** He repeated them as if he loved them, or at least deeply approved them.—**Is more than all whole burnt-offerings**—holocausts, offerings of animals to be wholly consumed, and thus the completest form of sacrifice—**and sacrifices.** Here the scribe went beyond the utterances of the law, technically so called, and took up the noblest tone of the prophets and psalmists. He had learned the lesson of such Scriptures as Ps. 40:6-8; 51:16, 17; 50:7-15; 1 Sam. 15:22; Isa. 1:11-20; Jer. 7:22, 23; Hos. 6:6; Mic. 6:6-8. In all these, obedience is set forth as better than sacrifice, and sacrifice is pronounced worthless apart from obedience in spirit. He had not learned the lesson so thoroughly as to be separated from the company of the Pharisees, but he was not ignorant of the great truth that religion is of the heart.

34. It was in this **that he answered discreetly,** or with understanding—namely, that he perceived the value of the religion of the heart. To perceive this was to touch the heart of Jesus. To prize love toward God and man is to be "discreet;" this is understanding. This is the "wisdom" of the book of Proverbs.—**Thou art not far from the kingdom of God.** Neither far from it, nor yet within it. This insight into spiritual things brought him near—very near; but he must act upon his insight, and part company with the perverters of Scripture and recognize the true King who stood before him, before he would be in the kingdom. The words are full of encouragement and of warning: Near! How easy, then, to enter! How terrible to go back!—We can neither repress nor answer the question, What became of the man? It is difficult to think that he turned back from the very gate. Yet what an opportunity just then for such a man to be "offended" in him! To how many can it be said, "The kingdom of God is come nigh unto you," to whom it cannot be said, "Thou art not far from the kingdom of God"!

This ended the questioning; no one ventured

35 ¶ And Jesus answered and said, while he taught in the temple, How say the scribes that Christ is the son of David?

36 For David himself said byᵇ the Holy Ghost, The Lord said to my Lord, Sit thou on my right hand, till I make thine enemies thy footstool.

37 David therefore himself calleth him Lord; and whence is he *then* his son? And the common people heard him gladly.

35 And Jesus answered and said, as he taught in the temple, How say the scribes that the Christ is the son of David? David himself said in the Holy Spirit,

The Lord said unto my Lord,
Sit thou on my right hand,
Till I make thine enemies ¹the footstool of thy feet.

37 David himself calleth him Lord; and whence is he his son? And ²the common people heard him gladly.

a Matt. 22 : 41 ; Luke 20 : 41....b 2 Sam. 23 : 2 ; 2 Tim. 3 : 16....c Ps. 110 : 1.——1 Some ancient authorities read *underneath thy feet*... 2 Or, *the great multitude*

to carry it farther. It is a sign of the independence of the narratives that Luke introduces this remark after the question of the Sadducees, Mark after the question of the scribe, and Matthew after Jesus' own question in return. But there is no contradiction here, for the remark stands in each evangelist at the end of the questioning, strictly so called, as that evangelist records it.

35-37. THE QUESTION OF JESUS IN RETURN. *Parallels*, Matt. 22 : 41-46 ; Luke 20 : 41-44.—Having repelled all their questions, he added to their defeat by asking one of his own, addressed, in Matthew, to the Pharisees, who were "gathered together," where also he draws out from them the statement that the Messiah **is the son of David.** In Mark and Luke he himself cites the statement—in Mark, from **the scribes,—That Christ is the son of David.** So he had been saluted the other day, at the entering of the city. That this name would rightfully belong to the Messiah, no one doubted in those days. (See Isa. 11 : 1-4 ; Jer. 23 : 5, 6, etc.)—The question of Jesus, **David therefore himself calleth him Lord; and whence is he then—**i. e. how can he be—**his son?** was not, of course, a denial of this, but a thrust intended to reveal the inadequacy of the current conception. The principle involved is that of comparing Scripture with Scripture; as if he had said, " Do not form your idea of the relation of the Messiah to David upon a single class of passages. Here is a passage that will modify your conception : have you thought of it? David speaks of him as his Lord ; there must therefore be something for you to add to your idea that he is David's son "—a necessary rule of interpretation, so self-evident that there ought to be no need of enforcing it. Yet there is need, for many influences conspire to lead Christians as well as Jews to forget it.

Concerning this passage (Ps. 110 : 1, quoted exactly from the LXX.), Jesus here affirms (1) that David was the author of it. His use of it turns upon this fact ; and thus he assents to the title that stands above the psalm, both in the Hebrew and in the LXX. (2) That David made

this utterance "in the Holy Spirit." This can mean only that the utterance was not solely David's own, but was made under an inspiration of the Spirit of God. No theory of inspiration is given here, but the fact is expressly stated. (3) That the passage was Messianic. Not for himself (1 Pet. 1 : 12), any more than for himself (2 Pet. 1 : 21), did David say this. It was one of those forward-looking utterances that found their full meaning only in him who was to come.—The passage, thus brought by the Lord himself to its application, took a powerful hold upon the faith and imagination of the church, and entered into the formation of doctrine. (See Acts 2 : 34-36 ; 1 Cor. 15 : 25 ; Eph. 1 : 20 ; Col. 3 : 1 ; Heb. 1 : 3 ; 8 : 1 ; 10 : 12 ; 12 : 2 ; 1 Pet. 3 : 22.) Here, however, the argument of Jesus turns on the word **Lord,** and implies the divinity of the Messiah. David's son would be a man ; but this Son of David was to be one whom David could also call his **Lord.** More than man, therefore, he must be. This is a warning that the scribes have their ideas of the Messiah still to mend and to conform to the teaching of the Scriptures.

And the common people—translate, " the great multitude " (*ho polus ochlos*)—**heard him gladly.** A touching testimony to his acceptance even on this last day of his ministry. It was a day of victory. How thankful all godly Jews ought to have been for such a voice as this, expounding the familiar Scriptures and revealing God!—The unhappy mistranslation, **the common people heard him gladly,** has been made the basis for inferences far too large—even if the text had been right—as to the character and popular effect of his ministry. It is a wonder that the revisers have retained it.

38-40. WARNING AGAINST THE SCRIBES. *Parallel*, Luke 20 : 45-47.—How much of Matthew's twenty-third chapter is parallel, as having been now uttered, it is perhaps impossible to say. A large part of that chapter has a close parallel in Luke 11 : 37-52, and Luke 13 : 34, 35 is identical with the conclusion of the discourse in Matthew. Accord-

12

38 ¶ And he said unto them[a] in his doctrine, beware[b] of the scribes, which love to go in long clothing, and love salutations in the market-places,

39 And[c] the chief seats in the synagogues, and the uppermost rooms at feasts:

40 Which devour widows' houses,[d] and for a pretence make long prayers: these shall receive greater damnation.

41 ¶ And[e] Jesus sat over against the treasury, and beheld how the people cast money into the treasury: and many that were rich cast in much.

42 And there came a certain poor widow, and she threw in two mites, which make a farthing.

---

38 And in his teaching he said, Beware of the scribes, who desire to walk in long robes, and to have [39] salutations in the marketplaces, and chief seats in the synagogues, and chief places at feasts; they who devour widows' houses, [1]and for a pretence make long prayers; these shall receive greater condemnation.

41 And he sat down over against the treasury, and beheld how the multitude cast [2]money into the treasury: and many that were rich cast in much. [42] And there came [3]a poor widow, and she cast in two

---

a ch. 4 : 2....b Matt. 23 : 1; Luke 20 : 46....c Luke 11 : 43... d 2 Tim. 3 : 6....e Luke 21 : 1.——1 Or, even while for a pretence they make....2 Gr. brass....3 Gr. one.

---

ing to Luke 11, the chief part of this discourse was spoken in a Pharisee's house, somewhere in Peræa. It seems most probable that Matthew, not having recorded the Peræan ministry, here combined several discourses of denunciation, which were actually delivered at various times. At the same time, the brief report in Mark and Luke may be only a fragment of what was said on this occasion. This appears to have been his last word with his enemies, as the discourse of John 14-16 was his last word with his friends.

Beware of the scribes, which love—correctly, desire—**to go in long clothing, and** (desire) **salutations in the market-places.** Luke inserts "love" before "salutations," but Mark carries the verb "desire" through the sentence.—**In long clothing.** Liddell and Scott render "in full dress"—i. e. in whatever official robes they were entitled to wear; not, as Jesus, in the clothing of common life.—**Salutations,** formal and prolix, forbidden by Jesus to his disciples on their journeys for work (Luke 10 : 4).—**Chief seats in the synagogues.** The seats nearest to where the sacred rolls of the law were kept.—**Uppermost rooms**—chief places, or couches—**at feasts.** The places of honor at the table. "Uppermost rooms" was once intelligible, but is strangely misleading now. "Room" meant "place," not apartment, when the translators used it thus. (For explanation of the allusion, see Luke 14 : 7-11.)—**Devour widows' houses.** As if this were what they fed upon in their first places at the feasts. Covetous designs that we cannot further specify are meant. "Insinuating themselves with defenceless women, as if they would truly be their defenders" (*Theophylact*).—**These shall receive greater**—or more abundant—**damnation,** or "condemnation." Greater, because they had misused their spiritual privileges, betrayed the trust of the simple, and brought reproach upon the name of God.—Our Lord's denunciations of the representatives of Judaism in his day seem terribly severe and

almost cruel; but what is known of the absurd and heartless refinements of the Pharisaism of that age fully supports the strong language that he used. What must have been the indignation of such a soul as his at such perversion of the religion of his Father!

41-44. THE POOR WIDOW AND HER OFFERING. Parallel, Luke 21 : 1-4.—**Jesus sat over against the treasury.** Peculiar to Mark. The treasury stood in the court of the women. Here were thirteen brazen chests, called *shopheroth*, or "trumpets," from the shape of the apertures for the reception of money. "Nine chests were for the appointed temple tribute and for the sacrifice tribute—that is, money-gifts instead of the sacrifices; four chests for freewill-offerings, for wood, incense, temple decoration, and burnt-offerings" (*Lightfoot*).—**Beheld**—as he sees now—**how the people cast money into the treasury.** Literally, "copper;" but the word had obtained the wider sense of money in general. That many of the gifts were large is an indication that it is used here in the wider sense.—**The verb beheld,** in the imperfect tense, seems to show that he was sitting and watching the stream of givers as it passed.

42. A certain poor widow—literally, "one poor widow"—coming alone; contrasted with the **many rich** who **cast in much.** Her gift evidently belonged among the freewill-offerings. The incident is fresh and striking after the mention of men who devour widows' houses. Even if this widow was not a victim of the scribes, she was one of the class whose misfortunes Jesus had freshly in mind.—**Two mites.** The *lepton* ("thin") was a very small copper coin. The *kodrantés*—which is the Latin *quadrans* transferred to Greek—was one-fourth of the Roman *as*. The *as*, originally of greater value, was worth at this time about eight mills; hence the *lepton*, "mite," was about one mill. She had not in her hand the single coin, the farthing, but the two that made up its value: "Of which the widow might have kept one" (*Bengel*). She freely gave both.

43 And he called *unto him* his disciples, and saith unto them, verily I say unto you, That* this poor widow hath cast more in, than all they which have cast into the treasury:

44 For all *they* did cast in of their abundance ;* but she of her want did cast in all that she had, *even* all her living.

---

43 mites, which make a farthing. And he called unto him his disciples, and said unto them, Verily I say unto you, This poor widow cast in more than all

44 they that are casting into the treasury: for they all did cast in of their superfluity; but she of her want did cast in all that she had, *even* all her living.

CHAPTER XIII.

AND as he went out of the temple, one of his disciples saith unto him, Master, see what manner of stones and what buildings *are here!*

2 And Jesus, answering, said unto him, Seest thou these great buildings? there* shall not be left one stone upon another, that shall not be thrown down.

---

1 AND as he went forth out of the temple, one of his disciples saith unto him, [1]Master, behold, what manner of stones and what manner of buildings!

2 And Jesus said unto him, Seest thou these great buildings? there shall not be left here one stone upon another, which shall not be thrown down.

---

a 2 Cor. 8: 2-12....*b* 1 Chron. 29 : 3, 17; 2 Chron. 24 : 10....*c* Deut. 24 : 6....*d* Matt. 21 : 1; Luke 21 : 5....*e* Luke 19 : 44.——1 Or, *Teacher*

---

43. He called unto him his disciples, that they might not miss such an opportunity to judge an act by its moral value. They were about to express their admiration of the splendor of the temple (chap. 13:1); but had they none for a beautiful action?—She **hath cast more in, than all they.** First stated, then proved. The standard is willingness, the inward grace of charity; but willingness cannot be measured apart from the standard of ability. She gave out of her penury; they, from their abundance. Nominally, they gave much and she gave little; but really they gave little and she gave much, for they gave their fragments and she her all. Their gifts were large, while hers was liberal.— "Liberality" is a much-misused word. Derived from the Latin *liber*, "free," it refers properly to the spirit of the gift, and not at all to its amount. Large givers may be illiberal, and liberal givers may not have much to give; but it is the cheerful giver, the liberal soul, that God loveth, whether his gift be large or small. There is a beauty in the great gifts of the rich, if the heart is right: the kingdom of God needs them, and the Master must esteem them valuable; but for the cheerful gifts of the poor he has a peculiar tenderness. With him quality is above quantity. (Compare Matt. 10 : 42, and an illustration of the genuine liberality in 2 Cor. 8 : 1–5.)

Here follow, probably, the request of the Greeks to see Jesus and the final utterance in the temple, ending at nightfall with the solemn appeal, "Yet a little while is the light with you. Walk while ye have the light, lest darkness come upon you" (John 12: 20-36). Then he went out of the temple, to enter it no more.

1-37. QUESTIONS CONCERNING THE DESTRUCTION OF THE TEMPLE, AND THE ANSWER. *Parallels,* Matt. 24 : 1-51; Luke 21 : 5-36.—The parallelism, however, is not perfect, verses 12, 13 having their precise parallel in Matt. 10 : 21, 22. Of the whole discourse, Matthew's report is the fullest, and Luke's is given in the most strongly-marked rhetorical style. The divergences in expression are very great, especially in Luke, but they probably give more of help than of difficulty in the interpretation.

1, 2. The time is the evening that followed Tuesday. In the Jewish reckoning it belongs to the next day, but we naturally connect it with Tuesday, the last day of the public ministry. The ministry was ended now, and this was the last departure of Jesus from his Father's temple.—**What manner of stones and what buildings.** Literally, "How great!" Luke adds the mention of the votive offerings with which the temple was decorated, the chief of which had been added by Herod the Great. (See allusions to, Josephus, *Ant.* 17. 6. 3.) The calling of our Lord's attention now to the splendor of the temple is commonly explained by reference to Matt. 23 : 37-39, where he had just implicitly announced the doom of the temple, whereby his disciples were led to wonder whether such buildings could be doomed. But it may be doubted whether the language of Matt. 23 : 37-39 was uttered at that time. It is found, almost word for word, in Luke 13 : 34, 35, in the record of the Peræan ministry, before the last arrival of Jesus at Jerusalem. At that time the language would be not only natural, but most solemn, and intelligible in a prophetic sense: "Ye shall not see me henceforth, till ye shall say, Blessed is he that cometh in the name of the Lord" (see Matt. 21 : 9); but on the last day of the ministry this would be an extremely obscure and strange prediction. Most probably, therefore, Matthew has here followed his custom of grouping, and brought in a remark that belongs to an earlier time.—But the admiration of the Galilean disciples for the splendid temple needs no special explanation. At this time the magnificence of the buildings struck them—or, as in Mark, **one of his disciples,** very likely Peter—and the exclamation came forth.—The

3 And as he sat upon the mount of Olives, over against the temple, Peter and James and John and Andrew asked him privately,
4 Tell us, when shall these things be? and what *shall be* the sign when all these things shall be fulfilled?

3 And as he sat on the mount of Olives over against the temple, Peter and James and John and Andrew
4 asked him privately, Tell us, when shall these things be? and what *shall be* the sign when these things are
5 all about to be accomplished? And Jesus began to

---

answer is a plain, unrelieved announcement of the coming total destruction of the temple and its buildings: **there shall not be left one stone upon another, that shall not be thrown down.**

3. These words were said as he went out from the temple and was going on his way (Matthew, according to the Revision). Going toward Bethany, **he sat upon the mount of Olives, over against the temple,** where the whole structure rose before him. By this time, probably, the dusk of evening was coming on. The questioners were **Peter and James and John and Andrew,** the special three, with the brother of Peter added; but it does not follow that no others were present.

4. [It is proper to remind the reader that neither the general editor nor the Society can be responsible for the interpretation of every passage in the Commentary. See General Introduction, p. 42 (2). For there are passages whose meaning, or whose full meaning, is doubtful; and the following must be regarded as one of them. Dr. Clarke has stated his own view ably, but has also in his concluding remarks presented the view which appears to the general editor correct. Yet the subject is so important that it may be well for those who can to read the following articles: "The Coming of Christ. Matt. 24: 29–31," by Dr. Edward Robinson, Bib. Sac., First Series (1843), pp. 531–537; "The Eschatology of Christ," etc., by Dr. C. E. Stowe, Bib. Sac., vol. vii (1850), pp. 452–478; "Observations on Matt. 24: 29–31, and parallel passages," etc., by Prof. M. Stuart, Bib Sac., vol. ix (1852), pp. 329–355 and 449–468.—A. H.] The actual contents of the inquiry must be carefully noted. There are two questions, of which the first is verbally identical in the three reports. **When shall these things be?** The second is, in Luke, literally, "What (will be) the sign when these things are about to come to pass?" In Mark, **What shall be the sign when all these things shall be fulfilled?** or, "When these things are all about to be accomplished." In Matthew, literally: "What (will be) the sign of thy coming, and of the consummation of the age?" The points of inquiry are, therefore, in Mark and Luke: (1) The time of the threatened destruction of the temple, and (2) the sign by which the

nearness of that time can be known. In Matthew they are (1) the time of the threatened destruction of the temple, and (2) the sign by which it can be known that the time of Christ's coming and the consummation of the age is near. There is no reason to doubt that the three evangelists intended to record the same question. Some suppose, however, that Matthew reports three questions instead of two: "When will the temple fall?" "What is the sign of thy coming?" "What is the sign of the end of the world?" But (1) "end of the world" is an unfortunate mistranslation, unfortunately retained by the Revisers, which has greatly obscured the whole discourse and the whole subject for readers of the English Bible. "The consummation of the age," on the lips of a Jew of that period, meant the completion of the ante-Messianic Jewish age, which completion was expected to come to pass in the establishment of the Messiah's kingdom. (2) That the questioners were thinking of only one event under the two forms of expression is plain from the fact that they conceived of one sign as answering for both: "What (will be) the sign (not signs) of thy coming and of the consummation of the age?" They thought that what would show them one would show them both. Jesus had spoken of his own coming in his kingdom (Matt. 16: 28; Mark 9: 1), and the disciples connected what he now said of the destruction of the temple with what he had already said on that subject; and both the destruction of the temple and the coming of his kingdom they associated with the ending of the ante-Messianic Jewish age. Matthew, with his Jewish coloring, gives more of the language of Messianic expectation, but the questions are the same in all. They are as simple as the inquiries of children. The disciples were innocent of doctrinal intention, because ignorant of the whole matter of inquiry; and we are not justified in drawing doctrinal inferences from the form of their questions. They asked simply, "When will the temple fall?" and "What will be the sign that the fall of the temple is near?"

5. The discourse that follows has proved one of the most perplexing in the Bible. The writer of this Commentary does not expect to reach an interpretation that is free from difficulties. He wishes faithfully to interpret the

5 And Jesus, answering them, began to say, Take⁴ heed lest any *man* deceive you:
6 For many shall come⁵ in my name, saying, I am *Christ*; and shall deceive many.

say unto them, Take heed that no man lead you 6 astray. Many shall come in my name, saying, I am

---

a Jer. 29: 8; Eph. 5: 6; 2 Thess. 2: 3; Rev. 20; 7, 8....*b* Acts 5: 36-39; 1 John 4: 1.

---

text, not to supplement it. Some relief from the perplexities may, perhaps, be found by regarding the following hints, which seem worthy to be followed. 1. It is to be presumed that Jesus meant to answer the questions that were asked him. 2. It is to be presumed that he meant, in general, to be understood, not that he intended to perplex his hearers. He may not have been able so to speak that they should perfectly understand him, but we can scarcely suppose that he intended to answer their sincere though ignorant inquiry by leading them into insoluble difficulties, especially new ones which they had not yet encountered. He often spoke in parables, but never in riddles. 3. Hebrew prophecy, not English prose, is the type upon which the discourse is formed, and by which it is to be interpreted. Modern readers easily forget into how prolific a seed-bed of Old Testament thought the words of Jesus fell when they entered the minds of his disciples. With the tone and language of Hebrew prophecy they were thoroughly familiar; and Hebrew prophecy differs widely from English prose in its modes of expression. 4. Such a discourse may be expected to contain notes of time that will serve as a key to its interpretation. A prophetic discourse in reply to a direct question as to time will probably not be left indeterminate as to the time of its fulfillment. Such notes of time, when found, must be carefully regarded, never explained away. 5. Upon any theory, it is no reproach to an interpreter if he cannot point out the exact fulfillment of every part. Even as to what is already past, it is impossible to assume the completeness of written history. How much should we know of that destruction of the temple which our Lord foretold, if it were not for a hundred pages of Josephus? 6. This discourse is not the whole of Scripture, and it is not to be assumed that what is not found here cannot be found anywhere in the word of God. The present duty is to study and interpret this discourse, not to unfold the entire scriptural doctrine on the points which it may suggest. That doctrine may be much larger than the teaching of this discourse.

OUTLINE.—The discourse divides itself into four parts: 1. *The signs of the coming*

event (5-23); 2. *The event itself Apocalyptically portrayed* (24-27); 3. *The time of the event* (28-32); 4. *Exhortation to vigilance* (33-37). These divisions are substantially the same in Matt. 24—viz.: The signs (4-28); the event (29-31); the time (32 36); exhortation (37-51). The same also in Luke 21: The signs (8-24); the event (25-28); the time (29-33); exhortation (34-36).

I. THE SIGNS OF THE COMING EVENTS. Verses 5-23.—A clear note of time is given in verse 14, where the Christians in Judea are commanded to flee thence to the mountains. This note of time distinctly places the signs in the period that preceded the fall of Jerusalem, for to no other period could such a command apply. Thus this section of the discourse (5-23) at least is in direct response to the question of the disciples concerning the destruction of the temple. Interpreters are generally agreed in this, though some would find a second application to events still future. This second application many would find in the latter part of the discourse, and some in the whole. On the question of such a double reference, see note at the end of the chapter. **Jesus, answering them, began to say**—or, as in the Revision, "Jesus began to say to them," a form of speech that corresponds to the promise of weighty utterance. Compare the opening of the sermon on the mount. (Matt. 5: 2.)

First Sign: The Coming of False Christs. Verses 5, 6.—A prediction that belongs by internal fitness to the Jewish period alone. In no other nation or period would the coming of false claimants to the Messiahship be a matter of importance to the destinies of the kingdom of God. In the present age, for example, the arising of such claimants among the Jews would not affect the kingdom—the Christ is too firmly enthroned. **In my name.** Not, of course, claiming to be Jesus the Nazarene, but claiming to be the Messiah. To come in that name, Jesus says, is to come in his name. How clear an assertion of his own right to it! Before the fall of Jerusalem, the land of the Jews was overrun with impostors, who sought to inflame religious zeal for political purposes. "These were such men as deceived the people under pretence of divine

7 And when ye shall hear of wars and rumors of wars, be ye not troubled: for *such things* must needs be; but the end *shall* not *be* yet.

8 For nation shall rise against nation, and kingdom against kingdom; and there shall be earthquakes in divers places, and there shall be famines and troubles: these *are* the beginnings of sorrows.

9 ¶ But take heed to yourselves: for they shall[b] deliver you up to councils; and in the synagogues ye

7 *he*; and shall lead many astray. And when ye shall hear of wars and rumors of wars, be not troubled: *these things* must needs come to pass; but the end is not yet. For nation shall rise against nation, and

8 kingdom against kingdom: there shall be earthquakes in divers places; there shall be famines: these things are the beginning of travail.

9 But take ye heed to yourselves: for they shall deliver you up to councils; and in synagogues shall

a a. 27: 3; 46: 1, 2; Prov. 3: 25; John 14: 1, 27....b Matt. 10: 17, etc.; Rev. 2: 10.

inspiration, but were for procuring innovations and changes of government; and these prevailed with the multitude to act like madmen, and went before into the wilderness, as pretending that God would show them there the signal of liberty." (Josephus, *Wars*, 2. 13. 4.) (See Acts 21 : 38 for an example.) The time of these pretenders, according to Josephus, was during the procuratorship of Felix (A. D. 53–60), and the trouble of Paul at Jerusalem fell in the midst of the period of these excitements. **Take heed**, says Jesus, **lest any man deceive you; for these shall deceive many.**

Second Sign: Wars and Calamities. Verses 7, 8.—Verse 8 is explanatory of the first part of verse 7, and the last part of verse 7 is the resulting word of counsel. They should hear of wars actual and terrible, **and rumors of wars,** threatening still more terrible things, but born of excitement and fear; actual troubles sore enough, but giving rise to fear of worse. There is no need to point out special wars and rumors as the ones that he had in mind, for it was a period of disturbance: four Roman emperors murdered in swift succession, and the world agitated by the changes; the Jews suffering in strifes and insurrections in various places; the Roman power threatening more and more in Palestine, and bringing home strong fear to the Jews who dwelt there. One chapter in Josephus (*Wars*, 2. 18) amply illustrates and confirms our Lord's warning. As for troubles in the realm of nature, **earthquakes** are known to have been more frequent in that century than in almost any other in the history of man, and **famines** afflicted many countries. The words **and troubles** are omitted in the best text. Luke adds, "and pestilences." These are true signs; but they are preliminary signs, not final. **Be ye not troubled, for such things must needs be; but the end shall not be yet.** Luke—"the end is not immediately." What **end?** Best interpreted by contrast with the word **beginning** in verse 8: **these are the beginnings of sorrows—**

literally, "The beginning of birth pangs are these." Not yet is the end of the birth pangs, not yet is the end of the preliminary signs and sorrows; for **nation shall rise against nation, and kingdom against kingdom;** there shall be earthquakes, there shall be famines,—and these are the beginning of birth pangs, not the end; **the end shall not be yet.** "The beginning of birth pangs." Both words are significant. This is only the beginning, and there is yet more to be endured—a word of warning. But these are not fruitless pains: they are like the pains of travail. By them the new spiritual kingdom is to be brought into the world. When they are ended, the Old Dispensation will be a thing of the past, but the new will be fully born. This is a word of hope. This caution against fear, and this thought that these were birth pains, may well have been watchwords of patience and courage among the Christians when the trouble came.

Third Sign: Persecution Against Christians. Verse 9.—**But take heed to yourselves.** The pronoun should be expressed, and that emphatically. " But do ye take heed to yourselves" is not too strong. You, in such troubles, must have an eye to your conduct. Here note, to be remembered through the whole discourse, that when our Lord uses the emphatic *you* (*humeis*), it is to be presumed that he refers to his immediate hearers. **Take heed** is not a caution to keep out of danger, but a warning against thoughtless and unworthy actions. **They shall deliver you up to councils.** The council was the local court attached to the synagogue, which had power in cases of religious offense. (Matt. 5 : 22.) The beating in synagogues is illustrated in Acts 22 : 19 and 26 : 11, Saul of Tarsus having a hand in the work. Thus far the persecution is Jewish, but the words that follow point to similar testimony before Gentile authorities. The word for **rulers,** "governors," is always applied in the New Testament to officers of the Roman Empire, as Pilate, Felix, Festus. It would seem that

shall be beaten; and ye shall be brought before rulers and kings for my sake, for a testimony against them.
10 Andᵃ the gospel must first be published among all nations.
11 But when they shall lead *you*, and deliver you up, take no thought beforehand what ye shall speak, neither do ye premeditate; but whatsoever shall be given you in that hour, that speak ye: for it is not ye that speak, butᵇ the Holy Ghost.
12 Now the brother shall betray the brother to death, and the father the son: and children shall rise up against *their* parents, and shall cause them to be put to death.
13 And ye shall be hatedᵈ of all *men* for my name's

ye be beaten; and before governors and kings shall ye stand for my sake, for a testimony unto them.
10 And the gospel must first be preached unto all the
11 nations. And when they lead you *to judgment*, and deliver you up, be not anxious beforehand what ye shall speak: but whatsoever shall be given you in that hour, that speak ye: for it is not ye that speak,
12 but the Holy Spirit. And brother shall deliver up brother to death, and the father his child; and
13 them to be put to death. And ye shall be hated of all men for my name's sake: but he that endureth to the end, the same shall be saved.

a Matt. 28 : 19; Rev. 14 : 6....*b* Acts 2 : 4; 4 : b, 31; 6 : 10....*c* Mic. 7　6....*d* Luke 6 : 22; John 17 : 14.—1 Or, *put them to death.*

under the word **kings** Roman emperors must be included, and the standing before governors and kings must be a standing there as "prisoners of the Lord." (Eph. 4: 1.) Yet it is to be **for a testimony unto them**—(not against them), whereby even governors and kings shall be made to know of him who is King of kings and Lord of lords. Paul is the most familiar example of all this, standing before Felix, Festus, Agrippa, Nero. Other apostles had similar experiences, though we see them mainly in their relation to Jews. Matthew adds here: "They will kill you." See Acts 12: 2 for the fate of one of the four questioners; concerning another, see Rev. 1: 9; another still, John 21: 19, 20.

Fourth Sign: Diffusion of the Gospel. Verse 10.—**And the gospel must first be published (preached) among all nations.** Literally, "unto all the nations"—*i. e.*, as far as to all the nations. Matthew has, literally, "in all the inhabited world." Luke omits. The natural meaning is, that the good news of the kingdom must, before the end of the birth pangs, be widely proclaimed among the existing nations. Until it could be reasonably said that this had been done, the end of the sorrows was not to be looked for. How long and how severe the pains would be, the disciples might infer from the fact that the whole inhabited world was to be visited with the message before they could end. It might seem enough that they must suffer "perils of their own countrymen," hatreds and cruelties of the Jews, but they must look forward to they knew not how many "perils of the Gentiles," in a field as wide as the known world. This word concerning all the nations is a step toward the great command written in Matt. 28: 19. See also Mark 14: 9. As to the fulfillment of the prediction, we find Paul affirming that the gospel is already known "in all the world." (Col. 1: 6.) See also Rom. 1: 8. He says, again, that it is "preached in all

creation under heaven" (so, correctly, in the Revision, Col. 1: 23), and, as if in explicit reference to this prediction, "made known to all nations for the obedience of faith." (Rom. 16: 26.) All this was written, of course, years before the fall of Jerusalem. The amazingly rapid diffusion of the gospel before the sweeping away of the Old Dispensation is a well-known matter of history.

Counsel to the persecuted. Verses 11-13.— Before coming to the fifth and last sign of the predicted event, Jesus makes a digression, specifying some details of persecution and instructing his disciples how to act. The case is that of actual arrest. **Take no thought beforehand what ye shall speak.** The best text omits **Neither do ye premeditate.** The word translated **take no thought** is the same as in Matt. 6: 25, and the sentence is properly rendered in the Revision "Be not anxious beforehand." The command is not against reflection or suitable preparation, but against anxiety about the defense that must be made before the tribunal. That defense should be provided for: the Holy Spirit should speak in them. In Luke—sublime self-assertion!—"I," the pronoun emphatic in the Greek—"I will give you a mouth and wisdom which all your adversaries shall not be able to withstand or to gainsay." Accordingly, they were to speak what might be given them; and with this promise they might dismiss all anxious fear. A fresh warning is now added of the intensity of the persecution. Not only in courts and synagogues should it be met with, but at home and among kindred. **The brother shall betray the brother to death**—*i. e.*, report him as a Christian and enter complaint that will result in his death. By the same means, parents shall cause the death of children, and children of parents. Compare Matt. 10: 34-37. **Ye shall be hated of all men.** A strong expression for the hatred that should meet them on every side,

sake: but he* that shall endure unto the end, the same shall be saved.

14 ¶ But when ye shall see the abomination of desolation spoken of[b] by Daniel the prophet, standing where it ought not (let him that readeth understand,) then let them that be in Judea flee to the mountains:

14 But when ye see the abomination of desolation standing where he ought not (let him that readeth understand), then let them that are in Judea flee

a Dan. 12 : 12 ; Rev. 2 ; 10....*b* Dan. 9 ; 27.

---

abundantly justified by the terms in which the early Christians were spoken of in literature, both by Jews and by Gentiles. For my name's sake. See 1 Peter 4: 16; Acts 5: 41. It was exactly for this that they did suffer. Tertullian says: "We are tortured when we confess our crime, and set free when we deny it; for the strife is about a Name." Hated by all, yet there is a promise to "him that overcometh." **He that shall endure unto the end, the same shall be saved**—*i. e.*, he that persists in faith and godliness and devotion to the kingdom until these calamities are overpast, or so long as God calls him to endure, he shall possess the salvation of which the kingdom has promise. Parallel, in spirit, are all the promises to the conqueror in Rev. 2, 3.

Fifth and Final Sign: The Invasion of the Sacred Place. Verse 14.—All the other signs have been preliminary, but this marks the coming of the actual end of the birth pangs. "Then shall the end come" (Matt.), complementary to "the end shall not be yet" (ver. 7), the end of these sorrows, which are sorrows of hope. At length the birth pangs are to be concluded. **Spoken of by Daniel the prophet** is rightly omitted here by the Revisers. The words are genuine in Matthew, but not in Mark. So the fifth sign is, in Mark, **When ye shall see the abomination of desolation standing where it ought not.** In Matthew, "When ye see the abomination of desolation, spoken of by Daniel the prophet, standing in the holy place." Luke says nothing of the abomination of desolation, but he perhaps retains a trace of the expression when he says, "Then know that her desolation is at hand." But Luke throws great light upon the obscure phrase by substituting for it, "When ye see Jerusalem compassed with armies." The discussion of the relation of this passage to the Book of Daniel belongs to the Commentary on Matthew, where alone the allusion to Daniel is genuine. The rendering of the Revisers, "Standing where he ought not," appears to be due to the fact that, in the text which they adopt, the participle "standing" is in the masculine gender (*heste-*

kota, instead of *hestos*, which is neuter). The participle thus fails to agree with the noun "abomination" (*bdelugma*), which is neuter; and the Revisers appear to have felt that such an irregularity must have been intentional, and must indicate that the abomination was conceived of, partly at least, in a personal manner.

The abomination of desolation—*i. e.*, the abominable thing, or power. whose work it is to make desolate. The parallel and explanatory language of Luke, already cited, proves that the phrase refers in some way to the Roman armies, half personified, perhaps, as indicated by the participle—the desolating, insulting heathen power, with its abominations of false worship. **Standing where it ought not** is equivalent to Matthew's "standing in the holy place"; and the holy place is, most naturally, the temple and its consecrated ground. The fifth sign is, therefore, "When ye see the invading Roman power pressing up to the temple, and even into it." This is the final sign that the time is at hand. It is not necessary to suppose that our Lord was referring exclusively to any one act in the history of the siege, so that the sign should be recognizable solely in some single moment. "When the siege is so far advanced that the enemy is closing around the temple"—this is the sign. The siege of Jerusalem began at about the beginning of the year 70 A. D.; operations against the tower of Antonia and the part of the city in which the temple stood began in the month of May; the tower was taken on the 11th of June; the temple was fired on the 16th of July; the siege of the upper city, enclosed within the ancient wall of David and Solomon. was soon after begun; and about the 12th of September the Romans entered through the breach they had made in that wall. See Smith's *Dictionary of the Bible*, Art. "Jerusalem." Thus, in the course of the siege, there was time for Christians to watch the progress of events toward the fulfillment of this sign.

Let him that readeth understand is parenthetical, commonly read as a remark of Jesus, meaning, "Let him that readeth the Book of

15 And let him that is on the house-top not go down into the house, neither enter *therein*, to take any thing out of his house.
16 And let him that is in the field not turn back again for to take up his garment.
17 But woe to them that are with child, and to them that give suck in those days!
18 And pray ye that your flight be not in the winter.

15 unto the mountains: and let him that is on the housetop not go down, nor enter in, to take any thing
16 out of his house: and let him that is in the field not
17 return back to take his cloak. But woe unto them that are with child and to them that give suck in
18 those days! And pray ye that it be not in the

Daniel understand it, so as to make this application of his language" ; but better read as a remark of the Evangelist, meaning, "Let him that readeth this forewarning from the Lord understand it, and be ready, when the sign appears, to act upon the accompanying command." In Mark there is no allusion to Daniel, and when he counsels **him that readeth,** he can address his words to no other than **him that readeth** this book. When the Gospels of Matthew and Mark were written, the time had not yet come, though the preliminary signs must have begun to appear. During the progress of those signs, until the last one should appear, the Lord had commanded nothing but brave endurance ; but the last sign was to be to them the signal for flight. Therefore it was especially important that this sign should be recognized and understood. It looks as if the preachers of the evangelical story had been in the habit of pointing this prediction by a sharp call to attention, and Matthew and Mark took it up in their written gospels with a kind of *nota bene:* "Let the reader understand." That Mark was writing for Gentiles is scarcely an objection, for this discourse had been made familiar to Jewish and Gentile believers alike before it was here written out. Luke, who seems to have written later, omits the appeal.

(1) *Command for the Time of the Fifth Sign.* Verses 15, 16.—The command is for the Christians who may be in Judea to flee instantly to the mountains when the sign appears. **To the mountains**—general, denoting any place of refuge in the wild country ; not unlikely with a slight, but intentional reference, to the story of Lot, and the command given him to "escape to the mountains" from the doomed city of Sodom. The command is given with more detail by Luke: "Then let them that are in Judea flee unto the mountains, and let them that are in the midst of her (Jerusalem) depart out ; and let not them that are in the country enter therein." Great emphasis is laid on the promptness of the flight. **On the housetop.** The houses were flat-roofed, and Christians might be on the roofs of their houses for prayer (Acts 10: 9), for rest, or for observation.

In some cases there were outside stairs, and the roofs of adjacent houses were sometimes connected, so that the nearest way to flee might be across the roof of another house. Instant flight was commanded, without so much as going down through the house to take anything ; and the man who might be at work in the field without his coat or outer garment, was to flee the shortest way, not going home for it. The one thing was to get away from Judea. Josephus (*Wars,* 4. 9. 1.) records the fact that during the earlier part of the siege of Jerusalem, many escaped from the city to places of safety. Eusebius (*Eccl. Hist.,* 3 5.) is our authority for the statement that the Christians seized the providential opportunity for escape, and withdrew from Judea to Pella, in the mountains of Gilead, where they found a safe refuge.

(2) *Further Warning of the Sorrows of that Time.* Verses 17-20.—**Woe** is an exclamation of pity here, not of condemnation. The tender heart of Jesus foresaw the sufferings of women with child, and with children in their arms. The sufferings of such in the siege were among its darkest horrors. These his friends would escape, but the flight would have its horrors too ; and that these might be alleviated as much as possible, he would have them pray. **Pray ye that your flight be not in the winter**—in the best text, "that it be not in winter." Matthew alone, writing for Jews, adds, "nor on the Sabbath day." Apart from any scruples of the Jewish Christians about the Sabbath of the law, there might be special difficulties in fleeing on that day through a land where the Sabbath was honored as in Judea. As for the winter, the hardships of hasty traveling in winter in Palestine are very great, as all who have tried it testify ; and these were bidden to flee without pausing to take with them even the most common comforts. Notice how perfectly unrevealed is the precise time of the event. It is proper matter for prayer. He intimates that it would not be in vain for them to pray concerning such matters as the time when the Roman armies should press into the holy place. They might pray concerning the season of the year, and even the day of the

19 For* *in* those days shall be afliction, such as was not from the beginning of the creation which God created unto this time, neither shall be.
20 And except that the Lord had shortened those days, no flesh should be saved; but for the elect's sake, whom he hath chosen, he hath shortened the days.
21 And then if any man shall say to you, Lo,*b* here *is* Christ; or, Lo, *he is* there; believe *him* not:
22 For false Christs and false prophets shall rise, and shall shew signs and wonders, to seduce, if *it were* possible, even the elect.

19 winter. For those days shall be tribulation, such as there hath not been the like from the beginning of the creation which God created until now, and
20 never shall be. And except the Lord had shortened the days, no flesh would have been saved: but for the elect's sake, whom he chose, he shortened the
21 days. And then if any man shall say unto you, Lo, here is the Christ; or, Lo, there; believe *it* not:
22 for there shall arise false Christs and false prophets, and shall shew signs and wonders, that they may

a Dan. 12 : 1 ; Joel 2 : 2....*b* Luke 17 : 23.——I Or, *him.*

week, in which the announcement of the final sign should reach them. As a matter of fact, it was not **in the winter.**

For in those days shall be affliction— correctly, in the Revision, "those days shall be tribulation," or, "a tribulation." The days shall be so heavy with woe as to be themselves an affliction, a burden of misery. **Such as was not from the beginning of the creation which God created unto this time.** Characteristic expansion by Mark of what is briefer in Matthew, "from the beginning of the world." A part of the same expression is found in 2 Peter 3 : 4. **Neither shall be.** Except, of course, in the case now mentioned. Compare the parallel language of Luke: "For these are days of vengeance, that all things that are written may be fulfilled. . . . And there shall be great distress upon the land, and wrath upon this people"— i. e., upon Israel. See 1 Thess. 2 : 14–16, where the same announcement of wrath is recorded. [Does not Paul refer to calamities that came upon the Jews before he wrote to the Thessalonians?—A. H.]

Except that the Lord had shortened those days, no flesh should be—or would have been—**saved.** No mortal man within the circle of which the context speaks would have been preserved alive. This limitation of the field of thought is obvious, and this is the only sense that the context will allow to the word **saved.** If the destruction had been permitted to go on as long as the passions of men would have continued it, the land would have been swept of people. **The Lord,** who **short·ned the days,** is Jehovah, the God of the old covenant. Jesus does not give this title to himself. The shortening of the days is mentioned in the past tense: **He hath short·ened the days**—i. e., they were shortened in the counsel of God, which in all this was to be fulfilled. Various causes conspired to shorten the siege: (1) Herod Agrippa had begun to strengthen the walls of Jerusalem in a way which, if finished, would have rendered them

"too strong for any human power" (Josephus), but was stopped by orders from Claudius (A. D. 42 or 43); (2) the Jews, being divided into factions, had totally neglected to make provision to stand a siege; (3) the magazines of corn and provisions had been burned just before the arrival of Titus with his besieging army; (4) Titus arrived suddenly, and the Jews voluntarily abandoned parts of the fortifications. (*Alford,* quoted from Greswell.) It is **for the elect's sake, whom he hath chosen,** that the Lord shortened the days. **The elect,** here, are the believers in Christ, who are concerned in these troubles— i. e., the Jewish Christians. These, like others who believed, he had chosen to be "heirs of the kingdom" (James 2 : 5), and these he would keep alive for further use on the earth; therefore in his providence the time of destruction was limited. This was the "remnant" existing then in Israel, as in the days of Elijah (1 Kings 19 : 18), and as when the other prophets spoke (Isa. 1 : 9; Ezek. 11 : 13) the faithful part, for the sake of which God's counsels were gracious. This "remnant" was the true Israel in the days of the prophets, and the Christians were the true Israel in this time of tribulation. See Phil. 3 : 3; also Rom. 2 : 28, 29. Here, then, was the outcome of our Lord's personal ministry; many were called among the Jewish people, but few were chosen (Matt. 12 : 14)—i. e., the elect were few. Compare 2 Peter 1 : 10: "Wherefore the rather give diligence to make your calling and election sure,"—make sure that you are found, not only among the many who are called, but among the few who are chosen. The many perished in the guilt of their rejection, while for the sake of the few the days of tribulation were shortened.

(3) *Repeated Caution, Concluding the First Division of the Discourse.* Verses 21–23.— **False Christs** and **false prophets** again, in the wilder and more terrible excitements of the "end" of the troubles. The culmination of the woe brings the climax of fanaticism

23 But take ye heed; behold, I have foretold you all things.
24 ¶ But in those days, after that tribulation,[b] the

23 lead astray, if possible, the elect. But take ye heed: behold, I have told you all things beforehand.
24 But in those days, after that tribulation, the sun

a 2 Pet. 3 : 17.....b Dan. 12 : 1 ; Zeph. 1 : 15, 17.

and fraud. The presence of the deceivers is still prominent in Josephus. As for the **signs and wonders**, that age was full of men who claimed supernatural power. See Acts 19: 13-19, and for examples within or near the Jewish circle, Simon Magus (Acts 8 : 9-24) and Elymas (13 : 6-12). The effort of these impostors would be, in the time now predicted, **to seduce—or lead astray—if it were possible, even** (the best text omits 'even') **the elect**—i. e., to rally the Christians, with others, to the standard of some false Christ. But they were expressly warned. **If any man shall say unto you, Lo, here is** (the) **Christ, or, Lo, he is there, believe him not.** Matthew adds: "If they shall say unto you, Behold, he is in the desert, go not forth; Behold, he is in the secret chambers, believe it not." 'In the desert': see passage from Josephus cited under verse 6. 'In the secret chambers': as if waiting in concealment till a force of supporters should be gathered. But the Master assured his disciples that he would not be there, to be found by any such seeking, and other Christ there was not, to be found by any seeking. The events of which he spoke were not to be searched out in deserts or in secret chambers; they would flash on the world like the lightning, and upon the sinful Jerusalem the woe would come like the eagle upon the prey. (Matthew.)

The signs of the fall of the temple, for which the disciples had asked, had now been given, five in number, namely: *The coming of false Christs; wars and calamities; persecution against Christians; the diffusion of the gospel; and the gathering of the Roman armies about the temple.* The first four were premonitory, being more general in their character; the fifth was to be a definite event, and was to serve to them, if they were near Jerusalem, as a signal or trumpet call to flight. Our Lord now repeated the caution given in verse 9. **But take ye heed**—rather, "But do ye take heed," ye being strongly emphatic. In saying **I have foretold you all things**, he affirmed that he had told them enough, so that they could know whenever the day was approaching. (Heb. 10: 25.) The first question (verse 4), "When shall these things be?" has not yet been answered; but

the second, "What shall be the sign when all these things shall be fulfilled?" has been answered.

II. The Event Itself, Apocalyptic-ally Portrayed. Verses 24-27.—Our Lord now advances from the signs to that which they foreshowed.

It is important to observe the prominence of Old Testament language in this paragraph. In the Greek text of Westcott and Hort, forty-four words, out of a total of seventy-one, are printed in the type that denotes quotation from the Old Testament; in the parallel paragraph in Matthew, fifty-five words, out of a total of ninety-two. The paragraph in Luke differs so largely that a count can scarcely be brought into comparison.

The great question here is that of time. The notes of time must therefore be carefully studied. In Mark's report, taken by itself, there is no difficulty in understanding them, or in determining the time to which the passage refers —it is, **In those days, after that tribulation.** No hearer of this language would think of any time but that next following the tribulation of Jerusalem just described. If our Lord referred to any other period, there must have been a large omission of important matter before these words in Mark's report, or else there must have been some unrecorded emphasis or gesture that would give to his words the meaning, **But in those days** (not these) **after that tribulation** (not this). But it is artificial and arbitrary to suppose such an unrecorded element in our Lord's discourse. Mark can scarcely have understood him to point away to some new and distinct period without indicating it in his words. As to the possibility of an omission in Mark's report, see below. Matthew's report, taken by itself, is still more definite, "Immediately after the tribulation of those days." It is difficult to see why Matthew introduced the word "immediately" (which certainly means "immediately"), if he did not understand that the event now to be predicted was at once to follow the events already foretold. Thus Matthew and Mark place the event that is now to be portrayed just after the tribulation that preceded the fall of Jerusalem. The theory of an omission is as follows: Luke has (²¹⁻²³), "But woe unto them that are with child, and to them that give suck, in those days! for there shall be great distress in the land, and wrath upon this people"; then he proceeds, adding to Matthew and Mark, "And they shall fall by the edge of the sword, and shall be led away captive into all the nations; and Jerusalem shall be trodden down of the Gentiles (or nations, same word as just above), until the times of the Gentiles (or nations) be fulfilled"; and then he returns to substantial parallelism with Matthew and Mark, saying, "And there shall be signs in the sun," etc. Here, in verse 24, it is often thought Luke opens to view a long period that is not recognized in Matthew and Mark. The clause "until the times of the Gentiles be fulfilled" is taken as equivalent to "until the fulness of the Gentiles be come in"—i. e., to the kingdom of Christ (Rom. 11: 25); and thus the prediction in Luke is supposed to stretch on to the end of the time which is a day of grace to the Gentiles. Then Luke is understood, at verse 25, to go on from the end of that time, and to place the signs in the sun, etc., beyond it; and then this "period of the Gentiles" is introduced, or assumed, in the reading of the record in Matthew and Mark, so that in those days shall refer to the distant future to which Luke has led us. Concerning this interpretation: (1) It rests upon what is probably a misunderstanding of the clause, "until the times of the Gentiles be fulfilled." This, probably, is not parallel to "until the fulness of the Gentiles be come in" (Rom. 11: 25)—more naturally, "until the times of the Gentiles be fulfilled" means simply "as long as God shall be pleased to use the Gentiles for this purpose"—not the "day of grace" of the Gentiles, but the time assigned to the Gentiles (i. e., to "the nations," among whom "the people" were to be led captive) for the execution of God's judgment upon Jerusalem, a time which is left wholly indeterminate as to length. So Meyer and Grimm. (2) It rests upon a wrong idea of the relation of statements concerning the lapse of time to continuous discourse. It assumes that after the mention of a given period the discourse goes on from the end of that period, whereas it may just as naturally return to the starting point. "I am going to Europe for a year; I will write to you," does not mean "I will write to you after the end of the year"—it means "I will write to you after going to Europe." So here. According to Luke, our Lord tells of the overthrow of Jerusalem, and leaves the ancient city to be "trodden down of the Gentiles, until the times of the Gentiles be fulfilled," and then goes on to speak of the significance of the overthrow in the progress of his kingdom. (3) It rests upon an incorrect theory of the harmony of the gospels. It does not recognize the evangelists as independent witnesses, each of whom is historically trustworthy, but assumes that a correct report of facts is to be obtained only by the process of combination. (4) It thus introduces great difficulties as to the inspiration and the trustworthiness of the evangelists. According to this theory, Matthew and Mark omitted an essential part of our Lord's discourse, and thereby distinctly applied a great prediction to the wrong period. If they conveyed an incorrect impression as to the meaning of our Saviour in so important a matter, it is difficult to see how they can be the inspired and trustworthy guides that they have been supposed to be in the knowledge of Jesus. (5) This interpretation can scarcely be reconciled with the solemn language of verse 30, reported by all the evangelists: Verily I say unto you, this generation shall not pass till all these things be done. The natural meaning of that language is perfectly at one with the natural meaning of the words, In those days, after that tribulation. Both predictions promise an early fulfillment. See note on verse 30.

Hence we are compelled to place the event that is now to be portrayed "immediately," as Matthew says, "after the tribulation of those days." From telling of the troubles that preceded the fall of Jerusalem, Jesus was proceeding to speak of what should follow them. But the portrayal of the event to which the tribulation led is made in a style quite unlike that of the preceding discourse. Thus far, all has been expressed in plain, literal terms; but the culminating event, being one of the great crises in the history of God's kingdom, is described after the manner of the ancient prophets, in lofty, apocalyptic language. It is portrayed first in its reference to the past (24, 25), and then in its reference to the future (26, 27). In reference to the past, the impending event is the overthrow of Jerusalem, and, with it, of the Old Dispensation. In reference to the future, it is announced as the coming, or, at least, as a coming, of the Son of man.

24, 25. If this were to be read as the language of English prose, founded on science—

sun shall be darkened, and the moon shall not give her light, 25 And⁴ the stars of heaven shall fall, and the powers that are in heaven shall be shaken.

shall be darkened, and the moon shall not give her 25 light, and the stars shall be falling from heaven, and the powers that are in the heavens shall be shaken.

a Isa. 13 : 10 ; 34 : 20, 23 ; Jer. 4 : 28 ; 2 Pet. 3 : 10, 12 ; Rev. 6 : 12-14 ; 20 : 11.

i. e., on facts as they are known to be—it would tell of astronomical wonders, and of impossibilities too: **The stars of heaven shall fall.** But it would be quite otherwise in Hebrew prophecy, to which the hearers would at once perceive that our Lord was alluding. The imagery of these verses is the familiar imagery of destruction, especially of national destruction. Closely similar language is used in Isa. 13 : 10, in denouncing destruction upon Babylon; in Isa. 24 : 19-23, in speaking of the enemies of Israel more generally; in Isa. 34 : 4, 9, 10, of Idumæa; in Ezek. 32 : 7, 8, of Egypt; in Amos 8 : 9, of the northern kingdom of Israel; in Joel 2 : 30, 31, of the events that attended the setting up of the kingdom of Christ. Compare Acts 2 : 19, 20, and Dr. Hackett's note. Ezekiel's language concerning Egypt is (32 : 7, 8), "When I shall put thee out"—*i. e.*, extinguish thee—" I will cover the heaven, and make the stars thereof dark: I will cover the sun with a cloud, and the moon shall not give her light. All the bright lights of heaven will I make dark over thee, and set darkness on thy land, saith the Lord God." Isaiah's language concerning Babylon is (13 : 10), "The stars of heaven and the constellations thereof shall not give their light: the sun shall be darkened in his going forth, and the moon shall not cause her light to shine." Concerning Idumæa (34 : 4), "And all the host of heaven shall be dissolved, and the heavens shall be rolled together as a scroll: and all their host shall fall down, as the leaf falleth off from the vine. and as a falling fig from the fig tree." The language of our Lord in verses 24, 25, is quoted almost exactly from the Septuagint of Isa. 13 : 10 and 34 : 4. It is almost impossible for readers trained in modern science to imagine how his language here would sound to hearers who had never heard of modern science, but were thoroughly familiar with this prophetic imagery; yet to such it was addressed, and from their point of view it must be interpreted. They would instantly perceive that it was the imagery of national overthrow, the extinguishing of the luminaries of heaven corresponding well to the destruction of all that is great and glorious in national life.

They would never look for the fulfillment of this prediction in the realm of physical nature; they would understand our Lord to say that Jerusalem and the Jewish nation must follow in the way of Babylon, Egypt, and Idumæa, and be utterly destroyed. Hence, it is not necessary, or possible, to point out what calamities corresponded to each symbolic prediction. The falling of the stars need not be defined here, any more than in Isaiah, nor the shaking of the powers of heaven. Such predictions were never intended for literal fulfillment, for the simple reason that they are incapable of it. Plumptre's remark is true: "Our Lord speaks here in language as essentially apocalyptic as that of St. John (Rev. 6 : 12), and it lies in the very nature of such language that it precludes a literal interpretation." Thus the impending event is described in its relation to the past and to existing institutions, as an event similar to the overthrow of Babylon and of Egypt, a visitation upon Jerusalem such as God formerly brought upon other ungodly cities. In this view, it is the destruction of Jerusalem—*i. e.*, the sweeping away of the Old Dispensation. The significance that made it worthy of so lofty a prophetic description resided in the latter name, not in the former—not in that it was the destruction of a city, but in that it was the abandonment of the city of the Great King, the withdrawal of all sanctity from what had been the seat of God's revelation, and the abolishing of a once sacred dispensation. It must not be supposed that the event was the mere fall of Jerusalem: it was the overthrow of a set of institutions once divine, but now abandoned. The fall of Jerusalem is an event greatly underestimated in the popular Christian judgment. In its connection with the old and with the new, it stands among the most important events in the history of revelation. Yet its significance, being spiritual, was spiritually discerned, and only as the progress of the kingdom revealed it. Luke abbreviates the reference to signs in heaven, and makes more prominent the confusion and the perplexity of men and of nations.

26. In place of the old comes the new.

26 And then shall they see the Son of man coming in the clouds, with great power and glory.

26 And then shall they see the Son of man coming in 27 clouds with great power and glory. And then shall

a ch. 14 : 62; Dan. 7 : 9-14; Matt. 16 : 27; 24 : 30; Acts 1 : 11; 1 Thess. 4 : 16; 2 Thess. 1 : 7, 10; Rev. 1 : 7.

Looking backward, the great event is the sweeping away of Jerusalem and the whole Jewish cult and system; looking forward, it is the coming, or, at least, a coming, of the Son of man—**the Son of man coming in the clouds, with power and great glory.** As before, we must inquire what the language would mean to hearers familiar with the language of Hebrew prophecy; and we must remember that we are still in the region of prophetic symbols. The language, which serves as the keynote of the Apocalypse of John (Rev. 1: 7), is borrowed directly from the Apocalypse of Daniel. See Dan. 7: 13, 14: "I saw in the night visions, and behold, one like the Son of man came with the clouds of heaven, and came to the Ancient of days, and they brought him near before him. And there was given him dominion, and glory, and a kingdom, that all people, nations and languages should serve him: his dominion is an everlasting dominion which shall not pass away, and his kingdom that which shall not be destroyed." Note two important facts: (1) That this scene represents, not the completing of a kingdom already established, but the establishing or "giving" of a kingdom; (2) that this scene has its place in the vision, not in the interpretation—so that, according to the method that prevails in Daniel, it is not a picture of a literal scene in human history, but a symbolic picture, to which a parallel in human events is to be shown the prophet. For the interpretation—i. e., for the corresponding fact in history, see Dan. 7: 27: "And the kingdom and dominion, and the greatness of the kingdom under the whole heaven, shall be given to the people of the saints of the Most High, whose kingdom is an everlasting kingdom, and all dominions shall serve and obey him." The kingdom thus represented is one of a succession of powers upon the earth. See the whole chapter. The preceding powers have been great world-powers, ungodly and tyrannical, but now the dominion is given to "the people of the saints of the Most High." The prominence of "the people" here is too important to be over-looked; what is foretold may not unfitly be called the *regime* of the godly people—i. e., after the reign of tyrants and ungodly powers there shall come a reign of the Son of man in

and through his people; and of the establish-ment of this reign the coming of the Son of man with the clouds of heaven was given to Daniel as the prophetic symbol. Into the midst of such prophetic imagery in the minds of his hearers did this prediction of Jesus fall, and by knowledge of this prophetic reference in Daniel would it be interpreted. It would seem that they must have understood him to mean, in verse 26, "After the tribulation of Jerusalem and the overthrow of the prepara-tory dispensation, they shall see the Messiah gloriously manifested in the establishment of his spiritual kingdom among men." For similar highly wrought imagery applied to interpositions of God in history, see Ps. 97: 1-5; 50: 1-4; Isa. 19: 1; 64: 1, 2; Zech. 9: 14, and specially Ps. 18: 5-16. Of course, this manifestation could not be a single event, occurring in a day; it must be a great historic work and process, stretching on he does not say how far, involving the use of innumera-ble natural and supernatural agencies, and including whatever manifestations of himself his purposes for the great future may contem-plate. Compare the very important passage, Matt. 24: 64: "Hereafter"—or, correctly, as in the Revision, "Henceforth"—"ye shall see the Son of man sitting on the right hand of power and coming in the clouds of heaven;" where our Lord says that the coming in the clouds shall begin from that time, "the hour when the Son of man shall be glorified," and shall be seen from that time on. What can it be but the establishment of his spiritual kingdom, begun from his death and glorifica-tion, and receiving, from the divine point of view, a vast impulse and extension when the Old Dispensation was swept off from the earth? "The sign of the Son of man" (Matt.), if it were on earth, might naturally mean the ensign, or standard, of his kingdom, set up that men might gather round it. Compare Isa. 11: 10-12; 49: 22; 62: 10. But since it is "in heaven," it will most naturally mean the pre-liminary tokens, the earliest forth-streaming, of the Messiah's spiritual glory; a sign which was seen in the work of Christ's Spirit before the time of the event that he had foretold. On the whole paragraph, see an article in "Our Lord's Use of the Old Testament" in *The Expositor*, April, 1881, where the relation

27 And then shall he send his angels, and shall gather together his elect from the four winds, from the uttermost part of the earth, to the uttermost part of heaven.

28 Now learn a parable of the fig tree; When her branch is yet tender, and putteth forth leaves, ye know that summer is near:

29 So ye in like manner, when ye shall see these things come to pass, know that it is nigh, even at the doors.

he send forth the angels, and shall gather together his elect from the four winds, from the uttermost part of the earth to the uttermost part of heaven.

28 Now from the fig tree learn her parable: when her branch is now become tender, and putteth forth 29 its leaves, ye know that the summer is nigh; even so ye also, when ye see these things coming to pass,

---

of the passage to the language of the Old Testament is plainly illustrated.

Thus the impending event is, in its relation to the future, the coming, or at least a coming, of the Son of Man. But this coming is not to be searched for as an instantaneous event. It did not consist in the destruction of Jerusalem. It was not an event recognizable by all men, and estimated by them at its true importance. No great movement of the kingdom of God has been so recognized and estimated. "The kingdom of God cometh not with observation." The coming that occurred within the limits of time here given was the placing of the new kingdom in the world free from all restraints and hindrances of the Old Dispensation. In the period of the gospel Christ reigns in and through men. After the removal of the earlier dispensation, the world was open and free to his spiritual kingdom, and his spiritual powers had the field to themselves, no longer contradicted by an opposing system that claimed to represent the same God. Those powers have ever since been throwing down and building up at the will of their Lord, destroying the works of the devil and bringing in the reign of God and righteousness. See (5) in note at the end of the chapter.

27. The consequence of this coming is to be the gathering of his chosen into his kingdom. His angels are not necessarily beings of one class alone, as Gabriel and Michael (of whom we speak as if we knew more about them than we do). John the Baptist is the "angel" of Mal. 3: 1. Yet undoubtedly there is allusion here to the ministry of superhuman holy beings, parallel to that of Heb. 1: 14. The comprehensive word seems to include all messengers and agencies, human and super-human, that help the Son of man to gather to him his elect—all "ministers of his that do his pleasure," of every kind, if only they serve the purpose of his kingdom. The "gathering" of his elect into the kingdom is for time and for eternity; the whole earthly work of God in man is included in it, and the final gathering of souls into his glory is an

indispensable part of it. The field from which they come shall be world-wide, now that all Jewish restrictions are gone; thus is fulfilled Luke 13: 28, 29. See also Matt. 8: 11, 12, where the believing Roman centurion is recognized by our Lord as the first fruits of this great Gentile multitude. Matthew adds that his angels shall be sent forth (literally) "with a great trump," which is naturally to be regarded as the symbol of proclamation. Observe the close and suggestive resemblance of Rev. 14: 6, 7. The mention of gathering God's people by the trumpet would remind the hearers of Isa. 27: 12, 13; Zech. 2: 6; Deut. 30: 4—passages that tell of the regathering of God's scattered ones for his service. The phrase 'from the uttermost part (literally, "corner") of the earth to the uttermost part ("corner") of heaven,' is sufficient proof, if proof were needed, of the complete absence from the discourse of modern forms of thought respecting the structure of the world. The earth is conceived of as a plain, upon the corners of which the corners of the heaven appear to rest.

111. THE TIME OF THE EVENT. Verses 28–32.—Here are three sayings: (1) The time is to be recognized from the fulfillment of the signs; (2) it will be within the present generation; (3) it cannot be more closely designated.

28, 29. The first thought is parabolically set forth: "Learn the nearness of the event from its signs, as you learn the nearness of the summer from the opening foliage of the fig tree. Only yesterday morning they had seen a fig tree in leaf just there on the Mount of Olives. (Mark 11:13.) Ye know that summer is near. The ye is not emphatic. Some manuscripts read, to the same effect: "It is known that summer is near." But the next ye is emphatic, precisely as in verses 9 and 23: No ye in like manner, when ye shall see these things come to pass—i. e., these that have been specified as signs. They might expect, therefore, to see them. The subject of is nigh is indeterminate. The translation preferred by the Revisers, "He is nigh," is favored by the context, since a per-

30 Verily I say unto you, that this generation shall not pass, till all these things be done.
31 Heaven and earth shall pass away: but* my words shall not pass away.

30 know ye that 'he is nigh, even at the doors. Verily I say unto you, This generation shall not pass away, until all these things be accomplished. Heaven and earth shall pass away: but my words shall not pass

a Isa. 40 : 8.—1 Or. it.

son rather than an event is said to be at the doors. Compare James 5: 9: "Behold, the judge standeth before the door." As the fig leaves assured them of the approach of summer, so these signs were to certify the disciples that Christ was at the doors, ready to enter in that "coming" of which he had spoken.

30. The second of the three sayings concerning the time is bare and literal. There is nothing apocalyptic, or even parabolic, here. It is the announcement of the limit of the time. **This generation shall not pass, till all these things be done**, or be accomplished, or come to pass. Introduced by our Lord's formal and solemn, **Verily, I say unto you. All these things** may be, as in verse 29, all that have been promised as signs; or, more comprehensively, all that have been mentioned in the discourse, including the impending event itself. The latter is the more natural, after the announcement of verses 24-27, but there is practically no difference between the two, for our Lord has already said that when the signs are completed the event itself will be in act of accomplishment. **This generation**—*i. e.*, the men now living. The teaching is the same as in Matt. 16: 28: "There be some standing here which shall not taste of death till they see the Son of man coming in his kingdom." See note on Mark 9: 1. That this is the natural sense of *genea*, "generation," all admit; and hence it has always been felt that this verse would have been more easily explained if the second advent had occurred within that generation. Other meanings have very naturally been proposed for the word here: by some, "the human race"; by others, "this class of people"—*i. e.*, the elect, or the believers on Christ, the class that has just been mentioned. Both meanings, however, are artificial, and unsupported by any usage of the word in Greek. Many others explain: "This nation, the Jewish race, shall not cease to exist till all these things are done." But this too is an unnatural use of the word, which has no valid support in Greek usage, only approximate parallels having been found. Meyer's remark ("*He genea haute*—*i. e.*, the present generation, which *genea* with *haute* means

throughout in the New Testament") may be proved correct by consulting the following passages, which are all in which the phrase occurs: Matt. 11: 16; 12: 41, 42, 45; 23: 36; 24: 34; Mark 8: 12, 38; 13: 30; Luke 7: 31; 11: 29, 30, 31, 32, 50, 51; 17: 25; 21: 32; Acts 2: 40; compare Heb. 3: 10. Unless this remark of our Lord forms a very striking exception, "the men now living" is the only sense that is given in the New Testament to the phrase, "this generation." Of the force of *genea* here, Alexander (whose interpretation of the discourse would find another meaning more congenial) says: "Unless we forge a meaning for the word in this place which is not only unexampled elsewhere, but directly contradictory to its essential meaning everywhere, we must understand our Lord as saying that the contemporary race or generation—*i. e.*, those then living—should not die till all these prophecies had been accomplished." There is no right way but to give the language its natural sense. Whether or not we recognize a double reference in the discourse, we must recognize the fact that it contemplated a genuine fulfillment of its predictions, worthy to be called such, to take place before all the men then living had passed away. This is required not only by this verse, with its strong affirmation, but by the structure of the discourse. Our Lord had been most carefully teaching his hearers to recognize the signs of a coming event. The event that was coming must therefore have been coming so soon that they might reasonably expect to see it. If we attempt to escape the admission that an early fulfillment was contemplated by our Lord, we introduce a greater difficulty than we avoid; we destroy the naturalness and intelligibility of our Saviour's speech. He certainly meant this solemn saying to be understood.

31. This statement of time is confirmed by one of the most solemn and sublime of all our Lord's self-assertions. **Heaven and earth shall pass away, but my words shall not pass away**. This utterance, he says, like all his utterances, is more to be trusted than the order of nature. That order is changeable, and will ultimately be changed, but his words are of unchangeable validity.

32 ¶ But of that day and *that* hour knoweth no man, no, not the angels which are in heaven, neither the Son, but the Father.

32 away. But of that day or that hour knoweth no one, not even the angels in heaven, neither the Son,

The direct reference is less to the everlasting duration of his doctrine than to the absolute certainty of his predictions. "What I say will be found true, more surely than heaven and earth shall stand." **Heaven and earth** —the Scriptural name for the universal frame of things. (Gen. 1: 1; Isa. 1: 2; Ps. 96: 11.) Compare Jer. 31: 35-37, where the apparent stability of nature is used as the type of the faithfulness of God, and Isa. 51: 6; 54: 9, 10; Ps. 102: 24-27; Heb. 1: 10-12, where his faithfulness is said to outlast the stability of nature. The language of verses 30 and 31 is almost verbally identical in the three reports. Note that this amazing assertion was made in order to confirm to the disciples, who were to be left without further knowledge till experience should give it to them, the prediction of verse 30. It was as if he had "confirmed it with an oath." (Heb. 6: 17.) Note also the moment at which this great word was spoken. It was at the end of a ministry in which he had been rejected, and in the brief pause that preceded his death at the hands of murderers—one of the many cases in which his tremendous self-assertion blazes out the more brightly by reason of the darkness about it. His estimate of himself was never changed by the experience of rejection. Compare John 12: 37-50.

32. The third saying about the time is that a closer designation was then impossible. Within that generation, the prediction should be fulfilled, but at what **day or hour**—*i. e.*, exactly when it should occur, was known only to the Father. Note the changes made by the Revisers in the translation of the verse. The words **neither the Son** were formerly found in Mark alone, but by the Revisers they have been inserted in Matthew on sufficient manuscript authority. Most naturally, the day is the day of the event for which the disciples had been prepared by the designation of the signs—the time concerning which they had been taught to pray that it might not be in winter, or on the Sabbath. To this the context naturally leads. Some have seen reason for a change of reference in the change of pronouns, from *tauta*, in verse 30, to *ekinos*, here: "*These* things shall soon be done, but of *that* day in the far future, only the Father knoweth." But the pronoun *ekinos* has already been used quite prominently in verse 24—" In those

days, after that tribulation"—where the reference is to time that is included under the *tauta* of verse 30. Thus there is no fresh change of pronouns at verse 32; *ekinos* is used there as in verse 24, in more demonstrative reference to something that has before been mentioned. That **the angels which are in heaven** should be ignorant of any "times and seasons" occasions no surprise, but what of such ignorance in **the Son?** There are various inadequate explanations. One is that the Son, as man, did not know the time; while, as God, he did know it. We are not justified in thus dividing the consciousness of our Saviour; nor, supposing it to be so divided, would he have been morally justified in speaking thus. Another, that he did not will to know it, and therefore excluded the subject from his thoughts, and had not the knowledge in possession. Another, that he did not know it with the intention of revealing it. So the note in the Douay Version: "He knoweth it not as our Teacher—*i. e.*, He knoweth it not so as to teach it to us, as not being expedient." Both of these it is impossible to reconcile with the fact that he is "the truth." We must never suppose ourselves obliged by reverence to accept an inconclusive argument on the Lord's side, or a misinterpretation of Scripture. (Job 13: 7, 8.) What we have before us is the plain statement that he did not know when the predicted event would occur. The fact rests upon his own authority. As to the explanation of the fact, Meyer's brief sentence is sufficient: "*Except the Father* excludes also the Son, who has become man." The human limitations into which he had entered were such that in them he did not at that time know the time of the event that he predicted. The fact is mysterious, as the incarnation is mysterious, but not otherwise. Surely it ought not to be necessary to prove that Jesus Christ was a man. The same limitations appear in Luke 2: 52, and elsewhere, and need not trouble a believer in his true deity. Indeed, any conception of him is radically defective that does not include the recognition of his true and genuine humanity. It is a very striking fact that this one unknown matter is a matter concerning which our Lord expressly directed his friends to pray. (verse 18.) Thus he intimated that even this was not a matter of arbitrary appointment.

33 Take^a ye heed, watch and pray: for ye know not when the time is.

34 *For the Son of man is* as a man taking a far journey, who left his house, and gave authority to his servants, and to every man his work, and commanded the porter to watch.

35 Watch ye therefore; for ye know not when the master of the house cometh, at even, or at midnight, or at the cock-crowing, or in the morning;

36 Lest coming suddenly, he find you sleeping.^b

37 And what I say unto you, I say unto all, Watch.^c

33 but the Father. Take ye heed, watch 'and pray:

34 for ye know not when the time is. *It is as when* a man, sojourning in another country, having left his house, and given authority to his ²servants, to each one his work, commanded also the porter to watch.

35 Watch therefore: for ye know not when the lord of the house cometh, whether at even, or at midnight,

36 or at cockcrowing, or in the morning; lest coming

37 suddenly he find you sleeping. And what I say unto you I say unto all, Watch.

---

a Matt. 24 ; 42 ; 25 : 13 ; Luke 12 : 40 ; 21 : 34 ; Rom. 13 : 11. 12 ; 1 Thess, 5 : 6 ; Rev. 16 : 15.....*b* Matt 25 : 5.....*c* ver. 33, 35.

1 Some ancient authorities omit *and pray*....2 Gr. *bondservants.*

IV EXHORTATION TO VIGILANCE, IN VIEW OF THE NEAR BUT UNCERTAIN DAY OF HIS COMING. Verses 33–37.

General Exhortation. **33. Take ye heed, watch and pray.** The words 'and pray' are of doubtful authority. Translate, "take heed, be vigilant." The latter verb means "be awake"; hence, "be attentive." It does not mean "watch," in the modern sense—*i. e.*, "look out," or "be in expectation." The command is, not to be in expectancy, but to be awake and ready, not overcome by the forgetfulness of spiritual slumber: **For ye know not when the time is.**

Parabolic Conclusion. Enforcing the Exhortation. Peculiar to Mark 34–37. The sentence is grammatically incomplete, and the Revisers have completed it in one of the possible ways, probably in the best. The picture is of a man setting out on a journey, first entrusting **authority to his servants** for the time of his absence, and assigning to each his **work;** and then, just as he goes, turning and speaking this final word to **the porter** to bid him be vigilant. It is implied that he bids him be vigilant, because it is uncertain or unknown when he himself will return. Thus, Jesus compares the present exhortation to the parting warning of the householder. In verse 35, the imagery of the parable is continued; it is still **the master of the house** (not Jesus, directly) that is spoken of, and he may come in any one of the four watches of the night. The night is mentioned, because it is then that the porter may most easily fall from his vigilance into sleep; and the lord of the house must not find him **sleeping** at his post. The verb in verses 35 and 37 is *gregoreite,* which, like *agrupneite,* above, means simply "be awake," or "be vigilant." The same word in 1 Cor. 16: 13; 1 Peter 5: 8; Rev. 3: 2, 3. In the four watches of the night there is no allusion to four periods of history, or to times of greater or less spiritual darkness. This was simply a vivid picture of the responsibility

that would be upon the disciples after the departure of their Master. Yet this counsel was not for the apostles alone: in this sense, "be vigilant," it was plainly for all Christians, in that age and in every other. **What I say unto you, I say unto all, Watch**—"be vigilant; live in wakefulness and readiness."

Here follow appropriately, in Matthew, chapter 25, (1) The parable of the Ten Virgins, showing how it would be with the spiritually wakeful and how with the spiritually drowsy when their Master should call them to account; (2) the parable of the Talents, illustrating the trust that the Lord had given to his servants (compare "authority to his servants, and to every man his work"), and the account that he would require of it from each of them; and (3) the judgment scene, in which the principles of final acceptance and rejection by Christ the King are vividly set forth. From these closing verses in the thirteenth of Mark (33-37), the Saviour could easily pass to the twenty-fifth of Matthew. How bright a contrast to this discourse shines out in that which was really the last, John 14-16! This is heavy with woe and warning—that is rich in divine peace and inexhaustible in spiritual promise. That was the true farewell.

Thus ends the long activity of Tuesday (reckoning the evening with the day), which occupies ninety-five verses in Mark, or one-seventh of the whole book. Such a record of a single day shows us how little we really know of our Lord's activity. Even this, enlarged as it is by the additions that are made by Matthew, is no doubt an incomplete record; and hundreds of his days must have been as full as this.

THE QUESTION OF DOUBLE REFERENCE in this discourse has been reserved to the end, because it is a question that ought to be decided in view of the whole discourse, rather than at the suggestion of some single passage in it. The majority of interpreters find a second meaning, and a reference to events still future—namely, to the visible coming of Christ in the clouds at last and the events attendant upon it. It is quite generally held that down to verse 23 the main reference is to the signs of the ruin of Jerusalem, while a secondary reference is found to events premonitory of the future coming of Christ; and that from verse 24 the main reference is to the future coming of Christ, while a secondary reference is admitted to the destruction of Jerusalem. Thus the prophetic delineation of the signs refers primarily to the earlier time, and of the event itself to the later. So Alford. The basis of this reference to the future is found in the conviction that the destruction of Jerusalem is a true type of the destruction of the world at Christ's coming, on which account the signs of the two events may well be similar, and the relation of Christ's people to the two must be substantially the same. Of this it may be said: (1) A second reference is quite in accordance with certain characteristics of prophecy. There is no certainty that a prophetic discourse will find its exhaustive fulfillment in a single event. Some predictions of the Messiah had an earlier reference and fulfillment, as well as a later. A prediction of the working-out of principles in history may be fulfilled again and again. If the destruction of Jerusalem illustrates the same principles as the final Advent, it may stand as a type of it, and a second reference in this passage may be justified as consistent with the facts. (2) Whether this discourse had a second reference or not, it had a first, which was to reach fulfillment within that generation. (Ver. 30.) The expectation of a second fulfillment does not forbid but encourages the recognition of the first. A second implies a first. Belief in a preordained parallelism in the meaning of prophecy should render one all the more diligent in searching out first fulfillments. No interpreter needs, therefore, to reject such an interpretation as has now been given because of his recognizing a second reference in the passage. (3) Interpreted in the light of current modern conceptions, the discourse may, indeed, appear to take a new turn at verse 24, and to refer thenceforth to events still future, but not if interpreted by the aid of Old Testament usage. Read in the light of prophetic usage, our Saviour's language in verses 24-27, almost quoted from the prophets, does not necessitate, or suggest, or even admit, a change of reference at verse 24 from the impending ruin of Jerusalem to the future coming of Christ. Interpreted according to prophetic use, the language unquestionably portrays a national overthrow. In the light of prophetic use, it would most naturally be understood by his hearers and conceived by Christ himself. To the present writer it seems certain, therefore, that the light of the Old Testament is the true light for interpretation here; hence he has felt that he had no authority for the admission of a reference to events still future. If he had admitted such a reference, it could have been only by introducing it himself, for in the discourse he does not find it. (4) There are grave difficulties, both Scriptural and moral, in regarding the destruction of Jerusalem as a true type of the ending of the Christian age. The New Testament does not predict such a ruin for humanity as that, with the saved a mere handful, snatched out as the "elect" of the first age were hurried out of the perishing Jerusalem. The typical interpretation of that event originated in the supposed necessities of this discourse. (5) The present interpretation does not imply, however, that the predicted coming of Christ occurred and was completed in the first Christian age, either in the overthrow of the Old Dispensation or in the inauguration of the New. The Scriptures seem to teach that no single event gathers into itself the whole of his predicted coming. A strongly-illuminative word on the subject is Christ's own authoritative "henceforth," in Matt. 26:64 (see Revision): "Henceforth ye shall see the Son of man sitting on the right hand of power, and coming on the clouds of heaven." Here our Saviour indicates that his coming on the clouds is to be a process beginning from that time, whose chief significance is spiritual, and in which are included many events in the progress of his kingdom. The "henceforth" indicates that the description is figurative, and that all intended manifestations of himself to his people and the world are included in the process that he calls his coming. The present state of things is not to last forever, and at its end there will be such a manifestation of Christ and of God's completed kingdom with him as has never been made before (1 Cor. 15:24-28), in which the coming of Christ will culminate and find completion. Forbidden, as he conceives, by the discourse itself, to find a second reference reaching on to events still future, the present writer finds this view of the teaching of the passage not only Scriptural, but abundantly rich and satisfactory.

AN ADDITIONAL VIEW.

BY PROF. J. C. LONG, D. D.

We have three reports of our Lord's prophetic discourse on Mount Olivet—Mark 13; Luke 21; Matt. 24-25. No one of these reports is absolutely complete; that is, no one of them contains all our Lord's words in the exact order in which they were spoken. But, a report not complete in one sense, may be so in another; that is, it may be complete and adequate to the purpose which the reporter had in view. In this latter sense, two reports of the same discourse may be equally true, although one of them may be much briefer and less comprehensive than the other. If, for example, it were Mark's chief purpose to report what our Lord said about the destruction of Jerusalem, we need not think his report untrue or untrustworthy because he did not fully give what was said about the Lord's second coming, or the end of the world. And if Matthew, with a wider purpose, should report things which Mark omits, we need not, therefore, infer that he includes, or is in the habit of including, in a report of things said at one time, things said at another. When we have several reports of the same conversation or discourse, the only essential thing is that they should not contradict each other. In that case, all might be false; all could not be true. The reports of the three Evangelists are, in some respects, different; in no respect contradictory. The case, then, is briefly this: 1. We have three reports of the same discourse; 2. No one of these reports is absolutely complete; and, 3. All of them are equally trustworthy. It might be desirable to consider any one of these by itself; to treat it as if it stood absolutely alone, and to forget or ignore the fact that there are other reports. And this is what we should do if it was our purpose to ascertain the value of each of the Evangelists as distinct and separate witnesses. But if our main object was to ascertain the meaning of the discourse reported, we should compare and combine the several reports of it. We might get from each an impression which we would not get from the others, and from all combined, an impression that no one by itself would make; and yet, each separate impression might be according to the truth. There

is no reason why an interpreter of gospel history should not compare and combine several reports of the same thing, in order to gain a broader and more comprehensive view of it than he could get from any one of the reports. This is what the historian does when he uses the reports of the several brigade or division commanders, to enable him to describe a battle; and what the judge does when he combines the testimony of several witnesses in order to get a complete understanding of the case before him. It is our present business to ascertain, not what Mark's report might mean to us if we had only his Gospel; but what it actually does mean when taken in connection with what Matthew and Luke have to say about the same things.

1. Master, see what manner of stones, etc. The reference to the stones and the buildings is apparently abrupt. Why should the disciples call Jesus' attention to them? Not because, as Jews, they took pride in their beauty and magnificence. They had none of the feeling of the Psalmist when he bid strangers walk about Zion, tell her towers, mark her bulwarks, and consider her palaces. (Ps. 48.) They were evidently thinking of the destruction of these great buildings, which, in their massive strength, seemed indestructible. In calling the Lord's attention to them, they would suggest an explicit declaration of what he had before more or less obscurely hinted. Such a hint was given just before (Matt. 23: 37-39); and also earlier. (Luke 13: 34, 35.) The fact that Luke gives earlier words that Matthew records later, does not justify us in saying that Matthew records them out of their order. That would be not to interpret, but to amend or reconstruct his narrative. The destruction of Jerusalem weighed heavily on the Lord's heart, and he probably spoke of it, not once or twice, but many times. If the disciples sought an explicit statement, they immediately got it. Ver. 2.

3. The scene is changed from the temple to the western slope of the Mount of Olives. Luke says nothing of the place; gives no hint that the Lord and his disciples are not still in Jerusalem, and mentions no names of the disciples present. He says, "they" asked him. (21:7.) Matthew mentions the place, but no names. (24:3.) Mark gives both place and names: Peter and James and John and Andrew, the brothers and partners, who, three years before, on the shores of the Galilean lake, had become disciples, and were to become apostles, asked him, etc. We have in this a good example of the way in which the three accounts mutually supplement each other.

4. THE DISCIPLES' QUESTIONS. Parallel, Luke 21: 7.

The questions reported by Mark and Luke (21:7), are substantially identical. They are: 1. When shall these things be? That is, When shall these great buildings be utterly destroyed? and, 2. What shall be the sign of the coming destruction? So far as appears from Mark and Luke, no other question was asked; and we might suppose that all that follows was definitely and exclusively in answer to these two questions. But even in their reports there are intimations that the great Prophet's vision extended beyond the judgment of the Jews to the judgment of the world. (See ver. 24-27.) If we turn to Matthew, these intimations rise to definite statements. As he reports the questions asked, they are: 1. When shall these things be? the same as given by the other writers; and, 2. What shall be the sign of thy coming, and of the end of the world? (24:3.) The second question is peculiar to Matthew. It refers to two distinct things—the coming of the Lord, and the end of the world; but, as these two things are closely related, they are considered as one; and the sign of the one is the sign of the other. The Revised Version has, in the margin, "Consummation of the age," instead of end of the world. The change in rendering obscures the meaning. The same expression is used in Matt. 28: 20, where our Lord says: "Lo! I am with you always, even to the end of the world," or consummation of the age. "The end of the world," conveys a definite idea. What is meant by the consummation of the age? Does it mean, as some have supposed, the end, or completion, of the Jewish Dispensation, which was to be marked by the destruction of the temple? In that case, the "always" of the promise meant about forty years, and so far as the promise signified, after the close of the

Jewish Dispensation the disciples were to be left to themselves. But the promise was of help and guidance during the whole period of Christian labor and suffering. The end of the world cannot, therefore, mean the end of the Jewish Economy. In the same way, the coming of the Lord must mean something more than the coming of the gospel age—that long period in which, with alternations of ebb and flood, the truth shall go on increasing in power and glory. It marks the end, rather than the beginning, of the gospel age. It is that time up to which the Lord would be with his people; the reckoning time, when the stewards shall give account of their stewardship. Luke 19: 22-27; Matt. 25: 14. But in reporting the same discourse, why does Matthew introduce a question which the other Evangelists omit? It was because his plan was larger and broader than theirs.

5-23. THE LORD'S DIRECT ANSWER.

Our Lord's direct answer to the disciple's questions, is divided into two parts. In the first (ver. 6-13) he warns them against mistaking things that are not signs for signs. In the second, he tells them explicitly what the sign is, and what they must do when they see it. (Ver. 14-23.) The disciples might be led astray by deceivers (ver. 6); they might be unnecessarily alarmed by political commotions. Wars and rumors of wars must needs arise in the conflict of nation with nation. In the same way, from natural causes, there would be earthquakes and famines. (Ver. 7, 8.) Take heed to yourselves. (Ver. 9.) In the general disorder, the disciples would have special trials. Their first sufferings would come directly from the Jews; they would be beaten in synagogues. As they grew in numbers they would attract the attention of the Roman authorities, and be brought before rulers and kings. It is not unlikely that the persecutions which the disciples suffered from the Romans before the destruction of Jerusalem, were brought upon them by their connection with the Jews, with whom they were confounded. For a long time before the conflict between the Jews and the Empire actually began, the Jews were in a ferment; and outbreaks were always imminent. Any time a popular leader might excite revolt. The Emperor Claudius (41-54. A.D.), expelled the Jews from Rome, because they had made insurrection under the leadership of a pretended Messiah. (Judæos impulsore Christo assidue tumultuantes Roma expulit. Suet., Claud. 25). Even in the Neronian persecution it is not impossible that the Christians suffered rather as Jews than as Christians. It is not conclusive against this view that Tacitus expressly states that the Christians were persecuted by Nero as Christians. He wrote forty years after the event; and in the meantime, the Roman government had learned to distinguish Christians from Jews, which was not done by the Emperor Vespasian, in whose reign the temple tax was exacted of Christians, unless they could prove that they were not Jews. (See Merivale's "Romans Under the Empire," vii: 122.) But even if Christians were not persecuted by the Romans with a distinct understanding of their character and profession, it is yet true that their sufferings were for Christ's sake. The name they bore (to them the synonym of all that was pure and noble), associated by the Romans with fanaticism and rebellion, brought upon them the hatred of people and government alike. Tacitus says, that they were detested because of their crimes; that they were haters of the human race, and deserved the extremest punishment. We know that at the time of which Tacitus writes the Jews were turbulent, haters of the Romans, and hated by them. As applied to the Christians, his statement was not true; they were not haters of mankind; and the only occasion which the Romans could then have for hating them was that they bore the name of Christ, which, to the Romans, had a political significance. (See Merivale, vi: 216–223.)

10. The gospel must first be published, etc. The statement here needs something to make it clear. Matt. 24: 14, supplies that something: "This gospel of the kingdom shall be preached in all the world for a witness unto all nations; **and then cometh the end.**" The **must** implies a necessity of fitness. It is in accordance with the merciful and holy character of the Judge of all the earth, that there should be sufficient warning before the coming of calamity. All nations should know that God had not lightly cast away his people. The destruction of Jerusalem was not something fated. If the Jews had not rejected their Messiah, they

might have been saved politically. The one thing that necessitated the destruction of the Jews as a nation, was their unwillingness to be incorporated with and assimilated to the Empire. This unwillingness was produced by their feeling that faithfulness to God required them to obey only their own God-given laws; that submission to the Emperor was treason to God. This feeling would have passed away if they could have accepted Jesus, in whom Jew and Gentile are made one, the middle wall of partition being broken down. The Apostle Paul was a Jew, a Christian, and a Roman; and all Jews might have become the same. The preaching of the gospel gave them their last opportunity. They rejected it; and their city fell. Alas, that they knew too late, or never knew, the things that made for their peace! "O Jerusalem, Jerusalem!" (See the Lord's lamentation over the city. Luke 19: 41–44.) The question has been raised whether the gospel was actually preached to all nations. To insist that all nations must literally mean **all** nations, is to trifle with language. It simply means that the divine offers of mercy, the coming of the new, all-embracing kingdom, must be widely proclaimed, and the sentence long be suspended, before it should finally fall. The preaching is for a witness. As this gospel must be preached, there must be men to preach it; and those to whom this duty was given, must not be turned away from it by suffering or death. It is to strengthen the disciples in the discharge of their necessary and dangerous duty that the words in the eleventh verse were spoken.

12. Brother shall betray the brother to death. All the tenderest, sweetest ties of life shall be to hatred of Christ's name as chaff and stubble to the consuming flame.

13. The end, here, is not the same as the end spoken of in Matt. 24: 14. There it is primarily, at least, the end of Jerusalem, and of the temple. Here the **end** is a movable point, and is different to different persons: it is the point at which the earthly trial ceases. The salvation promised to continued faithfulness is immortal life.

14. Without the warnings given in verses 6–13, the disciples might have been uselessly hindered in their work. But there would come a time when their work in Jerusalem would be done, and they must think alone of their own safety. This time would be indicated by an unmistakable sign—the **abomination of desolation standing where it ought not.** What this was, Luke states plainly: "When ye shall see Jerusalem encompassed with armies, know that the desolation thereof is nigh." (Luke 21:20.) Then the disciples must flee to the mountains. The flight must be prompt and unhesitating (ver. 15, 16), and in those awful times, everything that might retard flight was to be deprecated. (ver. 17, 18.) The destruction of the holy city, brought upon it by the blind, unbelieving stubbornness of her children, was to be the crowning calamity of the world's history. It is no exaggeration to say that nothing equal to it ever was seen on the earth. Neither before nor since were so much wickedness and desperation and human suffering ever crowded together in such narrow limits of time and territory. The horrors of Paris during the Reign of Terror, or during the siege of the German army in the spring of 1871, are not to be compared with what took place at Jerusalem at the time of its destruction. (See Smith's "Dict. of the Bible," pp. 1305–1308; Milman's "Hist. of the Jews," Bk. xvi; Merivale's "Hist. of the Romans," vi, 450–471; or, better, Josephus.)

19. Except the Lord had shortened those days. The wrath of God towards his enemies is tempered by mercy towards his friends. As long as the siege of Jerusalem lasted, it might have lasted longer; and after the capture of the city, the Roman commander might have wrought the same desolation elsewhere. The days actually were shortened by two things: 1. The reckless fanaticism of the Jews themselves hastened the work of destruction: the hotter the fire the sooner the fuel is consumed. 2. The natural mildness of Titus made him unwilling to prolong the wretchedness of the conquered. The Greek inhabitants of Antioch urged him to expel the hated Jews from that city. The Roman answered: "The country of the Jews is destroyed; thither they cannot return; it would be hard to allow them no home to which they can retreat. Leave them in peace." So the days were shortened. God works through natural agencies to accomplish his purposes.

21. And then if any man shall say to you, **Lo, here is Christ.** The *then* may refer to the time of the siege, or to that immediately succeeding. It was natural that the desperate, infatuated, overpowered, but not subdued people should expect false Christs, and that false Christs should come forth to meet their expectation. The disciples were warned not to be misled by them. If we could feel that the warning looked to the somewhat distant future, it might suggest the great rising of the Jews under Barcochab, the son of a star, which ended in the complete and final overthrow of the Jews by the Romans [130, A. D.]. (See Milman's "Hist.," Bk. xviii.) It is more natural to suppose that the Lord refers to a nearer time; and the very decided intimation is, that his disciples were not to expect him at or immediately after the fall of the city. In Matt. 24: 27, he tells them that his coming was to be public and notable. If it was to take place immediately after Jerusalem's fall, there was no occasion for the warning against pretended Christs, who were to come secretly.

23. Behold, I have foretold you all things. These words mark the close of one section of the discourse; and the finished answer to the questions asked, as reported by Mark.

24–27. The Coming of the Lord, etc. Parallels, Matt. 24: 29–31; Luke 21: 25–29.

24, 25. These verses introduce a new subject. There is no reason to suppose that the Lord, after giving plain directions for the practical guidance of his followers, repeats what he had already said in figurative, or prophetic language. Indeed, it is expressly stated that what follows is different from what went before. **In those days**—that is, in that same general time, yet **after,** or, as Matthew has it, **immediately after that tribulation,** the sun shall be darkened, etc. There is no pause in the development of God's plans. One great event is immediately succeeded by, or paves the way for others. According to the report of Luke (21:24), Jerusalem was to be trodden down by the Gentiles until the times of the Gentiles be fulfilled; and those things which go to make up the times of the Gentiles do not tarry. In the details, Mark's report and Matthew's very nearly coincide. Exactly what is meant by the darkening of the sun, the paling of the moon, and the falling of the stars, we do not know. (See Dr. Clarke's Notes on these points.) We may notice, however, that judgment seems to begin with the greatest, and descend to the least. First the sun, then the moon, and then the stars shall be extinguished, or fall. The powers of the heavens **shall be shaken.** We do not venture even to conjecture what these things may mean. But after these things, which were to take place after the tribulation of Jerusalem, the Son of man was to come in the clouds, with great power and glory. He was not coming to begin, but to finish up his Messianic work on earth. See ver. 27, and especially Matt. 25: 31–46: "When the Son of man shall come in his glory," etc. **In the clouds.** This recalls Acts 1: 9-11: "As they were looking, he was taken up, and a cloud received him out of their sight." . . . "This same Jesus. . . shall so come in like manner as ye have seen him going into heaven."

27. And then shall he send his angels, and shall gather together his elect. In the parable (Matt. 13: 24-30) we have the same thing taught: "In the time of the harvest, I will say to the reapers," etc. . . . . "The harvest is the end of the world (consummation of the age), and the reapers are the angels." (It is noteworthy that the phrase "end of the world," or, consummation of the age, is found only in Matthew's Gospel, and in that only three times (13: 39; 24: 3, and 28: 20.) The reader is invited to refer to it, and assure himself that it does not mean the end of the Jewish Economy.) The mention of the four winds and the uttermost parts of the earth, shows two things: 1. That the Lord's kingdom had been universally spread abroad; and, 2. That the ingathering was to be complete and final. How often has the thought of the glorious coming of the Lord stirred the imagination and strengthened the hearts of his people. See 1 Thess. 4: 13-18; 2 Tim. 4: 8; 2 Cor. 5: 10; Rev. 20: 11-13. In the very earliest creeds, the disciples were taught to profess their belief in our Lord's "passion and resurrection from the dead, and ascension into heaven in the flesh, and his future manifestation from heaven in the glory of the Father, to gather all things in one." The creed here quoted is in Irenæus' "Against Heresies," Bk. I. 10. It was written, prob-

ably, towards the close of the second century, but represents the belief of a much earlier time. The so-called Apostles' Creed tells us of the Son "who sits at the right hand of the Father, whence he will come to judge the living and the dead." So, too, the Nicene Creed. The coming of the Son of man to judge the world was one of the most general anticipations of the early church, and it is hardly possible that the view of it which early prevailed should not have been handed down by and from the apostles themselves.

As verse 23 closed the answer to the question in reference to the overthrow of the temple, so verse 27 closes the direct answer to the question about the coming of the Son of man, and the end of the world. The relations of the disciples to the two questions determined the character of the answers to them. In the first case, they were to be personally exposed to dangers, and needed instructions which they could easily understand. Such the Master gave them. On the other hand, the coming of the Son of man was something more remote. Like the **end** already mentioned, there was a sense in which it was a movable point. To some faithful soul there is, every hour, a coming of the Son of man. He comes to receive his own, and to lead them to their mansions in his Father's house. But, besides, there is a coming at the end of the world. In either sense, an exact knowledge of the time of the coming would serve no good purpose. Our Lord, therefore, spoke of it in the grand but indefinite language of prophecy.

28-37. Further Instruction. Parallels, Matt. 24: 32-51; Luke 21: 29-35.

With verse 27, the whole prophecy closes. But a further word of instruction was needed. It is given (ver. 28-31, and 32-37.) Even in that case, in which his words were needed for their personal guidance, our Lord did not speak with astronomical exactness. He did not mention a day or hour. By way of reminding them of this, he now adds the parable of the fig tree. We cannot tell from the greenness of the fig tree, or the purple lilac blooms, or the white cherry blossoms, the exact day of the month; but these things assure us that the summer is near. It is this certainty as to the indefinite, and uncertainty as to the definite, that lies at the bottom of our moral trial; and renders watchfulness necessary. The things definitely foretold would certainly happen, and they would happen before that generation should pass away; but the time of them should come as comes the summer—by sure but unmarked steps. The siege of Jerusalem began in the spring. Christ's words were surer than the order of nature. (Ver. 35.)

30. The **all these things** might include all the things before spoken of—the destruction of the temple, the darkening of the sun, the coming of the Son of man—all. There is no grammatical reason why they should not. But an interpreter who makes his grammar his only guide, must often be led astray. Two classes of things had been mentioned; one that would concern the hearers personally, that would be attended by an unmistakable sign, and require specific action; the other was to follow the first, attended, however, by no definite mark, and extending to an indefinite future. Between the consummation of the first and of the second class, Luke makes "the time of the Gentiles" intervene. Matthew, prolonging the discourse through his twenty-fifth chapter, indicates that the second class of events was to be prolonged in time. It is hardly probable that he and Luke were led to expect the end of the world before the passing away of that generation. The New Testament writers, in their general drift, indicate no such expectation. We come, therefore, to the interpretation of the words, **all these things,** with a logical presumption against their including both the classes of events before mentioned. If it be said that in interpreting the words of Mark we have no right to go beyond his record to ascertain the meaning he intended to convey; the reply is, that he was reporting the discourse of another, and if we would understand what that discourse meant to him, we must put ourselves as nearly as possible in his place. We must hear the Lord's words as he heard them, or as they were heard by the one who reported them to him. In order to do this, we have a right to use any helps within our reach. In this case, the general rule applies, that where the grammatical reference is obscure or ambiguous, it must be determined by the context, or by the nature of the case. The whole context, and the nature of the case, forbid the supposition that the disciples understood the Lord to teach that he would come, and the final account of the world be closed before the generation then living should pass away.

32. But of that day and hour. It is important to observe the pauses and breaks in the discourse; the changes from one point or subject to another. Verses 13, 23, 27, and 31, mark the close of subjects; new subjects begin with verses 14, 24, 28, 32. The **that day,** of this verse, stands somewhat in opposition to the **these things** of verse 30. Its reference is to the close of the Dispensation. To refer it to the coming of the Son of man, may at first seem arbitrary, and without sufficient reason. But notice that **that day** early came to represent the time of the coming of the Lord. The apostle speaks of the crown of righteousness which the righteous judge will give him at **that day;** and prays for mercy on the house of Onesiphorus at **that day.** But, should we hesitate to think that our Lord uses the phrase in its subsequent compendious sense, we turn to Matthew's record for light. In 24: 36, he says: "But of *that day* and hour knoweth no man, no, not the angels of heaven, but my Father only." Then follows: "But as the days of Noe were, so shall also *the coming of the Son of man be*"! It is then, the end, the consummation of the age, far off or near, like some nebulous star, seen through mists or rifts of storm clouds, of whose coming even the Son of man knows not the day. The destruction of Jerusalem should be preceded by a definite sign—the city surrounded by armies. But the coming of the Son of man should be sudden, unexpected. See Matt. 24: 37-39.

33. The discourse, as recorded by Mark, closes with an exhortation solemn and impressive; and yet so simple that a child may understand it. (Ver. 32-37.) **For ye know not when the time is.** If the Son of man knows not, how much less do we! The comparisons of this conclusion all bring before us the disciples of the Lord working or idling, watching or sleeping, liable at any moment to be startled by his coming. And our Lord did not speak to those before him alone. His words are: "What I say unto you, I say unto all—Watch."

CHAPTER XIV.

AFTER two days was *the feast of* the passover, and of unleavened bread: and the chief priests and the scribes sought how they might take him by craft, and put *him* to death.

2 But they said, Not on the feast-*day,* lest there be an uproar of the people.

1 Now after two days was *the feast of* the passover and the unleavened bread: and the chief priests and the scribes sought how they might take him with subtility, and kill him: for they said, Not during the feast, lest haply there shall be a tumult of the people.

1, 2. THE RULERS CONSPIRE TO KILL JESUS. *Parallels,* Matt. 26 : 1-5; Luke 22 : 1, 2.—Here Matthew's report is full, while Mark and Luke are compendious. Matthew quotes the remark as to the nearness of the passover from Jesus himself, who also adds here a fresh prediction of his betrayal to death by the cross. This prediction now becomes definite as to time: **After two days.** Matthew says, too, that these words were added at the end of the discourse on the Mount of Olives, immediately after the representation of the great judgment-scene, in which he appears as "the king," dispensing eternal destiny. From that discourse he rose to speak of his own betrayal.

The feast of the passover, and of unleavened bread. Two names for the same thing, though slightly differing in their representation of it. The passover was celebrated on a single day, and the seven days that followed were called "the days of unleavened bread," from the prohibition of leaven that continued through them (Ex. 12 : 18, 19). Of course it was the beginning of this period, the passover day itself, the fourteenth day of Nisan, that was now said to be **two days** off.

The plotting against the life of Jesus definitely began after the raising of Lazarus. See John 11 : 47-53. There Caiaphas appears in the plotting, in which were concerned "the Pharisees and chief priests;" here, a meeting is held at his house (Matthew), at which are present "the chief priests and elders of the people;" in Mark, **the chief priests and the scribes.** The Pharisees were prominent as opposers all through the ministry, but at the end, when the Passion approached, the chief priests became the leaders of opposition. The Pharisees are mentioned in the Gospels (as related to the history) seventy-four times before the completion of the triumphal entry to Jerusalem, and sixteen times after it; and nine of the sixteen allusions are found in the twenty-third chapter of Matthew, the chapter of "woes." The chief priests, on the contrary, are mentioned twelve times before the completion of the triumphal entry, five of these allusions being after the raising of Lazarus, and sixty-nine times after it. Thus the chief priests appear almost exclusively in connection with the Passion. The priestly element was mainly of the party of

the Sadducees. The meeting at the house of Caiaphas (Matthew) was either a formal or an informal meeting of the Sanhedrin, in which body both sects were represented, but the leading influence was that of the priests. The purpose was to find some way of taking Jesus **by craft** to kill him—some hidden plot for secret murder, with no open violence.—**But they said.** In the text of the revisers verse 2 begins with "for," and gives the reason of their desire for secrecy: they could not work openly, for fear of a disturbance.—**Not on the feast-day,** or "during the feast"—*i. e.* not till after the feast. The meaning is not that they would hasten to finish before the feast, for the throng of which they were afraid must already have filled the city. It was too late to finish before the feast; they would wait now till it was over.

3-11. THE ANOINTING OF JESUS AT BETHANY, AND THE TRAITOROUS PROPOSAL OF JUDAS, SUGGESTED BY IT. *Parallels,* Matt. 26 : 6-16; Luke 22 : 3-6; John 12 : 1-8.—But John is parallel only in the anointing, and Luke only in the visit of Judas to the plotting enemies. From this point we have, with many variations and omissions, a fourfold harmony. The time of the anointing is fixed by John at "six days before the passover"—*i. e.* on Saturday, or the Jewish Sabbath, the day before the triumphal entry to Jerusalem. The narrative is introduced by Matthew and Mark out of its order, having been omitted in its own place and reserved for insertion in company with the act to which it gave rise. The relations of this story furnish one of the best illustrations of undesigned coincidence and mutual confirmation in the Gospels, and at the same time of the fragmentariness of our records. Matthew, Mark, and John all tell of a complaint concerning the anointing and a rebuke from Jesus, but John alone tells us that Judas was the offended one; while Matthew and Mark tell us, as John does not, that he immediately went to the meeting of enemies with his traitorous proposal. Yet Matthew and Mark, by the act of putting the narrative just here, silently confirm the testimony of John, showing that they were aware that the feast at Bethany had something to do with the betrayal. But for John we should not have known what to make of their placing the story here.—

3 ¶ And being in Bethany, in the house of Simon the leper, as he sat at meat, there came a woman having an alabaster box of ointment of spikenard, very precious; and she brake the box, and poured *it* on his head.

4 And there were some that had indignation within themselves, and said, Why was this waste of the ointment made?

3 And while he was in Bethany in the house of Simon the leper, as he sat at meat, there came a woman having [1]an alabaster cruse of ointment of [2]pure nard very costly; *and* she brake the cruse, and 4 poured it over his head. But there were some that had indignation among themselves, *saying*, To what purpose hath this waste of the ointment been made?

a Matt. 26 : 6; Luke 7 : 37; John 12 : 1, etc.——1 Or, *a flask....* 2 Or, *liquid nard*

It is scarcely necessary to say that this is not the same anointing as that of Luke 7 : 37–50; or that this Mary is not Mary Magdalene; or that there is no evidence to connect Mary Magdalene with either of the anointings.

3. Being in Bethany—where he had just arrived on the last journey toward Jerusalem—**in the house of Simon the leper,** who is entirely unknown. From John we would infer that the family of Lazarus made the supper, and hence it has been conjectured that Simon must have been in some way connected with that family; but the facts are beyond our reach. It is a reasonable conjecture that Simon had been healed of leprosy by Jesus.—**There came a woman,** who was Mary, the sister of Lazarus. So John, who also informs us that Martha was serving and Lazarus was a fellow-guest at the table with Jesus. The traits of character that are thus illustrated are identical with those that appear in Luke 10 : 38–42. The various glimpses that are given us of this family convince us of their truth by their perfect consistency.—Only by John is the name of the woman given, but surely not because Matthew and Mark did not know it; the very record (verse 9) proves that they knew. Such a promise would not be recorded concerning an unknown person. The synoptists plainly had some reason for suppressing, as they did, all definite allusions to the family at Bethany. They have no mention of the raising of Lazarus; and Mary is here simply a woman, and there is no allusion to Lazarus or Martha. When Luke alludes to the household (10 : 38–42) there is nothing to indicate where they lived or that they had any closer connection with our Lord. Some reason, which was removed before John wrote, kept the synoptists silent.—**Having an alabaster box**—or "cruse" or "vase"—**of ointment of spikenard,** or rather "of nard." The word "spikenard," though it was originally *spica nardi,* "head" or "tuft of nard," has obtained a different meaning, and is not the best word here. Nard was an Indian plant, from the root and leaves of which was expressed an oil which was among the most highly prized of unguents. The translation in the Revised New Testament omits the Greek word *pistikos,* except as it seems

to be represented, by intention, in the first syllable of "spikenard." The word is a doubtful one, as the revisers indicate in their margin, but probably it means "pure" or "unadulterated." Adulteration of such unguents was frequent. The "pure nard" of the American revisers is doubtless right.—It was **very precious,** a fact that determines the standing of the family as among the comparatively rich. Not improbably, this one vase too much may have been purchased for the anointing of Lazarus for the grave.—**She brake the box.** Broke the neck of the vase, to pour out all that it contained. The mention of the act is peculiar to Mark.—**Poured it on his head.** So Matthew. John, "She anointed the feet of Jesus, and wiped his feet with her hair." The statements differ; John plainly intended to tell of an anointing of the feet, and Matthew and Mark of the head; but there is no reason to reject the idea that both are correct, and that Mary anointed both head and feet. From Luke 7 : 46 it is plain that anointing of the head of a guest was common and anointing of the feet was unusual, a rare and special tribute. It is not unlikely that Mary had heard the story of the earlier anointing in Simon's house in Galilee, and received from it the suggestion of her own act.

Her motive, so far as it was connected with the raising of her brother from death, is admirably expressed by Tennyson (*In Memoriam,* xxxii.) :

"Her eyes are homes of silent prayer,
  Nor other thought her mind admits
  But, 'He was dead, and there he sits,
And he that brought him back is there.'

"Then one deep love doth supersede
  All other, when her ardent gaze
  Roves from the living brother's face
And rests upon the Life indeed.

"All subtle thought, all curious fears,
  Borne down by gladness so complete,
  She bows, she bathes the Saviour's feet
With costly spikenard and with tears."

4, 5. The complaint is that of "the disciples" in Matthew; of *some* in Mark; of "Judas Iscariot, one of his disciples," in John; probably, in fact, of Judas, scattering his objections among the rest. One evil-whisperer

5 For it might have been sold for more than three hundred pence, and have been given to the poor. And they murmured against her

6 And Jesus said, Let her alone; why trouble ye her? she hath wrought a good work on me.

7 For ye have the poor with you always, and whensoever ye will ye may do them good: but me ye have not always.

8 She hath done what she could: she is come aforehand to anoint my body to the burying.

5 For this ointment might have been sold for above three hundred ¹shillings, and given to the poor.

6 And they murmured against her. Put Jesus said, · Let her alone; why trouble ye her? she hath

7 wrought a good work on me. For ye have the poor always with you, and whensoever ye will ye can do

8 them good: but me ye have not always. She hath done what she could: she hath anointed my body

a Deut. 15 : 11.——1 See marginal note on chap. vi, 37.

may poison many minds. The complaint was extremely plausible: this did indeed seem like waste; the poor certainly appeared to have a higher claim. The estimate of the value of the ointment, **more than three hundred pence**, or denarii, is a rough one, ill-natured, and not unlikely exaggerated, though the testimony of the word **very precious** remains. Three hundred denarii was a sum equal to about forty-five dollars, but practically, in that age, much greater than that. One denarius appears in Matt. 20 : 2 as a day's wages. The objection of Judas is expressly attributed by John to a dishonest motive, pleading the cause of the poor merely as a pretence.—**And they murmured against her,** or reproved her harshly. Peculiar to Mark. This seems to be the work of more than Judas: too many of the disciples fell in with his plausible but heartless cavil. This was a mistake of theirs similar to that about the coming of the little children to Jesus (Mark 10 : 13), a worldly divergence from the spirit of the Master. Not yet were they able to see beauty in pure spiritual excellence.

6-9. The answer of Jesus—an answer for which all ages do well to be thankful. In reply to the worldly complaint, it is the vindication of the unworldly heart. First he protects the woman, **Let her alone; why trouble ye her?**—Then he praises the act, paying tribute to its inward quality. **She hath wrought a good work on me** (*kalon ergon*), an act of moral beauty. The spectators had estimated it outwardly, after the manner of men, with reference merely to its practical effect in visible usefulness; he shows it to them as an act of spiritual quality, admirable in itself, lovely, and worthy of a tender reverence. It was all this, because it was a pure act of love to him. In his sight a pure love is precious for itself.—This high praise he next vindicates (verse 7) in view of the timeliness of the act. Kindness to **the poor**, he says, is always possible, for they are ever at hand; but anything that is to be done to him in person as an act of ardent love must be done quickly.—Yet how tender a way is this of mentioning the in-

evitable and impending loss! **Me ye have not always.** See how high an honor he thus puts upon love as love: he compares it with usefulness, and, at least for certain purposes, calls it the higher of the two. Helpfulness to the needy is no optional work: it is one of the duties, and not less one of the privileges, in his kingdom. See how he identifies his needy brethren with himself in Matt. 25 : 40. Yet even this he would have to be set aside for the time, when love finds such an opportunity to lavish itself on him. This is no selfishness of his, no love of anointings, no greediness of the heart for tributes of affection; this is recognition of the supreme worth of holy love. "Love did well," he says, "to seize the moment and do its utmost before I was away, even though the poor must wait." He was right: love did well, not only as bringing forth a deed of moral beauty, but even for the poor. Mary did infinitely more for the poor by the act of that day than she could have done by giving them the value of the ointment. That would have relieved only a few of them, and only for a little while; but the deed of love has been a blessing to the poor of all later ages. The selling of the alabaster box for charity's sake would soon have been forgotten, but the breaking of it for love's sake has inspired ten thousand deeds of unselfishness.

His high judgment of the act he further vindicates (verse 8) by showing it as an act of deep loving insight. He touches here upon a motive beyond that which Tennyson has recognized. **She hath done what she could.** It was the utmost that she had means of doing for a purpose that she held very dear—namely, **she is come aforehand to anoint my body to the burying.** Matthew, "in that she hath poured this ointment on my body, she did it for burial." Such words would scarcely have been spoken if they had not represented the purpose that was present in Mary's mind. The time was close upon his entrance to Jerusalem, when his disciples expected him to triumph. Mary, with deeper

9 Verily I say unto you, Wheresoever this gospel shall be preached throughout the whole world, *this also* that she hath done shall be spoken of for a memorial of her.

10 [a] And[a] Judas Iscariot, one of the twelve, went unto the chief priests to betray[b] him unto them.

11 And when they heard *it*, they were glad, and promised to give him[c] money. And he sought how he might conveniently betray him.

9 aforehand for the burying. And verily I say unto you, Wheresoever the gospel shall be preached throughout the whole world, that also which this woman hath done shall be spoken of for a memorial of her.

10 And Judas Iscariot, [d]he that was one of the twelve, went away unto the chief priests, that he might

11 deliver him unto them And they, when they heard it, were glad, and promised to give him money. And he sought how he might conveniently deliver him *unto them*.

a Matt. 26 : 14, etc. ; Luke 22 : 3, etc....b John 13 : 2....c 1 Kings 21 : 20; Prov. 1 : 10-16.——1 Gr. *the one of the twelve.*

insight, understood him at that time, perhaps, where no one else understood him, and felt that instead of triumph it must be death. She had lovingly looked forward to what must follow death : it would be death at the hands of enemies, and probably there would be no opportunity for her to do any service of affection for his body. But he was with her now, and while her thoughts were busy the impulse seized her to pour out upon his body this precious ointment now, anointing him beforehand for the burial. This was an act of fellowship with his sufferings. How contrary to the spirit of Peter in Matt. 16 : 22 : "Be it far from thee, Lord"! but like the *words* of Peter in Luke 22 : 33 : "I am ready to go with thee both into prison and to death."—What a tribute from Jesus! **She hath done what she could.** Do not spoil it by metaphysical or theological analysis; it is utmost Love recognizing love's utmost.

It is an exceptional act, and it gives to its doer an exceptional place (*verse 9*). Note the solemn **Verily I say unto you.** The woman is elevated to a place in the Gospel story—not only her deed, but herself. It shall be told everywhere **for a memorial of her**—*i. e.* as a means of keeping her in remembrance. No one else ever received from the Lord such a promise. No other act in his life is recorded to have so pleased him, for no other appears to have been so purely and profoundly an act of unselfish, holy, sympathetic love. After such a record of his estimate of love, we can understand the place he gives to love in John 13 : 35 as the badge of discipleship.—Notice the assumption that the gospel is to **be preached throughout the whole world.** The phrase (*eis holon ton kosmon*) is broader than the language of Matt. 24 : 14—literally, "all the inhabited world;" or of Mark 13 : 10, "among all the nations." That the gospel is to be thus preached he does not state, but assumes ; it is the woman's part that needs to be mentioned. Compare Luke 10 : 42 : "Mary hath chosen the good part, which shall not be taken away from her." By this unexpected promise of world-

wide and age-long fame Mary may well have been humbled, but the disciples who had found fault humiliated.

10, 11. The record now returns to the time of verses 1, 2. The conspirators are in session, and are unexpectedly joined by one of the company of Jesus. **Judas** is specified as "one of the twelve;" in Matthew, in Mark, literally, as "he that was one of the twelve;" Luke is still more emphatic : "being of the number of the twelve." His original honor is the special badge of his infamy. Angered by the rebuke at Bethany, and taking this as the climax of his reasons for such a step, he comes with his proposal to place Jesus in their hands. Note that the Greek word (*paradidōmi*) means "to deliver up," and does not in itself contain the idea of treachery that belongs to our word "betray"—a fact which the revisers have frequently, but not always, observed.--At the coming of Judas the conspirators, surprised and delighted, change their plan, cut short their delay, and close the bargain for the delivery of Jesus at any time, tumult or no tumult : for such an opportunity it is worth while to run some risks. In Matthew the proposal of pay comes from Judas : "What are ye willing to give me, and I will deliver him up to you?" There also the price is mentioned, thirty pieces of silver—*i. e.* shekels—about fifteen dollars intrinsically, but relatively much more, perhaps ten times as much. But it was not the money that induced Judas to the act : he was no such shallow man. Deeper motives—of dissatisfaction with Jesus—must long have been at work. From that time he was watching his opportunity, which soon came.

12-16. THE PREPARATION FOR THE PASSOVER. *Parallels*, Matt. 26 : 17-19; Luke 22 : 7-13.—The time, unquestionably, is Thursday, before sunset. The passover lamb was to be killed on the fourteenth day of Nisan, and to be eaten in the evening that followed that day ; this evening was counted, however, in the Jewish reckoning, as part of the next day. All the synoptists positively assert that this Thursday was the day for killing the passover.

12 ¶ And the first day ofᵃ unleavened bread, when they killed the passover, his disciples said unto him, Where wilt thou that we go and prepare, that thou mayest eat the passover?

13 And he sendeth forth two of his disciples, and saith unto them, Go ye into the city, and there shall meet you a man bearing a pitcher of water: follow him.

14 And wheresoever he shall go in, say ye to the good man of the house, The Master¹ saith, Where is the guest-chamber, where I shall eatᵈ the passover with my disciples?

15 And he will shew you a large upper room furnished and prepared: there make ready for us.

16 And his disciples went forth, and came into the city, and found as he had said unto them: and they made ready the passover.

12 And on the first day of unleavened bread, when they sacrificed the passover, his disciples say unto him, Where wilt thou that we go and make ready 13 that thou mayest eat the passover? And he sendeth two of his disciples, and saith unto them, Go into the city, and there shall meet you a man bearing 14 a pitcher of water: follow him; and wheresoever he shall enter in, say to the goodman of the house, The ¹Master saith, Where is my guest-chamber, where I shall eat the passover with my disciples? 15 And he will himself shew you a large upper room furnished and ready: and there make ready for us, 16 And the disciples went forth, and came into the city, and found as he had said unto them: and they made ready the passover.

---

a Ex. 12 : 6, etc....b ch 11 : 2, 3 ; Heb. 4. 13....c John 11 : 26; 13 : 13....d Rev. 3. 20....e John 16 : 4.——1 Or, Teacher

---

From early Christian times John has been supposed to differ from the synoptists here by representing that at the time of our Lord's trial—*i. e.* in the night between Thursday and Friday—the passover feast itself was still to be eaten, indicating thus that the true passover day, the fourteenth of Nisan, was Friday, and not Thursday. Accordingly, some have maintained that Jesus did not really eat the passover at all, but, as a substitute for it, partook of a similar meal one day in advance. This theory is favored by the desire to find our Saviour crucified on the very passover day, and thus accurately fulfilling the ancient type. But such a divergence among the evangelists upon a simple matter of fact concerning which they cannot have been ignorant would be very strange, even apart from all questions of inspiration ; for it could not possibly be unconscious on the part of John, who wrote last, yet his manner is totally unconscious of any purpose to correct the previous understanding on the subject. A more thorough examination of John's language shows, however, that the differences are by no means irreconcilable. John does not assert as positively as at first appears that the passover day was Friday. (See a good and satisfactory discussion of the subject in Andrews's *Life of our Lord.*) The result is that no serious difficulty remains in accepting the positive statements of the synoptists that Jesus really partook of the passover at the proper time.

12. The first day of unleavened bread— *i. e.* of the passover celebration. Leavened bread was to be put away from the houses for seven days, from the fourteenth of Nisan at evening to the twenty-first at evening (Ex. 12: 18-20). **—When they killed**—impersonal ; when it was customary to kill—**the passover.**—Matthew and Mark record, while Luke omits, the inquiry of the disciples as to the place of observance. Notice how they assumed that instead of scattering to family circles of their own they

were to keep the feast as a household with Jesus as the head. But the household had no home (Luke 9 : 58), and they did not know where to spread the table.—As to the necessary preparation, (1) originally the head of the household killed the lamb, which had been selected and kept four days beforehand ; but in later times the lamb was slain by the priests in the temple, some member of the household presenting it there and assisting. This was a part of the service proposed by the disciples on this occasion—to buy the lamb and attend to the sacrificing. (2) It was necessary to attend to the roasting of the lamb, to provide the bread, wine, bitter herbs, and sweet fruits, and to spread the table ; in this case, also, to provide a place.

13-16. He sendeth forth two of his disciples, who were Peter and John (Luke). Jesus himself still remained in Bethany. There is something omitted from this story, but what is it ? Is it a previous understanding with some disciple who had a house in the city, perhaps a secret disciple like Joseph of Arimathæa? or is it a superhuman knowledge and control of the movements of unseen men ? The message is, in Matthew, "The Master" (Teacher) "saith, My time is at hand ; I keep the passover at thy house with my disciples"—a message which seems to imply that the householder knew Jesus as "the Teacher," and would know something of what he meant by "my time is at hand." — **Where is the** (in the best text "my") **guest-chamber?** which naturally indicates either that he had arranged for the room or that he had used it for some purpose before. The man would seem, therefore, to have been more or less distinctly a disciple. The question about the guest-chamber does not ask for information : it is equivalent to "Show my messengers the place." It may therefore have been agreed that when Jesus was ready he would send some one to claim the

17 And in the evening he cometh with the twelve.
18 And as they sat and did eat, Jesus said, Verily I say unto you, One of you which eateth⁰ with me shall betray me.
19 And they began to be sorrowful, and to say unto him one by one, *Is* it 1? and another *said, Is* it 1?

17 And when it was evening he cometh with the 18 twelve. And as they ¹sat and were eating, Jesus said, Verily I say unto you, One of you shall betray 19 me, *even* he that eateth with me. They began to be sorrowful, and to say unto him one by one, Is it 1?

guest-chamber and prepare the passover, and the meeting with the servant bearing the pitcher may have been a chosen signal. On the other hand, we may recognize this as another instance (like John 11 : 14) of the superhuman knowledge that Jesus possessed; but with it we must recognize also a superhuman control of the movements of absent persons—something of which we have no other traces in his life except in the cases of his healing from a distance. There is no objection to recognizing both, but it is a good general principle not to suppose miracle where the ordinary course of life sufficiently explains the facts. In this case we may suppose a miracle, but it seems scarcely necessary. The pitcher-bearer was to be merely a silent guide: all the conversation was to be with the **good man**—*i. e.* master—**of the house.**—He, the master of the house, **will show you a large upper room, furnished** —*i. e.* supplied with table and couches—**and prepared: there make ready for us.** Matthew omits the sign by which they were to find the house, but he leaves room for it; and the narratives need no reconciliation.

17-26. THE EATING OF THE PASSOVER, AND THE INSTITUTION OF THE LORD'S SUPPER. *Parallels,* Matt. 26 : 20-30; Luke 22 : 14-39; John 13-17.—Matthew and Mark are closely parallel. Luke differs from them somewhat in arrangement, relates what was said during the eating of the passover, and records our Lord's tender and searching reproof of ambitious strife at the table. John 13-17 is placed here because it relates to the same hour, though it contains but very little that is strictly parallel to the record of the synoptists. But John confirms the order of Matthew and Mark where it differs from that of Luke; and their arrangement is generally followed.

17. The Paschal lamb was slain between the hour of prayer (three o'clock) and sunset. About sunset, which would be at that season at a little after six, Jesus may have come into the city. With this sunset began, according to the Jewish reckoning, the day of his death. **The twelve** were with him; Luke, "the apostles." There was a somewhat larger circle of near followers, but there is **no indication**

that any of these were now present. First came the passover itself, one "cup" of which is mentioned by Luke (22:17); meanwhile, or perhaps earlier, the rebuke of ambition, which probably manifested itself in connection with taking their places at the table. It is quite possible that the disciples were even expecting this passover season to witness the display of their Master's Messianic power; in which case, they would think, their relative nearness to his person would immediately be important. After the rebuke came the washing of the disciples' feet by their Master—matchless enforcement of the law of love and humility, which ought to have decided the character of his church for all time. After the rebuke, the passover still unfinished, came the pointing out and withdrawal of the traitor. If we had only the Gospel of Luke, we should suppose that Judas remained till after the establishment of the Supper. But Luke probably puts the record of the Supper out of its place, because he has just mentioned the "cup" of the Paschal meal—mentioned by him alone—and that suggests the bread and the other cup, which he at once proceeds to speak of.

18. According to John, Jesus was impelled now to point out his betrayer by his own inward trouble, the presence of the traitor weighing heavily upon his spirit. **Verily I say unto you**—no wonder that his solemn formula came forth now—**One of you which eateth with me shall betray me.** Literally, "One of you shall betray me, even he that eateth with me;" the last phrase peculiar to Mark in its form, though Luke preserves the idea. It is an allusion to Ps. 41 : 9, and it means, not "who is eating with me now," but "my companion, one who has been so near to me as to be my companion at table." The very words of the psalm, probably, had just been uttered (John 13 : 18). This was the first definite announcement that the betrayer was to be one of the twelve, though John 6 : 70 was a terrible hint of it.

19. They had not distrusted one another—so Luke and John expressly—and did not even now suspect the guilty one. But perhaps they had reason to suspect him, and would have done so if they had been less simple. **They**

20 And he answered and said unto them, *It is* one of the twelve, that dippeth with me in the dish.

21 The Son of man indeed goeth, as it is written of him: but woe to that man by whom the Son of man is betrayed! good⁰ were it for that man if he had never been born.

20 And he said unto them, *It is* one of the twelve, he 21 that dippeth with me in the dish. For the Son of man goeth, even as it is written of him: but woe unto that man through whom the Son of man is betrayed! good were it ¹for that man if he had not been born.

a Matt. 18 : 6, 7.——1 Gr. *for him if that man.*

---

began to be sorrowful. How could they be otherwise? Each heart sprang up to deny the charge, yet the denial admitted by its form that the Lord must be right in making it.—**Is it I?** or rather, since the interrogative word *mēti* expects a negative answer, " It is not I, is it? Thou canst not mean me?" No one denies the charge as a whole, but each, so far as he dares, repels it from himself. The clause, **and another said, Is it I?** is omitted from the best text : it certainly is superfluous.—John now asked, at the suggestion of Peter, who the betrayer was, and obtained privately (not otherwise) the sign of the morsel from the dish. It is not certain that the information thus given went even to Peter, who had sought for it (John 13 : 23-26).

20. For others of the company besides John there was a second answer, narrowing the circle more closely than that of verse 18. **One of the twelve, that dippeth with me in the dish.** The word is a diminutive, denoting probably a side-dish, perhaps containing the conserve of sweet fruits. A single dish might serve three or four of the company. Thus he diminished the circle in which the betrayer was to be found.—It is not certain (see below) that all this was heard and noticed by the entire circle. Apparently it was the intent of Jesus to make Judas aware that he was known, and to compel him to leave the company; yet he would do this half confidentially and by gradual approaches, for the sake of Judas himself. He would let him see exposure coming that, if such a thing were possible, he might even yet confess and repent. " As I live, saith the Lord God, I have no pleasure in the death of the wicked; but that the wicked turn from his way and live " (Ezek. 33 : 11).

21. The Son of man indeed goeth—departs, makes his exit from life; a softened expression for his death—**as it is written of him**—written (as he said at Mark 9 : 12) that he must suffer many things and be set at naught; written as in Isa. 53. In Luke, " Goeth as it hath been determined." Compare the record of his positive submission to the fulfilment of the Scriptures in the garden (Matt. 26 : 54). But the guilt of wilful human agents is unaffected by prophecies and predeterminations.

So it is said concerning Judas himself, in the prayer of the apostles (Acts 1 : 25); concerning the Jews, in the discourse of Peter (Acts 2 : 23).—Prophecy does not interfere with responsibility, nor was there any such preappointment of God as to diminish the guilt of **that man by whom the Son of man** was betrayed. His sin, our Lord says, makes of his life an utter failure, misfortune, curse; better for him never to have had it.—A brief but terrible saying. **Good were it for that man if he had never been born.** It implies that to most men it is better to have been born; it teaches that there is sinning that utterly forfeits the good of existence; it leaves Judas to a doom too fearful to be contemplated. This is the clearest scriptural illustration of that " forfeiting of one's self (Luke 9 : 25) and " loss of the soul " (Mark 8 : 36) which sin renders possible to man. There is no one but Judas, however, who is expressly said to have met with such an end—a grave hint to us to be very slow in passing explicit personal condemnation.

Here Matthew adds that Judas at last said, like the rest, " Is it I ?" and was definitely pointed out. Yet John says that even when he left the room his treason was not understood by the other apostles, but they supposed he was going out as the trusted servant of the company (John 13 : 27-30). If the two reports are to be harmonized, it must be by the very natural supposition that the conversation was carried on, partly at least, in groups, and many things passed half noticed, or noticed only by a few. Perhaps we often read such narratives too stiffly, and overlook the free and informal nature of the interviews that are recorded.—It must have been at this point that Judas withdrew. The weight of opinion was formerly in favor of the view that he was present at the Supper; but in more recent times the opposite view is more generally held.

22-26. Parallel to the synoptical narratives of the institution of the Lord's Supper is Paul's statement in 1 Cor. 11 : 23-25. The four narratives fall into two pairs, marked by some differences. Matthew and Mark are closely parallel, and so are Luke and Paul. John has no allusion to the Supper.

22. As they did eat, or " were eating."

22 ᶜ And⁴ as they did eat, Jesus took bread, and ǀ 22 And as they were eating, he took ᵇbread, and
blessed, and brake *it*, and gave to them, and said, ǀ when he had blessed, he brake it, and gave to them,
Take,ᵇ eat; this is my body. ǀ

a Matt. 26 : 26, etc. ; Luke 22 : 19 ; 1 Cor. 11 : 23, etc....*b* John 6 : 48-58.——1 Or, *a loaf*

Still engaged with the Paschal meal; there was
no special preparation or clearing of the table,
as if to do justice to a new beginning. All was
simple and quiet. Luke has already mentioned
(22 : 17, 18) the passing around of one "cup" of
the passover, and some expositors think they
can identify the place of the cup that entered
into the Supper in the order of the Paschal
feast. But it is not certain that the order of
the feast, as given by Jewish authorities, was
exactly that of our Lord's time, or that, if it
was, he strictly followed it. The foundation
for a definite judgment, therefore, is scarcely
adequate; and it is best simply to recognize
the fact that he took one of the cups of the
feast, as being ready to his hand, and turned
it to this new use and meaning.—**He took
bread.** The bread that was at hand on the
table, which was the unleavened barley-bread,
in thin flat loaves. As there was no special
preparation for the new institution, so there
was no providing of new materials. No special significance appears in the fact that the
bread was unleavened, and there is nothing to
make us doubt that he would have used leavened bread just as readily, if that had been
before him.—**And blessed, and brake it.**
Literally, "having blessed, he broke (it)." The
implied pronoun is governed by the verb, not
by the participle; it is not directly said that he
blessed the bread, but that he broke the bread.
The participle may mean either "having blessed God"—*i. e.* by giving thanks—or "having
invoked the blessing of God" upon the bread
and those who were to partake of it. In either
case this was no "prayer of consecration:" it
was the simple "grace" or "blessing" over
food, though the contents of the prayer may
have been modified by his thoughts, made
even unwontedly great and tender by the occasion. In Luke and Paul the word is "having
given thanks," the same word that Matthew
and Mark use when they speak of his prayer
over the cup.—He **brake** the bread into fragments; whether using one loaf or more does
not appear.—**And gave to them.** The apostles, as they reclined about the table. In that
position, it is most likely that he broke the
bread upon a plate and handed it to them.—
And said, Take. The word **eat** is omitted
here from the best text, though unquestioned
in Matthew; both words are omitted by Luke

and Paul.—**Take**—*i. e.* with the hand, in order
to eat it. There is no spiritual mystery in the
word, as if it related to some mystical appropriation.—**This is my body.** So Matthew
and Mark; Luke, "this is my body which is
given for you" (present participle, "is being
given"); Paul, "this is my body which is for
you." The word "broken" ("which is broken
for you," 1 Cor. 11 : 24), though ancient, is undoubtedly a gloss intended to complete the
sense. It must be omitted, and there is no
original scriptural authority for saying "which
is broken for you." Neither is the "breaking"
of our Saviour's body one of the facts that are
symbolized in the bread of the Supper.

All the four give the simple words **this is
my body.** There was no possibility of a literal acceptation of his words by the disciples,
for his body was visibly and tangibly among
them, as real to their senses as their own bodies. But there was no danger of such an acceptation of them, for the disciples were men
of Oriental mind, to whom such figurative language would not be perplexing; the Old Testament, with its manifold figures and resemblances (*e. g.* "the Lord God is a sun and a
shield," Ps. 84 : 11; "we are the clay, and
thou our potter," Isa. 64 : 8; "the seven good
kine are seven years," Gen. 41 : 26) and the
words of Jesus himself (*e. g.* "I am the door,"
John 10 : 9; "the field is the world; the good
seed are the children of the kingdom; but
the tares are the children of the wicked one,"
Matt. 13 : 38) would render this language perfectly plain. They would understand him to
mean, "this bread which I offer you is the
symbol of my body." Any suggestion of literalism, as if Jesus meant that the bread by
miracle *was* literally his body, would have
amazed the disciples beyond measure. How
absolutely inconsistent it would have been,
too, with the simple, earnest, natural character
of the whole occasion !

In Matthew and Mark it is merely "this is
my body"—words that convey the announcement of his death, but nothing more; Luke and
Paul add the destination of that body to the
good of men, for whose sake it is "given" to
death : "which is for you" or "which is given
for you." Thus the facts symbolized in the
bread of the Supper are (1) the giving of his
body to death, and (2) the fact that it was given

14

23 And he took the cup: and when he had given thanks, he gave *it* to them: and they all drank of it. 24 And he said unto them, This *is* my blood of the new testament, which is shed for many.

23 and said, Take ye: this is my body. And he took a cup, and when he had given thanks, he gave to them: and they all drank of it. And he said unto them, This is my blood of the *covenant, which

---

a 1 Cor. 10 : 16 John 6 : 53. ——1 Some ancient authorities insert *new.*

---

to death for men. In other words, (1) his sacrifice or self-giving, the completeness of it being the point first made prominent by the mention of death, and (2) his sacrifice or self-giving for the good of others—*i. e.* of men. Beyond these facts the symbolic teaching of the bread does not extend, the purpose of his sacrifice or the object to be gained by it being first suggested by the cup. Thus there is a progress of thought in the service, often overlooked, but evidently intended by our Saviour.—The offering of the symbol of his body would be eaten would remind the disciples of the "hard saying" of John 6 : 53–56. But that hard saying was a necessary one, and this symbol was intended to keep it constantly in mind—namely, that there is no true life without a personal appropriation of the Christ who died for men, and a personal assimilation of him in his self-sacrifice to the purpose of new life in the soul. The eating is the symbol of this appropriation and assimilation.

23. And he took the cup. Literally, "And taking a cup." So Matthew and Mark ; Luke and Paul say "the cup," by which, however, they mean the well-known cup of the ordinance. He took "a cup" of the red wine mingled with water with which the table was supplied. There is no mention of wine at the passover in the Pentateuch, but before our Lord's time the various "cups" of the feast—never less than four in number—had become a regular part of the service. The wine was the common wine of the country, and was mixed with water as it was drunk. Here, again, our Lord provided nothing new, but took what was before him.—**And when he had given thanks.** The same word that is used by Luke and Paul of the first prayer. Hence there was no new quality or character in the second. This too was a simple "grace before meat," though we cannot refrain from thinking that he who spake as "never man spake" gave it, out of his own heart, a quality for ever unmatched. There were Jewish forms of prayer and thanksgiving to be used over the cups of the passover, but it is hard to believe that our Saviour confined himself to them at this time, beautiful as they may have been.—**He gave it** (the cup) **to them: and they all drank of it** (or from it). **And he said unto them,** while they were drink-

ing; so the words naturally mean. In Matthew, "he gave it to them, saying, Drink from it, all of you ;" Luke and Paul, simply, "in like manner also the cup, after supper," in which the second prayer is not mentioned, except by implication in the phrase, "in like manner."

24. Testament (*diathēkē*) should be translated "covenant." It would be a great help to true understanding if our Bible were divided into "Scriptures of the old covenant" and "Scriptures of the new covenant ;" then such passages as this would readily fall into their true place. Here, however, on manuscript authority, the word **new** is to be omitted, both in Matthew and in Mark. Then we shall read, **This is my blood** of the covenant, **which is shed** (or poured out) **for many.** Matthew adds, "unto remission of sins ;" Luke and Paul, "This cup is the new covenant in my blood ;" Luke adds, "which is shed" (or poured out) "for you." There is a grammatical irregularity in Luke's sentence, however, which the revisers have attempted to represent by translating, "even that which is poured out for you." **Is,** as before, is "the copula of symbolic resemblance" (*Meyer*), and the saying, in Mark, means, "This which I offer you is the symbol of my blood," etc. But that which is symbolized is not merely "my blood :" it is "my blood of the covenant," or "my covenant-blood ;" which means, "my blood poured out in death, that it may be, in the spiritual realm, what the ancient blood of the covenant symbolized."—Here we reach the announcement of the purpose of his sacrifice. The word "new" is implied in the sense, though not expressed, for of course it is of the new covenant that he speaks. The new covenant was predicted in Jer. 31 : 31–34, and is identified with the gospel in Heb. 8 : 7–12. The blessings promised in it are (1) pardon of sin and acceptance with God, and (2) the writing of the law of God in the heart, and consequent knowledge of God on the part of men. These are the two great gifts of the gospel, restoration to God and assimilation to God. Now, Jesus calls his blood the "covenant-blood" of that covenant. For the significance of "the blood of the covenant," see Ex. 24 : 3–8, which our Lord evidently had in mind. The same scene is again alluded to, though perhaps not that scene exclusively, in Heb. 9 : 19, 20. See other references to the blood of the covenant (but now of the new covenant) in Heb. 10 : 29 and 13 : 20. The blood of the covenant was sacrificial blood, of burnt-offerings and peace-offerings, shed and made ready at the moment of the establishment and ratification of the covenant between Jehovah and Israel. It was divided into two parts, and half of it was sprinkled (or rather "cast," poured out) upon the altar of Jehovah ; then the book of the covenant was read in the hearing of the people, and they assented to it ; and then the remaining half of the blood was sprinkled (or "cast," poured out) on the people. The ceremony was a sacrificial act toward God and an act of self-dedication and consent to God on the part of man. It was the sealing of a covenant of fellowship and sacramental union between Jehovah and his people ; and the blood, offered to God and applied to man, was the means and the token by which the covenant was brought into full effect. Now, our Lord says the new and better covenant—the covenant of actual pardon and of law written in the heart—has its covenant-blood, as had the old ; and he says that he sheds his own blood as covenant-blood to bring God and man into the actual union and fellowship promised in the new covenant. His offering of himself is to be acceptable in the sight of God (Eph. 5 : 2), as the blood sprinkled on the altar was, and it is to be accepted by men, through faith, as the means by which they are brought into "the eternal covenant" of genuine fellowship with God. One of the objects of the new covenant (Jer. 31 : 34) is specified by our Lord here, according to Matthew, "unto remission of sins." To bring this to pass, his offering of himself reaches Godward and reaches manward.—This blood is **shed** (or poured out) **for many.** So Matthew and Mark. Paul interprets this to mean "for all" (2 Cor. 5 : 14 ; 1 Tim. 2 : 6), and so does John (1 John 2 : 2). As no "breaking" of our Saviour's body is symbolized by the breaking of the bread, so it would be hard to show that the "pouring out" of his blood is symbolized by the pouring out of the wine ; for the simple reason that the pouring out of the wine is not mentioned in the original service.—The drinking of that which represents the covenant-blood is itself significant ; it refers again to John 6 : 56 : "He that eateth my flesh and drinketh my blood dwelleth in me, and I in him." It is significant, also, in connection with the covenant. The old covenant-blood was externally sprinkled, for the covenant was largely external ; the new is to be drunk (in symbol), for the covenant is inward, spiritual,

dealing with the soul and its character and destinies. As the sprinkling marked the acceptance of the outward covenant, so the drinking signifies the acceptance of the inward covenant, and of Christ as the "Mediator" of it (Heb. 8 : 6). It implies consent of the soul to the new and better covenant, to its holiness, its unworldliness, its purpose of fellowship with God and likeness to him. Whoever "drinks this cup" pledges himself at once to reliance upon the Saviour whose reconciling death is here represented, and to that godly, Christlike life which the new covenant contemplates. To partake of his Supper is to accept, not only the saving benefit, but also the guiding light and the heavenly spirit, of his new covenant.

Luke and Paul add the words of permanent institution, "This do in remembrance of me." Paul uses them twice, both of the bread and of the cup, thus putting the two on the same level. He is not speaking, either, to the original eleven or to any set of office-bearers, but to the miscellaneous church at Corinth. So the withholding of the cup from the laity was unknown to Paul.—It is noticeable, also, that it is of **the cup,** not of the bread, that **all** are expressly said to have partaken (verse 23).

Concerning the institution of the Lord's Supper, note (1) the extreme simplicity of the event. The time chosen was at the simplest and most domestic of all the Jewish festivals; the passover was a household celebration. The materials were the simplest and most ordinary: he took, not the lamb of the passover, which had associations of a special and limited kind in the national history, but the simple, ordinary food and drink of man, and used them to express the ideas of his kingdom. The central ideas of his kingdom were expressed, too, in the simplest form, without amplification or doctrinal development. The vast structure of sacramental doctrine that has been built upon this act of his is like a pyramid upon its apex. No transubstantiation, and nothing that suggests it ; no "real presence," except of him who broke the bread ; no trace of a sacrificial idea : no pomp and show ; no hint that this was to be the centre of ceremonial worship, or of worship at all. It was simply the partaking, with vocal thanksgiving, of common bread and wine, in which a definite symbolic significance had been recognized. The celebration appears in like simplicity after the day of Pentecost. (See Acts 2 : 46 ; 20 : 11.) (2) The testimony of the Lord's Supper to the life and death of Jesus. From the day of Pentecost until now it has been observed, with great varieties of form and

25 Verily I say unto you, I will drink no more of the
fruit of the vine, until that day that I drink it^a new
in the kingdom of God.

25 is shed for many. Verily I say unto you, I shall no
more drink of the fruit of the vine, until that day
when I drink it new in the kingdom of God.

a Joel 3 : 18; Amos 9 : 13, 14.

of idea, but always "in remembrance of" him
in his death for sinners. Like the Lord's Day,
it is an omnipresent witness to the reality of the
facts which it commemorates. This testimony
is not weakened by any perversions of the
ordinance: it is the existence of the ordinance
that is significant. (3) Our Lord gave no name
to the ordinance. It was early called "the
breaking of bread" (Acts 2 : 42). Paul called it
"the Lord's Supper" (1 Cor. 11 : 20), using the adjective *kuriakos* that was coined for Christian
purposes and is applied in the New Testament
only to the Lord's Supper and (Rev. 1 : 10) to the
Lord's Day. The word *koinōnia*, "participa-
tion" or "communion," is used of it descriptively
(1 Cor. 10 : 16), but not in Scripture as a name; and
"communion" in its modern religious sense
does not represent the meaning of that word.
"The Communion" is not a good scriptural
designation of the ordinance. The name "Eu-
charist" is derived from the word *eucharistēsas*,
"having given thanks," by which our Lord's
act of prayer is described; but it is an accidental name, not scriptural, and not truly descriptive. "The Lord's Supper" seems to be the
best name for general use. (4) Why did the
apostles alone partake? The Lord's Supper
was to be a commemorative institution, and
depended for its significance upon his death.
His death, though near, was still future; the
time had not come, therefore, strictly, for the
institution to exist. Yet he himself must establish it. The fitting time was evidently at the
very end of his life; and he chose the very last
evening. The fitting company was evidently
the company that was closest about him; for
all that he could do was to leave the institution
as a trust, to be understood and used after he
was gone. It would not have suited such a
purpose to call in all who loved him; therefore
he instituted his Supper in the presence of the
apostles alone, and left it for them to establish
in the Christian churches when these should
come into being. This they did; and we find
the Lord's Supper, in the Acts and the Epistles,
existing in, and administered by, the various
churches (Acts 2 : 42, 46; 20 : 7; 1 Cor. 10 : 21; 11 : 20-34).

25. Introduced without a connective; introduced in Matthew by "But." Instead of **I will
drink no more,** translate, "I shall no more
drink." It is a simple future, predictive, not
expressive of will. **I** is not emphatic in any

of the records of this saying.—**Of the fruit—**
literally, offspring or product—**of the vine.**
A solemn and emphatic variation from the
ordinary form of speech.—**New** (*kainon*). Not
neon, "freshly made," "recent," like the new
wine (*oinos neos*) that will burst the bottles
(Matt. 9 : 17), but of new kind, corresponding to
the new covenant that has just been mentioned
or suggested (*hē kainē diathēkē*, Luke and Paul;
the thought, though not the word, present in
Matthew and Mark), and to the New Jerusalem
and the new heaven and the new earth. The
verse is the same in Matthew and Mark, save
that Matthew says "this fruit of the vine" and
"drink it new with you." "This fruit of the
vine"—*i. e.* the passover wine, which had been
used both in the old institution and in the new.
The verse has this peculiar difficulty, that Luke
has it in substance twice, but in connection
with the passover, and not at all with the Lord's
Supper; spoken once of the passover in general
(Luke 22 : 16): "For I say unto you, I will not any
more eat thereof, until it be fulfilled in the
kingdom of God;" and once of one of the cups
of the passover: "For I say unto you, I shall
not drink from henceforth of the fruit of the
vine, until the kingdom of God shall come."
Whether the saying was suggested by the passover or by the Lord's Supper must remain in
doubt. Connected with the passover, it would
occasion no difficulty; connected with the
Supper, it has occasioned much perplexity.
Alexander, on the one hand, is not satisfactory
when he says: "The simplest explanation of
these words is that which makes them a solemn
though figurative declaration that the Jewish
passover was now to be for ever superseded by
the Lord's Supper as a Christian ordinance."
On the other hand, the popular interpretation
which looks to an actual drinking by our Lord
of **new** wine with his people in ages yet to
come, the wine being a literal product of the
renovated earth, seems to sacrifice the characteristic style of scriptural prophecy for a
bald and barren literalism. Something of mystic
symbolism surely is here: our Lord was speaking of spiritual things. Whatever obscurity
may remain in the special form of expression,
the general thought appears to be, "I have done
with passover wine, I have done with symbols.
Hitherto has been the old, symbolic, preparatory; but from this hour, when the Son of

26 ¶ And when they had sung an hymn, they went out into the mount of Olives.
27 And Jesus saith unto them, All ye shall be offended because of me this night : for it is written,ᵃ I will smite the shepherd, and the sheep shall be scattered.
28 Butᵇ after that I am risen, I will go before you into Galilee.
29 Butᶜ Peter said unto him, Although all shall be offended, yet *will* not I.

26 And when they had sung a hymn, they went out unto the mount of Olives.
27 And Jesus saith unto them, All ye shall be ¹offended : for it is written, I will smite the shepherd, and the sheep shall be scattered abroad. Howbeit, after I am raised up, I will go before you into
29 Galilee. But Peter said unto him, Although all

---

a Zech. 13 : 7....*b* ch. 16 : 7....*c* Matt. 26 : 33, 34 ; Luke 22 : 33, 34 ; John 13 : 37, 38.——1 Gr. *caused to stumble.*

---

man is glorified, the new begins" (*to kainon*). "Henceforth to me—and to you with me—all is fulfilment; and the relation of men to God which my joy will henceforth commemorate is the new relation in which all these signs and symbols find their corresponding reality." Thus the Christian commemoration in the Lord's Supper is parallel to his drinking the wine new in the kingdom of God, and is to us, in its measure, an "entering into the joy of our Lord."—This saying does not prove that he did not then drink of the cup. Even if uttered at the Supper, it might be spoken in reference to a last partaking of the preparatory and symbolic.

26. The singing was the closing act in the celebration of the passover, and that which was sung was the latter part of the Hallel, or great song of praise (Ps. 113-118). The first two of these six psalms were sung earlier in the service, and Ps. 115-118 at this point, at the end. There is no reason to doubt that Jesus and his company followed the custom; and Jesus, as the celebrant, would not only sing, but lead in the singing. These holy songs obtain a special and most touching interest from being thus associated with the thoughts of our Saviour at that solemn moment. (See a strikingly eloquent and sympathetic portrayal of the scene in *Philochristus*, chap. xxviii.)—Before **they went out into the mount of Olives** the great conversation of John 14-16 took place, and the final intercessory prayer of Jesus was offered (John 17 : 1-26).

27-31. JESUS FORETELLS THE DISPERSION OF THE APOSTLES AND THE DENIALS OF PETER. *Parallels*, Matt. 26 : 31-35 ; Luke 22 : 31-38 ; John 13 : 36-38.—In Luke and John this warning seems to have been spoken before the going out ; in Matthew and Mark, after. The narratives differ, but the difference makes no difficulty.

27. All ye shall be offended because of me this night. In the best text simply "Ye shall all be offended "—*i. e.* surprised, shocked, disappointed, broken in faith. It is a pity that there is no English word that represents this

Greek word better than the literal but awkward "cause to stumble" which the revisers have usually adopted. "Offend," however, is certainly an inadequate rendering.—**I will smite the shepherd, and the sheep shall be scattered.** Freely quoted from Zech. 13 : 7 ; not exactly as in the Hebrew or as in the Septuagint, but not diverging essentially from either. He had called himself the Good Shepherd who would lay down his life for the sheep (John 10 : 11), and now the moment was at hand. The citation from Zechariah shows (see the context there) that he was thinking of his death in the spirit of Isa. 53 : 5, 6, 10.—**The sheep shall be scattered.** A sorrowful forewarning to them, but even more sorrowful to him who knew them so well and would gladly have saved them from temptation if he could.

28. A promise to re-collect the scattered apostolic body in Galilee. The promise of a resurrection is made incidentally, and appears to have made no impression whatever — not even to have awakened the remembrance of the previous prediction. But probably the accompanying announcement, implied in the smiting of the Shepherd, had passed lightly over them, scarcely understood. The promise of meeting in Galilee was recalled to them by the tidings that were brought from the deserted tomb (Mark 16 : 7).

29, 30. The assertion of the coming failure on the part of the disciples was resented, almost, by Peter ; he knew that he loved his Master, but did not know how little his love was yet able to bear. He knew that the spirit was willing, but was scarcely aware that the flesh was weak. This was boasting, and rash boasting ; yet there was a genuine love beneath it. **Although all shall be offended, yet will not I.** All may not be so sure as I of their own love. Compare the searching question, "Lovest thou me more than these?" (John 21 : 15). "Are you so much more sure of your own heart? Is your love that stronger love that you thought it was?" Here belongs, probably, the remarkable saying, "Simon, Simon, behold, Satan asked to have you" (or "obtained you by asking"

30 And Jesus saith unto him, Verily I say unto thee, That this day, *even* in this night, before the cock crow twice, thou shalt deny me thrice.

31 But he spake the more vehemently, If I should die with thee, I will not deny thee in any wise. Likewise also said they all.

32 And[a] they came to a place which was named Gethsemane: and he saith to his disciples, Sit ye here, while I shall pray.

30 shall be[1]offended, yet will not I. And Jesus saith unto him, Verily I say unto thee, that thou to-day, *even* this night, before the cock crow twice, shalt deny me thrice.

31 But he spake exceeding vehemently, If I must die with thee, I will not deny thee. And in like manner also said they all.

32 And they come unto[2]a place which was named Gethsemane: and he saith unto his disciples, Sit ye

—*i. e.*, all of you), "that he may sift you as wheat, but I have prayed for thee," etc.—a most impressive illustration of our Lord's thoughtfulness for the soul that is in danger, followed by the touching answer of sincerity and self-ignorance : "Lord, I am ready to go with thee both into prison and to death " (Luke 22 : 33).

30, 31. Solemnly emphatic is the Lord's forewarning. Matthew has "to-day," and Luke "in this night;" Mark gives both. All the other three have " before the cock crow ;" Mark, **before the cock crow twice.** This is his form of expression, differing from the others both in the prediction and in the narrative of the denial. (See verses 68 and 72.) There was a first cock-crowing recognized, though not so prominent as that which was commonly called "the cock-crowing." It occurred irregularly a little after midnight, while the well-known time of cock-crowing was at the earliest day-break. If, in any of the records, the statement of particulars here was to be completed by personal remembrance and a keen memory was to supply details, it would surely be in the Gospel that felt the influence of Peter.—The presence of the **twice** in Mark may be due to the fact that Peter remembered the sound of a cock-crowing, falling half noticed upon his ear in the midst of his danger and his sin—a sound that ought to have been a warning to him even then.—**Thou shalt deny me thrice.** No one can doubt the genuineness of this prediction ; if we were to doubt it, we should have to doubt the whole history. But was not this supernatural foresight? The definite announcement of three denials does not look like a forecasting of probabilities or an inference from Peter's weakness and danger. It is a claim of true foreknowledge.—As for Peter, he fell here, as at Matt. 16 : 22, into presumptuous contradiction of his Master; and he was not content with calm utterance : he **spake the more vehemently,** saying more than was necessary, making his professions too bold and open. Yet he was not alone in it ; all the disciples did the same, though the record seems to convey the impression that his boasting was deeper than that of his fellows. He alone denied ; and he

was the leader, at least in denying that he could deny.

32–42. THE AGONY IN GETHSEMANE. *Parallels,* Matt. 26 : 36–46 ; Luke 22 : 39–46 ; John 18 : 1.—Luke and John place here the going out to the garden, which Matthew and Mark have placed a little earlier. The only question involved in consequence is whether the conversation about the desertion and denial took place in the upper room or on the way—a question of no great importance. The hour of going out to the garden cannot be exactly known. The time of ending the Paschal meal was usually not far from midnight, and probably in this case it was at least not later than that ; more likely it was earlier.

32. A place which was named Gethsemane. The spot is assigned by all the evangelists to the slope of the Mount of Olives, eastward from the city. Matthew and Mark give the name ; John alone calls it a garden. Luke intimates, and John expressly asserts, that it was a frequent resort of Jesus, where he was often accompanied by his disciples. The name "garden" denotes an enclosed place, and is sometimes applied to what we would call an orchard. The traditional site of Gethsemane is a little way up the slope of the Mount of Olives ; it contains eight venerable olive trees, but, venerable as these are, they are probably of later date than the time of our Lord, for Josephus asserts that in the siege of Jerusalem all trees about the city were cut down and the Mount of Olives was used as a camp (*Wars,* 5. 2. 3). It was probably even then an olive-garden, however, the name "Gethsemane" ("oil-press") bearing testimony to the uses to which the place was put. The traditional site cannot be proved to be the true one, though the tradition is ancient ; but it is quite certainly near to the true one, to say the least.—Arrived at the place, he at once separated himself from the most of his company, saying to eight of the eleven, **Sit ye here, while I shall pray,** and adding, according to Luke, the counsel, "Pray that ye enter not into temptation," thus leaving them to pray while he also went to prayer.

33 And he taketh with him Peter and James and John, and began to be sore amazed, and to be very heavy;
34 And saith unto them, My^a soul is exceeding sorrowful unto death: tarry ye here, and watch.

33 here, while I pray. And he taketh with him Peter and James and John, and began to be greatly
34 amazed, and sore troubled. And he saith unto them, My soul is exceeding sorrowful even unto

a John 12 : 27.

33, 34. Peter and James and John. Now, as before, the chosen companions. (See Mark 5 : 37; 9 : 2.) The Master's knowledge of the certainty of Peter's fall did not lead him to change the choice and leave Peter behind. Indeed, was there not a certain tenderness toward Peter in thus keeping him near, as if he would protect him as much as possible? Yet, besides, who was there among the twelve on whom he could more rely? His motive in having them near him was the desire of companionship—not of immediate companionship, yet he

the order of a climax. Beyond the feeling of amazement, he began to be in deep and terrible anguish.—**My soul is exceeding sorrowful unto death. Unto,** expressive of degree: "This is an agony as of death; nay, this is an agony that human life cannot long endure. If it continues, I shall die." Remember that this was no loose, popular speech, exaggerated and only half true, such as we often use: he was the Truth.—Observe carefully, too, that in this agony there is absolutely nothing physical. It was his **soul** that was **sorrow-**

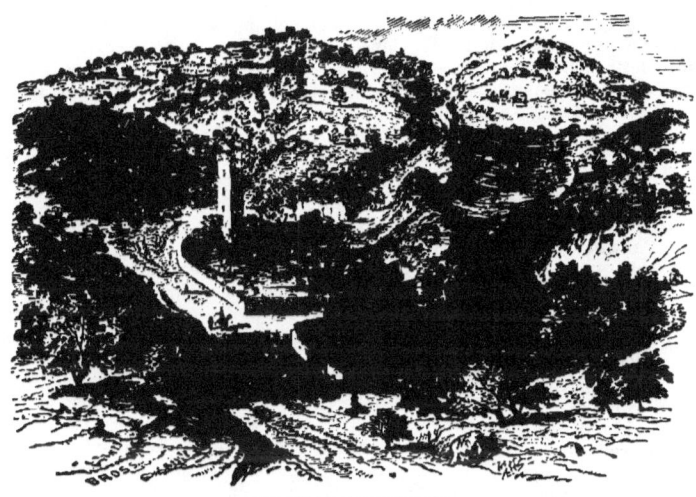

GARDEN OF GETHSEMANE.

would not be utterly alone; he would have friends at hand, though they might not be in sight. It was the true human impulse: his agony was coming, and alone he must meet it; yet wholly alone who could bear to be?—Two words describe the feeling that was coming upon him, **sore amazed, and very heavy.** The first tells not only of amazement, but even of stupefaction from amazement, as if an utterly unwonted feeling was taking possession of his soul, and he knew not what to make of it; the entrance upon a new stage of experience was overcoming him. The second tells of sore trouble, anguish of spirit; it is a stronger and sharper word than the first, and follows it in

ful; no bodily inflictions had anything to do with it. This was altogether an inward grief, a struggle of the spirit.—The physical sufferings of our Lord, as they were not the first occasion of his anguish, so were never the chief source of his pain. The true understanding of his agony has been kept away from many minds by a too exclusive attention to the physical part. Physical suffering is more easily understood than spiritual, yet a look at the cross merely in its physical aspects gives us no idea whatever of its true meaning.—Because of this agony coming upon him he said to the three, **tarry ye here, and watch.** Matthew, "watch with me." To watch is to keep

35 And he went forward a little, and fell on the ground, and prayed* that, if it were possible, the hour might pass from him.

36 And he said,[b] Abba, Father, all things *are* possible unto thee; take away this cup from me: nevertheless,[c] not what I will, but what thou wilt.

35 death: abide ye here, and watch. And he went forward a little, and fell on the ground, and prayed that, if it were possible, the hour might pass away from him. And he said, Abba, Father, all things are possible unto thee; remove this cup from me:

---

a Heb. 5 : 7....*b* Rom. 8 : 15; Gal. 4 : 6....*c* Ps. 40 : 8; John 4 : 34; 5 : 30; 6 : 38, 39; 18 : 11; Phil. 2 : 8.

---

awake, to be vigilant; he would have friends near, even though imperfect friends, and he would have them awake, not lost to him in unconsciousness. How touching an appeal! He had chosen them, taught them, guarded them, prayed for them; he had just spoken to them (John 14-16) in the tone of an infinite calmness concerning the coming trouble; but when had he leaned on them thus, and cast himself on their thoughtfulness and fidelity? It was a new form for the relation of Master and disciple, and so to be trusted with their Master's welfare ought to have made them watchful.

35. He went forward a little. By himself, perhaps farther into the shade.—There he **fell on the ground.** Luke, "kneeled;" Matthew, "fell on his face." No doubt it was full prostration.—His prayer was **that, if it were possible, the hour might pass from him.** It was **the hour,** with its untold horrors for his soul, that so oppressed him, and he pleaded that if he could possibly be spared this experience, the relief might come.—What was this agony, this sorrow **unto death?** It will never be fully explained, and we must not expect to understand it altogether. But some elements were certainly in it: (1) An incomparable sense of the horribleness of sin—such a sense of its abominableness and of its infinitely fearful issues as no sinner ever had, and as no lost soul, even, can ever have; such a sense of the horribleness of sin as none but a holy being can ever entertain; a sense, too, penetrated by an incomparable sympathy with the beings whom sin has ruined, and rendered terrible and poignant by the intensity of his love for man. Such a sense of the horribleness of sin was always with him, but **the hour** brought it in fresh intensity, because now was coming the supreme manifestation of the character and work of sin. Now was the manifested God to be utterly rejected; now was the incarnate Word to be spitefully murdered. (2) The personal shrinking of holy love from impending rejection and outrage. This rejection was to take place in his person; it was the rejection of God, of God's own character, of God's highest work and manifestation of himself. If human love cannot find itself rejected and insulted without pain, how can

divine—the more, since the divine love is infinitely unselfish, and had for its object the salvation of those who were now rejecting it? Included in the agony was the inconceivably painful recoil of infinitely tender love from murderous outrage at the hands of those whom it would save. (3) All this to be experienced by One who was man as well as God, and by whom every experience must be realized and sinlessly accepted in his human nature. All this, and whatever else may have been included in the agony, must be humanly endured; and nothing in his humanity must rebel or fail to fill its place in execution of the divine purpose. (4) As minor elements, but not less real, the shrinking of full, fresh, healthy human life from death; the honorable shrinking of human purity, personal dignity, perfect self-respect, from unmerited disgrace; the intolerableness of the seeming irony of events, in that such a life should be the one to have such an ending.—That the relation of his soul to his Father and of his Father to him was that of perfect amity and confidence we have proof in the filial tone of his prayer; in the assertion recorded in John 16 : 32 concerning this very time: "I am not alone, because the Father is with me;" in his question (Matt 26 : 53) asked in the midst of this time: "Thinkest thou that I cannot now pray to my Father, and he shall presently give me more than twelve legions of angels?" and in the fact that he was then perfectly and amid utmost difficulties doing his Father's will. (Note the principle of John 8 : 29). See also Heb. 5 : 7 as to the favorable hearing of his prayer.)

36. Abba. The Aramaic word for **Father,** the very word that Jesus used. (Compare Mark's citation of the very words, chap. 5 : 41; 7 : 34; 10 : 51.) He alone gives **Abba** here, and **Father** as a translation of it. The two equivalent words appear together in Rom 8 : 15 and Gal. 4 : 6.—**All things are possible unto thee.** Taking for his own encouragement what he had offered for the encouragement of his friends (chap. 10 : 27). He was made in all things like unto his brethren (Heb. 2 : 17), and showed us what comforts to lay hold upon.—**Take away this cup from me.** So, with request and yet with submission, John 12 : 27. The thoughts

•

37 And he cometh, and findeth them sleeping, and saith unto Peter, Simon, sleepest thou? couldest not thou watch one hour?
38 Watch ye, and pray, lest ye enter into temptation. The spirit truly is ready, but the flesh is weak.
39 And again he went away, and prayed, and spake the same words.
40 And when he returned, he found them asleep again, (for their eyes were heavy,) neither wist they what to answer him.

37 howbeit not what I will, but what thou wilt. And he cometh, and findeth them sleeping, and saith unto Peter, Simon, sleepest thou? couldest thou not
38 watch one hour? Watch and pray, that ye enter not into temptation: the spirit indeed is willing,
39 but the flesh is weak. And again he went away,
40 and prayed, saying the same words. And again he came, and found them sleeping, for their eyes were very heavy; and they knew not what to answer

a Rom. 7 : 18-25 ; Gal. 5 : 17.——1 Or, Watch ye, and pray that ye enter not.

of the Supper were still in his mind. The cup was the cup of sacrifice, the same that he had been drinking before (chap. 10 : 38) ; yet never had it been pressed to his lips as now. Now to drink it was to drain it and to die. It is not exact to say that his human nature asked for the withdrawal of the cup, but it is true that it was because of his human nature that he asked it. Now came the greatest task that had ever been laid upon his human nature in accepting and doing the divine will. The greatness of the task made him pause—not falter—and request that if it were possible, it might be made less.—Nevertheless, not what I will, but what thou wilt. Not expressive of a conflict between the wills, and yet honestly expressive of a moment's delay in the full acceptance by the God-man of the will of God. It was not a sinful delay; it only represented his sense of the inadequateness of humanity, even of perfect humanity, to the mystery of divine suffering; and it ended in the request that God's will might be done. (Compare Heb. 5 : 7, 8, which refers to this struggle.) He had to learn obedience, though not to unlearn disobedience, by the things which he suffered : that was a lesson that even he could not learn except by experience. Learn it he did, perfectly ; and "thy will be done" is the expression of his success. The writer to the Hebrews represents that it was through this learning of obedience that he became the Author of eternal salvation. This was the perfecting—nay, it was, in spirit, the offering—of the perfect sacrifice.

37, 38. The three were sleeping, weary and unthoughtful.—The remonstrance is addressed to Peter, as the most confident one in his professions of sufficiency, but it is really for them all. Couldest not thou watch—or "hadst thou not strength to watch" (Matthew, "with me")—one hour? Perhaps we may infer that he had been about an hour absent from them, though the conclusion must not be too confidently drawn.—The address is Simon, not "Peter."—Watch ye—i. e. awake, be wakeful—and pray, lest ye enter into tempta-

tion. If you cannot keep awake "with me," there is reason why you should do it for yourselves: trial is coming, and you are not strong enough to bear it safely. Therefore awake and offer the needful prayer. Here is an illustration of the occasion for his own prayer, "Lead us not into temptation." The trial must come, yet it was right for them, weak as they were, to shrink from it and to pray that it might not be too severe for them. The call to prayer was all the more significant from the fact that he himself was agonizing in prayer. If he needed it, how much more did they!—The spirit truly is ready—or, rather, "the spirit indeed is willing"—but the flesh is weak. Introduced without a connective as a remark of his own, almost as a meditation. It is a candid recognition of the good as well as the evil in his friends: their professions, though rash, were not empty. "The spirit is willing; you do desire to be true to your Master." But the spirit and the flesh are contrary to each other (Gal. 5 : 17), and the flesh would triumph if the spirit was not strengthened from above.—The flesh is weak—i. e. weak for the purposes of the spirit. In the great struggle for the spiritual unification of man the efficient means is prayer; but it must be the prayer of the spiritually wakeful. No other will guard from temptation. (See Eph. 6 : 18.)

39, 40. Yet he was not satisfied with his own praying. He had said, not what I will, but what thou wilt, yet apparently he had not said it as he would ; or, at least, he would say it again.—Spake the same words. Not necessarily the same form, but the same substance (ton auton logon). Yet in Matthew, where the prayer is quoted, there is a visible progress from the first. The one is, "O my Father, if it be possible, let this cup pass away from me : nevertheless, not as I will, but as thou wilt;" the other is, "O my Father, if this cannot pass away except I drink it, thy will be done." In the latter there appears a deeper conviction that the cup cannot pass away, and a more unconditional acceptance of it as the will of God.—Observe that in the repetition of prayer there was no formalism, but only intensity of desire.

41 And he cometh the third time, and saith unto them, Sleep on now, and take *your* rest: it is enough, the hour is come: behold, the Son of man is betrayed into the hands of sinners.
42 Rise up, let us go; lo, he that betrayeth me is at hand.
43 ⸿ And[b] immediately, while he yet spake, cometh Judas, one of the twelve, and with him a great multitude with swords and staves, from the chief priests[d] and the scribes and the elders.

41 him. And he cometh the third time, and saith unto them, Sleep on now, and take your rest: it is enough; the hour is come; behold, the Son of man is betrayed
42 into the hands of sinners. Arise, let us be going: behold, he that betrayeth me is at hand.
43 And straightway, while he yet spake, cometh Judas, one of the twelve, and with him a multitude with swords and staves, from the chief priests and

a John 7 : 30; 8 20; 13 : 1....*b* Matt. 26 : 47; Luke 22 : 47, etc.; John 18 : 3....*c* Ps. 3 : 1, 2....*d* Ps. 2 : 2.

He would not lay down the petition until he had offered it as he would.—**Again** he found the three **asleep.** Apparently they had been barely aroused when he returned before, and had again quickly sunk into sleep.—But this time they were awakened sufficiently to think of excuses, and found that they had none to give. **Neither wist they what to answer him.** The mention of it is peculiar to Mark—a natural reminiscence of Peter's. Luke (who tells the story briefly) attributes their sleep to sorrow—*i. e.* to the weariness of nature overstrained by grief. But this excuse did not occur to them at the time as suitable, nor did any other.

41, 42. Here Matthew adds that he went away the third time and prayed, using the same words (*logon*) again. Not even yet satisfied!—Mark implies the third retirement for prayer in mentioning the third return. That they were **the third time** asleep is implied, though not stated.—**Sleep on now, and take your rest.** Words of sorrowful irony. He wearily gives up all expectation of companionship from them—for which he has asked in vain—and will leave them to their slumbers. "Sleep on and rest yourselves, if that is the thing that you choose: I will not disturb you." Meyer well remarks: "The deepest sorrow of the soul, especially when it is joined with such mental clearness, has its irony; and by what apathy was Jesus confronted!" Does not our Saviour here come into a very deep and suggestive unity with habitual human feeling?

These words of irony stand by themselves. After he had spoken them there was a pause, though perhaps of only a moment, during which Jesus caught sight or sound of the betrayer and his band approaching. Then he turned quickly to the sleeping disciples and spoke hurriedly, in an altered tone. Now all was changed, and the time for allowing them to sleep was past. The remainder was uttered rapidly, and attended with whatever effort was necessary to waken the sleepers.—**It is enough** —*i. e.* enough of sleep—**the hour is come,** *the* hour, long foreseen, desired (Luke 12 : 50), yet dreaded, but now accepted in obedience to the

will of God.—**Behold, the Son of man is betrayed into the hands of sinners,** or, rather, " is delivered up:" there is no good reason for departing from the simple meaning here.—**Rise up, let us go**—*i. e.* back to our company, and out to meet those who are coming.—Nor have we far to go or long to wait. **Lo, he that betrayeth me**—or giveth me over to the wicked men—**is at hand.** Even during the brief time of this utterance he had been coming nearer, and there was not time for the little company to do more than turn their faces toward the sad future before **the hour** had indeed **come.**

43–52. JESUS IS MADE PRISONER. *Parallels.* Matt. 26 : 47-56; Luke 22 : 47-53; John 18 : 2-12.—The approach of the recreant disciple and his company was manifest to them all **immediately, while he yet spake.**—Again, as at Mark 14 : 10 (and parallel passages), all the reporters put the traitor on record as **one of the twelve,** John alone varying the phraseology. This, to the friends of Jesus, was the wonderful and horrible thing—that **one of the twelve** should do this deed. John adds to his infamy by noting that his familiarity with the habits of Jesus and his company led him to the right place, at Gethsemane.—The **great multitude** that was with him is said by all the four to have come **from the chief priests.** (See note on verse 1.) Their share in the sending of the crowd is recognized on all sides. The remaining part of the responsible body is " the elders of the people," in Matthew; **the scribes, and the elders,** in Mark; " the Pharisees " in John— various ways of describing the official body, the Sanhedrin. John's account of the approaching company is more full and exact, and tells us that Judas was accompanied by " the band," or cohort, of soldiers, which can be nothing else than some part of the Roman garrison of Jerusalem. The religious authorities, then, had made requisition for a military guard in making this arrest, for fear, or pretended fear, of tumult. Some Roman authority, therefore—Pilate or some one not much

44 And he that betrayed him had given them a token, saying, Whomsoever I shall kiss,*a* that same is he: take him, and lead *him* away safely.

45 And as soon as he was come, he goeth straightway to him, and saith, Master,*b* Master; and kissed him.

46 ¶ And they laid their hands on him, and took him.

47 And one of them that stood by drew a sword, and smote a servant of the high priest, and cut off his ear.

44 the scribes and the elders. Now he that betrayed him had given them a token, saying, Whomsoever I shall kiss, that is he; take him, and lead him 45 away safely. And when he was come, straightway he came to him, and saith, Rabbi; and ¹kissed 46 him. And they laid hands on him, and took him. 47 But a certain one of them that stood by drew his sword, and smote the ²servant of the high priest,

a 2 Sam. 20 : 9 ; Ps. 55 : 21 ; Prov. 27 : 6....*b* Luke 6 : 46.——1 Gr. *kissed him much*....2 Gr. *bondservant.*

lower—must have known what was in contemplation. The others, "officers," who are mentioned by John, were probably Levites or some other officers of the temple. This was no mob; both the civil and the religious authorities were directly active in the arrest.—The soldiers had the **swords,** and the officers from the temple were armed with **staves** (plural of "staff") or clubs. The night was lighted by the moon, but in going out into the shaded enclosure there would be need of lights, and John says that they were provided with torches and lanterns.—Such a company, military and miscellaneous, armed and lighted, quietly as it might wish to approach, was so considerable in size and appointments that it is not strange that Jesus saw or heard it on the way.

44, 45. John's account of what follows is by no means a recapitulation of what appears in the story of the synoptists. He omits all reference to the kiss of Judas, and inserts what they had omitted—namely, the question of Jesus, intended to shield his disciples, and the temporary retreat of his enemies before the glory of his presence. The most probable place for this seems, however, to be after the kiss and before the arrest. The kiss was a common form of salutation among the Jews (Luke 7 : 45; Acts 20 : 37), and became a sign of love in the Christian Church (Rom. 16 : 16; 1 Pet. 5, 14. etc.). It may have been the usual salutation from the disciples to their Master. The sign appears, in Matthew, to have been agreed upon just then, as they were drawing near. The verb in Mark (in the perfect tense) is capable of another sense, but the whole saying of Judas in verse 44 is an utterance of haste and agitation, indicating that it was spoken on the spot. To say **take him, and lead him away safely**—*i. e.* securely, that he may not escape—was utterly needless, and tells of the guilty man's excitement.—The proposal of the kiss was his own, not theirs. Was it necessary that such a sign should be used? Could they not find him? It seems a gratuitous insult, and a superfluous degradation of himself on the part of Judas.—**Lead him away safely** is peculiar to Mark; it is one of the sayings that no inventor would

ever think of putting in.—The traitor was prompt and ready: he came **straightway** to Jesus with his kiss.—Still in agitation, he gave him a fervent kiss. In the proposal it was *philéso;* in the act, *katephilésen,* a stronger word. He **kissed him** with all signs of heartiness; so that the emphatic nature of the kiss was noticed. —His words are, in Matthew, "Hail, Rabbi;" in Mark, simply **Master,** or "Rabbi," the repetition of the title being unsupported by the best authorities. Bengel remarks that Judas is never said to have called Jesus "Lord." Twice he is said to have called him "Rabbi," here and in Matt. 26 : 25; and some have inferred that this cooler and more distant form of address was customary with him—an inference precarious, but possible. Even if it was the colder title, the union of the title with the kiss made up an utterance of consummate hypocrisy.— No answer of Jesus is recorded in Mark, but one is given by Luke and another by Matthew. Luke, "Judas, betrayest thou the Son of man with a kiss?" Matthew, "Comrade," or companion ("friend" is a misleading word here), "do that for which thou hast come." So, correctly, in the Revision. One is the most searching and terrible of reproaches; the other is companion to the "What thou doest, do quickly," that sent Judas out from the circle of the disciples. The two are perfectly consistent, and no doubt both fell upon the ears of the guilty man.—After the double answer, probably, comes the wonderful scene of John 18 : 4-8, ending with the hint of Jesus to his disciples that they could help him no further: "If therefore ye seek me, let these go their way."

46, 47. Then the arrest was made, and Jesus was actually a prisoner.—The episode that follows is one of the most peculiar and touching in the Gospels. First, of the smiting with the sword. There were two swords in the company (Luke 22 : 38), of which Peter had one; he had had it at the Supper and during his sleep in the garden. Where he got it, or with what intent, we can scarcely guess. Who had the other? Was it Simon the Zealot? Perceiving that Jesus meant to make no resistance, these two with swords must needs volunteer their help (Luke),

48 And Jesus answered and said unto them, Are ye come out, as against a thief, with swords and *with* staves to take me?
49 I was daily with you in the temple, teaching, and ye took me not: but the scriptures* must be fulfilled,
50 And* they all forsook·him, and fled.
51 And there followed him a certain young man, having a linen cloth cast about *his* naked *body;* and the young men laid hold on him:
52 And he left* the linen cloth, and fled from them naked.

48 and struck off his ear. And Jesus answered and said unto them, Are ye come out, as against a robber, 49 with swords and staves to seize me? I was daily with you in the temple teaching, and ye took me not: but *this is done* that the scriptures might be 50 fulfilled. And they all left him, and fled.
51 And a certain young man followed with him, having a linen cloth cast about him, over *his* naked 52 *body;* and they lay hold on him; but he left the linen cloth, and fled naked.

a Ps. 22 : 1 ; Isa. 53 : 3, etc.; Luke 24 : 44....*b* ver. 27 ; Ps. 88 : 8 ; Isa. 63 : 3....*c* ch. 13 : 16.

though the unknown second one is not recorded to have struck a blow.—**One of them that stood by,** unnamed by the synoptists, is identified by John as Peter. A feeling of valor stirred in his heart, but yet again in contradiction to the spirit of his Master: "Minding the things of men, and not the things of God" (Mark 8 : 33). It was no longer, "Lord, I am ready to go with thee both into prison and to death" (Luke 22 : 33); now he must feebly strike, to prevent his Lord from going to death or to prison. It is another illustration of "the spirit indeed is willing, but the flesh is weak"—an illustration more significant than the falling asleep, and approaching in significance the one that was yet to come.—The blow was ill-directed, and struck only the **ear** of the man at whose head it was aimed, **a servant**—or rather the **slave**—**of the high priest**—*i. e.* of Caiaphas. As the synoptists omit the name of Peter, so they omit that of this man ; John gives it as Malchus.—Here, very singularly, Mark drops the story, Matthew and John proceed with our Lord's rebuke to Peter, and only Luke tells that he healed the wounded ear. Any explanation of these facts is impossible ; one would think all would have recorded the healing. In Luke the scene is very beautiful, the Lord saying, "Suffer ye thus far"—*i. e.*, probably, "Permit me thus far the use of my hands," and touching the ear with healing power. Here is a gentle apology for Peter's act; an astonishing act of submission to his captors, even asking them for the use of hands that had power to heal; a wonderful display of divine power at the very moment of his self-surrender, as if he would show that he was not yielding from weakness or necessity: the humble returning of his hands, nevertheless, to the custody of his foes; and, most wonderful of all, perhaps, the hardihood of the men who could take again the healing hands and bind them (John 18 : 12).—The rebuke to Peter contains, in John, the echo of his recent prayer: "The cup which my Father hath given me, shall I not drink it?" In Matthew it tells of the hopelessness of such resistance, asserts that

heavenly legions would come to his aid if he wished them, and declares that neither earthly rescue nor heavenly is to be thought of, since this is the counsel of God according to the Scriptures.

48-50. He submits to the fulfilment of the Scriptures, but it is impossible even for him not to be indignant at the senseless violence of wicked men. Literally, "As against a robber are ye come out with swords and clubs to take me?" They had opportunities in the temple every day, but they must needs wait till this midnight hour, and then come out thus armed, as if he were a violent and dangerous character. There is a true shame in this unwillingness to be treated as robbers are treated; to be "numbered with transgressors" cut him to the heart. But he fell back upon his former conviction: the Scriptures must be fulfilled; and "all this" (Matthew) was done, in order that they might be fulfilled—not merely that minute predictions might have something to correspond to them, but, more broadly, that he might endure and accomplish what the Scriptures had foretold. According to Luke, he ended with "but this is your hour"—the hour assigned to you by God's counsel—"and (this power which is gathering in upon me is) the power of darkness," of spiritual opposition to spiritual light.—The disciples, permitted by him to "go their way" (John 18 : 8), now **all forsook him, and fled.** But **forsook** is too strong a word for the original; "left" is better.—Nothing has been said of reunion with the eight whom he had left (verse 32), but undoubtedly the whole company had come together when the intruders came.

51, 52. Peculiar to Mark; manifestly, the reminiscence of an eye-witness. No inventor would have left a story so incomplete. This young man **followed** Jesus; literally, in the best text, "followed with him"—*i. e.* he was a companion with him in the garden; he was present there, and was no stranger. Yet he had not been with Jesus and the others at the Supper, for then he would have been clothed.—The **linen cloth** (*sindon*) in which he was wrapped was the garment of the night. The word, supposed to be akin to *ind*, *Indian*, first denoted a peculiar kind of delicate cloth; afterward it meant linen. In the New Testament it is used, besides this place, only of the cloth in which the body of Jesus was wrapped for burial. Sleeping near and hearing what events were in progress, this young man had risen from his bed and joined Jesus in the garden as he was.— It is added that they **laid hold of him. The young men** is to be omitted. Either the attempt to take him was due to a sudden impulse of mischief in some of the crowd upon seeing a man in so unwonted a guise, or he was some one whom the enemies of Jesus were anxious to secure even when they would let his disciples go. In the passage there is absolutely no hint as to who he was, and no help to conjecture. That he was Mark himself is purely a guess, and not a very probable one. Those who identify the rich young ruler (Mark 10 : 17; see note there) with Lazarus are inclined to think that he here again appears. There is considerable overstraining in some of the reasons as given in Plumptre's note; but a few reasons seem worth mentioning. He was **a young man**, again; if the officers were especially anxious to take him, the fact corresponds with the testimony of John 12 : 10, that the Jews were plotting to kill Lazarus as well as Jesus, and when they were taking Jesus they would certainly be sure to seize upon Lazarus if he was at hand; and this incidental and mysterious manner of mentioning the young man is in perfect accord with the practice of the synoptists in speaking of the family at Bethany. Of course these considerations do not amount to proof, but they perhaps open the way for a legitimate conjecture. The identification would be an extremely interesting one if it were true, for it would wonderfully illustrate the power of him to whom "all things are possible" (chap. 10 : 27), the unwilling man having been brought by his mighty working to be more faithful than the very apostles.—The young man was determined not to be taken, and escaped by leaving his only garment in the hands of his pursuers. Lazarus would know that capture meant certain death.

In this section we take leave of Judas, who appears no more in Mark's Gospel. Jesus foreknew his treason (John 6 : 64, 70, 71), and yet chose him to be an apostle. It has often been objected to our Saviour that in this treatment of Judas there was cruel irony; yet Jesus acted in good faith, knowing the better possibilities of Judas, as well as his evil heart. When a man of high possibilities and fearful dangers appeared among his disciples, it would be the impulse of the Saviour to have the man near himself for the man's own sake. Thus, though the personal contact with Christ made his privileges special, his case was not really exceptional. "Judas was treated," as Dr. Hovey has said, "very much as every bad man is treated who is enabled, in the providence of God, to have great light and to wield great influence for a time in a religious society." (See a pretty full discussion of this matter in Smith's *Dictionary of the Bible*, Am. Ed., art. "Judas Iscariot.") But for unwritten reasons of which the chief external reason doubtless was that Jesus proved not to be such a Messiah as he was thinking of—he became dissatisfied and rebellious in heart; and then the very association with Jesus that might have been to him a training in all holiness and heavenliness of mind became the means of deeper misunderstanding, dissatisfaction, and hatred. The process was a natural one: "From him that hath not shall be taken away even that which he hath." When once the real beauty of Jesus was no beauty to his heart, helps became injurious to him and light itself deepened his darkness. He is a fearful example of the darker possibilities that may dwell in men who are capable of great good (Matt 6 : 22 24).

53-65. JESUS IS EXAMINED BY CAIAPHAS AND THE SANHEDRIN, AND ADJUDGED WORTHY OF DEATH: AFTER WHICH HE IS MOCKED IN THE PRESENCE OF HIS JUDGES. *Parallels*, Matt. 26 : 57-68; Luke 22 : 54, 55, 63-65.

Jesus was subjected to three examinations before Jewish authorities: before Annas (John 18 : 13), before Caiaphas and the informal meeting of the Sanhedrin (in the present section, Matthew and Mark), and before the Sanhedrin formally assembled (Luke 22 : 66-71). Of these, Matthew and Mark narrate the second and allude to the third (Matt. 27 : 1; Mark 15 : 1); while Luke alludes to the second (Luke 22 : 54) and narrates the third (22 : 66-71). John, writing later, and having special familiarity with the first, narrates that, and alludes to the second (John 18 : 24). Thus the story is completed only by a careful comparison of all the records. Of these three examinations Farrar says (*Life of Christ*, 2. 327, 328) : "The first was the practical, the second the potential, the third the actual and formal, decision that sentence of death should be passed judicially upon him. Each of the three trials might, from a different point of view, have been regarded as the most fatal and important of the three. That of Annas was the authoritative *prejudicium*; that of

53 ¶ And[a] they led Jesus away to the high priest: and with him were assembled all the chief priests and the elders and the scribes.

54 And Peter followed him afar off, even into the palace of the high priest : and he sat with the servants, and warmed himself at the fire.

55 And the chief priests and all the council sought for witness against Jesus to put him to death; and found none.

56 For[b] many bare false witness against him, but their witness agreed not together.

53 And they led Jesus away to the high priest; and there come together with him all the chief priests 54 and the elders and the scribes. And Peter had followed him afar off, even within, into the court of the high priest; and he was sitting with the officers, 55 and warming himself in the light *of the fire.* Now the chief priests and the whole council sought witness against Jesus to put him to death; and found it 56 not. For many bare false witness against him, and

a Matt. 26 : 57, etc.; Luke 22 : 54, etc.; John 18 : 13, etc....*b* Ps. 35 : 11.

Caiaphas, the real determination; that of the Sanhedrin at daybreak, the final ratification." —The reports are all more or less fragmentary, and transactions that were simultaneous are detailed, now in one order, and now in another. The narratives of the trial have been regarded by many as a fruitful field for the sceptic who delights in discrepancies. On a superficial study discrepancies do appear; but the result of the closer investigations of recent times has been that a clear and consistent history thoroughly accordant with Jewish customs comes to light.

53. The high priest here is Caiaphas, who was actually in office. Annas had been high priest, though not since about seven years earlier. He was a man of high standing, constantly consulted in the affairs of the Jews; and to him Jesus had already been led, in the hope of eliciting something in a preliminary examination that might serve as material for use in a more formal trial. Accordant with the view of the three trials that is here maintained is the revised version of John 18 : 24 : "Annas therefore sent him bound" (in place of "now Annas had sent him bound") "unto Caiaphas the high priest." This verse, thus correctly translated, assigns the events of the trial that precede it, in John, to the house of Annas. That verse is parallel to the beginning of this verse 53.—If the words **with him** are genuine, of which there is some doubt, they refer to Jesus, as in the Revision: "There come together with him"—*i. e.* with Jesus, to the high priest—"all the chief priests and the elders and the scribes." This is an enumeration of the classes represented in the Sanhedrin. But this cannot have been a formal meeting of that body, for it was illegal to hold a meeting for the trial of capital cases by night. (Compare the language of Luke 22 : 66 about the formal meeting that took place at the first available moment.) The recorded non-consent of Joseph of Arimathaea to the condemnation (Luke 23 : 51), and the evident fact that Nicodemus also had taken no part in the proceedings, make it probable that this was a packed meeting arranged to suit the purpose of prejudgment.

54. Peter, whose last appearance was in ill-timed violence, appears again, following **afar** amid the crowd that moves after the officers and their prisoner; or perhaps the word may signify that he was at the rear of the throng. John was his companion (John 18 : 15); so Peter must not be blamed, as if this far-off following were almost a part of his denial. No disciple was with Jesus then; perhaps none was nearer than Peter and John: he was not anxious to have them near him.—The palace of the high priest was probably within easy distance of the temple: its exact site is unknown. It is an inference from the language of John that Annas may have had his home with Caiaphas, his son-in-law, in some part of the high priest's palace. The inference is a probable one; it is supported by the fact that in the "sending" from Annas to Caiaphas there appears to have been no change of place, Peter and the scene of his denials being all the time at hand.—Peter **sat with the servants**—or, rather, "with the officers"—**and warmed himself.** Luke and John mention the kindling of the fire; Luke says that it was in the midst of the hall, or, rather, of the court around which the house was built, and John mentions the "cold" that occasioned it, the chill of a night in spring. Peter had been sleeping on the ground in the chilly night.—Matthew says that Peter sat there "to see the end," waiting in such company and comfort as he could find. Mark alone adds the touch, **warmed himself at the fire,** or, literally, "in the light" (*pros to phōs*)—*i. e.* in the light of the fire. Was not this a remembrance of Peter himself? and did he not remember it because that same glow of the firelight was the means of his being recognized? He remembered the light on the circle of faces and the consequence of its shining upon him, and gave Mark the expressive phrase, "warming himself in the firelight."

55, 56. The judges were taking testimony in a capital case, although the meeting was informal and the trying of such a case was illegal. They were not only taking testimony, but seeking it; and seeking not only testimony, but

57 And there arose certain, and bare false witness against him, saying,

58 We heard him say, I will destroy* this temple that is made with hands, and within three days I will build another made without hands.

59 But neither so did their witness agree together.

60 And* the high priest stood up in the midst, and asked Jesus, saying, Answerest thou nothing? What is it which these witness against thee?

57 their witness agreed not together. And there stood up certain, and bare false witness against him, say-

58 ing, We heard him say, I will destroy this †temple that is made with hands, and in three days I will

59 build another made without hands. And not even

60 so did their witness agree together And the high priest stood up in the midst, and asked Jesus, saying, Answerest thou nothing? what is it which

a ch. 15 : 79; John 2 : 19....b Matt. 26 : 62, etc.———† Or, *sanctuary*

false testimony, with the definite purpose of conviction—a cruel parody upon justice. The statute-book of the Sanhedrin was the law of Moses, and that law required at least two witnesses in a case of life and death (Deut. 17 : 6; 19 : 15). The council was making a pretence of conformity to law and to the demands of justice—at least, in some details.—But they found nothing satisfactory—a surprising thing. One would think they needed to find no trouble in getting testimony if they were satisfied with false testimony. But it seems to have been necessary that the witnesses should agree; from which it looks probable that they were examined separately. Fragments of evidence that would suit them would be easily enough obtained, but they must have agreement; and in this court it must be evidence that had at least some shadow of relevancy to the law of Moses and the sacred things.—The change of persecutors from Pharisees to **chief priests** had something to do with the difficulty in securing evidence. The case was now in the hands of the authorities in Jerusalem, and the most of our Lord's utterances, and all his recent ones, up to within a few days, had been made in Galilee or Peræa. Moreover, the range of available evidence was limited by the jealousies between the chief priests, who were now managing the case, and the Pharisees. Many of the utterances of Jesus against the Pharisees were but too agreeable to the men of the priestly party; while any utterances that he had made against the priests might be only too satisfactory as evidence to the Pharisaic minority that was present.—The existing haste was also an element in the case: they could not wait to send for witnesses, but were obliged to do what they could with such as were at hand.

57–59. Two witnesses "at the last" (Matthew) in whose story there was more promise —a charge of blasphemy against the temple, a most serious charge, especially in the sight of this priestly party. Compare the accusation against Stephen (Acts 6 : 13, 14). Here the charge of disrespect toward the temple was coupled with that of claiming supernatural power, either divine or magical, power to **build**—in

place of the old—**another made without hands.** Misunderstanding or dim remembrance or wilful perversion of his language at the earliest passover of his ministry (John 2 : 19). The later cleansing of the temple, so horrible to the priestly party, had doubtless brought this language to mind again; and that work would render such an accusation as this more agreeable to them than almost any other could be. It is a striking fact that John, who records the early saying, makes no allusion to the charge, while Matthew and Mark, who record the accusation, have no allusion to the early saying—a cross-reference of some value.—But the testimony claimed to be that of ear-witnesses: **We heard him say.** And then, apparently, they did not quote alike. It is scarcely probable that the differences between the testimony, as given by Matthew and by Mark, represent the differences between the two witnesses, one alleging that he said "I can destroy," and the other that he said **I will destroy;** and one inserting, while the other omitted, **made with hands** and **made without hands.** Such differences, insisted upon, might invalidate testimony exactly as this was invalidated; but these differences are too much in the manner of the evangelists to be relied upon as intended for illustrative quotations.— The word for **temple** here, as in John 2 : 19, is the word that denotes the inner and more sacred part, the sanctuary, the "holy place."—Both here and at verse 56 it is Mark alone who points out that the witnesses were discordant. He leaves the impression, though he does not expressly say, that the council was aware of the discordance and insufficiency of the evidence.

60, 61. The effort to find evidence must have been considerably prolonged; probably there was search made through the whole of the throng that was present for some one whose testimony would avail. Witness after witness tried and failed, and Jesus was silent. He had no need to speak: his enemies were refuting themselves. But his silence was majestic, and his calmness contrasted with their agitation, te their great discomfiture. This silence was more

61 But he* held his peace, and answered nothing. Again the high priest asked him, and said unto him, Art thou the Christ, the Son of the Blessed?

62 And Jesus said, I am: and ye⁶ shall see the Son of man sitting on the right hand of power, and coming in the clouds of heaven.

63 Then the high priest rent⁶ his clothes, and saith, What need we any further witnesses?

61 those witness against thee? But he held his peace, and answered nothing. Again the high priest asked him, and saith unto him, Art thou the Christ, 62 the Son of the Blessed? And Jesus said, I am: and ye shall see the Son of man sitting at the right hand of power, and coming with the clouds of heaven. 63 And the high priest rent his clothes, and saith,

a Ps. 39 : 9 ; Isa. 53 : 7 ; 1 Pet. 2 : 23....*b* Dan. 7 : 13 ; Matt. 24 : 30 ; 26 : 64· Luke 22 : 69 ; Rev. 1 : 7....*c* Isa. 37 : 1.

---

powerful than speech to baffle and enrage them. —If the place was the ordinary place of meeting, the Sanhedrin sat in a semicircle, in the midst of which the accused was placed. Out to Jesus, in the midst, now came Caiaphas with his question. Some make it a single question : "Answerest thou nothing to that which these witness against thee?" But the punctuation of the English Bible and of the revisers corresponds better to the haste and excitement of the questioner : **Answerest thou nothing? What is it,** etc.—He was in a rage at his own failure and the calm silence of his prisoner. He himself could make nothing of the evidence, but in his wrath he could hurl it at Jesus as if it were of some importance. **What is it which these witness against thee?** As if Jesus must dispose of the testimony, nugatory though it was.—The picture of his rage confronting Jesus, who stood bound before him (John 18 : 19), renders the silence of Jesus all the more impressive. Mark expresses it now in doubled phrase after the question. **He held his peace, and answered nothing.**—But if nothing could be drawn from witnesses, something might be drawn from himself : he might be made to commit himself by a blasphemous utterance, or at least by one that would be so regarded ; and it was best to go at once to the main point, the question whether he was the Christ. A claim of the Messiahship would not necessarily be blasphemous : some one must one day make it, and rightfully ; but if such a one as Jesus should make it, after such life and words as his had been, and especially now, as he stood bound and friendless before the court of Jehovah's nation,—that might be condemned as blasphemous. Yet the high priest knew well enough what the answer would be, from words that Jesus had spoken in Jerusalem itself. (See John 5 : 18 ; 8 : 58 ; 9 : 37 ; 10 : 36 ; 12 : 32–37.)—**Art thou the Christ, the Son of the Blessed?** According to Matthew, it was a solemn oath that the high priest offered him : "I adjure thee by the living God that thou tell us." As much as to say, "I put you under oath, that you may clear yourself of the charge that you have made this claim," but meant as an opportunity for him to make the

claim afresh. The priest rejected the claim with his whole soul, yet wished Jesus to make it for the sake of punishing it.—**The Blessed.** A common title for God among the Jews, used absolutely, as a title, here only in the New Testament.

62. Caiaphas was not wrong in relying upon this appeal to break the silence. False charges and perversions of his words Jesus could leave to defeat themselves, but silence now would be unfaithfulness. So the answer came, clear and unqualified : **I am.** Matthew gives the answer in the rabbinical formula, "Thou hast said," which was perfectly identical in meaning with the simple "Yes." This was no popular or informal claim : it was a solemn assertion, in the presence of the religious court of the Jewish nation, in response to the formal oath of the high priest.—But the claim of Messiahship was expanded and rendered still more distinct by the memorable words that he added. **Ye shall see the Son of man sitting on the right hand of power, and coming in the clouds of heaven.** This, like Mark 13 : 26 (see notes there), is a reference to Daniel's vision (Dan. 7 : 13, 14). By this reference to well-known prophecy respecting the Messiah, Jesus made his claim as bold and plain as words could make it. This was a representation of the Messiah as the Founder of a kingdom that should take the place of the ancient world-powers, and should continue for ever. So his answer means, "I am the Messiah, and you shall see me acting as the predicted Founder of the everlasting kingdom." In Matthew, "Henceforth ye shall see," etc.—*i. e.* the founding of the kingdom represented in Daniel's vision is now to begin in your very presence ; not "hereafter," in some distant future.—Jesus was not really on trial, but Israel was ; this was the trial-moment of the theocracy. Had Israel eyes to recognize its King?

63, 64. Caiaphas was the mouthpiece of the nation at the moment of decision. Most unenviable distinction! It was his emotion that answered the formal appeal of the true King of Israel ; and his emotion was that of unspeakable horror and indignation. Now was the rejection of the Christ ; now was the rejection of Israel.—**The high priest rent his**

64 Ye have heard the blasphemy: what think ye?
And they all condemned him to be guilty of death.
65 And some began to spit on him, and to cover his
face, and to buffet him, and to say unto him, Prophesy:
and the servants did strike him with the palms of their
hands.

64 What further need have we of witnesses? Ye have
heard the blasphemy: what think ye? And they
65 all condemned him to be ¹worthy of death. And
some began to spit on him, and to cover his face, and
to buffet him, and to say unto him, Prophesy; and
the officers received him with ²blows of their hands.

a ch. 15 : 19; Isa. 50 : 6.——1 Gr. *liable to....2 Gr. strokes of rods*

clothes. An act forbidden to him as a sign of sorrow (Lev. 21 : 10); but, from the example in 2 Kings 18 : 37, it had become the rule to admit the act as a sign of horror at blasphemy. Plumptre says that "the judges in a Jewish trial for blasphemy were bound to rend their clothes when the blasphemous words were uttered; and the clothes so torn were never afterward to be mended." Accordingly, for the high priest to rend his clothes was "almost as much a formal sign of condemnation as the putting on of the black cap by an English judge." Maimonides, writing, in the thirteenth century, of Jewish customs and traditions, marks out the precise manner in which clothes should be rent in horror at blasphemy and the length of the rents that should be made. He says that all the garments that a man has on, except the outermost and the innermost, should be torn to a specified extent; and both the words that are used here in Matthew and Mark are plural—the outer garments (*ta himatia*) in Matthew, and the inner garments (*tous chitōnas*) in Mark.—What need we any further witnesses? Ye have heard the blasphemy. But the verb is in the aorist: "Ye *heard* it as he spoke." Certainly there was no need of witnesses, if this was what they were waiting for: the worst was on record.—What think ye? A call for the votes of those who had heard.—Matthew quotes the response directly; Mark, indirectly. Guilty (*enochon*) of death. When followed by the genitive of the crime, the word means "guilty of," as in Mark 3 : 29; when followed by the genitive of the penalty, as here, it means "worthy of" or "justly exposed to." It is a fit word to stand in a verdict. This was the expression of the determination of the council; not yet a legal decision, because the meeting was not a legal meeting, but lacking only the form of law.

65. The council has condemned him; he is hopeless of safety and life; therefore let loose upon him all who will insult and abuse him. He is bound; torment him.—Who are they that torment him? In Luke, "the men that held him;" in Mark, some, not further defined; in Matthew, the indefinite "they." He still stands in the midst of the Sanhedrin, and the members of that body must know and ap-

prove of the insulting, if they do not take part in it. That they take no part in the actual tormenting is more than can be affirmed.—Some began to spit on him. Matthew, "they did spit in his face" as he stood bound.—And to cover his face, and to buffet him, and to say unto him, Prophesy. Enlarged and explained in Luke: "When they had blindfolded him, they struck him on the face, and asked him, saying, Prophesy" (and tell), "who is he that smote thee?" This is trifling with him as a claimant to prophetic powers: "Can he tell, blindfolded, which of the wretches dancing round him it was that struck him? A fine Messiah if he cannot!" In Matthew, "Prophesy unto us, thou Christ."—After the first comers, including, probably, some of the Sanhedrists, had had their fill of this, the servants, "attendants" or "officers," followed the example, and had their turn at abusing him.—Did strike him with the palms of their hands. The original of this (*rhapismasin auton elabon*) is apparently a Latinism, meaning, substantially, "they took him to beat him"—*i. e.* took him into their hands to beat him, in their turn. It is hard to judge whether "blows of their hands" or "blows of rods" is better; in the indeterminate use of the word, perhaps simply "blows" is best. The word translated buffet, above, refers to blows with the fist.—So he stood, bound, blindfolded, spit upon, smitten, taunted, loaded with insult, first by one set of men and then by their imitators. This was no pretence or show; it was the real work of real passion—actual hatred and scorn doing their utmost in bitter earnest. This was violent and intense rejection, fulfilling in its intensity and violence all the prophecies of rejection and all the descriptions of righteous sufferers. (See Isa. 50 : 6; 53 : 3, 7.) This is the reception that is accorded to the Incarnate God by the people who have had the clearest revelation, and who consider themselves the special friends and allies of his government. This is the significance of the scene; it is the indignant and contemptuous rejection of perfect moral goodness by sinful men. This is the depth of sin; and this is the depth of humiliation for the Messenger who brings the saving love of God.—No word from his lips; he was

15

63 ¶ And[a] as Peter was beneath in the palace, there cometh one of the maids of the high priest: *67* And when she saw Peter warming himself, she looked upon him, and said, And thou also wast with Jesus of Nazareth.

68 But he denied, saying,[b] I know not, neither understand I what thou sayest. And he went out into the porch; and the cock crew.

66 And as Peter was beneath in the court, there 67 cometh one of the maids of the high priest; and seeing Peter warming himself, she looked upon him, and saith, Thou also wast with the Nazarene, even 68 Jesus. But he denied, saying, [1] I neither know, nor understand what thou sayest: and he went out into

---

a Matt. 26 · 69; Luke 22:55; John 18 : 16....*b* 2 Tim. 2 : 12, 13.——1 Or, *I neither know, nor understand: thou, what sayest thou?*

---

silent, as in the trial. The remembrance of his patience remained with his disciples, to be cited as the great example. (See 1 Pet. 2 : 20, 23.) How true and striking an illustration of his self-command under this torture is this! "When he suffered, he threatened not."

66–72. PETER THRICE DENIES HIS MASTER. *Parallels,* Matt. 26 , 69–75; Luke 22 : 56–62; John 18 : 17–27.—The synoptists relate the three denials together, as forming a connected whole; but John, whose narrative in this part is much more full of special details, places the three denials in their connection with other events that were occurring at the same time. The second and third he puts close together, but between the first and the second he introduces other matter. It scarcely needs to be said that this paragraph is parallel in time to the earlier part of the preceding, ending, perhaps, during the time of the abuse. The story of the denial suffers in the matter of tragic interest by being thus separated from the accompanying scenery and exhibited as a detached story. It is sad enough in itself, but its deepest and saddest significance comes from its connection with what else was going on at the same time. Of the two scenes, in the court and in the house, each was rendered sadder by the other.

THE FIRST DENIAL.—**66–68.** John expressly places this within the time of the preliminary examination before Annas. The first thought would be that this would require a change of place between the first and the second; but the simple and probable conjecture that Annas and Caiaphas occupied one house removes that apparent difficulty. It was probably merely from one part of the high priest's palace to another that Jesus was sent for the second examination; so that Peter remained near him throughout the trial.—**As Peter was beneath.** Not in **the palace,** but "in the court." The *aulē* was the court or quadrangle around which the house was built, although the word is sometimes used of the palace as a whole. The place is said to have been **beneath,** in contrast to the rooms of the house that was built about it. It was here that the fire was built (Luke 22 : 55). In Matthew, Peter is said to have been "without" in

the court. Here, in the light of the fire (Luke), Peter was sitting. Luke has here the same fresh descriptive language that Mark used at verse 54 (*pros to phōs*), "(turned) toward the light." It shows us the disciple standing in the circle around the fire with the strong glow shining upon his face.—In this light **one of the maids** (or maidservants) **of the high priest** easily recognized him. She was "the doorkeeper" (John), who had let Peter in, in company with John, who brought him and secured his admission. Mark says, and he alone, that **she saw Peter warming himself,** and then **looked upon him,** or "fixed her eyes on him," looked carefully; partial recognition, followed by a gaze that fully identified the man. —Her charge is a question in John; an affirmation in the synoptists; but of one effect in all. In Mark, **thou also wast with Jesus of Nazareth,** or, rather, "with the Nazarene, Jesus." The tone was doubtless sharp and scornful, perhaps keen with ridicule; for did not even the servants know what "the Nazarene" claimed to be, and in what state he now was? But what mattered the tone or the intentions of the questioner? It was a simple question of fact, to which friend or enemy ought never to look for any but a truthful answer.—But, though the questioner thought herself sure, she was surprised by a negative answer. In John, simply, "I am not;" in Luke, "Woman, I do not know him;" in Matthew, "I know not what thou sayest;" in Mark, at greater length, **I know not, neither understand I what thou sayest.** Thus he denied: Matthew, "in the presence of all." So far as we can judge, the motive must have been chiefly a sudden shame. It can scarcely have been definite and intelligible fear; it was rather a shrinking, a weakening of moral courage. It had been easy to profess bravery, but now it was easier to withdraw from all connection with him whom Annas was seeking to condemn: the false "No" was easier than the loyal "Yes." But the question and answer made him uneasy by the fire, **and he went out into the porch,** or vestibule, the passage from the street to the court within the house—went thither to escape observation, even if but a little

69 And a maid saw him again, and began to say to them that stood by, This is *one* of them.
70 And he denied it again. And a little after, they that stood by said again to Peter, Surely thou art *one* of them; for thou art a Galilæan,ᵃ and thy speech agreeth *thereto*.
71 But he began to curse and to swear, *saying*, I know not this man of whom ye speak.
72 And the second time the cock crew. And Peter called to mind the word that Jesus said unto him, Before the cock crew twice, thou shalt deny me thrice. And when he thought thereon, he wept.ᵇ

69 the ¹porch; ²and the cock crew. And the maid saw him, and began again to say to them that stood by, 70 This is *one* of them. But he again denied it. And after a little while again they that stood by said to Peter, Of a truth thou art *one* of them; for thou art 71 a Galilæan. But he began to curse, and to swear, I 72 know not this man of whom ye speak. And straightway the second time the cock crew. And Peter called to mind the word, how that Jesus said unto him, Before the cock crew twice, thou shalt deny me thrice. ³And when he thought thereon, he wept.

a Acts 2:7....*b* 2 Cor. 7:10.——1 Or, *forecourt*....2 Many ancient authorities omit *and the cock crew*....3 Or, And he began to weep.

while.—Mark alone records that as he went **the cock crew.** (See verse 30, and note there.) Peter remembered this sound, which ought to have been a warning; it was prominent in his memory, though not in any other disciple's reminiscences, and through him it came into the record. He was alone, apparently, when he heard it. Must he not often have said to himself, "Oh that I had heeded it"?

THE SECOND DENIAL.—**68-70.** The first was single and simple, a response to a single inquiry; before the moment of the second the questions came thicker, and the denial was a response to more than one. The place, if we had Mark alone, would seem to be the porch, with the female slave who kept the door again at her duty; but this would be only a probable interpretation, and John says expressly that Peter was standing by the fire and warming himself. He had returned, then; possibly the chill of the night had driven him back. In Mark, the questioner is **a maid**—*i. e.* the same maid as before, the doorkeeper; in Matthew, it is "another maid;" in Luke, "another" (masculine)—*i. e.* another, a man, in John, no subject is expressed; it is the indefinite "they."—In Mark the maid, seeing him, began to **say to them that stood by,** etc.; in which there is a suggestion of a more general conversation. The doorkeeper asked the question, and others took it up. The time, in Luke, is "after a little while."—The charge is virtually the same in all the synoptists: **This is one of them;** and in John, again, it is a question, almost identical with the first, and to the same effect with the charge in the synoptists. It was a simple question of identifying the man.—His response is merely characterized in Mark as a denial. **He denied it again.** In John, "I am not;" in Luke, "Man, I am not;" in Matthew it is said that "he denied with an oath, I know not the man," calling God to witness that Jesus was to him a stranger!—This second was apparently a single denial, as truly as the first; but it was made in reply to a group of inquiries.

THE THIRD DENIAL.—**70-72.** John says nothing of the time; in Matthew and Mark it is a **little after** (*meta mikron*)—not the same word as in Luke's account of the second denial (*meta brachu*); in Luke the time is specified as "about one hour" later. The place is not mentioned, and may most naturally be supposed to be, as before, by the fire.—Now, again, perhaps even more than before, the questions came in a group, from several persons. In Matthew and Mark, **they that stood by;** in Luke, "another;" in John the questioner is "one of the servants of the high priest, being kinsman of him whose ear Peter cut off."—As to the identification of Peter, the questioners proposed two reasons for being sure of their man. The synoptists all make them say that he is **a Galilæan,** and Matthew specifies, more closely, that his speech makes him manifest as such. The allusion to his speech in Mark is properly omitted by the revisers. In John the question of the servant, from whom Peter might well shrink, is, "Did I not see thee in the garden with him?" It is said that the Galilæan speech differed from that of Jerusalem in a certain thickness of utterance in the guttural sounds, and in a difficulty that Galilæans had in pronouncing *sh,* which they transformed into *th.* It has been suggested as possible that the peculiarity may have appeared in Peter's pronunciation of "Nazareth" or "Nazarene." In his excitement the native peculiarity would more decidedly appear.—Now that the recognition was so positive and well grounded, the unhappy man felt called upon for the stronger denial. First, the denial was simple; then, "with an oath;" now, **he began to curse and to swear.** So Matthew and Mark. The cursing, however, was not reckless and pointless profanity, as the use of the word in modern speech would suggest. Rather does the word suggest some such form as that of 2 Kings 6:31: "God do so, and more also, to me, if the head of Elisha the son of Shaphat shall stand on him this day." The swearing, or oath, would call God to witness, and the cursing would invoke evil from God upon himself if what he said was false. The statement which he would thus confirm was, **I know not this man of whom ye speak.** —In the midst of the final act of sin came the reproof. "Immediately the cock crew;" Luke, "while he was yet speaking." Mark notes that it was **the second** cock-crowing. (See above.) This time the warning was noticed; but Luke adds the mention of the other unspeakably touching reproof, that cut the sinful man to the heart: "The Lord turned and looked upon Peter." Standing, probably, in the midst of the abuse, with cruel enemies mocking him, he still had "leisure from himself" to know what his boastful follower was doing, and to turn to him with a heart-searching look. He was somewhere within the apartments of the house, and Peter was in the inner court; through some open door his piercing glance could be seen. With the cock-crowing and the look came back to his memory the Lord's prediction, which he had thought he could never fulfil, and his heart was broken. John says nothing of the result; in Matthew and Luke, he "wept bitterly;" in Mark the language is unusual, and not very plain (*epibalōn eklaien*): it is variously translated by interpreters, but probably best rendered as in the English Bible, **when he thought thereon, he wept.** He heard the cock, he saw the look of Jesus, he remembered the saying of Jesus, he thought of the saying and what it meant, he "went out," away from the fire and the questioners, and he "wept bitterly;" as well he might! But the tears were tears of penitence. Judas went away in the agony of despair to throw away his life; Peter went out in that "godly sorrow that worketh repentance unto salvation."—In these notes upon the denial the fourfold record has been brought together, in order to show that there is here no essential difference between the evangelists. Charges of contradiction have often been made; but they are shown to be vain as soon as we reproduce the scene and remember how many persons were present from whom the inquiries about this disciple would naturally proceed. Some (as Plumptre) have been inclined to change the order somewhat and make Mark's

second denial the third, while John's third is identified with the second. But each evangelist apparently intends to record three denials, and probably to record them in their order; and no considerable difficulties are met with in explaining the story as it stands. Therefore it seems best not to attempt changes of order.

The lessons of the denial are manifest and familiar—the folly and danger of self-confidence; the folly of relying upon the readiness of the spirit and forgetting the weakness of the flesh; the folly of disregarding friendly warnings from the best of friends; the folly of going into company where denial will be easier than acknowledgment; the folly of failing to anticipate the power of coming temptation; the certainty that one act of sin will call for another to protect it; the danger that the second sin will be more decided than the first, and the third more positive than the second; the power of man to act upon his worse nature even when a better is in him. On the other hand, the grasp of Jesus on Peter availed when the grasp of Peter on Jesus would never have availed to save him; the tenderness of Jesus, ready with his forewarning; his patience, not wearied out even by this; his thoughtfulness for his servant, and the timeliness of his reproachful look. Penitence is the best gift of God to a sinner. Peter delighted to say that Jesus was exalted "to give repentance to Israel, and forgiveness of sins" (Acts 5:31). Peter dared to say (Acts 3:14), "Ye denied the Holy One and the Just." "So did I," he might have added, "but he looked me into penitence; and now I am trying to show you the same pleading eyes fixed upon you to look you into penitence too. Will you not behold them?"—John was in the same company with Peter, but he stood while Peter fell. Hence, Peter could not plead necessity. What must have been the feelings of John, who had brought his fellow-disciple in, if he heard him disown their common Master? It seems as if he could not have heard it; for would he not have remonstrated and saved Peter the second and third denials?—But for such a triumph of grace in Peter the weak, the church might never have had Peter the strong, the genuine rock.

CHAPTER XV.

A ND straightway in the morning the chief priests
held a consultation[a] with the elders and scribes
and the whole council, and bound Jesus, and carried
him away, and delivered him to Pilate.

1 AND straightway in the morning the chief priests
with the elders and scribes, and the whole council,
held a consultation, and bound Jesus, and carried

a Ps. 2 : 2; Matt. 27 : 1, etc.; Luke 23 : 1; John 18 : 28; Acts 3 : 13; 4 : 26.

1-15. JESUS APPEARS BEFORE THE FULL SANHEDRIN, AND IS THEN SENT TO PILATE, WHO, AFTER VAIN EFFORTS TO RELEASE HIM, GIVES HIM UP TO BE CRUCIFIED. *Parallels,* Matt. 27 : 1-26; Luke 22 : 66-23 : 25; John 18 : 28-19 : 16.—Here Mark's narrative is briefest, omitting much that the others mention. Here, also, and from this point on through the story of the Passion, Mark is less rich than anywhere else in those graphic touches of description that are generally so characteristic of him. His narrative runs on much more closely than elsewhere in the course taken by the others, especially by Matthew; and the plain, unpicturesque character of his style in this part can scarcely fail to strike a student of the Greek text. A sufficient and very interesting explanation of the change is found in the fact that Peter, after his denial, was not a close observer of the progress of events. Whether he was present at all, we do not know; and if he was, it was with a broken heart that would scarcely venture near the Master whom he had so deeply wronged. Very few of his graphic reminiscences would Mark be able to obtain, and much more than elsewhere would he be dependent upon the common sources of information. This coincidence forms a very interesting confirmation of the opinion that Peter's influence was the leading one in the preparation of this book. Luke tells what was done at the official meeting of the Sanhedrin, and mentions the sending of Jesus to Herod; Matthew introduces the remorse and suicide of Judas, and tells of the dream of Pilate's wife and the effort of Pilate to throw off the responsibility of the condemnation of his prisoner; John speaks of the shrinking of the priests from the defilement of Pilate's judgment-hall, recounts most fully the interviews between Jesus and Pilate, describes the impression that the prisoner made upon the governor, and makes prominent the efforts of Pilate to secure his release. John had known the trial more accurately than the others, partly from the fact of his acquaintance with the high priest (John 18 : 15), and intentionally completed the reports already in existence. If Peter had been loyal, he would have known all that John knew (John 18 : 16). All the matters above men-

tioned Mark omits or passes over rapidly, and confines himself to facts that are common to him with other evangelists.

1. The meeting that is here mentioned is the one that could not be held till daybreak, the formal assembly of the Sanhedrin. **The whole council** took part in it—*i. e.* the whole Sanhedrin. The Aramaic word is a corruption of the Greek *sunedrion.*—For a meeting that could legally find their victim guilty, they seized the first possible moment. **Straightway in the morning.** Luke, "as soon as it was day." Of this meeting Mark tells nothing, except in the words **held a consultation;** Matthew tells nothing more, except that the consultation was "against Jesus, to put him to death." According to the most probable arrangement, this meeting is more fully reported in Luke 22 : 66-71. There are some difficulties in this grouping, but less, on the whole, than in any other. According to this, the witnesses were not called in at the formal meeting, but the council repeated the question that had elicited the desired blasphemy: "Art thou the Christ?" The answer of Jesus (Luke 22 : 67-70) well corresponds to the fact of a second questioning: he asserts his true Messiahship, but does it with a kind of protest against the unreasonableness and ungodliness of their demand. His confession is taken as sufficient evidence of blasphemy, and he is condemned by a formal vote.—Here first do Matthew and Mark speak of the fact that he was **bound;** John said that he was bound in the garden. Perhaps this later binding was a special binding in token of condemnation: so early tradition represents, affirming that he was led to Pilate with a cord around his neck.—**Delivered him to Pilate.** The Sanhedrin was not allowed, under the Roman Power, to execute the penalty of death, and the next step necessarily was to obtain the consent of the governor to the death of Jesus. Doubtless, no trouble was apprehended in obtaining it. Troops had been sent to aid in the arrest; the city was full of Jews; and the desire of the leaders at such a time, especially against one who had no visible claim upon the governor and could be accused of exciting the people by claiming royalty, seemed to them altogether likely to be successful. — **Pilate.**

2 And Pilate asked him, Art thou the King of the Jews? And he, answering, said unto him, Thou sayest *it*.
3 And the chief priests accused him of many things: but he answered nothing.
4 And Pilate asked him again, saying, Answerest thou nothing? behold how many things they witness against thee.
5 But Jesus*a* yet answered nothing; so that Pilate marvelled.

2 him away, and delivered him up to Pilate. And Pilate asked him, Art thou the King of the Jews? And he answering saith unto him, Thou sayest.
3 And the chief priests accused him of many things.
4 And Pilate again asked him, saying, Answerest thou nothing? behold how many things they accuse
5 thee of. But Jesus no more answered anything; insomuch that Pilate marvelled.

a Isa. 53 : 7 ; John 19 : 9.

Pontius Pilate, the Roman Procurator of Judæa. The procurator was primarily the collector of the imperial revenue, but he was invested also with judicial power. The residence of the Procurator of Judæa was ordinarily at Cæsarea, but at the great national festivals he was obliged, often much against his will, to be present at Jerusalem. Of Pilate's early history nothing definite is known. He came to Judæa about A. D. 26, and remained not far from ten years in office. His administration had been marked by frequent and needless insults to the Jews, especially in the way of outraging their religious prejudices, and the Jews had no love for him. His character was but too well illustrated in his relations with our Lord—not altogether bad, but weak even while stubborn; wilful, yet vacillating, and incapable of perceiving high truth and purity.

2. At first (John) they supposed that their mere assertion that Jesus was a malefactor would be sufficient; but Pilate remembered that he was a judge, and called for their case against him. Then (Luke) they made their charge—not at all the same as in their own council, but a fresh one suited to the governor's ears. Any charge would do, if only it would be successful. Three accusations appear in Luke: stirring up the people, forbidding to give tribute to Cæsar, and claiming to be Christ a King. Religious offences would be nothing here: their only hope lay in establishing political charges.—Upon this came Pilate's question, **Art thou the King of the Jews?** Thou is emphatic. The language is so reported by all four evangelists. We can imagine the question asked in the tone of scorn or of amusement or of pity. What a moment to inquire about his kingship! Bound, disgraced, apparently helpless, he stood where no Messiah could be conceived by a Jew to stand. The Messiah was to triumph over the Gentiles; but Jesus was at the mercy of the Gentile governor, who was asking him, **Art thou the King of the Jews ?**—But the answer was not withheld. **Thou sayest it.** The formula of the rabbis, equivalent to a positive "Yes ;" so Pilate would understand it,

and all hearers with him. From John we learn that this question and reply formed a part of a longer conversation in which Jesus set forth the nature of his kingdom as an unworldly kingdom and a kingdom of truth, intending, apparently, to relieve Pilate's fear of political complications on account of his claims, and at the same time to let him hear what his own claims really were.—In connection with this conversation, study the effect of his sufferings on the attitude of Jesus. See how steadily he maintained his own consciousness of his mission and claims ; how he never lost sight of his true position for a moment or spoke as any other than the Christ of God, the Judge of the world. This was true when he was before the high priest ; it was true in the presence of Pilate ; and it continued true on the cross.

3-5. The **chief priests** reiterated the accusations above quoted from Luke, and tried all that seemed to have any hope or promise in them. Yet we learn from John that they themselves did not enter into the judgment-hall, for fear of contracting defilement that would disqualify them for the remainder of the passover feast. No fear had they of the defilement of injustice, but ceremonial impurity they must shun as if it were death. He whom they would kill was the One who had pointed out to them this very thing, the vanity of external defilements and the true source of the evil that does defile. Such deeper secrets of defilement they did not wish to know ; even a burdensome outward law was easier for them to keep than an inward law of righteousness.—**But he answered nothing,** at the end of verse 3, is omitted in the best text ; his silence is implied in Pilate's question. As the accusations before the high priest had drawn out no reply from him, so this new set of charges, as empty as the first, brought no answer from his lips. We do not imagine the true majesty of this silence until we think of the excitement and feverishness of his opponents. The priests were outside the hall, whispering and agitating among the people, and accusation after accusation was brought to the governor. The prisoner may have had in mind

6 Now at *that* feast he released unto them one prisoner, whomsoever they desired.
7 And there was *one* named Barabbas, *which lay*
bound with them that had made insurrection with
him, who had committed murder in the insurrection.
8 And the multitude, crying aloud, began to desire
him to do as he had ever done unto them.

6 Now at ¹the feast he used to release unto them
7 one prisoner, whom they asked of him. And
there was one called Barabbas, *lying* bound with
them that had made insurrection, men who in
8 the insurrection had committed murder. And
the multitude went up and began to ask him

a Matt. 27 : 15 ; Luke 23 : 17 ; John 18 : 39.——1 Or, *a feast*

Isa. 53 : 7 : "He was oppressed, and he was afflicted, yet he opened not his mouth ;" but if he
had, he was not trying to fulfil the prophecy.
Rather would the prophecy comfort him and
keep him nerved for patience, as did the other
Scriptures when he knew "that thus it must
be " (Matt. 26 : 54).—Pilate's question implied that
Jesus could not afford to leave such accusations
unanswered. It was quite new to him as a judge
to see a prisoner so indifferent to defence. Little
did Pilate know how well his prisoner could afford to "commit himself to him that judgeth
righteously " (1 Pet. 2 : 23), or how morally impossible it was for him to condescend to answer
such accusations, even though they might put
his life in jeopardy.—The governor's appeal for
a defence was as powerless as the attacks of the
enemies, and the silence was unbroken : **Jesus
yet answered nothing.** "Jesus no more answered anything" (in the Revision) is not an
improvement on the old rendering. In Matthew, as in the Revision, "he gave him no answer, not even to one word"—*i. e.* no response
to a single word of what Pilate had been saying.—At the silence **Pilate marvelled ;** in
Matthew, "marvelled greatly." No doubt it
seemed to him reckless self-abandonment. He
saw no crime in Jesus, but, since the charges
were false, why did he not defend himself?
According to Luke, Pilate here reported to
the accusers that he found in Jesus nothing
worthy of death, and they thereupon renewed
the charge of popular agitation, begun in Galilee and prosecuted all the way to Jerusalem.
Well they knew how little dangerous this agitation was. If it had only been dangerous to Pilate and his masters, they would all have fallen
in with it ; but they chose to represent it as sedition, though they knew that they were lying.—
The mention of Galilee reminded Pilate of Herod, who had over Galilee a kind of authority,
and who was then in Jerusalem ; and he seized
the opportunity to rid himself of an unpleasant
responsibility by sending Jesus and his accusers
to Herod. Before him the accusations were renewed, and Herod himself asked Jesus many
questions ; but the majestic silence was still unbroken, and no ground of condemnation was
discovered. But the prisoner was there again

insulted, and thence he was sent back to the
original tribunal.
**6–8. Now at that feast he released unto
them one prisoner.** No other traces remain
of this custom of releasing a prisoner at the
feast on demand of the people. It is akin,
however, to certain Roman customs observed
at the festivals of the gods, and so it is not unlikely that Pilate may have introduced it among
the Jews, perhaps by way of atonement for his
wanton insults to the populace. Whether the
practice extended to any other festivals besides
the passover does not appear, but the language
of John renders it scarcely probable that it did.
—Of **Barabbas** nothing is known except what
is learned here. The name, "Bar-abbas," means
"son of his father," which may perhaps be
taken to mean that he was of distinguished
family and was named in family pride. But
the title " father" was given to rabbis, and it is
quite possible that it means in this case "son
of a rabbi," and that the religious connections
of the man are thus indicated. Matthew says
that he was a "notable," or distinguished, prisoner, which indicates that he was personally
well known, and at the same time that his case
was a remarkable one. The readiness with
which the people were united in calling for
him may be taken as a sign that he was in some
sense a popular favorite. Of his crime, we are
told that there had been an insurrection in the
city, that the insurgents had committed murder, and that the insurgents, who were also
murderers—among whom was Barabbas—were
now lying in prison. From the prominence of
his name, we should infer that he had been a
leader in the insurrection. One of the latest
insurrections had been occasioned by the act of
Pilate in taking the money from the sacred
treasury, dedicated to God under the name of
" Corban" (Matt. 15 : 5 ; Mark 7 : 11), for the construction of aqueducts, whereby he brought water
to Jerusalem from the distance of four hundred
furlongs (Josephus, *Wars,* 2. 9. 4). This, of
course, aroused the indignation of the Jews,
and in the tumult that ensued many lost their
lives. If Barabbas and his companions were
engaged in this insurrection, there was reason
why the people should be interested in them.

9 But Pilate answered them, saying, Will ye that I release unto you the King of the Jews?
10 For he knew that the chief priests had delivered him for envy.*
11 But the chief priests moved the people, that he should rather release* Barabbas unto them.

9 *to do* as he was wont to do unto them. And Pilate answered them, saying, Will ye that I release unto you the King of the Jews? For he perceived that for 11 envy the chief priests had delivered him up. But the chief priests stirred up the multitude, that he

a Prov. 27 : 4 ; Eccles. 4 : 4 ; Acts 13 : 45 ; Tit. 3 : 3....*b* Acts 3 : 14.

In such an insurrection, too, the "son of a rabbi" might easily be concerned, for all the religious passions of the people would then be on fire. Some ancient authorities, though not the most ancient or the most decisive, make his name, in Matt. 27 : 17, to be "Jesus Barabbas." "Jesus," which is the same as "Joshua," was a common name among the Jews, and this man may have been called "Jesus the rabbi's son." This would render plain and striking the language of Pilate in the passage cited : "Which will ye that I release to you, Jesus Barabbas, or Jesus who is called Christ?" But the contrast of verse 20, in Matthew, "that they should ask Barabbas, and destroy Jesus," seems to prove that the writer had no such second name for Barabbas in mind.—The mention of releasing a prisoner comes, in Mark, from the people, who—not **crying aloud,** but—"going up" (so the best text), thronged about the palace, and demanded that the governor should conform to the custom. All the other evangelists mention it first when it came as a proposal from the lips of Pilate. Probably the popular request was prepared by the counsel of the priests.

9-11. From this point, even in the extremely brief record of Mark, Pilate appears anxious to set Jesus at liberty. In none of the synoptic narratives does any adequate reason appear for this anxiety. It is only when we turn to the fuller record of John and are informed of the earlier interview (John 18 : 33-38), in which Jesus declared himself a King of truth, that we understand the governor's desire to save him. Not that Pilate was by that first interview profoundly awed, but after it he would feel that Jesus was at the worst a harmless enthusiast whose ideas were not of the kind that ought to bring him before the judgment-seat. With such a thought in mind, he remembered that he was a judge, and his sense of justice prompted him to shield his prisoner from wrong. Already was the better impulse present that might have saved Pilate from his crime.—The offer to release Jesus, according to the custom of releasing a prisoner, was intended to be favorable to him, and so was the form of the proposal—**Will ye that I release unto you the King of the Jews?**—which was an attempt to touch the national feeling. A very

ignorant attempt, however : these Jews would have none of a king who had stood bound before a Gentile ruler, unless, indeed, he took that as the opportunity to free himself, glorify Israel, and destroy the Gentile dominion.—But Pilate **knew that the chief priests had delivered him for envy**—*i. e.* because they feared his influence upon the people, which would certainly, if left alone, destroy theirs. Therefore he thought a direct appeal to the people might possibly meet with a favorable response.—Pilate's knowledge of the motives of the priests is an important element in the case. The certainty in his mind that this was an unjust prosecution made him without excuse in his vacillation and his final surrender. Just here also comes in, in Matthew, the story of the message from his wife warning him against taking part in the proceeding against Jesus. Her thoughts about Jesus may have sprung wholly from her dream, but it is at least as likely that her dream about Jesus was suggested by her previous anxious thoughts. Reinforced by such a special warning, Pilate's conscience ought to have been strong enough—nay, it was strong enough, if he had not tampered with it—to govern him.—The picture sketched so rapidly in verse 11 is full of dreadful meaning. The **chief priests** were outside, too conscientious to come into the hall, and they were going to and fro among the multitude, excited already, talking to this man and to that, exciting them still more, and suggesting the robber and murderer as the one for them to choose instead of Jesus. How deep was the fall of Judaism ! Its priests condescending to the work of demagogues, agitating for the acceptance of a murderer instead of the Holy One of God ! This was, as it were, an official degradation of the glory of Israel, a deliberate dragging of the sacred things in the mire. Thus for the final cry, which "prevailed" (Luke), the chief priests were directly responsible.—The first popular utterance that is recorded was, "Not this man, but Barabbas" (John) ; in Luke, still stronger, "Away with this man, and release unto us Barabbas."

12-14. The governor had put the question to the people, and would not take it back : if they would decide the matter, so much the

12 And Pilate answered, and said again unto them, What will ye then that I shall do *unto him* whom ye call the King of the Jews?
13 And they cried out again, Crucify him.
14 Then Pilate said unto them, Why, what evil[b] hath he done? And they cried out the more exceedingly, Crucify him.
15 ¶ And *so* Pilate, willing to content the people, released Barabbas unto them, and delivered Jesus, when he had scourged *him*, to be crucified.

12 should rather release Barabbas unto them. And Pilate again answered and said unto them, What then shall I do unto him whom ye call the King of
13 the Jews? And they cried out again, Crucify him.
14 And Pilate said unto them, Why, what evil hath he done? But they cried out exceedingly, Crucify him.
15 And Pilate, wishing to content the multitude, released unto them Barabbas, and delivered Jesus, when he had scourged him, to be crucified.

a Ps. 2 : 6; Jer. 23 : 5; Acts 5 : 31....*b* Isa. 53 : 9.

easier for him. He had proposed to please them, and so he continued in the same direction with his question, **What will ye then that I shall do unto him whom ye call the King of the Jews?** Matthew, "with Jesus, who is called Christ?"—**What will ye.** Was he there to find out what the mob willed? Luke says that he even now " wished to release Jesus," but what a way was this to seek that object!—An honorable official name he gave to Jesus—one according to Matthew, and another according to Mark: " Christ " and **King of the Jews ;** but by the hateful turn of speech, **whom ye call** the King of the Jews, he tried, in his vexation, to hint that this prisoner was, after all, the real King of the people with whom he was dealing—a fling at the Jews, by which he would insult them even while he humored them. But, though he was vexed with them and with himself, the deed was done; he had invited the crowd which the priests were making their tool to decide what should become of Jesus.—**And they cried out again.** The previous cry, of preference for Barabbas, is implied in this **again,** though Mark has not mentioned it before, as the others have.—**Crucify him!** Now the fatal suggestion came, "If I release Barabbas, what shall I do with Jesus?" " Let them change places. The punishment of the robber would be crucifixion ; let Jesus suffer it, while the robber goes free." It is true that the proposal of crucifixion was almost implied in the demand that Jesus should die at the hands of the Roman Government, for that was the ordinary penalty in cases where anything of infamy was involved. But with the crowd, with whom, apparently, Barabbas was something of a favorite, the proposal of an exchange of places would bring in the idea of crucifixion in the form most acceptable to their excited passions: " Let him die the death from which we save Barabbas."—The governor ought to have expected exactly this if he appealed to the people, yet he seems to have been shocked at it. **Why, what evil hath he done?** A sincere but ill-timed attempt to reason with an excited crowd, and that after the main question has been given

into their hands. The governor's resistance comes too late ; he has placed himself and his decision in the people's power, and it is vain to think of reasoning now. Luke notes that this is " the third time" that he has remonstrated. He seems to be much in earnest ; he adds again that he has found no cause of death in Jesus ; he proposes to " chastise him "—cowardly offer to compromise justice and half punish a guiltless prisoner!—and then to set him free. Here the sense of responsibility comes back upon Pilate, though he has tried to shake off the responsibility itself, and he shrinks from consenting to so unjust a deed, though he would consent to one that was only less extreme in its injustice.— But all in vain ; the voices that shocked him with their cry refuse to give over. **They cried exceedingly.** So Matthew and Mark. Not **the more or the more exceedingly.** They cried loud and long, unwilling to take refusal. Luke, " they were instant," or urgent, " with loud voices, asking that he might be crucified." Luke adds, in solemn and indignant strain, " and their voices prevailed." — But Pilate would still shrink from the responsibility of the act. Matthew, and he alone, tells how he washed his hands in symbol of his innocence of the condemnation, and how the Jewish multitude madly accepted and claimed the guilt for themselves and their children. Matthew wrote for Jewish Christians, for whom their nation's self-inflicted curse had an interest that it did not possess for the readers of Mark's Gospel. (Compare Acts 5 : 28, where this seems to have been forgotten.)—After this act Pilate considered his utmost to be done, and fully surrendered.

15. Here the final act is narrated. The motive is stated again. **Willing,** or wishing, **to content the people.** The phrase is a marked Latinism (*to hikanon poiēsai*), being an exact transference of the Latin *satisfacere,* " to satisfy." Such phrases may seem to confirm the traditional statements respecting the connection of Mark and his Gospel with the Christian community at Rome, but they do not really prove more than that the writer was influ-

16 And the* soldiers led him away into the hall called Prætorium; and they called together the whole band.
17 And they clothed him with purple, and platted a crown of thorns, and put it about his *head;
18 And began to salute him, Hail, King of the Jews!
19 And they smote him on the head with a reed, and did spit⁴ upon him, and, bowing *their* knees, worshipped him.

16 And the soldiers led him away within the court, which is the ¹¹Prætorium; and they call together the 17 whole ²band. And they clothe him with purple, and 18 plaiting a crown of thorns, they put it on him; and they began to salute him, Hail, King of the Jews! 19 And they smote his head with a reed, and did spit upon him, and bowing their knees worshipped him.

a Matt. 27 : 27 ; John 18 : 28, 33 ; 19 : 9....*b* ch. 14 : 65.——1 *Or, palace*....2 *Or, cohort*

enced by the idioms of the Latin language.— Of the act itself, both sides are presented: he **released Barabbas unto them,** giving him into the hands of those who would make great rejoicing over him, and he **delivered Jesus to be crucified.** Luke continues, in the same wondering and indignant strain, "And he released him that for sedition and murder had been cast into prison, whom they asked for; but Jesus he delivered up to their will."— But before the final delivering over of Jesus came the scourging. So all but Luke, who passes it by. The word is a Latin word again (*phragellōsas,* which is merely the word *flagellare,* "to whip," "scourge"), adopted into Greek. It is not peculiar to Mark here; Matthew has the same. It is just as well for us, and better, that this word fails now to bring to the imagination the full picture that it might suggest. Scourging was a Roman punishment, inflicted with knotted cords or thongs of leather, which were sometimes weighted with bones or metal. The victim was stripped, always as far as to the waist and sometimes altogether, and tied by the hands to a pillar, in a bent posture, in which the blows would fall with the greatest possible force upon his back. The Roman severity made no provision for limiting the number of blows that might be administered; the Jewish law, with characteristic tenderness, confined it to forty (Deut. 25 : 3), and in practice, for fear of accidental excess, the number was "forty stripes save one" (2 Cor. 11 : 24). Jesus was scourged under Roman regulations, not Jewish; and, as to the severity of the scourging, we can say only that there was nothing to prevent the rough soldier who performed the act from continuing till he was weary or till the prisoner fell exhausted. Imagination instinctively turns away from the scene, and we scarcely thank those who, by realistic descriptions, succeed in exhibiting before us its actual horrors.

16–23. JESUS IS MOCKED BY THE SOLDIERS, AND IS LED TO THE PLACE OF CRUCIFIXION. *Parallels,* Matt. 27 : 27–34; Luke 23 : 26–33; John 19 : 2–17.—Luke omits the mocking by the soldiers, and adds an ac-

count of what Jesus said to certain women who followed on the way to the place of death. John adds the last, but futile, effort of Pilate to secure the release of Jesus.

16–19. The soldiers are soldiers of the Roman army; not themselves Romans, but mercenary soldiers, of whatever kind or origin. Many of these, at least, were coarse and degraded in the extreme. Into their hands the prisoner condemned to crucifixion appears to have gone, that he might be **led** to his death; but in this case they resolved to have some sport out of him before he died. Such mockings were frequent, but this was a rare opportunity, for here was one who could be mocked as a disappointed and discrowned King.— **Into the hall called Prætorium.** Rather, "within the court, which is the Prætorium." The word originally denoted the tent or temporary abode of the prætor, the general; then the official residence of the governor of a province; then the barracks attached to the governor's residence. It was sometimes used of any fine house, as "palace" now is. Here it denotes the barracks, the place where the soldiers lived. Into this place (literally, "within" it) they took their victim for abuse.—How many were at first concerned we are not told; but they brought together **the whole band,** or cohort, so far as they were within reach and at liberty, to see the sport. This mocking resembles the earlier one (chap. 14 : 65) in outward appearance, but is to be distinguished from it. That was a Jewish mocking, this a Gentile; that was in the presence of the Sanhedrin, and perhaps some of the members had part in it—and in that the Jewish authorities rejected and insulted their own Messiah—but this was the reckless, unmeaning work of rough barbarians, executing the will of enemies to Jesus, but themselves simply stupid, heartless, and cruel. To Jesus himself, that was rejection, and this was abandonment; that had to do with the transactions that procured his death, this was but an incident, not a decisive element, in his way to death. In heart and motive the mocking of the soldiers was far less guilty than that of the Sanhedrists. In the same strain Jesus said to Pilate, "He that delivered me unto thee"—*i. e.* the high priest, representative of the theocracy and the highly-privileged — "hath the greater sin."—The **purple** robe was a soldier's cloak cast about him in mocking suggestion of the idea of royalty.—But more clearly was that idea satirized and ridiculed in the **crown**—a wreath woven or twisted from some thorny vine which cannot be very positively identified. It is commonly taken to be the *Zizyphus spina Christi*, "known locally as the *nebk*, a shrub growing plentifully in the valley of the Jordan, with branches pliant and flexible, and leaves of a dark glossy green like the ivy, and sharp prickly thorns. The shrub was likely enough to be found in the garden attached to the Prætorium" (*Plumptre*). Out of such material was made a caricature, but a painful one, of a kingly crown.—Matthew adds that they put a reed in his right hand. The word is too vague for close definition, but the reed was meant for a mock-sceptre.— All this was simply a mock-coronation for him who was understood to be claiming even yet to be a king. But is he less a King for having worn the crown of sorrow? Nay, but more. The **crown of thorns** is the crown of an endless dominion over men. "*Via crucis, via lucis*" ("The way of the cross, the way of light") (Phil. 2:5-11).—**And began to salute him**— "kneel to him," Matthew—**Hail, King of the Jews!** saluting with his title the newly-crowned Sovereign. In the Jewish derision the taunt was, "Prophesy unto us, thou Christ;" the Gentiles call him **King of the Jews**—a touch of truth and naturalness in the titles. The soldiers doubtless felt an additional delight in the name they chose, because by the use of it they were insulting the Jews as well as Jesus.—The sceptre they had given him they now took away, to abuse him with it. His tied hands could scarcely hold it, and they took it and struck him with it **on the head**, driving the thorns into his flesh.—Then they **did spit upon him** while they knelt before him with their false adoration.—All the verbs in verse 19 are in the imperfect tense, indicating that the acts were performed repeatedly: thus they smote him again and again on the head, and more than once knelt before him, spitting upon him as they did so, repeating their cruelty and insult as long as they would.

Is not the striking fact in all this mockery that we can see so little a way into the thoughts of Jesus? The scene is external to him. With the most vivid description (like that of Farrar), still he moves through the scene a silent figure, suffering in mysterious majesty. All that we really behold is One who is absolutely surrendering himself to endure all, even to the end, and who, "like a sheep dumb before his shearers, opened not his mouth." In Tischendorf's Greek text there is the record of fifty-three words spoken by him before Annas, of twenty-four before Caiaphas, of thirty-three before the full Sanhedrin, and of one hundred and two in two private interviews with Pilate. The whole could easily be spoken in the space of two minutes. Against these, remember the long silences before Caiaphas, Herod, Pilate, and the total silence through the scourging and the two derisions. By his own dignity and patience his thoughts are closed to us. We see the scene move on about him, and the men who wrong and torment him we can understand; but the soul of the sufferer himself is, as it were, veiled.

It is here that John (19:4-15) tells of a final effort on the part of Pilate to save the life of Jesus—an effort in which new motives appear, blended with the ones that are already familiar. First is pity: he leads forth the sufferer and shows him to the people, saying, "Behold the man," that they may feel that he has endured enough and may at last be willing to let him go. Then he hears that Jesus has claimed to be the Son of God; at which fears, half superstitious, arise in his mind, and he takes Jesus aside to question him as to whence and what he is. Jesus tells him nothing, but a strange fear abides with him and prompts fresh efforts for release. He again tries to rally the national feeling to Jesus as the King of the Jews, but is thwarted by their absolute renunciation of national hope and acceptance of Cæsar as their only king. They have already warned Pilate that to let Jesus go would be taken as disloyalty to Cæsar; and now, when they cry, "We have no king but Cæsar," he yields and gives Jesus over to their will. This entire effort on the part of Pilate took place some time after he had "washed his hands of the whole matter:" his conscience would not let him rest, even though he had seemed to clear himself of responsibility. The feeling of all later time—that Pilate could not, and did not, wash away his own responsibility and guilt—was already Pilate's own feeling. Of his subsequent history little is really known, but tradition has represented his later years as embittered by intolerable and incurable remorse for this one terrible act.

20. The soldiers were satisfied at length with their cruel sport, and **took off** the robes of mock-royalty, that they might proceed in earnest toward his death.—All that we know of **his**

20 And when they had mocked[a] him, they took off the purple from him, and put his own clothes on him, and led him out to crucify him.

21 And they compel one Simon a Cyrenian, who passed by, coming out of the country, the father of Alexander and Rufus, to bear his cross.

20 And when they had mocked him, they took off from him the purple, and put on him his garments. And they lead him out to crucify him.

21 And they [1]compel one passing by, Simon of Cyrene, coming from the country, the father of Alexander and Rufus, to go *with them,* that he might bear his

a ch. 10 : 34; Job 13 : 9 ; Ps. 35 : 16 ; Matt. 20 : 19 ; Luke 22 : 63 ; 23 : 11, 36.——1 Gr. *impress.*

own clothes, which they now put upon him again, relates to the under-coat (*chitōn*), which John tells us was seamless and " woven from the top throughout " (John 19 : 23). It was a coat, not a " robe," that was seamless. If we judge from the description that Josephus gives of a similar garment for the high priest (*Ant.* 3. 7. 4), we shall infer that this tunic, or under-coat, was intended to be drawn on over the head—a process how painful, after the scourging and the other abuse, we forbear to imagine.—When the victim was again dressed, they **led him out** on the way to death. But it was nothing new : to him the life of the last year had been avowedly the way to death (Matt. 16 : 21) ; and much longer, in his own heart, had he been looking toward the cross. He "came," in fact, "to give his life a ransom for many" (Mark 10 : 45). It was known from eternity that when God should be incarnate in a sinful race, the Incarnate One would be killed by the rage of sin. It was known, also, that only by means of such death could the counsel of saving love be fulfilled and the Incarnate God become a perfect Saviour. So the cross was no surprise to him who endured it, and the actual experience was only the fulfilment of his constant expectations.

21. John says that Jesus "went out bearing the cross for himself," the customary way for criminals to go to their death. (See Matt. 10 : 38, where this moment is anticipated and the lot of the disciple, in fellowship with the Master's sufferings, is pointed out.) But the synoptists all tell how the cross was laid upon another, to be borne after Jesus ; commonly explained by supposing that Jesus was sinking beneath the burden, so that it was feared that he could not carry it to the appointed place. The conjecture is perfectly reasonable, and may be accepted as probably the true explanation. —**They compel.** The word is used only here and at Matt. 27 : 32 (*parallel*) and 5 : 41. It is the word that refers to enforced service exacted by the government. This was an official party, being executioners of the Roman power, and they "impress" this man into their service. —**One Simon,** . . . **who passed by**—*i. e.* one whom they accidentally met.—**A Cyrenian.** Cyrene lay on the southern coast of the Mediterranean, westward from Egypt. Many Jews

dwelt there, who were represented in the assembly on the day of Pentecost (Acts 2 : 10), and among the pioneers of missionary work to the Gentiles (Acts 11 : 20). Men from the same place were among the opponents of Stephen (Acts 6 : 9). —**Coming out of the country** toward the city ; so that the company did not overtake him, but met him. No inferences can be drawn as to the place or the distance from which he had come, except that it is presumable that he was in the city at the time of the passover. on the previous evening.—**The father of Alexander and Rufus.** The only hint of any kind as to the personal life and relations of this Simon ; and this is peculiar to Mark. Whoever Alexander and Rufus may have been — and the names are so common as to reveal nothing of their personality—they must have been well-known men among the earliest readers of Mark's Gospel. There is no Alexander in the New Testament who can be identified with this one ; there is a Rufus in Rom. 16 : 13, whose name suggests some interesting possibilities. Somewhere he had been intimately associated with Paul, and so had his mother, who was regarded by Paul with a truly filial affection : "Salute Rufus chosen in the Lord, and his mother and mine." "Men of Cyrene" were among the founders of the church in Antioch (Acts 11 : 20), where Paul spent, immediately after the church was founded, the first year of his active Christian service. It is a reasonable conjecture that Rufus was one of these, well known among the Christians, and especially among the Gentile Christians, and that Paul's intimacy with him and his mother dated from that time. Moreover, it was to Antioch, just after the end of that first year, that Mark accompanied Paul (Acts 12 : 25) ; and there he may have familiarly known Rufus and his mother, and perhaps Alexander with them.—That Simon was at this time a disciple of Jesus and was laid hold of for that reason is a groundless conjecture ; but that he afterward became a disciple and was widely known as a Christian is implied in Mark's manner of speaking of him.—In the impressing of this man, met by chance, there was something of the same wantonness that had appeared in the derision : there were men enough who might bear the cross, but here

22 And they⁣ bring him unto the place Golgotha, which is, being interpreted, The place of a skull.
23 And they gave him to drink wine mingled with myrrh: but he received it not.

22 cross. And they bring him unto the place Golgotha, which is, being interpreted, The place of a skull.
23 And they offered him wine mingled with myrrh:

a Matt. 27 : 33; Luke 23 : 33; John 19 : 17, etc.

was a chance comer, perhaps odd in garb to the eyes of the soldiers—possibly a slave—and he was the man for their purpose. It would be pleasant to imagine that by this unexpected and unique relation to Jesus the man was brought into the faith.

Here Luke speaks of the multitude that followed, and especially of the women, whose hearts overflowed in tears of pity, and of the Lord's answer to them. He was still the conscious Messiah, knowing himself and knowing what all this meant. No pity would he accept; but he foresaw what this deed would cost, both to the guilty, and to the innocent whose destinies were wrapped up with theirs, and he called for pity upon these, in view of the impending woe.

22. The place of crucifixion is by Matthew and Mark called **Golgotha,** which is interpreted as meaning **The place of a skull.** In John the order is inverted: "A place called the place of a skull, which is called in Hebrew, Golgotha;" in Luke it is simply "the place which is called Calvary"—*i. e.* "The skull." From the Latin word used in the Vulgate to translate *kranion,* "skull"—namely, *calvaria;* used in all the Gospels—comes the popular name "Calvary," which is not, however, in any sense an original or a genuine name for the place.— Why it was called "Golgotha" or "The skull" can only be conjectured. It was not named "The place of skulls," and that fact refutes the theory that it was a spot where skulls of executed criminals lay about; yet the theory needs no refutation, for the Jews would not thus visit a locality so defiled. More plausible is the conjecture that it was a low, round, bare hill. The place is never called a hill, it is true; but this seems the most natural way to account for the name. It should be remembered, however, that localities are constantly named, in popular speech, from passing events or circumstances, and that the names remain when the occasions have long been forgotten. There is no evidence that Golgotha was the common place of execution, and there is a certain amount of evidence against it in the fact that Joseph's garden, or orchard, was close by, or, as John expresses it, "in the place where he was crucified." It has been suggested as possible that the spot was chosen by the priests as a deliberate insult to

Joseph, one of their own Sanhedrin, who had not consented to their deed and was perhaps suspected of a regard for Jesus.—The locality itself is altogether unknown. It was outside the city, as the language of John 19 : 20 proves, and as the writer to the Hebrews assumes that his readers know (Heb. 13 : 12). Researches on the subject have been numerous and persevering, but have developed nothing certain and trustworthy. "The data for anything approaching certainty are wholly wanting; and, in all probability, the actual spot lies buried under the mountainous rubbish-heaps of the ten-times-taken city" (*Farrar*).—The almost complete obliteration of sacred sites in connection with the ministry of our Lord is a fact that cannot fail to have a meaning. The identification of the general scenes of his work is perfect, but minute identifications of particular places fail, in almost every case, to be satisfactory. Christianity is a religion that does not need help from sacred places or from holy relics. The principle of John 4 : 20-24 sets it free from all dependence upon such means of attracting and attaching worshippers to itself. The natural interest of men in sacred places has been sufficiently served, in divine providence, by the remarkable preservation of Palestine in an unchanged state. As for the natural interest of men in relics, it is innocent until it interferes with the service of religion to man: there it is unchristian, and is to be driven out by better knowledge of Christ.

23. The draught that was now offered was a benumbing draught. It was rarely that the Romans did so merciful a deed to a dying criminal, but the Jews had it for a custom thus to relieve the final agonies; and it is said that the wealthy ladies of Jerusalem were accustomed to provide, at their own expense, the stupefying draught for all who were there to be crucified. Matthew calls it "wine mingled with gall;" Mark, **with myrrh.** It is likely that Matthew is more strictly correct, but either name would be understood to refer to the well-known aid to unconsciousness in the sufferer.—Probably the other two sufferers that day took it, but Jesus **received it not.** Matthew, "when he had tasted it, he would not drink." The tasting may have been the act of extreme physical exhaustion and thirst, in which any offer of drink was for the

24 And when they had crucified him, they parted*
his garments, casting lots upon them, what every man
should take.
25 And it was the third hour; and they crucified him.

24 but he received it not. And they crucify him,
and part his garments among them, casting lots
25 upon them, what each should take. And it was the

a Ps. 22 : 18.

moment welcome; in which case, the refusal to do more than taste followed upon the recognition of the purpose of the draught. Or the tasting may have been a recognition of the friendly purpose of those who offered the draught, while the refusal was a declaration that such kindness was not for him. In any case, the refusal expressed his determination to meet death with all his powers in exercise. No opiate should disqualify him either for suffering in obedience to the will of God or for looking up with undimmed vision into his Father's face. We speak of his refusal as "an act of the sublimest heroism" (*Farrar*) : such it is; and yet we may see how instinctively we associate all that is noblest with Jesus, and require it of him, if we ask ourselves how it would have been if he had been willing to die under the influence of some narcotic drug. Would not the whole significance of his death be gone? There would have been self-indulgence and self-sparing in the act, and no longer could we speak of him as giving himself, with perfect self-surrender, to do and suffer for the salvation of man. One who would consent to die that death in stupefaction could be no Saviour.

24-41. THE CRUCIFIXION AND DEATH OF JESUS. *Parallels,* Matt. 27 : 35-56; Luke 23 : 33-49; John 19 : 18-37.

24. Crucified him. Crucifixion was a common form of execution among the Romans, the Carthaginians, and some other nations, which confined it for the most part to slaves and to malefactors of the worst kind. The cross was of various forms, sometimes like an **X**, sometimes like a **T**, and sometimes prolonged like the Latin cross, which is familiar to all modern eyes. In this case the ordinary pictures correctly represent the form, as the fact that the inscription was put "over his head" assures us. The first act in crucifixion was to lay the cross on the ground and nail or bind the victim to it; "the latter was the more painful method, as the sufferer was left to die of hunger." The language of Thomas (John 20 : 25) proves that in this case the body was fastened to the cross by nails. Through the hands the nails were driven, and through the feet, either separately or crossed, Then the cross was raised and set in the hole in the earth that had been dug for it, and the victim was left to his agony. A wooden sup-

port between the legs partly sustained the weight of the body. The cross was not high, as in many pictures of the crucifixion : it was only so high that the victim was raised a little from the earth.—The physical agonies of crucifixion were such that we may well shrink from any attempt to portray them. Victims were sometimes known to linger for nine days on the cross, enduring such a complication of torments as we scarcely have power to imagine. (Whoever wishes a horribly realistic picture of the scene may find it in Farrar's *Life of Christ,* chap. lxi.)—The clothes of the victim were given to the soldiers who did the work of the hour. The soldiers must stay and guard the place, lest there should be even now a rescue of the Crucified One : such was the Roman custom, for rescues were not unknown. The soldiers were four in number (John 19 : 23). A centurion also was present, in charge of them. Whatever there may have been of his clothes they divided into four equal parts, but for the seamless coat (not "robe") they cast lots; in which John saw the fulfilment of David's language in Ps. 22 : 18.—To all the disciples, apparently, the twenty-second psalm stood as an inspired anticipation of this scene, even down to minute details. It is not necessary to suppose that they were at the time aware of the close and startling resemblance, but as they thought it over the fact became plain to them.

25. The mention of the hour is peculiar to Mark. In the Jewish reckoning the hours were counted and numbered from sunrise to sunset, and an hour was a variable division of time, being always a twelfth part of the natural or solar day, which varied with the season. The sixth hour was always at noon, but **the third hour,** *e. g.,* was nearer to noon in the winter than in the summer. In April it was a little earlier than 9 A. M.—Not much is known as to the appliances possessed by the Jews of that age for the measurement of time. It is certain, however, that no watches existed, and that clocks, even of an imperfect kind, were not very numerous. Perfect accuracy in the reporting of the time of day is not to be expected from such men as the apostles, in such circumstances; and there is no reason to suppose that they would be inspired to make more

26 And the superscription of his accusation was written over, THE KING OF THE JEWS.

27 And with him they crucify two thieves; the one on his right hand, and the other on his left.

26 third hour, and they crucified him. And the superscription of his accusation was written over, THE KING OF THE JEWS. And with him they crucify two robbers; one on his right hand, and one on his left.[1]

---

1 Many ancient authorities insert ver. 28 *And the scripture was fulfilled, which saith, And he was reckoned with transgressors.* See Luke xxii. 37.

---

exact statements of the time of day than they were naturally able to make.—John speaks of the hour differently from the synoptists, saying that "about the sixth hour" Jesus was still in the last interview with Pilate. The ordinary explanation is, however, that he was measuring time according to the Roman method, which numbered the hours from midnight to midday.

26. It is uncertain whether it was customary thus to append to the cross the statement of the offender's crime. John calls **the superscription** a *titlos*, the word being the Latin word *titulus* ("a superscription, or title") transferred to the Greek; but evidence is wanting to show that the word was commonly used of such an inscription. There is no indication that such a title was put over the other two crosses.—**The superscription of his accusation.** Rather, "of his crime" or of the cause of his death. The inscription is given in four forms by the four evangelists: Mark, **The King of the Jews;** Luke, "This (is) the King of the Jews;" Matthew, "This is Jesus the King of the Jews;" John, "Jesus the Nazarene the King of the Jews." The difference is partly due, perhaps, to the fact that the inscription was written in three languages (John)—in Hebrew, Latin, and Greek—and that it may thus have been present in various forms to various minds. It is partly due, also, to the fact that the evangelists were not writing in the style of legal documents, and were not striving for absolute accuracy in quotation. All that they cared to do was to record the substance of what was written over their Master's head. Each gave the substance of it as he remembered it, and all to the same effect.—If any one of the four reporters is to be regarded as the most correct here, we would naturally say that it was John, whom we know to have stood close beside the cross (John 19: 26). From him, also, we learn of the complaint of the enemies of Jesus at what Pilate had written for the inscription, as seeming to bear testimony to his real kingship, while they wished only his claim of kingship to go on record, and how Pilate, already angry both at them and at himself, would do nothing to please them and left the inscription as it was. Perhaps his refusal had in it something of the pitying spirit of his plea, "Behold the man;" as if he were unwilling to add anything to the terrible sum of insult that was already heaped upon Jesus. Perhaps, too, there was a lingering conviction that, after all, in a deep but mysterious sense, he truly was a king (John 18 : 37).

27. **And with him they crucify two thieves,** or, rather, "robbers." These have been mentioned already by Luke as conducted with Jesus to the place of crucifixion. He calls them merely "malefactors;" John does not say what they were; in Matthew and Mark, more specifically, they are "robbers," not **thieves,** under which inadequate and misleading name their true character has long been concealed. They were men with a record like that of Barabbas—men who had been engaged in some kind of violence, for which they were now suffering the penalty that according to law they had deserved (Luke 23 : 41).—It is possible, of course, that the violence in which they had taken part was not altogether of the most blameworthy kind, for impulses of the better class sometimes entered into the motives that caused the tumults of those days. In one of the two a better heart did appear, and in such manner as to suggest at least some degree of previous thoughtfulness in the man.—Doubtless it was considered by the priests a happy thought to complete the degradation of the dishonored "King" by thus placing him in death between two violent criminals. The central place was meant for a caricature upon the idea of a place of honor; not unlikely his cross was a little taller than the others. They were willing to exalt him among robbers and to let him enjoy a pre-eminence on the cross.—It is here, where mentioning the actual crucifixion, that Luke records the wonderful saying that fell from the lips of Jesus—"Father, forgive them, for they know not what they do"—uttered, apparently, as they were raising the cross to its position. It was the first of the seven words from the cross, and it was a new voice under the sun that spoke it. The long silence had betokened self-command, but the breaking of the silence showed that the self-command was spiritual and was perfect, no unlovely passion blending with the agony. But here was more than self-command: here was utmost Love, unaltered by utmost outrage and misery, breathing out the spirit of forgiveness even now, and

28 And the scripture* was fulfilled, which saith, And he was numbered with the transgressors.
29 And they* that passed by railed on him, wagging their heads, and saying, Ah, thou* that destroyest the temple, and buildest it in three days,
30 save thyself, and come down from the cross.
31 Likewise also the chief priests, mocking, said among themselves with the scribes, He saved others; himself he cannot save.

29 And they that passed by railed on him, wagging their heads, and saying, Ha! thou that destroyest 30 the ¹temple, and buildest it in three days, save (hy- 31 self, and come down from the cross. In like man- ner also the chief priests mocking *him among them- selves with the scribes said, He saved others; ²him-

a Isa. 53 : 12....*b* Ps. 22 : 7....*e* ch. 14 : 58; John 2 : 19.——1 *Or, sanctuary....*2 *Or, can he not save himself?*

recognizing the ignorance that rendered pardon possible (1 Tim. 1 : 13), though it did not alter the malignity of the sin. (See the same principle in 1 Cor. 2 : 8.)

It was by a natural thought that verse 28 was added, **And the scripture was fulfilled which saith, And he was numbered with the transgressors**, especially since Jesus had said, as he was about going to Gethsemane, that this saying was to be fulfilled in him (Luke 22 : 37). But the verse was unquestionably added by some later hand than that of Mark, and is rightly omitted by the revisers. The falling out of this verse from the text leaves the double quotation in chap. 1 : 2, 3 the only quotation from the prophets made by Mark himself in the whole Gospel.

29-32. Here is a third derision. First the Sanhedrists and then the soldiers mocked him —*i. e.* first the Jews and then the Gentiles— and now a miscellaneous crowd taunts him, in which Jews and Gentiles are both present, but with Jewish voices prevailing. The synoptists all describe this derision in detail, but John mentions it not at all. Luke begins with "the people stood beholding:" he makes the people to be spectators, of whose feeling he says noth- ing (so the best text, represented by the Re- vision), and makes the Sanhedrists and the soldiers the chief tormentors. There is noth- ing inconsistent with this in the other Gos- pels, but Matthew and Mark tell of passers-by who reviled him, picturing (as before us a careless, lounging multitude who seized the opportunity for cruel sport. We must remember that the cross was so low that the sufferer was actually among his tormentors, able to look directly into their eyes, and even liable to abuse from their hands; although of such abuse, in our Saviour's case, there is happily no record.— **They that passed by railed on him, wag- ging their heads.** Shaking their heads in scorn, and perhaps enforcing the expression of their triumph and contempt by gestures and grimaces. (See Ps. 22 : 7.) This, in many, was genuine passionate hatred, and in others it was unbridled wantonness. In either case there would be no limit to the intensity of

their derision.—The interjection (**Ah,** Greek *Oua*) is used here alone in the New Testament, and should perhaps be classed with Mark's quoting of "Ephphatha," and his other quo- tations of the very words. Perhaps the re- visers have represented it in the best way by "Ha!" In the classics, it expresses wonder; here, bitter irony.—The reproach is that which was present in the trial before the Sanhedrin informally assembled. **Thou that destroy- est the temple, and buildest it in three days.** Irony false as well as cruel; but that made no difference to the tormentors. If he had claimed such power, he surely need not be there upon the cross—unless, indeed, he was the deceiver that they called him. One who had made such claims could certainly save himself; and any one who could save himself from such a death would assuredly do it. Who would not **come down from the cross** if he had the power?—This was the taunt of the passers-by—sharp enough and cruel, but far surpassed in sharpness by the next, cutting and cruel both from its source and from its substance. The group is sketched by Matthew and Mark. **Likewise also the chief priests, mocking, said among them- selves with the scribes.** Matthew, "and elders." This was not addressed to Jesus; it was a mocking conversation, loud enough, no doubt, for him to overhear; an insulting by- play between the religious leaders of Israel, re- vealing their utter hardness and heartlessness by "mocking him among themselves," as in the Revision, for their common amusement. But sharper was their derision in itself than even their personality could have made it.— **He saved others; himself he cannot save** —a charge in which even the tenderness and the power that were so abundantly manifested in his works were turned against him. "Is all that power of no avail to him now in his ex- tremity?" To one who heard would arise the remembrance of his innumerable acts of heal- ing, and of those whom he had called back from death; "and yet he cannot save him- self"! There seems to be implied a suspicion that there must be something wrong about

32 Let Christ the King of Israel descend now from the cross, that we may see,* and believe. And they that were crucified with him reviled him.

32 self he cannot save. Let the Christ, the King of Israel, now come down from the cross, that we may see and believe. And they that were crucified with him reproached him.

a Rom. 3 : 3 ; 2 Tim. 2 : 13.

power that thus deserts its possessor in time of need—either a hint of fraud in the mighty works, or almost a renewal of the old accusation, "He casteth out demons through the prince of the demons." "If his power deserts him now, it is condemned as evil power." According to Matthew, the revilers added the appropriate conclusion to this charge, quoting loosely, but unmistakably, from the twenty-second psalm: "He trusted in God; let him deliver him now" (full emphasis on "now"), "if he desireth him: for he said, I am the Son of God." This desertion to suffering and death was, in their sight, a perfect proof that there could be no friendship or fellowship between the sufferer and God. This complete desertion could have only one significance; and the men who believed themselves to be God's favorites were gloating over God's conclusive desertion and rejection of the one who had claimed him as his Father.—And they added, according to Matthew and Mark, the specific demand, **Let Christ the King of Israel descend now from the cross, that we may see, and believe,** emphasizing again the **now,** as if this were the very moment when he might win their faith by such a display of power.—The demand that he should **come down from the cross** was not an unreasonable demand, from his enemies' point of view; that would be giving Israel something like what they wanted in their Messiah. He had persisted in giving them what they did not want; but this, being of the nature of a convincing sign, would be evidence of the kind that they delighted in. To refuse it, if it was within his power, would be to cast discredit, not only on his ability, but on his wisdom—even on his common sense—and on all his claims of connection with God. But this was only the renewal of the old demand for signs, of which a godly heart could feel no need in his presence (Matt. 12 : 38, 39; Mark 8 : 11, 12). Nay, it was a renewal of the temptation of Satan in the wilderness. The language, "If thou be the Son of God" (Matt. 27 : 40), must have instantly recalled that temptation to his mind; this was a new solicitation to prove his Divine Sonship by means of his enemies' choosing. Moreover, it was a renewal of the temptation to obtain power over men by unspiritual means: "If thou therefore wilt worship me,

all shall be thine." We must not think that he was unconscious of the solicitation and its meaning. He recognized, we may be sure, the familiar voice of the temptation, but he was "obedient, unto death."—Not the least touching and impressive part of our Saviour's endurance was his willing submission to total misunderstanding. The opinions concerning him that were present about the cross were absolutely false and amounted to complete misrepresentation. Little did any beholder know how morally impossible it was for him to come down from the cross; and the whole of that moral purpose which gave significance to this transaction was unknown or misjudged on every side. Yet he "opened not his mouth," either to remove the misapprehension or to plead for a delay of judgment. He knew himself, his purpose, and his future so well as to be content to wait for other times and better understanding.—Luke adds that the soldiers took part in the derision—i. e. the four who had crucified him, and whose office it was to "watch" him till death should relieve them (Matt. 27 : 36). These came to him, "offering him," or bringing him, vinegar, perhaps tauntingly, holding it out to him, but not putting it to his lips. It was the sour wine that the soldiers drank. Their words repeat the Gentile taunt, as in the second derision, "If thou be the King of the Jews, save thyself." The chief priests said, "the Christ, the King of Israel," but these, "the King of the Jews." —**And they that were crucified with him reviled him.** So Matthew and Mark, who say nothing of the great exception that Luke commemorates. There is no difficulty in supposing that the two began their reviling together, but that one of them came even then to a better mind under the influence of the dying Redeemer.—Throughout this last mocking, as in the others, the sufferer maintained his majestic and triumphant silence—the silence of perfect patience and self-command. It was broken by the second of the words from the cross, the sublime word to the penitent robber, "Verily I say unto thee, To-day shalt thou be with me in paradise" (Luke 21 : 43). What other ever broke such silence with such speech? Here was the Messianic consciousness, not only unclouded, but making the loftiest of its

16

33 And* when the sixth hour was come, there was darkness over the whole land until the ninth hour.
34 And at the ninth hour Jesus cried with a loud voice, saying, Eloi,*b Eloi, lama sabachthani? which is, being interpreted, My God, my God, why hast thou forsaken me?*c

33 And when the sixth hour was come, there was darkness over the whole ¹land until the ninth hour.
34 And at the ninth hour Jesus cried with a loud voice, Eloi, Eloi, lama sabachthani? which is, being interpreted, My God, my God, ²why hast thou forsaken me?

a Matt. 27 : 45; Luke 23 : 44....b Ps. 22 : 1....c Ps. 42 : 9; 71 : 11; Lam. 1 : 12.——1 Or, earth....2 Or, why didst thou forsake me?

utterances: no other word of the Christ surpasses this in directness and boldness of self-assertion. And there was never a passing doubt in the mind of Jesus that he was accepted in the sight of his Father and about to enter into his Father's glory and his own. In truth, he was making of the cross itself the throne and the judgment-seat. How triumphant a response to the hatred that wished to degrade him by placing him between two robbers!—Here, also, according to John, we are to place the third of the words from the cross: "Woman, behold thy son; behold thy mother," by which he completed the last duty that sprang from his personal human relations, giving his mother into the care of his disciple. Here was

"A heart at leisure from itself
To soothe and sympathize."

33. Of the **darkness,** mentioned by all the synoptists, no natural explanation is to be given, except that Matthew says there was a great earthquake; and such disturbances of nature are often accompanied by an unwonted gloom. This, however, is only a hint provided us, not an explanation. The evangelists apparently intend to represent it as a supernatural event, a silent expression of sympathy from inanimate nature, more tender than man. Here we must leave it. An eclipse of the sun it was not, since the passover fell at the time of the full moon, and such eclipses are impossible when the moon is at the full. It is best regarded simply as a work of God, a miracle of sympathy, intended to symbolize the divine estimate of the horribleness of this deed and to shame and silence the wicked license of men.—Of the extent of the darkness it is impossible to speak, for the phrase **over the whole land** is too indefinite to guide us. The meaning certainly is not "over the whole earth," or contemporary history would show some confirmatory evidence. Whatever ignorance may remain upon the subject, the heart feels the fitness of such a sign of sympathy. When we perceive the significance of this death—the Just for the unjust; the Good Shepherd giving his life for the sheep; the chastisement of our peace falling upon him; the Incarnate God dying to save

the race that he had made—we are ready to consent to such a sign, and say,

"Well might the sun in darkness hide,
And shut his glories in."

According to all the three, the darkness continued from **the sixth hour until the ninth hour**—i. e. from midday till about three o'clock. We must again remember the difficulty of making exact measurements of time, and must not assume that these are meant for mathematically correct statements.—Of what was said and done during the time of the darkness nothing is told. The natural impression is that with the darkness there fell a silence upon the place. It seems quite certain that during these hours Jesus suffered in silence, and almost equally certain that now his tormentors were still and the noise of the crowd was hushed. The darkness served as a mantle for the sufferer, to cover him from the scoffing and violence of his enemies. It came, we may almost say, as a response to the heartless taunt, "He trusted in God; let him deliver him now, if he desireth him." From their cruel hands and tongues at least, he did deliver him.

34. At the ninth hour the darkness ended, and just as it was departing it seems to have been that Jesus spoke again. More than once already had the language of the twenty-second psalm been brought to mind by the events of the day—to his mind, no doubt, as well as to other minds. The piercing of his hands and feet, the division of his garments among the soldiers, the casting of lots upon his coat, and the insulting words and looks about him, must have reminded him of it, but especially the quotation of his enemies from it, the making of which was itself a fulfilment of the prophecy of the psalm. (Compare the language of Ps. 22 : 7, 8.) The attitude of his tormentors around him and the nature of his own misery corresponded exactly to the imagery of the psalm, and it would have been strange if his mind were not by this time dwelling upon that familiar language, now terribly fulfilled.—His cry was a literal quotation of the first sentence of that psalm. **My God, my God, why hast thou forsaken me?** Matthew and Mark cite the Hebrew words, or rather the Aramaic. Mark gives **Eloi** instead of " Eli," Eloi being the Syriac form. Mark is accustomed to give the very words, but in this case it would seem, from the play upon the word mentioned in the next verse, that Matthew's form must have been the correct one. Luke and John omit this utterance, John, perhaps, because he was no longer present, having taken the mother of Jesus away from the scene of agony (John 19 : 27). While Matthew and Mark preserve it, it is singular that this is the only one of the words from the cross that they do record.

The cry itself reveals unfathomable depths. A full explanation of it is impossible to man, and must remain so; for the humanity of Christ himself is the only humanity that can ever be adequate to the mystery of divine suffering. This cry seems to represent the Saviour's spiritual agony at its very deepest, and as we study it its meaning and its mystery grow deeper before our eyes. Some things about it, however, are certain. It was not extorted from our Saviour by an actual desertion on the part of his Father, a changing of his Father's feeling toward him from love and approval to wrath. Note the meaning of the following passages: "I came down from heaven, not to do mine own will, but the will of him that sent me" (John 6 : 38); "He that sent me is with me; the Father hath not left me alone; for I do always those things that please him" (John 8 : 29); "Therefore doth my Father love me, because I lay down my life, that I might take it again" (John 10 : 17). This was the moment of that laying down of his life which his Father had appointed to him, and for which his Father loved him. It is morally impossible that at the supreme moment of his perfect obedience God turned away from him in wrath. Any wrath that could have been directed against him at that moment, or indeed at any other, could have been only a seeming wrath: God really approved of him. But the untrue appearance of anger is impossible to God, and so is real anger against a righteous being. We cannot say that God supposed him to be guilty and was therefore angry at him, this temporary anger being a part of the plan. God never supposes anything that is not true, and never feels anger at any one who does not deserve it. To suppose that such temporary anger against Jesus in the moment of his perfect obedience was planned is "to introduce the profoundest unreality into the relations of the Father and the Son" (A. M. Fairbairn's *Studies in the Life of Christ*, p. 325) and into the whole method of divine grace in saving sinners. No true heart can plan to be angry at a given time at a being who is only supposed to be deserving

of anger; least of all can God. Nor do the Scriptures assert that God was angry at Jesus then. His wrath is assumed by many as the explanation of this cry of sorrow, but the belief in it rests wholly upon inference.

What, then, is the explanation of the cry? We must seek it in such facts as the following. (1) There was then in his soul a suffering on account of sin sorer than any that ever was or can be endured by any other of woman born. No penal suffering can approach it in intensity. The sinfulness of the human race had brought him to the cross. Not merely the malice of individuals, but the entire sum of human sinfulness, had had to do with bringing him thither. He was suffering in order that he might remove the sinfulness of men; and, with the sensitiveness of perfect righteousness and of immeasurable pity, he felt the horribleness and curse of sin. But sin was now expressing itself against him in the form of extremest outrage against righteousness and love. It was a dreadful reality, forcing home its utmost malignity upon the manifested God. In penal suffering sin bears its fruit in souls that are morally corrupted and weakened; but here sin was forcing its evil on One who was the Incarnate Holiness and Love. The suffering that it caused him was not, strictly, penal suffering; but in his perfect righteousness, his intense sympathy of love toward man, and his sensibility to good and evil, never dulled by sin, there lay the secret of a suffering sharper than penal suffering can ever be. The driving of the nails through his flesh was but the outward symbol of what sin was doing to his soul. It surely was of God's will that he was suffering thus, and thus alone. This was a part of that which "it pleased the Lord" (Isa. 53 : 10) to lay upon him—a part of "the cup which his Father had given him" (John 18 : 11). A suffering that reached less far than this would not have sufficed to "make the Captain of our salvation perfect" (Heb. 2 : 10) or to complete his perfect offering of himself (Heb. 9 : 14). (2) If we look at the solitariness of this suffering, and ask how it was possible for Christ thus to feel himself forsaken as the Psalmist did, the general answer is that in this final agony our Saviour's sense of his unity with God was overpowered by his sense of his unity with sinful men. These two unities were the Godward and manward aspects of his essential being. His unity with God was due to his place in the Godhead as the Word which in the beginning was with God and was God; his unity with men was due to the fact that in him the Word had become flesh—*i. e.*, had entered into human life and limitations, so that he who was the Word was also truly and equally a human being. Such unity with men was possible because man was made in the image of God (Gen. 1 : 27; James 3 : 9). The Word was the image of God (Heb. 1 : 3; Col. 1 : 15), and therefore the archetype of man; hence the Word, when incarnate, was truly the brother of man (Matt. 25 : 40; John 20 : 17), while yet he did not cease to be the Son of God (Matt. 11 : 27; John 10 : 30). His unity with God and his unity with men were equal, and the very nature of his being constituted him the Mediator, uniting God and men, able to feel with both and act for both. Through his life these two unities seem to have remained, if one may so speak, in equipoise. But in this final agony his unity with God and his unity with men conspired so to roll upon his consciousness the whole burden of human sin as that the sense of the divine unity could scarce remain for his comfort. (a) His unity with men. They were killing him because he was good. Sin was doing its worst, breaking forth as uncontrollable rage against holiness and love. It was godlessness, malignity, deicide—the scornful, wrathful rejection of the character, kingdom, and work of God. The entire sum of human sinfulness had had to do with bringing him to the cross, and the vastness and guilt of that sinfulness were fearfully present to him. Yet it was not sin that was foreign to him, in which he felt no personal concern. He had cast in his lot with men in a unity so true and vital that by virtue of it he "bore our griefs, and carried our sorrows" (Isa. 53 : 4; Matt. 8 : 17), and "bore our sins" (1 Pet. 2 : 24). This unity with men, though undefinable in human terms, was terribly and gloriously real. It finds partial analogies in the closest human relations, especially in that of parent and child. Not mere sympathy, but unity of life, brought the whole burden of the world's sin upon his consciousness. What was ours was his that what was his might be ours. (b) His unity with God. At the same time, he was the image of the Godhead, in whom all the moral affections and judgments of God were most truly present. Hence he was perfectly one with God in his estimate of the sin that he was bearing. He shared to the full in God's just and necessary wrath against it. His whole being abhorred and condemned it, even while his unity with men had so terribly involved him in it. His filial relation, too, gave him a peculiar horror at the sin of man in violating a filial relation intended by the Creator to be perfected in a sonship so like his own. His perfect filial holiness was absolutely condemning, in unity with his Father, the sin with which, in unity with his brethren, his soul was weighed down. Thus his unity with God brought him no relief, but only intensified his woe and helped to take away the sense of its own preciousness, The sense of his unity with men overpowered the sense of his unity with God and brought the whole burden of the world's sin upon his consciousness, leaving him with no consciousness of the helpful presence of his Father. (3) This may be plainer if we remember that he was living, doing, and suffering within the limits of humanity. He was "in all things made like unto his brethren" (Heb. 2 : 17), and no divine power of his was ever called in to make his burden lighter. As the truth that he taught had to be apprehended by his human powers before he as Mediator was ready to declare it (see Dr. Hovey's God with Us, p. 75), so all the holiness, love, labor, humiliation, and agony that his mission involved had to be accepted and appropriated by human powers and sinlessly wrought out within the limits of humanity. The more naturally, therefore, might the sense of his unity with sinful men sweep away the sense of his unity with God in this dreadful time and leave him to feel himself alone in his agony. Thus our Saviour appears in real community of experience with the devoutest of his brethren, though suffering immeasurably beyond them. His suffering, mysterious though it was, was not endured in an essentially different world from ours. The cry that he borrowed from the Psalmist he used in essentially the same sense as the Psalmist, to whom it meant, "Why hast thou allowed me to suffer without the sense of thy helpful presence?" See also the experience of Job (18 : 6-9; 23 : 3-9) and of Jeremiah (20 : 7-9, 14-18), and compare what Paul says of "the fellowship of his sufferings" and conformity to his death. He stands as our great Example in his filial faithfulness in the darkness. Even this loneliness did not shake his confidence in his Father or weaken the claim of his heart upon him; still did he call him "my God, my God." Like the Psalmist, too, and Job and Jeremiah, he found the period of darkness short, the light of God quickly returning to the soul that in the darkness had been true.

The significance of the cross in connection with redemption has not been too much dwelt upon, but the significance of the cross by way of example has been too much overlooked. See 1 Peter 2 : 21-24 for the example of Christ in death as well as in the suffering that preceded. See also Phil. 2 : 5-8.

35 And some of them that stood by, when they heard *it*, said, Behold, he calleth Elias.

36 And one ran and filled a sponge full of vinegar, and put *it* on a reed, and gave² him to drink, saying, Let alone; let us see whether Elias will come to take him down.

37 And⁶ Jesus cried with a loud voice, and gave up the ghost.

35 me? And some of them that stood by, when they 36 heard it, said, Behold, he calleth Elijah. And one ran, and filling a sponge full of vinegar, put it on a reed, and gave him to drink, saying, Let be; let us 37 see whether Elijah cometh to take him down. And Jesus uttered a loud voice, and gave up the ghost.

a Ps. 69 : 21....*b* Matt. 27 : 50; Luke 23 : 46.

35, 36. To the soldiers the quoted words would be unmeaning, but to the chief priests and to others trained in the Hebrew Scriptures they were plain. No Sanhedrist failed to recognize the passage. But some pretended not to recognize it, and to think that the **Eli** was meant for **Elias**. The popular expectation of Elijah in connection with the Messiah made this another insulting thrust at Jesus as claiming the Messiahship: "The Christ is calling upon his predicted fellow-messenger!" So the scoffing voices had been stilled, but not silenced, by the darkness, and broke out afresh when it was removed.—Here, just as the scoffing was renewed, we must place that which John gives as the fifth word from the cross, "I thirst," uttered, as John asserts, in perfect self-possession, from the consciousness that this was a part of his predicted course.—It was in response to this utterance—not a cry, but uttered in tones of genuine physical exhaustion—that the **vinegar** was offered to him. The offering of it was an act of kindness by one unknown, probably one of the soldiers. It was no drugged wine, but the common sour wine that the soldiers drank. The coincidence with Ps. 69 : 21 is merely external.—**On a reed.** John, "upon hyssop"—*i. e.* the sponge was held out upon a stalk of hyssop, the mouth of Jesus being probably just too high to be reached by the hand.—**Gave him to drink.** And he did not refuse. (Compare John, "when he had received the vinegar.") —Matthew and Mark differ as to the source of the remark. **Let alone; let us see whether Elias will come to take him down,** Mark attributing it to the man himself, and Matthew to the bystanders who had already spoken of Elijah. No doubt the remonstrance arose, as Matthew says, from the bystanders. If the two accounts are to be harmonized, it is quite possible to suppose that the thoughtless soldier fell in with the taunt of the heartless spectators, even while he did a deed of mercy.—In Matthew the query is whether Elijah will come and save him; in Mark, whether Elijah **will come** to **take him down.** It is plain, they think, that he cannot come down from the cross himself, but perhaps when he is helpless he can have Elijah's help; and so they wish the sol-

dier to let him alone and put his supposed expectations to the test.

37. In Matthew and Mark only the utterance of a loud voice is mentioned; in Luke and John the sixth and seventh of the seven words from the cross are introduced. It is impossible to determine, except from internal probability, which of these was the last utterance, though it should be added that Luke's language, "and having said this, he expired," is a little more definite than that of John. Probably the saying recorded by John, "It is finished," was first uttered. It is retrospective and triumphant; it is the final echo of the word that he spoke by anticipation on the previous evening: "I have finished the work which thou gavest me to do." The word recorded by Luke was probably the last, the very dying word: "Father, into thy hands I commend my spirit." This again is a quotation from the Psalms (Ps. 31 : 5, cited almost exactly from the Septuagint, with the addition of "Father"). As an utterance now, it is prospective and trustful; it is the "Return unto thy rest, O my soul;" it is the expression of perfect faith at the moment of death. Remember that this, though it was more, was a genuine human death. As such it is the great example and comfort of the dying, and these final words of faith are an inestimable treasure. In the first recorded Christian death the spirit of this prayer reappears, but the petition is addressed to Christ himself: "Lord Jesus, receive my spirit" (Acts 7 : 59).—We would naturally think of this as a quiet breathing of faith; but it was uttered **with a loud voice.** After the agony and the cry of loneliness, it was fitting that all should know that he was dying in the peace of God.— **And gave up the ghost.** *Exepneusin*, used by Mark and Luke, is the exact equivalent of "he expired"—*i. e.,* simply, "he died." It is extremely unfortunate that the phrase in the received version should be retained in the Revision. The only other word of description is that of John, "he bowed his head."

Jesus died voluntarily. (See John 10 : 18: "No one taketh it"—*i. e.* my life—"from me, but I lay it down of myself.") In a real sense, his death was his own act. This is not to be taken, however, as meaning that on the cross

38 And the vail of the temple was rent in twain, from the top to the bottom.

38 And the veil of the ¹temple was rent in twain from the top to the bottom.

1 Or, *sanctuary*

he put an end to his life by an act of his will, or, in plain language, committed suicide. His death had its adequate physical causes, like any other death. He did not hasten it by miracle, and he could not have escaped or delayed it without miracle. He suffered unto death. But the shortness of the time that he spent on the cross proves (see note on verse 44) that he did not die the ordinary death of the crucified. The physical torture, severe as it was, was not the sole cause of his death. He died of his agony, the inward woe and struggle of his soul—that is to say, he died directly in consequence of his agony respecting sin. The suffering was accepted in perfect submission to the divine will, and was perfectly endured; but it was such as humanity could not endure without being rent asunder, spirit from body. He undertook to endure it, and did endure, until it killed him. He "became obedient, unto death."—As to the physical cause of his death, they are not to be envied who have fixed their eyes so closely upon it as to be able to write whole books on the subject; but there appears to be much in favor of the theory that he died directly from rupture of the vessels of the heart—a mode of death that is known in rare cases to result from extreme mental anguish. There is nothing gained, however, by saying to ourselves that "he died literally of a broken heart." That is a mere play upon words that means nothing and calls our attention away from the main point. That is the tendency, indeed, of the whole discussion of the physical cause of our Saviour's death. The spiritual cause of his death is better worth our days and years of study. He died on account of our sins, that he might be able to deliver us from them. His death is the culmination of the action of his incarnate life. It was all intended to reveal God perfectly, to condemn sin in the sight of the human heart and conscience, to provide efficient means of bringing sinners back to God, and thus to do that which was necessary to the nature of God before he could freely send forth his saving influence upon the world.

38. The object-lesson that corresponds, in the synoptists, to the spoken word in John, "It is finished." **The vail of the temple** was the heavy embroidered curtain that hung between the Holy Place and the Holiest of All. "The vail of the sanctuary" would be a more adequate and significant translation, for it was the

vail that concealed the inner sanctuary of the temple, even from the priests (Ex. 26 : 31–33). The rending of that vail in connection with the death of Jesus (Luke places it just before the death; Matthew and Mark, apparently at the very moment) could be nothing but a miraculous event; certainly it was not a result of the earthquake. The priests alone would see it, but such an event could not be effectually concealed, anxious as they might be to conceal it. It would find its way out among the rumors of the time, and the story would not have taken its place in the records of Christianity if it had not been confirmed by the priests who became obedient unto the faith (Acts 6 : 7). The event was a sign from God. The significance of the "first," or outer, "tabernacle" is set forth in Heb. 9 : 1–10. While it was standing, with the vail between it and the Holiest, "the way into the Holiest was not made manifest;" the symbolic dwelling-place of God was still shut away from men, and the only approach was symbolized by priestly and sacrificial services. The rending of the vail announced the end of the old sacrificial religion, told the priests that their work was done, and declared that the way to God was henceforth freely open to men. Jesus, passing "through the vail, that is to say, his flesh" (Heb. 10 : 20), which alone had intervened between him and the glory of his Father, had now entered as the true High Priest into the true Holy Place, and he had gone as the forerunner of all his people, leaving no vail behind him, no barrier, real or symbolic, in the way of man to God. The temple was henceforth no true sanctuary, and the rending of its vail proclaimed that the space within it was now common ground. (It is well to study here the entire passage in the Epistle to the Hebrews, from 4 : 14 to 10 : 25.)—Yet observe even in this miracle the rational and suggestive method of God with men. He did not destroy the temple, though its legitimate work was done. How easy it would have been to let the earthquake shatter the outer sanctuary just when the vail was rent that concealed the inner! And how ready men would have been to call it an appropriate interposition! He did not destroy the temple, but he did give to the nation that held it sacred, and especially to the priests who held it most sacred, a most significant and impressive hint, a help to thought and to conviction, a means of learning for themselves that the way to God

39 ¶ And when the centurion, which stood over against him, saw that he so cried out, and gave up the ghost, he said, Truly this man was the Son of God.
40 There were also women looking on afar[1] off; among whom was Mary Magdalene, and Mary the mother of James the less and of Joses, and Salome;
41 (Who also, when he was in Galilee, followed him, and ministered[a] unto him;) and many other women which came up with him unto Jerusalem.

39 the top to the bottom. And when the centurion, who stood by over against him, saw that he so gave up the ghost, he said, Truly this man was the Son of God. And there were also women beholding from afar: among whom were both Mary Magdalene, and Mary the mother of 40 James the less and of 41 Joses, and Salome; who, when he was in Galilee, followed him, and ministered unto him; and many other women that came up with him unto Jerusalem.

a Ps. 38 : 11....b Luke 8 : 2, 3.——1 Many ancient authorities read so cried out, and gave up the ghost....2 Or, a son of God....3 Gr. little.

was open. He spoke to them in symbol that they might think and understand, appealing, as he always does, to the rational power in man. —No one of the evangelists offers any explanation of this symbol, whence some have inferred that they did not understand it. Better infer that they supposed every one would understand it; although this is not to deny that even to them it might seem still more profoundly significant after the overthrow of Jerusalem.

Here Matthew speaks of the earthquake, the rending of the rocks, and the opening of the graves, and adds the unexplained record of the coming forth of saints from their graves after the resurrection of Jesus.

39. The centurion. Here is one of Mark's Latinisms, for he borrows the Latin word *centurio* (*kenturion*), while Matthew and Luke use the customary Greek word. He was the officer in charge of the crucifixion, who had **stood over against him**, where he could see everything, as his duty was.—The best text omits **that he so cried out**, and reads, "when the centurion . . . saw that he thus expired"—*i. e.* with such more than human dignity, and with such amazing signs in nature about him. Matthew, "seeing the earthquake, and the things that were done;" Luke, simply, "seeing that which was done." Matthew joins with the centurion the others who were watching Jesus with him—*i. e.* the soldiers. Luke, in the following verse, tells of the profound impression that was made on the spectators generally by the awful scene.—**Truly this man was the Son of God.** Luke, "Really righteous was this man;" Matthew like Mark, with the omission of "man." The revisers rightly give "a son of God" as an alternative translation. The centurion probably spoke in Latin, where there is no definite article; the *Filius Dei* (**Son of God**) that he uttered would bear either meaning. It is impossible to tell exactly what his thought was—whether he meant "the Son" or "a son," "God" or "a god." Possibly, Luke, aware of this ambiguity in the language of the heathen Roman, but knowing that he meant it as a genuine tribute of reverence, may have intention-ally given the moral significance of the remark instead of its precise form. The centurion had been hearing the title **Son of God** applied in scoffing to the sufferer, and, though ignorant, yet with a truer heart than that of the Jews, he assented to it as a title that was well deserved. Yet with him it could scarcely mean much more than "this man was righteous."—It has been observed that all the centurions in the New Testament appear at good advantage, candor and kindness having been manifested in some form by them all.

40, 41. All the synoptists mention this group of women, Luke without enumeration of their names. Luke has a similar group (or, more strictly, the same) at chap. 8 : 2, 3, with some names enumerated. Here three are mentioned as belonging to the company that **followed him, when he was in Galilee, and ministered unto him** (Luke 8 : 3, "ministered to him of their substance"), and **many other women** are mentioned (by Mark alone) as having come **up with him unto Jerusalem.** —They stood **afar off** (so all the synoptists), looking on, and with them (Luke) were "all his acquaintance"—*i. e.* the group contained generally those of his friends who were present in Jerusalem. Of course the mention of this group, being introduced after the record of his death, relates to no single moment, and does not imply that the same persons were together during the whole time of the crucifixion. John has already spoken of all whose names are given here as standing earlier "beside the cross." It is a touching fact that the mother of Jesus appears only there, beside the cross, and not among those who stood **afar off.—Mary Magdalene.** Now earliest mentioned, except in Luke 8 : 2. Her connection with her Lord began, as that passage leads us to believe, with his act in casting out of her "seven demons"— *i. e.* in relieving her of some specially severe form of demoniacal possession; for there is no good reason to spiritualize the healing, as James Freeman Clarke has done (*The Legend of Thomas Didymus*) into the deliverance from falsehood, murder, pride, luxury, selfishness, unbe-

42 ᶜ And now when the even was come, because it was the Preparation, that is, the day before the sabbath,

43 Joseph of Arimathæa, an honorable counsellor, which also waited* for the kingdom of God, came, and went in boldly unto Pilate, and craved the body of Jesus.

42 And when even was now come, because it was the
43 Preparation, that is, the day before the sabbath, there came Joseph of Arimathæa, a councillor of honorable estate, who also himself was looking for the kingdom of God; and he boldly went in unto Pilate,

a Luke 2 : 25; Tit. 2 : 13.

lief, and despair. There is no evidence for identifying her with any other Mary of the Gospels or to cast doubt on the purity of her life. The most probable derivation of her name is from " Magdala," or " Migdol," " the watch-tower," a town on the shore of Lake Gennesaret. After the healing she became one of the " ministering women ;" but her recorded connection with her Lord has to do mainly with the scenes of his death and resurrection.— **Mary the mother of James the less,** or the little. Probably a descriptive name, given because he, like Zacchæus, was small of stature. —**And of Joses.** (See note on Mark 3 : 18.) There are unanswered questions about this family group, but it seems most probable that the James and Joses here mentioned are not to be identified with those who appear among the " brethren of the Lord " at Mark 6 : 3.—**Salome** is to be identified with "the mother of Zebedee's children " in the parallel passage in Matthew, and probably with the sister of our Lord's mother in John 19 : 25. (See note on Mark 3 : 17.)

Between the record of the death and that of the descent from the cross John inserts the narrative, which he alone has preserved, of the breaking of the legs of the two robbers, in order to hasten their death before the beginning of the Jewish Sabbath, and of the piercing of the side of Jesus with the soldier's spear, in order to test the reality of his death, or rather to decide the question, if there was any doubt. It is from the outflow of "blood and water" that the inference is drawn respecting the physical cause of his death.

42–47. THE DESCENT FROM THE CROSS, AND THE BURIAL OF JESUS. *Parallels,* Matt. 27 : 57–61; Luke 23 : 50–56; John 19 : 38–42.

42. The natural inference is that the death occurred not long after the ninth hour—*i. e.* at between three and four o'clock by our reckoning. The Sabbath would begin at sunset. It was common enough for the Romans to leave the bodies of the crucified on the cross—indeed, they often remained there till they were devoured by birds or fell to pieces in decay—but this execution had taken place under Jewish auspices, and the Jews would not be willing, in

view of the prohibition in Deut. 21 : 23, that the body of Jesus should remain all night on the cross, and still less over the Sabbath, which, as the Sabbath of the passover week, was "a great day" (John 19 : 31).—**The Preparation, that is, the day before the sabbath.** A valuable definition, because it removes the suspicion that the same word may elsewhere mean the day before the passover.—The time, **when the even was come,** cannot be more closely defined, but it cannot have been long after the death of our Saviour.

43. Joseph of Arimathæa, or " who was from Arimathæa." Mentioned on this occasion only, his name and residence being given by all four evangelists.—Arimathæa is of uncertain site. It is commonly identified with Ramah, or Ramathaim-zophim, the home of Elkanah, the father of Samuel (1 Sam. 1 : 1; 2 : 11)—a place which is known in the Septuagint as "Armathaim." The identification is probably correct, but the site of Ramah has long been in doubt. The best modern theory follows a somewhat ancient tradition in locating it at *Neby Samuel,* about four miles north-west from Jerusalem. This site would satisfy all the requirements of the history, and may be regarded as probably the true one.—Concerning Joseph himself, we learn from Matthew that he was a rich man; from Mark, that he was **an honorable counsellor,** or, more probably, "a counsellor of honorable estate," a rich and prosperous man. Luke as well as Mark calls him a counsellor, which means, here, a member of the council, or Sanhedrin, of the Jews. Luke further calls him " a good man and a just," and adds that " he had not consented to their counsel and deed." Apparently, he had been absent from the meeting; perhaps intentionally omitted from the call, perhaps absent at daybreak, when the meeting was held, at his home in Arimathæa.—Concerning his relations to Jesus, we have in Mark and Luke that he **waited,** or was looking, **for the kingdom of God** (compare Luke 2 : 25, 38), by which is meant that he was a devout Jew who delighted in the promises of God concerning his coming kingdom and was expecting their early fulfilment. The phrase does not declare that he was a disciple of Jesus, but it does represent him as

44 And Pilate marvelled if he were already dead: and calling *unto him* the centurion, he asked him whether he had been any while dead.
45 And when he knew *it* of the centurion, he gave the body to Joseph,
46 And he bought fine linen, and took him down, and wrapped him in the linen, and laid him in a sepulchre which was hewn out of a rock, and rolled a stone[a] unto the door of the sepulchre.

44 and asked for the body of Jesus. And Pilate marvelled if he were already dead: and calling unto him the centurion, he asked him whether he [had] been 45 any while dead. And when he learned it of the cen-46 turion, he granted the corpse to Joseph. And he bought a linen cloth, and taking h..ı down, wound him in the linen cloth, and laid him in a tomb which had been hewn out of a rock; and he rolled

---

a ch. 16 : 3, 4.——l Many ancient authorities read *were already dead.*

---

one of those who were ready for discipleship. Matthew says, however, that he "was a disciple of Jesus," and John says the same, adding, " but secretly, for fear of the Jews." Thus he belonged to the class mentioned in John 12 : 42, 43. Not until now, apparently, had his convictions in favor of Jesus brought him to frank confession. His position was a trying one, and he had not had moral power to conquer its difficulties. But now, "the Lord being merciful unto him," as he was to Lot in Sodom (Gen. 19 : 16), he was brought forth out of his false position, love and sorrow being the messengers that led him forth.—He **came**—*i. e.* to the place of crucifixion. Perhaps the word, standing where it does, indicates that he arrived at the place when Jesus was dying or dead, having only then come into the city from his home. If he had been at Arimathaea since the night before, he may have known nothing of what was going on ; in which case the sudden amazement would swell the tide of his indignation and horror, and easily lead him beyond his former self in devotion to the Crucified One.—The participle does not merely mean **boldly :** it means, "waxing bold," coming to new boldness. The word is peculiar to Mark.— In this new boldness he **went in unto Pilate,** to his house or place of judgment, whither the chief priests would not go for fear of defilement (John 18 : 28). There he **craved**—or, literally, "asked"—**the body of Jesus.** So, identically, the synoptists; John, "asked that he might take away the body of Jesus."

44, 45. The mention of Pilate's wonder and inquiry is peculiar to Mark. Plainly, Pilate did not know of the breaking of the legs of the robbers. Only a few hours had passed, and it seemed impossible that Jesus was dead. Not improbably, there was a shock to Pilate's mind in the tidings : he had honestly wished to save him, and so soon all was over! **Calling unto him the centurion, he asked him whether he had been dead** long (*palai*), not **any while.**—There is a certain rough tenderness in Pilate here ; he would do what he could to preserve the Crucified One from insult and help him to honorable burial ; so, the death being

officially confirmed, **he gave the body** (or, rather, "granted the corpse") **to Joseph.** So the best text : *ptōma,* instead of *sōma.*—Here John adds, " he came therefore, and took away his body." Here, also, John tells of the coming of a helper to Joseph—a man of the same class, a fellow-member of the Sanhedrin, another secret disciple—Nicodemus, who came to Jesus by night (John 3 : 1). His accession now is a surprise to us, but it may not have been to Joseph. He has appeared before only in that nightly conversation, and as pleading for candor in the judgment respecting Jesus, and taunted by his companions as if they already suspected him of a kind of discipleship (John 7 : 50–52). He now brought "a mixture of myrrh and aloes" —*i. e.* of the aromatics used in preparing the dead for burial — "about a hundred pounds weight." This was not necessarily bought beforehand ; speedy burials were common in that land, and rapid preparation must have been common too. Moreover, there is no reason to doubt that Nicodemus knew all the day what was going on. He may have been preparing while Jesus was dying. So there is no reason to suppose, as some have done, that his preparation was parallel to that of Mary of Bethany, made beforehand (Mark 14 : 8).—There is something extremely touching about the coming of these two men to bury the body of him whom they had not publicly confessed when he was alive. The shock of sorrow and indignation quickened love and rendered secret discipleship no longer possible. If the two men were thus drawn to Jesus in his extremest humiliation, it seems likely that by his resurrection their faith would be confirmed and rendered permanent.

46. The **fine linen** was the *sindon,* the same as that mentioned at chap. 14 : 51—a foreign fabric, probably Indian, said to have been used in Egypt as a wrapping for mummies. In later Greek, however, the word means "linen." It can scarcely be said to define positively the nature of the cloth. Mark alone says that it was **bought** now, at the very time when it was to be used.—**Wrapped him in the linen.** The wrapping in this cloth was not a mere enfolding of the body, but, at least in part, the closer

47 And Mary Magdalene and Mary *the mother* of Joses beheld where he was laid.

47 a stone against the door of the tomb And Mary Magdalene and Mary the *mother* of Joses beheld where he was laid.

wrapping or binding (John, "they took the body of Jesus, and wound it in linen clothes with the spices") which was customary among the Jews. When Lazarus came forth, he was "bound hand and foot with grave-clothes" (John 11:44), each limb wrapped up by itself. This wrapping, however, in the case of Jesus, was left unfinished because of haste, the Sabbath coming quickly on.—Observe that the very thought of preparing the body thus for burial was inconsistent with all thought of a resurrection.—Of the site and ownership of the sepulchre Mark tells us nothing, saying merely that

STONE AT MOUTH OF SEPULCHRE.

it was **hewn out of a rock,** or, rather, "out of the rock"—*i. e,* not a natural cavern, such as were frequently used for tombs. Matthew and Luke note the same fact, Luke using a word (*laxeutos*) that points a little more definitely to the skilful workmanship of which the tomb gave evidence. It was no rude cave in which he was laid, but a carefully-made **sepulchre.** Luke and John tell us that it was new and had never before been used; Matthew, by a single word, that it was the property of Joseph. From John we learn that it was in a "garden" or orchard, an enclosed and cultivated place—the same word that is used of Gethsemane—and

that the garden was "in the place where he was crucified"—*i. e.* close at hand. The nearness of the spot is given by John, who says nothing of Joseph's ownership as the reason for selecting it, the approach of the Sabbath requiring haste.—Having thus placed the body, Joseph **rolled a stone unto,** or against (*epi*) **the door of the sepulchre.** Matthew, "a great stone." The illustration represents the tomb described in the following passage: "In Jerusalem has been found a peculiar tomb. The sloping ground has been cut down perpendicularly and the rock is cut out, so that the front wall is of perpendicular rock. There is a chamber within, containing a table of stone on which to prepare the body for burial and a stone bowl for water. Within this is the tomb itself, an inner chamber, with shelves to receive the bodies. The entrance to this is an opening in the upright rock-wall three feet square. Running across before this opening, at the foot of the wall in which it is made, is a groove in the floor, one foot deep and six inches wide. In this groove is a round stone, six inches thick, just fitting the groove, and four feet or more in diameter—a stone like a grindstone. This runs in the groove, and can be rolled up before the square opening so as to cover it, and rolled away from it so as to give entrance. It is so heavy that the full strength of a man is required to roll it away. If Joseph's new tomb were like this, the women might well ask who should roll away the stone for them." The date of this tomb, however, seems to be unknown, and so high an authority in Jewish customs as Dr. Edersheim appears to know nothing of such structures. (See *Bible Educator,* vol. iv., p. 332.) It is certain that rock-hewn tombs usually had doors of stone that turned on hinges. (See Hackett's *Illustrations of Scripture,* p. 108; Van Lennep's *Bible Lands,* p. 580.) If Joseph's new tomb, perhaps unfinished, had such a door, with its fastenings yet uncompleted, he may, for additional security, have caused a stone so large as to be moved only with difficulty to be rolled up against it, on the outside.

47. The women had remained at the cross when no apostle was there, and now they followed to the sepulchre, where new friends were doing the work that belonged to old. Only two are mentioned here and in Matthew; in

CHAPTER XVI.

AND when the sabbath was past, Mary Magdalene, and Mary the *mother* of James, and Salome, had bought sweet spices,[b] that they might come and anoint him.

2 And very early in the morning, the first *day* of the week, they came unto the sepulchre at the rising of the sun.

1 AND when the sabbath was past, Mary Magdalene, and Mary the *mother* of James, and Salome, bought 2 spices, that they might come and anoint him. And very early on the first day of the week, they come

a Matt. 28 : 1 ; Luke 24 : 1, etc. ; John 20 : 1....*b* Luke 23 : 56.

Luke, the women generally who had followed from Galilee. Matthew shows them "sitting over against the sepulchre;" Mark says that they **beheld where he was laid ;** and Luke shows them present and watchful during the entombment. He also shows them going home and preparing spices to finish the embalming, but not till after the Sabbath. (See the true division of paragraphs in Luke, in the Revision.)—That Sabbath was to be "a high-day" with the Jews; to the disciples it was a day of despair. In truth, it was the turning-point of time, though neither Jews nor disciples knew it. The crime of the Jews and of sinful humanity was completed; the revelation of God as Saviour had been made; the work of preparatory dispensations was ended; all was ready for the breaking forth of the new power of God unto salvation. But that Jewish Sabbath before the dawning of the first Lord's Day was the time of pause and silence; the Prince of Life lay dead, and all hopes seemed disappointed; the new power was as yet unknown and undreamed of in the world. No day was ever like that, or ever shall be.

Matthew adds the record of what was done after the night had passed: the enemies of Jesus secured the placing of the official seal of the governor on the door of the tomb and the setting of a guard there, under pretence of fear that his friends might steal his body and declare that he had risen.

1-8. THE MEETING OF THE WOMEN WITH AN ANGEL AT THE SEPULCHRE, AND THE ANNOUNCEMENT OF THE RESURRECTION OF JESUS. *Parallels*, Matt. 28 : 1-8; Luke 24 : 1-8.—The narrative of John is so different in form that definite parallelism can scarcely be indicated. Concerning the narratives of the resurrection generally, it is to be remarked that they are fragmentary and not easily combined into a continuous story. Instead of insisting upon a complete and detailed harmony in this part of the history, it is better to recognize the fact that we have four fragmentary records of this great event, and to study them rather by comparison than by combination. In the fragmentary character of the narratives objectors have often thought

they found reason for doubt of the reality of the resurrection. But a wiser view of the matter would regard the brevity and simplicity of the narratives as a sign of the perfect honesty of the writers and of the unquestionableness of the event. It is plain that the evangelists were unconscious of any necessity for special effort in proving that the Lord had arisen. Their narratives are those of men to whom the resurrection of Jesus is an absolute and unquestionable certainty.

1. When the sabbath was past—*i. e.* after sunset of Saturday. Here again the three women are mentioned, as at chap. 15 : 40; two of them, Salome being omitted, were mentioned again at verse 47.—The second **Mary** is here **the mother of James :** in the preceding verse she was called the mother of Joses; at chap. 15 : 40, "the mother of James the less and of Joses." No reason can be given for the variation.— **Bought sweet spices.** Not **had bought.** The places of business in Jerusalem were opened after sunset of the Sabbath, and it was then that they went to buy.—**That they might come and anoint him.** Complete the embalming. Why, after what Nicodemus had done? We can answer only by remembering the great importance of sepulture in the esteem of the Jews, the interest that attached to it, and the unutterable personal affection that in the present case impelled the women to insist upon having a share in whatever was done for Jesus. Observe, again, that their purpose implied the full conviction that his death was real and final, like any other death. The wretched Sabbath that had intervened brought no new thoughts to their minds and no convincing remembrance of the Master's prediction. No disciple, apparently, had been able even to suggest to another the thought of a resurrection. In this blank despair of theirs we have a most valuable confirmation of the event. If they had been expecting a resurrection, we might have thought them less trustworthy in their declaration that it occurred; but they came to the tomb to complete the embalming.

2-4. Here we reach the region where the four narratives, being fragmentary, cannot be combined without the help of hypothesis.— **At the rising of the sun.** Rather, "the sun

3 And they said among themselves, Who shall roll us away the stone from the door of the sepulchre?
4 And when they looked, they saw that the stone was rolled away, for it was very great.
5 And entering into the sepulchre, they saw a young man sitting on the right side, clothed in a long white garment; and they were affrighted.
6 And he saith unto them, Be not affrighted: ye seek Jesus of Nazareth, which was crucified: he is risen: *he is not here: behold the place where they laid him.

3 to the tomb when the sun was risen. And they were saying among themselves, Who shall roll us
4 away the stone from the door of the tomb? and looking up, they see that the stone is rolled back:
5 for it was exceeding great. And entering into the tomb, they saw a young man sitting on the right side, arrayed in a white robe; and they were
6 amazed. And he saith unto them, Be not amazed: ye seek Jesus, the Nazarene, who hath been crucified: he is risen; he is not here: behold, the place

a Ps. 71 : 20.

having risen," which is the literal translation of Mark's designation of the time. The suggestions in the other Gospels of an earlier coming may possibly be referred to the time of setting out, and the state of the morning light as the women recalled it in remembering their walk as a whole. Mark certainly places their arrival at or just after the rising of the sun.— The conversation is perfectly natural. **They said,** or were saying, **among themselves,** as they approached the place, **Who shall roll us away the stone?** It is not at all strange that in the agitation of the time they should prepare themselves, and even find themselves almost there, without ever thinking of the great stone, especially if the rolling of it up to the door was something that was not always done. As for the guard (Matt. 27 : 62-66), there is no evidence that the women knew of its existence. It was placed there on the morning of the Sabbath, on which day they had been quietly at home (Luke 23 : 56). Mark's graphic account of their surprise is, literally, "And looking up, they see that the stone hath been rolled away."—**For it was very great** is commonly taken as an explanation of the question of the women; by some, as an explanation of the fact that when their eyes were lifted, having been downcast before, they could not fail to notice that the stone had been rolled away. The rolling away of the stone is mentioned by all the evangelists; the conversation of the women about it, by Mark alone.

5. The women are three in Mark, two (the two Marys) in Matthew, of indeterminate number in Luke; John speaks only of Mary Magdalene. According to Mark's report, they entered at once into the tomb and found **a young man sitting on the right side, clothed in a long white garment,** or, more literally, "arrayed in a white robe." The description all peculiar to Mark.—The **young man** is not called, in Mark, an angel, and neither here nor in any other of the reports is there any indication that he was endowed with wings, as angels are by the hands of artists;

rather is it denied by implication. Matthew describes the angel with the thought of his splendor in mind; Mark much more simply, representing him almost like one of the young Levites that ministered in the temple; Luke, who speaks of two messengers, mentions only the brilliancy of their raiment: he calls them "two men." (Compare the same language at Acts 1 : 10.)

6, 7. The first words were addressed to the fear of the women, or rather to their amazement, for such is the meaning of the word; they were overwhelmed with wonder.—The words of the **young man,** in Mark, are calm and measured; the utterance in Luke is much more rapid and exultant: "Why seek ye him that liveth, among the dead?" But here (literally), "Be not amazed: ye seek Jesus, the Nazarene, who hath been crucified."—The words that follow are the same in all three, only the order and connectives being changed. **He is risen: he is not here.** The Living One is not among the dead; this is not the place to find the Crucified.—**He is risen.** How few words tell the story! No one on earth was able yet to understand it and rejoice, but the angel's voice must have been tremulous with the joy of heaven over the triumph of the Son of God.—Matthew and Mark add the request to the women to come and see **the place where they laid him,** the now vacant place, described by John (20 5-7) as he saw it a little later—a request intended, apparently, to bring conviction and assurance to their minds. Yet here was reproof. They had come to see that very place, and to find him in it and to prepare his body to remain there—come, after all that he had said, with never a thought that they could find it empty. They had come to seek him as the Nazarene who had been crucified; but the tone of the heavenly messenger suggests that they might have been prepared to find him the Conqueror of death.—The women had been at hand, both at the cross and at the tomb, when the apostles were absent, and now they were to be the messengers who should

7 But go your way, tell his disciples and Peter that he goeth before you into Galilee: there shall ye see him, as he said unto you.

7 where they laid him! But go, tell his disciples and Peter, He goeth before you into Galilee: there shall

call the apostles back. **Go your way, tell his disciples and Peter.** Peter, as the leader of the apostolic band; still marked and treated in this message as the leader. If the message was dictated directly by Jesus, the introduction of Peter's name may have been intended directly to reassure him after his fall. Unquestionably it would have that effect, and perhaps we have a record of the impression it made upon his anxious mind in the fact that it is here, in the Petrine Gospel, that the message is recorded in this form. With this exception, however, the record of John, or even that of Luke, after the resurrection, contains more that would naturally be suggested by Peter's memory than that of Mark. (Compare note at the beginning of chap. 15.)—The women were bidden, **go your way, tell his disciples.** If John's narrative is to be harmonized with this, we must suppose that Mary Magdalene had arrived before the others, and had already gone to tell Peter and John that some strange thing had happened at the sepulchre, though she knew not yet that it was the resurrection of the Lord.—**That he goeth before you into Galilee: there shall ye see him, as he said unto you.** (See Matt. 26 : 32.) Yet he did not go at once to Galilee, but met the apostles, as well as the women, at Jerusalem. The explanation probably lies in the fact that Galilee was appointed to be the scene of his manifestation of himself to the largest assembly of witnesses, and of his most decisive instructions. (See Matt. 28 : 16, with 1 Cor. 15 : 6.) He did precede the apostles thither, and there they saw him, although he was pleased to show himself to them earlier in Jerusalem.—Verse 7 contains the utterance as given in Matthew; in Luke, the angel reminds the women, instead, of Jesus' own prediction of his death and his rising again on the third day. Luke adds, "and they remembered his words."—Such was the earliest announcement of the resurrection. No glimpse, not even the faintest of the resurrection itself was granted to any human being, friend or foe, or is permitted to us. Like other events of spiritual significance, it "came not with observation." Doubtless it occurred in quietness, as it did in the solitude and darkness of the fast-closed sepulchre.

The evidence of the reality of the resurrection may here be summarized. As preliminary to it, it may be well to restate also the proofs of the reality of our Saviour's death.

In evidence of the reality of the death we have (1) the positive, natural, and evidently sincere assertions of all the evangelists. (2) The fact of a hostility in the Jews that would not rest satisfied without the completion of its work in the death of Jesus, and that could not be deceived as to the question whether he was really dead or not. (3) The inquiry on the part of Pilate, occasioned by wonder at the announcement of so speedy a death (Mark 15 : 44). (4) The testimony of the centurion in charge of the crucifixion (Mark 15 : 45), and the further testimony implied in the act of the soldiers under his command in not breaking the legs of Jesus (John 19 : 32, 33). It was the duty of these soldiers to watch the victim of crucifixion until death had occurred. (5) The record (John 19 : 34) of a spear—thrust into the Lord's side, which would of itself be sufficient to produce death, if it had not already occurred. (6) The full and detailed account of embalmment and entombment in all the Gospels. (7) The intention of the women to complete, after the Jewish Sabbath had intervened, the process thus begun (Luke 23 : 56; 24 : 1). (8) The complete despair that appears in the conduct of the disciples, so far as it is shown to us. (9) The absence of any suspicion to the contrary in the proposal of his enemies to guard the sepulchre (Matt. 27 : 63, 64). (10) The omission of denial of the reality of his death from the plan that was devised to protect the unfaithful guards (Matt. 28 : 11-15).—In these points we have the evidence, not only that the disciples of Jesus believed him to be really dead, but that all who bore an important part in his crucifixion were thoroughly convinced of the reality of his death.

In evidence of the reality of the resurrection we have (1) the direct assertions of all the evangelists. It is absolutely unquestionable that they intended to assert the reality of the resurrection; and there is no reason for rejecting their testimony here, if there is reason for receiving it anywhere. From the Gospels in general, overwhelming evidence of their personal honesty can be gathered, and every item of this evidence is valuable as confirming the truthfulness of this part of their story. (2) Since, in all candor, we must accept this testimony, we have, conveyed by means of it, the risen Lord's deliberate testimony to the reality of his own resurrection. In Luke (24 : 38-43) and in John (20 : 27) we see him deliberately offering to his disciples physical proof of his own real bodily

8 And they went out quickly, and fled from the sepulchre; for they trembled and were amazed; neither said they any thing to any *man;* for they were afraid.

8 ye see him, as he said unto you. And they went out, and fled from the tomb; for trembling and astonishment had come upon them: and they said nothing to any one; for they were afraid.

presence among them. (Compare the language of Acts 1 : 3.) (3) The fact that the Christian religion immediately sprang up, having the assertion of this fact for one of its two central doctrines. Compare 1 Thess. 5 : 14: "If we believe that Jesus died and rose again." In preaching the new faith, the apostles constantly made these two assertions with equal confidence, beginning from the day of Pentecost (Acts 2 : 24; 3 : 15; 4 : 10; 10 : 40; 1 Pet. 1 : 3). It has already appeared that at the time of Jesus' death his disciples were entertaining no hope of a resurrection (Luke 24 : 21). It is impossible to suppose them dishonest in their subsequent proclamation of the resurrection as a fact. The fact of this proclamation in the spiritual power that was attendant upon it cannot be legitimately accounted for, except on the ground that the resurrection was real. (4) The testimony of the apostle Paul to the reality of the event. Paul was not one of the original disciples, but was at first an implacable enemy. His testimony has a special value, therefore, as that of a separate and independent witness. He became convinced that the resurrection of Jesus was real (1 Cor. 15 : 20), and accepted it as a vital point in his system of Christian truth (Rom. 1 : 2-5; 1 Cor. 15 : 12-17). After some twenty-five or thirty years had elapsed, he carefully and minutely rehearsed the evidence of the resurrection (1 Cor. 15 : 4-8), and was able to appeal to more than five hundred witnesses, the most of whom he declared to be still alive. In his preaching, as well as in his writing, he constantly asserted and made use of the fact (Acts 13 : 33-37; 17 : 31; 24 : 15; 26 : 23). (5) The existence in all Christian ages of the Lord's Day (Rev. 1 : 9), the first day of the week (Acts 20 : 7). As we have in the Lord's Supper a visible proof of our Saviour's death, so in the Lord's Day we have an historical proof of the reality of his resurrection.

8. Mark shows us only the fear of the women; Matthew, the "fear and great joy." In Mark the women say nothing to any one; in Matthew they run to bring word to his disciples. Hence some have inferred that the group of women separated, some returning to the city by one way in joy, and others by another way in terror. But it scarcely seems possible that Matthew or Mark can have had in mind the idea of a division of the company of women, for Matthew mentions only two women as present, and Mark only three. Others place

the fear before the meeting with Jesus (Matt. 28 : 9) and the joy after it. But it is well to remember that we are dealing with fragmentary reports of an hour of intense excitement and agitation. If such reports vary as to particulars, the presence of so amazing a fact as that of which they tell is the best explanation of the variety, and so the best harmony for the narratives.

For they were afraid (*ephobounto gar*). Here Mark's direct and continuous narrative, in parallelism with Matthew, ceases; for whatever we may think of the verses that follow, as to their source and authority, it is certain that from this point there is a change of tone and of method. There is no longer a narrative of events, but rather a summary, brief and compendious, and apparently so by intention. Where we expect the story to go on and tell of the meeting of the disciples with the Lord we meet with a new paragraph, starting in a new style, and dealing in a new way with a part of the events that are given in detail by the other evangelists. It is incredible, however, that Mark desired to close his Gospel with verse 8. Ending there, it would be incomplete, not only in a rhetorical sense, but historically also, for it would contain no proof of the resurrection, beyond the announcement of it by the angels. Some conclusion beyond the eighth verse the author must at least have had in contemplation.

9-20. SUMMARY OF EVENTS AFTER THE RESURRECTION OF JESUS. The *Parallel Passages* will be noted verse by verse.

By the revisers these verses are set by themselves with the remark, "The two oldest Greek manuscripts, and some other authorities, omit from verse 9 to the end. Some other authorities have a different ending to the Gospel." Doubtless the revisers would not be understood to mean that the "different ending" was of any value. They would only cite its existence in some ancient authorities as a sign of uncertainty as to the genuineness of the present ending. The majority of modern authorities regard these verses as the work of some other person than Mark. The most elaborate defence of their genuineness is by the Rev. J. W. Burgon (*The Last Twelve Verses of St. Mark's Gospel Vindicated*). The argument in their favor may be found clearly stated in Scrivener's *Introduction to the Criticism of the New Testament* (second edition, pp. 507-513). Dr. J. A. Broadus has argued on the same side in the *Baptist Quarter-ly*, July, 1869. The reasons for regarding the passage as the work of another hand than that of Mark are given by Alford in his *Commentary*, and by Meyer. The possible conjectures as to the history of the passage are given by Dr. Plumptre in Ellicott's *New Testament Commentary for English Readers*. It is to be noticed that the revisers do not enclose the passage in brackets as they do John 7 : 53–8 : 11, evidently regarding the argument against it as less conclusive than the one against that passage.

The reasons against it are, briefly, as follows: (1) The passage is omitted from the two oldest manuscripts, the Sinaitic and the Vatican. In the latter a blank space is left, as if the writer knew that the Gospel was incomplete, but was not in possession of the conclusion. It is omitted also from a few other manuscripts, of much less authority than these two, and in a few copies of four ancient versions. (2) Eusebius, in the fourth century, making more or less use of the work of Ammonius in the second, arranged the four Gospels in parallel passages on the principle of a harmony, and from this arrangement these verses are omitted. Eusebius says, moreover, that they are not found in 'the correct copies'"—a statement in which he is followed by Jerome and others, whose names are of less weight. (3) As to the internal evidence, there is no good connection between the passage and what precedes it, and no allusion in it to the context; the purpose of it is not a continuation of the purpose of Mark's record; it has the character of an epitome, in which it is unlike anything else in Mark; it contains certain additions to the statements of the other Gospels, but they are not in the least like Mark's characteristic additions; the peculiar words and phrases of Mark are absent, and about twenty words and phrases are found that occur nowhere else in his Gospel.

The reasons in favor of the passage are as follows: (1) It is contained in all the ancient manuscripts except those mentioned above, and in all the versions. (2) The nineteenth verse is quoted by Irenæus (about A. D. 170) with the introduction, "Mark says, at the end of the Gospel." From that time on the passage is freely cited by Christian writers generally, who treat it as they do other Scripture. (3) It has a place in the lectionaries, or selections of Scripture for public reading, which were in use in the Eastern Church "certainly in the fourth century, very probably much earlier" (*Scrivener*). It held a place of honor, indeed, in being taken as the Scripture for a special service

at matins on Ascension Day. There is no question that the passage came down, to say the least, from very nearly the same date as the Gospel of Mark, or that it was generally, though not universally, accepted in the church as a part of that Gospel.

If the passage is not Mark's, the problem is to account for its almost universal acceptance from the earliest times as a part of his Gospel; if the passage is Mark's, the problem is to account for the fact that his Gospel was known and received in some parts of the church without it; and the further problem remains to tell why Mark so suddenly broke off his narrative in the midst and epitomized the remaining history, doing it, moreover, in a style so unlike that of his ordinary writing. It may be said, in general, that external evidence is mainly, but with important exceptions, in favor of the acceptance of the passage as the production of Mark, and that internal evidence is mainly, and without important exceptions, against it. The difficulties on account of internal evidence would remain, somewhat diminished, perhaps, but not destroyed, if it were supposed that Mark himself at a later time added this concluding paragraph; and the abrupt ending of his original Gospel would still have to be accounted for.

The writer of this Commentary is unable to treat these verses as if they were the work of the same hand that produced the Gospel of Mark. The best explanation of the peculiar state of facts about the passage, in his judgment, is that which is proposed in the article "Gospels" in the *Encyclopædia Britannica* (Ninth Edition, vol. x., p. 801): "Few Greek scholars will be induced to believe that the author of the second Gospel deliberately chose to end a book on the good news of Christ with the words *ephobounto gar*. From a literary point of view, the *gar*, and from a moral point of view the ill-omened *ephobounto*, make it almost incredible that these words represent a deliberate termination assigned by an author to a composition of his own. Others have suggested that the last page of the manuscript may have been accidentally destroyed. But this suggestion seems to overlook the consideration that the manuscript was in all probability written, not for a private library, but for use in the church, and that it would immediately be multiplied by copies. Again, we know, from reference to Matt. 28 : 8 and Luke 24 : 9, that the common tradition ceases with the return of the women from the Lord's tomb." (That is to say, whatever any one of the three evangelists records

9 ¶ Now when *Jesus* was risen early the first *day* of the week, he appeared first to Mary Magdalene, out of whom he had cast seven devils.
10 *And* she went and told them that had been with him, as they mourned and wept.
11 *And* they, when they heard that he was alive, and had been seen of her, believed not.

9 [1]Now when he was risen early on the first day of the week, he appeared first to Mary Magdalene, 10 from whom he had cast out seven demons. She went and told them that had been with him, as they 11 mourned and wept. And they, when they heard that he was alive, and had been seen of her, disbelieved.

1 The two oldest Greek manuscripts, and some other authorities, omit from ver. 9 to the end. Some other authorities have a different ending to the Gospel.

after that point is peculiar to himself; material common to all extends no farther.) "But it is precisely at this point that the genuine Mark (16:8) also terminates. Now, that a page should have been torn out containing just that part of Mark which followed after the close of the common tradition would be a most remarkable and unlikely coincidence. It seems far more probable that Mark ends his Gospel here because the common tradition ended here, and because he scrupled to add anything to the notes and traditions which he knew to rest upon a higher authority than his own. If this be the true explanation, it stamps with the seal of a higher authority such traditions as have been preserved to us by so scrupulous an author.

From the historical and ecclesiastical point of view, the passage is canonical—*i. e.* it is a part of a book that the church has received as a whole into the Canon. But the question remains for the interpreter whether its testimony is to be received as of equal authority with that of the Gospels in general. This question must be answered in the negative. The suggestion above cited seems to afford a sufficient account of the fact that the original document of Mark was so abruptly terminated. If it was so terminated, and was in circulation with so abrupt an ending, it would be most natural that some one should add a conclusion to complete so unfinished a work. That conclusion would be added at a very early date, and would naturally be, exactly as we find it, an epitome, a summary without details, of events subsequent to the ones already recorded. Such a conclusion represents the tradition of the church, or of some part of the church, respecting the events of which it speaks; but the transcript of the tradition is anonymous, and the one thing that we know about it is that it is to be separated from the Gospel to which it has been attached. Therefore its testimony is to be regarded as testimony of the second class, one degree removed from testimony of the first authority. It will be observed, however, that there are some indications that this summary was not made wholly by compilation from the other Gospels, some statements being introduced here that are found nowhere else in the Scriptures—

a fact that would give to its testimony a certain additional value as that of an independent witness to what was believed in the church.

9. The word for **first day of the week** (*prōtē sabbatou*) is different from the one that is used by Mark at verse 2 (*tē mia tōn sabbatōn*).— **First to Mary Magdalene.** In agreement with John (20:1-18). Matthew speaks first of his appearing to "the women," of whom he makes Mary Magdalene to be one; Luke omits this appearing, and mentions none before the one that occurred on the way to Emmaus.— **Out of whom he had cast seven devils.** A fact alluded to elsewhere only in Luke (8:2), and not in John, with whose statement the first part of the sentence coincides. It is a singular fact that this reference to Mary Magdalene's personal history, evidently introduced as a mark of identification upon her, stands where it does. This is the fourth mentioning of her within twenty verses (see verse 1 and chap. 15: 40 and 47), and it is the last that occurs in the book. A continuous writer would scarcely introduce this mark of identification only at the fourth and last recurrence of her name. The presence of it here cannot be taken otherwise than as a sign that at verse 9 a new hand has taken the pen.—The appearing to Mary Magdalene is recounted at length by John, and few scenes in the life of our Lord are more profoundly natural and touching. The relations of Mary Magdalene to the resurrection have immortalized her, even as the relations of Mary of Bethany to the death and burial of the Saviour have immortalized her (Matt. 26:13).

10, 11. In these verses are found no less than six words or constructions that occur nowhere in the Gospel of Mark, except in this closing passage; and four of them — *ekeinos,* "that," used not emphatically; *poreuomai,* "went;" *theaomai,* "seen;" and *apisteō,* "unbelieving"— are found in this passage more than once. Inferences from the employment of unaccustomed words, it is true, are somewhat precarious; but the group of new expressions in this paragraph is certainly too remarkable to be overlooked, especially in connection with the other signs of a change of author.—Verse 10 is parallel to John 20 : 18; but the final words, **as they**

12 ¶ After that he appeared in another form unto two° of them, as they walked, and went into the country.
13 And they went and told *it* unto the residue; neither believed they them.
14 ¶ Afterwards he^b appeared unto the eleven as they sat at meat, and upbraided them with their unbelief° and hardness of heart, because they believed not them which had seen him after he was risen.

12 And after these things he was manifested in another form unto two of them, as they walked on 13 their way into the country. And they went away and told it unto the rest: neither believed they them.
14 And afterward he was manifested unto the eleven themselves as they sat at meat; and he upbraided them with their unbelief and hardness of heart, because they believed not them who had seen him

a Luke 24 : 13....*b* Luke 24 : 36 ; 1 Cor. 15 : 5....*c* Luke 24 : 25.

mourned and wept, are additional, as is the whole of verse 11, John having said nothing of the reception that the tidings of Mary Magdalene met with. This statement cannot have been derived from any of the other Gospels. It is noticeable that in this paragraph the slowness of the disciples to believe in the resurrection of their Master is much insisted upon—almost as if the author desired to show that no anticipation of such an event was present in their minds. The early unbelief of those who so soon afterward were preaching the resurrection of Jesus with perfect assurance has an evidential value of the greatest importance. The testimony of this passage to the fact of the unbelief is scarcely less valuable, historically, than any other testimony ; for it comes from a time when the truth as to the original thoughts of the disciples on the subject was well known in the circle from which it proceeded.

12. Parallel to Luke 24 : 13–32, but, like the preceding verses, it is only a bare statement of what the other writer tells with a tender and loving particularity—in this respect, not at all in Mark's manner.—**Unto two of them.** Unnamed here, and only one of them, Cleopas, is named in Luke.—**As they walked, and went into the country**—*i. e.* to Emmaus, "threescore furlongs from Jerusalem," but of unknown site. The time appears to have been in the afternoon of the first Lord's Day.—**In another form.** Slight variation from Luke, who makes the failure to recognize him reside in them, not in him : "Their eyes were holden, that they should not know him." Luke's expression, "Jesus himself drew near and went with them," seems to imply, not merely a hidden identity, but an identity so true and so manifest that they might have recognized him. This way of stating the matter, however (**in another form**), would be a natural popular mode of expression to one who was telling the story briefly.—The opening phrase in this verse, after these things (*meta tauta*) " is not found in Mark, though many opportunities occurred for using it " (*Alford*). Neither is it found in Matthew.

13. Parallel as to the event, but not other-

wise, to Luke 24 : 33–35. There, as here, the two return from their journey and report that they have met the Lord, but the reception of their tidings is not the same. Here it is said, **neither believed they them**—*i. e.* the disciples generally, to whom the report was made, did not believe. In Luke they were already saying among themselves, "The Lord is risen indeed, and hath appeared unto Simon." (Compare 1 Cor. 15 : 5, where alone the appearing to Simon— *i. e.* to Peter (Cephas)—is again mentioned.) Harmonists have tried by all possible expedients to reconcile these two statements, but their results are not satisfactory. A not impossible conjecture is that of Westcott (*The Gospel of the Resurrection*), which is, substantially, that they had believed the testimony of Peter (though they had not believed that of Mary Magdalene), but were now perplexed at hearing that he had appeared to some one else at a distance, and in such a way as to make them doubt the possibility of it under the conditions of time and space. The doubt would thus be the result of the peculiarity of his resurrection-life—a life in which he was not with them as before, but came and went in unexpected and inexplicable manifestations; a not impossible conjecture, but only a conjecture. Yet doubtless belief and disbelief alternated in their minds through all that day and through days that followed.

14. First, according to this paragraph, he was manifested to Mary Magdalene, then to the two disciples, then to the eleven ; a climax—one, two, eleven—completed by the emphatic pronoun, according to the Revision, " unto the eleven themselves," as if this completed the course of manifestations. From this point to the end of verse 18 the passage reads as if the writer was thinking of only one interview. If he had more than one occasion in mind, he has not indicated it. Apparently, however, the testimony of the other Gospels distributes these occurrences to several occasions. Verse 14 appears to be parallel to Luke 24 : 36–43 ; although, if it is, we again have only the most compendious account of an event that is elsewhere given in fuller detail. It is possible, however, that

17

15 And he said unto them, Go[a] ye into all the world, and preach the gospel to every creature.[b]
16 He[c] that believeth, and is baptized, shall be saved; but he[d] that believeth not, shall be damned.

15 after he was risen. And he said unto them, Go ye into all the world,. and preach the gospel to the 16 whole creation. He that believeth and is baptized shall be saved; but he that disbelieveth shall be[e]

a Matt. 28 : 19; John 20 : 21....b Rom. 10 : 18; Col. 1 : 23....c John 3 : 18, 36; Acts 16 : 31-33; Rom. 10 : 9; 1 Pet. 3 : 21....d John 12 : 48; 2 Thess. 2 : 12.

some other interview, otherwise unrecorded, is meant. The Lord came to his disciples when they were reclining at the table—a fact that appears in no other record—and he **upbraided them** (*ōneidisen*, a very strong word; see chap. 15 : 32; Matt. 11 : 20) **with their unbelief and hardness of heart, because they believed not them which had seen him after he was risen**—another fact that does not elsewhere appear. Possibly, therefore, this may not be the meeting of the first evening; but we cannot be certain.

15. At first sight one would say that this verse was certainly parallel to Matt. 28 : 19; but it is impossible to prove it parallel, the two contexts being by no means the same. It is quite possible that the command as cited here was uttered on another occasion, earlier than that of the command as cited by Matthew. It may be that verses 14-18 preserve the remembrance of some interview, not elsewhere recorded, at which our Lord spoke to the apostles of their mission substantially as he spoke a little later to a larger company gathered on the appointed mountain in Galilee. It is commonly thought that the meeting of Matt. 28 : 16-20 is to be identified with that of 1 Cor. 15 : 6, when more than five hundred brethren were present. The supposition gives a richer significance to the great command that he there delivered, making it a command to the whole body of his followers, and not merely a commission to his apostles. Whether the command as given here is quoted from that occasion, or, as now suggested, from an earlier one, must be left in doubt. If it is quoted from that occasion, there is a long break between verses 14 and 15. The interview of the second Lord's Day intervened; so did the departure to Galilee and the meeting of seven disciples with the Lord at the Lake of Gennesaret.—The command as cited here is broader, if possible, than in Matthew, though less full in details. **Go ye into all the world, and preach the gospel,** or glad tidings, "to the whole creation," not **to every creature,** which is not an allowable translation of *pasē tē ktisei*. The broad phrase is limited, of course, by the sense of the passage. "The whole creation" is not spoken of because, as Bengel and Alford have it, the whole creation is redeemed by Christ, and by Christianity the lower creatures

are to be benefited and the face of the earth is to be renewed. That thought has no fitness in this connection. Paul claimed (Col. 1 : 23) that the gospel had already been "preached in all creation which is under heaven" (Revision)—*i. e.* everywhere. Both there and here the phrase is broader than the "all the nations"—*i. e.* Gentiles—of Matt. 28 : 19 and Rom. 16 : 26. It is the broadest possible designation of the field in which the Christian teachers could find human beings to listen to their message. Under this commission the field of the gospel is wherever the gospel can be received, and the place appointed for Christian labor is literally everywhere. Contrast this with the exclusiveness required during our Lord's personal ministry. Matt. 10 : 5, 6 : "Go not into any way of the Gentiles, and into any city of the Samaritans enter ye not, but go rather to the lost sheep of the house of Israel." See a limitation still more sharp and startling in Matt. 15 : 24.— Very significant is our Saviour's widening of the field for his servants after his resurrection. The wider purpose was announced on the first evening as ready for fulfilment (John 20 : 21). In Luke 24 : 47, as in Matt. 28 : 19, he gave them "all the nations" for their field, and here "the whole creation." Again, just before the Ascension, he told them (Acts 1 : 8) that their mission was to carry them "unto the uttermost part of the earth." Thus the commission was as plain as words could make it; yet the national narrowness required time and further training before it would allow the Christians to recognize the world as their field.

16. **He that believeth, and is baptized, shall be saved.** Broad announcement of the purpose and result of the proclamation. It was the preaching of a Saviour, and the promise was that salvation should follow for every one who accepted the glad tidings and obeyed the Saviour. The first step is believing—*i. e.* believing the message and believing on the Saviour. To believe the message intellectually, without the faith that trusts the soul to the Saviour, is by no means the "believing" of the Scriptures. (See John 5 : 24; 6 : 40; Acts 16 : 31.)—The second step is baptism. **He that believeth, and is baptized.** Baptism was with the apostles a first and natural result of believing, an expression of loyalty to Jesus

17 And these signs shall follow them that believe: In my* name shall they cast out devils; they shall speak* with new tongues;
18 They shall take up serpents;* and if they drink any deadly thing, it shall not hurt them: they* shall lay hands on the sick, and they shall recover.

17 condemned. And these signs shall follow them that believe: in my name shall they cast out demons;
18 they shall speak with ¹new tongues; they shall take up serpents, and if they drink any deadly thing, it shall in no wise hurt them; they shall lay hands on the sick, and they shall recover.

a Luke 10 : 17 ; Acts 5 : 16 ; 8 : 7 ; 16 : 18 ; 19 : 12....b Acts 2 : 4 ; 10 : 46 ; 1 Cor. 12 : 10, 28....c Luke 10 : 19 ; Acts 28 : 5....d Acts 5 : 15, 16 ; 28 : 8.——1 Some ancient authorities omit new.

that almost formed a part of the original act of faith. Any thought of separating baptism from believing, whether by anticipation or by delay, would have seemed to them a perversion of its meaning. (Study especially, in its connection, the exhortation of Peter on the day of Pentecost, Acts 2 : 38.) It is on this principle that these expressions were made by which Christians who reject all ideas akin to baptismal regeneration have sometimes been perplexed. Baptism was regarded as almost a part of the receiving of Christ, so closely was it connected with the beginning of the new life in him. This promise, which is, substantially, " believe and confess — accept Christ inwardly in the heart, and outwardly before the world — and thou shalt be saved," well represents the thought of the apostolic age on the subject. (Compare Rom. 10 : 10 ; Gal. 3 : 27.)—**But he that believeth not,** or disbelieveth, **shall be damned,** condemned. The ground of the condemnation is (John 3 : 19) that " light is come into the world, and men loved darkness rather than light, because their deeds were evil." Thus he who disbelieves the gospel shall by reason of that very fact "be condemned;" his own act condemns him, implies and reveals a character in which he is condemned as a person of evil heart. "The wrath of God abideth on him" (John 3 : 36), and will continue to abide upon him so long as his disbelieving the gospel continues. The ground of the condemnation is essentially moral ; the ground, indeed, is the character of God ; and hence the condemnation is necessary and inevitable. In the final judgment upon the disbelieving soul God will affirm this righteous condemnation, and will, without an arbitrary decree, assign the soul to the destiny that the condemnation requires.—The substitution by the revisers of "condemned " for **damned** is a gain to clearness and correctness of thought, since it associates this terrible judgment of God more distinctly with the moral considerations that justify it, and helps to show how far his judgment is from being an arbitrary judgment. (See Acts 17 : 31 ; Rom. 2 : 5 ; 2 Cor. 5 : 10.)

It has often been remarked that baptism is not mentioned in the second or condemnatory clause ; so that disbelief stands alone as the ground of condemnation. True ; but baptism could not be mentioned in that clause. "He that believeth not and is not baptized " would be unmeaning, and " he that believeth not, or (believing) is not baptized," would misrepresent the spirit of the gospel. Faith and baptism are not strictly co-ordinate in their relation to saving grace, though by divine appointment they are companion acts to the Christian. Yet in a modified sense it is true that " he that, believing, is not baptized, shall be," or rather is, thereby "condemned," provided that the instruction of his Lord in the matter has been made known to him.

17, 18. These verses are without parallel in the words of our Saviour, and they contain the nearest approach that we find in the New Testament to the tone and coloring of the Apocryphal Gospels. In the existing uncertainty as to the source of this entire paragraph it is difficult to know exactly how they should be judged—whether as a citation of our Saviour's very words, or as the interpretation current in the church, and justly attributed to him, in substance if not in precise form, of the **signs** that did **follow them that believe.** That such signs did exist in the early church — though doubtless not in the case of every believer—is unquestionable ; and such a prediction as this would be sufficiently fulfilled by the general diffusion of them in the body, though all believers did not possess them.—**In my name shall they cast out devils**—a power already granted to the apostles when in service (Matt. 10 : 8), and supposed, at least by some, to be constantly with them (Mark 9 : 18, 19), and abundantly continued in the church (Acts 8 : 7 ; 16 : 18 ; 19 : 15, 16).—**They shall speak with new tongues.** (See Acts 2 : 4-11, of the speaking on the day of Pentecost ; also Acts 10 : 46 ; 19 : 6 ; 1 Cor. 12 : 10 ; 14 : 1-28.) There is much that remains unexplained about the gift of tongues, but of the reality of the endowment there is no room for doubt.—**They shall take up serpents.** (Compare the language addressed to the seventy disciples at Luke 10 : 19, and see Acts 28 : 5 for the nearest approach to a fulfilment.)—**If they drink any deadly thing, it shall not hurt them.** (See again Luke 10 : 19.) Tradition relates the occurrence of fulfilments of this prediction, as in the case

19 ¶ So then* after the Lord had spoken unto them, he was received up into heaven, and sat^b on the right hand of God.
20 And they went forth, and preached every where, the Lord^c working with *them*, and confirming the word with signs following. Amen.

19 So then the Lord Jesus, after he had spoken unto them, was received up into heaven, and sat down at the right hand of God. And they went forth, and preached everywhere, the Lord working with them, and confirming the word by the signs that followed. Amen.

a Acts 1 : 2, 3 ; Luke 24 : 51....*b* Ps. 110 : 1 ; 1 Pet. 3 : 22....*c* Acts 5 : 12 ; Heb. 2 : 4.

of the apostle John, but there are no cases recorded in Scripture.—**They shall lay hands on the sick, and they shall recover.** Abundantly illustrated in the early Christian history (Acts 3 : 7 ; 5 : 15 ; 9 : 34 ; 14 : 10 ; 28 : 8). From James 5 : 14, 15 and 1 Cor. 12 : 9 it is apparent that healing was regarded by the Christians, apart from the apostles, as a gift that resided in some of their number. Only in Acts 28 : 8 is there any allusion to the laying on of hands for the purpose of healing; in James 5 : 14 the means is anointing with oil.—The only things peculiar in this enumeration of "signs" are the promises respecting the taking up of serpents and the drinking of deadly things. According to the analogy of all evangelical miracles, such promises on the lips of our Saviour would be limited, by the nature of the gospel, to occasions when they would serve the real purpose of the gospel. The power of miracles was never entrusted to men to be used for their own ends. There is reason to believe that if an apostle had tried to serve some selfish personal purpose by miracle, he would have found the power failing him.

19. The last two verses form a kind of special conclusion, dealing in general terms alone, and not picturing any single events. Authorities are divided between **the Lord** and "the Lord Jesus," the revisers adopting the latter. The title **Lord,** applied absolutely to Jesus, is not of frequent occurrence in the Gospels, and the use of it here and in the following verse has been taken as a sign of the later date of this paragraph, "after that had become the almost uniform way in which the Church spoke of her Divine Head" (*Plumptre*); but the inference is doubtful.—**After the Lord had spoken unto them**—*i. e.* after he had given them such commands and promises as have just been recorded. If verses 19, 20 did not form a separate generalizing paragraph, we might feel compelled to say that these words placed the Ascension immediately after the interview just mentioned; but, as it is, there is no such necessity.—**Was received up into heaven.** There is no pictorial representation in this such as we find at Acts 1 : 9. There is no reason to think that the writer had the visible scene of the Ascension at all in mind with any purpose of pre-

senting it to the imagination of his readers. The assertion is simply that he was received to heaven, according to his own prediction (John 6 : 62 ; 20 : 17).—**And sat on the right hand of God.** Regarded as the seat of honor and of administration. His sitting there appears in the New Testament as the fulfilment of the prophetic promise in Ps. 110 : 1, where is given the assurance of full power and victorious dominion. (See note on Mark 12 : 36 ; also Rom. 8 : 34 ; 1 Pet. 3 : 22 ; Heb. 1 : 3 ; 8 : 1 ; 10 : 12 ; 12 : 2.) The mention of his sitting down at the right hand of God is the appropriate close for the record of his life, and especially, perhaps, for the record of Mark, in which his intense activity is so clearly exhibited. Not that his sitting there is a symbol of rest : the throne is not a seat of repose, but the seat of unceasing administrative action. Our Saviour's sitting down at the right hand of God is a symbol of his cessation from the toil that occupied him before, but it is still more profoundly a symbol of continued activity—the activity that follows upon attainment to the possession of universal sovereignty. This brief assertion, therefore, **he was received up into heaven, and sat on the right hand of God,** tells of the complete success of our Saviour's mission to the earth and the full certainty that the results that remained to be wrought out in human history will be accomplished. He humbled himself and became obedient, unto death ; wherefore God also highly exalted him, and gave him the name that is above every name, that in the name of Jesus every knee should bow.

20. Between the preceding verse and this there is an untranslated antithesis: *ho men kurios . . . ekeinoi de.* **The Lord . . . was received up into heaven, . . . and they went forth, and preached every where.** Here came to pass the exact fulfilment of his word in Matthew : "All power is given unto me in heaven and in earth ; go ye therefore and make disciples of all the nations." The triumphant Saviour was ready to send out the heralds of his completed salvation, and at his bidding they went forth.—**Every where.** Not to be taken, of course, as a declaration that the word had already been preached everywhere, and not as a basis for any conclusion as to the date at which the statement was committed to writing. The apostles and their companions did go every where as rapidly as the Lord opened the way for them.—**The Lord working with them.** The unseen Lord Jesus, now glorified, recognized as working with his humble servants on the earth. Their activity was his activity, and his strength was the means of their triumph. The life of the church on the earth is the continued life of Christ. Compare the relation of the Acts of the Apostles to the Gospel of Luke as stated in the opening sentence: "The former treatise have I made, of all that Jesus began both to do and to teach," the verb "began" being in the emphatic position. What was done in the church was that which Jesus continued "both to do and to teach." (See Bernard's *Progress of Doctrine in the New Testament.*)—He is still **working with** his people through the agencies that were brought into use by his Spirit, but the means that were most distinctly in the writer's mind were the miracles. **Working with them, and confirming the word with signs following,** or "by the signs that followed." (Compare Heb. 2 : 3, 4.)—This testimony to the presence and working of the Saviour came, evidently, out of the midst of the age of miracles, when the visible supernatural **signs** were recognized among the most striking tokens of his presence. Even then, however, the best signs of his presence were perceived by some to be the spiritual operations of his gospel. (See 1 Cor. 12 : 29-13 : 13.) Graces are better than gifts. Of graces, the abiding graces are the best; and of these, "the greatest is love." "God is love, and he that abideth in love abideth in God, and God in him." Love is the Lord's own sign (John 13 : 35) : "By this shall all men know that ye are my disciples, if ye have love one to another."

THE END.